Cisco Unified Customer Voice Portal

Building Unified Contact Centers

Rue Green

D1608570

Cisco Press

800 East 96th Street

Indianapolis, IN 46240

Cisco Unified Customer Voice Portal

Building Unified Contact Centers

Rue Green

Copyright © 2012 Cisco Systems, Inc.

Published by:
Cisco Press
800 East 96th Street
Indianapolis, IN 46240 USA

First Printing December 2011

Library of Congress Cataloging-in-Publication data is on file.

ISBN-13: 978-1-58714-290-1

ISBN-10: 1-58714-290-2

Warning and Disclaimer

This book is designed to provide information about Cisco Unified Customer Voice Portal. Every effort has been made to make this book as complete and as accurate as possible, but no warranty or fitness is implied.

The information is provided on an "as is" basis. The author, Cisco Press, and Cisco Systems, Inc., shall have neither liability nor responsibility to any person or entity with respect to any loss or damages arising from the information contained in this book or from the use of the discs or programs that may accompany it.

The opinions expressed in this book belong to the author and are not necessarily those of Cisco Systems, Inc.

Trademark Acknowledgments

All terms mentioned in this book that are known to be trademarks or service marks have been appropriately capitalized. Cisco Press or Cisco Systems, Inc. cannot attest to the accuracy of this information. Use of a term in this book should not be regarded as affecting the validity of any trademark or service mark.

Corporate and Government Sales

The publisher offers excellent discounts on this book when ordered in quantity for bulk purchases or special sales, which may include electronic versions and/or custom covers and content particular to your business, training goals, marketing focus, and branding interests . For more information, please contact: **U.S. Corporate and Government Sales 1-800-382-3419 corpsales@pearsontechgroup.com**

For sales outside of the U.S. please contact: **International Sales international@pearsoned.com**

Feedback Information

At Cisco Press, our goal is to create in-depth technical books of the highest quality and value. Each book is crafted with care and precision, undergoing rigorous development that involves the unique expertise of members from the professional technical community.

Readers' feedback is a natural continuation of this process. If you have any comments regarding how we could improve the quality of this book, or otherwise alter it to better suit your needs, you can contact us through e-mail at feedback@ciscopress.com. Please make sure to include the book title and ISBN in your message.

We greatly appreciate your assistance.

Publisher: Paul Boger

Associate Publisher: Dave Dusthimer

Executive Editor: Brett Bartow

Managing Editor: Sandra Schroeder

Project Editor: Seth Kerney

Editorial Assistant: Vanessa Evans

Cover Designer: Sandra Schroeder

Composition: Mark Shirar

Business Operation Manager, Cisco Press: Anand Sundaram

Manager Global Certification: Erik Ullanderson

Development Editor: Marianne Bartow

Copy Editor: Apostrophe Editing Services

Technical Editors: Gary Ford, Jeff Spronk, Rahul Manikitala,and Lou Yao

Proofreader: Language Logistics LLC, Christal White

Indexer: Tim Wright

Americas Headquarters	Asia Pacific Headquarters	Europe Headquarters
Cisco Systems, Inc.	Cisco Systems (USA) Pte. Ltd.	Cisco Systems International BV
San Jose, CA	Singapore	Amsterdam, The Netherlands

Cisco has more than 200 offices worldwide. Addresses, phone numbers, and fax numbers are listed on the Cisco Website at **www.cisco.com/go/offices.**

CCDE, CCENT, Cisco Eos, Cisco HealthPresence, the Cisco logo, Cisco Lumin, Cisco Nexus, Cisco StadiumVision, Cisco TelePresence, Cisco WebEx, DCE, and Welcome to the Human Network are trademarks; Changing the Way We Work, Live, Play, and Learn and Cisco Store are service marks; and Access Registrar, Aironet, AsyncOS, Bringing the Meeting To You, Catalyst, CCDA, CCDP, CCIE, CCIP, CCNA, CCNP, CCSP, CCVP, Cisco, the Cisco Certified Internetwork Expert logo, Cisco IOS, Cisco Press, Cisco Systems, Cisco Systems Capital, the Cisco Systems logo, Cisco Unity, Collaboration Without Limitation, EtherFast, EtherSwitch, Event Center, Fast Step, Follow Me Browsing, FormShare, GigaDrive, HomeLink, Internet Quotient, IOS, iPhone, iQuick Study, IronPort, the IronPort logo, LightStream, Linksys, MediaTone, MeetingPlace, MeetingPlace Chime Sound, MGX, Networkers, Networking Academy, Network Registrar, PCNow, PIX, PowerPanels, ProConnect, ScriptShare, SenderBase, SMARTnet, Spectrum Expert, StackWise, The Fastest Way to Increase Your Internet Quotient, TransPath, WebEx, and the WebEx logo are registered trademarks of Cisco Systems, Inc. and/or its affiliates in the United States and certain other countries.

All other trademarks mentioned in this document or website are the property of their respective owners. The use of the word partner does not imply a partnership relationship between Cisco and any other company. (0812R)

About the Author

Rue Green, CCIE No. 9269, is a Technical Leader for the Customer Collaboration Service Line within Cisco Advanced Services focusing on Unified Contact Center architectures and deployment methodologies. He currently acts in a delivery architect role over sighting deployment architectures for Unified CVP, Unified ICM, and Cisco Unified Communications Manager for Unified Contact Center Solutions. Rue has spent the last 21 years working within different roles covering software development to network architecture, design, and implementation for large voice and data networks. Rue has a B.S. degree in computer science and mathematics from Colorado Mesa University. He is also a dual Cisco Certified Internetwork Expert (CCIE #9269) in Routing & Switching and Voice, and a Certified Information System Security Professional (CISSP #75393). He also carries many other vendor and industry certifications such as the Microsoft Certified Systems Engineer with Exchange 2003 emphasis and the newer Microsoft Certified IT Professional: Enterprise Administrator certification on Server 2008.

About the Technical Reviewers

For more than 13 years, **Gary Ford** has been privileged to work for many large systems integration companies, Cisco Advanced Technology Partners, and end customers, designing, deploying, and maintaining Cisco telephony and contact center solutions. His introductory role to contact centers started in 1997 while working for British Telecom (BT) as a test engineer tasked with integrating the GeoTel ICR platform into BT's core telephony network. Over the following years, Cisco acquired GeoTel and rapidly transformed the ICR product set to include solutions from other Cisco acquisitions and a great deal of in-house innovation. His role has changed over the years from test engineer to contact center and unified communications consultant. Gary spends much of his time designing and deploying Cisco unified communications solutions for a wide range of customers. Gary also holds a Bachelor's of Engineering degree in computer systems engineering, the status of Chartered Engineer, and several Cisco, Microsoft, and business-related professional qualifications.

Jeff Spronk, CCIE No. 20437, has been working in Advanced Services at Cisco as a Network Consulting Engineer for three years. As a member of the Customer Collaboration Service Line, his focus is to design, deploy, and test Cisco Unified Contact Center solutions for large enterprise customers. Jeff's role also includes the creation of UCC-related intellectual property and documentation. Prior to joining Cisco, Jeff worked as part of the UCC deployment team, assisting a Cisco Partner and Cisco sales teams with designing and troubleshooting contact center solutions.

Dedications

This book is dedicated first to my family, my wife Marcy and my two awesome children, Kyla and Jake. Without their support, encouragement, and patience, it would not exist. Secondly to my Mom and Dad, who instilled in me strong work ethics and a will to never doubt myself. Lastly, to my sister, who has always been the big sister with a big heart. I think they will be proud of what follows.

Acknowledgments

I would like to thank the following teams for helping me create this book.

First, my manager and colleague, Aaron Chaskelis from Cisco, for his support and guidance on this project. I could not have done it without it.

Secondly, Janet Byron, formerly a principal engineer at Cisco, for her deep technical knowledge on Unified CVP and guidance on content found throughout the book. I want to wish Janet well in her newly found freedom and hope to have the pleasure of working with her again in the future.

Scott Hogg, a principal consultant at GTRI, for convincing me to step up and take a swing at the book. Without his words of encouragement and guidance, this book would not exist.

Chris Chandler and Tom Armstrong from Cisco for their contributions pertaining to sizing and mitigation techniques for high-latency networks and Unified CVP. Their work, illustrated in this book, is a superb example of their deep technical expertise in solution architecture and Unified CVP.

Jason Kuo, formerly an engineer at Cisco , for his contribution around media files and Unified CVP's IVR and HTTP caching techniques. His content was a great addition to this book, and I am grateful for his insight.

Rahul Manikitala, a Systems Engineer at Cisco Systems, Inc., for his great insight pertaining to the layout and content of this book.

Lou Yao, Network Consulting Engineer at Cisco, for his friendship and honest opinions pertaining to the technical content found in this book.

Andrew Marc-Aurele, Network Consulting Engineer at Cisco, for gathering some great examples pertaining to troubleshooting TDM and VXML conversations.

The technical reviewers, Gary Ford and Jeff Spronk, who provided excellent technical coverage and kept this book accurate and easy to navigate.

Finally, the Cisco Press team: Brett Bartow, the executive editor, for seeing the value and vision provided in the original proposal and believing enough to provide me the opportunity to build this book. In addition, Marianne Bartow, development editor, for her relentless push to develop my rough manuscript into a fine piece of technical literature and pushing the entire team to meet our deadlines. Lastly, everyone else in the Cisco Press team who spent countless hours normalizing the manuscript, its technical drawings and content; their effort can be seen throughout the book pertaining to my ideas, words, and pictures, presented in ways that I could never have imagined.

Contents at a Glance

Contents

Icons Used in This Book

Command Syntax Conventions

The conventions used to present command syntax in this book are the same conventions used in the IOS Command Reference. The Command Reference describes these conventions as follows:

- **Boldface** indicates commands and keywords that are entered literally as shown. In actual configuration examples and output (not general command syntax), boldface indicates commands that are manually input by the user (such as a **show** command).

- *Italic* indicates arguments for which you supply actual values.

- Vertical bars (|) separate alternative, mutually exclusive elements.

- Square brackets ([ ]) indicate an optional element.

- Braces ({ }) indicate a required choice.

- Braces within brackets ([{ }]) indicate a required choice within an optional element.

Introduction

Once upon a time I was told that Unified CVP is both a product and a solution. At the time, I didn't understand the significance of that statement and chalked it up as another one of those fancy analogies that actually didn't mean much. However, as time went by I started to examine that statement and understand how correct it truly is. To understand and appreciate Unified CVP, you must first understand it as a product and then graduate to understanding it as a solution. In other words, Unified CVP requires a solution-level mind set. This means to master Unified CVP and it integrations, you must visualize it at the solution level and not just at the product level.

Cisco provides an enormous amount of documentation for Unified CVP. This documentation covers the design, installation, configuration, and administration aspects of Unified CVP. So why write a book on Unified CVP? The answer is fairly simple. With all the great documentation available from Cisco, not a single document provides the important details of Unified CVP. Those important details are scattered throughout numerous Cisco technical documents or buried in training manuals provided by training partners. Up until the construction of this book, an engineer would need to attend some classes and dig through several hundred if not thousands of pages of documentation to just get a good architecture understanding of Unified CVP. This approach created a perception that Unified CVP is a complicated product with a decent learning curve for an engineer to become proficient at implementing it. Hence, the goal of this book is to boil down and simplify the architectural details and collect and present them in one reference without trying to replace the existing design, installation, and configuration guides already available from Cisco.

Currently, Cisco has released version 8.5 of Unified CVP and has a release date for version 8.7 and even 9.0. However, quite a few customers may still use version 7.x or even 4.x, so there is a compelling need for a book that can capture the best technical content sampled from different Cisco documents, white papers, best practices, and brain dumps from senior engineering resources such as the author to present it in a simplified manner for ease of consumption.

Objectives of This Book

Many organizations are currently working to transform their existing legacy TDM Contact Centers to feature-rich, IP-based unified contact centers. Although some organizations are working on these huge transformational projects, several are still contemplating how this transformation can impact them and what solutions exist to enable them to move to a true IP-based unified contact center solution.

Cisco Unified Customer Voice Portal (CVP), formally Internet Service Node or ISN, is quickly becoming a strong replacement technology for legacy TDM IVR solutions. Cisco Unified CVP integrates with Cisco Unified Contact Center Enterprise and Cisco Unified Call Manager to produce a feature-rich replacement for legacy components ailing from scalability, functionality, and proprietary IVR languages. Because of the numerous options and integrations available for designing next generation contact center solutions with Unified CVP, outlining best practices and architectures pertaining to these options becomes an even greater challenge for contact center and network engineers. This book intends to provide architecture guidelines and proven deployment best practices for mitigating design and sizing challenges when deploying Unified CVP.

This book covers the Unified CVP architecture first, outlining its key advantages and design considerations. When the underlining architecture and integration points are defined, the book focuses on key architecture and solutions to address some the most common, yet complex, design challenges existing in today's unified contact center deployments. Where appropriate, the book provides working configurations and examples that support the deployment of the architectures discussed. The book concludes by covering topics such as upgrades, troubleshooting, and the virtualization of Unified CVP.

This book does not cover introductory concepts on how a contact center functions. It is based on the assumption that you have a fundamental understanding of contact centers and their requirements both from a technical standpoint and from a business perspective. In addition, although the audience level for this book may not be expert on Unified CVP, it is assumed that basic unified contact center components such as UCCE via Unified ICM and CUCM are understood. It covers the design architectures for Unified CVP but at the same time gives practical examples on how to implement those architectures. In that way this book provides a good mix of the design concepts with implementation examples for Unified CVP.

Who Should Read This Book?

The book is targeted to a technical audience composed of information technology staff responsible for designing and deploying Unified Contact Centers. In addition, Contact Center mangers that are curious of the design benefits and considerations with Unified CVP could also be likely candidates. Application consultants that provide UCCE scripting support can also benefit from this book, simply because it offers the underlining architecture for how applications are handled in the network and how calls are delivered for queuing, treatment, and delivery. This book assumes some knowledge of IP-based or legacy-based contact centers and is geared to a technical audience. Therefore, people with either a CCVP or CCIE can value the technical content of this book.

The secondary target is the actual end customers in charge of day-to-day maintenance and troubleshooting of their own platform.

How This Book Is Organized

This book contains nine chapters that cover the core areas of Unified Customer Voice Portal. An overview of each chapter follows.

- **Chapter 1, "Introduction to Unified Customer Voice Portal":** Provides a history lesson about Unified CVP and its advantages. This chapter also provides a technical overview of VoiceXML.

- **Chapter 2, "Unified CVP Architecture Overview":** Covers Unified CVP native components including the Call Server, VXML Server, Reporting Server, Operations Console Server, and Cisco Unified Call Studio. This chapter also covers non-native components including IOS devices, Cisco Unified ICM, Cisco Unified Call Manager, content load balancers and third-party servers. This chapter discusses different deployment models and licensing requirements.

- **Chapter 3, "Functional Deployment Models and Call Flows":** Includes a discussion regarding the Standalone, Call Director, Comprehensive, and VRU-only deployment models and their detailed call flows.

- **Chapter 4, "Designing Unified CVP for High Availability":** Covers different Unified CVP geographic models, edge queuing techniques, and call survivability. Includes detailed discussions about the creation of high-availability architectures for SIP, H.323, and content present by load balancers and media servers.

- **Chapter 5, "Working with Media Files":** Covers the architecture of the IOS-based IVR and HTTP Client with discussions pertaining to streaming, caching, and various types of HTTP connections and interactions.

- **Chapter 6, "Sizing, Networking, and Security Considerations":** Covers Sizing, Quality of Service, Network Latency, and Security considerations for Unified CVP.

- **Chapter 7, "Upgrading":** Provides guidance for Unified CVP upgrade strategies and methodologies including approaches to migration H.323 deployments to SIP.

- **Chapter 8, "Troubleshooting":** Provides a framework that you can use to isolate faults with a Unified CVP deployment, followed by continued discussion about how to determine device status and detailed troubleshooting steps for native and non-native components.

- **Chapter 9, "Virtualization":** Covers the history of virtualization and how it applies to Unified CVP deployments, followed by some best practice guidance for designing a virtualized Unified CVP deployment using UCS. This chapter concludes with some use cases for deployments using Unified ICM, Unified CVP, with Unified CCE agents.

Chapter 1

Introduction to Unified Customer Voice Portal

This chapter covers the following subjects:

- **The History of unified CVP:** In the beginning there was Internet Service Node (ISN).

- **What is Unified Customer Voice Portal?** This is not your Grandma's IVR.

- **What is VoiceXML?** How does CVP exploit VoiceXML?

- **Advantages of Deploying CVP:** What is the IVR problem?

The History of Unified CVP

In early 2000, Cisco initiated a new project with the code name YoYo. This project focused on the creation of a multi-media interactive voice response (IVR) solution using web technologies as its base. For many years businesses invested in the deployment and utilization of Time-Division Multiplex (TDM) or legacy-based IVRs from which customers would place a call to and interact with for automation of everyday business functions. These front-end IVRs handed calls off to legacy Automated Call Distribution (ACD) systems for further call routing and treatment.

Legacy IVR farms were typically implemented in a centralized fashion both from the call termination to the equipment placement. Because these farms were centralized, no capability existed to treat a call at the edge or the origination point of the call. This means that a call sourced at a coast or border location had to be taken back by a carrier and transferred to the correct location of the IVR farms for treatment. These transfers generated take back and transfer fees for the carriers and were a significant source of cost for contact centers; until technologies such as ISN, they would continue to plague legacy IVR/ACD deployments. Further implications from this centralized model arose from the inability of an IVR farm to transfer a call back to a different location for further treatment or agent routing. Typically, the IVR farms would be located close to the ACD systems, which would provide intelligent agent routing. However, when the call was placed on an ACD, that's where it would typically remain because the legacy ACD systems did not have call control mechanisms to initiate a network transfer or transfer the call to another IVR or ACD site. From a business continuity-perspective, this was a drawback to the legacy solutions. The ultimate deficiency was the inability of the legacy ACD and IVR systems to embrace and support convergence. These systems were usually implemented to support TDM technologies and would not permit the convergence of calls over Internet Protocol (IP).

Over the past 10 years, ISN has grown and established its place in the IVR market. As the supported features grew, the product name and version also changed. Internet Service Node soon became known as Customer Voice Portal and has more recently been branded as Unified Customer Voice Portal. This 10-year evolution also brought new protocol support such as Session Initiation Protocol (SIP), a slew of new integrations, and most important an established set of call flow models that quickly became a conversation piece for partners and customers working to implement the right call flow for their business.

Note   The terms interactive voice response (IVR) and Voice Response Unit (VRU) are essentially referencing the same element. Throughout this book these two terms are used interchangeably and reference either the same component or application leg of a call serviced by such a component.

What Is Unified Customer Voice Portal?

Unified Customer Voice Portal is both a product and a solution. Although this is quite accurate, the latter part of that statement is critical; it is a solution that in itself is significant to the entire contact center solution. All aspects of Unified CVP require a solution-level mindset whether it is designing for or troubleshooting a deployment. From a product-perspective, Unified CVP has specific software products delivered as part of the media kit purchased from Cisco. However, from a solution-perspective, Unified CVP relies on several key software components to provide a VoiceXML-based solution that addresses carrier class IVR and IP switching services via Voice over IP (VoIP) networks. Following is a list of the feature set included with Unified CVP:

- **IP Based IVR Services:** Unified CVP can perform prompt-and-collect or even advanced self-service applications interacting with CRM Databases. Automated Speech Recognition (ASR) and Text to Speech (TTS) can also be invoked using the Media Resource Control protocol (MRCP). Applications can be developed using Micro-Application technology with Cisco Unified Contact Center Enterprise software or created by using Unified CVP Call Studio development tools.

- **IP-based queuing treatment:** Using VoiceXML technologies, Unified CVP provides call treatment at the edge with personalized prompts and queue music and can even prioritize calls based on call data or CRM profiles.

- **Integration with Cisco Unified Contact Center:** Unified CVP integrates with the Cisco Unified Contact Center via a VRU Peripheral Gateway (PG). This integration enables the Unified Contact Center Enterprise (Unified CCE) to control VoIP switching, IVR services, and agent selection, enabling Unified CVP to intelligently connect the call to an available agent using its call control capabilities and the Real-Time Transport Protocol (RTP) for bearer traffic. This RTP stream connects via the ingress gateway to an agent selected by Unified CCE. However, for true VoIP implementations, the traditional Cisco Unified Communications Manager (CUCM) PG must be used and integrated with Unified CCE.

■ **IP-based call switching:** Using H.323 or SIP, Unified CVP can perform call routing and switching between IP endpoints. These endpoints are typically gateways integrated with legacy TDM networks such as the PSTN, ACDs, or PBXs. In addition, Cisco IOS-based H.323 gatekeepers, CUPS, and CUSP (an IOS-based proxy server) are supported to enable the centralization and management the dial plan.

Note   At the time of this writing, Unified CVP supports two different SIP proxy servers. The first is referred to as Cisco Unified Presence Server (CUPS) and is deployed via a server component that requires the existence of a Cisco Unified Communications Manager cluster. Because of the complexity and cost of this requirement, Cisco also released the support for the second type of proxy server named Cisco Unified Sip Proxy (CUSP), which is deployed via an IOS gateway module. Each have their advantages and caveats, as shown in Chapter 4, "Designing Unified CVP for High Availability."

■ Unified CVP Operations Console: Unified CVP has a web-based management portal for performing administrative and configuration tasks. This interface enables all components in the solution to be centrally managed by a single interface. In addition Cisco Contact Center Support Tools is also integrated with Unified CVP.

■ **VRU reporting:** Unified CVP provides a centralized database for access to real-time and historical reporting.

■ **VoiceXML custom application development:** Unified CVP provides a powerful IDE for building and deploying VoiceXML applications with Unified CVP branded Unified CVP Studio.

■ **Serviceability enhancements:** Starting with version 8.0.1 of Unified CVP, an integrated system CLI feature was added to enable administrative and maintenance-related queries to be normalized for all components in the solution. This basically means that a single **show run** command could produce the running configuration for disparate technologies by returning the equivalent of individually running the same command on all components in the Unified CVP solution. By integrating a Web Services Manager (WSM), tools such as the new Analysis Manager and system CLI can interact with this service. It enables WSM to normalize the request per technology and return the expected results to the user.

■ **Call control enhancements:** Beginning with version 8.0.1 of Unified CVP, several significant call control enhancements were introduced into the product. The following includes a few highlights:

  ■ Unified CVP is now location- and bandwidth-aware, meaning that issues in previous versions concerning Call Admission Control (CAC) have now been addressed. In addition, this integration with CUCM also enables Unified CVP to be aware of the edge location when transferring a call from an agent to a skill group queue.

  ■ Unified CVP now supports outbound dialing in the vein of supporting the new courtesy call back feature. This feature enables the Unified CVP to track calls that request a call back via a call studio application. When an agent is available, it reserves the agent and calls the originating caller back rather than keeping them in the queue while listening to music.

  ■ Post Call Survey is now supported. This enables a contact center customer to configure the platform to transfer the originating caller after the agent hangs up to a DNIS that enables a post call survey to be conducted.

  ■ SIP Server Groups are now supported. These replace the previously cumbersome configuration of local SRV files on individual call servers and instead enables the SRV configuration to occur via the Operations Console, which are then stored in the centralized configuration database. They are pushed to all Unified CVP Call Servers in the solution. In addition, a heartbeat mechanism was implemented to enable Unified CVP to verify the availability of an endpoint before a SIP INVITE is sent.

  ■ Trunk utilization metrics such as the status of memory, trunks, and CPU are sent to CVP not only for reporting but also for ICM reporting and scripting purposes. Scripts created in UCCE can now make intelligent routing decisions based on trunk metrics where prior this was not the case.

Note   Unified ICM refers to the Cisco Intelligent Contact Management suite of products that provide intelligent call routing to either legacy TDM- or IP-based endpoints. When Unified ICM is integrated with CUCM and agents are deployed as IP-based endpoints, the term Unified CCE is used to describe a Unified Contact Center Enterprise deployment with IP-based agents. Both Unified ICM and Unified CCE are used to describe these products and relationships throughout this book.

  ■ User To User Info (UUI) is applied for passing the ISDN data of an incoming call from the PSTN to ICM and from ICM to third-party ACDs in CVP transfers or disconnects. Unified CVP can now UUI in hex encoded format onto the outbound direction of CVP, such as to an agent or even an IVR.

  ■ Unified CVP now supports the Cisco IOS- based proxy branded as CUSP by Cisco. This enhancement enables CVP to support more than just a single proxy implementation for environments that do not have a CUCM implementation or a Cisco Unified Proxy Server (CUPS).

- Unified CVP now supports an additional media load balancer, ACE, and ACE load balancers are now supported along with the legacy Cisco Content Service Switch (CSS).

- Unified CVP now supports out-of-band DTMF using the SIP KPML DTMF method. Typically, CVP deployments using the SIP protocol use inband RFC2833 DTMF configuration on endpoints. However, some endpoints support only out-of-band DTMF, such as the Cisco 7985 video phone and CTI ports used in IPCC Mobile Agent deployments.

- Unified CVP now supports hookflash transfers using SIP. This feature permits a legacy PBX to frontend an ingress gateway but still enable hookflash signaling followed by DTMF to be sent via SIP to the PBX through the ingress gateway.

- In addition to flat G.711 codec support, version 8.0.1 of Unified CVP also supports the use of a flat G.729 codec. However, all prompts must also be converted to G.729. The term flat refers to the use of a single codec on all call legs with no call legs using different codecs. Future releases of Unified CVP enable the mixing of codecs for different call legs.

- **Virtualization Support:** The supported hardware for virtualization is the Cisco UCS B-Series and C-Series using VMware. This feature is covered later in the book in Chapter 9, "Virtualization."

What Is VoiceXML?

As mentioned earlier in this chapter, the creation of ISN and its eventual evolution into Unified CVP required the use of web-based technologies. A protocol had to exist to enable a Unified CVP call server the capability to send instructions to a voice browser or gateway where it could be rendered and executed providing call treatment. VoiceXML was the protocol used to do exactly this.

Voice eXtensible Markup Language, or VoiceXML, is a markup language designed for creating audio dialogs that feature synthesized speech, digitized audio, recognition of speech or dual-tone multifrequency (DTMF) key input, and recording of spoken input. It is a common language for content providers, tool providers, and platform providers to promote service portability across implementation platforms. With a syntax similar to HTML, VoiceXML is easy to use for simple interactions. It provides language features to support complex IVR dialogs while at the same time shields the application developer from low-level, platform-specific IVR and call control details.

VoiceXML programs are rendered (or executed) by a VoiceXML browser; much like an HTML program is rendered via an Internet browser (such as Internet Explorer). A Cisco Voice Gateway (or router) can provide the VoiceXML browser function. For small deployments, the functions of the Ingress Voice Gateway and VoiceXML Gateway are typically deployed in the same router. The Cisco IOS VoiceXML Gateway provides both gateway and VoiceXML browser functions.

In the most simple call-processing scenario, a new call arrives, and the gateway matches a dial peer to an available VoiceXML gateway port. The VoiceXML gateway port represents a VoIP endpoint and can be logically thought of as a voice response unit (VRU) port. Upon arrival of the new call, the VoiceXML gateway (that is, the VRU) sends an HTTP request to a Cisco Unified CVP VoiceXML Server for instruction. The URL contained in the HTTP request correlates to a specific VoiceXML doc. In response to the HTTP request, the Unified CVP VoiceXML Server sends the requested, dynamically generated VoiceXML doc to the VoiceXML gateway (that is, the voice browser) to be rendered. A typical VoiceXML doc is short and prompts the caller for some input and then includes the results in a new HTTP request that redirects the caller to another URL and VoiceXML doc. Because a typical call requires numerous prompts and caller inputs, numerous VoiceXML documents need to be rendered and a large number of possible paths are made through these VoiceXML documents. Figure 1-1 illustrates this process with Unified CVP in comprehensive mode using SIP as the call control protocol.

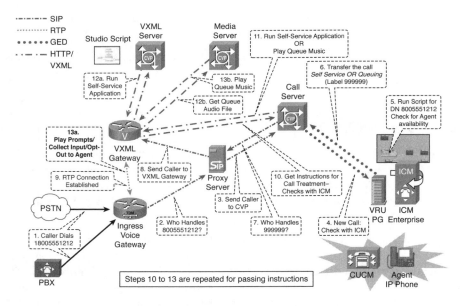

Figure 1-1 *Unified CVP Comprehensive Call Processing*

To logically link the many different VoiceXML documents that might need to be rendered and to simplify the task of creating VoiceXML documents, a graphical scripting tool is often used to enable the IVR service developer to easily develop complete IVR services with conditional logic and customer relationship management (CRM) database integration. Cisco Unified Call Studio is one such scripting tool. The Cisco Unified CVP VoiceXML Server can execute scripts developed with Cisco Unified Call Studio. Both were designed to work with Cisco Unified CVP Server, Cisco Voice Gateways, Cisco VoiceXML Gateways, CUCM, Cisco Unified Contact Center, and Cisco VoIP-enabled LAN/WAN.1

Advantages of Deploying Unified CVP

To fully appreciate the advantages of deploying Unified CVP, you should first revisit and outline a topic coined the "IVR Problem."

Legacy PBX/ACDs, ands TDM-based IVR solutions, are limited by proprietary technology. As mentioned earlier, TDM-based IVRs tend to be site-specific and are deployed in IVR farms with little to no "edge" design or treatment capability. Furthermore, no concept of centralized call control is in these legacy systems. TDM-based IVRs typically rely on the voice carrier's capability around take back and transfers incurring costs on a call-by-call basis. In addition, after the transfer has left the IVR, call control is lost to the PBX/ACD, causing further loss in call continuity around reporting. Finally, most if not all voice systems deployed today support convergence. Technologies that do not support the concept of convergence create significant operational and scalability challenges for businesses looking to use their bandwidth.

Unified CVP addresses all these shortcomings simply by the nature in which it was designed. It was created around open architectures such as web-based VoiceXML and uses a converged IP infrastructure for its bearer and nonbearer traffic. Because VoiceXML is used as an instruction vehicle, Unified CVP can furnish enterprise edge IVR treatment and further reduce the transport costs with a legacy centralized solution. Because Unified CVP also provides centralized call control, it can also accommodate IP switching services to enable a call to be transferred using the IP network, which affords significant flexibility and cost-savings by eliminating expensive carrier take back and transfer fees. Cradle-to-grave reporting is also achieved by Unified CVP with its integration with Cisco Intelligent Contact Management (ICM) software.

Chapter 2, "Unified CVP Architecture Overview," demonstrates how the Unified CVP architecture provides excellent scalability to meet business needs.

Summary

Unified CVP has evolved over the past 10 years to address several shortcomings of legacy IVR and ACD systems. Unified CVP is both a product and a solution. Understanding the solution component of Unified CVP is the focus of this book.

By understanding the problem for which Unified CVP was created to solve, it should be a simple mental transition to comprehend why and how its architecture resolved these issues. Although there have been quite a few releases of Unified CVP over the past ten years, this book focuses on the current major release of 8.x and provides solution-level guidance on the design and implementation process for a scalable 8.x Unified CVP solution.

Although this book provides design, configuration, and sizing examples where appropriate, it should not be considered as a replacement for the design, configuration, and administration guides for Unified CVP produced by Cisco and available at cisco.com. Furthermore, this book covers areas pertaining to Unified CVP that are not well understood or documented by the current Cisco documentation. This book expands on those topics where appropriate in an attempt to help the reader garnish a deeper understanding of how this technology works and cover topics found only in tribal knowledge or on the rarely visited dirt roads.

Reference

1. Cisco Documentation, *Cisco Unified Customer Voice Portal(CVP) 8.x Solution Reference Network Design (SRND)*, 2010: 1–2.

Recommended Reading and Resources

Cisco Documentation, *Cisco Unified Customer Voice Portal (CVP) 8.x Solution Reference Network Design (SRND)*, http://www.cisco.com/en/US/docs/voice_ip_comm/cust_contact/contact_center/customer_voice_portal/srnd/8x/cvp8xsrnd.pdf.

Schulzrinne, H. RFC 2388, "RTP Payload for DTMF Digits, Telephony Tones and Telephony Signals," http://tools.ietf.org/html/rfc2833, May 2000.

Chapter 2

Unified CVP
Architecture Overview

This chapter covers the following subjects:

- **Unified CVP functional deployment models:** Brief introduction to these models and components used in each.

- **Unified CVP core components:** Call Server, VXML Server, Reporting Server, Operations Console Server, and Cisco Unified Call Studio.

- **Unified CVP solution-related components:** IOS Devices, Cisco Unified Intelligent Contact Management (ICM), Cisco Unified Communications Manager, SIP Proxy Servers, content load balancers, and third-party servers.

- **Unified CVP licensing:** Core component licensing.

What Are the Unified CVP Functional Deployment Models?

A basic understanding of the functional deployment models should be established because they are referenced in this chapter. Following is a list and brief definition of each Unified CVP Functional Deployment model:

- **Standalone:** Deployed to accomplish self-service IVR requirements only, this model does not invoke any call control and or have integration with Unified ICM or CCE for queuing or call delivery to available agents. It provides a standalone VRU implementation for CVP.

- **Call Director:** Mostly deployed to accomplish IP switching services only. This model is useful if you want to accomplish the following:

  - Only interested in using Unified CVP to provide Unified ICME with VoIP call switching

  - Prompt/collect to be performed by third-party VRUs and ACDs

- Not interested in using a Unified CVP VoiceXML Server for delivering custom VXML applications

- **Comprehensive:** As the name indicates, this is the most comprehensive deployment model providing IVR services, queue treatment, and IP switching services. This model is useful if you want to accomplish the following:

  - Use Unified CVP to provide Unified ICME or CCE with VoIP call switching capabilities.

  - Use Unified CVP to provide Unified ICME or CCE with VRU services, which include integrated self-service applications, queuing, and initial prompt and collect.

  - Support Video integrations for video IVR, video queuing, and video agent capabilities. Sometimes the video integration is referred to as a separate deployment model called Basic Video. However, because the Basic Video call flow is identical to Comprehensive using Voice (with the only difference being the use of video endpoints in place of voice), it is considered part of the comprehensive deployment model.

  - Deploying and supporting the option Unified CVP VoiceXML Server component.

  - Deploying and supporting the integration to optional ASR/TTS servers for prompting and collecting using Automatic Speech Recognition (ASR) or Text to Speech (TTS).

- **VRU-only:** Provides IVR services, queuing treatment, and switching for SS7/IN PSTN endpoints. This model relies on the PSTN to transfer calls between call termination endpoints. It is useful if you want to accomplish the following.[1]

  - Use Unified CVP to provide Unified ICME or CCE with VRU services, which would include integrated self-service applications and initial prompt and collect.

  - Do not want to use Unified CVP for call switching.

  - Deploying and supporting the option Unified CVP VoiceXML Server component.

  - Deploying and supporting the integration to optional ASR/TTS servers for prompting and collecting using Automatic Speech Recognition or Text to Speech.

Note   Chapter 3, "Functional Deployment Models and Call Flows," examines the models in more detail.

Unified CVP Solution Overview

As an introduction to the Unified CVP solution set, begin with an illustration of the products, either native or non-native to Unified CVP that interact in the overall solution. Figure 2-1 provides a high-level diagram of these relationships.

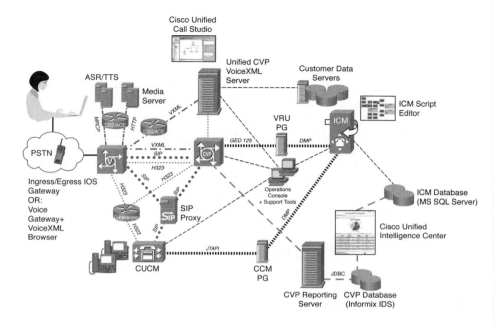

Figure 2-1 *CVP Solution Overview*

Native Unified CVP components consist of the following:

■ CVP Call Servers

■ CVP VoiceXML Servers

■ CVP Reporting Servers

■ Operations Console Servers

■ CVP Call Studio

They are referenced as native because they are included in Unified CVP product set. Later in this chapter each native component is discussed in detail prior to a discussion about non-native components.

Non-native components consist of the following:

■ IOS devices

■ SIP Proxies

■ Gatekeepers

■ Cisco Intelligent Contact Management (ICM)

■ Cisco Unified Communication Managers

- Media Servers

- Content load balancers such as CSS and ACE

- Third-party server integration for features such as ASR and TTS

Figure 2-1 illustrates several communication protocols used between different native and non-native components. Depending on the state of the call and what is commonly referred to as the *leg of the call*, certain protocols might or might not be engaged. In addition, not all the non-native components are required for the solution to work. Depending on customer requirements for load balancing, centralized dial plans, and high availability, different non-native components might or might not exist. For example, the use of a content load balancer such as the Cisco CSS or ACE devices might not be a required component to the solution. Whether it exists depends on the load balancing strategy required for Media Servers, which have the responsibility to provide media to calls during treatment. In later chapters strategies around high availability for native and non-native components are provided.

Unified CVP Architecture

Prior to a deep dive on the native and non-native components for Unified CVP, take a closer look at the overall architecture of Unified CVP for its native components. Figure 2-2 provides a detailed illustration of how native components are architected and their interaction with non-native components.

The CVP VXML Server and CVP Call Server do not need to be standalone installations. It is quite common for these components to be co-resident and running on the same server. Figure 2-2 breaks them out as separate servers to illustrate their relationship both with native and non-native components. The Message Bus is a critical vehicle that moves messages between the native components.

Note   The call legs of a Unified CVP call are commonly referred to as "switch" and "VRU" or "Application" legs. The switch leg of a call is defined by the originating call leg from the Ingress Gateway and its termination to the CVP Call Server. This leg of the call uses call control protocols such as SIP and H.323 to set the call up and enable the CVP Call Server to gain call control. Some deployment models use the switch leg differently depending on what role the CVP Call Server plays in that particular model. However, understanding the basic concept of a call's switch leg is critical to all elements of the Unified CVP solution.

After the call connects to the CVP Call Server and instructions have been received on what to do with the call, the VRU or application leg of the call is initiated. The VRU leg is where the VoiceXML instructions are sent to the IOS VXML Gateway either as a result of a micro-application running on ICM or a studio application served up by the CVP VXML Server. The switch and VRU legs of a call usually exist in parallel, each one performing either call control responsibilities or call treatment instructions, respectively. When call treatment has completed and the call is ready to be transferred to an agent or other endpoint, the VRU leg of the call is interrupted by the CVP Call Server, and the switch leg completes the transfer based on instructions from ICM or the result of a studio application.

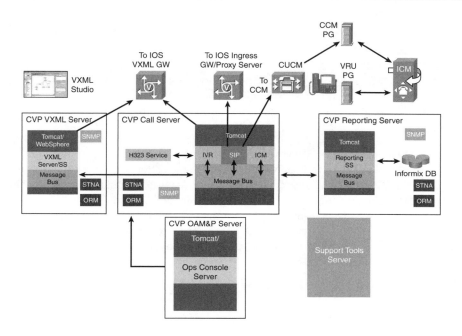

Figure 2-2   *Unified CVP Architecture*

For the CVP Call Server, it participates in both the switch and VRU legs of the call. For the switch leg, it communicates with the IOS Ingress Gateway, either a gatekeeper or a proxy server (depending on your call control protocol) or router, and even a Call Manager, depending on what is required during the switch leg. In addition the CVP Call Server participates with the IOS VXML gateway using its built-in IOS Voice Browser to both terminate the switch leg of the call and begin the VRU leg of the call for treatment. In situations in which micro-applications are built in ICM and are used to provide CVP with instructions for either call treatment on the IOS VXML gateway or direction on where to kick off an external VXML application on the CVP VXML server, the CVP Call Server uses the ICM subsystem to interact with an ICM Peripheral Gateway or PG using a VRU PIM, which communicates directly with ICM. This PG and its software-based VRU PIM is how the CVP Call Server requests and receives instructions from ICM. These instructions can be in the form of a label or a dialed number (DN) for which the call should be transferred to, or they can be instructions for call treatment.

Tip   The creation of the micro-applications required to direct CVP to perform certain call control functions such as transfers and so on and call treatment functions that include playing media files, collecting DTMF, and such live in either an ICM script maintained by the ICM script editor or are built via the Unified Call Studio application and hosted by the CVP VoiceXML Server. CVP does not have a scripting engine. It simply asks ICM for instructions on what its next move should be. This is why the Comprehensive call flow model for CVP uses ICM heavily for scripting logic acts as the brain of the operation.

In the CVP Self-Service call flow model, a CVP Call Studio application is invoked directly from the IOS Voice Browser during the switch leg of the call; Unified CVP participates only as a VoiceXML Server during the VRU leg of the call providing a Self-Service application developed with Cisco Unified Call Studio and not the ICM script editor. In the next chapter the functional deployment models are discussed in greater detail.

The CVP VoiceXML Server is invoked if during the VRU leg of a call Unified CVP receives instructions from Unified ICM via a micro-application to invoke a studio application. The CVP VoiceXML Server delivers the Studio application and renders its logic into VoiceXML instruction documents that are then sent to and executed by the Cisco VoiceXML Gateway using its built-in Voice Browser capabilities. The deployment models discussed earlier in this chapter determine how and which component is invoked. However, a majority of this discussion is focused around the self-service and comprehensive models.

The Operations Console server provides a centralized web management interface for managing and configuring all elements in the Unified CVP solution. A Unified CVP deployment can have only one server configured as an Operations Console, and typically this is an additional role to the CVP Call Server. So in general, a complete solution may have multiple Reporting Servers, Call Servers, and VoiceXML Servers but only one Operations Console Server. The support ratio should be x (VoiceXML server) connected to y (Call Server) connected to z (Reporting server), where x > y > z with one Operations Console and one Support Tools. The Support Tools Server is also a shared component with Unified ICM.

The next few sections cover the native components in the Unified CVP solution in much greater detail. The term *native* refers to components that are truly core to the CVP solution and are not optional for its operation. Covered later in this chapter are the non-native components that are mostly optional depending on the deployment model exercised and the customer's solution requirements.

Call Server

Figure 2-3 provides a detailed look at the Call Server, its subsystems, and how it interacts with other native and non-native Unified CVP components.

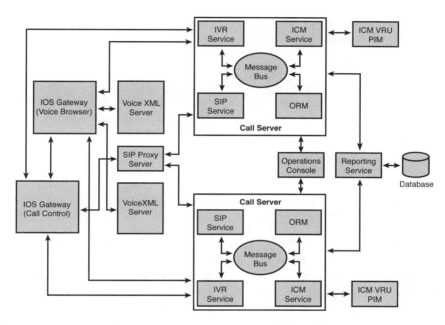

Figure 2-3   *Unified CVP Call Server Subsystem Relationships*

SIP Service

The SIP service communicates with a SIP proxy whether it is a Cisco Unified Presence Server (CUPS) or the IOS-based Cisco Unified SIP Proxy for dial plan resolution (refer to Figure 2-3). However, the SIP service does not need to communicate via a SIP Proxy; the Call Server supports non-proxy configurations using static routes. In addition, the SIP service also communicates with Ingress Gateways and Unified Communications Manager SIP Trunks. The SIP service implements a Back-to-Back User Agent (B2BUA) that accepts SIP invite messages from other SIP components and typically directs them to an available VoiceXML Gateway for call termination. When the Call Server has completed the call setup, the Call Server continues to handle subsequent call control requirements. Although the Call Server does have call control, this service does not touch or see any of the RTP or bearer traffic. The SIP service is also fully integrated with the ICM service via the Message Bus. This integration enables the SIP service to request routing instructions via the ICM service and permits the ICM service to initiate subsequent call control requests to perform transfers of calls from a queue to an agent or between agents. As detailed in Chapter 4, "Designing Unified CVP for High Availability," the differences between the supported SIP Proxy servers, CUPS, and CUSP are compared and contrasted against each other and, using static routes, are directly configured on the Unified CVP call servers, providing advantages and disadvantages to each approach.

ICM Service

The ICM service directly communicates with a VRU PIM located on the ICMPG and is responsible for communications between the Unified CVP components and ICM (refer to Figure 2-3). The ICM service sends and receives messages on behalf of the SIP service, and the IVR service to PIM software process uses the GED-125 protocol. This protocol enables the Call Server to interact with ICM in a manner similar to how legacy ACDs interacted with ICM before integrations with Unified CVP or ISN existed. The ICM service is responsible for all communication between Unified CVP components and Unified Intelligent Contact Management Enterprise (ICME).[2]

IVR Service

The IVR service functions as part of the VRU leg of the call (refer to Figure 2-3). Calls are provided to this service via the SIP service, which results in a micro-application being executed (Comprehensive Call Model) from Unified ICM. This service then produces VoiceXML pages based on the results of the micro-application and are sent to the Cisco VoiceXML Gateway for execution via its built-in Voice Browser. In addition, a micro-application can be configured to instruct the IVR service to generate a special VoiceXML page, which informs the Cisco VoiceXML Gateway to invoke an application hosted by a CVP VoiceXML Server. These types of applications are usually developed using the Unified Call Studio application. The IVR service also plays a significant role in implementing Unified CVP's native failover mechanism. For media servers, ASR/TTS Servers, and VoiceXML Servers, the IVR service orchestrates retries and failover attempts between these servers and the Cisco VoiceXML Gateway. However, this mechanism is only available when deploying CVP in the Comprehensive call flow model because other models do not use the IVR service. For example, the Self-Service call flow model does not interact with the IVR service. It does not enable the IVR service to perform retry and failover attempts when certain servers cannot be contacted by the Cisco VoiceXML Gateway. As detailed in Chapter 4, this feature is key to designing and deploying a content load-balancing strategy for CVP across geographically distinct data centers.

Note All CVP Services are not represented as Windows Services. For example, the SIP, ICM, and IVR CVP subsystems run as part of one Windows service named Cisco CVP Call Server. The H.323 Service known previously as the CVP Voice Browser is also a Windows service. Keep this in mind as you look at the Windows Services mmc console. There is not a one-to-one relationship with the CVP subsystem services and Windows services.

H.323 Service

Previous versions of CVP called this service the CVP Voice Browser, and although it is not shown in Figure 2-3, it still exists in Unified CVP 8.x mostly to support migrations to SIP. This service interacts with the IVR service to relay call arrival, departure, and transfer instructions between it and other H.323 components.[3]

Warning   H.323 protocol supported in Unified CVP 8.x exists only for upgrades from previous versions of CVP. Greenfield deployments of Unified CVP 8.x do not support the use of the H.323 protocol, and it is highly probable that the next major releases of CVP will not have any H.323 support. The underlining reason for this departure falls into two major areas. First, the standards are clearly moving away from H.323 to SIP. Secondly, the capability to maintain the support for two voice protocols within the Unified CVP footprint considering all the solution features and integrations is a monstrous feat. If your enterprise is currently using H.323, you should consider migrating to SIP sooner rather than later.

Unified CVP VoiceXML Server

Figure 2-4 illustrates the placement of this component for the call server. Although Figure 2-4 represents separate servers, the VoiceXML Server can be installed as co-resident with the Call Server. Applications are built using the Unified Call Studio application, which is then deployed onto the VoiceXML Server. The Voice Browser located on the Cisco VoiceXML Gateway accesses these hosted applications, which causes the Unified CVP VoiceXML Server to execute these complex IVR applications by exchanging VoiceXML pages.

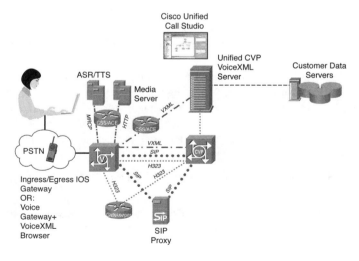

Figure 2-4   *CVP VoiceXML Server and Studio*

In the Unified CVP comprehensive call model, these VoiceXML studio applications are invoked on an as-needed basis by a special Micro-Application executed from within the Unified ICM routing script. In addition to the comprehensive model, the VoiceXML Web Server can also be deployed in a standalone configuration, which does not include any Unified ICM components. In this model, applications are invoked by calls arriving directly on the Cisco VoiceXML Gateways, invoking a dial-peer that kicks off a set of self-service TCL scripts, which instructs the gateway to fetch and process the hosted application on the VoiceXML Server.

Unified Call Studio (Formerly Unified CVP VoiceXML Studio)

As shown in Figure 2-4, Unified Call Studio is an integrated development environment (IDE) for the creation and deployment of VoiceXML applications with Unified CVP. It is based on the open source Eclipse framework that provides advanced drag and drop Rapid Application Development (RAD) with graphical editing features. In addition, custom plug-ins can be developed and used within studio applications to further expand the application's capability to interact with other services within the network. Unified Call Studio is used as an offline tool with the capacity to compile and deploy consolidated applications to the VoiceXML Server for hosting and delivery to Cisco VoiceXML Gateways. Most customers designate multiple workstations for the deployment of Unified Call Studio and the development and modifications of VoiceXML applications.

Unified CVP Reporting Server

Figure 2-5 continues to build on Figure 2-4 by showing the Reporting Server placement in the Unified CVP solution.

The Reporting Server receives data from the IVR Server, the SIP service (if used), and the VoiceXML Server. However, the Reporting Server depends on the Call Server to receive call records. In Standalone Unified CVP VoiceXML Server deployments, one Call Server is needed per Reporting Server. The Reporting Server must be local to the Call Servers and VoiceXML Servers that it is accommodating. Deploying the Reporting Server at a remote location across the WAN is not supported; therefore, multiple Reporting servers should be used and placed at each site when Call Servers and VoiceXML Servers exist at multiple locations. Database administration and maintenance activities such as backups and purging are accomplished using the Unified CVP Operations Console Server.[4]

The following changes to the Reporting Server were added in release 8.0.1 of Unified CVP:

■ **Increase in database sizes:** Although the size for the small (lab) database remained the same, the medium and large database sizes were increased, as shown in Table 2-1.

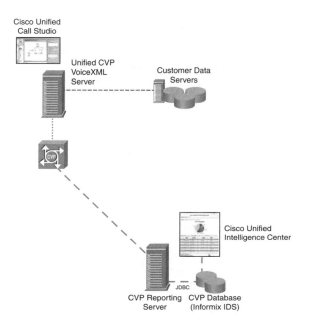

Figure 2-5   *Unified CVP Reporting Server Relationship*

■ **Data modeling changes:** You can find the complete and updated schema for the reporting database in the *Reporting Guide for Cisco Unified Customer Voice Portal*, May 2010, listed in the "References" and "Recommended Reading and Resources" sections at the end of this chapter.

■ **Simplified installation and upgrade:** After running the CVP Reporting Server installer, prior to CVP 8.0(1) end users had to run two batch files, ReportingRunAsInformix.bat and ReportingRunAsCVPDBAdmin.bat (in that order). As of 8.0(1), users are not required to run the ReportingRunAsCVPDBADMIN script; they can run a new script named CVP_Database_Config.bat file. This script can handle either an install or an upgrade. An upgrade to the reporting server can be made from CVP 4 or CVP 7.

Table 2-1   *Unified CVP Reporting Server Database Sizing*

Size	Previous Version Size	CVP 8.x Size
Small	2 G	2 G
Medium	50 G	100 G
Large	100 G	200 G

Unified CVP Operations Console Server (Operations Console)

Figure 2-6 continues to build on Figure 2-5 by showing how the Operations Console Server is injected into the solution and communicates to native and non-native components.

Figure 2-6   *Operations Console Server*

The Operations Console Server provides a web-based dashboard for the management and configuration of all components in the Unified CVP solution. Only one Operations Console Server is necessary per Unified CVP deployment, and it is a required component. The Operations Console Server must be run on a separate physical machine or virtually if Cisco Unified Computing System is deployed from other Unified CVP devices. However, beginning with Unified CVP 8.0(1), it can be co-resident with Support Tools. The Operations Console provides a direct link to Support Tools, which collects diagnostic and instrumentation content for many of the solution components.

The Operations Console can be configured with a map of the deployed solution network. This map and subsequent configurations of the solution components are stored locally on the server and can be backed up with off-the-shelf backup tools. Administrators can access the configuration of the solution via a browser-based interface, as illustrated in Figure 2-7.

This interface can display two views for configuration parameters for solution components. The first view is a runtime view, which shows the status of all configuration parameters as the solution components are currently using them. The second view is an offline view, which illustrates the configuration parameters as they are stored in the Operations Console Server's database and will be deployed to a component the next time a Save and Deploy operation is executed. This offline feature enables configuration parameters to be updated or preconfigured even if the solution component does not exist or is offline. When the solution component comes back online or is installed, without its services running, an administrator can deploy these settings to the component. When the services for that component are active, the configuration parameters are applied.

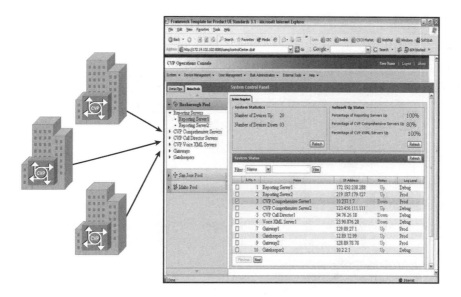

Figure 2-7   *Web Interface of the Operations Console*

> **Caution**   The Operations Console Server is not a redundant solution component. You cannot deploy more than one, nor can its content be duplicated within a deployment. Backups of the configuration database should be performed regularly or whenever changes are made.[5]

Unified CVP Non-Native Solution Components

Most of this chapter has focused on the Unified CVP architecture from a native component perspective, meaning components that are natively part of the Unified CVP solution. The next few sections target the solution components that are not native to the Unified CVP solution with most being optional to a deployment. However, their significance in the solution depends on the deployment model exercised and the customer requirements around the solution's scalability and availability. In either case, a solid understanding of these non-native components is critical in connecting the dots for future chapters. Non-native solution components consist of the following:

- Cisco Ingress Voice Gateway (TDM or CUBE)

- Cisco VoiceXML Gateway (Voice Browser)

- Cisco Egress Gateway

- Video Endpoints

- Cisco Unified Communication Manager (CUCM)

- Cisco Unified Contact Center Enterprise (Unified CCE)

- Cisco Gatekeeper

- Cisco SIP Proxy (CUPS and CUSP)

- Domain Naming Server (DNS)

- Cisco Content Load Balancers (CSS and ACE)

- Third Party Media Servers (IIS and Apache)

- Third Party Automatic Speech Recognition (ASR) and Text-to-Speech (TTS) Servers

Cisco Ingress Voice Gateway

Figure 2-8 introduces the Cisco Ingress, Egress, and Cisco VoiceXML Gateways into the solution.

The Cisco Ingress Voice Gateway terminates an incoming call from the PSTN and provides a pivot point between TDM/SIP Services and VoIP using H.323, SIP, or MGCP. This gateway currently supports H.323 and SIP. Media Gateway Control Protocol or MGCP can be supported as long as the gateway is registered with a Cisco Unified Call Manager. This is mostly because the Call Server for Unified CVP does not support MGCP natively, and using this protocol has implications on CVP's capability to gain and maintain call control. Cisco Unified Border Element (CUBE) implementations, previously known as IP-to-IP Gateway, are also supported on this gateway to support SIP trunking from the service provider in place of TDM technologies. It enables customers to maximize their connection options provided by today's carrier networks. Some Unified CVP deployment models enable the Ingress Gateway to also function as a Cisco VoiceXML Gateway (refer to Figure 2-8). However, this model is more typical in the branch deployment model than in the centralized model, where standalone VoiceXML routers are usually deployed in a centralized farm for call treatment. Combining the Ingress and VoiceXML roles into a single router is a supported and common configuration option. However this has sizing and other survivability implications on the solution. For a current list of supported Ingress, Egress, or Cisco VoiceXML Gateways, always consult the *Hardware and System*

Software Specifications for Cisco Unified CVP (formerly called the *Bill of Materials*) available on Cisco.com.[6]

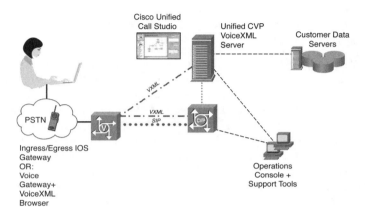

Figure 2-8   *(Non-Native) Cisco Ingress, Egress, and Cisco VoiceXML Gateways*

Note   Previous versions of Unified CVP referred to a document that was coined the "Bill of Materials" for CVP. Each version of Unified CVP was released with an updated version of this Bill of Materials that listed the hardware and software compatibility guidelines for IOS devices and third-party hardware and software for the respective release of Unified CVP. The term Bill of Materials was and still is confusing because it uses a term that most integration partners associate to a customer's Bill of Materials or items that they have purchased for a solution. Do not get the usage of these two terms confused: One is a compatibility document generated by Cisco, and the other relates to a customer purchased list of components. Always make sure before generating a customer Bill of Materials for acquisition that the Cisco Hardware and System Software Specifications guide for CVP is consulted to ensure the correct hardware and software components are purchased.

Cisco VoiceXML Gateway

The Cisco VoiceXML Gateway (refer to Figure 2-8) hosts the Cisco IOS Voice Browser. Chapter 1, "Introduction to Unified CVP," defines VoiceXML and indicates that there is a Voice Browser component that acts in a similar fashion as a web browser for its interpretation of VoiceXML commands sent in a VoiceXML document from a VXML Server. The IOS-based Voice Browser found in the Cisco VoiceXML Gateway performs this function during the VRU leg of a call. After it executes the VoiceXML instructions, it returns the results to the Unified CVP Call Server controlling application script asking for further instructions. This conversation continues until either the call is transferred to an endpoint such as an agent or the caller hangs up.

The Cisco VoiceXML Gateway can be installed co-resident with the Ingress Gateway component, but doing so reduces the overall capacity of both components. This type of deployment is usually found in a branch model where there is a need to perform edge queuing and call treatment. In addition, the Cisco VoiceXML Gateway can be installed as a standalone router. This greatly increases the number of calls that it can treat. This type of deployment is usually found in a centralized model where potentially Unified CVP calls are sharing an Ingress Gateway infrastructure where not all calls are for Unified CVP, but many additional calls could be for just plain old voice traffic. This model also enables a much cleaner separation of switch and VRU traffic and enables easier troubleshooting and support. Unless the Cisco VoiceXML Gateway is deployed in a co-resident mode with an Ingress Gateway, it does not require any TDM hardware because VoiceXML instructions use the WAN and LAN to directly deliver its instructions to the LAN interface on the router.

The Cisco VoiceXML Gateway has the capability to play .WAVeform Audio Format (wav) files stored in the router's flash memory or on a third-party media server. When prompts are retrieved from a third-party media server, they are cached by the router to reduce WAN bandwidth consumption and prevent poor voice play back quality. The VoiceXML document provided to the Cisco IOS Voice Browser via Unified CVP and CCE have pointers embedded in the instructions on where to locate the media server. These pointers can point directly to a media server URL, or they can point to an ASR/TSS server. The Cisco VoiceXML Gateway is also responsible for interacting with ASR and TTS servers via the MRCP protocol.

Tip   When considering which Cisco VoiceXML Gateway to deploy and their capacity in either standalone or co-resident mode, always consult the *Hardware and System Software Specifications for Cisco Unified CVP*, (formerly called the *Bill of Materials*) available on CCO at Cisco.com.

Cisco Egress Gateway

In the Unified CVP solution, the Egress Voice Gateway is typically used during transfers to the PSTN or legacy ACDs and IVRs. Although there is an RTP stream terminating on the egress gateway, which commonly originates from the Ingress Gateway ports, the signaling stream logic is typically handled by a Unified CVP server, depending on the call flow model used. This call control stream enables Unified CVP to work closely with Unified CCE to control and handle transfers to legacy systems. Refer to Figure 2-8 to see this egress gateway as co-resident with the ingress and Cisco VoiceXML Gateway.

However, this might make sense only in branch deployments. Larger centralized deployments tend to support either ingress/egress routers with standalone Cisco VoiceXML Gateways or standalone Ingress, Egress, and Cisco VoiceXML Gateways. This is all dependent on the customer requirements, budget, and call volume.

Video Endpoints

Although video endpoints are supported as part of the Unified CVP solution, adoption and use of video with Unified CVP has been sluggish and nearly non-existent. This could be because of other, more popular multichannel options, such as web co-browsing, chat, and email. However for sake of reference and completeness, Unified CVP does support basic video endpoints such as the following:

■ Cisco Unified IP Phone

■ Cisco Unified Video Advantage

■ Cisco TelePresence

SIP Proxy

To further build out the solution overview illustration, the SIP proxy component is added. Figure 2-9 shows the placement of the SIP Proxy within the Unified CVP solution.

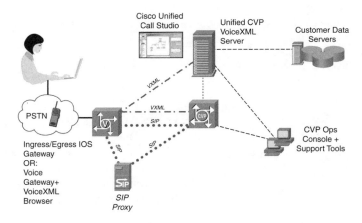

Figure 2-9   *(Non-Native) SIP Proxy*

The SIP Proxy is the component that routes individual SIP messages among SIP endpoints. It plays a key role in accomplishing high-availability requirements pertaining to call switching, balancing, and failover as covered in Chapter 4. Several SIP endpoints are supported, and the SIP proxy is responsible for load balancing and providing failover among these endpoints. With release 8.0(1) of Unified CVP, two different proxy servers are supported: Cisco Unified Presence Server (CUPS) and an IOS-based SIP proxy server named Cisco Unified SIP Proxy (CUSP). CUPS require the installation of a Cisco Unified Communications Manager Cluster (CUCM) for a CUPS server to be installed. This requirement can create additional costs and overhead for the overall solution, especially in deployment models where CUCM is not used or required. Because CUSP is IOS-based and runs on a Cisco gateway, its implementation has a much smaller footprint and greatly reduces the operational overhead of managing a SIP proxy server farm. In general, CUSP costs less to deploy than CUPS.

Note   Previous versions of CUSP such as 1.1.x depended entirely on an IOS-based CLI for configuration. This interface was difficult to navigate and had a substantial learning curve. However, with the current version of CUSP, 8.5, a Graphical User Interface (GUI) has been provided along with the old CLI interface for configuring CUSP. This GUI interface has reduced the learning curve for CUSP implementations. Most Unified CVP deployments use the CUSP proxy simply because of its smaller footprint and ease of placement. You can find the documentation for the newer version of CUSP on Cisco.com or via the following links:

■   **CLI Configuration Guide for Cisco Unified SIP Proxy Release 8.5:**
    http://www.cisco.com/en/US/docs/voice_ip_comm/cusp/rel8_5/cli_config/cusp_cli_
    config.html

■   **GUI Configuration Guide for Cisco Unified SIP Proxy Release 8.5:**
    http://www.cisco.com/en/US/docs/voice_ip_comm/cusp/rel8_5/OLH/gui_config_
    olh.html

Finally, at the time this was written, previous versions of CUSP stopped at version 1.1.4, whereas the newer version has been released as 8.5. This does not mean there are seven major releases between version 1.1.4 and 8.5. For Unified CVP, Cisco has bypassed major release numbers in the past to normalize the version of the software with other non-native components. If you recall, Unified CVP started out and moved through releases as 1.x, 2.x, 3.x, 4.x, 7.x, and now 8.x, so don't be fooled by the gaps in release number for native and non-native components.

Following are the benefits of implementing a SIP proxy component into the Unified CVP solution:

■   To provide load balancing and sharing, priority and weight attributes can be configured for SIP routes placed into the SIP Proxy Server for Unified CVP components.

- If one of the supported SIP Proxy Servers already exists in your current SIP network, Unified CVP and its respective components can simply be added to this infrastructure as an additional SIP endpoint.

- Centralized dial plan management can be achieved by implementing a SIP Proxy Server. Without using a SIP Proxy Server, each Unified CVP SIP component must be independently configured to support the overall SIP dial plan.

- If a Cisco Unified Presence Server is chosen as the SIP Proxy Server, an enterprise is better positioned to take advantage of Presence as a compliment to Unified CVP.[7]

Gatekeeper

As mentioned earlier in this chapter, the support for the H.323 protocol is diminishing with each new release of Unified CVP. However, sections throughout this book continue to touch briefly on this subject. As shown in Figure 2-10, the Gatekeeper is to H.323 call flows as the SIP Proxy Server is to SIP call flows.

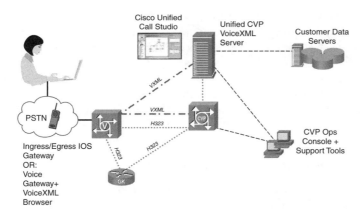

Figure 2-10 *(Non-Native) H.323 Gatekeeper*

The Gatekeeper is critical in achieving high-availability designs in the H.323 protocol arena. For Unified CVP, it is used only for designs that use H.323 for call control. The Gatekeeper provides directory lookup services, load balancing, and even failover capabilities for clustered Gatekeepers. However, the Gatekeeper is different than a SIP Proxy in the sense that control messages do not pass through it. It is more of a request/response implementation. In the Unified CVP solution, Gatekeepers provide dialed number mapping, load balance H.323 call requests, and final agent dialed number resolution for completing transfers to agents. Gatekeepers support the following failover mechanisms:

■ **Hot Standby Routing Protocol (HSRP):** This mechanism enables two Gatekeepers to share a virtual IP address. One Gatekeeper can actively respond to requests on this virtual IP address while the second Gatekeeper is in standby mode waiting to preempt or assume the active virtual IP address if the first Gatekeeper were to fail. This mechanism does not enable any call requests to be passed to the passive Gatekeeper, leaving it in a standby or passive mode.

■ **Alternative Gatekeepers:** This mechanism enables a CVP Call Server or H.323 gateway to have the capability to use two Gatekeeper IP addresses with one configured as primary and one as secondary. These H.323 endpoints can then switch to the secondary IP address and Gatekeeper if the first failed. This is the preferred and most common implementation of Gatekeepers with Unified CVP.

■ **Gatekeeper Update Protocol (GUP):** This protocol enables Gatekeepers to be clustered, performing updates and keepalive monitoring. However, Unified CVP does not natively support the GUP protocol between its call servers and the Gatekeeper, so the use of this mechanism is strictly to permit all registered endpoints, call admissions, active calls, and statistics to flow within the Gatekeeper cluster. Unified CVP would still use the Alternative Gatekeeper mechanism to access the clustered Gatekeepers. GUP would run between the Gatekeepers in the cluster to keep them updated and current.

Unified Contact Center Enterprise (Unified CCE)

If advanced call control (IP Switching, transfers to agents, and so on) is required with Unified CVP, either Cisco Unified CCE or Cisco Unified Intelligent Contact Management Enterprise (ICME) becomes a required component. Unified CCE provides software that manages contact center agents with call scripting capabilities. Essential Unified CCE becomes the brains of the Unified CVP solution directing transfers and call treatment requirements by executing call routing scripts such as Micro or Studio Applications. Because Unified CVP is directly connected to Unified CCE, these call scripts direct the Unified CVP solution to perform call treatment and agent transfers during non-stand-alone deployments of Unified CVP. As illustrated in Figure 2-11, Unified CVP communicates directly with Unified CCE via the GED-125 protocol using a PIM configured on the VRU PG.

GED-125 is a Cisco proprietary control protocol in which a single socket is used to control many telephone calls. Unified CVP is treated as a Voice Response Unit (VRU) for Unified CCE just as other GED-125 VRUs are connected. Unified CVP is simply a VRU Peripheral to Unified CCE or Unified ICME.

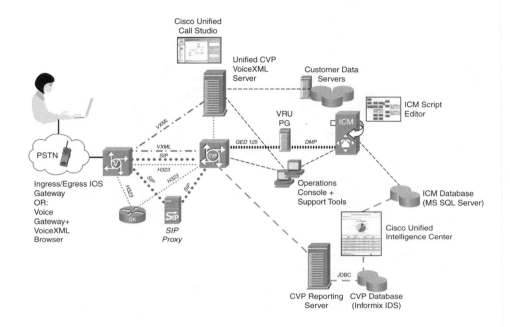

Figure 2-11   *(Non-Native) Cisco Unified Contact Center*

Note   A Unified CCE Peripheral Gateway or PG, is an intermediate server and process that communicates directly with an ACD, PBX, VRU, or other peripherals such as a Unified Communications Manager. A peripheral is an ACD, VRU, or any other device that distributes contacts (calls, email, web, or chat). The PG reads status information from the peripheral and sends it to the Unified CCE Central Controller. The PG is also capable of sending routing requests to the Unified CCE Central Controller and receiving route responses back. The PG also converts peripheral language to Unified CCE language and vice versa, which is why it is called a "Gateway." A standard PG can support up to 32 Peripheral Interface Managers (PIM) for similar devices. However, a Generic PG can connect to one of any support ACDs and one of any supported VRU/IVRs. The PIM is a software process running on the PG responsible for the detailed interaction with the peripheral.

Cisco Unified Communications Manager (CUCM)

Figure 2-12 shows the Cisco IP-based PBX. This component is responsible for managing and switching VoIP calls among IP phones. If this component is combined with Unified ICME, the solution becomes Unified CCE.

Cisco Unified Communications Manager (Unified CM) is the main call processing component of a Cisco Unified Communication system. Unified CVP interacts with Unified CM to deliver customer originated calls to Unified CCE agents. SIP Gateways deliver these

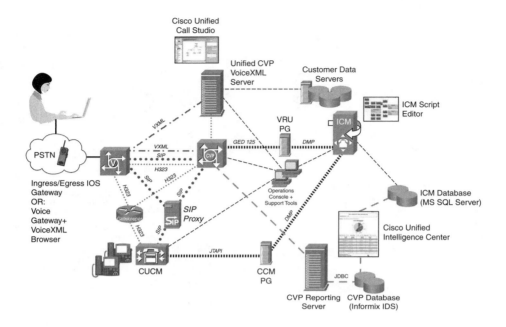

Figure 2-12   *(Non-Native) Cisco Unified Communications Manager*

calls via available Unified CM SIP trunks, whereas H.323 gateway calls are routed via available Unified CM H.323 trunks. Although most customer calls originate from a PSTN, TDM, or SIP trunk connection, situations exist in which Unified CM could also originate a call such as the following:

- An office user (non-agent) dials an internal help-desk number serviced by Unified CVP.

- An agent initiates a consultative transfer to a skill group serviced by Unified CVP.

PSTN calls can arrive on MGCP-controlled gateways and be transferred to Unified CVP using either SIP or H.323, depending on what deployment model is used. Because Unified CM is a non-native component in the Unified CVP solution, it depends on the deployment model used as to whether Unified CM plays any role at all in the call flows. For example, in pure TDM-based deployments with Legacy ACDs, it is unlikely that a Unified CM will be deployed unless the purpose of implementing one would be to migrate to Unified CCE. Similarly, in a Unified CVP Standalone Self-Service deployment, calls never need to be routed or switched to an agent IP phone and usually are handled by the VoiceXML Gateway with instructions from the VoiceXML server. There are some hybrid models where a call may start in a self-service mode, but when IVR treatment has been exhausted, they could be sent into a more comprehensive model requiring a Unified CVP queue point with Unified CCE agents. In this case, Unified CM makes a great deal of sense because calls would eventually require live agents.

Caution   Only certain versions of Unified CM are compatible with Unified CVP solutions. For example, Unified CVP is supported with SIP only if Cisco Unified CM 5.0 or later is deployed. Unified CVP is supported with H.323 for Unified CM 4.x or later releases. However, it is important to verify version compatibility using the *Hardware and System Software Specifications for Cisco Unified CVP Release 8.x*, (formerly called the *Bill of Materials*) available on CCO at Cisco.com. Whenever possible, try to use the most current software releases available and compatible with respect to Unified CM to ensure that issues and bugs found in older releases do not find their way into your deployments.

Third-Party DNS, Media and ASR/TTS Servers

Third-party servers play a critical role in providing supplementary services for the Unified CVP solution. Although they might be non-native and even optional depending on the deployment model used, they are still important to understand for the overall solution and what services they typically provide. This section touches on three of the most important third-party servers: Media, DNS, and ASR/TTS. Figure 2-13 illustrates the placement of media and ASR/TTS servers. DNS servers are not illustrated but covered in detail as to their impact on the solution. In addition, two new load balancers are also illustrated in Figure 2-13, which are covered in the next section.

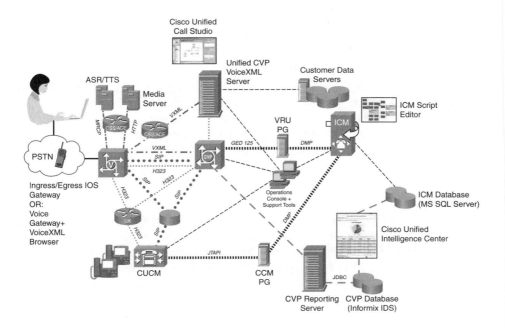

Figure 2-13   *(Non-Native) Third-Party Servers and Load Balancers*

DNS Server

The use of a DNS server in the Unified CVP solution is completely optional. A DNS Server is used to resolve hostnames to IP addresses. However, multiple hostnames can be configured in a DNS server zone to provide a form of load balancing using round-robin DNS. Successive requests from a host can return unique IP addresses for similar components, like the Unified CVP Call Server SIP Service.

Warning   Although DNS servers can provide a simple load-balancing feature using round-robin name resolution, DNS servers do not recognize if the IP address returned for a host is alive and available. The implication of this is that DNS could return an IP address of a call server that is not available or down, meaning that a SIP proxy or gateway would then need to ask again for a different name resolution and hope that the IP address returned at that time was alive and receiving calls. Remember the old saying, "Hope is not a strategy."

DNS Servers are significant in the following SIP components:

- **Ingress Gateway:** When a call arrives at an Ingress Gateway, the gateway can use a DNS Server to distribute the calls to different SIP Proxy Servers. In addition, if no SIP Proxy Servers are used, DNS can also be used to load balance the switch leg of the call to different CVP Call Servers' SIP Service.

- **SIP Proxy Server:** During the switch leg of the call, the SIP Proxy Servers can use a DNS Server to load balance calls to different CVP Call Servers' SIP Service or to Cisco VoiceXML Gateway routers for treatment.

- **CVP Call Server SIP Service:** The CVP Call Server SIP Service can use a DNS server to distribute calls to different SIP Proxy Servers. If a SIP Proxy Server is not used, DNS can be used to directly to distribute VRU legs among multiple Cisco VoiceXML Gateways for the outbound VRU leg of a call. This configuration assumes that Send to Originator is not configured or used by the CVP Call Servers to service the VRU leg of the call. Send to Originator or StO, is discussed in the next chapter.

Media Server

The media server component is a simple web server, such as Microsoft IIS or Apache, and is an optional component. The role of the media server is to serve up access to prerecorded audio files, external VoiceXML documents, or even external ASR grammars to the Cisco VoiceXML Gateway. Because some of these files can be stored in the gateway's local flash, the media server is an optional component. However, in most deployments, media servers deploy at a central location, which provides a streamlined approach to managing and updating customer prerecorded audio files. Without the use of media servers, updating audio files stored locally on Cisco VoiceXML Gateways would be an operational challenge. In addition, media servers can be deployed in redundant pairs. Devices such as the Cisco Content Service Switch or the Cisco Application Content Engine can be used to load balance traffic to redundant and geographically separated media servers as described in the next section. The Cisco VoiceXML Gateway uses the HTTP protocol to communicate and fetch files from the media servers.

Note   A Cisco VoiceXML Gateway when deployed in Unified CVP comprehensive mode can be configured with two media server IP addresses per gateway. These addresses can either be the IP address of a media server or a Virtual IP Address or VIP of a set of load balancers. If you recall the Unified CVP IVR service and its role for the CVP Call Server were defined. The IVR Service can insert different hostnames into the URLs found in the VoiceXML instructions originating from an ICM micro-application, thus exploiting the use of these two media server host entries on the Cisco VoiceXML Gateway for basic high-availability requirements. In simple terms, the gateway attempts to fetch audio files from a host entry on the VoiceXML instructions. If that fetch fails, the IVR service identifies this failure from the Cisco VoiceXML Gateway's communication and instructs the gateway to try the backup host entry for the media server. The use of mediaserver and mediaserver-backup as the media server hostnames is simply an example of a possible name that is completely configurable in ICM to be any hostname. The IVR service simply adds -backup to the hostname configured in the script and instructs the Cisco VoiceXML Gateway to retry fetching the media using the -backup hostname.

Although this is a nice feature when operating under the comprehensive model for Unified CVP, it does not exist when working with the Unified CVP Standalone Self-Service deployment model simply because the IVR service is never part of the call flow. This has significant impact on how redundant media servers can be deployed when operating in standalone self-service mode with or without load balancers.

This poor man's failover mechanism built into the IVR service can be simply replicated in the Standalone Deployment model by implementing a load balancer by which the IP address of the mediaserver on the Cisco VoiceXML Gateway would point to a load balancer, which in turn would deliver a redirect message with one of many available media server IP addresses, assuming redirects are configured on the load balancer. The use of redirects enables the load balancer to remove itself from subsequent fetch messages placing the Cisco VoiceXML Gateway and media server in direct communication. However, in the extreme case in which a load balancer VIP were not accessible, the secondary hostname mediaserver-backup could be configured to point to a different VIP address for a completely separate set of clustered load balancers. The bottom line: The IVR service with a set of load balancer clusters can provide a robust availability plan around media and ASR/TTS servers from the Cisco VoiceXML Gateway's perspective.

ASR/TTS Server

This component is truly optional in the sense that unless a deployment requires ASR or TTS functionality during the VRU leg of a call, there is no need to deploy this server. Typically, this component is deployed in a farm, and load balancers are used to direct Cisco VoiceXML Gateways to different servers in these farms for better utilization of server ports and licenses. However, if load balancers are not deployed in the solution, as noted previously with the media servers, the Cisco VoiceXML Gateway can support up two of these servers configured as host entries in a similar but different fashion as for the media server. Furthermore, the servers must be installed and licensed following the manufacturer guidelines. MRCPv1 should be configured on the Cisco VoiceXML Gateway if you expect to render instructions sent by either Micro-Applications or the Unified CVP VoiceXML Server. However, you can use MRCPv2 if no Micro Applications are in use (Standalone Self-Service mode) and only Unified CVP VoiceXML Server applications are used. Cisco does not manufacturer, sell, or even support any ASR/TTS Servers. However, Unified CVP is tested and certified with products such as ScanSoft, Nuance, and IBM offerings.[8]

Caution   Because ASR/TTS servers are continuously tested for compatibility with Unified CVP, always be sure to consult the *Hardware and System Software Specifications for Cisco Unified CVP Release 8.x*, (formerly called the *Bill of Materials*) available on CCO at Cisco.com to be sure the version you plan to purchase and deploy is supported by Unified CVP 8.x.

Load Balancers: CSS and ACE

Two load balancers are supported by Cisco in the Unified CVP solution (refer to Figure 2-13): Cisco Content Services Switch and Cisco Application Content Engine. Although both can load balance traffic from the Cisco VoiceXML Gateways to media and ASR/TTS servers, neither can load balance SIP or H.323 call control or bearer traffic.

The CSS is an older product with ACE being the roadmap product to replace it. However, as of this writing, the ACE product seemed to have the upper hand with respect to supporting advanced features around high availability. Both products provide high availability pertaining to a Virtual Router Redundancy Protocol (VRRP) implementation using a Virtual IP Address (VIP). The idea is that a VIP is an IP address shared by every load balancer in a cluster. Each load balancer also has a local IP address within the same subnet as the VIP, from which they communicate the status and owner of the VIP. Although the implementation of this feature is more complicated with the ACE product, it does provide more flexibility around high-availability configurations and the usage of backup server farms. The supportability of a VRRP or VIP implementation is powerful when considering that Cisco VoiceXML Gateways can support only the configurations of two media servers and two ASR/TTS servers. So in a situation where the load balancers are centrally located in two different data centers, providing local failover between them in a pair requires the use of a VIP. Without this basic feature, you cannot set up a Cisco VoiceXML Gateway to use a load balancer and still provide N+1 redundancy per data center simply because there would be too many IP addresses and no capacity to configure them on the Cisco VoiceXML Gateway. This type of load balancer implementation provides a box-to-box redundancy with pairs located in different data centers, which are completely addressable by the Cisco VoiceXML Gateways. In addition, the use of a load balancer is supported in all deployment models except for the Call Director call flows, which do not require the use of Unified CVP VoiceXML Servers, Media Servers, or ASR/TTS Servers.

Where ACE load balancers are deployed, the minimum license requirements for ACE follow:

■   1-Gbps throughput license (ACE-AP-01-LIC)

■   A nondefault SSL feature license if you plan to use ACE for SSL (a CSS switch requires a SSL module for the chassis to use SSL with CSS)

■   Application Acceleration License (ACE-AP-OPT-LIC-K9), which enables more than 50 concurrent connections on ACE[9]

Unified CVP Licensing

An important but confusing part of the Unified CVP solution is how individual components are licensed for use. This section summarizes the licensing approach for native components and illustrates which types of licenses are required to operate the solution. Understanding the requirements and enforcement model around licensing the solution become critical when designing and sizing a Unified CVP solution. How licensing is procured and applied to the solution depends entirely on what the components in the solution accomplish and how the overall architecture was designed. This section does not dive into the details around licensing non-native components because each of those products has different licensing requirements than Unified CVP. However, taking a solution-level mindset, all native and non-native components should be correctly licensed for their roles. Documentation does exist for all non-native components on how they should be licensed.

The licensing information for Cisco Unified CVP has been consolidated and moved into the *Cisco Customer Contact Solutions Ordering Guide*. The Ordering Guide provides a single, frequently updated source for all the Unified CVP licensing information. Cisco employees and Partners with a valid login account can access the Ordering Guide at http://www.cisco.com/web/partners/downloads/partner/WWChannels/technology/ipc/downloads/CCBU_ordering_guide.pdf.

If you need licensing information for Unified CVP but cannot access the Ordering Guide, contact your local Cisco Systems Engineer (SE) or Partner.[10] The following sections are from this document and have been summarized and formatted for your reference.

Types of CVP Licenses

The following list defines the elements that make up the Unified CVP licensing strategy. Depending on the deployment model used, some or all these elements could be implemented to license and run the solution.

Unified CVP Server-SW

The CVP Server-SW license is required for each Unified CVP Call Server and VoiceXML Server. The CVP Server-SW licenses for the CVP Call Servers are tied to the IP address of the servers. The CVP Server-SW licenses for the CVP VXML Servers are tied to a unique

System ID. However, you do not need a CVP Server-SW license for the Operations Console or Reporting Servers.

Unified CVP Ports

This component is the number of CVP ports (nonredundant) required, which is the total number of simultaneous voice and video sessions that require self-service (with the Unified CVP VoiceXML Server) or queuing.

- A single port license is used when a VoiceXML session is established. Therefore, one port license is consumed, whether the call is serviced by a self-service application or is queued.

- If a customer will have X number of calls queued and Y number of calls receiving self-service treatment, one must order a minimum of X+Y ports to ensure sufficient ports are ordered.

  - If the ports you ordered are for Unified CVP Call Server SKU

    - A port license file automatically generates and contains 1000 ports.

    - Although you are allowed to use only the number of Port Licenses purchased when retrieving the licenses keys via the licensing tool on Cisco.com, you always receive a license key for 1000 port licenses. This is to prevent product deficiency in license use when it is either supporting queuing or self-service or providing call control. Without providing a maximum number, there would be no way to support UCCE customers with CVP call control if the number of ports were limited to what was ordered.

  - If the ports you ordered are for a Unified CVP VoiceXML Server

    - In your deployment, you receive a pool made up of CVP Ports and CVP Redundant Ports of licenses for your servers. This pool must be divided among each of the servers. This allocation is accomplished by the customer using the licensing tool on Cisco.com.

    - Typically, you would want to divide your pool licenses evenly between your VXML Servers. For example, if your Port License SKU includes 500 licenses, and you have five CVP VXML Servers, you would license each server for 100 licenses.

Unified CVP Redundant Ports

This component is the number of redundant CVP ports required to accomplish adequate business continuity if a Unified CVP server outage occurs. Following are some additional characteristics.

- Similar to CVP ports.

- From a purchasing perspective, you can use these licenses when an unexpected burst of calls occurs.

- From a licensing perspective, these will be part of the same pool (previously mentioned) as your regular CVP Ports.

Unified CVP Call Directors

A Call Director server license provides call control for non-Unified Contact Center solutions. Call Director licensing is determined by the server, with the number of sessions limited by the capacity available for the protocol used on the server. Following are some additional characteristics:

- Similar to the CVP Server-SW licenses, yet no queuing or self-service is enabled for this part number.

- Required only for non-Unified Contact Center ACDs and other devices frontended by an Egress Gateway.

- Not required for Unified CCE agents. Call Director Licenses are implicitly provided with Cisco Unified Contact Center Enterprise and do not have to be separately ordered.

- When CVP operates in a comprehensive model (that is, with queuing/self-service) and there are ACD agents/TDM IVR transfers involved, CVP Call Director Server licenses are required unless the transfer to ACD agents use a method that takes the call away from the Unified CVP Servers (such as with SIP Refer, H.323 Blind/Refer, *8 TNT, hookflash, or TBCT). However, when CVP operates in a sole Call Director model with release port transfer to the ACD agents, the base call Director Server license still applies. Furthermore, in a sole Call Director model without using release port transfer-to ACD agents, call Director Server licenses are required. You can choose from four packages depending on the required number of call director ports.

Unified CVP Reporting Servers

This component provides the reporting repository for the Unified CVP data. Following are some additional licensing characteristics:

- They provide the reporting repository for Unified CVP data. Included with the license is a relational database for querying of data to build reports. The Cisco Unified Intelligence Center client has the capability to report from data stored in the Report Server. Two options are available with the Report Server, a standard version and a premium version. The standard version supports a dual processor server with a maximum of a 50 GB database for basic reporting. The premium version supports a 100 GB database on a four-way processor.

- Licensed by the IP address of the Report Server.

- One CVP Report Server license per Report Server.

Cisco Unified Call Studio

This component provides a development environment to build Cisco Unified Call Studio VoiceXML applications. Following are some additional considerations when licensing this component:

- Call Studio is licensed for each developer machine where Call Studio is installed, which is typically at least one per CVP deployment. Customers that use CVP for queue and transfer purposes only do not require a Call Studio license, assuming Micro-Applications are used and not custom VXML applications. Even though Call Studio is used by developers, a full license must be purchased by any partner or customer to develop applications for use on production systems. For this software only, the term "production use" means "use for development" and "use for production" for any type of application. Lastly, it should be noted that Call Studio can be installed and used for up to 30 days with an actual product license key.

- Licensed by a unique node key, known as the System ID.

Licensing Native Unified CVP Components

This section contains a breakdown of requirements and contents the user receives when using the Product Authorization Keys (PAK) to retrieve the CVP licenses.

Unified CVP Call Server

The following items outline what is required and received when a user activates a PAK Code for a Unified CVP Call Server.

- Requirements:

  - IP Address of the Unified CVP Call Server

  - Software license instructions packaged with the PAKs or PAK codes

  - Cisco.com login ID

- Contents received:

  - One CVP Server-SW license file

  - One CVP Port license file, which automatically generates and contains 1000 ports

Note   You are legally allowed to use only the number of purchased Port Licenses. When retrieving the licenses keys via the licensing tool on Cisco.com, you always receive a license key for 1000 port licenses. The reason for this is to overcome a product deficiency in which a license is used when it is either supporting queuing or self-service, or when providing call control. Without providing a maximum number, it would be impossible to support UCCE customers with CVP call control if there were a limitation on the number of ports ordered.

Unified CVP VoiceXML Server

As with the Unified CVP Call Server, a PAK code is also provided that should be used to activate the Unified CVP VoiceXML Server license. Following are the required items and what the user should expect to receive.

- Requirements:

    - System ID from the Unified CVP VoiceXML Server, which is found in the properties for the Unified CVP VoiceXML Server in the Operations Console.

    - Software license instructions packaged with the PAKs or PAK codes.

    - Cisco.com login ID.

    - Estimate of the number of ports to be licensed to each Unified CVP VoiceXML Server.

- Contents Received:

    - One CVP Server-SW license file for the Unified CVP VoiceXML Server.

    - One CVP Server-SW license file for a Unified CVP Call Server. This Call Server license is automatically generated for each ordered CVP Server-SW. For servers running only as Unified CVP VoiceXML servers (and are not co-resident with a Unified CVP Call Server), this Call Server license does not need to be applied.

    - One CVP Port license file, which contains the number of ports that have been "assigned" to this server. This number is then deducted from the pool of ports (previously mentioned).

Cisco Unified Call Studio

As with the Unified CVP Call Server, a PAK code is provided when licensing Cisco Unified Call Studio. Following are the requirements to activate the PAK code and what the user should expect to receive when the activation is complete.

- Requirements:

    - System ID from the Call Studio, which is found in the About menu.

    - Software license instructions packaged with the PAKs or PAK codes.

    - Cisco.com login ID.

- Contents Received:

    - One CVP Call Studio license file

Unified CVP Reporting Server

The last native component discussed in this section follows the same activation procedure as the Unified CVP Call and VoiceXML Server. Following are the requirements to activate the license and what the user should expect to receive from the transaction:

■ Requirements:

■ IP address of the CVP Call Server

■ Software license instructions packaged with the PAKs or PAK codes

■ Cisco.com login ID

■ Contents Received:

■ One CVP Reporting Server license file

Caution   Unified CVP Upgrades and Licensing

When upgrading Unified CVP from version 4.0, 4.1, and even 7.0, only new media is required; new licenses are not required. However, if you upgrade from an older version of CVP such as 3.1 or earlier, new licenses are required, and you must work with Cisco licensing and product management to obtain them. In a situation in which you currently have Queue and Transfer capabilities or pre-CVP 3.x versions, you are eligible only for Call Server licenses, which can provide the same capability that was available in your older versions. The good news is that if you use CVP 4.1 and migrate to CVP 8.x, the CVP installation converts the licenses to the new format, with upgrades provided with the Product Upgrade Tool or PUT tool.

Determining What You Need

To adequately evaluate the licensing requirements for a Unified CVP solution, each component must be sized to accommodate how the solution will be deployed and used. This sizing exercise drives the quantity and type of licenses required for Unified CVP components in the solution. The next few sections provide some guidelines for this effort. In addition, Chapter 6, "Sizing, Networking, and Security Considerations," provides more details about sizing best practices that can directly impact how the solution is licensed.

Sizing Unified CVP Server Licenses

A CVP Server software license permits the use of CVP Call Server software and a CVP VXML Server on a server. In other words, in the case of CVP Call Server and VXML Server (co-resident), there will be only one server software license needed. However, multiple license files will be generated. One license file is used for CVP Call Server software, and another one is used for CVP VXML Server software. Sizing depends entirely upon the number of servers required for the solution and how many are in a co-resident mode with both the Call Server and VXML Server software installed on the same machine. If you decide to deploy standalone CVP VXML Servers, you are required to purchase a server license for those standalone servers and one for any CVP Call Servers. In addition the total number of ports required is equivalent to the Unified CVP ports plus Call Director ports (even if the Call Director ports are free of charge) plus redundant ports. The total number of ports required is used to calculate the number of servers needed. Servers must exist for regular port licenses, and additional servers must exist for the redundant port licenses. The next component outlines the difference between regular and redundant port licensing. As noted earlier, although there is no charge for Call Director calls when an agent is a Unified CCE agent, you still must be sure to size the Unified CVP solution to handle the number of concurrently transferred calls directed by CVP to Unified CCE Agents, which depending on those call volumes could lead to the purchase of additional Unified CVP Server Software licenses. For example, assume that you need to support 400 IVR ports. Although CVP Call Server can support that you must also consider the transfers to Unified CCE agents by CVP. Making it simple, you had 800 Unified CCE agents that might all be taking calls transferred by CVP in a worst case. Doing the math, 400 + 800 = 1200 calls/ports simultaneously handled by CVP in the peak time. Assuming you use SIP for call control and have deployed CVP Call and VXML Servers in a co-resident model, two CVP SIP-based Call Servers would be required. (Each SIP Call Server can handle 750 ports or 750 * 2 = 1500 > 1200) and therefore two CVP Server Software licenses are needed instead of one server license.

Sizing Unified CVP Port Licenses

To size Unified CVP Port licenses, you must first determine the number required of port licenses. Establish the busiest point in the most active hour of the contact center. The focus should be on what the calls are actually doing at the busiest moment in the day. The Unified CVP Port License is only for calls receiving IVR treatment, such as in self-service or in queue. Calls that connect to agents do not use a Unified CVP Port License. They use a Call Director server bundled with Call Director ports license, which may or may not be included free of charge. So take the busiest moment of the day as a snapshot and determine call characteristics such as waiting in queue, simple self-service without the use of ASR/TTS, or a VXML Server and which calls perform self-service with the use of ASR/TTS or a VXML Server. The total number of these calls corresponds to the number of regular (non-redundant) Unified CVP Port Licenses required for your deployment. Understanding how many calls are transferred via IP switching to agents is equally important because this information is used in sizing a CVP server and does not apply to port licenses except indirectly for the Call Director Server licensing case.

Sizing Unified CVP Redundant Port Licenses

Redundant licenses are purchased by port. You can order as many redundant ports as required based on the desired level of redundancy, up to the number of primary ports purchased. So if your redundancy model is N+N, you would order the same number of Unified CVP redundant port licenses as primary port licenses ordered. If your redundancy model is N+1, you would order the number of redundant port licenses necessary for a single redundant server. A server license must also be ordered for each additional redundant server ordered.

Sizing Unified CVP Call Director Licenses

As described previously in the port licenses section, you must determine the number of calls that CVP directs or transfers to the agents and remains in call control after the initial transfer. This function is called *call director*, which is used interchangeably with the term *call control* and is free of charge when the agent is a Unified CCE agent. (That is, no port and server licenses are required additionally for Unified CCE agent call control function usage in CVP.)

Unified CVP Call Director Licenses are required when Unified CVP is used for IP switching to agents who are not on Cisco Unified CCE systems, such as agents on ACD systems. In Unified CVP 4.1 and later releases, Call Director is licensed per server and per the wanted number of Call Director ports or calls on each server. The number of wanted Call Director ports or calls is limited by the capacity available for the protocol used on the server.

The number of required Call Director ports or calls corresponds to the maximum number of simultaneous calls active in the Unified CVP Call Servers and are connected to ACD agents as envisioned in the busiest moment of the day.

If you have a mix of Unified CCE agents and ACD agents, this is the continuing step required after calculating the required port and server licenses as described in the previous sections. Focus on the latter phase of the call after the IVR session, which is the agent transfer or talking phase. Again, for calls connected to Unified CCE agents, there is no Call Director Server license required. For calls connected to ACD agents, Call Director Server licenses are required as an addition to the regular server software licenses on each server.

If using only pure Call Director application with CVP (neither self-service nor queuing included), it is not necessary to calculate the required port licenses for queuing or self-service during IVR phase. To obtain the corresponding Call Director Server software licenses, the only concern should be the required call director ports.

There is a unique situation in the pure Call Director application with CVP. This is the case when you choose to use release port transfer with a sole call director application (that is, no self-service and queuing usage in the deployment; just pure IP Call Directing or Switching). The Call Director Server software licenses on each server is required. However, because the port is released, you do not need to include these ports in sizing CVP Call Director Servers. Instead rely on the cps to size the CVP servers. This implies you need to select the base Call Director Server software license for this unique Call Director deployment.

Note   All Unified CVP software is "node locked," which means that users must register their licenses and provide a server ID to receive a license. For a CVP Call Server and CVP 8.0 VXML server, the IP address is used as a node lock mechanism. For CVP 8.0 Studio, the MAC address is used. Although for the CVP 7.0 VXML Server and studio, it is based on System ID. (Refer to the CVP Administration and Configuration guide on how to obtain the system ID from the CVP Operations Console to submit to Cisco to fetch license key to operate the CVP VXML Server.

Ports are enforced on the Unified CVP VXML Server, and the Unified CVP Call Server licenses are set to the maximum number of sessions allowed per server; however, customers are required to comply with the number of sessions purchased, not the number of sessions provided in the license file.

A single port license is used when a VoiceVXML session is established. Therefore, one port license is consumed, where the call is serviced by a self-service application or queued.

Unified CVP Licensing Use Cases

The following examples illustrate how to size and license CVP based on customer requirements and a deployment model.

Use Case 1: CVP Co-Resident Call Server+VoiceXML Servers and Unified CCE Agents

A unified CCE customer with 1000 agents wants 400 ports for queuing, 300 ports for self-service, and 100-percent redundancy across two sites. The deployment model uses SIP for call control with Unified CVP support for both a self-service and comprehensive model.

Solution:

Because queuing and self-service ports use the same license, this customer requires 700 Unified CVP ports and 700 redundant ports, with three server licenses. Each site requires three servers with co-resident Call and VoiceXML Servers due to 700 + 1000 / 750 = ~3.

Following are the Unified CVP components required:

- Three Server licenses

- 700 Port licenses

- 700 Redundant Port licenses

- Minimum of one Studio license

- Reporting Server license (optional)

Note No Call Director Server licenses are required for the 1000 agents because they are Unified CCE agents and already have the Call Director license.

Use Case 2: CVP Standalone

A customer wants a standalone (without Unified ICM or Unified CCE) self-service solution of 450 ports and 100 percent redundancy.

Solution:

The Customer would require 450 ports of Unified CVP, 450 redundant ports, and 2 Unified CVP Server Licenses.

Following are the Unified CVP Components required:

- Two Server licenses (one server for primary, one server for redundancy)
- 450 Port licenses
- 450 Redundant Port licenses
- Minimum of one Studio license
- Reporting Server license (optional; if reporting is wanted and additional Server license is required for the Call Server used for Reporting)

Summary

In this chapter the Unified CVP architecture was examined with both native and non-native components. The Unified CVP native components are tightly coupled together and thoughtfully engineered to provide a robust solution addressing several different functional deployment models and their integrations with non-native components such as Unified CCE. The most significant list of non-native components was examined, detailing their roles and integrations with Unified CVP. This should provide a deeper understanding of how the solution is licensed and enforced, adding more understanding around important considerations when architecting and designing a Unified CVP solution. This chapter also illustrated how the licensing guidance could be applied to common customer scenarios.

The next chapter takes a closer look at the different functional deployment models supported by Unified CVP. Detailed call flows are provided and discussed for implications on customer requirements. From this point forward, you should have a strong understanding of both native and non-native components and their roles in the Unified CVP solution.

References

1. Cisco Documentation, *Cisco Unified Customer Voice Portal (CVP) 8.x Solution Reference Network Design (SRND)*, 2010: 1–21.

2. Cisco Documentation, *Cisco Unified Customer Voice Portal (CVP) 8.x Solution Reference Network Design (SRND)*, 2010: 1–6.

3. Cisco Documentation, *Cisco Unified Customer Voice Portal (CVP) 8.x Solution Reference Network Design (SRND)*, 2010: 1–6.

4. Cisco Documentation, *Cisco Unified Customer Voice Portal (CVP) 8.x Solution Reference Network Design (SRND)*, 2010: 1–7.

5. Cisco Documentation, *Cisco Unified Customer Voice Portal (CVP) 8.x Solution Reference Network Design (SRND)*, 2010: 1–8.

6. Cisco CVPI Training, "Technical Overview."

7. Cisco Documentation, *Cisco Unified Customer Voice Portal (CVP) 8.x Solution Reference Network Design (SRND)*, 2010: 1–12.

8. Cisco Documentation, *Cisco Unified Customer Voice Portal (CVP) 8.x Solution Reference Network Design (SRND)*, 2010: 1–16.

9. Cisco Documentation, *Cisco Unified Customer Voice Portal (CVP) 8.x Solution Reference Network Design (SRND)*, 2010: 1–15.

10. Cisco Documentation, *Cisco Unified Customer Voice Portal (CVP) 8.x Solution Reference Network Design (SRND)*, 2010: 15–1.

Recommended Readings and Resources

Cisco Documentation, *Cisco Unified Customer Voice Portal (CVP) 8.x Solution Reference Network Design (SRND)*, http://www.cisco.com/en/US/docs/voice_ip_comm/cust_contact/contact_center/customer_voice_portal/srnd/8x/cvp8xsrnd.pdf.

Cisco Documentation, *Reporting Guide for Cisco Unified Customer Voice Portal 8.0(1)*, http://www.cisco.com/en/US/docs/voice_ip_comm/cust_contact/contact_center/customer_voice_portal/cvp8_0/configuration/guide/cvp_801_report.pdf.

Cisco Documentation, *User Guide for Cisco Unified CVP VXML Server and Cisco Unified Call Studio, Release 8.0(1)*, http://www.cisco.com/en/US/docs/voice_ip_comm/cust_contact/contact_center/customer_voice_portal/cvp8_0/user/guide/cvp_801_vxml.pdf.

Cisco Documentation, *Hardware and System Software Specification for Cisco Unified Customer Voice Portal (Unified CVP), Release 8.0(1)*, http://www.cisco.com/en/US/docs/voice_ip_comm/cust_contact/contact_center/customer_voice_portal/cvp8_0/reference/guide/cvp_801_bom.pdf.

Cisco Documentation, *Cisco Customer Contact Solutions Ordering Guide*, http://www.cisco.com/en/US/partner/prod/collateral/voicesw/custcosw/ps5693/ps1844/CCBU_ordering_guide.pdf.

Cisco Documentation, *Cisco ACE 4700 Series Appliance Server Load-Balancing Configuration Guide*, http://www.cisco.com/en/US/docs/app_ntwk_services/data_center_app_services/ace_appliances/vA3_1_0/configuration/slb/guide/slbgd.pdf.

Cisco Documentation, *Cisco CSS 11500 Series Content Services Switches Configuration Guides*, http://www.cisco.com/en/US/partner/products/hw/contnetw/ps792/products_installation_and_configuration_guides_list.html.

Chapter 3

Functional Deployment Models and Call Flows

This chapter covers the following subjects:

- **Functional deployment models:** Standalone, Call Director, Comprehensive, VRU-only.

- **Detailed call flows:** Call flow details for each Functional Deployment Model.

- **Unified CCE interactions:** Network VRUs in Cisco Intelligent Contact Management Enterprise and IP originated calls with Cisco Unified Communications Manager.

Functional Deployment Models

As discussed briefly in the previous chapter, Unified CVP has some well-defined and commonly referenced functional deployment models. This chapter provides more details for these models and examines what each model accomplishes, its call flow, and even which native and non-native components are used. Understanding these models is critical to designing, implementing, and troubleshooting a Unified CVP solution. The chapter ends with a discussion that encompasses Unified CVP and its relationship and interactions with Unified CCE components, such as Unified ICM and Cisco Unified Communications Manager.

Standalone Model

Although this model is the simplest of all the functional deployment models, the flexibility available in Unified Call Studio applications is astounding. This model gives an organization the capability to replace legacy IVR systems using applications built using Unified Call Studio and hosted via the Unified CVP VoiceXML Server. The standalone model provides a standalone, automated self-service IVR solution that callers can access via TDM and VoIP terminating at Unified CVP's Ingress voice gateways. In addition callers could also access this solution via VoIP endpoints. Figure 3-1 shows the components used with this solution and their protocols.

Table 3-1 identifies which components are required, optional, and not used by this model. In addition, the Native column identifies components native to the Unified CVP solution.

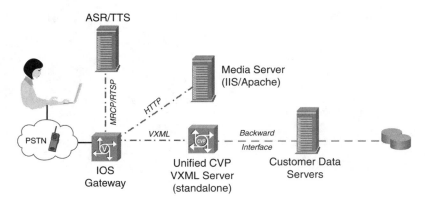

Figure 3-1   *Unified CVP Standalone Functional Deployment Model*

> **Note**   Although Figure 3-1 does not show all the optional components, this model can also use content service switches to load balance both media fetch requests and VoiceXML connections requested from the VoiceXML Gateway. In addition, transfers such as bridged, blind, and even release trunk transfer types (TNT, hookflash, TBCT, and SIP REFER) are supported in this model, which also means that both Egress Gateways and CUCM endpoints are also optional, depending entirely on the customer call flow requirements.

Component and Protocol-Level Call Flow

This section examines how components interact with each other at the protocol level. Figure 3-2 illustrates the steps of a typical standalone call flow with each step detailed.

Following are the details of each step referenced in Figure 3-2:

Step 1.   The call arrives from either the PSTN or a VoIP connection to the gateway. In this illustration, the gateway is functioning as both an Ingress Gateway and as a VoiceXML Gateway. The reason an Ingress Gateway is optional in Table 3-1 is because this initial call could be just a VoIP connection, which would require only a VoiceXML Gateway to terminate it and kick off the self-service application.

Step 2.   The gateway sends an HTTP request to the Unified CVP VoiceXML Server. Prior to this occurring, the gateway performs the following actions:

   a. The gateway matches an incoming Dialed Number Identification Service (DNIS) against its dial-peer configuration and kicks off a preconfigured application dial-peer. Example 3-1 provides a sample of how this dial-peer is configured for DNIS 1931 on the VoiceXML Gateway:

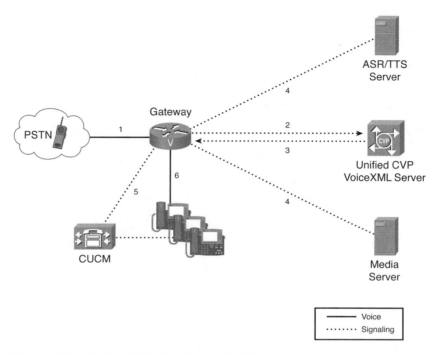

Figure 3-2 *Unified CVP Standalone Call Flow*

Example 3-1 *Incoming Dial-Peer for Kicking Off a Self-Service Application*

```
dial-peer voice 1 voip
 description — — Self Service SIP Calls from IP — —
 service myapp
 codec g711ulaw
 incoming called-number 1931
 dtmf-relay rtp-nte h245-signal h245-alphanumeric
 no vad
```

      b. The application dial-peer invokes a self-service TCL script located in the router's flash memory, which invokes the Unified CVP standalone bootstrap VoiceVXML document. Example 3-2 provides a sample of how this is configured on the VoiceXML Gateway.

Example 3-2 *Self-Service Application Configuration on Gateway*

```
application
 service myapp flash:CVPSelfService.tcl
  paramspace english language en
  paramspace english index 0
  param CVPSelfService-port 7000
  param CVPSelfService-app MyApp
```

```
   param CVPPrimaryVXMLServer 192.168.1.100
   param CVPSecondaryVXMLServer 192.168.1.101
   paramspace english location flash
   paramspace english prefix en
 !
service CVPSelfService flash:CVPSelfServiceBootstrap.vxml
 !
```

Table 3-1 *Unified CVP Standalone Native and Non-Native Component Usage*

Component	Required	Optional	Not Used	Native
SIP Service (Call Server)	—	—	Yes	Yes
IVR Service (Call Server)	—	—	Yes	Yes
ICM Service (Call)	—	Yes		Yes
H323 Service (Call Server)	—	—	Yes	Yes
VoiceXML Server	Yes	—	—	Yes
Unified Call Studio	Yes	—	—	Yes
Ingress Gateway		Yes	—	—
VXML Gateway	Yes	—	—	—
SIP Proxy	—	—	Yes	—
Gatekeeper	—	—	Yes	—
Operations Console	Yes	—	—	Yes
Reporting Server	—	Yes	—	Yes
ASR/TTS	—	Yes	—	—
Media Server	—	Yes	—	—
DNS Server	—	Yes	—	—
Content Services Switch	—	Yes	—	—
Unified ICM	—	Yes	—	—
Unified Call Manager	—	Yes	—	—
Egress Gateway	—	Yes	—	—

Note Example 3-2 also exposes the configuration for primary and secondary VoiceXML Servers using a parameter field. This approach illustrates an important consideration when deploying more than two standalone VoiceXML Servers. When more than two Unified CVP VoiceXML Servers are deployed, the VoiceXML Gateways must either be manually configured to use different pairs as primary and secondary servers, or a content load balancer switch would need to be deployed. If the latter approach is taken, the IP addresses configured in Example 3-2 would simply be the VIP addresses for the service load balanced by the content load balancers.

    c. This VoiceXML document, also located in the router's flash memory, performs an HTTP request to the configured IP address of the Unified CVP VoiceXML Server. This IP address is preconfigured as a parameter when the self-service application is set up (refer to Example 3-2).

Step 3. The Unified CVP VoiceXML Server runs the application specified in the HTTP URL provided in Step 2. The result of running the application returns a dynamically generated VoiceXML document to the VoiceXML Gateway. Prior to building this dynamic VXML document, the Unified CVP VoiceXML Server can access backend systems as instructed by the application to incorporate personalized data into the VoiceXML document.

Step 4. The VoiceXML Gateway parses and renders the VoiceXML document. Following are the details pertaining to the rendering of this VoiceXML document:

    a. If the VoiceXML instructions require a media file fetch operation, prior to fetching a prerecorded media file from a media server, the gateway first determines if the required prompt file is already cached in the gateway's http client cache. If so, that file is played to the caller; if not, the gateway resolves the media server name located in the fetch URL provided by the VoiceXML document. This media server name can either be a locally configured ip host entry or resolved via DNS.

    b. If the VoiceXML instructions require the use of an ASR or TTS server, the VoiceXML Gateway sets up a connection to an ASR/TTS Server and streams media from the server. Caller input can be captured via DTMF detection on the Ingress Gateway or via DTMF/speech recognition on an ASR Server.

    c. As defined by the VXML document, the VoiceXML submits an HTTP request containing the results of the caller input to the Unified CVP VoiceXML Server. The Unified CVP VoiceXML Server again runs the application specified in the HTTP request URL, passing it the results provided by the previous VoiceXML Gateway request and dynamically generates another VoiceXML document for rendering by the VoiceXML Gateway. This dialog continues until either the call is deemed as treated by the Unified Call Studio application or the caller terminates the call.

Step 5.　The Ingress Gateway can, optionally, transfer the call to any destination that it can deliver a call to, such as Cisco Unified Communications Manager (CUCM).

Step 6.　UCM can set up the call between an agent phone and the Ingress Gateway using a specific agent DNIS or a DNIS that corresponds to a hunt group or IP-IVR port. For this call flow this transfer is purely bridged, blind, or released trunk in nature and has no agent selection intelligence other than what CUCM can provide.

A slight variant of this call flow model is the use of Unified ICM to provide a lookup and return a label via the Unified CVP PG integration. Figure 3-3 illustrates this call flow followed by a detailed discussion about the involved steps.

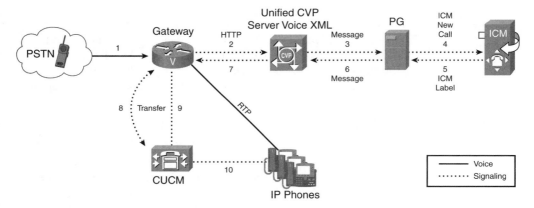

Figure 3-3　*Unified CVP Standalone with ICME Lookup Call Flow*

Step 1.　The call arrives from either the PSTN or a VoIP connection to the gateway. In this illustration, the gateway is functioning as both an Ingress Gateway and as a VoiceXML Gateway.

Step 2.　The gateway sends an HTTP URL request to the Unified CVP VoiceXML Server. The same configurations and substeps apply that were covered in the previous call flow.

Step 3.　As a result of executing the application hosted by the Unified CVP VoiceXML Server, the server sends a message to the Unified CVP Call Server requesting that Unified CVP requests a label from Unified ICM.

Step 4.　The Unified CVP Server sends Unified ICM a new call request via its Voice Response Unit (VRU) Peripheral Interface Manager (PIM), which is configured and hosted by the Peripheral Gateway (PG). This new route request invokes a new incoming route response that in turn invokes a routing script in Unified ICM.

Step 5.　Unified ICM returns a Unified ICM routing label to the Unified CVP Call Server via the Unified CVP VRU PIM hosted by the PG.

Step 6. The Unified CVP Server returns a message to the VoiceXML Server with the routing label returned by Unified ICM.

Step 7. As in the previous call flow, the VoiceXML returned to the VoiceXML Gateway can include references to ASR/TTS, Media Servers for playing media, and the collections of digits or can be transfer instructions based on the Unified ICM label.

Step 8. The Ingress Gateway can, optionally, transfer the call to any destination that it can deliver a call to, such as CUCM.

Step 9. The Ingress Gateway signals the CUCM server for connection to either an IP Phone or IP IVR Port.

Step 10. CUCM can set up the call between an agent phone and the Ingress Gateway using a specific agent DNIS or a DNIS that corresponds to a hunt group or IP-IVR port. For this call flow this transfer is purely bridged, blind, or released trunk in nature and has no agent selection intelligence other than what CUCM can provide.

Caution This particular call flow returns only a routing label from the results of executing a routing script invoked by the new call dialog between Unified ICM and CVP. Running an external script or providing queuing is not supported with this variant. If call queuing is a requirement, you should use the comprehensive call flow model. In addition, this variant assumes the following:

- A Unified CVP Call Server has been defined using the Operations Console.

- A Unified Call Studio application has been created that contains a Unified ICM request label element.

- A Unified ICM script must be set up to handle the new call dialog request returning a correct routing label to Unified CVP.

The Unified Call Studio application must be deployed on the Unified CVP VoiceXML Server.

Call Flow Ladder Diagram

Figure 3-4 illustrates the call flow by showing the interaction between native and non-native CVP components. In addition, both call flows previously discussed are illustrated. However, the interaction with Unified ICM would not exist for the Unified CVP Standalone without ICME lookup call flow.

By examining the previous ladder diagram, it is obvious that the Unified CVP call server services such as the Session Initiation Protocol (SIP), H.323, or Interactive Voice Response (IVR) service are not used with this deployment model. The Intelligent Contact Management (ICM) service is engaged only in the execution of a Unified ICM lookup, and at no point in the call flow does CVP have any call control responsibilities.

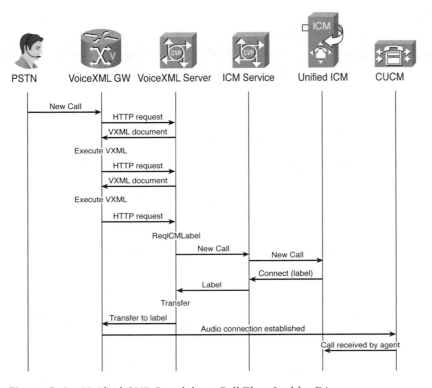

Figure 3-4   *Unified CVP Standalone Call Flow Ladder Diagram*

Transfers and Subsequent Call Control

In addition to providing self-service, the Standalone VoiceXML Deployment model can transfer callers to another endpoint, either VoIP (for example, Cisco Unified Communications Manager) or TDM (for example, Egress Voice Gateway to PSTN or TDM ACD). However, IVR application data cannot be passed to the new endpoints with this deployment model. Therefore, there will be no agent screen pop if the endpoint is a TDM ACD.

As noted earlier, this model supports the following types of transfers:

VoiceXML Bridged Transfer: The outcome of the transferred leg (that is, transfer failed, transfer call leg released, and so forth) is submitted back to the Unified CVP VoiceXML Server. The VoiceXML session is then resumed, and further iterations of the IVR call treatment and transfers can be performed. During the period of time that a call is transferred, a Unified CVP VXML Server port license is used if it is a bridged transfer.

VoiceXML Blind Transfer: With VoiceXML 2.0 Blind Transfers, the call remains connected through the Ingress Voice Gateway, but Unified CVP does not have any method to provide any subsequent call control.

Release Trunk Transfer (TNT, hookflash, TBCT, SIP Refer):   As with VoiceXML 2.0 Blind Transfers, the Ingress Gateway port is released, and no subsequent call control is possible.

Note   The VoiceXML transfers are invoked using Cisco Unified Call Studio's **transfer** element. Release Trunk Transfers are invoked by providing specifically formatted return values in Cisco Unified Call Studio's **subdialog_return** element.[1]

The Call Director Model

The purpose of this functional deployment model is to give organizations the ability to route and transfer calls across their existing VoIP networks. Because this functional deployment is often found in organizations preparing for or migrating to a VoIP contact center, it is no surprise that its strengths lie in its capability to switch calls to multiple TDM-based ACDs and IVRs without having to use PSTN prerouting or release trunk transfer services. When the organization is ready to implement CVP-based IVR services and Cisco Unified Contact Center Enterprise, it can migrate its Unified CVP deployment to the comprehensive functional deployment model discussed later in this chapter.

Furthermore, this particular deployment model gives Unified CVP and Unified ICM the capability to pass call data between these ACD and IVR locations. Unified ICM can also provide cradle-to-grave reporting for all calls. Although a customer can have a Unified CVP Reporting Server in this deployment model, it is optional because there is little call information stored in the Unified CVP reporting database. Both TDM and VoIP call originations are supported in this deployment model.[2] Figure 3-5 shows the components used with this solution and their protocols.

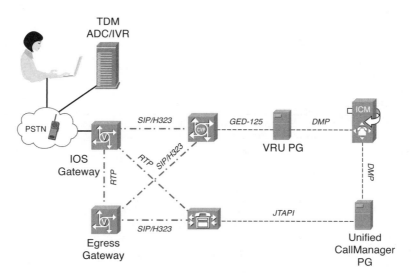

Figure 3-5   *Unified CVP Call Director Functional Deployment Model*

Table 3-2 identifies which components are required, optional, and not used by this model. In addition, the Native column identifies components that are native to the Unified CVP solution.

Table 3-2   *Unified CVP Call Director Native and Non-Native Component Usage*

Component	Required	Optional	Not Used	Native
SIP Service (Call Server)	Yes (if SIP)	—	—	Yes
IVR Service (Call Server)		—	Yes	Yes
ICM Service (Call Server)	Yes	—	—	Yes
H323 Service (Call Server)	Yes (If H323)	—	—	Yes
VoiceXML Server	—	—	Yes	Yes
Unified Call Studio	—	—	Yes	Yes
Ingress Gateway	Yes	—	—	—
VXML Gateway		—	Yes	—
SIP Proxy	Yes (if SIP)	—	—	—
Gatekeeper	Yes (If H323)	—	—	—
Operations Console	Yes	—	—	Yes
Reporting Server	—	Yes	—	Yes
ASR/TTS	—	—	Yes	—
Media Server	—	—	Yes	—
DNS Server	—	Yes	—	—
Content Services Switch	—	—	Yes	—
Unified ICM	Yes	—	—	—
Unified Call Manager	—	Yes	—	—
Egress Gateway	—	Yes	—	—

Note   Although Figure 3-5 does not show all the optional components, this model can use SIP proxy servers and gatekeepers depending on what call control protocol is used in the deployment.

SIP-Based Protocol-Level and Component Call Flow

This section examines how the components interact with each other at the protocol level. As illustrated for the Unified CVP Standalone model, Figure 3-6 reviews the steps of a typical call director call flow.

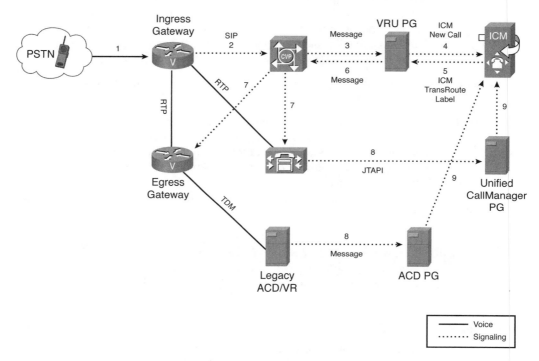

Figure 3-6   *Unified CVP Call Director SIP Call Flow*

Step 1.   The call arrives from either the PSTN or a VoIP connection to the gateway.

Step 2.   The Ingress Gateway sends a SIP INVITE message either directly to the Unified CVP call server or to a SIP Proxy Server, which forwards the request to the Unified CVP Server SIP Service.

Step 3.   The Unified CVP Server SIP Service sends a route request to Unified ICM via the Unified CVP Server ICM Service and the PG.

Step 4.   The Unified CVP Server sends Unified ICM a new call request via its VRU PIM that is configured and hosted by the PG. This new call request invokes a new incoming dialed number that in turn invokes a routing script in Unified ICM.

Step 5.   The Unified ICM routing script selects a target and returns a translation route label to the PG via the Unified CVP VRU PIM hosted by the PG.

Step 6.   The Unified CVP Server's ICM Service processes the instructions provided by the VRU PIM and hands the label over to the SIP Service for call setup.

Step 7.   The Unified CVP Call Server's SIP Service signals either the Ingress Gateway or the proxy server, depending on its configuration. This enables the call to be set up between either an Egress Gateway or a Unified Communications Manager cluster. Depending on the solution requirements, the call server can connect calls to either an Egress Gateway or Unified Communications Manager. As depicted in Figure 3-6, Real-time Transport Protocol (RTP) or voice bearer traffic flows directly between the Ingress Gateway and an Egress Gateway or a Unified Communications Manager IP Phone. Call control signaling continues to flow through the Unified CVP to enable subsequent call control.

Step 8.   When the call arrives at the selected termination, the termination equipment sends a request to its PG for routing instructions.

Step 9.   When the call arrives at the selected termination, the termination equipment sends a request to its PG for routing instructions. This step involves the translation route and enables any call data from the previously run Unified ICM script to be passed to the selected termination. In the case of a TDM-based IVR, the self-service can occur with the caller either being released or transferred to a live agent. In the case of a TDM-based ACD, the call may be queued until an agent is available.

Note   In either of these cases, the IVR self-service or ACD treatment is not handled by Unified CVP but configured and delivered via the legacy TDM-based IVR or ACD. VRU Scripts and transfer to a VRU leg are not available in this call flow model.

VoIP Transfers Using SIP

Figure 3-7 illustrates how VoIP transfers using SIP are accomplished within this model. Because the Unified CVP call server still maintains call control, it has the capability to signal the Ingress Gateway to move the call from one termination point to another. This is accomplished via PG messages from the original termination point, which may have been a legacy ACD/IVR or Unified Communications Manager. Although Figure 3-7 illustrates this transfer using a second Egress Gateway, this transfer could occur to the same or a different Egress Gateway or Unified Communications Manager cluster.

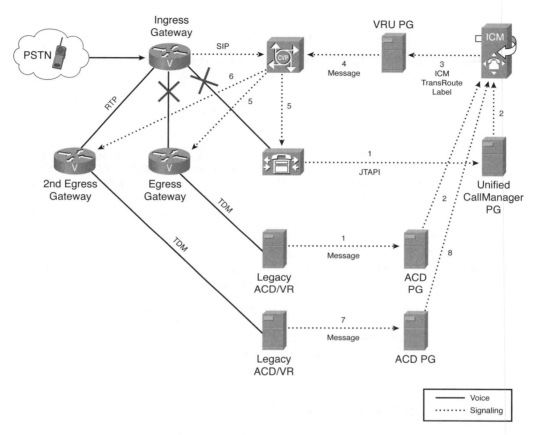

Figure 3-7 *Unified CVP Call Director SIP Transfers Call Flow*

Following are the details for the steps previously referenced:

Step 1.   A caller from a previously routed call, which is currently controlled by the Unified CVP Call Server, requests to be transferred to another location.

Step 2.   The TDM IVR, ACD, or Unified Communications Manager sends a post-route request with call data (via its PG) to Unified ICM.

> **Note**   Regardless of whether the call was initially routed to a TDM IVR, ACD, or Unified Communications Manager cluster location, the call can request to be transferred to another location as long as the Unified CVP Call Server still has call control with the Ingress Gateway.

Step 3.   When Unified ICM receives this post-route request, it runs an associated routing script based on the transferred dialed number. The Unified ICM routing script selects a target and returns a translation route label to the PG via the Unified CVP VRU PIM hosted by the PG.

Step 4. The Unified CVP Server's ICM Service processes the instructions provided by the VRU PIM and hands the label over to the SIP Service for call setup.

Step 5. The Unified CVP Server's SIP Service releases the call leg to the originally selected termination devices. In Figure 3-7, these devices were either an Egress Gateway or a Unified Communications Manager.

Step 6. The Unified CVP Call Server's SIP Service signals either the Ingress Gateway or the proxy server, depending on its configuration, which enables for the call to be set up between either the second Egress Gateway or a different Unified Communications Manager cluster. The call can also be extended to the same devices that the originating call terminated on. However, Steps 1 through 6 are still required. Existing RTP streams are torn down and brought back up with the second termination device, as depicted in Figure 3-7.

Step 7. When the call arrives at the second termination device, the termination equipment sends a request to its PG for routing instructions.

Step 8. This step involves the translation route and enables any call data from the previously run Unified ICM script to be passed to the selected termination. In the case of a TDM-based IVR, self-service can occur with the caller either being released or transferred to a live agent. In the case of a TDM-based ACD, the call may be queued until an agent is available.

Note   Calls can continue to be transferred between locations using the same VoIP-based transfer call flow previously described.

SIP Call Flow Ladder Diagram

Figure 3-8 illustrates the call flow showing the interaction between native and non-native CVP components. Expanding from Figure 3-3, additional services are engaged with this deployment model than what was illustrated for the standalone model. For example, the SIP Service is now used with a SIP proxy server, Egress Gateways, and even a Unified Communications Manager cluster.

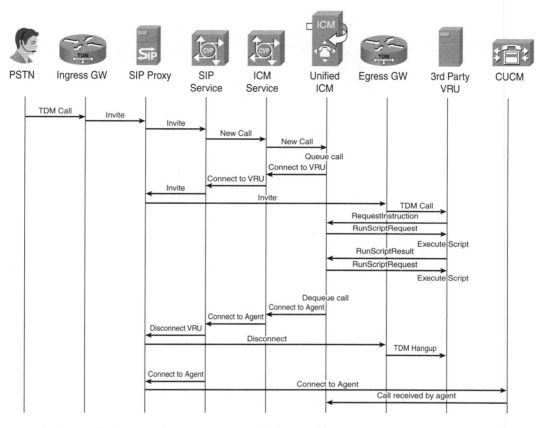

Figure 3-8   *Unified CVP Call Director SIP Call Flow Ladder Diagram*

> **Note**   Figure 3-8 also depicts the overlapping agent connect conversations, which are mutually exclusive and presented on the same ladder diagram to provide a comparison between a transfer that occurs to an Egress Gateway versus the same transfer to a Unified Communications Manager cluster with agent IP Phones.

H.323 Protocol-Level and Component Call Flow

Although it has been mentioned a few times in this book that H.323 is still supported for upgrades and not for green-field deployments, you need to understand the basic protocol call flow and component interaction for H.323. Migrations require engineers to migrate these call flows to SIP. Understanding how they currently operate can provide important insight for performing migrations. Figure 3-9 illustrates the H.323 call flow, which has striking similarities to the previous SIP call flow shown earlier in Figure 3-6.

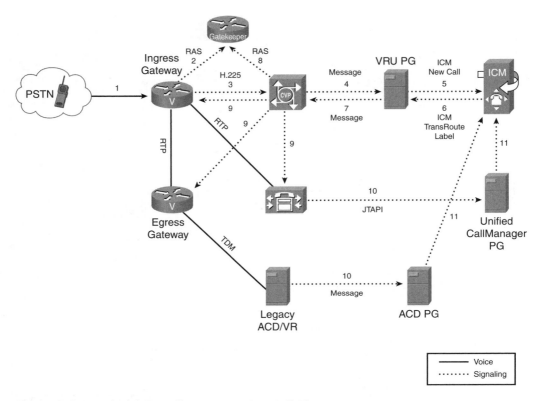

Figure 3-9   *Unified CVP Call Director H.323 Call Flow*

Following are the details for the steps previously referenced:

Step 1.   The call arrives from either the PSTN or a VoIP connection to the gateway.

Step 2.   The Ingress Gateway sends an H.225 Registration, an Admission, and a Status (RAS) request to the H.323 gatekeeper to find the IP address of an appropriate Unified CVP Server for the incoming dialed number.

Step 3.   The Ingress Gateway sends an H.225 call setup message to the Unified CVP Server's H.323 Service.

> **Note**   During the initial call setup between the Ingress Gateway and the CVP Call Server, a brief G.711 voice stream exists and is immediately torn down when the Unified CVP Call Server gains call control.

Step 4.   The Unified CVP Server's H.323 Service sends a route request to Unified ICM via the Unified CVP Server's IVR Service, the Unified CVP Server's ICM Service, and the PG.

Step 5.   The Unified CVP Server sends Unified ICM a new call request via its VRU PIM that is configured and hosted by the PG. This new call request invokes a new incoming dialed number that in turn invokes a routing script in Unified ICM.

Step 6.   The Unified ICM routing script selects a target and returns a translation route label to the PG via the Unified CVP VRU PIM hosted by the PG.

Step 7.   The Unified CVP Server's ICM Service processes the instructions provided by the VRU PIM and hands the label over to the H.323 Service for call setup.

Step 8.   The Unified CVP Call Server's H.323 Service sends a RAS request to the H.323 gatekeeper to find the IP address of the appropriate termination (an Egress Voice Gateway to the PSTN, an Egress Voice Gateway front-ending a TDM peripheral or a Unified Communications Manager Cluster).

Step 9.   The Unified CVP Server's H.323 Service then sends an H.225 call setup message to the termination location (Egress Voice Gateway or Unified Communications Manager cluster) and makes an Empty Capability Set (ECS) request to the Ingress Voice Gateway to redirect the call. RTP or voice bearer traffic flows directly between the Ingress Gateway and the selected termination point (refer to Figure 3.9). Call control signaling continues to flow through the Unified CVP call server to allow subsequent call control.

Step 10.   When the call arrives at the selected termination, the termination equipment sends a request to its PG for routing instructions.

Step 11.   This step involves the translation route and enables any call data from the previously run Unified ICM script to be passed to the selected termination. In the case of a TDM-based IVR, self-service can occur with the caller either being released or transferred to a live agent. In the case of a TDM-based ACD, the call may be queued until an agent is available.

> **Note**   Although a SIP Proxy Server is optional for both the switch and VRU leg of a SIP call with Unified CVP, an H.323 gatekeeper is not for H.323 calls. The H.323 service running on a Unified CVP Call Server requires a registration with a gatekeeper; without this configuration and subsequent registration, the call server from an H.323 perspective remains in a down state. The implication of this requirement on SIP and H.323 call flows is that a SIP configuration can exclude the use of a SIP proxy server relying on static SIP routes, whereas an H.323 configuration requires a gatekeeper to have the call server up and processing H.323 calls. Even with edge queuing architectures that use the H.323 Set Transfer Label configuration, an active gatekeeper registration must still exist on the call server for the label to be sent back to the originating H.323 Gateway, even though the architecture ignores the gatekeeper lookup during the VRU leg of a H.323 call.

VoIP Transfers Using H323

Figure 3-10 illustrates how VoIP transfers work with H.323. The call flow is similar to SIP; however, a gatekeeper lookup using RAS is required in the middle of the call flow.

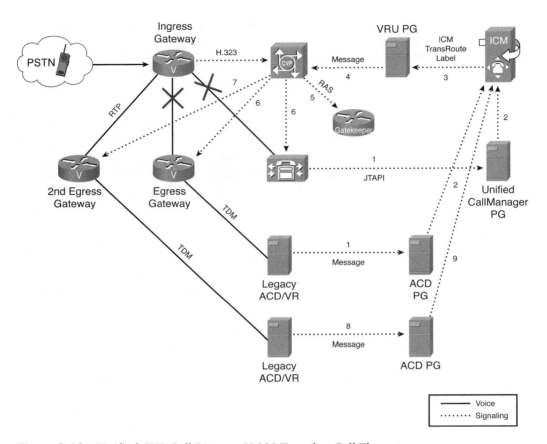

Figure 3-10   *Unified CVP Call Director H.323 Transfers Call Flow*

Following are the details for the steps previously referenced:

Step 1.   A caller from a previously routed call, which is currently controlled by the Unified CVP Call Server, requests to be transferred to another location.

Step 2.   The TDM IVR, ACD, or Unified Communications Manager sends a post-route request with call data (via its PG) to Unified ICM.

Note   Regardless of whether the call was initially routed to a TDM IVR, ACD, or Unified Communications Manager cluster location, the call can request to be transferred to another location as long as the Unified CVP Call Server still has call control with the Ingress Gateway.

Step 3.   When Unified ICM receives this post-route request, it runs an associated routing script based on the transferred dialed number and other criteria. The

Unified ICM routing script selects a target and returns a translation route label to the PG via the Unified CVP VRU PIM hosted by the PG.

Step 4. The Unified CVP Server's ICM Service processes the instructions provided by the VRU PIM and hands the label over to the H.323 Service for call setup.

Step 5. The Unified CVP Server's H.323 Service queries the H.323 gatekeeper to get an IP address for the new termination.

Step 6. The Unified CVP Server's H.323 Service releases the call leg to the originally selected termination devices. These devices were either an Egress Gateway or a Unified Communications Manager (refer to Figure 3-10).

Step 7. The Unified CVP Call Server's H.323 Service signals the original termination device, which enables the call to be set up between either the second Egress Gateway or a different Unified Communications Manager cluster. The call could also be extended to the same devices that the originating call terminated on. However, Steps 1 through 6 are still required. Existing RTP streams are torn down and brought back up with the second termination device (refer to Figure 3-10).

Step 8. When the call arrives at the second termination device, the termination equipment sends a request to its PG for routing instructions.

Step 9. This step involves the translation route and enables any call data from the previously run Unified ICM script to be passed to the selected termination. In the case of a TDM-based IVR, self-service can occur with the caller either being released or transferred to a live agent. In the case of a TDM-based ACD, the call may be queued until an agent is available.

Note   Calls may continue to be transferred between locations using the same VoIP-based transfer call flow previously described.

Transfers and Subsequent Call Control

In addition to the transfers managed by Unified ICM, the Call Director Deployment model can transfer calls to non-ICM terminations or invoke a Release Trunk Transfer to the PSTN. However, if a call is transferred to a non-ICM controlled termination, call data cannot be passed to the termination, further call control is impossible for the call, and the cradle-to-grave call reporting that Unified ICM gathers is complete. In the case of a Release to Trunk Transfer on the Ingress Voice Gateway, call data or call control cannot be maintained. However, if the call is a translation routed to another ICM peripheral, call data and cradle-to-grave reporting can be maintained.

If a transfer fails or the termination device returns a busy status, or if the target rings for a period of time that exceeds the Unified CVP Call Server's ring-no-answer (RNA) timeout setting, the Unified CVP Call Server cancels the transfer request and sends a transfer failure indication to Unified ICM. This scenario causes a Router Re-query operation within Unified ICM, enabling a different target to be selected or execution of a remedial action.[3]

Comprehensive Model

This next function deployment model provides organizations with a mechanism to route and transfer calls across a VoIP network, offers IVR services, and queues calls before routing to a selected agent. These features are usually found in situations in which an organization is interested in providing a pure IP-based contact center. A caller can initially be directed into an IVR service, exit, and be queued for the next available agent. In addition, transfers are supported between Unified CCE Agents. The passing of data between Unified CVP and ICM is fully supported, and cradle-to-grave reporting for all calls is also supported. Figure 3-11 shows the components used with this solution and their protocols.

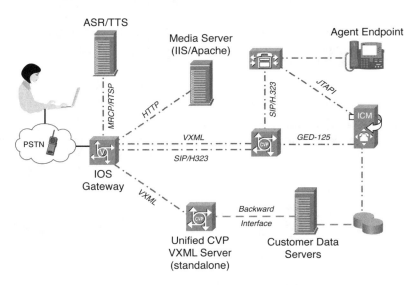

Figure 3-11 *Unified CVP Comprehensive Functional Deployment Model*

Note Although some documentation identifies Basic Video as a potential fifth deployment model, Basic Video is nothing more than a comprehensive deployment model with video endpoints replacing voice endpoints; therefore, the call flows provided in this section also apply to the implementation of Basic Video with Unified CVP. The use of Cisco Unified Videoconferencing hardware, Radvision IVP, and Radvision iContact are not required for the implementation of the Basic Video Service and are out of the scope of this book.

Table 3-3 identifies which components are required, optional, and not used by this model. In addition, the Native column identifies components native to the Unified CVP solution.

Table 3-3   *Unified CVP Comprehensive Native and Non-Native Component Usage*

Component	Required	Optional	Not Used	Native
SIP Service (Call Server)	Yes	—	—	Yes
IVR Service (Call Server)	Yes	—	—	Yes
ICM Service (Call Server)	Yes	—	—	Yes
H323 Service (Call Server)	Yes (If H323)	—	—	Yes
VoiceXML Server	—	Yes	—	Yes
Unified Call Studio	—	Yes	—	Yes
Ingress Gateway	Yes	—	—	—
VXML Gateway	Yes	—	—	—
SIP Proxy	—	Yes	—	—
Gatekeeper	Yes (If H323)	—	—	—
Operations Console	Yes	—	—	Yes
Reporting Server	—	Yes	—	Yes
ASR/TTS	—	Yes	—	—
Media Server	—	Yes	—	—
DNS Server	—	Yes	—	—
Content Services Switch	—	Yes	—	—
Unified ICM	Yes	—	—	—
Unified Communications Manager	—	Yes	—	—
Egress Gateway	—	Yes	—	—

Note   Although Table 3-3 lists the Unified Communications Manager and Egress Gateway as optional components, at least one of these components should exist to enable a call to be transferred to either a legacy ACD Agent via an Egress Gateway or to a Unified CCE Agent hosted by a Unified Communications Manager cluster. Which component is deployed depends entirely on the organization's requirements. In addition, the use of load balancers, media servers, and even an ASR/TTS Server are also optional because the VXML Gateways can be configured in such a way to allow them to operate without these components. In the case of ASR/TTS, this would be true only if the organization has no requirement to perform the ASR/TTS treatment for incoming calls.

SIP-Based Protocol-Level and Component Call Flow

This section examines the detailed call flow steps performed in a typical comprehensive call flow. As its name indicates this model is the most complex from a call flow perspective. Figure 3-12 illustrates a typical comprehensive call flow with a SIP proxy server as part of the solution. Figure 3-13, provided later in this section, covers a similar SIP call flow without a proxy server.

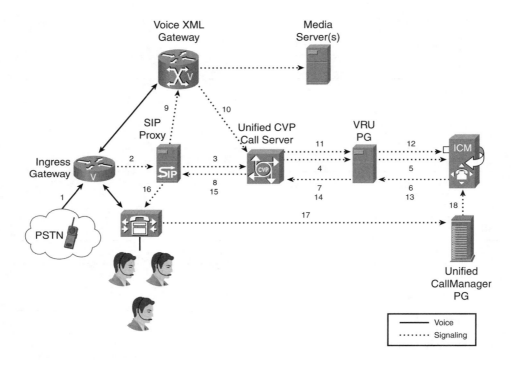

Figure 3-12 *Unified CVP Comprehensive SIP Call Flow with a SIP Proxy Server*

Following are the details for the steps previously referenced:

Step 1.   The call arrives from either the PSTN or a VoIP connection to the gateway.

Step 2.   The Ingress Gateway sends a SIP INVITE message the SIP Proxy Server.

Step 3.   The SIP Proxy Server forwards this SIP INVITE to the Unified CVP Server's SIP Service.

Step 4.   The SIP Service sends a new call request to Unified ICM via the Unified CVP Server ICM Service and the PG.

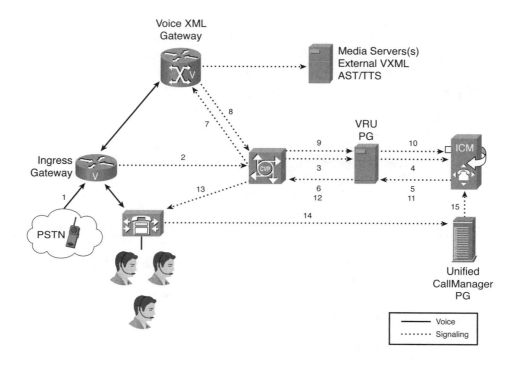

Figure 3-13 *Unified CVP Comprehensive SIP Call Flow Without a SIP Proxy Server*

Step 5.   The Unified CVP Server sends Unified ICM a new call request via its VRU
PIM that is configured and hosted by the PG. This new call request invokes a
routing script in Unified ICM based on the dialed number provided by
Unified CVP.

Step 6.   The Unified ICM routing script determines that the caller must be transferred
to the VRU and passes a Connect to VRU request to the PG, which will be forwarded to the ICM Service on the Unified CVP Call Server.

Step 7.   PG passes the information provided in Step 6 to the ICM Service on the
Unified CVP Call Server.

Step 8.   Invitation to Connect to VRU goes from SIP Service back to the SIP Proxy
Server requiring the SIP Proxy Server to determine which VXML Gateway
based on its routing table should handle the Connect to VRU and subsequent
call treatment session for the VRU leg of the call.

Step 9.   Invitation (including information about Ingress Gateway) is sent from the SIP
Proxy Server to a VXML Gateway, which then connects the audio path back
to the Ingress Gateway.

Step 10.   The VRU label causes the VXML Gateway to fire off an application dial-peer,
which starts the VRU or application leg of the call. The VXML Gateway con-

nects to the Unified CVP Call Server via HTTP and requests instructions for treating the connected call. This HTTP new call request is handled by the Unified CVP Server's IVR Service, which then passes this request to the Unified CVP Server's ICM Service.

Step 11. ICM Service sends Request Instructions to Unified ICM via the PG.

Step 12. Unified ICM continues the script that was started in Step 5 and processes additional nodes that produce Run Script requests to the Unified CVP Server's ICM Service. It hands these instructions over to the Unified CVP Server's IVR Service that converts them into VXML pages that are forwarded back to the VXML Gateway for rendering and execution. This process can also include prompt and collect instructions and continues between Unified ICM, Unified CVP, and the VXML Gateway until an agent becomes available. The VoiceXML Gateway also fetches any media files requested in the VXML pages from the media server (refer to the top of Figure 3-12).

Step 13. The agent becomes available, so Unified ICM dequeues the call and asks to be disconnected from the VXML Gateway. Unified ICM passes a connect-to-agent request to the Unified CVP Server's ICM Service via the VRU PG.

Step 14. PG passes the information provided in Step 13 to the ICM Service on the Unified CVP Call Server. The ICM Service passes this connect request to the Unified CVP Server's SIP Service.

Step 15. The Unified CVP Server's SIP Service passes this VRU disconnect request to the SIP Proxy Server.

Step 16. The SIP Proxy Server passes a disconnect message to the VXML Gateway. SIP Service passes a connect-to-agent request to the SIP Proxy Server. The SIP Proxy Server passes this connect-to-agent request back via a SIP INVITE to the Cisco Unified Communications Manager Subscriber server responsible for handling the configured SIP Trunk. Because the audio path was torn down between the Ingress Gateway and the VXML Gateway, a new one is established between the Ingress Gateway and the Unified CCE Agent IP Phone hosted on the CUCM cluster.

Step 17. Unified Communications Manager informs the PG that a call was delivered to a Unified CCE Agent.

Step 18. PG notifies Unified ICM that a call has been delivered to the Unified CCE Agent.

Note   It is common for the Unified CCE Agent IP Phone to be registered with a subscriber server in the Cisco Unified Call Manager cluster that is not the same server configured to communicate with PG and ICM. The Computer Telephony Integration (CTI) Manager service, which should be running on all servers in the cluster that control agent IP Phones, is cluster-aware and forwards updates for agent state, and so on to the CTI Manager service running on the subscriber server connected to the Communications Manager PG via JTAPI. This enables a pair of Communications Manager PGs to service an entire CUCM cluster, even when IP Phones are registered to different servers in the cluster. However, there are still limitations on how many Unified CCE Agents can be serviced via a single pair of Communication Manager PGs. For additional agent and PG sizing considerations please refer to the Unified Contact Center Enterprise Solution Reference Network Design (SRND) or Bill of Materials located at Cisco.com.

Although a previous call flow detailed how the Comprehensive model uses a SIP Proxy Server, a SIP Proxy Server is an optional non-native component. This indicates that a second call flow can occur when a SIP Proxy is not part of the solution. Figure 3-13 provides a look at this call flow, which is similar to the previous call flow (refer to Figure 3-12).

Following are the details for the steps previously referenced:

Step 1.   The call arrives from either the PSTN or a VoIP connection to the gateway.

Step 2.   The Ingress Gateway sends a SIP INVITE message to the Unified CVP Call Server's SIP Service.

Step 3.   The SIP Service sends a new call request to Unified ICM via the Unified CVP Server ICM Service and the VRU PG.

Step 4.   The Unified CVP Server sends Unified ICM a new call request via its VRU PIM configured and hosted by the PG. This new call request invokes a new incoming dialed number that invokes a routing script in Unified ICM.

Step 5.   The Unified ICM routing script determines that the caller must be transferred to the VRU and passes a Connect to VRU request to the PG, which will be forwarded to the ICM Service on the Unified CVP Call Server.

Step 6.   PG passes the information provided in Step 5 to the ICM Service on the Unified CVP Call Server.

Step 7.   The Unified CVP Server's SIP Service determines which VXML Gateway should handle the Connect to VRU and the subsequent call treatment session by examining it's local static SIP routing table configured on the all Server.

Step 8.   The VRU label causes the VXML Gateway to fire off an application dial-peer, which starts the VRU or application leg of the call. The VXML Gateway connects to the Unified CVP Call Server via HTTP and requests instructions for treating the connected call. This HTTP new call request is handled by the Unified CVP Server's IVR Service, which then passes this request to the Unified CVP Server's ICM Service.

Step 9.   The ICM Service sends Request Instructions to Unified ICM via the PG.

Step 10.   Unified ICM continues the script that was started in Step 5 and processes additional nodes that produce Run Script requests to the Unified CVP Server's ICM Service, which then hands these instructions over to the Unified CVP

Server's IVR Service that converts them into VXML pages forwarded back to the VXML Gateway for rendering and execution. This process can also include prompt and collect instructions and continues between Unified ICM, Unified CVP, and the VXML Gateway until an agent becomes available. The VoiceXML Gateway also fetches any media files requested in the VXML pages from the media server (refer to the top of Figure 3-13).

Step 11.   The agent becomes available, so Unified ICM dequeues the call and requests to be disconnected from the VXML Gateway. Unified ICM passes a connect-to-agent request to the Unified CVP Server's ICM Service via the PG.

Step 12.   PG passes the information provided in Step 11 to the ICM Service on the Unified CVP Call Server. The ICM Service passes this connect request to the Unified CVP Server's SIP Service.

Step 13.   The Unified CVP Server's SIP Service passes disconnect to the VXML Gateway. The SIP Service then passes the connect-to-agent request via a SIP INVITE to the Cisco Unified Communications Manager Server responsible for handling the configured SIP Trunk for the cluster. Because the audio path was torn down between the Ingress Gateway and the VXML Gateway, a new one is established between the Ingress Gateway and the Unified CCE Agent IP Phone hosted on the CUCM cluster.

Step 14.   Unified Communications Manager informs the PG that a call was delivered to a Unified CCE agent.

Step 15.   PG notifies Unified ICM that a call has been delivered to the Unified CCE Agent.

Caution   The key takeaway from the previous call flow is that by choosing not to use a SIP Proxy Server, critical elements required for redundancy do not exist. By using a supported SIP Proxy Server, a solution can achieve a high-level of redundancy and increase efficiency pertaining to configuration management and troubleshooting. The call flow (refer to Figure 3-13) requires that each Unified CVP Call Server to be configured with static SIP routes for all VRU and transfer labels. In addition, the Ingress Gateways also must be configured with multiple dial-peers to enable it to choose which Unified CVP Call Server to connect via the switch leg of the call. Although you can use DNS to ease some of this configuration pain, it is best practice in medium or large Unified CVP deployments to use a supported SIP Proxy Server.

VoIP Transfers using SIP

Figure 3-14 illustrates how a VoIP transfer is handled when a Unified CCE agent initiates the transfer via its agent desktop application.

The following detailed steps cover two options supported in the configuration of this transfer: the use of an ICM Dialed Number Plan and Unified Communications Manager

Route Points. Both options follow the same call flow but are quite different in how they engage during a transfer.

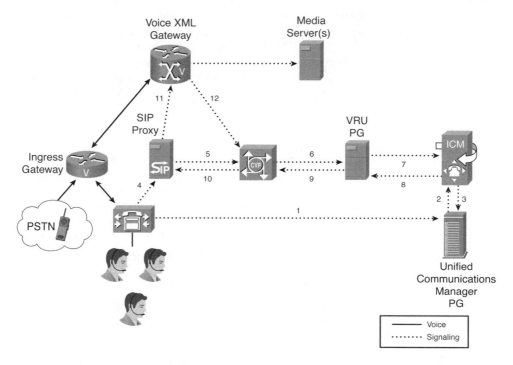

Figure 3-14 *Unified CVP Comprehensive SIP Transfer Call Flow Using an ICM Dialed Number Plan*

The ICM Dialed Number plan is configured within Unified ICM and enables a dial plan matrix to exist where translations can be configured and scripts can be executed before the Unified Communications Manager is asked to decide how to route the label returned by Unified ICM. This enables a transfer to be intercepted as soon as it is initiated on the agent desktop and keeps the dial plan for the contact center stored inside the Unified ICM database and not entirely within the CUCM database.

A second approach is to use Route Points configured within CUCM. This approach is far less desirable simply because of the amount of provisioning and that the dial plan exists both in Unified ICM and Unified Communications Manager. It increases the difficulty around provisioning and troubleshooting the solution.

Note   The ICM Dialed Number Plan (DNP) can be used only if the Unified CCE agents use their agent desktop software to initiate the transfers. If the Unified CCE agents elect to use their IP phones for the transfer, the solution must be configured with CTI Route Points in Unified Communications Manager. This is because agent desktop software queries the ICM DNP for a label on where the call should be sent based on the number dialed by the agent. This is an important consideration, especially if the solution requires transfers to be initiated from both the IP Phone and the agent desktop software. The ladder diagrams provided in Figures 3-18 and 3-19 illustrate this interaction.

The details are included in these steps:

Step 1.   The Unified CCE Agent initiates a transfer, either by dialing a route point configured on CUCM or dialing a number that has been configured in the ICM Dialed Number Plan. For the route point, because it is under the control of the Communications Manager PG, ICM is notified when the route point is called, which kicks off a routing script. For the ICM Dialed Number Plan, the agent desktop application sends the dialed digits via the Computer Telephony Integration Object Server (CTIOS) Server, which interacts with ICM without CUCM knowing yet that a transfer has been initiated.

Step 2.   Unified ICM executes a transfer script associated with either the route point dialed or the result of the number mapping configured in the ICM Dialed Number Plan.

Step 3.   The Unified ICM script executed in Step 2 either finishes by finding an available Unified CCE agent and returns the DN of that agents phone, or it returns a label that is then sent by CUCM to a Unified CVP Call Server to gain call control on the new call transfer leg.

Step 4.   CUCM matches the label returned by Unified ICM in Step 3 and determines that it must be sent to the SIP Proxy Server via the SIP trunk configured for the CUCM cluster.

Step 5.   The SIP Proxy Server consults its routing table and determines that the label dialed by CUCM in Step 4 must be sent to a Unified CVP Call Server and processed by its internal SIP Service.

Step 6.   The Unified CVP Call Server's SIP service accepts the SIP INVITE from the SIP Proxy Server and hands the existing call request over to the ICM Service, which forwards it to the VRU PG.

Step 7.   The Unified CVP Server sends Unified ICM an existing call request via its VRU PIM that is configured and hosted by the PG. This existing call request causes Unified ICM to continue the execution of the script that began in Step 2.

Note   The label referenced in Step 6 and VRU labels used during the VRU leg of a call are two different labels because the routing client from Unified ICM's perspective during this transfer is actually the CUCM PG and not the Unified CVP VRU PG. A Routing Client is used to determine what label should be returned and to whom the label should go to. Later, this chapter discusses interaction with Unified ICM in much greater detail when VRU types and their significance are covered. The key takeaway is that a different routing client label is used during Steps 6 and 7, than the VRU label that will be returned in Steps 8 and 9. Also both of these labels have a correlation ID appended to the end of the label that was configured for the routing client. The Correlation ID is generated by ICM when it returns a label for the requesting routing client. Unified CVP uses its maximum DNIS setting within the call server to determine when the length of the received label signifies a new call or an existing call. For example, the default setting for the maximum DNIS in Unified CVP is ten digits. So for new calls originating on the switch leg, the total DNIS value of the incoming call should be ten digits or less, for Unified CVP to set up a new call dialog with Unified ICM. However, when a transfer or VRU label is provided to CVP as noted in the preceding Steps 6 and 7, the label for both routing clients, Unified CVP and CUCM, should be at least ten digits in length (that is, 9999999999 and 8888888888, respectively).

This ensures that when Unified ICM adds the call's Correlation ID to the routing client label, it will always be greater than ten digits and therefore always instructs Unified CVP to open an existing call dialog with Unified ICM to continue executing the transfer script started in Step 2. The maximum DNIS setting in Unified CVP can be modified to a lower or higher number, but it is critical to understand the relationship between this setting and which call dialog gets invoked based on the label presented to CVP.

Step 8.   The Unified ICM routing script determines that the caller must be transferred to the VRU and passes a Connect to VRU request to the PG, which will be forwarded to the ICM Service on the Unified CVP Call Server. The new label generated here is for the Unified CVP Server because it is now the routing client. A single SendToVRU Node can be used to generate two labels: one from execution in Step 3 and one from its continued script execution in this step. Unified ICM is smart enough to determine which routing client label to return, and it accomplishes this with a single node in the script.

Step 9.   VRU PG passes the information provided in Step 8 to the ICM Service on the Unified CVP Call Server.

Step 10.   The Invitation to Connect to VRU goes from SIP Service back to the SIP Proxy Server requiring the SIP Proxy Server to determine which VXML gateway, based on its routing table, should handle the Connect to VRU and subsequent call treatment session for the VRU leg of the call.

Step 11.   The Invitation (including information about the Ingress Gateway) goes from SIP Proxy Server to a VXML Gateway, which then connects the audio path back to the transferring the Unified CCE Agent's phone. The transferring Unified CCE Agents' Phone establishes audio connection with the VXML Gateway.

Step 12.   The VRU label causes the VXML Gateway to fire off an application dial-peer on the VXML gateway, which starts the VRU or application leg of the call. The VXML Gateway connects to the Unified CVP Call Server via HTTP and requests instructions for treating the connected call. This HTTP new call request is handled by the Unified CVP Server's IVR Service, which then passes this request to the Unified CVP Server's ICM Service. Steps 11–18 (refer to Figure 3-12) continue to execute enabling the new transfer leg to either be treated on the VXML Gateway or connected to an agent in the new skill group.

Note   IP initiated transfers from a CUCM are always a new call leg. This explains why a Unified CVP Call Server must be contacted during this transfer to enable its SIP Service to gain call control. A transfer leg is no different than a new switch leg, other than the DNIS called is treated as if it were an existing call from the ICM's perspective. The call control provided by the CVP on this new transfer call leg is completely different than the call control provided for the originating call leg that is being transferred.

SIP Call Flow Ladder Diagram

Figure 3-15 illustrates this model's call flow, which provides details on how comprehensive it truly is.

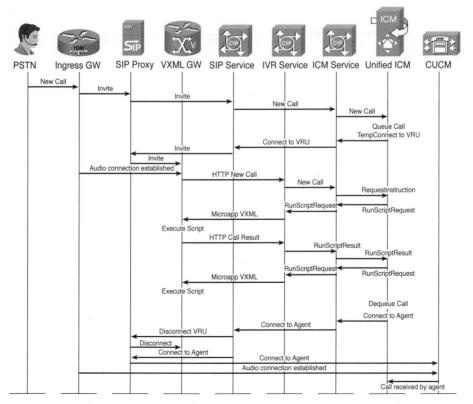

Figure 3-15   *Unified CVP Comprehensive SIP Call Flow Ladder Diagram*

In addition to this SIP call flow ending with the call being received by an agent, Figures 3-16 and 3-17 provide a ladder diagram for warm transfers using a CUCM route point to an available agent and to a queue treated by the VXML Gateway, respectively.

Dialing the CUCM route point initiates a connection to the CUCM PG that causes it to immediately execute a script within Unified ICM based on the dialed number of the route point (refer to Figures 3-16 and 3-17). The interaction when an agent is available and the call does not need to be queued to the VRU leg after the CVP has call control and has communicated with Unified ICM on what its next steps should be (refer to Figure 3-16).

Unified ICM discovers that a Unified CCE Agent is unavailable to take the call and instead makes a decision that the call should be queued and treated at the VRU (refer to Figure 3-17). Further communication is illustrated for the subsequent VRU or application leg of the call with conversations firing off between the VXML router and the Unified CVP Call Server.

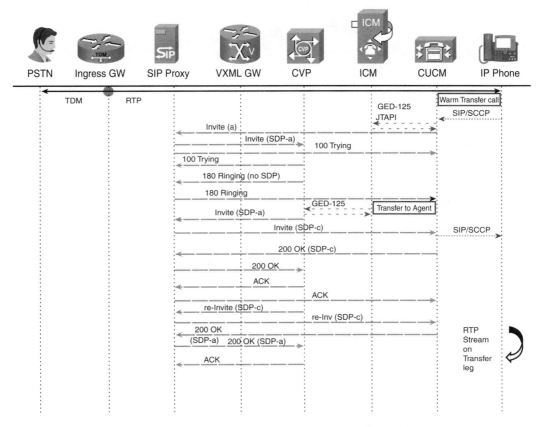

Figure 3-16 *Unified CVP Comprehensive SIP Warm Transfer to Agent via CUCM Route Point*

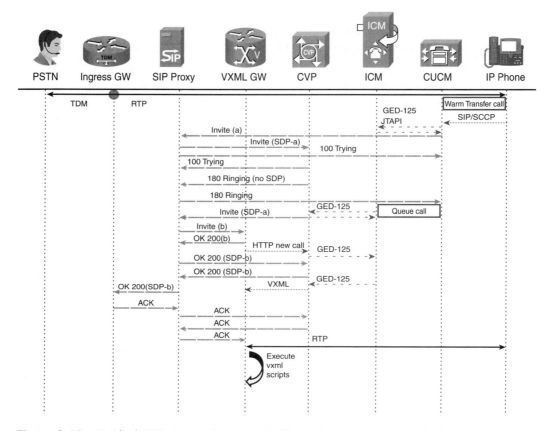

Figure 3-17   *Unified CVP Comprehensive SIP Warm Transfer to Queue via CUCM Route Point*

Transfers initiated by using ICM's Dialed Number Plan are similar except for how they are initiated. Figures 3-18 and 3-19 provide the equivalent ladder diagrams for transfer to an agent or a queue when initiating the transfers using an ICM Dialed Number Plan configuration.

The most important observation with respect to these ladder diagrams is how the transfer actually begins. When an Unified CCE Agent initiates the warm transfer via their agent desktop application, the ICM DNP application is engaged before CUCM must resolve and route the dialed number. ICM DNP enables the dialed number to translate within ICM and even have a script that executes the process of returning a completely different dialed number than the one the agent dialed. This is passed to CUCM for routing. The remainder of the ladder diagram displayed in Figures 3-18 and 3-19 are identical to the previous ones provided in Figures 3-16 and 3-17.

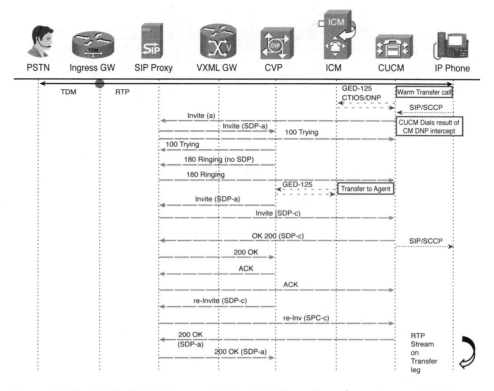

Figure 3-18 *Unified CVP Comprehensive SIP Warm Transfer to Agent via ICM Dialed Number Plan*

H.323 Protocol-Level and Component Call Flow

Figure 3-20 illustrates how the comprehensive call flow works when using H.323 as the call control protocol. The call closely resembles the previous SIP call flows presented in Figure 3-12. However, because H.323 is a peer-to-peer call control protocol, the gatekeeper provides only admission control services, which is different than how a SIP proxy handles the SIP invites in the SIP call flow. In the H.323 call flow for comprehensive, the gatekeeper replaces the SIP proxy from a call flow perspective. However, it is a mandatory component for H.323. In other words, there is no capability for Unified CVP to bypass the use of a gatekeeper as in the previously illustrated SIP without proxy call flow. Even if a Set transfer label configuration is used with H.323, enabling calls to be sent to the originating gateway during the switch leg of the H.323 call flow, the H.323 service does not go into an UP state unless a gatekeeper is configured. Without the H.323 service active on the call server, H.323 connections cannot be made during the switch leg of a call or connected to a VXML gateway after the VRU leg of the call is engaged. This creates a classic "chicken before the egg" stalemate situation.

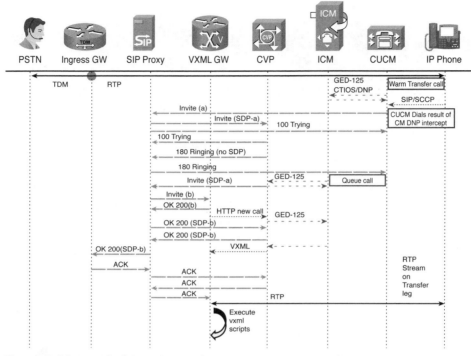

Figure 3-19 *Unified CVP Comprehensive SIP Warm Transfer to Queue via ICM Dialed Number Plan*

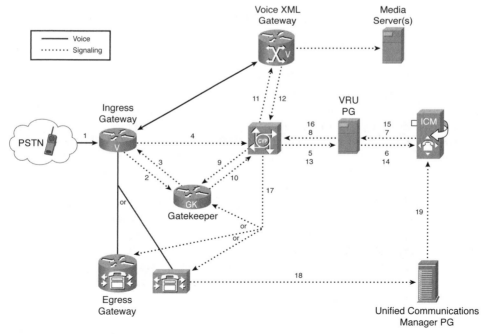

Figure 3-20 *Unified CVP Comprehensive H.323 Call Flow*

Following are the details for the steps previously referenced:

Step 1. The call arrives from either the PSTN or a VoIP connection to the gateway.

Step 2. The Ingress Gateway sends a Registration, Admission, and Status (RAS) request to the H.323 Gatekeeper to find the IP address of the Unified CVP Call Server.

Step 3. The H.323 Gatekeeper executes its call routing decision tree and matches the E.164 number (DNIS) to a registered Unified CVP Call Server. The gatekeeper returns an Admission Confirm (ACF) message containing the IP address of the Unified CVP Call Server to the Ingress Gateway.

Step 4. The Ingress Voice Gateway sends a H.225 call setup message to the Unified CVP Server's H.323 Service.

Step 5. The Unified CVP Server sends Unified ICM a new call request via its VRU PIM configured and hosted by the PG.

Step 6. This new call request invokes a new incoming dialed number that in turn invokes a routing script in Unified ICM.

Step 7. The Unified ICM routing script determines that the caller must be transferred to the VRU and passes a Connect-to-VRU request to the PG, which will be forwarded to the ICM Service on the Unified CVP Call Server.

Step 8. PG passes the information provided in Step 6 to the ICM Service on the Unified CVP Call Server.

Step 9. The H.323 Service sends a RAS Request to the H.323 Gatekeeper to find the IP Address of the VoiceXML Gateway associated with the VRU label returned by Unified ICM.

Step 10. The H.323 Gatekeeper executes its call routing decision tree and matches the VRU label to a registered VoiceXML Gateway. The gatekeeper returns an Admission Confirm (ACF) message containing the IP address of the VoiceXML Gateway to the Unified CVP Call Server.

Step 11. The Unified CVP Server's H.323 Service sends an H.225 setup message to the VoiceVXML Gateway returned in Step 10 by the Gatekeeper's ACF message.

Step 12. The VRU label causes the VXML Gateway to fire off an application dial-peer on the VXML Gateway, which starts the VRU or application leg of the call. The VXML Gateway connects to the Unified CVP Call Server via HTTP and requests instructions for treating the connected call. This HTTP new call request is handled by the Unified CVP Server's IVR Service, which then passes this request to the Unified CVP Server's ICM Service.

Step 13. ICM Service sends Request Instructions to Unified ICM via the PG.

Step 14. Unified ICM continues the script that was started in Step 7. It processes additional nodes that produce Run Script requests to the Unified CVP Server's

ICM Service, which then hands these instructions over to the Unified CVP Server's IVR Service that converts them into VXML pages forwarded back to the VXML Gateway for rendering and execution. This process can also include prompt and collect instructions and continues between Unified ICM, Unified CVP, and the VXML gateway until an agent becomes available. The VoiceXML Gateway also fetches any media files requested in the VXML pages from the media server (refer to the top of Figure 3-20).

Step 15.   An agent becomes available, so Unified ICM dequeues the call and asks to be disconnected from the VXML Gateway. Unified ICM passes a Connect-to-Agent request to the Unified CVP Server's ICM Service via the VRU PG.

Step 16.   PG passes the information provided in Step 15 to the ICM Service on the Unified CVP Call Server. The ICM Service passes this connect request to the Unified CVP Server's IVR Service.

Step 17.   The Unified CVP Server's IVR Service requests the H.323 Service to transfer the caller to the dialed number of the selected agent or Egress Gateway. The H.323 service then sends a RAS message to the H.323 Gatekeeper to find the desired endpoint, either an Egress Gateway or a H.323 CUCM trunk. The gatekeeper then returns an ACF message containing the IP address of the termination point. This causes the Unified CVP Server's H.323 service to send a H.225 call setup message to the termination point. Because the audio path was torn down between the Ingress Gateway and the VXML Gateway, a new one is established between the Ingress Gateway and an Egress Gateway or a Unified CCE Agent IP Phone hosted on the CUCM cluster.

Step 18.   The Unified Communications Manager notifies its Call Manager PG that the agent has received the call.

Step 19.   The Call Manager PG informs Unified ICM that the call was received by the agent.

VoIP Transfers Using H.323

As discussed earlier with VoIP transfers using SIP, H.323 implements the same call flow when using ICM DNP or CUCM Route Points. The only difference in the two call flows is the use of a SIP Proxy for SIP and a gatekeeper for H.323 transfers. In addition, the CUCM server that sets up the transfer call leg also uses a H.323 trunk connected to a gatekeeper versus a SIP trunk connected to a SIP Proxy. Other than these two small differences, the call flow is essentially the same. The SIP INVITE messages are replaced with H.323 ACF messages enabling the Unified CCE agents to connect to either a VoiceXML Gateway for treatment, an Egress Gateway connected to TDM endpoints, or an H.323 CUCM trunk passing the transfer call to an available agent handling a different Unified ICM skill group. The fundamentals that enable Unified CVP to gain call control for the transfer leg exists both in SIP and H.323 transfers. Only the component that holds the dial plan and decision on where the call is transferred changes, in this case from a SIP Proxy to a H.323 Gatekeeper. Figure 3-21 outlines a VoIP transfer when using H.323.

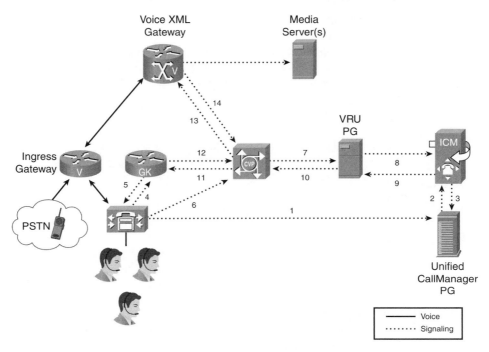

Figure 3-21 *Unified CVP Comprehensive H.323 Transfer Call Flow Using ICM DNP*

Following are the details for the steps referenced in Figure 3-21:

Step 1.   The Unified CCE Agent initiates a transfer, either by dialing a route point configured on CUCM or dialing a number that has been configured in the ICM Dialed Number Plan. For the route point, because it is under the control of the Communications Manager PG, ICM is notified when the route point is called, which invokes a routing script. For the ICM Dialed Number Plan, the agent desktop application sends the dialed digits via the CTIOS server, which interacts with ICM without CUCM knowing yet that a transfer has been initiated.

Step 2.   Unified ICM executes a transfer script associated with either the route point dialed or the result of the number mapping configured in the ICM Dialed Number Plan.

Step 3.   The Unified ICM script executed in Step 2 either finishes by finding an available Unified CCE agent and returns the label of the agents extension, or it returns a label that must then be sent by CUCM to a Unified CVP Call Server to gain call control on the new call transfer leg.

Step 4.   CUCM matches the label returned by Unified ICM in Step 3 and determines that it must be checked against the gatekeeper accessible via a RAS message over an H.323 trunk configured for the CUCM cluster.

Step 5. The H.323 Gatekeeper executes its call routing decision tree and matches the E.164 number (DNIS) to a registered CVP Call Server and processed by its internal H.323 Service. The H.323 Gatekeeper returns an ACF message to the CUCM subscriber processing the H.323 trunk information, which contains the IP address of the Unified CVP Call Server.

Step 6. CUCM sends a H.225 setup message with the Unified CVP Call Server's H.323 service.

Step 7. The Unified CVP Call Server's H.323 service hands the existing call request over to the ICM Service, which forwards it to the PG.

Step 8. The Unified CVP Server sends Unified ICM an existing call request via its VRU PIM configured and hosted by the PG. This existing call request causes Unified ICM to continue the execution of the script started in Step 2.

Step 9. The Unified ICM routing script determines that the caller must be transferred to the VRU and passes a Connect-to-VRU request to the PG. This is forwarded to the ICM Service on the Unified CVP Call Server. The new label generated here is for the Unified CVP Server because it is now the routing client. You can use a single SendToVRU Node to generate two labels: one from execution in Step 3 and one from its continued script execution in this step. Unified ICM is smart enough to determine which routing client label to return, and it accomplishes this with a single node in the script.

Step 10. PG passes the information provided in Step 9 to the ICM Service on the Unified CVP Call Server.

Step 11. The message to connect to VRU travels from the H.323 Service back to the H.323 Gatekeeper. Based on its prefix table, it requires the gatekeeper to determine which VoiceXML Gateway should handle the Connect to VRU and subsequent call treatment session for the VRU leg of the call.

Step 12. The Unified CVP Call Server's H.323 Service sends an H.225 setup message with the VoiceXML Gateway, which then connects the audio path back to the transferring Unified CCE Agent's phone. The transferring Unified CCE Agents' phone establishes audio connection with the VXML Gateway.

Step 13. An ACF message is returned to the Unified CVP Call Server's H.323 service that contains the IP address of the VoiceXML Gateway that should handle the VRU leg of the call.

Step 14. The VRU label causes the VXML Gateway to fire off an application dial-peer on the VXML Gateway, which starts the VRU or application leg of the call. The VXML Gateway connects to the Unified CVP Call Server via HTTP and requests instructions for treating the connected call. This HTTP new call request is handled by the Unified CVP Server's IVR Service, which then passes this request to the Unified CVP Server's ICM Service. As shown in Figure 3-20, Steps 13 through 19 continue to execute enabling the new transfer leg to either be treated on the VXML Gateway or connected to an agent in the new skill group.

H.323 Call Flow Ladder Diagram

Figure 3-22 illustrates a call flow ladder diagram when the H.323 protocol is engaged by a Unified CVP comprehensive deployment. This ladder diagram is similar to the diagram presented in Figure 3-15, with the SIP Proxy server replaced by an H.323 Gatekeeper. As noted in the previous section, H.323 transfers using ICM DNP or a CUCM Route Point are exactly the same as they are when using SIP, with the exception of the use of an H.323 trunk and a gatekeeper for admission control.

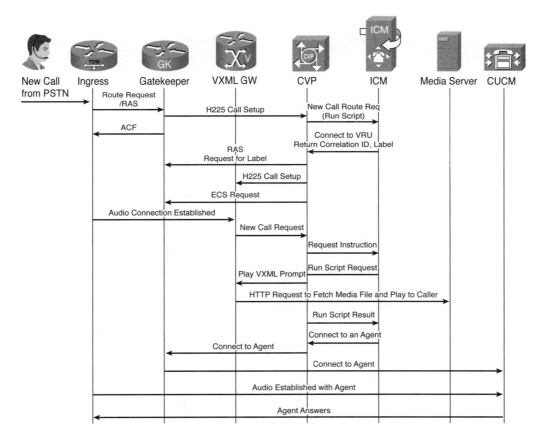

Figure 3-22   *Unified CVP Comprehensive H.323 Call Flow Ladder Diagram*

Figures 3-23 and 3-24 provide a ladder diagram for warm transfers using a CUCM route point to an available agent and to a queue treated by the VXML Gateway, respectively.

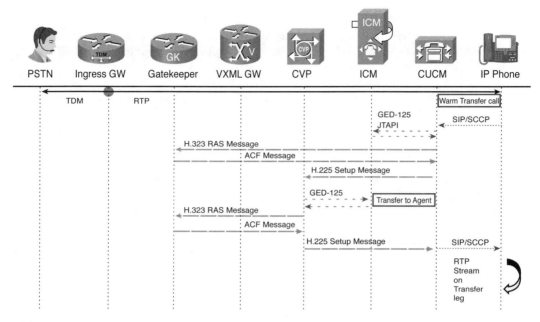

Figure 3-23 *Unified CVP Comprehensive H.323 Warm Transfer to an Agent via CUCM Route Point*

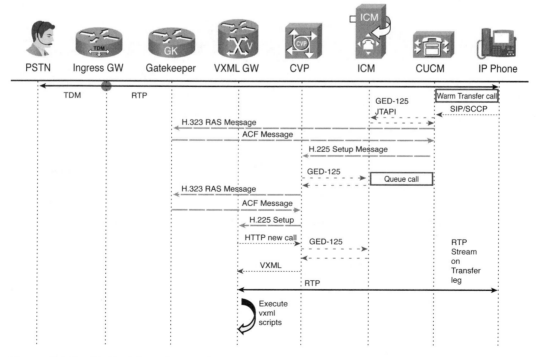

Figure 3-24 *Unified CVP Comprehensive H.323 Warm Transfer to Queue via CUCM Route Point*

All the observations noted for similar ladder diagrams found in Figures 3-16 and 3-17 for SIP-based transfers also apply here. One additional but equally significant observation with H.323 is how the H.323 Gatekeeper is never involved in call setup or control, only providing registration, access, and status services. Because H.323 is a peer-to-peer call control protocol, when the ACF messages are received, the endpoints set up calls between each other. They do not require a proxy or broker to complete on their behalf.

For consistency, Figures 3-25 and 3-26 provide the equivalent ladder diagrams for transfer to an agent or a queue when initiating the transfers using an ICM Dialed Number Plan configuration and H.323.

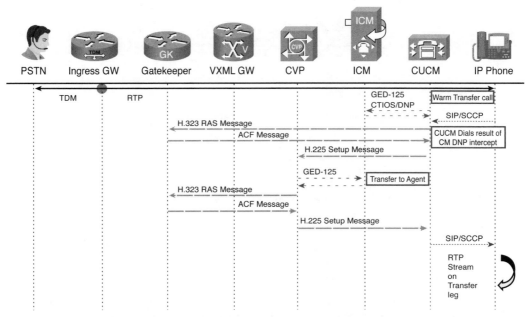

Figure 3-25 *Unified CVP Comprehensive H.323 Warm Transfer to an Agent via ICM DNP*

As in SIP transfers that use ICM DNP, the transfer starts and ends the same way. The usage of the gatekeeper (refer to Figures 3-22 and 3-23) is also identical when employing this type of transfer.

Transfers and Subsequent Call Control

In addition to the transfers managed by Unified ICM, the Comprehensive Deployment model can transfer calls to non-ICM terminations or invoke a Release Trunk Transfer to the PSTN. However, if a call is transferred to a non-ICM controlled termination, call data cannot be passed to the termination, further call control is impossible for the call, and the cradle-to-grave call reporting that Unified ICM gathers is complete. For a Release to Trunk

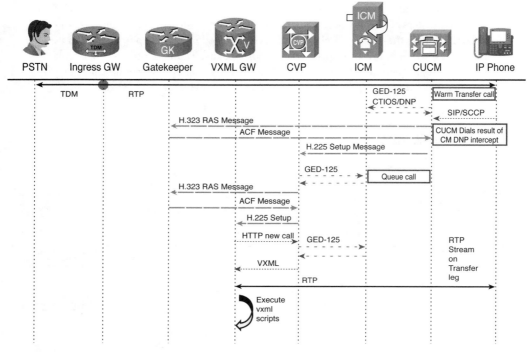

Figure 3-26 *Unified CVP Comprehensive H.323 Warm Transfer to Queue via ICM DNP*

Transfer on the Ingress Voice Gateway, call data or call control cannot be maintained. However, if the call is translation routed to another ICM peripheral, call data and cradle-to-grave reporting can be maintained.

If a transfer fails or the termination device returns a busy status, or if the target rings for a period of time that exceeds the Unified CVP Call Server's ring-no-answer (RNA) timeout setting, the Unified CVP Call Server cancels the transfer request and sends a transfer failure indication to Unified ICM. This scenario causes a Router Requery operation within Unified ICM, enabling a different target to be selected or execution of a remedial action.[4]

The VRU-Only Model

The last functional deployment model for Unified CVP exists for organizations that use advanced PSTN switching services controlled via a Cisco Unified ICM PSTN Network Interface Controller (NIC). There are two Unified ICM PSTN NICs available that enable subsequent call control of calls in the PSTN: the SS7 NIC and the Carrier Routing Service Protocol (CRSP) NIC. These NICs provide Unified ICM the capability to preroute calls intelligently to Unified ICM peripherals (such as ACDs and IVRs) and perform mid-call transfers in the PSTN.[4] Figure 3-27 shows the components used with this solution and their protocols.

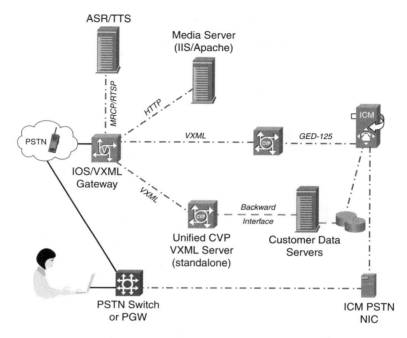

Figure 3-27 *Unified CVP VRU-Only Functional Deployment Model*

Table 3-4 identifies which components are required, optional, and not used by this model. In addition, the Native column identifies components that are native to the Unified CVP solution.

Table 3-4 *Unified CVP VRU-Only Native and Non-Native Component Usage*

Component	Required	Optional	Not Used	Native
SIP Service (Call Server)	—	—	Yes	Yes
IVR Service (Call Server)	Yes	—		Yes
ICM Service (Call Server)	Yes	—		Yes
H323 Service (Call Server)	—	—	Yes	Yes
VoiceXML Server	—	Yes	—	Yes
Unified Call Studio	—	Yes	—	Yes
Ingress Gateway	—	Yes	—	—
VXML Gateway	Yes	—	—	—
SIP Proxy	—	Yes	—	—
Gatekeeper	—	Yes	—	—

Table 3-4   *Unified CVP VRU-Only Native and Non-Native Component Usage*

Component	Required	Optional	Not Used	Native
Operations Console	Yes	—	—	Yes
Reporting Server	—	Yes	—	Yes
ASR/TTS	—	Yes	—	—
Media Server	—	Yes	—	—
DNS Server	—	—	Yes	—
Content Services Switch	—	Yes	—	—
Unified ICM	Yes	—	—	—
Unified Call Manager	—	Yes	—	—
Egress Gateway	—	Yes	—	—

Although Table 3-4 lists the Unified Communications Manager and Egress Gateway as optional components, typically at least one of these components exists to enable a call to be transferred to either a legacy ACD agent via an Egress Gateway or to a Unified CCE Agent hosted by a Unified Communications Manager cluster. The component to be deployed depends entirely on the organization's requirements. In addition, the use load balancers, media servers, and even an ASR/TTS Server are also optional because the Unified CVP VXML Gateways can be configured in such a way to enable them to operate without these components. For ASR/TTS, this would be true only if the organization does not have requirements to perform ASR/TTS treatment for incoming calls. If the IOS Ingress Gateway does not perform VoiceXML Gateway duties, a SIP Proxy or H.323 Gatekeeper can be used to route the VRU label to an available VoiceXML Gateway. The most important takeaway for this model is that Unified CVP does not perform call control for the switch leg of the call. The PSTN Switch or a Cisco Packet Data Network Gateway PGW with Unified ICM handles all call control and prerouting for the switch leg of the call leaving Unified CVP to handle only the VRU leg of the call—therefore the name for this model. Unified ICM can pass call data between termination points (for screen pop or other intelligent treatment) and provide cradle-to-grave reporting for all calls.

Component Call Flow

This section details the call flow steps performed in a typical VRU-Only implementation. As the name indicates, this call flow focuses on the VRU leg of the call. It leaves the call control and switch leg the responsibility of the PSTN's carrier switch and Unified ICM. Figure 3-28 illustrates this call flow with an optional SIP Proxy injected to load balance the VRU leg of the call.

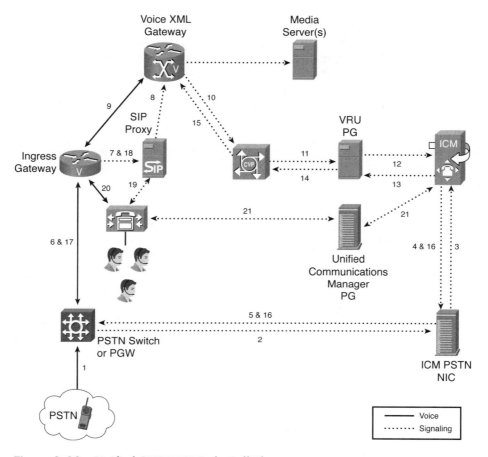

Figure 3-28   *Unified CVP VRU-Only Call Flow*

Following are the details for the steps referenced in Figure 3-28:

Step 1.   The call arrives at the PSTN Switch or PGW.

Step 2.   The PSTN Switch sends a new-call message to Unified ICM via either a CRSP NIC or a SS7 NIC.

Step 3.   The NIC forwards the request to Unified ICM where a routing script is invoked based on the dialed number provided by the PSTN Switch.

Step 4.   This routing script uses either a Send to VRU node or a Translation Route to VRU node to send a result back to the ICM PSTN NIC.

Step 5.   The NIC sends the result back to the PSTN Switch to have the call routed to the Unified CVP Ingress Voice Gateway. Depending on the PSTN capability and Unified ICM VRU type for the Unified CVP deployment, the response returned to the PSTN is either a translation route label (dialed number) or a dialed number plus a correlation ID.

Note   In most legacy ACD and IVR cases, translational routing is used to enable the call data to survive when the PSTN switch connects to these peripherals for further instructions from Unified ICM. These peripherals pass these translation route labels to their respective Unified ICM PGs, which then "marry" the call up with ICM for further processing and the extraction of call data. For Unified CVP, both translational routing and the use of a dialed number plus a correlation ID is supported. The one used depends on how the VRU type is defined. However, if translational routing is wanted or required, the translational route label ranges must be configured on all Unified CVP Call Servers that will be processing these labels. This is done via the Unified CVP Call Server's ICM Service using the Operations Console. Failure to correctly build these label ranges results in failed calls during the VRU leg of the call.

Step 6.   The PSTN routes the call to an available Ingress Voice Gateway port. At this point in the call flow, the VRU leg is beginning because the switch leg was completed when Step 5 was executed.

Step 7.   The Ingress Voice Gateway performs normal inbound POTS dial-peer matching to deliver the call to an available VoiceXML Gateway port. It is at this point that the use of a SIP Proxy or H.323 Gatekeeper can be used to aid in the load balancing and routing of the call. Figure 3-28 illustrates the use of a SIP Proxy. It also assumes that the Ingress Gateway and VoiceXML Gateway are separate devices.

Step 8.   The SIP Proxy extends an INVITE message to the VoiceXML Gateway to terminate the call between it and the Ingress Gateway.

Step 9.   The SIP INVITE is forwarded from the SIP Proxy Server to a VXML Gateway, which then connects the audio path back to the Ingress Gateway.

Step 10.   The VRU label causes the VXML Gateway to fire off an application dial-peer on the VXML Gateway, which starts the VRU or application leg of the call. The VXML Gateway connects to the Unified CVP Call Server via HTTP and requests instructions for treating the connected call. This HTTP new call request is handled by the Unified CVP Server's IVR Service, which then passes this request to the Unified CVP Server's ICM Service.

Note   The VRU-Only model at this point in the call flow supports the use of content load balancers such as ACE or CSS to load balance this HTTP request to a Unified CVP Call Server. Without the use of a content load balancer, the VoiceXML Gateway can have up to two Unified CVP call servers configured. This is accomplished by configuring two parameters for the application on the gateway, param cvpserverhost and param cvpserverhostbackup. If a content load balancing pair is used, these parameters would reference the VIP for the primary and backup load balancers, respectively. In other models like comprehensive, the default behavior for the VoiceXML Gateway is to extract the call server information from the signaling and use that information to connect its VRU leg back to the same call server that processed the switch leg of the call. However, in a VRU-Only deployment, there is no switch leg handled by a Unified CVP call server setting this signaling information to null, causing the VoiceXML Gateway to use the configured application parameters. This is a requirement in VRU-Only deployments, and if this configuration step is omitted from VoiceXML Gateway configurations, calls fail during the start of the VRU leg on the VoiceXML Gateway.

Step 11.   The Unified CVP Call Server's ICM Service sends a Request Instructions message to the VRU PG.

Step 12.   The Unified CVP Server sends the Unified ICM a new call request via its VRU PIM configured and hosted by the PG.

Step 13.   Unified ICM continues the script that was initiated in Step 3 and processes additional nodes that produce Run Script requests to the Unified CVP Server's ICM Service via the VRU PG.

Step 14.   The VRU PG provides Run Script requests produced in Step 13 to the ICM Service located on the Unified CVP call server.

Step 15.   The ICM Service hands these instructions over to the Unified CVP Server's IVR Service that converts them into VXML pages that are forwarded back to the VXML Gateway for rendering and execution. This process can also include prompt and collect instructions and continues between the Unified ICM, Unified CVP, and VXML Gateway until an agent becomes available. The VoiceXML Gateway also fetches any media files requested in the VXML pages from the media server (refer to the top of Figure 3-28). Steps 10 through 15 continue until the call is handled or needs to be transferred to an agent or other termination point.

Note   The use of a VXML Server and ASR/TTS services can also be invoked by the VoiceXML Gateway at this point in the VRU leg of the call.

Step 16.   When a Unified CCE Agent or a TDM ACD Agent becomes available, Unified ICM immediately sends a connect message to the PSTN via the PSTN NIC. This connect message contains either a translation route label or a dialed number plus correlation ID (depending on the PSTN switches capabilities).

Step 17.   Upon receipt of the connect message, the PSTN releases the existing call leg with Ingress Gateway and connects the call to the new termination point. In this example call flow, the same Ingress Gateway is used to connect the call to a Unified CCE Agent, so the PSTN connects back to the Ingress Gateway with a different dialed number.

Step 18.   The Ingress Voice Gateway performs normal inbound POTS dial-peer matching to deliver the call to an available Unified Communications Manager SIP trunk. It is at this point that the use of a SIP Proxy or H.323 Gatekeeper can be used to aid in the load balancing and routing of the call. Figure 3-28 illustrates the use of a SIP Proxy. It also requires that a SIP trunk be configured on the CUCM cluster pointing at the SIP Proxy server. If a H.323 Gatekeeper is used instead, a H.323 trunk must be configured and registered between the gatekeeper and the CUCM cluster.

Step 19.   The SIP Proxy forwards an INVITE message to the CUCM SIP trunk to terminate the call between the SIP trunk and the Ingress Gateway.

Step 20.   The Ingress Gateway sets up an audio path with the Unified CCE Agent.

Step 21.   CUCM notifies Unified ICM that an agent has received the call.

VoIP Transfers

VoIP transfers in this model are quite similar to the Comprehensive model with the exception of the component that has call control. In the Comprehensive model, Unified CVP has call control, and as illustrated earlier in this chapter, Unified ICM instructs Unified CVP to move the call to a new termination point. However, in the VRU-Only model, the PSTN has call control, so Unified ICM instructs the PSTN via the NIC to move the call to the new termination point. The previous call flow illustrated this beginning at Step 16, when a Unified CCE Agent became available and the call needed to be delivered to that agent. In addition, if a transfer is initiated by a Unified CCE Agent to another Unified CCE Agent on the same CUCM cluster, Unified ICM instructs Unified CM via its PG to transfer the call. As shown in the comprehensive model, this warm transfer leg is a new call leg, and the PSTN does not have call control scope over that type of transfer.

Call Flow Ladder Diagram

Figure 3-29 illustrates a call flow ladder diagram without the use of a SIP Proxy or gatekeeper. The PSTN connects directly to the VoiceXML Gateway, which kicks off the VRU leg of the call.

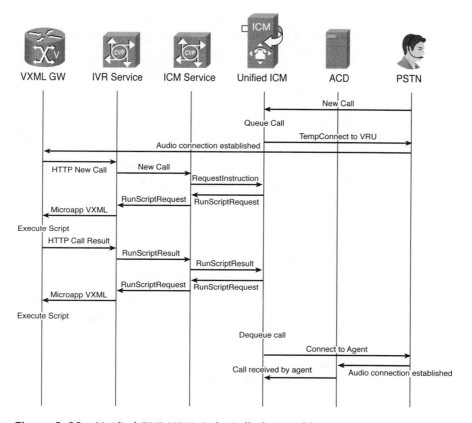

Figure 3-29   *Unified CVP VRU-Only Call Flow Ladder Diagram*

Network VRU Types

This section examines the different Network VRU types defined within Unified ICM and how they each relate to Unified CVP deployments. It begins with an overview of Unified VRU Types and then details how Unified CVP operates as a Type 10, 5, 3 and 7, or 8 and 2. The terms Voice Response Unit (VRU) and Interactive Voice Response (IVR) are used interchangeably in the following sections.

Overview of Unified ICM Network VRUs

This section describes the types of Unified ICM VRUs used for Unified CVP applications. Unified ICM perceives calls that need IVR treatment as having two portions: the Switch leg and the VRU leg. The Switch is the entity that first receives the call from the network or caller. The VRU is the entity that plays audio and performs prompt-and-collect functions. Unified CVP can participate in the Switch role or the VRU role, or both, from the perspective of Unified ICM. In a network deployment, multiple Unified CVP devices can also be deployed to independently provide the Switch and VRU portions.

The call delivery to a VRU can be based on either a Correlation ID or a translation route mechanism, depending on the network capability to pass the call reference identification to the VRU. Call reference identification is needed because Unified ICM must correlate the two legs (Switch and VRU) of the same call to provide instructions for completing the call. In the Unified ICM application, the VRU must supply this call reference ID to Unified ICM when the VRU asks for instructions on how to process the incoming call that it receives from the switch. This mechanism enables Unified ICM to retrieve the appropriate call context for this same call, which at this stage is to proceed to the IVR portion of the call. These two correlation mechanisms operate as follows:

■ **Correlation ID:** This mechanism is used if the network can pass the call reference ID to the VRU. This is usually the case when the VRU is located in the network with the switch and the call signaling can carry this information. (For example, the Correlation ID information is appended to the dialed digits when Unified ICM is used). This mechanism usually applies to calls being transferred within the VoIP network.

■ **Translation Route ID:** This mechanism is used when the VRU is reachable across the PSTN (for example, the VRU is at the customer premise) and the network cannot carry the call reference ID information in delivering the call to the VRU. A temporary directory number (known as a translation route label) must be configured in Unified ICM to reach the VRU. The network routes the call normally to the VRU as with other directory number routing in the PSTN. When the VRU asks for instructions from Unified ICM, the VRU supplies this label (which could be a subset of the received digits), and Unified ICM can correlate the two portions of the same call. Normally, the PSTN carrier will provision a set of translation route labels to be used for this purpose.

The deployed VRU can be located in the network (Network VRU) or at the customer premises. In the latter scenario, a Network Applications Manager (NAM) would be deployed in the network and a Customer ICM (CICM) would be deployed at the customer premises. The corresponding Correlation ID or Translation Route ID should be used accordingly, as described earlier, depending on the location of the VRU.[5]

Unified CVP as a Type 10 VRU

Figure 3-30 shows the relationship between the switch and VRU leg of a call when using a Type 10 VRU.

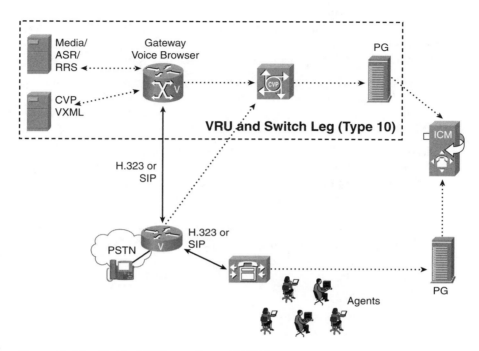

Figure 3-30   *Unified CVP as a Type 10 VRU*

Type 10 was designed to simplify the configuration requirements in Unified CVP Comprehensive Model deployments. The Type 10 VRU is the preferred VRU Type for all new installations, but it requires Cisco Unified ICM 7.1. Unified ICM 7.0 deployments should use the VRU types outlined in subsequent sections of this chapter.

- Type 10 Network VRU has the following behavior:

- There is a Handoff of routing client responsibilities to the Unified CVP switch leg.

- There is an automatic transfer to the Unified CVP VRU leg, resulting in a second transfer in the case of calls originated by the VRU, ACD, or Cisco Unified Communications Manager.

- For calls originated by Cisco Unified Communications Manager, the Correlation ID transfer mechanism is used. The Correlation ID is automatically added to the end of the transfer label defined in the Type 10 Network VRU configuration.

- The final transfer to the Unified CVP VRU leg is similar to a Type 7 transfer, in that a RELEASE message is sent to the VRU prior to any transfer.

In Unified CVP implementations, a single Type 10 Network VRU should be defined, and all Unified ICM VRU scripts should be associated with it. It requires one label for the Unified CVP Switch leg routing client, which transfers the call to the Unified CVP VRU leg. If calls will be transferred to Unified CVP from CUCM, it also needs another label for the CUCM routing client. That label transfers the call to the Unified CVP Switch leg. The Unified ICM Router sends that label to CUCM with a Correlation ID concatenated to it. CUCM must be configured to handle these arbitrary extra digits.

The Unified CVP Switch leg peripheral should be configured to point to the same Type 10 Network VRU. Also all incoming dialed numbers for calls to be transferred to Unified CVP should be associated with a Customer Instance that points to the same Type 10 Network VRU.

For calls that originate at a Call Routing Interface VRU or at a TDM ACD, a TranslationRouteToVRU node should be used to transfer the call to Unified CVP's Switch leg peripheral. For all other calls, use either a SendToVRU node, a node that contains automatic SendToVRU behavior (such as the queuing nodes), or a RunExternalScript.[6]

Note   Cisco Unified ICM 7.1 introduces the Type10 Network VRU. This VRU should be used for all new implementations of Unified CVP using Unified ICM 7.1 or greater, except as VRU-Only (Model #4a, described next). The Type 3 or 7 VRU can still be used for existing customer deployments that have upgraded or for deployments that are not running Unified ICM 7.1 or later.

Unified CVP as Type 5 VRU

Types 5 and 6 are similar in the sense that the VRU entity functions both as a switch (call control) and as the VRU (IVR). However, they differ on how they connect to the VRU. In Type 6, the Switch and the VRU are the same device; therefore, the call is already at the VRU. There is no need for a Connect and Request message sequence from Unified ICM's perspective. Figure 3-31 illustrates a Type 5 VRU with a Type 7.

On the other hand, in Type 5, the Switch and the VRU are different devices even though they are in the same service node from the viewpoint of Unified ICM. They both interact with Unified ICM through the same PG interface. Therefore, Unified ICM uses a Connect and Request Instructions sequence to complete the IVR call.

Note   As noted in Chapter 2, "Unified CVP Architecture Overview," there are two legs of the call as perceived by Unified ICM: the Switch leg and the VRU leg. Where Unified CVP acts as the service node application (that is, when Unified CVP receives the call directly from the network and not via pre-routing as in the VRU-Only model) Unified CVP appears to Unified ICM as Type 5 because the call control (Unified CVP) and the VRU devices are different. Hence, Unified CVP must be configured as VRU Type 5 in the Unified ICM and NAM configuration for the Switch leg. The VRU leg requires a different configuration depending on the deployment model (for example, the VRU leg could be Type 7 in the Comprehensive Unified ICM Enterprise deployment model as illustrated in Figure 3-31). However, the preferred VRU type for all new implementations of Unified CVP is Type 10.

For configuration examples of the Unified CVP application with VRU Type 3 or Type 7, refer to the latest version of the Cisco Unified CVP Configuration and Administration Guide, available on Cisco.com.

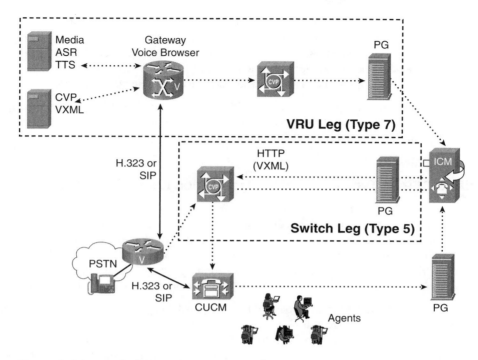

Figure 3-31   *Unified CVP as a Type 5 VRU*[6]

Neither Correlation ID nor Translation Route ID is needed when Unified CVP acts as a Type 5 VRU to Unified ICM and the NAM.[7]

Unified CVP as Type 3 or 7 VRU (Correlation ID Mechanism)

When the VRU functions as an IVR with the Correlation ID mechanism, Unified ICM uses Type 3 and Type 7 to designate sub-behaviors of the VRU via the PG in the Correlation ID scheme. Both Type 3 and Type 7 VRUs can be reached via the Correlation ID mechanism, and a PG is needed to control the VRU. However, the difference between these two types is in how they release the VRU leg and how they connect the call to the final destination.

In Type 3, the switch that delivers the call to the VRU can take the call from the VRU and connect it to a destination (or agent). In Type 7, the switch cannot take the call away from the VRU. When the IVR treatment is complete, Unified ICM must disconnect or release the VRU leg before the final connect message can be sent to the Switch leg to instruct the switch to connect the call to the destination. When used as an Intelligent Peripheral IVR, Unified CVP can function with either Type 3 or 7. It is somewhat more efficient under Type 7 because it gets a positive indication from Unified ICM when its VRU leg is no longer needed (as opposed to waiting for the VoiceXML gateway to inform it that the call has been pulled away).

As stated previously, there are two legs of the call: the Switch leg and the VRU leg. Different Unified CVP hardware can be used for each leg, but from the perspective of Unified ICM functionality. There will be a Unified CVP via PG acting as VRU Type 5 (that is, a service node) along with potentially a different Unified CVP via another PG acting as VRU Type 7 to complete the IVR application (self-service, queuing, and so forth)[8]

For configuration examples of the Unified CVP application with VRU Type 3 or Type 7, refer to the latest version of the Cisco Unified CVP Configuration and Administration Guide, available at Cisco.com.

Unified CVP as Type 8 or 2 VRU (Translation Route ID Mechanism)

When the VRU functions as an IVR with the Translation Route ID mechanism, Unified ICM uses Type 8 or Type 2 to designate sub-behaviors of the VRU via the PG in the translation route scheme. Both Type 2 and Type 8 VRUs can be reached via the Translation Route mechanism, and PG is needed to control the VRU. However, they differ in how they connect the call to the final destination. In Type 8, the switch that delivers the call to the VRU can take the call from the VRU and connect it to a destination/agent.

Type 2 is used when the switch does not have the capability to take the call away from the VRU to deliver it to an agent. In that case, when the IVR treatment is complete, Unified ICM sends the final connect message to the VRU (rather than to the original switch) to connect the call to the destination. The VRU effectively assumes control of the switching responsibilities when it receives the call. This process is known as a handoff. Similarly to the Correlation ID case, there are two legs of the call: the Switch leg and the VRU leg.

Unified CVP can be used for either the Switch leg or the VRU leg. For example, when a Network Interface Controller (NIC), NAM, or CICM is involved, Unified CVP should be configured as Type 2 or Type 8 in the VRU leg.[9]

For configuration examples of the Unified CVP application with VRU Type 8 or Type 2, refer to the latest version of the Cisco Unified CVP Configuration and Administration Guide, available at Cisco.com.

Network VRU Types and Unified CVP Call Flow Models

In Unified ICM, Network VRU is a configuration database entity. It is accessed using the ICM Configuration Manager's Network VRU Explorer tool. A Network VRU entry has two pieces of information:

Type: This is a number from 2 to 10 and corresponds to the types previously described.

Labels: This is a list of labels, which Unified ICM can use to transfer a call to the particular Network VRU that is being configured. These labels are only relevant for Network VRUs of Types 3, 7, and 10 (that is, those that use the Correlation ID mechanism to transfer calls). They are also required but never used in the case of Type 5. (Labels for Types 8 and 2 are defined in the ICM Configuration Manager's Translation Route Explorer tool and invoked via a Translation RouteToVRU node.) Each label is made up of two parts:

■ A digit string, which becomes a DNIS that can be understood by the gatekeeper (when using H.323), by a SIP Proxy Server or static route table (when using SIP without a Proxy Server), SIP, or by gateway dial-peers.

■ A routing client (also known as a switch leg peripheral). In other words, each peripheral device that can act as a switch leg must have its own label, even if the digit strings are the same in all cases.

As noted earlier, Unified ICM Release 7.1(1) introduced Network VRU Type 10, which simplifies the configuration of Network VRUs for Unified CVP. For most call flow models, a single Type 10 Network VRU can take the place of the Types 2, 3, 5, 7, or 8 Network VRUs, which were associated with the Customer Instance and the Switch and VRU leg peripherals. The VRU-Only call flow models still require Type 8. However, in one specific case Types 3 or 7 is still required.

Network VRU configuration entries have no value until they are associated with active calls. There are three places in Unified ICM where this association is made:

■ Under the Advanced tab for a given peripheral in the ICM Configuration Manager's PG Explorer tool

■ In the customer Instance configuration in the ICM Configuration Manager's ICM Instance Explorer tool

■ In every VRU Script configuration in the ICM Configuration Manager's Network VRU Script List tool

Depending on the call flow model, Unified ICM looks at either the peripheral or the customer instance to determine how to transfer a call to a VRU. Generally speaking, Unified ICM examines the Network VRU, which is associated with the switch leg peripheral when the call first arrives on a switch leg, and the Network VRU, which is associated with the VRU leg peripheral when the call is transferred to VRU using the Translation Route mechanism. It examines the Network VRU, which is associated with the Customer Instance or the default Network VRU from the System Information tool, when the call is transferred to the VRU using the Correlation ID mechanism.

Unified ICM also examines the Network VRU associated with the VRU Script every time it encounters a RunExternalScript node in its routing script. If Unified ICM does not believe the call is currently connected to the designated Network VRU, it does not execute the VRU Script.[10]

To examine how these VRU types interact with the previously defined Unified CVP Functional Deployment models, it is necessary to define the different variances of these models as such:

Model #1:   Standalone Self-Service
Model #2:   Call Director

Model #3a: Comprehensive Using ICM Micro-Applications

Model #3b: Comprehensive Using Unified CVP VXML Server

Model #4:   VRU-Only

Model #4a: VRU-Only with NIC Controlled Routing

Model #4b: VRU-Only with NIC Controlled Pre-Routing

Model #1: Standalone Self-Service

As mentioned earlier in this chapter, this model does not interact with Unified ICM VRU scripts, so a Network VRU setting is not relevant. Even in the hybrid case in which the Standalone Self-Service model used Unified ICM for a label lookup, a VRU script is not invoked, only a simple Route Request to the VRU PG Routing Client. Therefore a Network VRU is not needed.

Model #2: Call Director

An earlier discussion pertaining to the Call Director model explained that Unified ICM (via Unified CVP) is responsible for call switching only. Because this model does not provide queuing or self-service, there is no VRU leg. Therefore, a Network VRU setting is not required.

Model #3a: Comprehensive Using Micro-Apps

In this model however, Unified CVP devices act as both the Switch and VRU leg, but interestingly enough, the call does not need to be transferred from the switch leg to the VRU leg before a call treatment can occur. Because this is the classic example of a Type 10 VRU, one should be associated to all the Unified CVP peripherals.

Note   Deployments using Unified ICM 7.0 and earlier configured these peripherals as a Type 2, creating interesting challenges about which CVP servers processed the Switch leg of a call and which were expected to handle the VRU leg.

In addition, all incoming dialed numbers should be associated to Customer Instance associated with a Type 10 Network VRU. All the VRU Scripts that will be executed by the incoming call must be associated with the same Type 10 VRU. Although it is not always necessary, the best practice is for the Unified ICM routing script to execute a SendToVRU node prior to the first RunExternalScript node. This enables a VRU label to be generated and verify that the VoiceXML router can kick off and start the VRU leg of a call. By using this node in the routing script, an incremental step is provided testing the viability of the VRU components of the solution.[11]

Model #3b: Comprehensive Using Unified CVP VXML Server

From a call routing and Network VRU perspective, this model is identical to Model #3a previously described.

Model #4: VRU Only

In this model, the call first arrives at Unified ICM through an ICM-NIC interface, not through Unified CVP. At least initially, Unified CVP is not responsible for the Switch leg; its only purpose is as a VRU. However, depending on which kind of NIC is used, it might be required to take over the Switch leg when it receives the call. This model actually has two submodels, which are described separately in the following sections.

Model #4a: VRU-Only with NIC Controlled Routing

This submodel assumes a fully functional NIC capable of delivering the call temporarily to a Network VRU (that is, to Unified CVP's VRU leg) and then retrieving the call and delivering it to an agent when that agent is available. It further assumes that if the agent is requesting that the call be retransferred to another agent or back into queue or self-service, the NIC can retrieve the call from the agent and redeliver it as requested.

There are two variants of this submodel, depending on whether the Correlation ID or the Translation Route mechanism is used to transfer calls to the VRU. Most NICs (actually, most PSTN networks) cannot transfer a call to a particular destination directory number and carry an arbitrary Correlation ID along with it, which the destination device can pass back to Unified ICM to make the Correlation ID transfer mechanism properly function. For most NICs, therefore, the Translation Route mechanism must be used. There are a few exceptions to this rule, in which case the Correlation ID mechanism can be used.

The NICs that can transmit a Correlation ID include Call Routing Service Protocol (CRSP), SS7 Intelligent Network (SS7IN), and Telecom Italia Mobile (TIM). However, because this capability also depends on the PSTN devices that connect behind the NIC, check with your PSTN carrier to determine whether the Correlation ID can be passed through to the destination. If the NIC can transmit the Correlation ID, the incoming dialed numbers must all be associated with a Customer Instance associated with a Type 7 Network VRU. The Type 7 Network VRU must contain labels associated to the NIC routing client, and all the VRU Scripts must also be associated with that same Type 7 Network VRU. The peripherals need not be associated with any Network VRU. Although it is not always necessary, the best practice is for the Unified ICM routing script to execute a SendToVRU node prior to the first RunExternalScript node.

If the NIC cannot transmit a Correlation ID (the usual and safe case), the incoming dialed numbers must all be associated with a Customer Instance not associated with any

Network VRU. The Unified CVP peripherals must, however, be associated with a Network VRU of Type 8, and all the VRU Scripts must also be associated with that same Type 8 Network VRU. In this case it is always necessary to insert a TranslationRouteToVRU node in the routing script prior to the first RunExternalScript node. If the call is going to the VRU leg because it is being queued, generally the TranslationRouteToVRU node should appear after the Queue node. In that way, an unnecessary delivery and removal from Unified CVP can be avoided when the requested agent is already available.[12]

Model #4b: VRU-Only with NIC Controlled Prerouting

This submodel assumes a less capable NIC that can deliver the call only once, whether to a VRU or to an agent. When the call is delivered, the NIC cannot be instructed to retrieve the call and redeliver it somewhere else. In these cases, Unified CVP can take control of the switching responsibilities for the call. From the perspective of Unified ICM, this process is known as a *handoff*.

Calls that fit this particular submodel must use the Translation Route mechanism to transfer calls to the VRU. There is no way to implement a handoff using the Correlation ID mechanism.

To implement this model with Unified ICM 7.1, the incoming dialed numbers must all be associated with a Customer Instance associated with a Type 10 Network VRU. The VRU labels are associated with the Unified CVP routing client, not the NIC. The Unified CVP peripherals and VRU Scripts must be associated with the Type 10 Network VRU. In this case, it is always necessary to insert a TranslationRouteToVRU node in the routing script, followed by a SendToVRU node, prior to the first RunExternalScript node. If the call is going to the VRU leg because it is being queued, generally these two nodes should appear after the Queue node. In that way, an unnecessary delivery and removal from Unified CVP can be avoided if the requested agent is already available.

To implement this model with Unified ICM 7.0, the incoming dialed numbers must all be associated with a Customer Instance associated with a Type 7 Network VRU. The VRU labels are associated with the Unified CVP routing client, not the NIC. The Unified CVP peripherals must be associated with a Network VRU of Type 2, but all the VRU Scripts must be associated with the Type 7 Network VRU. In this case, it is always necessary to insert a TranslationRouteToVRU node in the routing script, followed by a SendToVRU node, prior to the first RunExternalScript node. If the call is going to the VRU leg because it is being queued, generally these two nodes should appear after the Queue node. In that way, an unnecessary delivery and removal from Unified CVP can be avoided if the requested agent is already available.[13]

Note Two different VRU transfer nodes are required. The first one transfers the call away from the NIC with a handoff. It establishes Unified CVP as a Switch leg device for this call. Physically the call is delivered to an Ingress Gateway. The second transfer delivers the call to the VoiceXML Gateway and establishes Unified CVP as the call's VRU device as well.

Summary

Unified CVP has a significant amount of flexibility in how it is deployed as discovered in this chapter. The different functional deployment models discussed provide a simple set of architectural starting points for engineers to understand these deployments and to discuss their strengths and differences with their customers. This chapter also discussed interactions with Unified ICM to provide some basic integration concepts about the switch and VRU leg of a call and how Unified ICM deals with each.

In addition, this chapter provided a detailed overview of the different call flows supported by each function deployment model solidifying this knowledge for use in future chapters pertaining to high-availability designs and troubleshooting the solution. As mentioned earlier, it is critical that engineers understand the solutions components, different deployment models, and their respective call flows to have a solid base of solution architectural knowledge to build upon with more advanced features found in later chapters.

The next chapter explores how CVP handles different geographical deployments such as centralized and distributed branches. It also illustrates how a distributed branch or edge design can be accomplished using different techniques supported by Unified CVP with SIP and H.323. It also acknowledges the importance of understanding the geographical deployments supported by CVP and how to build high availability into each of these components depending on their geographical placement.

References

1. Cisco Documentation, *Cisco Unified Customer Voice Portal (CVP) 8.x Solution Reference Network Design (SRND)*, 2010: 2–3.

2. Cisco Documentation, *Cisco Unified Customer Voice Portal (CVP) 8.x Solution Reference Network Design (SRND)*, 2010: 2–4.

3. Cisco Documentation, *Cisco Unified Customer Voice Portal (CVP) 8.x Solution Reference Network Design (SRND)*, 2010: 2–6.

4. Cisco Documentation, *Cisco Unified Customer Voice Portal (CVP) 8.x Solution Reference Network Design (SRND)*, 2010: 2–11.

5. Cisco Documentation, *Cisco Unified Customer Voice Portal (CVP) 8.x Solution Reference Network Design (SRND)*, 2010: 5–3.

6. Cisco Documentation, *Cisco Unified Customer Voice Portal (CVP) 8.x Solution Reference Network Design (SRND)*, 2010: 5–3.

7. Cisco Documentation, *Cisco Unified Customer Voice Portal (CVP) 8.x Solution Reference Network Design (SRND)*, 2010: 5–4.

8. Cisco Documentation, *Cisco Unified Customer Voice Portal (CVP) 8.x Solution Reference Network Design (SRND)*, 2010: 5–5.

9. Cisco Documentation, *Cisco Unified Customer Voice Portal (CVP) 8.x Solution Reference Network Design (SRND)*, 2010: 5–6.

10. Cisco Documentation, *Cisco Unified Customer Voice Portal (CVP) 8.x Solution Reference Network Design (SRND)*, 2010: 5–7.

11. Cisco Documentation, *Cisco Unified Customer Voice Portal (CVP) 8.x Solution Reference Network Design (SRND)*, 2010: 5–8.

12. Cisco Documentation, *Cisco Unified Customer Voice Portal (CVP) 8.x Solution Reference Network Design (SRND)*, 2010: 5–8, 9.

13. Cisco Documentation, *Cisco Unified Customer Voice Portal (CVP) 8.x Solution Reference Network Design (SRND)*, 2010: 5–9.

Recommended Reading and Resources

Cisco Documentation, *Cisco Unified Customer Voice Portal (CVP) 8.x Solution Reference Network Design (SRND)*, http://www.cisco.com/en/US/docs/voice_ip_comm/cust_contact/contact_center/customer_voice_portal/srnd/8x/cvp8xsrnd.pdf.

Cisco Documentation, *Cisco Unified Contact Center Enterprise Solution Reference Network Design (SRND)*, http://www.cisco.com/en/US/products/sw/custcosw/ps1844/products_implementation_design_guides_list.html.

Cisco Documentation, *Cisco Unified Customer Voice Portal Configuration Guides*, http://www.cisco.com/en/US/partner/products/sw/custcosw/ps1006/products_installation_and_configuration_guides_list.html.

Cisco Documentation, *User Guide for Cisco Unified CVP VXML Server and Cisco Unified Call Studio, Release 8.0(1)*, http://www.cisco.com/en/US/docs/voice_ip_comm/cust_contact/contact_center/customer_voice_portal/cvp8_0/user/guide/cvp_801_vxml.pdf.

Cisco Documentation, *Hardware and System Software Specification for Cisco Unified Customer Voice Portal (Unified CVP)*, Release 8.0(1), http://www.cisco.com/en/US/docs/voice_ip_comm/cust_contact/contact_center/customer_voice_portal/cvp8_0/reference/guide/cvp_801_bom.pdf.

Cisco Documentation, *Cisco Customer Contact Solutions Ordering Guide*, http://www.cisco.com/en/US/partner/prod/collateral/voicesw/custcosw/ps5693/ps1844/CCBU_ordering_guide.pdf.

Cisco Documentation, *Cisco ACE 4700 Series Appliance Server Load-Balancing Configuration Guide*, http://www.cisco.com/en/US/docs/app_ntwk_services/data_center_app_services/ace_appliances/vA3_1_0/configuration/slb/guide/slbgd.pdf.

Cisco Documentation, *Cisco CSS 11500 Series Content Services Switches Configuration Guides*, http://www.cisco.com/en/US/partner/products/hw/contnetw/ps792/products_installation_and_configuration_guides_list.html.

Chapter 4

Designing Unified CVP for High Availability

This chapter covers the following subjects:

- **Unified CVP geographic models:** Single site, multisite, multisite with distributed call processing and clustering over the WAN.

- **Edge queuing techniques and call survivability:** Edge queuing techniques including Set Transfer Label, Send to Originator, H323/SIP Significant Digits, and LBCAC configuration and call survivability options for edge devices.

- **SIP high-availability architectures:** HA designs for SIP-related components such as Ingress Gateways, proxies, and the Unified CVP SIP Service.

- **H.323 high-availability architectures:** HA designs for H.323-related components such as Ingress Gateways, gatekeepers, and the Unified CVP H.323 Service.

- **Content services high-availability architectures:** HA designs for content services components such as Content Services Switch, Application Content Engine (ACE), media servers, and VoiceXML Servers.

Unified CVP Geographic Models

The previous chapter examined the functional deployment models of Unified CVP. However, you need to understand how these models are overlaid onto a geographic and physical architecture. In other words, what are some of the most popular and supported physical deployments that accomplish different geographical challenges? This chapter focuses on these physical models. Building and understanding different high-availability architectures for each native and non-native component in the Unified CVP solution are analyzed in subsequent sections. This approach provides a stronger appreciation for the different options available for a highly available Unified CVP solution.

Documentation provided by Cisco and some training partners tend to reference the physical and geographical deployments by different names. To that end, this chapter discusses the following models using these names:

- **Single site:** All calls ingress into a single site and stay within the site.

- **Multisite with centralized call processing:** Calls may ingress at branch locations; however, only call control and VoiceXML protocols transverse the WAN, keeping call processing centralized.

- **Multisite with distributed call processing:** Calls may ingress at branch locations; however, only Unified CVP call control and VoiceXML protocols transverse the WAN. A local Cisco Unified Call Manager (CUCM) cluster is provided locally to provide agent phone registrations, call control for those phones, and transfers.

- **Clustering over the WAN:** Calls may ingress at each data center location or even at a branch location. However, call processing is split over a WAN connection between different data centers for maximum redundancy and high availability.

It's now time to take a closer look at each of these models, their illustrations, advantages, disadvantages, and routing considerations required to implement the specific model.

Single Site

As the name implies, this model supports Unified CVP, Unified Contact Center Enterprise (CCE), and Unified Communications Manager clusters placed into a single site. All the high-availability and redundancy architectures covered later in this chapter apply only to a single site. This makes the physical location of this type of deployment the single point of failure; meaning if the site is compromised, so is the solution. Additionally all functional deployment models for Unified CVP are supported with this physical model. Figure 4-1 illustrates how this site is deployed from a physical perspective.

The Unified CCE infrastructure is also located in the single site with the Unified CVP components as depicted. Non-native components are also located within the single site. However, how they are deployed depends on specific High Availability (HA) requirements for the solution. For example, typically when a single site deployment is used, the Ingress and VoiceXML Gateways are separated and deployed as separate physical gateways. This enables better redundancy for the ingress voice traffic sourced on the switch leg of the call and the treatment of the call during the Voice Response Unit (VRU) leg. It also simplifies the dial plan because the VRU label can simply be load balanced to a farm of VoiceXML Gateways without the need to use edge queuing techniques to place the call back on a specific router during the VRU leg of the call. In addition, by separating the Ingress and VoiceXML Gateways, simplified sizing and troubleshooting the solution also become huge advantages. They usually out-weigh the disadvantages of equipment costs.

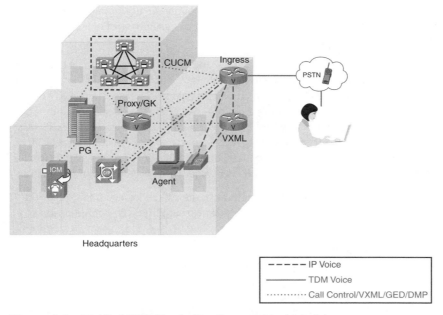

Figure 4-1 *Unified CVP Single Site Geographical Model*

Note *Edge queuing* refers to the ability to park calls at their origination or ingress locations for call treatment. This feature is powerful for Unified CVP because the solution can keep the call local to its ingress location and use the WAN to send and receive VoiceXML instructions to the edge VoiceXML Gateway treating the call. These keep the voice bearer traffic from traversing the WAN and using critical and expensive bandwidth. Edge queuing is a great improvement over legacy Automatic Call Distribution (ACD) and Interactive Voice Response (IVR) call treatment approaches because the call can now be treated at its point of entry or "edge" location, not requiring it to be sent to and terminated at a centralized ACD or IVR farm.

Following are these advantages for this model followed by its disadvantages:

Single site geographical model advantages:

- All components are located in the HQ location, without dependencies on a WAN.

- All calls ingress into HQ location enable Public Switched Telephone Network (PSTN) and trunk connections to be terminated in a single location.

- Each Cisco Unified Communications Manager (CUCM) cluster located in HQ can support up to 4000 agents, assuming two sets of CUCM Peripheral Gateways (PG) are deployed (2000 agents per set of PGs).

- Typical Call Admission Control (CAC) and transcoding are not required because the WAN is not used for voice bearer traffic and codec is usually G.711.

- Ingress and VoiceXML Gateways are typically deployed as separate devices enabling a simpler dial plan for the VRU leg of the call. A single VRU label can be generated for all Unified CVP Servers communicating to Unified Intelligent Contact management (ICM) as routing clients. This VRU label can then be load balanced across all VoiceXML routers in the farm using a Session Initiation Protocol (SIP) proxy server or gatekeeper, depending on the call control protocol that is in use. Edge queuing techniques such as send to originator (SIP), set transfer label (H.323), or the use of Location Based Call Admission Control (LBCAC) is not required because there is a single edge and farm for VoiceXML treatment. These edge queuing techniques are covered later in this chapter.

- Troubleshooting the solution is simpler because the switch leg and VRU leg of the call reside on different physical routers, which also simplifies the configuration of ingress and VoiceXML routers.

- Initial solution sizing and adding capacity to the deployment is easier because ingress and VoiceXML Gateway sizing can be accomplished separately, both initially and when you need to add capacity. This approach also enables you to add capacity to Ingress Gateways without having to add capacity to the VoiceXML Gateway farms at the same time, depending on the call volumes of the contact center. You can also use the Ingress Gateways for this type of deployment for incoming nonagent calls and outgoing PSTN calls. Combining ingress and VoiceXML router functionality into a single router reduces the overall capacity of the router when it acts as an Ingress Gateway. By keeping them separated, it enables the ingress to be scaled without also taking a capacity hit on the same router for VoiceXML services.

Single site geographical model disadvantages:

- Single point of failure exists with the physical site location.

- Single point of failure could also exist with the PSTN carrier and termination at a single site.

- Increase in ingress and VoiceXML Gateway costs exist because typically they are separated for this model.

- The model is designed for small-to-medium size enterprise contact centers and is not a good choice for larger enterprise deployments.

Multisite with Centralized Call Processing

The multisite with centralized call processing model is similar to the single site model with the exception that the incoming call can now be terminated locally at a remote branch office with agents residing in those offices. This model is also referred to as a classic Centralized Branch model. This is where the call processing function still resides in the HQ location, but the VoiceXML Gateway functions and agent location has changed. The obvious advantage of this model is the ability to locally terminate calls to where agents reside and only use the WAN for transporting Call Control and VoiceXML traffic between the HQ and branch locations. Figure 4-2 illustrates this model in more graphic details.

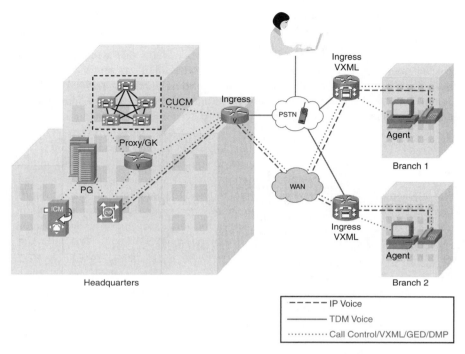

Figure 4-2 *Unified CVP Multi-site with Centralized Call Processing Geographical Model*

Although only call control and VoiceXML traffic is sent across the WAN, voice bearer traffic also transverses the WAN (refer to Figure 4-2). Referring back to previous chapters, during the switch leg of the call where the branch ingress router contacts the Unified CVP call server based on the incoming number dialed by the customer via the PSTN, a G.711 voice channel connects between the ingress router and the Unified CVP Call Server for a brief moment, which is quickly dissolved after call control has been established by the call server. This voice channel occurs only in H.323 deployments. When using SIP, this voice channel is never created. Following are these advantages for this model followed by its disadvantages:

Multisite with centralized call processing geographical model advantages:

■   A majority of Unified CVP solution components are located in HQ. This maximizes the use of Unified CVP licensing, call server farms, load balancers, SIP Proxy servers, Unified Communications Manager cluster servers, and so on without having to replicate the hardware infrastructure in each branch location.

■   Each CUCM cluster located in HQ can support up to 4000 agents, assuming two sets of CUCM PGs are deployed (2000 agents per set of PGs). Be sure to reference the Unified ICM's Solution Reference Network Design (SRND) or Hardware and System Software Specification (Bill of Materials [BOM]) for sizing details because they are dependent on the version of Unified ICM deployed.

■ Backup and recovery operations also benefit from this model because solution back-up and recovery can be done locally within the HQ location. It does not require the use of the WAN to restore large amounts of configuration data.

■ All calls ingress into remote branch locations enabling PSTN and trunk connections to be locally terminated to where the call originated. Call treatment occurs at the "edge" saving WAN bandwidth unless a call needs to be transferred to a different agent located in a different branch.

■ Ingress and VoiceXML Gateways are typically deployed as combination ingress and VoiceXML routers. This architecture can reduce the overall cost of a solution with a large number of branch locations because each branch does not need a standalone ingress and VoiceXML router. However, because a single VRU label is still typically returned for all Unified CVP Call Servers during the VRU leg of the call (one VRU label per routing client, with each call server being a routing client), you must use edge queuing techniques such as send to originator (SIP), set transfer label (H.323), significant digits (SIP/H.323), and even the use of LBCAC to identify the edge. Without these techniques, a single VRU label would not suffice when determining which edge device you should use to treat a call. In other words, a static route in the Unified CVP Call Server in a SIP Proxy server or even in a gatekeeper could not dis-tinguish one VRU label against multiple edge devices. This results in the call being incorrectly queued at the wrong combo ingress/VoiceXML router forcing voice bearer traffic across the WAN and defeating the purpose of edge queuing.

■ Troubleshooting the solution is simple because the switch and VRU leg of the call is terminated on the same combo ingress/VoiceXML router located at the branch loca-tion. However, depending on which edge queuing technique you use, additional con-figurations and steps exist in the configuration and troubleshooting of calls.

■ Initial solution sizing and the ability to add capacity is decentralized to what the branch call volumes are. Sizing the solution for switch and VRU leg interactions be-comes an exercise of understanding how much capacity is required per branch and sizing the combo ingress/VoiceXML routers accordingly.

Multisite with centralized call processing geographical model disadvantages:

■ Single point of failure exists with physical site location.

■ If a WAN failure occurs, the remote branches are cut off from the contact center components; more specifically there will be no connections to Unified CVP for call control, Unified CCE for agent availability and routing decisions, and a loss of call control for agent phones registered with CUCM. Unified CVP provides some simple survivability options that you can configure on the combo Ingress/VoiceXML Gateways to "reroute" a call if WAN connectivity is interrupted. However, this option does not provide the ability to queue a call, select an available agent, and so on. In addition, agent desktops and IP Phones also disconnect from the contact cen-ter with no survivability options for the agent desktop software. Agent IP Phones can still participate in SRST or register to a CME module on the IOS gateway, but this does not provide enterprise contact center services as when the WAN is available.

■ Depending on the WAN requirements pertaining to codec, transcoding may be required in the branch locations. For example, some customers require that all voice bearer traffic that transverses a WAN use a more compressed voice codec such as G.729. However, the call within the local branch office's LAN infrastructure can use G.711 codec. To compress the voice stream to G.729, the combo Ingress/VoiceXML Gateway located in the branch office would engage a transcoder resource located either on the gateway or a local DSP farm configured as part of the branch deployment. This transcoder resource would deliver the call to the HQ site using the compressed G.729 codec. This disadvantage would prevail only if agents were colocated in the HQ site, which is not shown in Figure 4-2 but definitely in Figures 4-3 and 4-4. However, if a transfer is initiated from a branch to a second branch to access a secondary skill group because the WAN is used to transport the transfer leg of a call to Branch 2, a transcoder would be engaged.

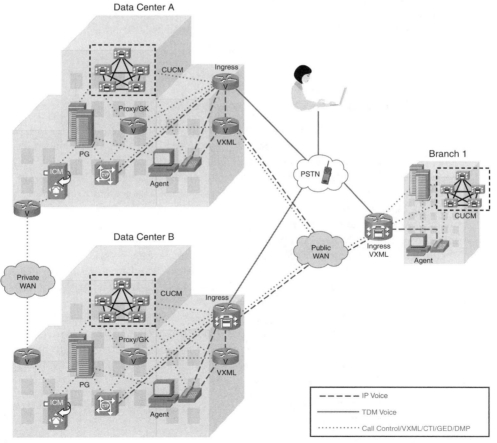

Figure 4-3 *Unified CVP Multisite with Distributed Call Processing Geographical Model*

- In addition to the requirement to transcode voice streams to G.729, the customer's WAN requirements state that a maximum number of voice streams cannot exceed some predetermined number of G.729 calls. If this requirement exists then Gatekeeper CAC or Location Based Call Admission Control (LBCAC) must be configured. With the newer releases of Unified CVP 8.x, LBCAC you can use to solve classic CAC issues and provide an edge queuing strategy by using location IDs configured within CUCM as site IDs. This ensures that the VRU label is returned to the edge router location that originated the call, keeping the call queued at the edge and meeting the WANs CAC requirements. LBCAC is discussed in detailed later in this chapter.

- Because the PSTN is terminated in each branch office and not centrally, the overall PSTN costs can be higher than those of the single site or clustered over the WAN models. The use of SIP trunk offerings from carriers can still be exploited. However, additional hardware might be required to terminate the SIP trunk at each branch office, separate from the VoiceXML router functionality. The use of SIP trunk is more common in other models such as the single site and clustering over the WAN model or as a hybrid to this model where the PSTN is terminated into HQ and not at each branch location for contact center-related numbers.

- This model is designed for large enterprise contact centers and depends heavily on the availability of the WAN.

Multisite with Distributed Call Processing

Multisite with distributed call processing is similar to the previous model with the exception that the call processing function provided by the CUCM cluster has now been distributed to the secondary data center and the branch locations. This model assumes that each of these CUCM clusters are independent clusters hosting their own set of agents and integrating with the Unified ICM solution deployed in data centers A and B. This is also why a PG is located at each branch office to provide the communication of agent availability and state to the Unified ICM components. Unified CVP call control is not distributed to each branch office but provided via farms located in data center A and B. Other non-native components such as SIP Proxy servers, Gatekeepers, load balancers, and media servers are also replicated only in data center A and B and are not typically placed in the branch offices. Unified CVP VoiceXML Servers usually reside in data center A and B. However some deployments may require local VoiceXML servers in the branch offices in special cases in which the voice application requires local VoiceXML resources for performance issues. This special use case would require additional application segmentation within Unified ICM's scripts to correctly direct incoming calls that need to be treated back to the correct VoiceXML server farm servicing and located in a specific branch. Figure 4-3 illustrates this physical model and provides the most likely scenario for its use.

Another interesting caveat with this model is the requirement to provide two separate WAN connections. First, don't get the usage of words such as "Public" and "Private" confused with WAN terminology used to describe public Internet connections and private network connections. There is no direct correlation between these terms. To deploy Unified ICM over a WAN, two WAN links must exist. Ideally, they should be physically separate networks that do not share any routing or transport infrastructure. The Private WAN illustrated on the left side of Figure 4-3 is used purely for private Unified ICM Router traffic and not PG traffic because this model would typically have duplexed PGs located with each Unified Communication Manager cluster, in which case a crossover cable between the two PGs would be used for private traffic. The PGs provide connections to the Unified CVP farm and CUCM cluster located in that respective data center. The private network is also used for heartbeat traffic between Unified Intelligent Contact Management (ICM) routers and for state transfers when a platform is recovering from a shutdown. The Public network is used for intracluster communications, Unified ICM public network traffic defined as traffic between the PGs and the Unified ICM routers and data replication from the Unified ICM Loggers to Distributors, including configuration changes. The next model provides similar requirements, except the CUCM PGs are actually split between the data centers using the private WAN network for heartbeats and status rather than a local cross-over cable. Following are the advantages and disadvantages of this model:

Multisite with distributed call processing geographical model advantages:

■   A majority of Unified CVP solution components are located in each data center and branch location. A single site failure does not impact any of the other locations. However, care must be taken to provide adequate Unified CVP licensing and replicated native and non-native components available for use in each data center.

■   Depending on customer requirements, PSTN calls could ingress in each data center and branch location. Call treatment occurs at the edge, saving WAN bandwidth unless a call needs to be transferred to a different agent located in a different data center or branch.

■   Each CUCM cluster location can support up to 4000 agents, assuming two sets of CUCM PGs are deployed (2000 agents per set of PGs). Be sure to reference the Unified ICM's SRND or Bill of Materials for sizing details because they are dependent on the version of Unified ICM deployed.

■   The Ingress and VoiceXML Gateways are typically deployed as separate devices because this model is designed to support a significant number of agents with the potential of high call volumes ingressing into the data centers and even larger numbers of branches. As with the single site model, ingress and VoiceXML farms are created, but rather than having them reside in a single location, they would exist in each location, that is, each data center and large branch locations. Because this is a slight variation of the single site model, an edge queuing technique such as LBCAC or significant digits must be used to allow the Unified CVP solution to get the VRU leg of a call back to the correct edge VoiceXML router farm. Other edge queuing techniques such as send to originator (SIP) or set transfer label (H.323) would not suffice because they assume that the source of the call origination (Ingress Gateway) can also perform VoiceXML duties, which won't work if the ingress and VoiceXML routers are separated. However, combining the ingress and VoiceXML functions into routers at these locations is supported, meaning other edge queuing techniques could be applied. You need to pick a technique that works with all edge devices.

Warning   Using SIP or Set Transfer Label (H.323) configurations to achieve edge queuing and routing assumes that *all* edge devices are combination ingress and VoiceXML routers. Because this is configured globally on the Unified CVP Call Servers, you need to be careful when picking an edge queuing technique. Make sure this requirement is met. If a customer has some branch offices that have combination ingress and VoiceXML routers while some other branches or data centers have separate VoiceXML router farms, they must use a different edge queuing technique such as LBCAC or significant digits to assign each location a site ID. Otherwise, some calls will fail for the VRU leg of the call (such as sites that do not have combo ingress and VoiceXML routers). In addition, IP-initiated transfers in Unified CVP from CUCM can be equally tricky because they do not use any Send to Originator or Set Transfer Configurations. Instead, they look to the local SIP Proxy or Gatekeeper respectively to route the call. This implication means that VRU labels must be placed in SIP Proxy or Gatekeepers to provide access to VoiceXML router farms in each location for treating calls that were transferred via CUCM. LBCAC and significant digit configurations are a bit more elegant in how they handle this because they always place the correct site ID in front of the VRU label during the VRU leg of the call. This allows it to be delivered to the correct VoiceXML router farm for local treatment. Refer to the sections later in this chapter where each of these edge queuing techniques are illustrated and analyzed in greater detail.

- Troubleshooting the solution may be simplified if the Switch and VRU legs of the call are terminated on the same combo ingress/VoiceXML router located in the data center or the branch location. However, depending on which edge queuing technique is deployed, additional configurations and steps would exist in the configuration and troubleshooting of calls.

- Initial solution sizing and the ability to add capacity is decentralized depending on the data center and volume of branch calls. Sizing the solution for switch and VRU leg interactions becomes an exercise of understanding how much capacity is required per location and sizing the ingress and VoiceXML router(s) accordingly.

Multisite with distributed call processing geographical model disadvantages:

- Overall solution cost is much greater than other models because the infrastructure must be replicated between data centers and branch locations.

- A physically separated private network is required for conversations between the A and B sides of the Unified ICM cluster.

- Because multiple CUCM clusters exist, at least one per location, multiple dial plans must also exist from a CUCM perspective. This increases the manageability and decreases the supportability of the solution.

■ If a WAN failure occurs, the remote branches are cut off from the contact center. More specifically, there will not be any connection to Unified CVP for call control, Unified CCE for agent availability, and routing decisions. Unified CVP provides some simple survivability options that you can configure on the Ingress Gateways to reroute a call if WAN connectivity has been interrupted. However, this option does not provide any ability to queue a call, select an available agent, and so on. In addition, agent desktops are also disconnected from the contact center with no survivability options for the agent desktop software.

■ Depending on the WAN requirements pertaining to codec, transcoding may be required in each location. For example, some customers require that all voice bearer traffic that transverses a WAN use a more compressed voice codec such as G.729. However, the call within the data center or local branch office's LAN infrastructure can use G.711 codec. To compress the voice stream to G.729, the Ingress Gateway located in the data center or branch office engages a transcoder resource located either on the gateway or a local DSP farm configured as part of the location's deployment. This transcoder resource delivers the call to other sites using the compressed G.729 codec. The disadvantage would prevail only if agents are colocated in data centers or other branch sites. However, if a transfer is initiated from a branch to a second branch to access a secondary skill group, because the WAN is used to transport the transfer leg of a call to Branch 2, a transcoder is engaged.

■ In addition to the requirement to transcode voice streams to G.729, the customer's WAN requirements can state that a maximum number of voice streams cannot exceed some predetermined number of G.729 calls. If this requirement exists, you must configure Gatekeeper CAC or LBCAC. With the release of Unified CVP 8.x, you can implement LBCAC to solve classic CAC issues and provide an edge queuing strategy. You can accomplish this by using location IDs configured within CUCM as site IDs to ensure that the VRU label is returned to the edge router location that originated the call. It keeps the call queued at the edge and meets the WANs CAC requirements. LBCAC is discussed in detailed later in this chapter.

■ Because the PSTN terminates in each data center and branch offices, the overall PSTN costs can be higher than those of the single site or clustered over the WAN models. The use of SIP trunk offerings from carriers can still be exploited. However, you might need additional hardware to terminate the SIP trunk at each location, separate from the VoiceXML router functionality. The use of SIP trunk is more common in other models, such as the single site and clustering over the WAN model or as a hybrid to this model where the PSTN is terminated into Data Center A/B and not at each branch location for contact center-related numbers.

■ This model is designed for large enterprise contact centers and depends heavily on the availability of the public and private WAN for contact center related services.

Clustering over the WAN

This model is a combination of the Multisite with centralized call processing and the multisite with distributed call processing models. The difference is that although the call processing is still centralized via a single CUCM cluster, the cluster and its respective PGs connect over the WAN. Both the Public WAN (CUCM intracluster communication) and the Private WAN (PG Communication) are used to achieve this process. In addition, agent phones are registered with a primary data center's CUCM subscriber and another CUCM subscriber in the secondary data center to provide redundancy. The CUCM PGs are also separated between the data centers with one having an active Protocol-Independent Multicast (PIM) communicated via JTAPI to the CUCM subscriber also located in the same data center as the PG. The second PG in the pair is configured to communicate with a different subscriber also located in the same data center as the second PG. The CTI Manager service mentioned in earlier chapters is responsible for routing agent phone requests between the subscriber that the agent phone is actually registered to and the subscriber that the active PG communicates with. You accomplish this via the intercluster communication between data center A and B. Furthermore, the Private WAN also includes Unified ICM Router private traffic and PG private traffic. Only one Unified CM PG is ACTIVE at any one time; the second PG in the previously noted pair is IDLE. Figure 4-4 illustrates this model and is followed by a list of advantages and disadvantages.

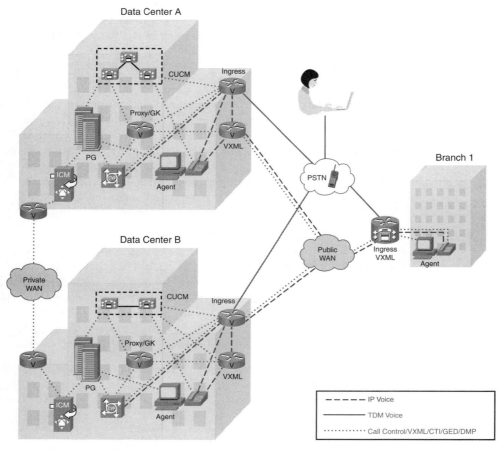

Figure 4-4 *Unified CVP Clustering over the WAN Geographical Model*

Clustering over the WAN geographical model advantages:

■ A majority of Unified CVP solution components are located in the data centers. This maximizes the use of Unified CVP licensing, call server farms, load balancers, SIP Proxy servers, Call Manager cluster servers, and so on without having to replicate the hardware infrastructure in each branch location.

■ The CUCM cluster located between data center A and B can support up to 4000 agents, assuming two sets of CUCM PGs are deployed over the WAN. (2000 agents per set of PGs). Typically in this model a single pair of PGs is deployed. Each PG has PIM for the Unified CM cluster and a PIM for each Unified CVP Call Server located in each data center. By deploying a single PG pair (rather than two sets of PG pairs) the Agent Targeting rule feature in Unified ICM can be used to simplify agent configuration because there is no longer a need to configure Device Targets for each IP Phone and associated label for every peripheral.

■ Backup and recovery operations also benefit from this model because solution backup and recovery is accomplished locally within the data center locations. It does not require the use of the WAN to restore large amounts of configuration data.

■ All calls ingress into branch locations allowing PSTN and trunk connections to terminate locally to where the call originated. Call treatment occurs at the edge-saving WAN bandwidth unless a call needs to be transferred to another agent located in a different branch. However, the calls could also ingress into each data center, which would be treated as another edge location (refer to Figure 4-4).

■ Ingress and VoiceXML Gateways are typically deployed as combination ingress and VoiceXML routers. This architecture reduces the overall cost of a solution with a large number of branch locations because each branch does not require a standalone ingress and VoiceXML router. However, the branch locations use combination ingress/ VoiceXML routers but the data centers have them separated (refer to Figure 4-4). This implies you must deploy an edge queuing technique such as LBCAC or significant digits to accommodate both types of ingress and VoiceXML router deployments.

■ Troubleshooting the solution is simple. The Switch and VRU leg of the call is terminated on the same combo ingress/VoiceXML router located at the branch location.

■ Initial solution sizing and the ability to add capacity is decentralized depending on the volume of branch and data center calls. Sizing the solution for switch and VRU leg interactions becomes an exercise of understanding the amount of capacity required per branch and sizing the combo ingress/VoiceXML routers accordingly.

Clustering over the WAN geographical model disadvantages:

■ A physically separated Private network is required for conversations between the A and B side of the Unified ICM cluster.

■ If a WAN failure occurs, the remote branches are cut off from the contact center. More specifically, there are no connections to Unified CVP for call control, Unified CCE for agent availability and routing decisions, and a loss of call control for agent phones registered with CUCM. Unified CVP provides some simple survivability options that you can configure on the combo Ingress/VoiceXML Gateways to reroute a call if WAN connectivity is interrupted. However, this option does not provide any ability to queue a call, select an available agent, and so on. In addition, Agent desktops and IP Phones are also disconnected from the contact center without survivability options for the agent desktop software. Agent IP Phones can still participate in SRST or register to a CME module on the IOS gateway, but it does not provide enterprise contact center services as when the WAN is available.

■ Depending on the WAN requirements pertaining to codec, transcoding may be required in the branch and data center locations. This disadvantage prevails only if agents colocate in the data center sites. However, if a transfer is initiated from a branch to a second branch or data center to access a secondary skill group, because the WAN is used to transport the transfer leg of a call, a transcoder would be engaged.

■ In addition to the requirement to transcode voice streams to G.729, the customer's WAN requirements might state that a maximum number of voice streams cannot exceed some predetermined number of G.729 calls. If this requirement exists, you must configure Gatekeeper CAC or LBCAC.

■ Because the PSTN terminates in each branch office and not centrally, the overall PSTN costs can be higher than those of the single site or clustered over the WAN models. The use of SIP trunk offerings from carriers can still be exploited. However, you might need additional hardware to terminate the SIP trunk at each branch office, separate from the VoiceXML router functionality. The use of SIP trunk is more common in other models such as the single site and clustering over the WAN model or as a hybrid to this model where the PSTN terminates into HQ and not at each branch location for contact center-related numbers.

■ A maximum of 80 ms round-trip delay is required for the Unified Communication Manager servers to be clustered over a WAN. Refer to Chapter 6, "Sizing, Networking and Security Considerations," and the Cisco Unified Communications System Release 8.x SRND noted at the end of this chapter for additional network considerations when clustering CUCM and deploying Unified CVP over a WAN.

■ This model is designed for large enterprise contact centers and depends heavily on the availability of the WAN.

Edge Queuing Techniques and Survivability

As previously discussed, Unified CVP supports the placement of distributed VoiceXML Gateways and provides a powerful feature in supporting edge queuing. This enables the call to be parked on the local VoiceXML Gateways with treatment, such as queue music, provided without voice bearer traffic traversing the IP WAN. In this scenario, only voice signaling and HTTP requests use the IP WAN to interact with the Unified CVP call servers and media servers. However, the manner in which edge queuing is designed and deployed is locally-dependent on the VoiceXML Gateways and centrally-dependent on the Unified CVP call servers, gatekeepers, and SIP proxy servers. Understanding these different techniques, their call flows, and survivability options is key to building a design with high availability. This next section focuses on the following edge queuing techniques and concludes with a discussion about the configuration of call survivability for high availability.

Edge queuing techniques used for high-availability designs fall into these categories:

- **Set Transfer Label (H323 Only):** The simplest way to accomplish edge queuing when using H.323; however, also has the most implications for co-resident Ingress and VoiceXML Gateways.

- **Send to Originator (SIP Only):** The simplest way to accomplish edge queuing when using SIP. However, as with the previous option, this also has the most implications for co-resident Ingress and VoiceXML Gateways.

- **Technology Prefix Stripping (H323 Only):** More complex approach to edge queuing using a technology prefix prefixed to the incoming Dialed Number Identification Service (DNIS) and saved by the Unified CVP call server. This approach is far more complex than using Set Transfer Label but is also more flexible with what it can accomplish from a high-availability perspective.

- **Significant Digits (SIP Only):** This technique is similar to Technology Prefix Stripping except a site code is prefixed to the incoming DNIS number and saved by the Unified CVP call server for subsequent call treatment requests. This technique is also more complex to configure than Send to Originator (StO) but is more flexible for achieving high availability in the edge VoiceXML Gateway farm.

- **Location Based Call Admission Control:** This technique is similar to how Significant Digits works with SIP. However, a Location and site code is configured between Unified CVP call servers and a Cisco Unified Communications Manager, allowing CVP to "pull" the site codes from the locations in CUCM providing a more seamless solution for providing high-availability edge queuing options for VoiceXML Gateways.

Set Transfer Label (H.323)

Set Transfer Label (H.323) is the simplest H.323 edge queuing technique available with Unified CVP. Basically, the Unified CVP H.323 Service is modified to indicate which labels returned by ICM, such as the VRU label, should be sent directly back to the gateway that originated the switch leg of the call for treatment during the VRU leg. This technique also requires that the Ingress Voice Gateway be configured as a functioning VoiceXML Gateway because it will be required to treat calls during the VRU leg of a call. Interestingly, this technique ignores the gatekeeper lookup during the VRU leg of a call, which presents some challenges for high availability. If the same router that sources the switch leg of a call fails and cannot process the VRU leg of the same call, Unified CVP cannot route the VRU leg of the call to a different VoiceXML Gateway. In most situations, if the VRU leg of a call cannot be processed by a combo ingress/VoiceXML router, chances are the router is down and the switch leg for the call has also failed. This chapter examines how you can configure routers' local survivability scripts to help provide a high-availability option when using this edge queuing technique.

Figure 4-5 provides a visual representation of this technique when using an H.323 comprehensive call flow model. Following the figure, a step-by-step procedure outlines the detailed configurations and process to deploy this technique.

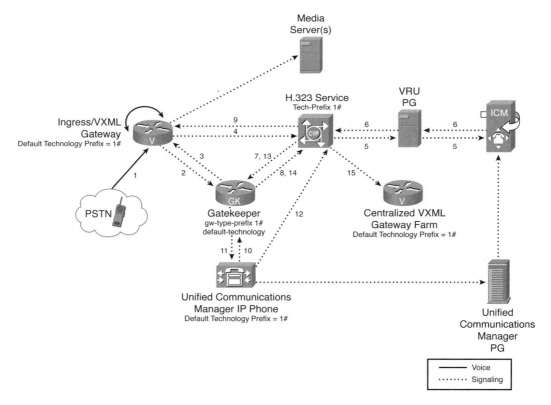

Figure 4-5 *H.323 Set Transfer Label Edge Queuing Technique*

Prior to understanding the detailed call flow steps (refer to Figure 4-5), you must place the following configuration on any Unified CVP H.323 Service to process calls using this technique. By accessing the VBADMIN utility, you can add the following configuration:

```
SetTransferLabel "9999*"
SetExcludeIP "10.1.1.10"
```

The SetExcludeIP option authorizes Unified CVP to ignore the SetTransferLabel directive if the source IP address of the request is found in the SetExludeIP list, which is 10.1.1.10 in the preceding example. This enables IP initiated transfers sourcing from a CUCM server to be ignored because that same CUCM server cannot treat the VRU leg of a call. The Unified CVP call server can process the call by asking the gatekeeper for endpoint guidance and send the call to where that endpoint resides. This brings up an interesting consideration:, When using this technique with H.323, it is a best practice to design a centralized VoiceXML Gateway farm to handle IP-initiated calls or transfers when the edge location for the originating or transferring device is difficult to identify. This ensures that these types of calls get treated via a centralized VoiceXML Gateway farm, which can then be correctly sized. Arbitrarily sending calls to any edge is not advised because it creates unwanted WAN traffic, land on edge devices that may not be correctly sized to handle these types of calls or transfers and a nightmare when it comes to troubleshooting call legs.

Following are the detailed steps for Figure 4-5:

Step 1. The call arrives from either the PSTN or a VoIP connection to the gateway.

Step 2. The Ingress Gateway sends a Registration, Admission, and Status (RAS) request to the H.323 Gatekeeper to find the IP address of the Unified CVP Call Server.

Step 3. The H.323 Gatekeeper executes its call routing decision tree and matches the E.164 number (DNIS) to a registered Unified CVP Call Server. The gatekeeper returns an Admission Confirm (ACF) message containing the IP address of the Unified CVP Call Server to the Ingress Gateway.

Step 4. The Ingress Voice Gateway sends a H.225 call setup message to the Unified CVP Server's H.323 Service. For a brief instance, a G.711 voice stream exists between the Ingress Voice Gateway and the Unified CVP Server's H.323 Service.

Step 5. The Unified CVP Server sends Unified ICM a new call request via its VRU PIM configured and hosted by the Peripheral Gateway (PG). This new call request corresponds to an ICM dialed number that in turn invokes a routing script in Unified ICM.

Step 6. The Unified ICM routing script determines that the caller must be transferred to the VRU and passes a Connect to VRU request to the PG, which is forwarded to the ICM Service on the Unified CVP Call Server.

Step 7. The H.323 Service sends a RAS Request to the H.323 gatekeeper to find the IP Address of the VoiceXML Gateway associated with the VRU label returned by Unified ICM.

Step 8. The H.323 Gatekeeper executes its call routing decision tree and matches the VRU label to a registered VoiceXML Gateway. The gatekeeper returns an ACF message containing the IP address of the VoiceXML Gateway to the Unified CVP Call Server. Per design, the only VoiceXML Gateways configured in the gatekeeper for the VRU label are located in the centralized VoiceXML farm. This becomes more obvious in Step 11.

Step 9. The Unified CVP H.323 Service determines that the VRU label provided by Unified ICM in Step 6 is configured as part of the SetTransferLabel directive in the Voice Browser administration utility. The results of the H.323 RAS request sent in Steps 7 and 8 are ignored with the VRU label being returned directly to the voice gateway that initiated the switch leg of the originating call. The Ingress Gateway then sets up the call with itself and kicks off the VRU leg for call treatment.

The following steps outline what occurs when initiating an IP-originated call or a subsequent transfer:

Step 10. An IP call is initiated via a CUCM cluster, or an IP originated transfer is initiated by an Agent. ICM is contacted and determines that a VRU leg is warranted as described in Step 6. The CUCM subscriber via its H.323 trunk sends a Registration, Admission, and Status (RAS) request to the H.323 Gatekeeper to find the IP address of the Unified CVP Call Server.

Step 11. The H.323 Gatekeeper executes its call routing decision tree and matches the E.164 number (DNIS) to a registered Unified CVP Call Server. The gatekeeper returns an ACF message containing the IP address of the Unified CVP Call Server to the CUCM subscriber.

Step 12. The CUCM subscriber sends a H.225 call setup message to the Unified CVP Server's H.323 Service. For a brief instance, a G.711 voice stream exists between the IP Phone and the Unified CVP Server's H.323 Service. Steps 5 and 6 are repeated for the transfer and VRU label, respectively.

Step 13. The H.323 Service sends a RAS Request to the H.323 gatekeeper to find the IP Address of the VoiceXML Gateway associated with the VRU label returned by Unified ICM. Per design, the only VoiceXML Gateways configured in the gatekeeper for the VRU label are located in the centralized VoiceXML farm.

Step 14. The H.323 Gatekeeper executes it call routing decision tree and matches the VRU label to a registered VoiceXML Gateway located in the centralized VoiceXML Gateway farm. The gatekeeper returns an ACF message containing the IP address of the VoiceXML Gateway to the Unified CVP Call Server.

Step 15. Even though the VRU label is configured as part of the SetTransferLabel directive in the Unified CVP H.323 service, the IP address of the Unified Communications Manager server initiating the call has also been configured as part of the SetExcludeIP directive located in the Unified CVP H.323 service. The Unified CVP H.323 service ignores the SetTransferLabel directive and connects the transfer to the centralized VoiceXML Gateway farm as directed by the gatekeeper.

Send to Originator or StO (SIP)

This technique is exactly the same as the previous example for H.323; however, the configuration is a bit simpler. The configuration of the VRU label is handled via the Operations console by accessing the SIP service configuration for all Unified CVP call servers that provide StO processing. Figure 4-6 shows where the StO configuration lives within a Unified CVP call server SIP configuration tab. The VRU labels are placed into dialog list box and wildcards are supported, just as in the previous example.

Figure 4-6 *Send to Originator Configuration via Operations Console*

With Set Transfer Label, you do not need to configure any excluded IP addresses because the SIP service actually checks the SIP header to determine what type of device has sourced the IP originated call or transfer. If the Unified CVP SIP Service determines that the IP originated call or transfer began via a CUCM cluster, it automatically knows to ignore the StO configurations for the VRU label and invoke the SIP proxy to determine where the centralized VoiceXML Gateway farm lives. This provides the same feature as the SetExcludeIP directive does for H.323. However, as shown in the Gatekeeper, you must configure the VRU labels as static routes in the SIP proxy and resolve to a centralized VoiceXML server farm for treating calls that originate or transfer from an IP endpoint unable to process VoiceXML instructions. Figure 4-7 illustrates this call flow and is followed by detailed steps pertaining to this technique.

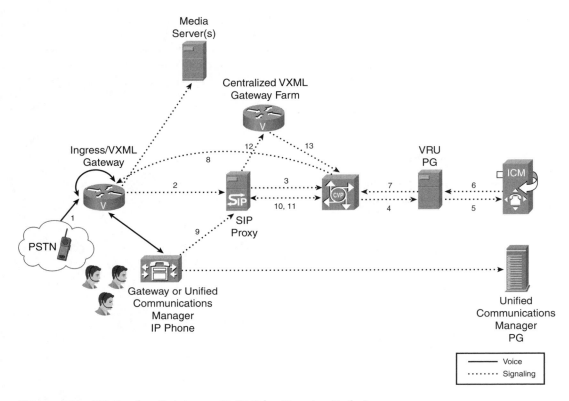

Figure 4-7   *SIP Send to Originator (StO) Edge Queuing Technique*

Obviously, this is similar to the previous example but for completeness, consider the following steps:

Step 1.   The call arrives from either the PSTN or a VoIP connection to the gateway.

Step 2.   The Ingress Gateway sends a SIP INVITE message the SIP Proxy Server.

Step 3.   The SIP Proxy Server forwards this SIP INVITE to the Unified CVP Server's SIP Service.

Step 4.   The SIP Service sends a new call request to Unified ICM via the Unified CVP Server ICM Service and the PG.

Step 5.   The Unified CVP Server sends Unified ICM a new call request via its VRU PIM configured and hosted by the Peripheral Gateway (PG). This new call request invokes a new incoming dialed number that in turn invokes a routing script in Unified ICM.

Step 6.   The Unified ICM routing script determines that the caller must be transferred to the VRU and passes a Connect to VRU request to the PG, which is forwarded to the ICM Service on the Unified CVP Call Server.

Step 7.   PG passes the information provided in Step 6 to the ICM Service on the Unified CVP Call Server.

Step 8.   The Unified CVP Call Server SIP Service determines that the VRU label provided by Unified ICM matches a label configured for Send to Origination. The SIP header has also been inspected, which identifies the source of the call to be capable of processing VoiceXML instructions for call treatment during the VRU leg. Because of these conditions, the Unified CVP Call Server SIP Service bypasses the SIP proxy and instructs the Ingress Gateway to connect to itself for VRU leg call treatment, kicking off the VRU leg of the call.

The following steps outline what occurs when initiating an IP originated call or a subsequent transfer:

Step 9.   An IP call is initiated via a CUCM cluster, or an IP originated transfer is initiated by an Agent. CUCM matches the label returned by Unified ICM from the transfer scripts and determines that it must be sent to the SIP Proxy Server via the SIP trunk configured for the CUCM cluster.

Step 10. The SIP Proxy Server consults its routing table and determines that the label dialed by CUCM in Step 4 must be sent to a Unified CVP Call Server and processed by its internal SIP Service.

Step 11. The Unified CVP Call Server's SIP service accepts the SIP INVITE from the SIP Proxy Server and releases the existing call request to the ICM Service, which forwards it to the VRU PG. The Unified CVP Server sends Unified ICM an existing call request via its VRU PIM configured and hosted by the PG (repeating Steps 4 through 7 for this existing call or transfer). This existing call request causes Unified ICM to continue the execution of the script that began in Step 9. When the VRU label is returned to the Unified CVP call server, the call server inspects the SIP header for the call origination and determines that the endpoint cannot process VoiceXML instructions and is indeed a CUCM subscriber. At this point the Send to Originator configuration is ignored, and the SIP proxy server is engaged to determine which VoiceXML Gateway farm should be used to treat the call.

Step 12. The SIP INVITE (including information about CUCM Subscriber) is forwarded from SIP Proxy Server to a VoiceXML Gateway located in the VoiceXML Gateway farm, which then connects the audio path back to the IP Phone registered with the CUCM Subscriber. The IP Phone establishes audio connection with the VoiceXML Gateway.

Step 13. The VRU label causes the VoiceXML Gateway to fire off an application dial-peer on the VoiceXML Gateway, which starts the VRU or application leg of the call. The VoiceXML Gateway connects to the Unified CVP Call Server via HTTP and requests instructions for treating the connected call. This HTTP new call request is handled by the Unified CVP Server's IVR Service, which then passes this request to the Unified CVP Server's ICM Service.

Technology Prefix Stripping (H.323 Only)

So what exactly is a technology prefix? A technology prefix is a discriminator that can distinguish between gateways having specific capabilities within a given zone. In the exchange between the gateway and the gatekeeper, the technology prefix selects a gateway after the zone has been selected. Currently, no standard defines what the numbers in a technology prefix mean; by convention, technology prefixes are designated by a pound (#) symbol as the last character. The technology prefix used with this edge queuing technique identifies the point of call origination or edge.

The idea with this edge queuing technique is to prepend incoming DNIS numbers with a technology prefix value that will be stripped and stored by the Unified CVP call server that handles the switch leg of the call. This can be tricky because the technology prefix prepended to the front of the DNIS value is the technology prefix for which the VoiceXML Gateway uses when registering with the gatekeeper. This implies that not only does each edge VoiceXML Gateway require a unique technology prefix, but also any H.323 endpoint to which the Unified CVP call server will transfer a call to must also have the same technology prefix, which was saved by the Unified CVP call server during the switch leg of the call. For example, if the intention is to transfer a call from an edge Ingress Gateway after call treatment has completed to a Unified CCE Agent hosted by a CUCM cluster, a H.323 trunk must be configured and registered with the gatekeeper for every technology prefix used by all Ingress Gateways. This is a requirement and can be cumbersome when an enterprise has several Ingress Gateways using this technique to provide edge call treatment. Unified CVP stores this embedded technology prefix for the entire duration of the call and uses it for both VRU and final destination transfer instructions. Without these CUCM H.323 trunks registered to the gatekeeper using the same technology prefix as the gateways that start the switch leg of the call, a transfer from CVP using the prepended technology prefix will fail due because the gatekeeper cannot match a CUCM H.323 trunk with the same technology prefix.

This requirement forces a great deal of design considerations about the technology prefixes that are going to be used. In addition, troubleshooting this solution requires a good understanding of how a gatekeeper routing decision is made and the significance of the technology prefix. However, in a pure H.323 environment in which complete routing flexibility is wanted and the Set Transfer Label technique is not an option, this technique can be valuable. With proper configuration and planning, the Set Transfer Label technique discussed earlier can accomplish everything that this technique provides. However in larger environments, having to maintain an exhaustive list of excluded IP addresses and transfer labels in every Unified CVP call server's H.323 service can become cumbersome and time-consuming versus setting up extra CUCM H.323 trunks and centralizing the dial plan in the gatekeepers.

This technique is similar to the SIP Significant Digit technique discussed later in this chapter. The main differences pertain to the use of significant digits removed from the front of the incoming DNIS number. In this technique, the digits stripped off are used as a technology prefix, whereas SIP uses them purely as digits indicating a site code. Figure

4-8 illustrates the call flow using this technique. In addition, a detailed discussion is provided that outlines the specific configurations required for implementation.

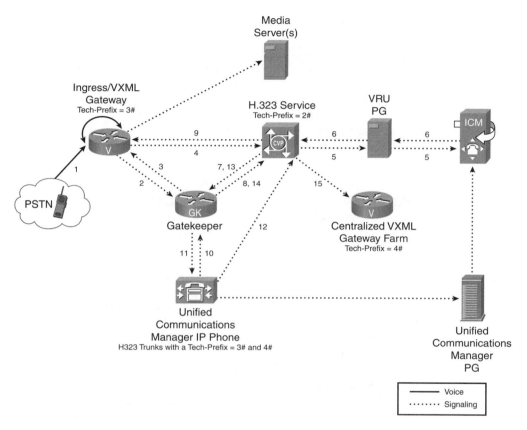

Figure 4-8   *H.323 Technology Prefix Stripping Edge Queuing Technique*

The following steps provide a walkthrough and where appropriate include details pertaining to required configuration.

Step 1.   The call arrives from either the PSTN or a VoIP connection to the gateway. The Ingress Gateway is configured to register with the gatekeeper using a technology prefix of 3#. Following is the command used to set this on the Ingress/VoiceXML Gateway:

```
myrouter(config-if)#h323-gateway voip tech-prefix 3#
```

There are more h323-gateway commands required to register to a gatekeeper; however, this is the particular one necessary to set the technology prefix. This same technology prefix is prepended to the DNIS string to allow Unified CVP to strip and save it for use during the VRU leg of a call or during a transfer.

Assume the DNIS is 8005551212. The Ingress Gateway would need a voip dial-peer configured as follows:

```
myrouter(config)#dial-peer voice 1212 voip
myrouter(config-dial-peer)#tech-prefix 2#3
```

This may look a bit odd, but this trick also enables the return technology prefix of a 3 to be embedded in front of the DNIS string without using a separate outgoing translation rule. The gatekeeper pays attention to only digits presented before the # as a technology prefix; the rest is treated as the DNIS. The 2# is the technology prefix used by the Unified CVP Call Server when it registers with a gatekeeper. However, this example shows how to accomplish the same task using a translation rule.

```
myrouter(config)#dial-peer voice 1212 voip
myrouter(config-dial-peer)#tech-prefix 2#
myrouter(config-dial-peer)#translate-outgoing called 99

myrouter(config)#voice translation-rule 99
myrouter(config-translate)#rule 1 /\(2#\)\(8005551212\) /\13\2/
```

This approach requires that a translation rule exists for each incoming DNIS for which you send toward Unified CVP or a rule built with a universal regular expression to represent multiple incoming DNIS values. The technology prefix is always applied to the DNIS value before the outgoing translation profile is applied. This requires the construction of a translation profile and rule to account for the prepended technology prefix. However, a single dial-peer could be used to match all 800 numbers using the previous example, without building and maintaining any translation rules. Both approaches result in the final DNIS string routed to Unified CVP as 2#38005551212. The 3 following the # is actually the technology prefix saved by Unified CVP and used to route calls back to the edge for treatment. In this case the router acts as an Ingress and VoiceXML Gateway, so you are interested in sending the VRU leg back to the same router that sourced the switch leg. Therefore embed this router's technology prefix for Unified CVP to strip and reuse during VRU treatment or transfers.

Step 2. The Ingress Gateway sends a RAS request to the H.323 Gatekeeper to locate the IP address of the Unified CVP Call Server to process the DNIS string of 2#38005551212. Because most likely all the Unified CVP Call Servers have registered with the gatekeeper using a technology prefix of 2#, the gatekeeper processes the RAS message and load balances this request to any of the registered Unified CVP call servers.

Step 3. The H.323 Gatekeeper executes its call routing decision tree and matches the E.164 number (DNIS) to a registered Unified CVP Call Server with a technology prefix of 2#. The gatekeeper returns an ACF message containing the IP address of the Unified CVP Call Server to the Ingress Gateway.

Step 4.   The Ingress Voice Gateway sends a H.225 call setup message to the Unified CVP Call Server's H.323 Service. For a brief instance, a G.711 voice stream exists between the Ingress Voice Gateway and the Unified CVP Server's H.323 Service. The Unified CVP Call Server strips the original DNIS string of 2#38005551212 by first removing the technology prefix of 2# and saving one digit, the 3, leaving a DNIS string of 8005551212 to be sent to ICM. The following configuration via the VBADMIN utility sets the parameters for this behavior on the H.323 Service:

```
setTechPrefix 2#  (Registers CVP with GK using 2#)
setSigDigits 1    (Tells CVP to save 1 digit)
```

Step 5.   The Unified CVP Server sends Unified ICM a new call request via its VRU PIM that is configured and hosted by the PG. This new call request references the incoming DNIS string of 8005551212, which in turn invokes a routing script in Unified ICM.

Step 6.   The Unified ICM routing script determines that the caller must be transferred to the VRU and passes a Connect to VRU request to the PG, which will be forwarded to the ICM Service on the Unified CVP Call Server.

Step 7.   Assuming that a VRU label of 999999999912345 was returned by ICM to be used the VRU for call treatment, the Unified CVP Call Server prepends the digit that was saved in Step 4 to this VRU label resulting in the following label: 3#999999999912345. If you recall in Step 1, the only device registered with the gatekeeper using a technology prefix of 3# is the Ingress Gateway and potentially a CUCM H.323 trunk. The H.323 Service sends a RAS Request to the H.323 gatekeeper to find the IP Address of the device associated with this newly constructed VRU label.

Step 8.   The H.323 Gatekeeper executes its call routing decision tree and matches the VRU label to a registered VoiceXML Gateway. It uses both the technology prefix of 3# and the zone prefix of 999* to find the edge VoiceXML router. The gatekeeper returns an ACF message containing the IP address of the VoiceXML Gateway to the Unified CVP Call Server.

Step 9.   The Unified CVP H.323 Service signals the Ingress Gateway directing it to connect to itself using the VRU label of 3#999999999912345. For this label to be processed and an application dial-peer matched, the following configuration must exist on the ingress/VoiceXML Gateway:

```
!Removes the Technolgy Prefix of 3#

myrouter(config)#voice translation-rule 1
 myrouter(config-translate)#rule 1 /3#/ //
 !Build a profile to use the translation rule above
myrouter(config)#voice translation-profile techprefix
 myrouter(cfg-translation-profile)#translate called    1
```

```
!Setup the application or VRU dial peer
 myrouter(config)#dial-peer voice 999 voip
  myrouter(config-dial-peer)#description VoiceXML Label dial-peer
  myrouter(config-dial-peer)#service bootstrap
  !Apply the translation profile to strip the technology prefix 3#

  myrouter(config-dial-peer)#translation-profile incoming techprefix
  myrouter(config-dial-peer)#incoming called-number 3#T
  myrouter(config-dial-peer)#dtmf-relay rtp-nte h245-signal h245-
alphanumeric
  myrouter(config-dial-peer)#no vad
  myrouter(config-dial-peer)#codec g711ulaw
```

This sample set of commands enables the Ingress/VoiceXML Gateway to match voice dial peer 999, strip off the prepended technology prefix of 3#, and kick off the VRU leg of the call. Furthermore, after a Unified CCE agent becomes available, the Unified CVP Call Server prepends the technology prefix saved in Step 4 before the agent label returned by Unified ICM. For example, if Unified ICM determined that agent at extension 1000 should get the call, the resulting label sent to the gatekeeper would be 3#1000. This is exactly why an H.323 trunk must be registered by a CUCM cluster for every technology prefix configured for a VoiceXML Gateway. Without this configuration the transfer to an agent would fail because a registered device would not be found by the gatekeeper with the expected technology prefix. All the other VoiceXML Gateway configuration commands are still required and are not illustrated with the previous example. Refer to the "Configuration and Administration Guide for Cisco Unified Customer Voice Portal" available at Cisco.com for details on configuring a VoiceXML Gateway.

The following steps outline what occurs when initiating an IP originated call or a subsequent transfer:

Step 10. An IP call is initiated via a CUCM cluster, or an IP originated transfer is initiated by an Agent. Unified ICM is contacted and determines that a VRU leg is warranted as described in Step 6. However, the label returned by Unified ICM to CUCM must be modified to embed the correct destination technology prefix and the technology prefix that Unified CVP has been configured to strip and save. Assume the label returned by Unified ICM is 888888888812345. Because it is required for the label to go into the Unified CVP Call Server to allow it to gain call control and the CUCM subscriber setting up the call cannot process VoiceXML instructions, it is necessary to embed a technology prefix of the centralized VoiceXML Gateway farm (refer to Figure 4-8). CUCM matches a route pattern for the label, which resolves to an H.323 trunk registered with the gatekeeper using a technology prefix of 2#. This is the same technology prefix as the Unified CVP Call Servers. It enables the 2# to be placed in front of the label. However, a translation pattern also needs to exist in the CUCM configuration to enable the prepending of a 4 (the technology prefix of the centralized VoiceXML Gateway farm) after the route pattern is matched. The resulting label sent to the gatekeeper would look like this: 2#4888888888812345. The CUCM subscriber sends a RAS request to the H.323 Gatekeeper to locate the IP address of the Unified CVP Call Server to process the DNIS string of 2#4888888888812345.

Step 11. Most likely all of the Unified CVP Call Servers have registered with the gatekeeper using a technology prefix of 2#, so the gatekeeper processes the RAS message and load balances this request to any of the registered Unified CVP call servers. The H.323 Gatekeeper executes its call routing decision tree and matches the E.164 number (DNIS) to a registered Unified CVP Call Server with a technology prefix of 2#. The gatekeeper returns an ACF message containing the IP address of the Unified CVP Call Server to the CUCM Subscriber.

Step 12. The CUCM subscriber sends a H.225 call setup message to the Unified CVP Call Server's H.323 Service. For a brief instance, a G.711 voice stream exists between the IP Phone and the Unified CVP Server's H.323 Service. The Unified CVP Call Server strips the original DNIS string of 2#4888888888812345 by first removing the technology prefix of 2# and saving one digit, the 4, leaving a DNIS string of 888888888812345 to be sent to ICM. Steps 5 and 6 are repeated using the DNIS string of 888888888812345.

Step 13. Unified ICM continues executing the transfer script that began in Step 10. Assume that a VRU label of "999999999912346" was returned by ICM to be used for the VRU for call treatment. The Unified CVP Call Server prepends the digit that was saved in Step 12 to the VRU label resulting in the following label: "4#999999999912345". If you recall in Step 10, the only device registered with the gatekeeper using a technology prefix of 4# is the centralized VoiceXML Gateway farm and a third CUCM H.323 trunk. The H.323 Service sends a RAS Request to the H.323 gatekeeper to find the IP Address of the device associated with this newly constructed VRU label.

Step 14. The H.323 Gatekeeper executes the call routing decision tree and matches the VRU label to a registered VoiceXML Gateway located in the centralized farm. It uses both the technology prefix of 4# as well as the zone prefix of 999* to find the centralized VoiceXML router. The gatekeeper returns an ACF message containing the IP address of the VoiceXML Gateway to the Unified CVP Call Server.

Step 15. The Unified CVP H.323 Service signals the CUCM subscriber directing it to connect to the standalone VoiceXML Gateway located in the central farm by using the VRU label of 4#999999999912346. For this label to be processed and an application dial-peer matched, the following configuration must exist on the VoiceXML Gateway:

```
!Removes the Technolgy Prefix of 4#
myrouter(config)# voice translation-rule 1
 myrouter(config-translate)# rule 1 /4#/ //
!Build a profile to use the translation rule above
myrouter(config)# voice translation-profile techprefix
 myrouter(cfg-translation-profile)#translate called 1
!Setup the application or VRU dial peer
myrouter(config)# dial-peer voice 999 voip
 myrouter(config-dial-peer)# description VRU or  Application Label
dial-peer
 myrouter(config-dial-peer)# service bootstrap
 myrouter(config-dial-peer)# translation-profile incoming techprefix
 myrouter(config-dial-peer)# incoming called-number 4#T
 myrouter(config-dial-peer)# dtmf-relay rtp-nte h245-signal h245-
alphanumeric
 myrouter(config-dial-peer)# no vad
myrouter(config-dial-peer)# codec g711ulaw
```

As discussed previously, when a CCE agent becomes available, the Unified CVP Call
Server prepends the technology prefix saved in Step 12 to the agent label returned by
Unified ICM. For example, if Unified ICM determines that the agent at extension 1001
should get the transferred call, the resulting label sent to the gatekeeper would be 4#1000.
Basically, its rinse and repeat from this point forward with a key take away still residing as
the need for matching CUCM H.323 trunks for each unique technology prefix, even when
using a centralized VoiceXML Gateway farm to treat IP initiated calls or transfers.

Significant Digits (SIP)

This technique is similar to the previous Technology Prefix approach, but it applies for
SIP only. There is no such animal as a technology prefix in SIP, so the technology prefix is
substituted with a site code prefix. This approach is much easier than H.323 because it is
using only a site code and does not have the constraints placed on it by a gatekeeper and
its relationship with the technology prefix. In addition, the CUCM cluster still requires
SIP trunks for sending and receiving calls. However, it is a single set of trunks and not a
trunk for each site prefix. This greatly simplifies the CUCM design and configuration. It
keeps the dial plan focused on site prefixes only. The CUCM cluster still requires to prefix the correct site code before the outgoing DNIS, and there still exists the challenge to
determine where the edge is when a call is transferred by a CCE agent. Because the
CUCM cluster provides CCE agents to be virtualized and placed at numerous edge locations, during a transfer there is no way that CUCM can signal Unified CVP with this particular technique to assure that a valid edge location is chosen for the transferring agent's
call treatment. As with the previous example, best practice states that call transfers
should be treated by a centralized VoiceXML Gateway farm allowing the CUCM cluster
to prepend the outgoing transfer DNIS label with the site code assigned to such a farm.

This section provides a closer look at an example call flow using this technique. It also
discuss how transfers are handled with the centralized VoiceXML Gateway farm.

Figure 4-9 illustrates this technique in more detail and is followed by a step-by-step configuration and call disposition discussion.

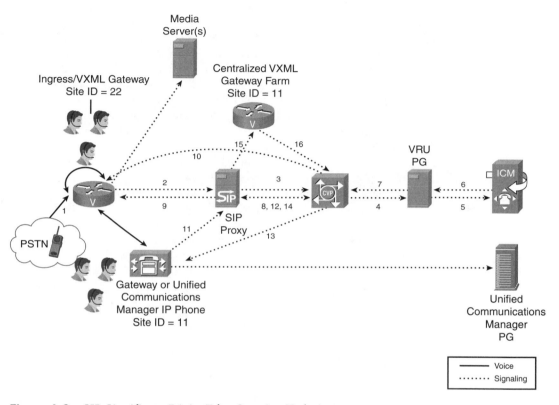

Figure 4-9 *SIP Significant Digits Edge Queuing Technique*

Step 1. The call arrives from either the PSTN or a VoIP connection to the gateway. Assume the incoming DNIS is 8005551212. The Ingress Gateway needs to prepend the DNIS with its preassigned site code. In this example the site code would be a 22. This enables the VRU leg of the call to be correctly routed back to this edge for treatment, as shown here. This example illustrates the configurations for modifying the incoming DNIS value with a site code.

```
myrouter(config)# dial-peer voice 1212 voip
 myrouter(config-dial-peer)# translate-outgoing called 99
 !Rest of dial-peer commands will follow

myrouter(config)# voice translation-rule 99
 myrouter(config-translate)# rule 1 8005551212 228005551212
```

The resulting DNIS is 228005551212 and then sent to the SIP Proxy server for routing.

Step 2.   The Ingress Gateway sends a SIP INVITE message to the SIP Proxy Server.

Step 3.   The SIP Proxy Server forwards this SIP INVITE to the Unified CVP Server's SIP Service. The Unified CVP Call Server must be configured to strip and store two significant digits for use during the duration of this call. The two digits saved in this example would be the site code prepended by the Ingress Gateway, which is 22. This site code is then prepended by Unified CVP for all subsequent labels returned by ICM for either returning the call to the edge for VRU treatment or delivering the call to a CCE agent. There are a couple caveats that should be discussed here. First, all resulting labels that include a site code + VRU label and a site code + CCE Agent Ext. must exist in the SIP proxy server as a static route to correct endpoint. The second caveat is that all edge endpoints and CUCM clusters receiving these labels must be configured to remove the site code from the incoming label to correctly route the call to either the application dial peer on the VoiceXML Gateway or a CCE agent extension on a CUCM cluster. The SIP proxy does not remove this site code when it resolves and identifies the endpoints. Figure 4-10 shows a Unified CVP Call Server's SIP Configuration tab. This provides the location for setting the value for stripping significant digits. In this example, you need to save two digits.

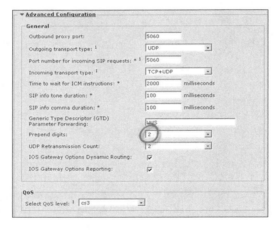

Figure 4-10   *Setting Significant Digit Value in a Unified CVP Call Server*

Note   All Unified CVP Call Servers in the farm must have the same value for the Prepend digits field because any one of them could be processing calls.

Step 4.   The SIP Service sends a new call request to Unified ICM via the Unified CVP Server ICM Service and the VRU PG.

Step 5. The Unified CVP Server sends Unified ICM a new call request via its VRU
PIM configured and hosted by the PG. This new call request invokes a new
incoming dialed number that in turn invokes a routing script in Unified ICM.

Step 6. The Unified ICM routing script determines that the caller must be transferred
to the VRU and passes a Connect to VRU request to the PG, which is forwarded to the ICM Service on the Unified CVP Call Server.

Step 7. PG passes the information provided in Step 6 to the ICM Service on the
Unified CVP Call Server.

Step 8. Assuming that a VRU label of 999999999912345 was returned by ICM to be
used for the VRU for call treatment, the Unified CVP Call Server prepends
the digit saved in Step 3 to this VRU label resulting in the following label:
22999999999912345. The SIP Proxy Server is contacted by the Unified CVP
Call Server and asked which endpoint handles 22999*, resulting in a SIP
INVITE extended to the Ingress/VoiceXML Gateway that sourced the switch
leg of the call.

Step 9. The SIP Proxy Server extends SIP INVITE to the Ingress/VoiceXML Gateway
that sourced the switch leg of the call.

Step 10. The Unified CVP SIP Service signals the Ingress Gateway, directing it to connect to itself using the VRU label of 22999999999912345. For this label to
be processed and an application dial-peer matched, the following configuration must exist on the Ingress/VoiceXML Gateway as shown here:

```
myrouter(config)# application
  myrouter(config-app)# service bootstrap flash:bootstrap.tcl
  !Strips the 22 from the VRU Label 999*
  myrouter(config-app)# param sigdigits 2
  !Configure the VRU or Application Leg Dial Peer
 myrouter(config)# dial-peer voice 999 voip
  myrouter(config-dial-peer)# description VRU or Application  dial-peer
  myrouter(config-dial-peer)# service bootstrap
  myrouter(config-dial-peer)# incoming called-number 22999T
  myrouter(config-dial-peer)# dtmf-relay rtp-nte h245-signal h245-
alphanumeric
  myrouter(config-dial-peer)# no vad
 myrouter(config-dial-peer)# codec g711ulaw
```

Furthermore, after a Unified CCE agent becomes available, the Unified CVP
Call Server prepends the site code (saved in Step 3) before the agent label is
returned by Unified ICM. For example, if Unified ICM determines that the
agent at extension 1000 should get the call, the resulting label sent to the SIP
Proxy is 221000. This exposes the need to have a static route in the SIP proxy
resolving to the CUCM Cluster's SIP trunk where the CCE Agent is hosted.

The following steps outline what occurs when initiating an IP originated call or a subsequent transfer:

Step 11. An IP call is initiated via a CUCM cluster, or an IP originated transfer is initiated by an Agent. Unified ICM is contacted and determines that a VRU leg is warranted as described in Step 6. However, the label returned by Unified ICM to CUCM must be modified to embed the correct site code. Assume the label returned by Unified ICM is 888888888812345. Because this label must go into the Unified CVP Call Server to allow it to gain call control and because the CUCM subscriber setting up the call cannot process VoiceXML instructions, a site code of the centralized VoiceXML Gateway farm must be embedded, as shown in Figure 4-9. CUCM matches a route pattern for the label, which resolves to a SIP trunk pointing to the SIP Proxy Server. However, a translation pattern must exist in the CUCM configuration to allow the prepending of a 11 (the site code of the centralized VoiceXML Gateway farm) after the route pattern was matched. The resulting label sent to the SIP Proxy would look like this: 11888888888812345. The CUCM subscriber uses its SIP trunk to ask the SIP Proxy who is the endpoint for the DNIS string of 11888888888812345.

Step 12. The SIP Proxy will most likely have several static routes for this DNIS, all resolving to different Unified CVP Call Servers, allowing this DNIS to be load balanced to different call servers. How these static routes are configured can determine which Unified CVP Farm processes switch and VRU legs. This implies that by correctly configuring the SIP Proxy routes, local data center call processing can be achieved. This approach is discussed later in this chapter as a strategy for load balancing calls locally to where they source. The SIP Proxy static routes are key factors for success.

Step 13. The CUCM server connects to the Unified CVP Call Server's SIP Service. For a brief instance, a G.711 voice stream exists between the IP Phone and the Unified CVP Server's SIP Service. The Unified CVP Call Server strips the original DNIS string of 11888888888812345 by first removing the site code 11 and storing it, leaving a DNIS string of 888888888812345 to be sent to ICM. Steps 5 and 6 are repeated using the DNIS string of 888888888812345.

Step 14. Unified ICM continues executing the transfer script, which began in Step 11. Assume that a VRU label of 999999999912346 was returned by ICM to be used for VRU for call treatment. The Unified CVP Call Server prepends the digit that was saved in Step 13 to this VRU label resulting in the following label: 11999999999912345. If you recall in Step 11, the SIP Proxy would have a set of static routes resolving to the VoiceXML Gateways located in the central farm by using a pattern of 11999*. This enables the VRU label to be load balanced across all VoiceXML Gateways in the farm. Unified CVP contacts the SIP Proxy with this label looking for an available VoiceXML Gateway in the centralized farm.

Step 15. The SIP Proxy resolves the VRU label and matches an available VoiceXML Gateway from the centralized farm and extends an invite to the gateway.

Step 16. The Unified CVP SIP Service signals the CUCM subscriber directing it to connect to the standalone VoiceXML Gateway located in the central farm by using the VRU label of 11999999999912346. As seen in Step 10, the following configurations must exist on the standalone VoiceXML Gateway:

```
myrouter(config)# application
 myrouter(config-app)# service bootstrap flash:bootstrap.tcl
 !Strips the 11 from the VRU Label 999*
 myrouter(config-app)# param sigdigits 2
!Configure the VRU or Application Leg Dial Peer
 myrouter(config)# dial-peer voice 999 voip
  myrouter(config-dial-peer)# description VRU or Application  dial-peer
  myrouter(config-dial-peer)# service bootstrap
  myrouter(config-dial-peer)# incoming called-number 11999T
  myrouter(config-dial-peer)# dtmf-relay rtp-nte h245-signal h245-
  alphanumeric
  myrouter(config-dial-peer)# no vad
  myrouter(config-dial-peer)# codec g711ulaw
```

As discussed previously, after a Unified CCE agent becomes available, the Unified CVP Call Server prepends the site code saved in Step 13 before the agent label returned by Unified ICM. For example, if Unified ICM determines that the agent at extension 1001 should get the transferred call, the resulting label sent to the SIP Proxy is 111000. Basically, its rinse and repeat from this point forward with a key take away still residing as the need for a matching static route in the SIP Proxy for the label 111001 resolving to the CUCM subscriber processing the SIP trunk, even when using a centralized VoiceXML Gateway farm to treat IP initiated calls or transfers.

Locations-Based Call Admission Control (LBCAC)

At first glance, you might think that discussing CAC as an edge queuing technique seems odd. However, LBCAC not only addresses CAC issues but also provides an additional benefit around edge queuing.

First, Unified CVP Branch office deployments requirements might exist that dictate control over the total number of calls that can transverse the WAN. This usually occurs in a centralized queuing model or for subsequent transfers. In either case a mechanism must exist to correctly calculate or control the total number of calls allowed to consume a predetermined WAN's bandwidth. CAC computations must be correct and representative of the bandwidth used by an individual call. These computations must work whether it is an IP call between two phones within CUCM cluster, calls over SIP/H.323 trunks, or calls originated from TDM-IP gateways.

Second, as noted in previous edge queuing techniques, determining where the edge exists during a subsequent transfer is problematic. It was addressed by providing a centralized farm for queuing such transfers. Because LBCAC requires siteID definitions in Unified CVP and is integrated with the CUCM locations, a transferring agent's location can be determined. In addition, an adequate and local VoiceXML Gateway can also be chosen for call treatment during the transfer. In summary, following are the two areas that LBCAC addresses when configured with Unified CVP:

■ Bandwidth miscalculations in CAC with IP originated callers and with any post transfers from agents

■ Fixes the inability to deterministically select a local VoiceXML Gateway for VRU treatment at the branch office during warm transfers from an agent because of lack of correlation between the two calls at consult

Next, define the issue around CAC, and illustrate how LBCAC addresses it. Figure 4-11 shows in simplistic terms why the CUCM cluster is unaware of calls and bandwidth consumption that occur prior to the call being sent to a CCE agent. From the CUCM cluster perspective, the gateways are "hidden" or "behind" the Unified CVP call server. The CUCM subscriber treats every call as if it came from the same device (SIP Proxy/Unified CVP/Gatekeeper) based entirely on the source IP. This problem directly impacts locations-based CAC configuration and calculations performed by the CUCM cluster.

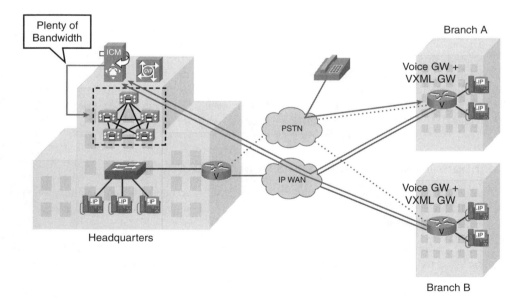

Figure 4-11   *Locations Call Admission Control Issue*

This issue does not present a problem when using edge queuing techniques such as SetTransferLabel (H.323) and Send to Originator (SIP) for the initial switch and VRU leg of a call. This is because the call is never sent to the CUCM cluster until a CCE agent is available to handle a call. Unified CVP handles all the call control, ICM interaction, Gatekeeper and SIP proxy interactions, and VRU processing. However, the switch leg of the call never becomes part of the CUCM locations-based CAC calculation until a CCE agent receives the call.

With H.323 CAC based call flows, Unified CVP provides a command **setlocationsbasedcac on** that causes the Unified CVP call server to populate the sourceCallSignalAddress field with the real Ingress Gateway IP address. In addition, the CUCM cluster service parameter Accept Unknown TCP Connection should be set to True because its default is false. These simple changes allow the CUCM cluster to perform locations-base CAC calculations for originating gateway and agent phone locations. SIP CAC-based call flows are easier because the Unified CVP call server populates the Call-info header by default with the originating devices IP address, such as the source Ingress Gateway. The CUCM cluster can look beyond the source IP address and inspect this Call-info header in the SIP INVITE enabling it to correctly perform locations-based CAC calculations for originating gateway and agent phone locations. However, the issue resurrects itself when the first CCE agent attempts to perform a warm transfer to a second CCE agent or skill group.

Note   Unified CVP should never be configured as a gateway in the CUCM cluster; instead, for H.323 a gatekeeper controlled trunk should be used.

Figure 4-12 illustrates yet another issue when dealing with multiple CUCM clusters because locations-based CAC calculations are local to the cluster and not transferred between CUCM clusters.

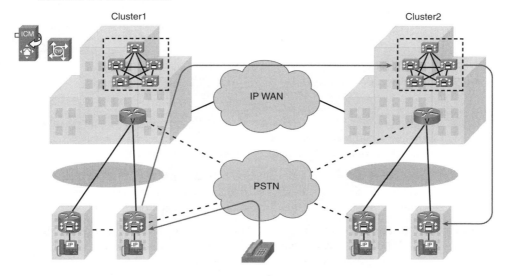

Figure 4-12 *Locations-based Call Admission Control Multiple CUCM Cluster Issue*

Each CUCM cluster imitates its own CAC mechanism providing an interesting dilemma. In the "normal" operation of Unified CVP, the call is sent directly to the destination cluster hosting the CCE Agent. However, this is undesirable simply because Cluster1 is in charge of the source Ingress Gateway and needs to recognize the active call to enable it to correctly perform locations-based CAC. To solve this issue, Unified CVP must be configured to route the destination CCE Agent DN through the CUCM cluster that controls the Ingress Gateway that is sourcing the switch leg of the call. This is achieved by prefixing a cluster ID to the originating DNIS using the "significant digit" edge queuing technique to route the call into CUCM Cluster1 and then over to CUCM Cluster2. Figure 4-13 provides a visual representation for this technique with a sample clusterID.

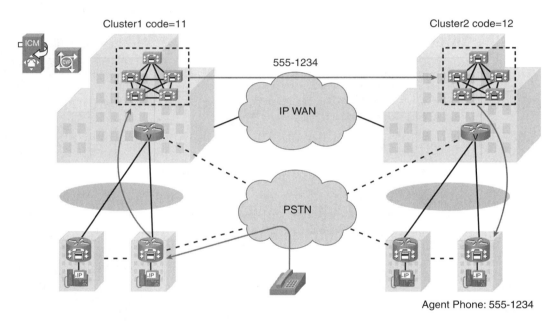

Figure 4-13   *Sig Digits with ClusterID for Multiple CUCM Cluster Routing*

In classical Significant Digit form, the site code is prefixed at the Ingress Gateway, saved by the Unified CVP call server and routed to Cluster1. It then reroutes to Cluster2, enabling Cluster1 to maintain accurate locations-based CAC calculations.

As noted earlier, the challenge to maintain accurate locations-based CAC calculations becomes increasingly more difficult after subsequent warm transfers enter the picture. Figure 4-14 frames up the issue that existed in previous version of Unified CVP.

Location bandwidth is deducted twice for IP originated hair-pinned calls (refer to Figure 4-14). The CUCM cluster believes that there are two active calls between Branch A and HQ. The problem is that Unified CVP is not sending the location information of the actual originating call because prior to Unified CVP 8.x there was no ability for Unified CVP to embed this information. So in Unified CVP 8.x and beyond, Locations-based CAC or

LBCAC was integrated between the Unified CVP call server and the CUCM cluster, solving this problem.

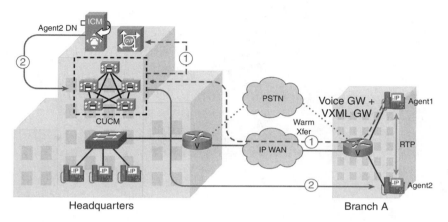

Figure 4-14   *Pre-unified CVP 8.x IP Originated Call LBCAC Calculation Limitation*

Locations-Based Call Admission Control Call Flow

Detailed configuration steps for setting up and implementing LBCAC is detailed in Chapter 12 of the *Configuration and Administration Guide for Cisco Unified Customer Voice Portal, Release 8.0(1)*. In addition, the steps for implementing legacy LBCAC are also provided for reference. Each is not be detailed in this book for sake of redundancy. Assuming that these configurations have been implemented and are complete, the following call flow would occur between the edge routers, Unified CVP, and the CUCM cluster. Figure 4-15 illustrates this call flow with detailed steps to follow. The process is similar to the Significant Digits technique that was implemented, with the major difference being the absence of edge translation patterns and significant digit stripping configurations within the Unified CVP call server.

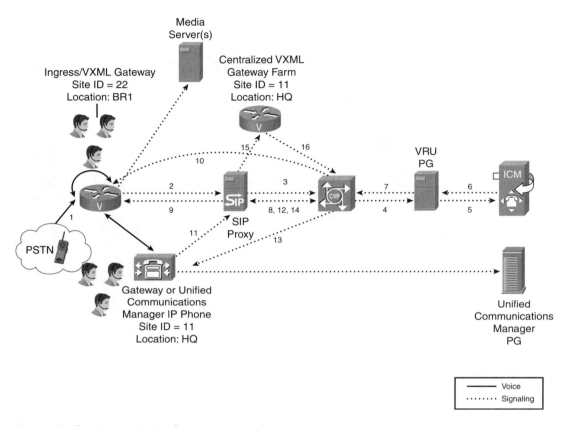

Figure 4-15   *SIP LBCAC Edge Queuing Technique*

Note   This technique also works for H.323, assuming the specific H.323 configurations are also completed.

Step 1.   The call arrives from either the PSTN or a VoIP connection to the gateway. Assume the incoming DNIS is 8005551212.

Step 2.   The Ingress Gateway sends a SIP INVITE message to the SIP Proxy Server. In the case of H.323, a gatekeeper is contacted with a RAS message.

Step 3.   The SIP Proxy Server forwards this SIP INVITE to the Unified CVP Server's SIP Service.

Step 4.   The SIP Service sends a new call request to Unified ICM via the Unified CVP Server ICM Service and the PG.

Step 5.   The Unified CVP Server sends Unified ICM a new call request via its VRU PIM configured and hosted by the Peripheral Gateway (PG). This new call request invokes a new incoming dialed number that in turn invokes a routing script in Unified ICM.

Step 6. The Unified ICM routing script determines that the caller must be transferred to the VRU and passes a Connect to VRU request to the PG, which is forwarded to the ICM Service on the Unified CVP Call Server.

Step 7. PG passes the information provided in Step 6 to the ICM Service on the Unified CVP Call Server.

Step 8. Because the Unified CVP call server has been configured to recognize this Ingress/VoiceXML Gateway as having been assigned a siteID and location, it is capable of adding the siteID to the VRU label after it is received from Unified ICM.

This site code is either prepended to VRU label, inserted into the VRU label between the label and the Correlation ID or appended to the end of the VRU label after the Correlation ID. The behavior exhibited by Unified CVP is dependent on how the server is configured during the configuration of LBCAC in the CVP Operations Console. As with the Significant Digits technique, the resulting label must exist in the SIP proxy server or gatekeeper as a static route to the correct endpoint. In addition, all edge endpoints and CUCM clusters receiving these labels must be configured to remove the site code from the incoming label to correctly route the call to either the application dial peer on the VoiceXML Gateway or a CCE agent extension on a CUCM cluster. The SIP proxy or gatekeeper does not remove this site code when it resolves and identifies the endpoints. The technique used to remove this siteID by the end devices completely depends on where and how it is inserted. In other words, the param setting for the application configuration on the VoiceXML Gateway works well for siteIDs prepended to the VRU label. However, a translation profile using a rule may be more suited for the removal of siteIDs buried in the middle or at the end of a VRU label. Presume that during LBCAC configuration, the Unified CVP call server was configured to prepend the site code to the VRU Label.

Assuming that a VRU label of 999999999912345 was returned by ICM to be used for the VRU call treatment, the Unified CVP Call Server prepends the siteID configured when setting up LBCAC for this gateway. This results in a VRU Label of 22999999999912345. The SIP Proxy Server is contacted by the Unified CVP Call Server and asked which endpoint handles 22999*.

Step 9. This results in a SIP INVITE being extended to the ingress/VoiceXML Gateway located in the BR1 location. In the case of H.323, a gatekeeper is contacted via a RAS message.

Step 10. The Unified CVP SIP Service signals the Ingress Gateway located in BR1 location directing it to connect to itself using the VRU label of 22999999999912345. For this label to be processed and an application dial-

peer matched, the following configuration must exist on the
Ingress/VoiceXML Gateway:

```
myrouter(config)# application
 myrouter(config-app)# service bootstrap flash:bootstrap.tcl
 !Strips the 22 from the VRU Label 999*
 myrouter(config-app)# param sigdigits 2
 !Configure the VRU or Application Leg Dial Peer
 myrouter(config)# dial-peer voice 999 voip
 myrouter(config-dial-peer)# description VRU or Application  dial-peer
 myrouter(config-dial-peer)# service bootstrap
 myrouter(config-dial-peer)# incoming called-number 22999T
 myrouter(config-dial-peer)# dtmf-relay rtp-nte h245-signal h245-
alphanumeric
 myrouter(config-dial-peer)# no vad
 myrouter(config-dial-peer)# codec g711ulaw
```

Furthermore, after a Unified CCE agent becomes available, the Unified CVP
Call Server prepends the siteID before the agent label returned by Unified
ICM. For example, if Unified ICM determines that the agent at extension
1000 should get the call, the resulting label sent to the SIP Proxy would be
221000. This exposes the need to have a static route in the SIP proxy resolving to the CUCM Cluster's SIP trunk where the Unified CCE Agent is hosted.

The following steps outline what occurs when initiating an IP originated call or a subsequent transfer:

Step 11.   An IP call is initiated via an IP Phone registered with a CUCM cluster, or an
IP originated transfer is initiated by an Unified CCE Agent. Unified ICM is
contacted either using a route point or invocation of the ICM Dialed Number
Plan (DNP). It determines that a VRU leg is warranted as described in Step 6.
Because Unified CVP has been synchronized with the CUCM cluster to rec-
ognize all locations configured for the cluster, and a correlation between the
locations and a siteID was completed, Unified CVP can correctly apply this
SiteID to the incoming label provided by CUCM.

Assume the label returned by Unified ICM is 888888888812345. This label
must go into the Unified CVP Call Server to allow it to gain call control The
CUCM subscriber setting up the call cannot process VoiceXML instructions.
So Unified CVP uses its LBCAC configurations to assign the correct siteID
for the VoiceXML Gateway closest to the Unified CCE agent transferring or
initiating the call. For example, if in Figure 4-15 the Unified CCE agent initiating the call or transfer were located in the HQ location with a respective
SiteID of 11, Unified CVP call server would place this siteID in front of the
resulting VRU label discussed in Step 14. For now, CUCM matches a route
pattern for the label, which resolves to a SIP trunk pointing to the SIP Proxy
Server. This SIP trunk must be configured with the "Phantom" location per
the LBCAC configuration instructions. Unlike the Significant Digit technique,

a translations pattern is not required to prepend any siteID because that responsibility is now solely in the hands of Unified CVP.

The CUCM subscriber uses its SIP trunk to ask the SIP Proxy who is the endpoint for the DNIS string of 888888888812345.

Tip What Is a Phantom Location?

It is when a call is hairpinned over an H323 or SIP trunk, or a SIP/H323 CVP call is queued at the local branch. Even though RTP is point-to-point within the local branch, Locations CAC is still double-counted as an outbound and inbound call. So bandwidth is deducted (twice) even though there is actually no WAN traffic.

The Phantom location is created by default. This location has unlimited bandwidth and cannot be modified by administrator. When this Phantom location is assigned to a trunk, call information is passed across the trunk so that CUCM correctly deducts bandwidth regardless of whether hairpins exist. This Phantom location should be assigned to the gateway/trunk for CVP.

CVP adds a special indicator header in the SIP/H323 signaling to indicate the real location of the call, using a SiteID. This enables the bandwidth to be deducted on the correct location.

Step 12. The SIP Proxy most likely has several static routes for this DNIS, all resolving to different Unified CVP Call Servers. This enables the DNIS to be load balanced to different call servers. The configuration of these static routes can determine which Unified CVP Farm processes switch and VRU legs. This implies that by correctly configuring the SIP Proxy routes, local data center call processing can be achieved. This approach is discussed later in this chapter as a strategy for load balancing calls locally to where they source. The SIP Proxy static routes is key factor.

Step 13. The CUCM subscriber connects to the Unified CVP Call Server's SIP Service. Steps 5 and 6 are repeated using the DNIS string of 888888888812345.

Step 14. Unified ICM continues to execute the transfer script that began in Step 11. Assume that a VRU label of 999999999912346 was returned by ICM to be used for VRU call treatment. Based on the location and SiteID configurations for Unified CVP and CUCM, a siteID is prepended to the VRU label resulting in the following label: 11999999999912345. As mentioned in Step 11, the SIP Proxy has a set of static routes resolving to the VoiceXML Gateways located in the central farm by using a pattern of 11999*. This enables the VRU label to be load balanced across all VoiceXML Gateways in the farm. Unified CVP contacts the SIP Proxy with this label and searches for an available VoiceXML Gateway in the centralized farm.

Step 15. The SIP Proxy resolves the VRU label and matches an available VoiceXML Gateway from the centralized farm and extends an invite to the gateway.

Step 16. The Unified CVP SIP Service signals the CUCM subscriber. It directs it to connect to the standalone VoiceXML Gateway located in the central farm by using the VRU label of 11999999999912346. As seen in Step 10, the following configurations must exist on the standalone VoiceXML Gateway:

```
myrouter(config)#application
 myrouter(config-app)# service bootstrap flash:bootstrap.tcl
 !Strips the 11 from the VRU Label 999*
 myrouter(config-app)# param sigdigits 2
 !Configure the VRU or Application Leg Dial Peer
 myrouter(config)# dial-peer voice 999 voip
  myrouter(config-dial-peer)# description VRU or Application  dial-peer
  myrouter(config-dial-peer)# service bootstrap
  myrouter(config-dial-peer)# incoming called-number 11999T
  myrouter(config-dial-peer)# dtmf-relay rtp-nte h245-signal h245-
alphanumeric
  myrouter(config-dial-peer)# no vad
 myrouter(config-dial-peer)# codec g711ulaw
```

As discussed previously, after a Unified CCE agent becomes available, the Unified CVP Call Server prepends the SiteID to the agent label returned by Unified ICM. For example, if Unified ICM determined that agent at extension 1001 should get the transferred call, the resulting label sent to the SIP Proxy would be 111000. Basically, its rinse and repeat from this point forward with a key take away still residing as the need for a matching static route in the SIP Proxy for the label 111001 resolving to the CUCM subscriber processing the SIP trunk. The process is identical when using H.323. The difference is only in the use of the gatekeeper in place of the SIP Proxy.

By moving the configuration of the SiteIDs into the Unified CVP call servers, the configuration required by the edge devices is greatly simplified. However, with any technique, there are a few caveats that should be listed:

■   A trunk configured with "MTP required" will not work with the LBCAC edge queuing technique. The primary reason is when the MTP is inserted into the media stream, the media is terminated between the endpoint and the MTP resource, not between the two endpoints. This is a significant limitation when a solution requires transcoding between different voice codecs and must also adhere to locations-based CAC requirements.

■   If a MTP/Transcoder/TRP media resource is inserted by the UCM layer, the incoming location information is not used.

■   If the intercluster call is not hair-pin/looped back to the same cluster, the former behavior of location based CAC logic applies.

In addition, during a CAC failure, meaning that bandwidth is unavailable to set up the call, Unified CVP returns a failure code to Unified ICM that triggers a router requery event.

Call Survivability

After discussing distributed deployments and edge queuing techniques for treating calls at their edge location, the obvious question is, so what happens when the WAN goes down? How does the voice services survive? It would be completely unacceptable to provide a solution that supports edge queuing without some mechanism to allow a call to survive during a WAN outage, Unified CVP call server outage, and so on. Unified CVP provides Tool Command Language (TCL) files located on the Ingress Gateways that are responsible for monitoring the current calls. They take over a call if a WAN or Unified CVP failure occurs allowing the call to survive with several options. This survivability is handled by a combination of services from a TCL script (survivability.tcl) and SRST functions. The survivability TCL script monitors the H.225 or SIP connection for all calls that ingress through the remote gateway. If a signaling failure occurs, the TCL script takes control of the call and redirects it to a configurable destination. These destinations are configurable via parameters in the Cisco IOS Gateway configuration.[1] Figure 4-16 provides a simple call flow for what occurs during a survivable event. However, while the figure outlines sending the call back out to the PSTN, the survivability TCL script has many options at its disposal to provide a multitude of survivability configurations.

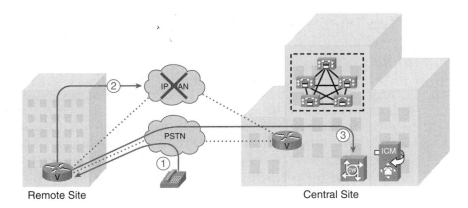

Figure 4-16 *Unified CVP Distributed Branch Call Survivability*

In addition, when the call arrives at the central site, it is treated as a new call. The existing call treatment and queue position are all lost and are not maintained during a survivability event. Following is a list outlining the capabilities available and supported as configurable parameters with the survivability TCL file and application:

■ Perform multiple types of transfers in call failure conditions:

■ *8 transfer connect (outpulse)

■ Hairpin

■ SRST

- ■ Hookflash Relay

- ■ Two B-Channel Transfer (TBCT)

■ Differentiate call recovery behavior by incoming DNIS.

■ Differentiate call recover behavior by incoming DNIS and how long the call had been in Unified CVP prior to failure.

■ Hand off to an auto-attendant type application in the event of some downstream failure (for example, WAN failure, Unified ICM failure, and Unified CVP failure). This auto-attendant functionality could be CME's Basic Automatic Call Distribution (B-ACD), a Unified CVP Standalone call flow model, a VoiceXML Server application, or a custom-written VoiceXML application.[2]

Following are the installation steps documented in the "Configuration and Administration Guide for Cisco Unified Customer Voice Portal," Chapter 12, page 388–389, referencing Call Survivability and presented here for reference. This guide should be used to explore additional configuration parameters and their options.

Tip   Configuration help for survivability parameters and their options are well documented via code commentary at the beginning of the survivability.tcl file located on each Ingress Gateway.

Step 1.   Access the Unified CVP Operations Console. Copy and deploy all script/prompt files to the gateway. Figure 4-17 provides shows this activity using the Operations Console and assumes the user deploys the script/prompt files to a combination ingress/VoiceXML Gateway using the Bulk Administration > File Transfer > Scripts and Media option. However, depending on the role of the gateway, not all files are required. Following is a list of files needed for VoiceXML and Ingress roles for a SIP comprehensive deployment model:

- ■ Ingress Gateway

- ■ Handoff.tcl

- ■ Survivability.tcl

- ■ Recovery.vxml

- ■ Ringtone.tcl

- ■ Cvperror.tcl

- ■ Ringback.wav

- ■ Critical_error.wav

- ■ VoiceXML Gateway

- ■ Cvperror.tcl

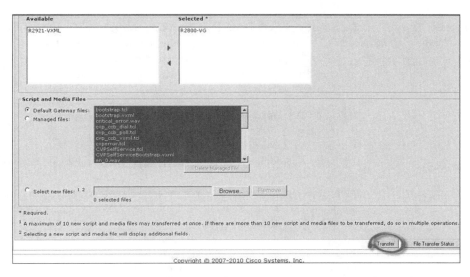

Figure 4-17 *File Transfer Using Unified CVP Operations Console's Bulk Administration*

- Ringback.wav

- Critical_error.wav

- Bootstrap.tcl

- Bootstrap.vxml

Step 2. On the gateway, do the following:

For a **Unified CVP Comprehensive** call flow model, first define two services:

```
myrouter(config)# application
 myrouter(config-app)# service survive flash:survivability.tcl
   myrouter(config-app-param)# paramspace callfeature med-inact-def
enable
 myrouter(config-app)# service handoff flash:handoff.tcl
```

Now add the following IOS commands to the gateway configuration:

```
mygateway(config)# ip rtcp report interval 2000
mygateway(config)# gateway
 mygateway(config-gateway)# timer receive-rtcp 6
```

Note The IOS gateway configurations invoke survivability between 8 and 16 seconds for an active call after a WAN failure. If IOS detects the absence of both RTP and RTCP packets after (2000*4)*2 ms = 8 to 16 seconds, it raises an error event and survivability is invoked. (The factor of 2 is a built-in IOS factor that cannot be configured. *Do not* adjust these values lower because this could cause the survivability event to be prematurely invoked.) The **timer receive-tcp** command configures a media activity timer that is the command for both H.323 and SIP. If set, it affects both H.323 and SIP calls.

For a **Unified CVP Standalone** call flow model, first define one service:

```
myrouter(config)# application
myrouter(config-app)# service survive-service flash:survivability.tcl
```

Now you must associate this service as a parameter on the CVPSelfService.tcl service associated with the incoming POTS dial-peer. Note the text param survive must be entered exactly as shown:

```
mygateway(config)# dial-peer voice 100 pots
 mygateway(config-dial-peer)# service my-CVP-service
 mygateway(config-dial-peer)# incoming called number 8005551212
mygateway(config)# application
 myrouter(config-app)# service my-CVP-service flash:CVPSelfService.tcl
  myrouter(config-app-param)# param CVPPrimaryVoiceXMLServer {IP of
Primary VoiceXML Server}
  myrouter(config-app-param)# param CVPBackupVoiceXMLServer {IP of
Backup VoiceXML Server}
  myrouter(config-app-param)# param CVPSelfService-app {Name of
VoiceXML Application}
  myrouter(config-app-param)# param keepalive my-CVP-service
 myrouter(config-app-param)# param survive survive-service flash:sur-
vivability.tcl
```

Step 3.   On the gateway, issue the following IOS commands: **call application voice load survive** and **call application voice load handoff**.

Step 4.   On a Unified CVP Comprehensive call flow model, create a dial-peer on the gateway, placing the Unified CVP called number on an incoming-called-number parameter. Assign the survive service to this dial-peer.

Note   As of version 8.x of Unified CVP, survivability is now supported with Cisco Unified Border Element (CUBE) and SIP. The configuration is similar; however, it can now be applied to a voip dial peer and not just a pots dial-peer.

On a Unified CVP Standalone call flow model, no special survivability dial-peer needs to be created. However, the parameter illustrated in Step 2, **param survive survive-service** must be included in the CVPSelfService.tcl service definition. This parameter indicates which service to run if a system failure occurs. This implementation provides different survivability services that can be invoked depending on the incoming pots dial-peer invoked.[3]

For a complete step-by-step process in configuring these different survivability options, refer to the "Configuration and Administration Guide for Cisco Unified Customer Voice Portal," Chapter 12, page 387, referencing Call Survivability. However, without providing an exhaustive list of configuration parameters provided in the Cisco documentation, this chapter examines some simple use cases that might provide more insight on how the parameters for a survivability solution can be configured. Assume that the last configuration noted in Step 2 has been completed for a Unified CVP comprehensive call flow. This chapter examines what happens when specific parameters are added to the survivability.tcl service to influence its behavior.

Use Case 1: Specific After Hours/ Holiday Priority Versus Open Hours

A customer wants to use time-of-day routing to distinguish between a WAN failure that occurs on the Thanksgiving holiday versus a failure that occurs during normal business hours. If the failure occurs during the holiday or after hours, a different DNIS must be dialed by the survivability script than if the failure occurs during normal operating hours. Example 4-1 provides a sample of this code.

Example 4-1 *Solution to Use Case 1*

```
myrouter(config)# application
 myrouter(config-app)# service survivability flash:survivability.tcl
  myrouter(config-app-param)# param open-hours-agent0 8005551010
  myrouter(config-app-param)# param open-hours-time0 12345:0900-1730
  myrouter(config-app-param)# param after-hours-agent0 8005551313
  myrouter(config-app-param)# param after-hours-agent1 8005551414
  myrouter(config-app-param)# param after-hours-time0 11/25
  myrouter(config-app-param)# param setup-timeout 7
  myrouter(config-app-param)# param alert-timeout
 myrouter(config)# dial-peer voice 800555 pots
 myrouter(config-dial-peer)# application survivability
 myrouter(config-dial-peer)# incoming called-number 8005551515
 myrouter(config-dial-peer)# direct-inward-dial
```

Assume that today is a holiday, Thursday, 11/25 at 1300 hours, and a call is made to DNIS 8005551515. Because 11/25 is defined as a specific after-hours-time, it will be selected before the 12345:0900-1730 open-hours-time (12345 equates to the days of the week, Monday through Friday), which also falls on a Thursday. If the WAN or communication to the Unified CVP solution fails, this configuration notifies the survivability script to first try to transfer the failed call to 8005551313 and then to 8005551414. This is because a date or time was matched in the after -hours-time definition for 11/25, which overrides and ignores the open-hours-agentX DNIS values.

Use Case 2: Specific Open Hours/ Holiday Priority Versus After Hours

This use case is similar to the first, except switched completely around. The failure for this use case occurs on Saturday, which is normally an after-hours-time. But because it is a special holiday and the contact center is open, a survivability configuration must be provided to handle the one-off open hours failure versus treating the call as a closed or after hours call. Example 4-2 provides a sample of this code.

Example 4-2 *Solution to Use Case 2*

```
myrouter(config)# application

 myrouter(config-app)# service survivability flash:survivability.tcl
  myrouter(config-app-param)# param open-hours-agent0 8005551010
  myrouter(config-app-param)# param open-hours-agent1 8005551111
  myrouter(config-app-param)# param open-hours-time0 12345:0900-1730
  myrouter(config-app-param)# param open-hours-time1 12/18:0600-2300
  myrouter(config-app-param)# param after-hours-agent0 8005551313
  myrouter(config-app-param)# param after-hours-agent1 8005551414
  myrouter(config-app-param)# param setup-timeout 7
  myrouter(config-app-param)# param alert-timeout
myrouter(config)# dial-peer voice 800555 pots
 myrouter(config-dial-peer)# application survivability
 myrouter(config-dial-peer)# incoming called-number 8005551515
 myrouter(config-dial-peer)# direct-inward-dial
```

Assume that today is Saturday, 12/18 at 0900 hours, peak of the holiday shopping season. Because 12/18 is defined as a specific open-hours-time, it will be selected for an open-hours agent, even though it falls on a Saturday that would normally be an after-hours time. If the WAN or communication to Unified CVP fails, this script first tries a transfer to 8005551010 (open-hours-agent0), tries 8005551111 (open-hours-agent1), tries 8005551313 (after-hours-agent0) and finally tries 8005551414 (after-hours-agent1).

Use Case 3: One DNIS for All Failures, No Time of Day Routing

This use case assumes that time of day routing and priority is not a requirement but that simply put, a last resort DNIS should be used to transfer all failures to. Example 4-3 provides a sample of this code.

Example 4-3 *Solution to Case 3*

```
myrouter(config)# application
 myrouter(config-app)# service survivability flash:survivability.tcl
  myrouter(config-app-param)# param after-hours-agent0 8005551313
  myrouter(config-app-param)# param after-hours-agent1 8005551414
  myrouter(config-app-param)# param setup-timeout 7
```

```
    myrouter(config-app-param)# param alert-timeout
myrouter(config)# dial-peer voice 800555 pots
 myrouter(config-dial-peer)# application survivability
 myrouter(config-dial-peer)# incoming called-number 8005551515
 myrouter(config-dial-peer)# direct-inward-dial
```

Incoming calls on DNIS 8005551515 that experience a WAN failure or a loss of communication to Unified CVP are transferred to 8005551313 (after-hours-agent0) and then attempt 8005551414 (after-hours-agent1). The key to this configuration is to not define any times either open or closed. This allows any call that fails to use the after-hours-agentX definitions for target DNIS values during a failure.

Use Case 4: Use DNIS to Organize Call Survivability Functionality

This use case illustrates a fairly common technique that requires multiple application definitions to handle different DNIS values used for Service and Sales. Although this technique works, as shown in Use Case 5, local router translation profiles and rules simplify the number of survivability applications configured and running on the Ingress Gateway. However, for now, here are the requirements for the Service and Sales survivability applications:

- Service calls dial a DNIS of 8005551212.

- If the service call fails somewhere in the course of the call, the following behavior is provided by the survivability application:

  - If the service call fails and the call had been in Unified CVP less than 30 seconds (which also includes the case in which the call never made it to Unified CVP, that is, 0 seconds), send the caller back through the PSTN via a *8 takeback to 8005551313.

  - If the call fails and the call had been in Unified CVP greater than or equal to 30 seconds, send the caller back through the PSTN via a *8 takeback to 8005551414.

- Sales calls dial a DNIS of 8005551515.

  - If the call fails (ignoring the amount of time the call had been in Unified CVP), send the caller back through the PSTN via a hairpin transfer to 8005551616.

  - Assume the PSTN switch is sending Automatic Number Identification (ANI) and DNIS in such a way that the ANI and DNIS are concatenated together in the DNIS field. Also assume that the ANI length is 10 and the DNIS length is 4. In addition, the ANI can be blank, for example, blocked callerID.

Example 4-4 *Solution to Use Case 4*

```
myrouter(config)# dial-peer voice 1 pots
 myrouter(config-dial-peer)# application services
 myrouter(config-dial-peer)# incoming called-number 8005551212
 !Rest of dial peer configurations
myrouter(config)# dial-peer voice 2 pots
 myrouter(config-dial-peer)# application sales
 myrouter(config-dial-peer)# incoming called-number 8005551515
 !Rest of dial peer configurations
myrouter(config)# dial-peer voice 3 pots
 myrouter(config-dial-peer)# destination-pattern 8005551616
 !Configure the specific POTs port
 myrouter(config-dial-peer)# port 7/0:D
myrouter(confif)# dial-peer voice 4 voip
 myrouter(config-dial-peer)# destination-pattern 8005551616
 ! Force the call to g711ulaw on hairpin
 myrouter(config-dial-peer)# codec g711ulaw myrouter(config)# application
myrouter(config-app)# service services flash:survivability.tcl
 myrouter(config-app-param)# param after-hours-agent0 DTMF*8,,,8005551313
 myrouter(config-app-param)# param after-hours-cvptime0 <30
 myrouter(config-app-param)# param after-hours-agent1 DTMF*8,,,8005551414
 myrouter(config-app-param)# param after-hours-cvptime1 >29
 myrouter(config-app-param)# param ani-dnis split 10:4
 myrouter(config-app)# service sales flash:survivability.tcl
 myrouter(config-app-param)# param after-hours-agent0 8005551616
 myrouter(config-app-param)# param ani-dnis split 10:4
```

The obvious disadvantage and limitation to this configuration is the requirement to build and load into memory different survivability services for each incoming DNIS applied to their respective dial-peers. This can become confusing and cumbersome for situations in which tens of hundreds of incoming DNIS values exist and must be configured for survivability. Use Case 5 provides a secondary approach to reduce the number of survivability applications configured and running when dealing with multiple incoming DNIS values.

Use Case 5: Single Survivability Application for Multiple Incoming DNIS Values

This use case solves the problem to build different survivability applications because unique incoming DNIS values exist. Based on the original incoming DNIS value for which the call failed, a new DNIS is built using the <retry> parameter in combination with a local translation profile and rules to modify the outgoing DNIS to a hunt group on a CUCM cluster, IP IVR controlled CTI Route Point, or any other routable endpoint, specifically for a skill group. Assume there are two separate DNIS numbers: one for Services using 8005551212 and one for Sales using 8005551515. When a failure occurs, the number that survivability should transfer to should be a unique hunt group DNIS values of 1111212 for Services and 1111215 for Sales, hosted by a CUCM Cluster. Example 4-5 shows the configuration for this use case.

Example 4-5 *Solution to Use Case 5*

```
myrouter(config)# voice translation-rule 10
!Services DNIS translation
myrouter(cfg-translation-rule)# rule 1 /8880055512\(..\)/ /11112\1/
!Sales DNIS translation
myrouter(cfg-translation-rule)# rule 2 /8880055515\(..\)/ /11112\1/
myrouter(config)# voice translation-profile DR
 myrouter(cfg-translation-profile)# translate called 10
!myrouter(config)# application
 myrouter(config-app)# service survivability flash:survivability.tcl
  myrouter(config-app-param)# paramspace english index 0
  myrouter(config-app-param)# paramspace english language en
  myrouter(config-app-param)# paramspace english location flash:
  myrouter(config-app-param)# paramspace english prefix en
  !Add Originating DNIS to end of retry number
  myrouter(config-app-param)# param open-hours-agent0 88<retry>
  myrouter(config-app-param)# param open-hours-time0 0123456:0000-2359
!myrouter(config)# dial-peer voice 1 voip
 myrouter(config-dial-peer)# description *** SEND CALL TO PRIMARY SIP PROXY ***
 myrouter(config-dial-peer)# preference 1
 myrouter(config-dial-peer)# destination-pattern 800555....$
 myrouter(config-dial-peer)# progress_ind setup enable 3
 myrouter(config-dial-peer)# session protocol sipv2
 myrouter(config-dial-peer)# session target ipv4:10.1.1.1
 myrouter(config-dial-peer)# dtmf-relay rtp-nte
 myrouter(config-dial-peer)# codec g711ulaw
 myrouter(config-dial-peer)# no vad
 !
myrouter(config)# dial-peer voice 2 voip
 myrouter(config-dial-peer)# description *** SEND CALL TO SECONDARY SIP PROXY ***
 myrouter(config-dial-peer)# preference 2
 myrouter(config-dial-peer)# destination-pattern 800555....
 myrouter(config-dial-peer)# progress_ind setup enable 3
 myrouter(config-dial-peer)# session protocol sipv2
 myrouter(config-dial-peer)# session target ipv4:10.1.1.2
 myrouter(config-dial-peer)# dtmf-relay rtp-nte
 myrouter(config-dial-peer)# codec g711ulaw
 myrouter(config-dial-peer)# no vad
 !
myrouter(config)# dial-peer voice 3 voip
 myrouter(config-dial-peer)# description ** SURVIVABILITY TO PRIMARY SUBSCRIBER"
 myrouter(config-dial-peer)# translation-profile outgoing DR
 myrouter(config-dial-peer)# destination-pattern 88.......$
 myrouter(config-dial-peer)# session protocol sipv2
```

```
myrouter(config-dial-peer)# session target ipv4:10.1.1.3
myrouter(config-dial-peer)# dtmf-relay rtp-nte
myrouter(config-dial-peer)# codec g711ulaw
myrouter(config-dial-peer)# no vad
!
myrouter(config)# dial-peer voice 882 voip
myrouter(config-dial-peer)# description ** SURVIVABILITY TO SECONDARY SUBSCRIBER"
myrouter(config-dial-peer)# translation-profile outgoing DR
myrouter(config-dial-peer)# destination-pattern 88.......$
myrouter(config-dial-peer)# session protocol sipv2
myrouter(config-dial-peer)# session target ipv4:10.1.1.4
myrouter(config-dial-peer)# dtmf-relay rtp-nte
myrouter(config-dial-peer)# codec g711ulaw
myrouter(config-dial-peer)# no vad
!ONE DIAL PEER FOR ALL
myrouter(config)# dial-peer voice 10 pots
!ONE SURVIVABILITY APPLICATION
myrouter(config-dial-peer)# service survivability
!MATCH ALL INCOMING DNIS VALUES
myrouter(config-dial-peer)# incoming called-number .
myrouter(config-dial-peer)# direct-inward-dial
myrouter(config-dial-peer)# forward-digits all
```

Assume that a call came in for Services on DNIS 8005551212. It matches the POTS dial-peer 10 further routing to VOIP dial-peers 1 and 2, respectively for the initial connection to Unified CVP via a proxy server. If a failure occurs on the WAN or communication is interrupted with Unified CVP at any time during this call, survivability is invoked. These configurations instruct the survivability script to place 88 in front of the originating DNIS that was saved during the first connection to Unified CVP. In this case the resulting retry string would be 888005551212. The survivability script then sends this DNIS value back through the configurations in the Ingress Gateway matching dial-peers 3 and 4. Prior to setting up the call with the CUCM Subscriber handling the hunt groups, the Ingress Gateway executes the outgoing translation profile named DR, which modifies the outgoing DNIS from 888005551212 to the hunt group number of 1111212. This basically saves the last two digits of the originating DNIS from the failed call. The ingress router rings this new number on a local CUCM subscriber, IP IVR, and so on to enable a specific survivability call treatment for customers looking for Services. The exact same process occurs for the Sales DNIS. However, the outcome is a different hunt group number set up specifically for Sales. By using this technique, the amount of configuration required on an Ingress Gateway servicing multiple inbound DNIS values can be greatly simplified into a single Plain Old Telephone Service/System (POTS) dial-peer and survivability application, leaving the complexity and DNIS mapping to the router's translation profile and rules.

Tip   Always try to keep the incoming DNIS ranges within a contiguous block of values. Also if you use a different range of DNIS values for failover, try to allocate them into a contiguous block. This would allow use of the technique previously described to map failed DNIS values into failover DNIS numbers using an intelligent mapping. For example, you could always say that if an originating DNIS number fails over, it always retains the last three numbers of the originating number. This allows for easier logic when mapping the failover numbers to applications that should provide unique call treatment and mapping based on the originating DNIS values. For example, if a Services DNIS were 8005551212 and it fails to a hunt group of 11111212, and the Sales DNIS is 8005551515 and it fails to a hunt group of 11111215. It's simple to examine the last two digits of the failed DNIS to know what kind of treatment the failover numbers provide. This reduces the number of translations and their complexity on the Ingress Gateway. It induces some logic into the application mapping exercises between the originating and failover calls. Although this can sometimes be difficult for organizations that currently use UCCE with IP IVR and are migrating to Unified CVP, there should still be some effort spent around performing this type of "housekeeping" before the deployment to migrate the contact center dial plan into a contiguous range.

SIP High-Availability Architectures

In the previous sections a closer examination was provided for distributed deployment models, different techniques to provide edge queuing support for these models, and call survivability at the edge in the unfortunate event of a WAN or communication failure with Unified CVP. This section focuses on components configured for a SIP call flow and provides details for the configuration of those components to support different requirements around high availability. Revisiting the solution-level mindset required to successfully design, deploy, and troubleshoot Unified CVP, you must individually examine each native and non-native component in the SIP architecture to understand the options available around high availability. Figure 4-18 provides a good starting picture for discussing these components. This discussion begins with the Ingress Gateways and progresses inward toward the Unified CVP Call Servers. The ACME deployment is a basic two data center deployment with Ingress and VoiceXML Gateways existing in each respective data center which represents the edge of the solution. After each component is discussed, a use case is provided at the end of this section to illustrate how the call progresses and survives depending on what type of failure occurs in each data center.

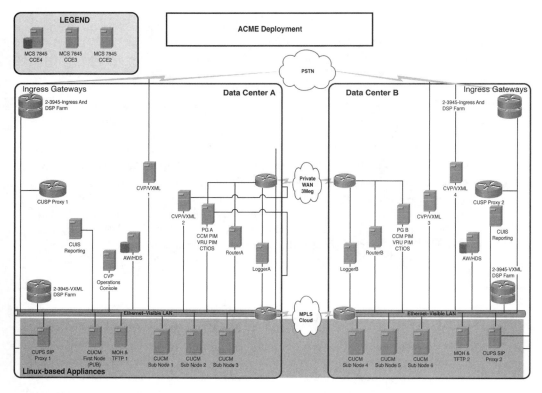

Figure 4-18 *ACME Company SIP Sample Deployment High-Level Architecture*

Layer 2 Switch Considerations

Refer to Figure 4-18 to see a high-level layout for a fault-tolerant Unified CVP system. Each component is duplicated for redundancy with the quantity of each of these components varying based on the expected busy hour call attempts (BHCA). Although the figure does not illustrate the details around Layer 2 and 3 redundancy, the basic premise is that the Layer 2 switches provide the first layer of redundancy for the Unified CVP components. Both LAN segments illustrated feeding into the Private WAN and MPLS Cloud should be configured with Layer 2 redundancy. Following are some additional considerations for Layer 2 switches:

- If one switch fails, only a subset of the components becomes inaccessible, allowing the components connected to the remaining switch to be available to process calls.

- If you use a Content Services Switch (CSS), its redundant partner must reside on the same VLAN to send keep-alive messages to each other via Virtual Router Redundancy Protocol (VRRP), a protocol similar to Hot Standby Router Protocol (HSRP). If one of the switches fails, the other CSS is still functional. ACE also has a similar requirement for the VLAN. It also uses HA keepalives.

■ Network Interface Card (NIC) Teaming is not currently supported in the Unified CVP solution.

■ The NIC card and Ethernet switch should be set to 100-MB full duplex for 10/100 links and set to auto-negotiate for gigabit links.

Originating Ingress and VoiceXML Gateways

Each datacenter provides PSTN access via localized Ingress Gateways (refer to Figure 4-18). Configuring each of these Ingress Gateways to use their local SIP proxy servers as primary and the other data centers proxy servers as secondary provides call routing redundancy across data centers. In addition, it is best practice to configure the Ingress Gateway to bind SIP signaling to the virtual loopback interface; following is how to accomplished that in SIP:

```
myrouter(config)# voice service voip
 myrouter(conf-voi-serv)# sip
  myrouter(conf-serv-sip)# bind control source-interface loopback0
  myrouter(conf-serv-sip)# bind media source-interface loopback0
```

This sample configuration enables the SIP signaling to operate independently of the physical interfaces. Assuming that Ingress Gateway is provisioned with multiple LAN interfaces implemented with a redundant Layer 2 and Layer 3 design, the loopback interface should be accessible from any physical interface, allowing SIP signaling and media packets to always be available regardless of what physical interface fails.

Note The IP routers for the network must provide redundant routes to this loopback interface and correctly propagate those routes to the rest of the routers in both data centers. How this is accomplished is beyond the scope of this book; however, the point is to be aware of this requirement when using loopback interfaces.

In addition to the tactical configurations used on an Ingress Gateway, PSTN routing decisions must be taken into consideration. For example, refer to Figure 4-18 to see how the PSTN connects to both Datacenter A and B. This implies that calls can be sourced at either location from the PSTN and delivered to Unified CVP. However, because the switch leg of the call is routed purely on the incoming DNIS, understanding what DNIS values are presented at each PSTN ingress location is critical when designing how the switch leg of a call is routed to Unified CVP. Following are a few options pertaining to this concept:

■ The same DNIS is delivered to each PSTN ingress router, regardless of which data center sources the call. This is actually a feature that must be discussed with the PSTN carrier, simply because there may be limitations on whether a call delivered to Datacenter A with a DNIS of 8005551212 can also be delivered to Datacenter B via the PSTN with the same DNIS. If this is possible, care must be taken to how the proxy servers are deployed and configured to localize the call treatment in each data center. This concept is discussed and illustrated in the SIP proxy section.

- Different DNIS values are delivered for Datacenter A calls as compared to Datacenter B calls. For example, a call to the Services department is delivered to the Datacenter A Ingress Gateways with a DNIS of 8005551212, and the same type of call is load balanced to Datacenter B Ingress Gateways with a DNIS of 8005551313. As noted in the previous bullet point, this provides two distinct DNIS values per data centers, which implies that how the static routes are configured in the SIP Proxy determines how the switch leg of the call is routed and treated by local Unified CVP farms in the respective data center.

- Datacenter A sources all DNIS values with Datacenter B existing as a PSTN backup connection. This implies that all DNIS values are delivered to the Datacenter A Ingress Gateways, and the SIP proxy devices either load balance the call between the Unified CVP farms in either data center or favor Datacenter A Unified CVP farms with failover only sent to Datacenter B. Both of these options do not allow either the Datacenter B Ingress Gateways or Unified CVP farms to be used until either a PSTN or Unified CVP failure occurs, respectively.

Configuration and deployment models used by the SIP proxy impact the routing behavior for both the switch and VRU legs of a call. These routing choices are listed here.

Additional high-availability configurations exist for the Ingress Gateway pertaining to how it routes the switch leg of a call toward Unified CVP. Following are a few options for creating high availability in these areas:

- **sip-server definition:** On the gateway, define the **sip-server** value in the user agent section for SIP configuration. This definition can either point to an IP address of a SIP Proxy or its hostname. Following is the configuration:

```
myrouter(config)# sip-ua
  myrouter(config-sip-ua)# sip-server ipv4:10.1.1.1:5060
myrouter(config)# dial-peer voice 1 voip
  myrouter(config-dial-peer)# session target sip-server
```

- Obviously, this configuration points only to a single SIP Proxy, so it does not accomplish much in the realm of high availability. By using a hostname, DNS could be used to allow a DNS server to load balance to multiple SIP Proxy servers using a round-robin approach:

```
myrouter(config)# sip-ua
  myrouter(config-sip-ua)# sip-server dns:proxy.acme.com
myrouter(config)# dial-peer voice 1 voip
  myrouter(config-dial-peer)# session target sip-server
```

- **Multiple SIP Proxy dial-peers:** On the gateway, define multiple SIP dial-peers with either the same preference or different preferences. If the desired behavior is to use all proxy servers equally for routing calls to Unified CVP, the preference for each of the dial-peers would be the same. However, Datacenter A ingress routers are more inclined to use their local proxy servers for call routing before they ask the Datacenter B proxy servers for assistance (refer to Figure 4-18). This enables the switch leg of the call to potentially be treated locally by the Datacenter A Unified CVP farm over the farm located in Datacenter B, eliminating unnecessary WAN traffic. For this latter configuration, Example 4-6 show how the ingress routers in Datacenter A must be configured:

Example 4-6 *Multiple SIP Proxy Dial Peers*

```
myrouter(config)# dial-peer voice 1 voip
 !SIP Proxy 1 located in DC A
 myrouter(config-dial-peer)# session target ipv4:10.1.1.1
 myrouter(config-dial-peer)# preference 1!
myrouter(config)# dial-peer voice 2 voip
 !SIP Proxy 2 located in DC B
 myrouter(config-dial-peer)# session target ipv4:10.2.1.1
 myrouter(config-dial-peer)# preference 2
  !
```

■ You can modify these examples depending on the routing behavior wanted for the solution. However, these configurations assume that the SIP proxies will be configured with static routes for both the switch leg DNIS values pointing to Unified ICM and VRU labels pointing to their respective VoiceXML Gateways (refer to Figure 4-18).

■ **Multiple Unified CVP dial-peers (no proxy):** Although it is best practice to always have a SIP proxy deployed as part of the solution whether its Cisco Unified Presence Server (CUPS) or Cisco Unified SIP Proxy (CUSP), you can configure an Ingress Gateway to send calls directly to the Unified CVP call servers, as shown in Example 4-7.

Example 4-7 *Multiple Unified CVP Dial Peers*

```
myrouter(config)# dial-peer voice 1 voip
 !Unified CVP Server 1 located in DC A
 myrouter(config-dial-peer)# session target ipv4:10.1.1.10
 myrouter(config-dial-peer)# preference 1!
myrouter(config)# dial-peer voice 2 voip
 !Unified CVP Server 2 located in DC B
 myrouter(config-dial-peer)# session target ipv4:10.2.1.10
 myrouter(config-dial-peer)# preference 2
  !
```

■ DNS SRV records via a DNS server: DNS Service records (SRV) enable an administrator to configure redundancy and load balancing with finer granularity than with DNS round-robin redundancy and load balancing. A DNS SRV record enables you to define which hosts should be used for a particular service; in this case the service is SIP. The configuration provided in the last bullet can be replaced with the following configuration, but assume that the Unified CVP servers have been defined in the name server as SRV records:

```
myrouter(config)# ip name-server 10.1.1.20
myrouter(config)# dial-peer voice 1 voip
 myrouter(config-dial-peeer)# session target dns:cvp.acme.com
```

■ **DNS SRV records via local static SRV records:** Similar to the previous bullet, you can also define SRV records locally on the Ingress Gateway to avoid using a DNS server. This simplifies the dial-peer configuration but also achieves DNS SRV load balancing and redundancy without relying on a DNS server. The obvious disadvantage of this approach is that if an SRV record must be modified, it has to be changed on all the Ingress Gateways. If a DNS server were used, the change would need to occur only in the zone on the DNS server. This is illustrated in Example 4-8.

Example 4-8   *DNS SRV Records via Local Static SRV Records*

```
!DC A SIP Proxy
myrouter(config)# ip host proxy1.acme.com 10.1.1.1
!DC B SIP Proxy
myrouter(config)# ip host proxy2.acme.com 10.2.1.1
!SRV Records for SIP/TCP
myrouter(config)# ip host _sip._tcp.cvp.acme.com srv 1 50 5060 proxy1.acme.com
myrouter(config)# ip host _sip._tcp.cvp.acme.com srv 10 50 5060 proxy2.acme.com
!SRV Records for SIP/UDP
myrouter(config)# ip host _sip._udp.cvp.acme.com srv 1 50 5060 proxy1.acme.com
myrouter(config)# ip host _sip._udp.cvp.acme.com srv 10 50 5060 proxy2.acme.com
```

■ Example 4-8 was designed for ingress routers located at Datacenter A. It favors the SIP Proxy located in Datacenter A because the priority provided for the SRV record is lower than the proxy located in Datacenter B (1 is lower than 10). A similar configuration exists on the ingress routers located in Datacenter B. However, the SRV priority field would switch to favor Datacenter's B proxy servers.

Caveats

If the originating gateway fails, the following conditions apply:

■ Calls in progress are dropped. There is nothing that can be done to preserve these calls because the PSTN switch has lost the D-Channel to all T1/E1 trunks on the gateway.

■ New calls are directed by the PSTN carrier to a T1/E1 at an alternative gateway, provided the PSTN switch has its trunks and dial-plan configured to do so.[4]

SIP Proxy Servers

In addition to redundant Ingress Gateways, Figure 4-18 illustrates the use of redundant SIP proxies. As discussed in earlier chapters, Cisco currently offers two different SIP proxy servers: CUPS and CUSP. The CUPS server is implemented as a Linux-based appliance, whereas the CUSP is implemented as a module running on a Cisco IOS router. Regardless of which proxy is used with the Unified CVP solution, there are some considerations pertaining to high availability you need to examine.

Cisco Unified Presence Server (CUPS)

The deployment of CUPS depends entirely on the existence of an existing CUCM cluster. CUPS integrates into the CUCM cluster and establishes IDS Global User Data Replication directly with the CUCM cluster's publisher. However, CUPS also uses its own subclustering technology to enable a CUPS implementation to have its own publisher for replication within its subcluster. Multiple servers can exist in a subcluster and multiple subclusters per CUPS implementation. The tricky part about this subcluster culture is that from a static SIP route perspective, CUPS replicates only static SIP routes between servers in the same subcluster and not between different subclusters. This small caveat can sometimes be overlooked during implementation forcing the routing of switch and VRU call legs to different data center locations, which may not be local to where the call originated, simply because the static route was replicated to all proxy servers in the subcluster. Factors such as unique incoming DNIS ranges per data centers should dictate whether CUPS deploys with a single subcluster spanning data centers or if it should be implemented using different subclusters per data center. Figure 4-19 shows CUPS replication behavior when separate subclusters deploy per data center.

One key take away from Figure 4-19 is that static routes are not replicated to other servers located in different subclusters. This is important because if an incoming DNIS sourced in Data Center A has a static route in Data Center A's CUPS server for the Unified CVP farm also located in Data Center A, and a failure occurs on the Ingress Gateway located in Data Center A and its secondary dial-peer was to use the CUPS server located in Data Center B, c static routes would need to be added manually to the CUPS subcluster located in Data Center B. In addition, if unique DNIS values could be sourced between data centers, it would make sense to add static routes in the Data Center A and Data Center B CUPS servers to always favor Data Center A for DNIS values sourced from the ingress router also located in Data Center A. However, secondary static routes with different priorities should still exist in both proxy servers enabling the Data Center B Unified CVP infrastructure as a secondary route in case the gear in Data Center A completely fails. DNIS values sourcing at the ingress router for Data Center B would have static routes favoring the Data Center B infrastructure as a priority with the secondary routes favoring the Data Center A infrastructure. This approach enables the call to always use the local infrastructure first for both the switch and VRU leg of the call.

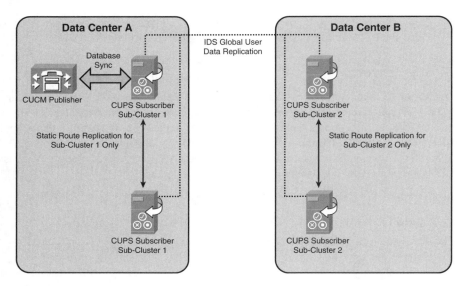

Figure 4-19 *CUPS Subclustering and Replication Behavior*

In conclusion, if the DNIS values sourced per data center are not unique and are one in the same, CUPS must be implemented using separate subclusters. If this is not the case, the static routes for the same DNIS placed in the Data Center A and B CUPS servers would always replicate to each other, overwriting the last route. This further implies that best practice would be accomplished with a single CUPS subcluster using the same DNIS and favor either Data Center A's or Data Center B's Unified CVP infrastructure as primary for the incoming DNIS. Using unique DNIS values per data center enable CUPS to be implemented either as a single subcluster spanning both data centers or as independent subclusters, one per data center. Because Unique DNIS values exist per static route, replication does not play havoc with how calls would then be routed.

Caution The routing challenges with replication and DNIS values visible during the switch leg of the call are specifically outlines. However, if the SIP proxy is engaged during the VRU leg of the call, the same challenge would apply. If unique DNIS values are presented during the switch leg of a call and a single subcluster is used between both data centers, the Unified CVP Call Servers must also be grouped by data center with each grouping provided a unique VRU label for its specific farm. For example, Data Center A's Unified CVP Call Servers could be handed a VRU label of 9111111111<correlation ID> and Data Center's B Unified CVP Call Servers receiving a VRU label of 9222222222<correlation ID>. This would enable static routes in each data center's CUPS servers to favor local VoiceXML Gateways and so on without the subcluster replication of these static routes from over-writing these configurations in each of the respective Datacenter CUPS servers.

Figure 4-20 shows how a single CUPS subcluster using two CUPS servers is configured with the first server implemented in the subcluster acting as the publisher for CUPS. One issue with a CUPS subcluster is that a subcluster supports only a maximum of two servers. This further implies that if a design warrants redundant CUPS servers per data center, two subclusters must be created, one per data center. Static routes must be manually added into each subcluster for the switch and VRU legs of a call. Remember, there is no replication of routes between CUPS servers in different subclusters.

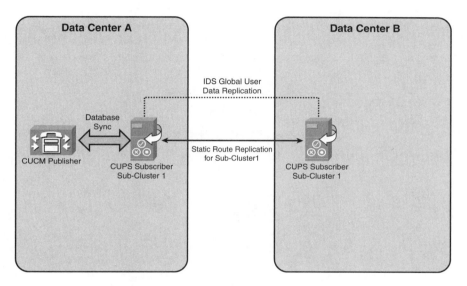

Figure 4-20   *Single CUPS Subcluster Design*

Tip   The publisher referenced for a CUCM cluster and the publisher referenced for the CUPS subcluster are not the same server or role. The publisher for the CUPS subcluster is the first server built when setting up a subcluster. There is always one of these servers per subcluster. The CUPS publishers directly communicate with the CUCM publisher for IDS Global User Data Replication and are also responsible for handling subcluster replications.

Again, static routes are replicated between all CUPS servers in a single subcluster even if the route is added to a CUPS server in Data Center B. Its route replicates to the CUPS server in Data Center A, implying that there is basically one routing table per CUPS subcluster. For more details on CUPS subclustering and design, refer to the Cisco Unified Communications Solution Reference Network Design SRND Release 8.x at Cisco.com.

Cisco Unified SIP Proxy (CUSP)

Earlier versions of CVP supported only CUPS as a SIP proxy, which forced all SIP imple-mentations to have at least a single CUCM cluster deployed. (CUPS must have a CUCM cluster to be installed.) In other words, to have a single CUPS server running, without a redundant server, at least one CUCM publisher had to exist, even if the agent phones were not hosted by CUCM. To achieve redundancy, more CUCM servers and CUPS servers had to purchased and deployed.

The current version of CVP now supports CUSP in addition to CUPS as a SIP proxy. As noted in earlier chapters, CUSP exists as a module hosted in a Cisco Integrated Service Router (ISR). Figure 4-21 shows the first redundancy model where a single CUSP router is deployed in each data center with each router hosting a single CUSP proxy module.

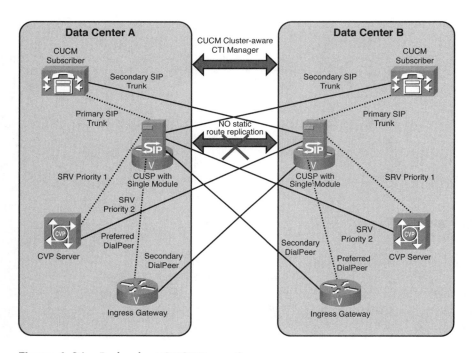

Figure 4-21   *Redundant CUSP Proxy Servers*

A couple of items about Figure 4-21 include the following:

■ It consists of two gateways for redundancy, geographically separated, one proxy module each, using SRV priority for redundancy of proxies, no HRSP.

■ The ISR is dedicated to the proxy blade functionality and is not colocated as a VoiceXML or Time Division Multiplexing (TDM) gateway because of platform vali-dation restrictions for CUSP.

■   TDM or Ingress Gateways are configured to use some form of SRV or with Dial Peer
    Preferences to use the primary and secondary CUSP proxies.

■   CUSP is configured with Server Groups to find primary and backup Unified CVP,
    Unified CM, and VoiceXML Gateways.

Note   This implementation of Server Groups is specific to the CUSP module configuration and should not be confused with Unified CVP's Server Group configuration via the
Operations Console.

■   Unified CVP is set up with Server Group to use the primary and secondary CUSP
    proxies during outbound call routing.

■   CUCM is configured to use Route Groups with multiple SIP Trunks resolving to the
    primary and secondary CUSP Proxies. Although a redundant trunk is not absolutely
    necessary because the CUCM Cluster's CTI Manager service is cluster-aware, having
    a redundant secondary trunk defined allows the call processing to continue on the
    subscriber in the respective data center where the CUSP Proxy router failed. In some
    larger deployments in which call control is load balanced and separated for sizing rea-
    sons, keeping the call control on a subscriber makes quite a bit of sense versus using
    a single trunk per data center and forcing the other data center's subscriber to handle
    its load in addition to the load from the failed CUSP module in the first data center.

Figure 4-22 shows a similar high-availability design for CUSP. However the overall capacity has been doubled because of the additional CUSP module placed in each ISR router.
This design essentially provides two CUSP modules at each location hosted by one
router. Although the capacity has been doubled and there is some redundancy with
respect to the dual module approach, for absolute redundancy you should consider four
ISR routers, each having a single CUSP module with two located at each data center. This
enables a data center to continue to provide CUSP proxy services if a complete ISR
router were to fail. These additional ISR routers can also be configured in an active-stand-
by design using HSRP on the ISR router, enabling one router in each data center to stay in
standby mode until the first ISR fails.

Unlike the CUPS proxy implementation, CUSP currently does not have the capability to
replicate static routes between different ISR routers or CUSP modules. All server groups
and static routes must be added to all modules each time a new route is added or updated.

Caveats

If the SIP Proxy fails, whether its CUPS or CUSP, call disposition remains the same for a
proxy failure:

■   If the primary SIP proxy server fails, all active calls are still preserved. Subsequent
    transfers of calls are also successful provided the backup SIP Proxy is available and

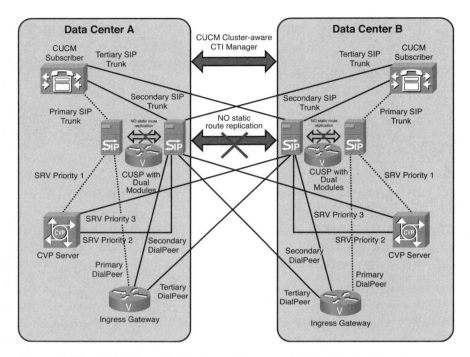

Figure 4-22 *Redundant CUSP Proxy Servers with Double the Capacity*

the RecordRoute header is not populated by the SIP Proxy. If the RecordRoute header is populated, signaling to the gateway is not possible and subsequent transfers will fail. In CUPS, the RecordRoute header is set to On by default, whereas CUSP has this option set to Off.

■   Because of potential long delays when DNS is used with CUPS, Cisco recommends disabling the DNS Server on CUPS. Refer to CUPS release notes for more information.

■   If all SIP proxy servers fail or are unavailable, new calls arriving at the gateway are default-routed using the previously cover call survivability options.

Unified CVP Call Server's SIP Considerations

When discussing high-availability designs for the Unified CVP Call Servers with SIP, there are two areas to consider. The first pertains to the call disposition around the Unified SIP Service running on the call servers. The second is the use of Server Groups to create static SRV records for Unified CVP to use when routing a SIP call toward the enterprise.

When configuring the SIP service within the Unified CVP Call Server using the operations console, multiple SIP Proxy servers should be configured for outbound redundancy. The proxy server should be configured as a DNS name with the resolution of this name either provided by a DNS server or using local DNS SRV records, which is now deemed a

Server Group configuration within Unified CVP. Figure 4-23 shows how to accomplish this via the Unified CVP operations console.

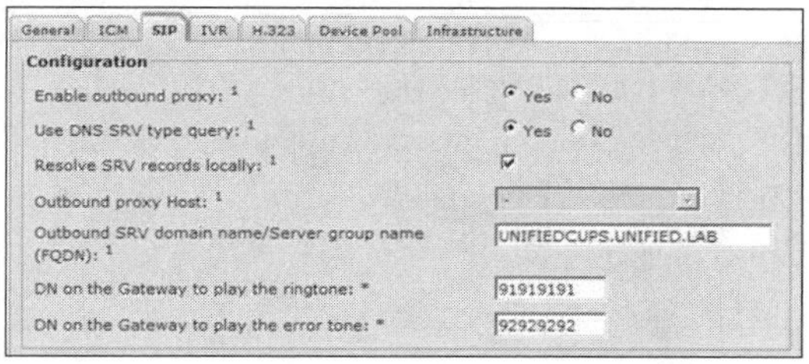

Figure 4-23 *Unified CVP SIP Service Configuration for Outbound Proxy*

If an Outbound proxy Host is used instead of a Server Group, the proxy server used must be set up via the Operations Console as a SIP Proxy Server prior to assigning it to the Unified CVP SIP Service. A Server Group can be configured instead of a single proxy hostname, enabling the local SRV records to override any DNS query (refer to Figure 4-23).

Note The options for static routes using a SRV resolved via a DNS Server, or using Server Groups, can introduce some unexpected, long delays during failover and load balancing with UDP transport on the Unified CVP Call Server when the primary destination is shut down or is off the network. With UDP, the per-hop delay is 3.5 seconds (assuming retry count is 2) or 7.5 seconds (with retry count of 3) by default. This delay is on every call or every other call (on average) during failover, depending on load balancing.[5]

A Server Group is a dynamic routing feature that enables the originating endpoints to have knowledge of the status of a destination address before attempting to send the SIP INVITE. Whether the destination is unreachable over the network or is out of service at the application layer, the originating SIP user agent can have foreknowledge of the status through a heartbeat mechanism. While in H.323, there exists an endpoint registration mechanism with the gatekeeper. Until now, one didn't exist for SIP endpoints. This feature enables faster failover on call control by eliminating delays due to failed endpoints. The Server Groups configured in Unified CVP and CUSP work the same way. However, in terms of just configuring Server Groups in Unified CVP, it refers to the creation and propagation of local SRV files to all Unified CVP Call Servers. Figure 4-24 shows the definition of local SRV records that are then propagated to all call servers.

If Server Groups are configured with heart beats, Unified CVP can provide dynamic routing capability and preemptively monitor the status of endpoints. This feature works only for outbound calls from Unified CVP. To cover the inbound calls to Unified CVP, the CUSP proxy server can send similar heartbeats to Unified CVP, which can respond with status responses.[6] All endpoints for which heartbeats need to be sent should be config-ured in a Server Group. However, as stated earlier, endpoints for which CUSP needs to make a routing decision to exist in a CUSP Server Group and not in a Unified CVP Server Group. This is because ultimately CUSP must make the decision on whether a VoiceXML Gateway is available to handle the VRU leg of a call that it then extends the SIP INVITE that implies that CUSP must be aware of the VoiceXML routers status before it attempts to send it a SIP INVITE for communication to a Unified CVP Call Server. However, when using CUPS as a proxy server, it makes more sense to place these endpoints in separate Unified CVP Server Groups specifically set up for gateways, and so on.

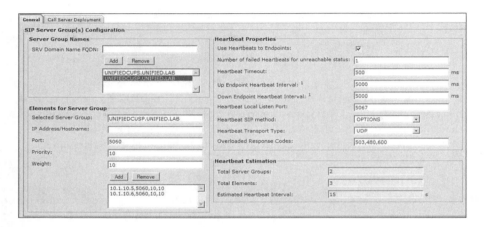

Figure 4-24   *Server Groups Created in Unified CVP*

Note   To turn off pinging when the element is *up*, set the Up Endpoint Heartbeat Interval to zero (reactive pinging). To Turn off pinging when the element is down, set the Down Endpoint Heartbeat Interval to zero (proactive pinging). You can achieve adaptive pining setting either of these fields to a value greater than zero regardless of whether the element is up or down (refer to Figure 4-24).

Any endpoint that CVP may route calls to should respond to OPTIONS with some response, either a 200 OK or some other response. Any response to a heartbeat indicates the other side is alive and reachable. CUPS and CUSP may return a 483 Too Many Hops response because the max-forwards header is set to zero in an OPTIONS message. Sometimes the endpoints may not enable OPTIONS or PING and may return 405 Method Not Allowed, which is fine as well.[7]

Caveats

Following are some additional caveats for the call disposition when using Unified CVP with SIP:

- If the Unified CVP SIP Service fails after the call has been transferred (transfers include transfer to an IP Phone, VoiceXML Gateway, or other Egress Gateway), the call continues normally until a subsequent transfer activity (if applicable) is required from the Unified CVP SIP Service. If the caller has not hung up and is awaiting further activity, there is a period of 9 to 18 seconds of silence before the caller is default-routed by survivability to an alternative location. The same applies for calls that have not been transferred.

- If a new call arrives and the Unified CVP SIP Service has failed, the SIP proxy redirects the new call to another Unified CVP Call Server with an active SIP Service. If call servers are unavailable, the call is default-routed to an alternative location by survivability.

- Server Groups are not automatically created during an upgrade to Unified CVP 8.0(1). All Server Groups must be explicitly configured and turned on after upgrading.

- TLS transport is not supported with Server Groups and Heartbeating.

- Duplicate Server Group Elements, such as proxy servers and gateways, are excluded for heartbeating because the heartbeating is already established for that element.

- When using hostnames as part of static routes in Unified CVP, those hostnames must be resolvable using a DNS lookup. If they fail resolution, those static routes will be disabled, and an error will be placed into the Unified CVP error log; only hostnames in the local SRV Server Groups configuration as an SRV name bypass this check. IP addresses always pass this validation.[8]

Use Case: High Availability Routing with Unified CVP and SIP

This section examines how this redundancy works with a simple use case. You accomplished this by using the architecture (refer to Figure 4-18) that depicts how Data Centers A and B behave when routing calls during normal operations and during an outage. Following are a few requirements and assumptions for this use case:

- Each Data Center (DC A and DC B) receives unique DNIS values from the PSTN.

- Each data center expects to use local resources first to treat the switch and VRU leg of incoming calls, with failover to the other data center if a Unified CVP resource is not available.

- Static routes in each of the data center proxy servers favor local Unified CVP components.

- CUPS is the referenced proxy and is deployed using a single subcluster between Data Centers A and B.

Figure 4-25 provides a call flow for Data Center A, illustrating the normal operation for calls ingressing into Data Center A's Ingress Gateways.

Refer to Figure 4-25 to see a decent base line for how calls are normally routed and treated without any infrastructure outages as detailed in the following steps:

Step 1.   A DNIS unique to Data Center A is delivered at the SIP Ingress Gateways from the PSTN.

Step 2.   The gateway sends a SIP INVITE message to the Data Center A CUPS Proxy Server.

Step 3.   The Data Center A CUPS Proxy Server then forwards the INVITE to the Data Center A CVP Call Server.

Step 4.   The Data Center A CVP Call Server sends a route request to ICM via the VRU PIM process on the ICM PG.

Step 5.   ICM runs a routing script, which initiates a transfer of the call to the VoiceXML Gateway.

Step 6.   ICM returns a Network VRU label of 9111111111<correlation ID> to the Data Center A CVP Call Server. This VRU label is unique for Data Center A's VoiceXML routers. The Unified CVP call server farm in Data Center B would have a unique VRU label associated to them as 9222222222<Correlation ID>. This enables the single routing table stored in the single CUPS subcluster to keep the VRU legs of each call local to the data center by routing them to the VoiceXML routers found in each data center, respectively.

Step 7.   The Data Center A CVP Call Server sends a SIP INVITE message to the Data Center A CUPS proxy server.

Step 8.   The Data Center A CUPS Proxy Server then forwards the INVITE to the Data Center A VoiceXML Gateway.

Step 9.   Based on instructions the VoiceXML Gateway receives from ICM (via the CVP Call Server), the gateway treats the call (plays media, queues the call, and so on). If the agent is in queue and an agent becomes available, ICM sends a message to the Data Center A CVP Server, which forwards a message via the SIP Proxy Server to the SIP Ingress Gateway and to Call Manager to transfer the call away from the VoiceXML Gateway and deliver it to the agent's IP Phone.

So what happens when a Unified CVP call server fails in Data Center A? Figure 4-26 shows how the solution kicks in its high availability configurations and uses Data Center B's Unified CVP components to handle the switch and VRU leg of the call.

An Unified CVP Farm outage in Data Center A has been identified (refer to Figure 4-26). The next steps provide details on how this outage is handled for call routing and treatment.

Step 1.   A DNIS unique to Data Center A is delivered at the SIP Ingress Gateways from the PSTN.

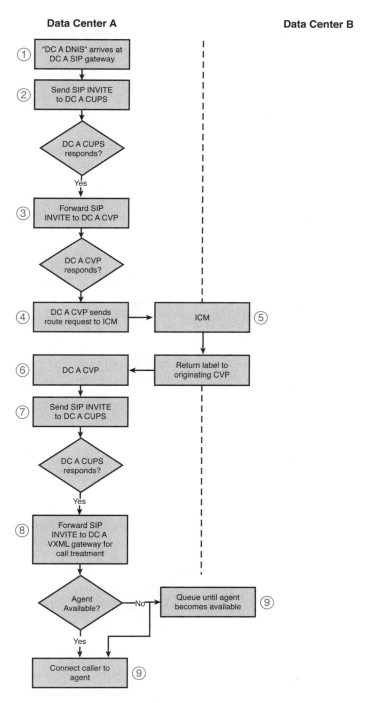

Figure 4-25   *Queue and Transfer Call at Data Center A Under Normal Circumstances (No Outages)*

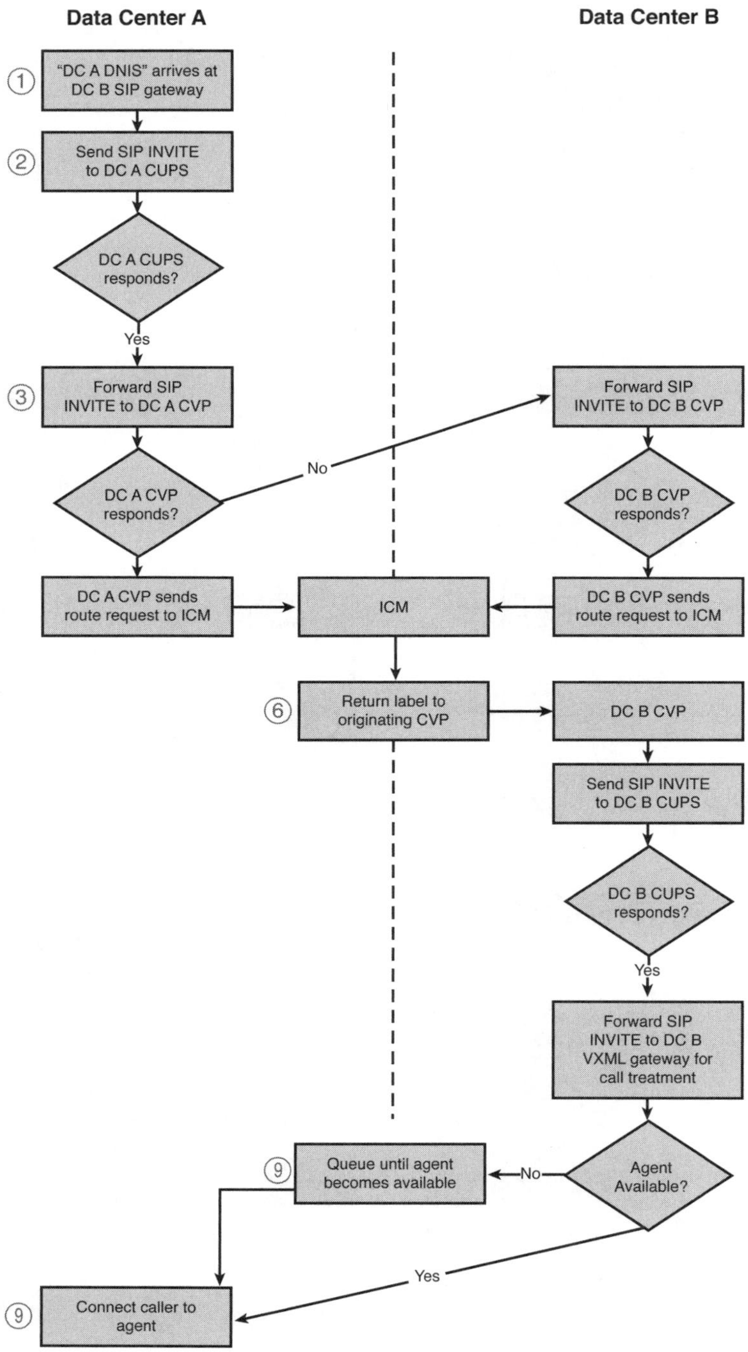

Data Center A **Data Center B**

Figure 4-26 *Queue and Transfer Call at Data Center A with Data Center A Unified CVP Farm Down*

Step 2.   The gateway sends a SIP INVITE message to the Data Center A CUPS Proxy Server.

Step 3.   The Data Center A CUPS Proxy Server then forwards the INVITE to the Data Center A CVP Call Server.

Step 4.   The Data Center A CVP Call Server does not respond, and a second SIP INVITE is sent to the Data Center B CVP Call Server.

Step 5.   The Data Center B CVP Call Server sends a route request to ICM via the VRU PIM process on the ICM PG.

Step 6.   ICM returns a Network VRU label of 9222222222<correlation ID> to the Data Center B CVP Call Server. This VRU label is unique for Data Center B's VoiceXML routers. The Unified CVP call server farm in Data Center A would have a unique VRU label associated to them as 91111111111<Correlation ID>. This enables the single routing table stored in the single CUPS subcluster to keep the VRU legs of each call local to the data center by routing them to the VoiceXML routers found in each data center, respectively.

Step 7.   The Data Center B CVP Call Server sends a SIP INVITE message to the Data Center B CUPS proxy server. Notice how the Data Center B Unified CVP Call Server actually uses the SIP proxy server located in Data Center B and does not connect to the SIP Proxy server located in Data Center A. This enables the unique VRU label returned in Step 6 to resolve to the local VoiceXML routers in Data Center B. Because only one VRU label can be returned per routing client from the VRU PG, there is no way to return a VRU label based on where the call originated, just where Unified CVP was engaged. This implies that the VRU leg of the call must be treated in the same data center as the Unified CVP call server for this routing design.

Step 8.   The Data Center B CUPS Proxy Server forwards the INVITE to the Data Center B VoiceXML Gateway.

Step 9.   Based on instructions the VoiceXML Gateway receives from ICM (via the CVP Call Server), the gateway treats the call (plays media, queues the call, and so on). If the agent is in queue and an agent becomes available, ICM sends a message to the Data Center B CVP Server, which forwards a message via the SIP Proxy Server to the SIP Ingress Gateway and to Call Manager to transfer the call away from the VoiceXML Gateway and deliver it to the agent's IP Phone.

In the rare case that Data Center A was to completely go down from a PSTN and routing perspective, and assuming the carrier was configured to route calls to Data Center B, a full disaster recovery call flow is executed, as shown in Figure 4-27.

With Data Center A completely offline, Data Center B must now take over the call routing and treatment. The following steps detail how that occurs.

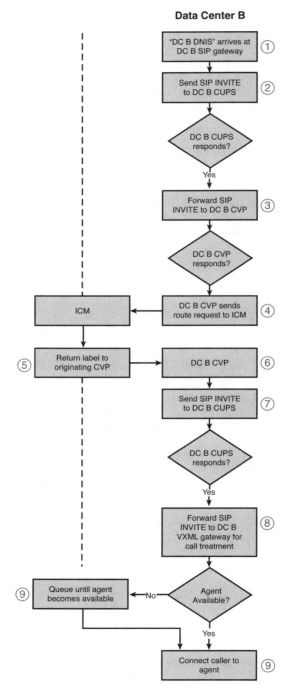

Figure 4-27 *Queue and Transfer Call at Data Center B During DR Situation*

Step 1.   A DNIS unique to Data Center B is delivered at the SIP Ingress Gateways from the PSTN.

Step 2.   The gateway sends a SIP INVITE message to the Data Center B CUPS Proxy Server.

Step 3.   The Data Center B CUPS Proxy Server then forwards the INVITE to the Data Center B CVP Call Server.

Step 4.   The Data Center B CVP Call Server sends a route request to ICM via the VRU PIM process on the ICM PG.

Step 5.   ICM runs a routing script, which initiates a transfer of the call to the VoiceXML Gateway.

Step 6.   ICM returns a Network VRU label of 9222222222<correlation ID> to the Data Center B CVP Call Server. This VRU label is unique for Data Center B's VoiceXML routers.

Step 7.   The Data Center B CVP Call Server sends a SIP INVITE message to the Data Center B CUPS proxy server.

Step 8.   The Data Center B CUPS Proxy Server then forwards the INVITE to the Data Center B VoiceXML Gateway.

Step 9.   Based on instructions the VoiceXML Gateway receives from ICM (via the CVP Call Server), the gateway treats the call (plays media, queues the call, and so on). If the agent is in queue and an agent becomes available, ICM sends a message to the Data Center B CVP Server, which forwards a message via the SIP Proxy Server to the SIP Ingress Gateway and to Call Manager to transfer the call away from the VoiceXML Gateway and deliver it to the agent's IP Phone.

After the DR event has been corrected and normal routing and operation are restored to Data Center A, Figure 4-28 provides the normal call flow for this high availability use case and illustrates critical decision points during a call.

Putting previous illustrations back together, a complete picture of how components in Data Centers A and B work together to provide a high availability design for Unified CVP and SIP is detailed in the following steps:

Step 1.   A DNIS unique to either Data Center A or Data Center B is delivered to the SIP Ingress Gateways from the PSTN.

Step 2.   The gateway sends a SIP INVITE message to the local CUPS server.

Step 3.   If the local CUPS server does not respond, a second SIP INVITE is sent to the remote CUPS server.

Step 4.   The CUPS server then forwards the INVITE to its local CVP Call Server.

Step 5.   If the local CVP Call Server does not respond, a second SIP INVITE is sent to the remote CVP Call Server.

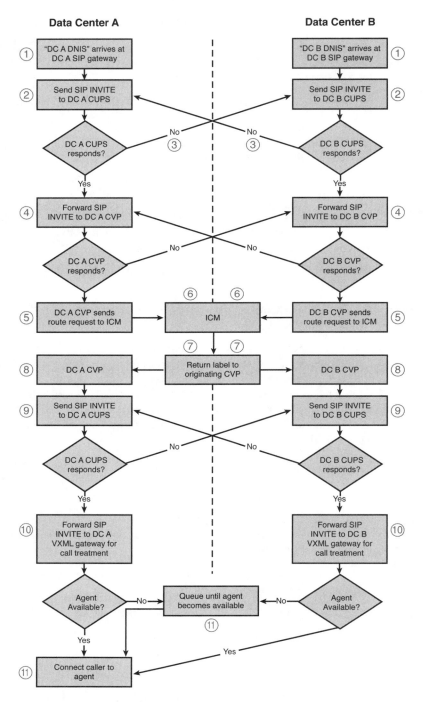

Figure 4-28 *Queue and Transfer Call Flow Under Normal Circumstances (No Outages)*

Step 6.   The CVP Call Server sends a route request to ICM via the VRU PIM process on the ICM PG.

Step 7.   ICM runs a routing script, which initiates a transfer of the call to the VoiceXML Gateway.

Step 8.   ICM returns a Network VRU label to the originating CVP Call Server.

Step 9.   The CVP Call Server sends a SIP INVITE message to the local CUPS proxy server.

Step 10.   The Data Center A CUPS Proxy Server forwards the INVITE to the local VoiceXML Gateway.

Step 11.   Based on instructions that the VoiceXML Gateway receives from ICM (via the CVP Call Server), the gateway treats the call (plays media, queues the call, and so on). If the agent is in queue and an agent becomes available, ICM sends a message to the Data Center A CVP Server, which forwards a message via the SIP Proxy Server to the SIP Ingress Gateway and to Call Manager to transfer the call away from the VoiceXML Gateway and deliver it to the agent's IP Phone.

The call can cross over a few times between each data center depending on what failures occur and whether they impact the switch or VRU leg of a call. This presents some operational and troubleshooting challenges, which continue to place emphasis on why it is critical to completely understand the Unified CVP solution and its underlying call flows.

H.323 High-Availability Architectures

The previous section concentrated on HA efforts pertaining to Unified CVP and the SIP protocol. This section examines the same architecture (refer to Figure 4-18) with SIP and the proxy components replaced with H.323 and gatekeepers. The use case provided in the previous section also applies as-is with only the H.323 interactions with the gatekeeper replacing the SIP interactions with the proxy server. This section is not a comprehensive configuration section on H.323 and gatekeepers. However, it provides some simple examples on how to configure each component for H.323 with high availability in mind. The format of this section is similar to the previous section on SIP. It begins with the Ingress and VoiceXML Gateways moving on to gatekeepers and concludes with specifics pertaining to the Unified CVP H.323 service.

Originating Ingress and VoiceXML Gateways

The configuration of Ingress Gateways to support H.323 is similar to how SIP is configured. As with SIP, use a virtual loopback interface wherever possible. In addition to binding the H.323 protocol to the interface, you must provide other parameters to enable this device to register with a gatekeeper. Unlike SIP, H.323 requires devices to be registered in the gatekeeper before a gatekeeper can advise an available Ingress Gateway, Unified CVP, or an egress endpoint. Example 4-9 shows how to configure a gateway to register with a gatekeeper using a zone name of acme-gk-A and a H.323 ID of ING-ACME-GW1:

Example 4-9   *Registering a H.323 Gateway with Alternative Gatekeeper*

```
myrouter(config)# Interface loopback0
 myrouter(config-if)# ip address 10.1.1.10 255.255.255.255
 myrouter(config-if)# h323-gateway voip interface
!IP Address of GK in DC A
 myrouter(config-if)# h323-gateway voip id acme-gk-A ipaddr 10.1.1.7 priority 120
!IP Address of GK in DC B
 myrouter(config-if)# h323-gateway voip id acme-gk-B ipaddr 10.2.1.7
 myrouter(config-if)# h323-gateway voip h323-id ING-ACME-GW1
 myrouter(config-if)# h323-gateway voip bind srcaddr 10.1.1.10
```

In addition to the Data Center A gatekeeper having a high priority for registration, Example 4-9 illustrates how an alternative gatekeeper is configured in the Ingress Gateway. Data Center B's gatekeeper would be registered with and used if the higher priority gatekeeper in Data Center A failed.

Tip   Using standardized prefixes for the H.323 ID on devices that perform different functions can deliver dividends when searching and filtering these registrations on the gatekeeper. For example, using prefixes such as ING=Ingress Gateway, VoiceXML=VoiceXML Gateway, VB=CVP H.323 Service, TR=CUCM Trunk, and so on, can create a simple yet decodable H.323 ID by device function. Issuing the command **show gatekeeper endpoints | include ING** on a gatekeeper, would filter and show all the Ingress Gateways registered with the gatekeeper, which quickly reveals the status of a gateway in question.

As with SIP, there are additional high availability configurations for H.323 for the Ingress Gateway pertaining to how it routes the switch leg of a call toward Unified CVP. Following are a few options for creating high availability in these areas:

■ **Single H.323 dial-peer:** Because a H.323 dial-peer uses RAS to communicate to the gatekeeper that it is currently registered with, there is no need to have multiple RAS dial-peers with different preferences. As illustrated in the previous section, when the primary gatekeeper fails, the Ingress and VoiceXML Gateways would then activate the alternative registration with the gatekeeper located in Data Center B at IP address 10.2.1.7. This enables a cleaner dial-peer configuration for the ingress router. Example 4-10 illustrates what the dial-peers for the Ingress Gateways located in Data Center A would look like, assuming that the H.323 registration configurations previously listed were completed.

Example 4-10   *Single H.323 Dial Peer*

```
myrouter(config)# dial-peer voice 1 voip
 myrouter(config-dial-peer)# destination-pattern 8005551212
 myrouter(config-dial-peer)# session target ras
 myrouter(config-dial-peer)# tech-prefix 2#
 myrouter(config-dial-peer)# dtmf-relay h245-alphanumeric
 myrouter(config-dial-peer)# codec g711ulaw
 myrouter(config-dial-peer)# preference 0
 myrouter(config-dial-peer)# no vad
```

■ In addition, the tech-prefix of 2# assumes that the Unified CVP H.323 services have been configured to register with the primary and alternative gatekeeper with a tech-prefix of 2#. Depending on where the Unified CVP call servers are located, their primary and alternative gatekeeper addresses are located in the data center serving as a backup. For example, the Unified CVP call server located in Data Center A, uses the gatekeeper in Data Center A as their primary gatekeeper with the gatekeeper in Data Center B as their alternative gatekeeper. As with SIP, this enables the dial plan configured in each gatekeeper to route the call to local resources first to avoid unnecessary WAN traffic during the switch and VRU leg of the call.

■ **Single H.323 dial-peer with Unified CVP dial-peer:** Although all H.323 installations require the use of a gatekeeper for the Unified CVP H.323 service to transition into an UP state, there is an option to enable calls to be sent directly to a Unified CVP call server as a backup to the RAS dial peer. Example 4-11 provides a backup dial peer if the gatekeeper rejects the RAS request.

Example 4-11   *Single H.323 Dial Peer with Unified CVP Dial Peer*

```
myrouter(config)# dial-peer voice 1 voip
 myrouter(config-dial-peer)# destination-pattern 8005551212
 myrouter(config-dial-peer)# session target ras
 myrouter(config-dial-peer)# tech-prefix 2#
 myrouter(config-dial-peer)# dtmf-relay h245-alphanumeric
 myrouter(config-dial-peer)# codec g711ulaw
 myrouter(config-dial-peer)# preference 0
 myrouter(config-dial-peer)# no vad
!
myrouter(config)# dial-peer voice 2 voip
 !Unified CVP Server 1 in DC A
 myrouter(config-dial-peer)# session target ipv4:10.1.1.10)
 myrouter(config-dial-peer)# preference 1
```

Additional Cisco IOS Gateway and VoiceXML Configurations

In addition to building high availability dial-peers and gatekeeper registrations, there are other considerations that should exist on any H.323 gateway:

- **Disable TCP timeout for H.225 signaling:** For the gateway to retain the active call when it loses the connection with either a Unified CVP call server or a CUCM subscriber, the following commands must exist on the gateway:

```
myrouter(config)# voice service voip
 myrouter(conf-voi-serv)# h323
  myrouter(conf-serv-h323)# no h225 timeout keepalive
```

  - If these commands do not exist on the gateway, calls still active that are otherwise unaffected by the failure (that is, the RTP stream still streams between endpoints) disconnect when the TCP session times out.

- **Setting RTP media timeout:** The following commands set the RTP media timeout:

```
myrouter(config)# ip rtcp report interval 2000
myrouter(config)# gateway
 myrouter(config-gateway)# timer receive-rtcp 4
```

  - These commands ensure that when the gateway detects that RTCP messages have not been received in the specified interval, the call is disconnected.

- **VoiceXML Gateway maximum connections:** Depending on what type of deployment and router is being used to provide VoiceXML Gateway services, the maximum number of connections that the gateway can service should always be configured on the VRU dial-peer. This avoids a situation in which more calls are sent to the gateway than what it can service from a VRU perspective. Without this simple configuration, as shown in Example 4-12, the routers overall performance can be impacted and all calls currently serviced by this VoiceXML Gateway are put into jeopardy:

Example 4-12 *Configuring a VoiceXML Gateway's Maximum Connections*

```
myrouter(config)# dial-peer voice 999 voip
 myrouter(config-dial-peer)# description VRU or Application Leg
 myrouter(config-dial-peer)# service bootstrap
 !Next command depends on the router and deployment model
 myrouter(config-dial-peer)# max-conn 240
 myrouter(config-dial-peer)# incoming called-number 999T
 myrouter(config-dial-peer)# dtmf-relay rtp-nte h245-signal h245-alphanumeric
 myrouter(config-dial-peer)# codec g711ulaw
 myrouter(config-dial-peer)# no vad
```

  - The value used with the **max-conn** command should be verified against the router version and how it has been deployed (co-resident, standalone, and so on) by using the *Cisco Unified Customer Voice Portal (CVP) 8.x Solution*

Reference Network Design (SRND), Gateway Sizing, 7-6. The previous example assumes a dedicated 3925 VoiceXML Gateway running IOS version 15.1.1T. This with Resource Allocation Indicator (RAI) and Alternative Endpoint configurations noted next can ensure that existing calls parked on a VoiceXML Gateway are not placed into jeopardy because of an oversubscription of calls received by the gateway.

■ **IOS Gateway Resource Allocation Indicator (RAI) :** Another feature rarely used when configuring either an Ingress or VoiceXML Gateway is RAI, which enables the gatekeeper to be signaled when a gateway is out of resources, which subsequently flags the H323 ID of that resource as being Out of Resource or "O" in the gatekeeper. This removes it from receiving calls unless all resources for a zone or technology prefix are also flagged as Out of Resources. Refer to the *Understanding, Configuring, and Troubleshooting Resource Allocation Indicator* white paper available at Cisco.com. Following are some common commands to enable this on the gateway:

```
myrouter(config)# gateway
myrouter(config-gateway)# resource threshold high 70 low 60
```

■ These commands set the high water mark to 70 percent and the low water mark to 60 percent. This means that when the gateway exceeds 70 percent of its available resources, it uses UDP to signal the gatekeeper as being Out of Resources. When the utilizations falls below 60 percent, a second message is sent asking the gatekeeper to unflag it as being Out of Resources and available to accept calls.

■ **VoiceXML Gateway H.323 alternative endpoints:** A common mistake when completing H.323 configurations for VoiceXML Gateway is to exclude configuring H.323 alternative endpoints. These configurations are used when a call is received by a VoiceXML Gateway but immediately rejected because of possible overloading not detected by RAI at the gatekeeper. When this occurs, the gatekeeper has already completed its routing decision and does not have the capability to reroute the call. As a fail-safe configuration, providing an alternative endpoint that the VoiceXML Gateway can provide at the time it rejects the call enables the device controlling the incoming call to reconnect to the alternative endpoint:

```
myrouter(config)# gatekeeper
myrouter(config-gk)# endpoint alt-ep h323id VXML-ACMEA-GW1 10.1.1.20
myrouter(config-gk)# endpoint alt-ep h323id VXML-ACMEA-GW2 10.1.1.21
myrouter(config-gk)# endpoint alt-ep h323id VXML-ACMEB-GW1 10.2.1.20
```

■ This by no means ensures that the alternative endpoint provided won't also reject the call. By staggering the alternative endpoints provided by a VoiceXML Gateway farm, looping the call back to endpoints that have already rejected it can be avoided.

Caveats

If the originating gateway fails, the following conditions apply:

- Calls in progress are dropped. There is nothing that can be done to preserve these calls because the PSTN switch has lost the D-Channel to all T1/E1 trunks on the gateway.

- If the gatekeeper rejects the RAS request, but the Unified CVP H.323 service is still in an UP state, the use of a dial-peer with a different preference can be used to connect the Unified CVP Call Server's H.323 service.

- New calls are directed by the PSTN carrier to a T1/E1 at an alternative gateway, provided the PSTN switch has its trunks and dial plan configured to do so.[9]

Tip   Dial-peer preferences on an IOS router are prioritized as the lower the preference the higher the priority. For example a dial-peer with a preference of 1 is preferred over a dial-peer with a preference of 2, so the lower the preference value, the more preferred the dial-peer is.

H.323 Gatekeepers

In early versions of Unified CVP, it was standard practice to deploy gatekeepers using Hot Standby Router Protocol or HSRP. However, although a Cisco gatekeeper still supports HSRP, it is no longer advised to deploy gatekeepers in this fashion to accomplish high availability. Instead, gatekeeper clustering and alternative gatekeeper configuration on Unified CVP is now the preferred and best practice approach to accomplishing high availability with gatekeepers. If however, a particular H.323 design wants to implement HSRP, there are some good configuration examples located in the SRND and configuration guides referenced at the end of this book for further reading.

Although Unified CVP does support alternative gatekeepers, Unified CVP does not support gatekeeper clustering in the sense that it cannot send, receive, or understand the Gatekeeper Update Protocol or GUP. However, this does not mean that a gatekeeper cluster used for creating zone redundancy between different gatekeepers cannot be configured. Unified CVP would simply tap into a primary and secondary gatekeeper using its standard alternative gatekeeper configuration added via the Voice Browser Administration CLI (VBADMIN). The most obvious question is, "Why is a CLI interface used for H.323 configurations and SIP is handled via the Operations Console?" The answer to this question lies in the vision for the product. Simply put, SIP is where it has been headed for several releases, and eventually H.323 will no longer be a supported call control protocol. So why enable it in the Operations Console if it doesn't fit the vision? To be fair, there is a small interface option in the Operations Console to execute VBAdmin CLI commands, but it definitely is not as rich as the SIP configuration user interfaces.

Chapter 13, "Configuring the H.323 Devices and VoIP," in the *Configuration and Administration Guide for Cisco Unified Customer Voice Portal, release 8.0(1)* provides a step-by-step process for setting up a gatekeeper cluster and how HSRP can be configured (page 464).

Unified CVP Call Server's H.323 Considerations

Regardless of which gatekeeper design is deployed, some specific commands and considerations exist for the Unified CVP call server's H.323 Service. Following are the specific commands for configuring Unified CVP to register with a primary and alternative gatekeeper. These commands are issued via the VBAdmin CLI interface:

```
setH323ID VB-ACMEDCA-CVP1
setgk "10.1.1.7:acme-gk-A, 10.2.1.7:acme-gk-B"
```

The preceding configuration sets the H323 ID for the Unified CVP Call server to VB-ACMEDCA-CVP1 before any gatekeepers are configured. With the **setgk** command, the gatekeeper in Data Center A(10.1.1.7) is preferred to the gatekeeper(10.2.1.7) in Data Center B, which is configured as the alternative gatekeeper. As mention earlier, Unified CVP does not support GUP. However, this configuration does enable the call server to register with an existing gatekeeper cluster that has been set up between Gatekeeper A and Gatekeeper B acting simply as an alternative gatekeeper client. If an outage occurs in the gatekeeper cluster, forcing Unified CVP's active gatekeeper to fail over to Gatekeeper B, Unified CVP does not restore its active gatekeeper registration to gatekeeper A even when gatekeeper A is restored. The only way to force this realignment is to bring down Gatekeeper B, forcing the active registrations back over to Gatekeeper A, which prior to performing this action would have been the alternative gatekeeper for the Unified CVP call server. Restarting the call server also forces this realignment to its primary gatekeeper. However, the key point here is that it is not automatically done by the H.323 service. Ingress, Egress, and VoiceXML Gateways also suffer from this alignment issue, meaning they too will not realign to their primary gatekeeper without restarting the H.323 gateway service on the gateway. Keep this caveat in mind when attempting to build high available H.323 designs because a shift in the primary and secondary gatekeepers can also mean that resource usage and routing changes depending on which gatekeeper handles the RAS requests and which H.323 IDs exist for those zone and technology prefixes. It can quickly get complicated.

Caveats

These caveats apply to both HSRP and alternative gatekeeper configurations.

The primary gatekeeper fails in the following situations:

■   Some calls in progress may not be transferred during the period that the endpoints are re-registering back to the backup gatekeeper. After the failed transfer, an error is returned to the ICM. If the ICM script is coded to return an error (an END node does this) and survivability is configured on the gateway, the call is default-routed.

- If the primary gatekeeper is restored, re-registration does not occur for H.323 endpoints back to the primary gatekeeper, unless those endpoints completely support GUP.

- New calls arriving at the incoming gateway and Unified CVP are correctly serviced; although, some of the calls might invoke survivability during the period that the endpoints are re-registering to the backup gatekeeper.

All gatekeepers fail in the following situations:

- The Unified CVP H.323 service goes out of service. This implies that even dial-peers that directly point to a Unified CVP IP address would not deliver calls simply because the H.323 service on the call server is down.

- Calls in progress are not transferred. After the failed transfer, an error is returned to the ICM. If the ICM script is coded to return an error (an END node does this) and survivability is configured on the gateway, the call is default-routed.

- New calls arriving at the gateway are default-routed if survivability is configured on the gateway.

The primary gatekeeper degrades but does not fail in the following situations:

- Two conditions can cause this: low memory due to memory leaks or excessive debug levels causing CPU overload.

- In this situation, call processing behavior is unpredictable because there might be no clean failover to the backup gatekeeper. If survivability is configured on the gateway, calls are default-routed.[10]

Content Services High-Availability Architectures

Content services are critical to delivering call treatment in a Unified CVP solution. Therefore, it comes as no surprise that enabling redundancy on the content switches and configurations for load balancing content fetch requests is equally important to building any high-availability solution for Unified CVP. This section takes a closer look at how you can deploy Content Switches such as ACE and CSS to provide redundancy at the appliance level. It also covers how the deployment of a Content Switch provides a critical load balancing service for Unified CVP. This section begins with the content switches, examining their appliance redundancy features and configurations to load balance traffic to media and VoiceXML Server farms.

Application Control Engine

Application Control Engine (ACE) can provide load balancing for HTTP, Media Resource Control Protocol (MRCP), and RTSP traffic; however, it cannot load balance call control traffic such as H.323 or SIP. ACE can determine which server in a set of load-balanced servers should receive the client request for service. Load balancing helps fulfill the client request without overloading either the server or the server farms as a whole. Because ACE can monitor the state of each server and provide failover services by transferring a server's load to a working server during a server failover, ACE provides a decent amount of high availability support.

You can deploy the ACE services as a standalone appliance or as a switch module. However, providing redundancy between the appliance version and a switch module is not supported at this time. to configure on appliance redundancy between ACE appliances, each ACE must be the same type of device and software release. You can configure a maximum of two ACE appliances (peers) for redundancy. Each peer can contain one or more fault-tolerant (FT) groups. Each FT group consists of two members: one active context and one standby context. The FT group has a unique group ID that is assigned by the user. (For a closer look at redundant context configuration, check out *Cisco 4700 Series Application Control Engine Appliance Virtualization Configuration Guide* at Cisco.com.) One virtual MAC address (VMAC) is associated with each FT group. The format of this VMAC is 00-0b-fc-fe-1b-*groupID*. Because the VMAC does not change upon switchover, the client and server Address Resolution Protocol (ARP) tables do not require updating. For addition information about VMACs, see the *Cisco 4700 Series Appliance Control Engine Appliance Routing and Bridging Configuration Guide* at Cisco.com.

Each FT group acts as an independent redundancy instance. During a switchover, the active member of the FT group becomes the standby member, and the original standby member becomes the active member. The following events can cause a switchover to occur:

■   The active member becomes unresponsive.

■   A "tracked" host or interface fails.

■   Enter the **ft switchover** CLI command to force a switchover.

Figure 4-29 illustrates how to configure context redundancy between two ACE appliances. Letters A, B, C, and D represent the active contexts in each redundancy group, whereas the primed letters A', B', C', and D' are standby contexts. The contexts are evenly distributed between the two ACEs. Configuration of the active and standby contexts on different ACEs is recommended.[11]

To outside nodes (clients and servers), the active and standby FT group members appear as one node for their IP addresses and associated VMAC. The ACE provides active-active redundancy with multiple-contexts only when multiple FT groups are configured on each appliance and both appliances contain at least one active group member (context). With a single context, the ACE supports active-backup redundancy, and each group member is an Admin context. For details about configuring contexts, see the *Cisco 4700 Series Application Control Engine Appliance Virtualization Configuration Guide* available at Cisco.com.

The ACE sends and receives all redundancy-related traffic (protocol packets, configuration data, heartbeats, and state replication packets) on a dedicated FT VLAN. You cannot use this dedicated VLAN for normal traffic.

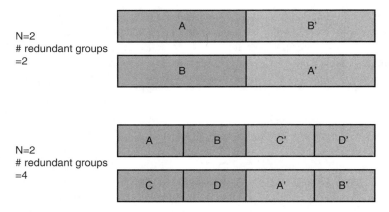

Figure 4-29   *Even Distribution of Contexts*

To optimize the transmission of heartbeat packets for multiple FT groups and to minimize network traffic, the ACE sends and receives heartbeat messages using a separate process. The ACE uses the heartbeat to probe the peer ACE, rather than probe each context. If an ACE does not receive a heartbeat from the peer ACE, all the contexts in the standby state become active. The ACE sends heartbeat packets over UDP. Frequency can be set with which the ACE sends heartbeat packets as part of the FT peer configuration. For details about configuring the heartbeat, see the "Configuring a FT Peer" section of the *Cisco 4700 Series Application Control Engine Appliance Administration Guide* at Cisco.com.[12]

The election of the active member within each FT group is based on a priority scheme. The member configured with the higher priority is elected as the active member. If a member with a higher priority is found after the other member becomes active, the new member becomes active because it has a higher priority. This behavior is known as preemption and is enabled by default. A user can override this default behavior by disabling preemption. To disable preemption, use the **preempt** command. Entering this command causes the member with the higher priority to assert itself and become active. For details about configuring the FT Group, see the "Configuring a FT Group" section of the *Cisco 4700 Series Application Control Engine Appliance Administration Guide* at Cisco.com.

Stateful Failover

The ACE replicates flows on the active FT group member to the standby group member per connection for each context. The replicated flows contain all the flow-state information necessary for the standby member to take over the flow if the active member becomes unresponsive. If the active member becomes unresponsive, the replicated flows on the standby member become active when the standby member assumes mastership of the context. The active flows on the former active member transition to a standby state to fully back up the active flows on the new active member.

After a switchover occurs, the same connection information is available on the new active member. Supported end-user applications do not need to reconnect to maintain the same network session.

Fault-Tolerant (FT) VLAN

Redundancy uses a dedicated FT VLAN between redundant ACEs to transmit flow-state information and the redundancy heartbeat. Do not use this dedicated VLAN for normal network traffic. The user must configure this same VLAN on both peer appliances and configure a different IP address within the same subnet on each appliance for the FT VLAN.

The two redundant appliances constantly communicate over the FT VLAN to determine the operating status of each appliance. The standby member uses the heartbeat packet to monitor the health of the active member. The active member uses the heartbeat packet to monitor the health of the standby member. Communications over the switchover link include the following data:

■ Redundancy protocol packets

■ State information replication data

■ Configuration synchronization information

■ Heartbeat packets

For multiple contexts, the FT VLAN resides in the system configuration file. Each FT VLAN on the ACE has one unique Media Access Control (MAC) address associated with it. The ACE uses these devices MAC addresses as the source or destination MACs for sending or receiving redundancy protocol state and configuration replication packets.

Note   The IP address and the MAC address of the FT VLAN do not change at switchover.[13]

Caveats

The following configuration requirements, restrictions, and caveats apply when configuring on appliance redundancy:

■ Redundancy is not supported between an ACE appliance and an ACE module operating as peers. Redundancy must be of the same ACE device type and software release.

■ In bridged mode (Layer 2), two contexts cannot share the same VLAN.

■ To achieve active-active redundancy, a minimum of two contexts and two FT groups are required on each ACE.

■ When configuring redundancy, the ACE keeps all interfaces that do not have an IP address in the Down state. The IP address and the peer IP address assigned to a VLAN interface should be in the same subnet but at different IP addresses. For more information about configuring VLAN interfaces, see the *Cisco 4700 Series Application Control Engine Appliance Routing and Bridging Configuration Guide*.[14]

ACE Load Balancing

Now that a good understanding of how to design and configure ACE for on appliance redundancy has been established, now focus on how ACE accomplishes high-availability services via load balancing of media and VoiceXML servers. Figure 4-30 provides a Layer 4 representation of how you can use ACE to load balance different server farms. More typical deployments cluster ACE appliance devices together, using a localized FT VLAN via a switch or cross-over cable. This provides redundant ACE appliances similar to how the Cisco Content Services Switches (CSS) deploy.

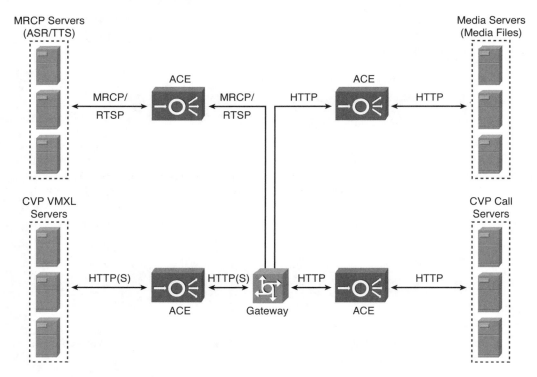

Figure 4-30   *Overview of ACE Load Balancing*

From a load balancing perspective, ACE is used primary to direct the initial session requests for a particular service. Four types of services ACE load balance when deployed with a Unified CVP solution:

■   HTTP prompts typical of media fetch requests targeted at Media Servers during VRU leg

- Adaptive Session Redundancy/ (Automatic Speech Recognition/Text To Speech [ASR/TTS]) for voice recognition and text to speech services

- Unified CVP Call Server request for instructions during VRU leg

- Unified CVP VoiceXML Server application request for instructions also during the VRU leg

To successfully configure an ACE appliance to load balance these services, the following Unified CVP components must be established:

- **Real servers:** Real servers for the ACE configuration represent the actual servers that ACE will be expected to load balance requests to. These servers are typically ASR/TTS, Media, VoiceXML, and CVP Call Servers (refer to Figure 4-30).

- **Server farms:** Typically in data centers, servers are organized into related groups called server farms. Servers within server farms often contain identical content (referred to as mirrored content) so that if one server becomes inoperative, another server can immediately take its place. After a server farm is created and named, existing real servers can be added to it. Other server-farm parameters, such as the load-balancing predictor, server weight, backup server, health probe, and so on can be configured as well.

- **Health monitoring:** ACE servers can be instructed to check the health of servers and server farms by configuring health probes (sometimes referred to as keepalives). After a probe is created, it can be assigned to a real server or a server farm. A probe can be one of many types, including TCP, ICMP, Telnet, or HTTP. The ACE server sends out probes periodically to determine the status of a load-balanced server, verifies the server response, and checks for other network problems that may prevent a client from reaching a server.

- **Class map and policy map:** The ACE server uses several configuration elements to filter traffic and then to perform various actions on that traffic before making the load-balancing decision. These filtering elements and subsequent actions form the basis of a traffic policy for server load balancing.[15]

For details around configuring ACE load balancing specifically for Unified CVP, refer to the *Configuration and Administration Guide for Cisco Unified Customer Voice Portal,* Chapter 14, starting on page 507, available at Cisco.com. In addition, more details about the general configuration of real servers, server farms and probes, and class and policy maps can be found in the *Cisco ACE 4700 Series Appliance Server Load Balancing Configuration Guide* located at Cisco.com.

Cisco Content Services Switch (CSS)

Similar to the ACE, CSS provides load balancing for HTTP and MRCP traffic. However, it cannot load balance call control traffic such as H.323 or SIP. A CSS provides three types of on appliance redundancy:

- **Virtual IP (VIP) and virtual interface redundancy:** Provides redundant VIP addresses and redundant virtual interfaces for fate sharing (the redundant interfaces and redundant VIPs fail over together to the backup CSS) and server default gateways

- **Adaptive Session Redundancy (ASR):** Provides session-level redundancy (stateful failover) to continue active flows without interruption if the master CSS fails over to the backup CSS

- **Box-to-box redundancy:** Provides chassis-level redundancy between two identically configured CSSs[16]

Although each of these on appliance redundancies have their advantages and disadvantages, this section examines the most common appliance redundancy used with Unified CVP deployments: VIP and Virtual Interface redundancy. Figure 4-31 shows how VIP redundancy is architected for a pair of CSS appliances. In this illustration, the client in a Unified CVP deployment would most likely be a VoiceXML Gateway and the web servers could be media, VoiceXML, or CVP call servers.

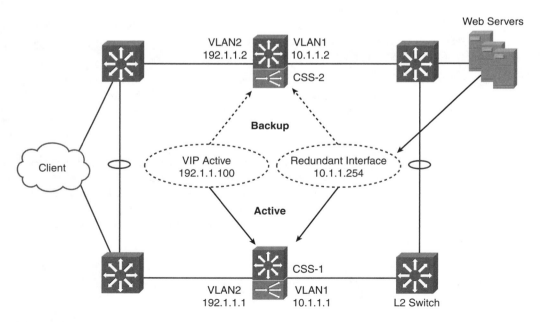

Figure 4-31 *Example of CSS VIP and Virtual Interface Redundancy*

When a pair of CSSs is configured to process client requests for the same VIP address, the VIP address is considered redundant. A typical use of VIP redundancy is with a virtual interface redundancy configuration where the master CSS processes all client requests to a VIP with a web server farm behind the CSSs and connected to the CSSs through a Layer 2 switch (refer to Figure 4-31). If the master CSS becomes unavailable, the backup CSS becomes master and processes all client requests for the VIP.

To set up CSSs for VIP redundancy, a virtual router must be configured on each CSS that can participate in the redundant configuration. A virtual router is an entity within a CSS to that a user associates with an existing VIP. A VIP becomes redundant when it associates with a virtual router. A maximum of 255 virtual routers for each VLAN can be configured.

Virtual routers providing redundancy for a VIP address are considered peers. Each virtual router peer has the same virtual router identifier (VRID) and runs on the same VLAN but runs on a different CSS. When the virtual routers are configured, the CSSs negotiate for mastership using Virtual Router Redundancy Protocol (VRRP). A virtual router in a redundant VIP configuration has the following characteristics:

■ The master processes all client requests directed to the VIP.

■ The backup may be either a

   ■ Backup virtual router, which forwards all client requests directed to the VIP to the master CSS

   ■ Shared backup virtual router, which processes all client requests it receives and does not forward requests for the VIP to the master CSS

A CSS designated as the master of a VIP automatically sends a gratuitous ARP for the VIP when the CSS becomes the master, either at startup or upon failover. This process enables the Layer 2 switch to learn where to forward packets that are directed to the VIP from clients. The CSS transmits one ARP request packet and one ARP reply packet for every gratuitous ARP invocation.[17]

Virtual Interface Redundancy

Virtual interface redundancy is a form of IP address redundancy that applies only to IP interfaces (not VIPs). A typical interface IP address on a CSS defines the interface in use on a particular VLAN. In a virtual interface redundancy configuration, the CSS designated as master maintains control over the redundant virtual interface. Each CSS also has its own circuit IP address that can be used for Telnet, Simple Network Management Protocol (SNMP), or the Device Management User Interface software.

The typical use for virtual interface redundancy is with a VIP redundancy configuration in which

■ Web servers are positioned behind a Layer 2 switch.

■ CSSs with the redundant virtual interface are positioned in front of the Layer 2 switch.

■   The servers are configured with a default route (gateway) pointing to the redundant virtual interface IP address.

A virtual router must be configured with the same VRID on the two CSSs on the backside subnet that is common to both CSSs. This VRID must be different from the VRID configured for VIP redundancy. When the new VRID associates with the virtual redundant interface IP address, the CSSs uses VRRP to negotiate mastership of the virtual redundant interface.

A CSS designated as the master of a virtual interface automatically sends out gratuitous ARPs for the virtual interface's IP address when the CSS becomes the master, either at startup or upon failover. This process enables the Layer 2 switch to learn where to forward packets that are directed to the virtual interface from the servers. It enables a server's default route to always point to the CSS designated as the master of the virtual interface. The CSS transmits one ARP request packet and one ARP reply packet for every gratuitous ARP invocation.

Virtual interface redundancy can also be configured on the uplinks of the CSSs when the VIPs reside on a subnet different from that of the uplinks. In this case, VIP redundancy on the public side of the CSSs cannot be configured. Static routes must be configured on the upstream routers pointing to the redundant virtual interface on the CSS as the router's next-hop gateway to the subnet where the VIPs reside.

Fate Sharing

Fate sharing means that, when the redundant VIP fails over on the public side of the network from the master to the backup CSS, the redundant virtual interface on the private side of the network also fails over from the master to the backup CSS. If virtual interface redundancy is not configured with VIP redundancy, asymmetric flows may result, as shown in Figure 4-32. Asymmetric flows occur when a CSS is master on the public side but backup on the private side, which breaks the connection between the client and the server.

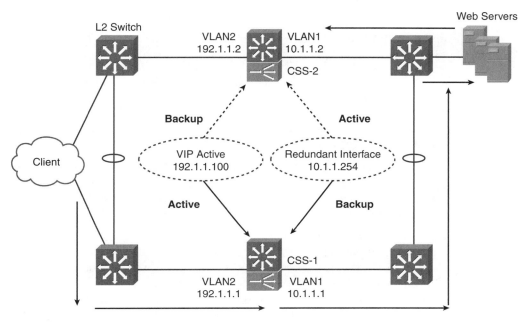

Figure 4-32 *Asymmetric Flows Without Fate Sharing*

To ensure that the redundant VIP and the redundant virtual interface fail over at the same time, the front and the back instances of VRRP (the virtual routers) must be bound so that the same CSS processes both inbound and outbound flows. This is accomplished by defining the IP addresses of the upstream router (the CSS default gateway) and the downstream Layer 2 switch that connects to the servers as critical services.

For example, the CSS provides a scripted keepalive (ap-kal-pinglist) that checks the health of the upstream router and the downstream Layer 2 switch. When this keepalive is configured, if either device fails, the critical service goes down, and the VIP and the virtual interface fail over together to the backup CSS. You can find further details on configuring Critical Services in the *Cisco Content Services Switch Advanced Configuration Guide* available at Cisco.com.[18]

CSS Load Balancing

From a load balancing perspective, CSS performs the same duties minus the RTSP protocol (refer to Figure 4-30). As noted earlier for ACE, there are four types of services that CSS also load balances when deployed with a Unified CVP solution:

■ HTTP prompts typical of media fetch requests targeted at Media Servers during VRU leg

■ ASR/TTS for voice recognition and text to speech services

- Unified CVP Call Server request for instructions during VRU leg

- Unified CVP VoiceXML Server application request for instructions also during the VRU leg

To successfully configure a CSS appliance to load balance these services, the following Unified CVP components must be established:

- **Services:** One CSS Service is configured for each Unified CVP component that needs CSS load balancing.

- **Rules:** A content rule should be established for each Unified CVP component type. To define a content rule, a content owner must be defined on the Content Switch. Media Servers, Call Servers, ASR/TTS Servers, and VoiceXML Servers might each have their own content rules defined.

- **Groups:** You might need to define source groups for each service. Group configuration can vary depending upon whether a single VLAN or multiple VLANs are used for the CSS' inbound and outbound traffic from the voice gateway and the Unified CVP component servers. If the servers and the voice gateway clients are on the same VLAN, destination services need to be specified. This configuration is sometimes referred to as a one-arm configuration because all traffic passes through one interface.

- **Keepalives:** Each Unified CVP component type also has a varying type of keepalive defined. The CSS keepalive definitions enable an appropriate method to determine whether the component is functional and can participate in receiving requests.[19]

For details about configuring CSS load balancing specifically for Unified CVP, refer to the *Configuration and Administration Guide for Cisco Unified Customer Voice Portal*, Chapter 14, starting on page 479, available at Cisco.com. In addition, you can find more details about the general configuration of services, rules, groups, and keepalives in the *Cisco Content Services Switch Advanced Configuration Guide* at Cisco.com.

Caveats

If the master CSS fails, the following conditions apply to the call disposition.

Calls in progress encounter various behaviors, depending on the type of service the VoiceXML Gateway client requested:

- **Media server requests are unaffected:** The VoiceXML Gateway has a short-lived interaction with the CSS for audio files. Upon receiving a media server request from the gateway, the CSS simply provides an HTTP redirect IP address for the VoiceXML Gateway. At that point, the gateway fetches the audio file directly from the media server, bypassing any further interaction with the CSS. In addition, media file requests to the CSS are infrequent because the VoiceXML Gateway caches previously retrieved media files.

- **Unified CVP IVR Service requests are unaffected:** Only the initial VoiceXML document request to a Unified CVP IVR Service uses the CSS. The CSS first picks a Unified CVP IVR Service to service the request. The first document passes through the CSS on its return to the VoiceXML Gateway. However, subsequent VoiceXML requests are made directly from the VoiceXML Gateway client to the Unified CVP IVR Service. If the CSS fails during the brief period that the first VoiceXML document is returned, the VoiceXML Gateway simply retries the request. If the backup (now primary) CSS selects the same Unified CVP IVR Service as the previous one, there is an error because of a duplicate call instance. In that case, the caller is default-routed by survivability on the originating gateway.

- **ASR/TTS requests typically fail but might be recoverable:** When the VoiceXML Gateway first makes an ASR/TTS request to the CSS, a TCP connection is opened from the VoiceXML Gateway to the Media Resource Control Protocol (MRCP) server. That TCP connection goes through the CSS and persists until the caller disconnects or is transferred to an agent. If the primary CSS fails, that TCP connection is terminated. The VoiceXML Gateway returns an error code, which the user can write a script to work around. The worst-case scenario is that the caller is default-routed to an alternative location by survivability on the originating gateway.

- **Unified CVP VoiceXML Server requests may fail:** The VoiceXML Gateway is "sticky" to a particular Unified CVP VoiceXML Server for the duration of the VoiceXML session. It uses CSS cookies to provide that stickiness. Configuring Adaptive Session Redundancy (ASR) on CSS peers in an active-backup VIP redundancy and virtual interface redundancy environment provides a stateful failover of most existing calls. ASR ensures that if the master CSS fails, the backup CSS has the necessary flow-state information to continue most active calls without interruption when the backup CSS assumes mastership. For the few cases in which the existing call cannot continue, the VoiceXML Gateway returns an error code, which the user can write a script to work around. The worst-case scenario is that the caller is default-routed to an alternative location by survivability on the originating gateway. The Adaptive Session Redundancy (ASR) feature of CSS ensures that port licenses are not temporarily and needlessly unavailable on the VoiceXML Server. The VoiceXML Server is stateful, and the ASR feature minimizes VoiceXML Server license port usage during a CSS failover. New calls are transparently directed to the VIPs on the backup CSS, and service is unaffected.[20]

Media Server

You can store audio files locally in flash memory on the VoiceXML Gateway or on an HTTP/TFTP file server. By definition, files stored locally to the gateway are highly available. However, HTTP/TFTP file servers provide the advantage of centralized administration of audio files.

When using Unified ICM Microapplications, the VoiceVXL Gateway sends an HTTP request to an HTTP media server to obtain audio files not already cached locally on the gateway. The following VoiceXML Gateway configuration is used when a load balancer, such as ACE or CSS, has not been deployed with the solution:

```
myrouter(config)# ip host mediaserver {ip-address-of-primary-media-server}
myrouter(config)# ip host mediaserver-backup {ip-address-of-secondary-media-server}
```

In comprehensive mode, the Unified CVP IVR service invokes the backup server only if the primary server is not accessible, and this is not deemed a load balancing mechanism. Each new call attempts to connect to the primary server. If failover occurs, the backup server is used for the duration of the call. The next call attempts to connect to the primary server. This redundancy feature is specific to the Unified CVP IVR service and not a media server per say. Other Unified CVP deployment models that do not use the Unified CVP IVR service, such as the standalone model, do not provide this type of behavior, simply because it does not use the Unified IVR service.

In standalone VoiceXML deployments with Unified CVP, all the best the script writer can do is to point Properties > AudioSettings > Default Audio Path URI in the application to a single media server or the load balancer VIP address for a farm of media servers. Obviously, this approach does not provide a means to access different media servers unless a load balancer with a VIP has been deployed and is considered a significant disadvantage for standalone deployments. To combat this oversight it is a good idea to always provide a load balancer for standalone deployments where highly available media servers are required.

Note   The *mediaserver* name used in the *ip host* statement previously listed is not a fixed name, and it needs to match whatever name was assigned to the media_server ECC variable assigned to the ICM script.

Where a load balancer has been deployed, such as ACE or CSS, the VoiceXML Gateway also uses the following VoiceXML Gateway configuration parameters to locate a server when using a content load balancer:

```
myrouter(config)# ip host mediaserver {ip-address-of-ACE/CSS-VIP-for-media-server}
myrouter(config)# ip host mediaserver-backup {ip-address-of-Second ACE/CSS-VIP-
for-media-server}
```

Because the CSS locates a viable media server on the first request, a backup server is rarely invoked. However, when deploying Unified CVP across several data centers, the backup server IP address could be a locally paired load balancer VIP or even a VIP of a load balancer located in a different data center.

Tip   Be sure when using load balancers with HTTP media servers that an HTTP redirect service is configured and enabled. This feature found in most supported load balancers enables load balancers to remove themselves from the HTTP conversation after the first redirect has been sent to the client. This enables the VoiceXML Gateways to directly communicate with the HTTP media servers by placing a load balancer in the middle of each transaction. This can significantly reduce the load on the load balancer and the number of streams for media transactions.

Caveats

If the media server fails, the following conditions apply to the call disposition:

- Calls in progress should automatically recover. The high-availability configuration techniques previously described should make the failure transparent to the caller. If the media request does fail, use scripting techniques to work around the error. (For example, retry the request, transfer to an agent or label, or use TTS.)

- New calls are transparently directed to the backup media server, and service is not affected.

- If the media server is located across the WAN from the VoiceXML Gateway and the WAN connection fails, the gateway continues to use prompts from the gateway cache until the requested prompt becomes stale, at which time the gateway attempts to refetch the media and the call fails if survivability is not enabled. If survivability is enabled, the call is default-routed.[21]

Unified CVP VoiceXML Server

Example 4-13 shows how to configure a primary and backup VoiceXML server for the VoiceXML Gateway to use when the standalone application has been invoked.

Example 4-13 *Configuring a Primary and Backup VoiceXML Server*

```
myrouter(config)# application
 myrouter(config-app)# service CVPSelfService flash:CVPSelfServiceBootstrap.vxml
 myrouter(config-app)# service {gateway application name} flash:CVPSelfService.tcl
  myrouter(config-app-param)# param CVPPrimaryVXMLServer 10.1.1.15
  myrouter(config-app-param)# param CVPSelfService-port 7000
  myrouter(config-app-param)# param CVPSelfService-app {name of application on the
VoiceXML Server}
  myrouter(config-app-param)# param CVPBackupVXMLServer 10.2.1.15
```

It is the **CVPPrimaryVXMLServer** and the **CVPBackupVXMLServer** parameters on the VoiceXML Gateway that control high availability for characteristics of the Unified CVP VoiceXML Server. However, if Unified CVP VoiceXML Server load balancing and more robust failover capabilities are required, you should use a load balancer such as ACE or CSS. The only change to these configurations to use a load balancer would be to set the IP address used in the param field to the VIP of the load balancer servicing the Unified CVP VoiceXML Server farm.

When using Unified CVP VoiceXML Servers with Unified ICM, the ICM script passes a URL to the VoiceXML Gateway to invoke the VoiceXML applications. You can configure the ICM script to first attempt to connect to Unified CVP VoiceXML Server A, and if the application fails out the X-path of the Unified CVP VoiceXML Server ICM script node, try the Unified CVP VoiceXML Server B. The IP address in the URL can also represent a VIP address serviced by a load balancer resolving to a Unified CVP VoiceXML Server Farm.

Caveats

If the Unified CVP VoiceXML Server fails, the following conditions apply to the call disposition:

- Calls in progress in a standalone deployment disconnect. You can recover calls in progress in an ICM-integrated deployment using scripting techniques to work around the error, as shown in the previous script. (For example, retry the request, transfer to an agent or label, or force an error with an END script node to invoke survivability on the originating gateway.)

- New calls are directed transparently to an alternative Unified CVP VoiceXML Server.[22]

Note   Without a CSS or ACE device, callers might experience a delay at the beginning of the call and need to wait for the system to timeout while trying to connect to the primary Unified CVP VoiceXML Server.

Summary

This chapter emphasized that building a highly available Unified CVP solution requires a deep understanding of how each of the native and non-native components achieve high availability. It is equally important to understanding how each component in the solution integrates with other components to further the high-availability story.

Edge queuing strategies play an important role for garnishing one of Unified CVP's more powerful features: queuing at the edge. Keeping the call at the edge presents its own challenges around survivability and the call's current location when warm transfers enter the picture. These are all critical concepts to understand and design for if you want to provide a highly available edge queuing design.

Determining where to route the call during switch and VRU conversations plays another significant role when considering how to provide redundancy. Without a highly available SIP or H.323 architecture, switch and VRU legs won't complete, and the user experience greatly suffers. Understanding how to provide redundant SIP and H.323 configurations ensures that redundancy is provided for each component in the solution, leaving no rock unturned and no opportunity for a component to fail during a DR event.

Content Services provide critical media and VoiceXML content during call treatment. Without highly available content services providing load balancing, the chance for a critical failure to occur in the solution is highly likely. However, by understanding the options available for on appliance redundancy and load balancing options for content servers lessens the chance that an outage can significantly impact the solution.

The next chapter takes a closer look at media files and how the Unified CVP solution uses them to deliver call treatment. It provides a detailed look at how the VoiceXML Gateway streams, processes, and caches media files.

References

1. Cisco Documentation, *Cisco Unified Customer Voice Portal (CVP) 8.x Solution Reference Network Design (SRND)*, 2010: 3–5.

2. Cisco Documentation, *Configuration and Administration Guide for Cisco Unified Customer Voice Portal*, 2010: 387–388.

3. Cisco Documentation, *Configuration and Administration Guide for Cisco Unified Customer Voice Portal*, 2010: 388–389.

4. Cisco Documentation, *Cisco Unified Customer Voice Portal (CVP) 8.x Solution Reference Network Design (SRND)*, 2010: 4–4, 4–5.

5. Cisco Documentation, *Cisco Unified Customer Voice Portal (CVP) 8.x Solution Reference Network Design (SRND)*, 2010: 4-6.

6. Cisco Documentation, *Cisco Unified Customer Voice Portal (CVP) 8.x Solution Reference Network Design (SRND)*, 2010: 4–14.

7. Cisco Documentation, *Cisco Unified Customer Voice Portal (CVP) 8.x Solution Reference Network Design (SRND)*, 2010: 4–14.

8. Cisco Documentation, *Cisco Unified Customer Voice Portal (CVP) 8.x Solution Reference Network Design (SRND)*, 2010: 4–15.

9. Cisco Documentation, *Cisco Unified Customer Voice Portal (CVP) 8.x Solution Reference Network Design (SRND)*, 2010: 4–4, 4–5.

10. Cisco Documentation, *Cisco Unified Customer Voice Portal (CVP) 8.x Solution Reference Network Design (SRND)*, 2010: 4–19.

11. Cisco Documentation, *Cisco 4700 Series Application Control Engine Appliance Administration Guide*, November 2007: 7–2, 7–3.

12. Cisco Documentation, *Cisco 4700 Series Application Control Engine Appliance Administration Guide*, November 2007: 7–4.

13. Cisco Documentation, *Cisco 4700 Series Application Control Engine Appliance Administration Guide*, November 2007: 7–7.

14. Cisco Documentation, *Cisco 4700 Series Application Control Engine Appliance Administration Guide*, November 2007: 7–8.

15. Cisco Documentation, *Configuration and Administration Guide for Cisco Unified Customer Voice Portal*, 2010: 508.

16. Cisco Documentation, *Cisco Content Services Switch Advanced Configuration Guide*, 2003: 6–3.

17. Cisco Documentation, *Cisco Content Services Switch Advanced Configuration Guide*, 2003: 6–5, 6–6.

18. Cisco Documentation, *Cisco Content Services Switch Advanced Configuration Guide*, 2003: 6–6, 6–7.

19. Cisco Documentation, *Configuration and Administration Guide for Cisco Unified Customer Voice Portal*, 2010: 480.

20. Cisco Documentation, *Cisco Unified Customer Voice Portal (CVP) 8.x Solution Reference Network Design (SRND)*, 2010: 4–29, 4–30.

21. Cisco Documentation, *Cisco Unified Customer Voice Portal (CVP) 8.x Solution Reference Network Design (SRND)*, 2010: 4–31.

22. Cisco Documentation, *Cisco Unified Customer Voice Portal (CVP) 8.x Solution Reference Network Design (SRND)*, 2010: 4–32.

Recommended Reading and Resources

Cisco Documentation, *Cisco Unified Customer Voice Portal (CVP) 8.x Solution Reference Network Design (SRND)*, http://www.cisco.com/en/US/docs/voice_ip_comm/cust_contact/contact_center/customer_voice_portal/srnd/8x/cvp8xsrnd.pdf.

Cisco Documentation, *Cisco Unified Contact Center Enterprise Solution Reference Network Design (SRND)*, http://www.cisco.com/en/US/products/sw/custcosw/ps1844/products_implementation_design_guides_list.html.

Cisco Documentation, *Cisco Unified Customer Voice Portal Configuration Guides*, http://www.cisco.com/en/US/partner/products/sw/custcosw/ps1006/products_installation_and_configuration_guides_list.html.

Cisco Documentation, *User Guide for Cisco Unified CVP VXML Server and Cisco Unified Call Studio, Release 8.0(1)*, http://www.cisco.com/en/US/docs/voice_ip_comm/cust_contact/contact_center/customer_voice_portal/cvp8_0/user/guide/cvp_801_vxml.pdf.

Cisco Documentation, *Hardware and System Software Specification for Cisco Unified Customer Voice Portal (Unified CVP)*, Release 8.0(1), http://www.cisco.com/en/US/docs/voice_ip_comm/cust_contact/contact_center/customer_voice_portal/cvp8_0/reference/guide/cvp_801_bom.pdf.

Cisco Documentation, *Cisco Unified Communications System Release 8.x SRND, January 2011,* http://www.cisco.com/en/US/partner/docs/voice_ip_comm/cucm/srnd/8x/uc8x.html.

Cisco Documentation, *Cisco ACE 4700 Series Appliance Server Load-Balancing Configuration Guide,* http://www.cisco.com/en/US/docs/app_ntwk_services/data_center_app_services/ace_appliances/vA3_1_0/configuration/slb/guide/slbgd.pdf.

Cisco Documentation, *Cisco CSS 11500 Series Content Services Switches Configuration Guides,* http://www.cisco.com/en/US/partner/products/hw/contnetw/ps792/products_installation_and_configuration_guides_list.html.

Chapter 5

Working with Media Files

This chapter covers the following subjects:

- **IOS-based IVR and HTTP client architectures:** Configuration and how clients interact with these architectures.

- **To stream or not to stream:** Call flows will be provided with focus on streaming and its relationship with caching.

- **Caching:** HTTP and IVR caches, their aging process, and how to load, clear, and verify that prompts are cached.

- **The HTTP connection:** Persistent connections, timeouts, and secure HTTPS connections.

- **FAQs:** Answers to some of the most common questions that exist pertaining to media files and Unified CVP.

IOS-Based IVR and HTTP Client Architectures

In previous chapters architecture was discussed pertaining to how media servers are positioned in the Unified CVP solution to deliver media files that address various call treatment requirements. Prior chapters mentioned the process to provide load balancing services to ensure that these media servers were highly available any time that a VoiceXML Gateway required a media file for call treatment. This chapter focuses on how the VoiceXML Gateway retrieves, caches, and plays the media to the caller. It examines the configuration of the VoiceXML Gateway to efficiently perform these functions and discuss IVR and HTTP caches. It also provides guidance on how the HTTP client and the IVR Media subsystems are architected and interact with each other. Understanding this relationship and how each is configured is essential to correctly designing and configuring the VoiceXML Gateway in the Unified CVP solution.

IVR and HTTP Client

The HTTP client subsystem is mostly responsible for fetching application documents from the HTTP server. However, it is also responsible for playing the fetched audio prompts for Interactive Voice Response (IVR) applications, such as Tool Command Language (TCL) and Voice Extensible Markup Language (VoiceXML). Figure 5-1 provides an architecture overview of this IVR and HTTP client interface.

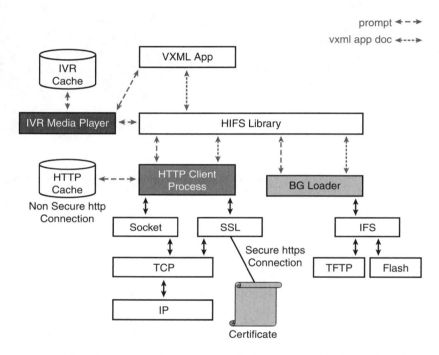

Figure 5-1   *Functional Block Diagram for IVR and HTTP Client Interface*

Taking a closer look at Figure 5-1 there are a few observations that should be pointed out. The HTTP client runs in the background, enabling the IVR Media Player and VXML Application process to make threaded fetch requests; releasing these processes from having to wait for the HTTP fetch to complete before processing other application requests. This is commonly referred to as *non-blocking requests*, which essentially means that after a file loading request has been sent over to the HTTP client, the IVR Media Player and VXML Application can continue servicing other callers, such as playing voice prompts or interpreting VXML instructions. As soon as the file has been loaded, the HTTP client process notifies the requestor using a callback function that inserts an event, which enables the parent or owner of the thread to pick-up the File Load Complete message asynchronously, thus providing a robust multithreaded application.

However, there is another critical process called the BG Loader or Background File Loader (refer to Figure 5-1). Because the HTTP client can provide only HTTP URL access, the BG

Loader process is critical for file loading from TFTP or Flash. Remember, media files can also be stored locally in the VXML gateway's flash or retrieved from a TFTP server. In these situations the IVR Media Player and VXML Application send a child process request to the BG Loader. When this process is complete, the BG Loader process executes a callback function that inserts an event complete message for processing by the parent or requestor. This occurs exactly as described for the HTTP client process.

There exists a process called the HIFS library (refer to Figure 5-1). HIFS is a combination of HTTP and IOS File System functions, hence HIFS. It has the responsibility for parsing the URLs and redirecting the file requests to the appropriate services, either HTTP or IFS. This library provides a clean and simple application interface for consistent integrations.

There are two key concepts when discussing how Unified CVP delivers and plays audio prompts: caching and streaming. Although these two concepts are related internally and may affect the solutions performance when the VXML gateway is under load, they actually are two completely different configuration elements. You need to know that caching and streaming are two independent properties, are orthogonal to each other, and can be configured in any way without affecting the other. For example, you can configure a router to play audio prompts in any of the following modes:

- Streaming from cache

- Streaming without cache

- Nonstreaming from cache

- Nonstreaming without cache

Later in this chapter, each of these calls flows are examined by providing their respective call flow ladder diagrams. Regardless of which mode the VXML gateway uses to play an audio prompt, some of the interaction between the IVR Media Player (IVR Voice Player) and the HTTP client remain the same. The HTTP client fetches audio files from an HTTP Server on behalf of the IVR Media Player. The IVR Media Player controls the streaming modes and transmits the audio data whether the caching is either totally controlled by the HTTP client or co-controlled by both subsystems.

To Stream or Not to Stream

By definition, streaming is delivering content that is continuously received by, and normally displayed to, the end user while it is being delivered to the provider. The name refers more to the delivery method of the content rather than the content itself. Examples of streaming multimedia could be content streamed over telecommunications networks such as radio, television, and so on. Nonstreaming examples might fit content such as books, audio CDs, and so on. How they are accessed and delivered defines whether they are streamed. By its definition, streaming media is nothing more than multimedia data transferred in a stream of packets that are interpreted and rendered, in real time, by a software application as the packets arrive.

The IOS Voice Browser plays the role of the application that renders and presents the stream. It can stream media files from a variety of different media servers, such as HTTP, TFTP, Real Time Streaming Protocol (RTSP), flash, and so on. RTSP streaming does not require the HTTP client or even the IVR Media Player on the VXML Gateway to be involved. However, if you plan to stream from a TFTP Server or flash, the IVR Media Player is the only process required. Furthermore, streaming from an HTTP Server requires both the IVR Media Player and the HTTP client.

In situations where nonstreaming is used to deliver the audio file to the VXML Gateway and subsequently to the caller, the entire audio file must be downloaded before it is played to the caller. The implication of using nonstreaming mode is that there will be a small delay or period of silence while the caller waits for the audio file to be downloaded prior to it being played for the caller. If the audio file is relatively small and delivered over a network-acceptable latency, it will most likely go unnoticed by the caller because this delay could be as small as a few milliseconds. Also this delay occurs if the media file requested by the VXML instructions has been cached, meaning the fetch does not need to occur and the file is immediately played from cache.

Obviously the advantage of streaming mode is that the file is immediately played when the first "chunk" of data has been retrieved and handed over to the IVR Media Player from the HTTP client. For large audio files, this creates a decent advantage because the caller does not hear any noticeable delay or period of silence. In addition, if a large audio file is already saved inside the HTTP client cache, the file can also start playing, even though nonstreaming may be used. This illustrates the separation between the IVR Media Player and the HTTP cache as discussed earlier.

From a simplistic perspective, nonstream wins every time simply because as soon as the entire file is downloaded, the HTTP client notifies the IVR Media Player. Then the IVR Media Player takes over and plays the entire prompt without any interaction with the HTTP client. Streaming mode however is much more complicated because a great deal of back-and-forth signaling occurs between the HTTP client and the IVR Media Player subsystems. For each chunk of audio downloaded from the HTTP server, the HTTP client notifies the IVR Media Player that a new "chunk" of audio is now ready to play for the caller. If for any reason subsequent chunks of audio content do not become ready in time for the IVR Media Player to play for the caller, the caller could be disconnected or experience quality issues with how the prompts are played. Delays in networks and outages with media servers can all contribute to an extended timeout. Because the actually timeout is approximately 10 seconds, the likelihood of the call being completely disconnected is remote.

What are the guidelines pertaining to the size of the media files? How do they ensure that they are classified as small? Although there is no absolute answer to this question, there are some general best practices that seem to keep VXML Gateways out of trouble. First, any audio file longer than 1 minute must be broken into multiple media files with the script stringing together these media files for a logical user experience. The following calculation illustrates how a bit rate representing a codec of g711ulaw is used to determine how large a 1-minute audio file will be:

```
64 Kbits/sec = 8 Kbytes/sec (bit rate for G711uLaw)
8 Kbytes/sec * 60 seconds = 480 Kbytes or ~0.5Mbytes
```

Similarly, the following calculation illustrates how a bit rate representing a codec of G.729 is used to determine how large a 1-minute audio file will be:

```
8 Kbits/sec = 1 Kbytes/sec (bit rate for G.729)
```

1 Kbytes / sec * 60 seconds = 60 Kbytes

Secondly, error and critical Waveform Audio (wav) files should be stored locally in the VXML gateway flash, which ensures that if a failure to fetch or access content from a media server occurs, the error or critical message can still be played for the caller.

Configuring streaming or nonstreaming is straightforward on the VXML gateway and is accomplished as illustrated in Example 5-1.

Example 5-1   *Configuring IVR Streaming*

```
myrouter(config)# ivr prompt streamed ?
  all     Stream all prompts
  flash   Stream flash sourced prompts
  http    Stream http sourced prompts
  none    Stream no prompts
```

By default, all streaming modes on a IOS gateway are disabled. To turn on streaming from a HTTP source, do the following:

```
myrouter(config)#ivr prompt streamed http
```

Logically, to turn on all streaming sources, issue the following command:

```
myrouter(config)#ivr prompt streamed all
```

Note   Although VXML gateways support streaming and nonstreaming configurations for HTTP, it is advised to disable all streaming sources including HTTP unless a customer requirement such as large file sizes requires streaming to be enabled. There have been several documented performance issues with the VXML gateways in earlier versions of Unified CVP pertaining to call quality when HTTP streaming is used. To ensure that streaming from all sources has been disabled, issue the command

myrouter(config)#ivr prompt streamed *none*

Caching

There are two types of caching when storing media files on a VXML Gateway: the IVR Media Player cache and the HTTP client cache. As mentioned earlier, the HTTP client cache stores media files downloaded from a HTTP server. In nonstreaming mode the entire media file is downloaded and stored in the HTTP client cache before it is played by the IVR Media Player. However, in streaming mode, the first chunk of the media file is stored inside the HTTP client and IVR cache. All subsequent chunks of the file are saved in the IVR cache-only.

HTTP Client Cache

The HTTP client Cache can store files downloaded only from HTTP servers. There have been some suggestions that the HTTP client cache also stores files fetched from the VXML Gateways flash memory or a TFTP Server; this is incorrect. Some engineers have decided to store media files locally in each VXML Gateways flash memory as a way to save network bandwidth and utilization. This approach comes with a different price, one that is more taxable against the administration team and not the network team. If the contents of the flash media files change, an administrator of the solution is required to access all the VXML Gateways and update the locally stored media files with the changes. This creates significant administrative overhead for large Unified CVP deployments. However, by storing the media files on HTTP servers and building an adequate load balancing and high-availability design for the hosting and delivery of these media files, this administrative overhead can be mitigated. If the media files change, the administrator must update the HTTP servers with the new files. The next time a caller needs to hear these new prompts, the HTTP client will access the new files, download them accordingly, thus refreshing its HTTP client cache.

So why use caching? The answer to this question lies in the chain of events that occurs when you don't use caching. First, the HTTP client must request a copy of a media file from an HTTP server for every caller that requires it. Secondly, each of those requests must download the file using separate HTTP conversations, each consuming identical bandwidth. The HTTP client must also "check out" memory from the VXML Gateway's IOS and save this file to that "borrowed" memory. After the IVR Media Player plays the prompt, the HTTP client must "check in" the memory it "borrowed" from the VXML gateway's IOS. So obviously having an audio file cached saves network traffic, CPU cycles, and file copying operations, boosting the performance of the VXML Gateway.

A cached file can be shared among several callers. This is accomplished by a reference counter (ref count) being assigned to the number of IVR Media Players that use the same file. If a file cannot be cached, that file will not be shared. The memory storage for that will be used exclusively for just one single IVR Media Player. When that player is done with the audio prompt, the file is immediately removed from the noncached storage.

HTTP Client Cache Control

The HTTP client cache is controlled mainly with two configuration parameters from the client and some parameters sent by the server.

A file can be saved in the http client cache if it meets the criteria of two router configuration parameters: file size limit and cache memory pool size. On the other hand, if the file is larger than the file size limit or the cache memory pool is out of space, the file will not be cached. Example 5-2 shows how these two parameters are configured to control HTTP client caching.

Example 5-2   *Configuring HTTP Client Caching*

```
myrouter#configure terminal
Enter configuration commands, one per line. End with CNTL/Z.
myrouter(config)#http client cache memory ?
  file  Configure maximum file size allowed for caching
  pool  Configure maximum memory pool allowed for HTTP Client Cache

myrouter(config)#http client cache memory pool ?
  <0-100000> Memory size in K bytes. Zero to disable HTTP caching.
myrouter(config)#http client cache memory file ?
  <1-10000 Memory size in K bytes. Any single file larger than
  this size will not be cached.
```

The default memory file size is 50 Kbytes. The recommended file size is 600 Kbytes. Any file with a size larger than the configured HTTP client memory file size will *not* be cached.

Similarly, the default memory pool size for the HTTP client cache is 10 Mbytes. However, the recommended cache memory pool size depends on the available system memory and the user's applications. To determine what this value should be for a deployment, all the most common used application and media file sizes need to be added up, which should then be used as the value for setting the cache memory pool size using the preceding command. Using a value of zero for this pool size will effectively turn off caching.

In addition, when configuring a portion of the VXML Gateway memory as a cache pool for the HTTP client, it does not mean that amount of memory is immediately allocated for the HTTP client. The HTTP client dynamically grows its cache memory pool size on an as-needed basis. As more and more HTTP URLs are fetched into the router, more and more memory is allocated to cache them.

Example 5-3 provides a model of the results from executing the **show http client cache** IOS command, which illustrates how to verify the configuration and operation of the HTTP client.

Example 5-3   *Verifying the HTTP Client*

```
myrouter#show http client cache
HTTP Client cached information
==============================
!Configured cache memory and maximum file sizes in bold
Maximum memory pool allowed for HTTP Client caching = 20000 K-bytes
Maximum file size allowed for caching = 400 K-bytes
!Sum of the overhead (e.g. http message headers from the server) plus the first
chunk !of the files in bold.
Total memory used up for Cache = 3558 Bytes
Message response timeout = 10 secs
Total cached entries     = 4
Total non-cached entries = 1


          Cached entries
          ==============


entry 141,   1 entries
!"Ref" indicates how many applications are referencing this URL
!"context" is just a pointer link to the application handler
Ref    FreshTime    Age          Size         context
—-     ————-        —-           — —          ———-
0      86400        126358 *     465          67518CDC
url: http://mymediaserver/script/test.vxml



entry 156,   1 entries
!"FreshTime" is he life expectancy of this URL
!"Age: is how long it has been since it was downloaded
!"Size" stands for the number of bytes in the first chunk that the HTTP Client has
!received from the server
Ref    FreshTime    Age          Size         context
—-     ————-        —-           — —          ———-
1      3031573      208          151          0
url: https://mymediaserver/script/firstpage.vxml

entry 158,   1 entries
Ref    FreshTime    Age          Size         context
—-     ————-        —-           — —          ———-
1      3334260      63           0            0
url: http://mymediaserver/audio/dir_menu.au



entry 167,   1 entries
Ref    FreshTime    Age          Size         context
—-     ————-        —-           — —          ———-
```

```
2      49982      208        455        0
url: http://mymediaserver/script/playprompt.vxml


          Non-cached entries
          ==================


!File is too large to cache > 400kb, "324" is only the size of the first chunk of
data !sent by the server to the HTTP Client, not audio file size.
Ref    Size
—·     — —
1      324
url: http://mymediaserver/audio/toolongprompt.au
```

Following are some observations from the output illustrated in Example 5-3:

1. The **show http client cache** output shows the cache memory pool size and maximum files size configured.

2. **Total memory used up for cache** is the actual memory that is needed to store all the management information for the files listed here. It is not the total size of all the cached files. Rather, it is the sum of the overhead (e.g., http message headers from the server) plus the first chunk of the files.

3. In the **Cached entries**, the "Ref" number indicates the number of applications that are currently referencing this URL. Usually, most audio files have a ref count 1 on them, meaning that the IVR Voice Player is holding them. If two calls are requesting to play the same cached URL simultaneously, that entry will have a ref count of 2. A zero (0) ref count means that no one is using this URL. URLs cannot be removed from the cached entry until the ref count is zero.

4. "FreshTime" is the "life expectancy" of this URL. "**Age**" is how long it has been since this URL was last downloaded. If the Age of the file is older than its FreshTime, the URL will be flagged with an **asterisk (*)** next to its Age number to indicate that the file is already **stale**, such as the previous "test.vxml" listed.

5. "Size" stands for the number of bytes in the first chunk that the http client has received from the server. This number could be either zero (0), which means that the server has not sent any data for this file yet, or a number that is less than or equal to the size of the audio file, depending on the size of the audio file and the streaming mode.

6. "**Context**" is just a pointer link to application handler. It is for internal use only.

7. **URL** shows the entire URL that the data is retrieved from. The URL starts with either **http:** or **https:**. Naturally, there is a distinction between the following two URLs: http://www.myserver.com/app.vxml and https://www.myserver.com/app.vxml.

8. Occasionally, two or more identical URLs may appear together. This happens when the file downloading process overlaps each other. In this case, the URL in the later download becomes a child of the previous one. When the later URL download is

complete, its parent URL is removed from the cached entry. The child URL is saved in the cache because its age is "younger" than its parent.

9. In the **Noncached entries**, we see a file called toolongprompt.au, which is too large (> 400 Kb) and cannot be saved in the cache. Again, the size 324 is not the actual size of the file; rather, it means the server sends only 324 bytes in the first chunk for this file. The remainder of the file is sent in subsequent chunks, and they are all forwarded to the IVR Voice Player by the http client.

10. All entries in the Noncached Entries are temporary. They will be removed immediately after the application is done with the URL.

The caching of a file can also be controlled by the server as to whether this file should be cached and if so, how long it should be kept in the cache. These parameters are sent from the server either via http message headers or through vxml application scripts.

So what happens to HTTP Query Data with respect to caching? A query is a URL that has a question (?) mark followed by one or more **name-value** attribute pairs in it. By default, the HTTP client cache does not cache query data returned from the HTTP server. For security reasons this has been the behavior since the release of the VXML feature; however, there was a need to cache the query data to improve the system performance. To maintain backward compatibility, the HTTP client does not cache any query data unless the following is configured:

```
http client cache query
```

Naturally two different callers with two different query URLs show up as though they both have identical URLs in the **show http client cache** output. This is because their different values in the attributes are all masked out, but the http client cache is caching two different URLs. Following is an example of a bank URL where the username and password are masked out for security reasons:

```
https://www.mybank.com/scripts/login.php?user=*******&password=***
```

Figure 5-2 outlines how caching works for the HTTP client and also provides insight as to what occurs when multiple VXML applications fetch media files.

An interesting observation from Figure 5-2 is how the call flow proceeds when different applications fetch media files. If the application is requesting a reload of the media file, it must first be validated as being more recent than the current cache entry. If it is not, it is discarded and the cache contents are returned to the VXML application. Later, this chapter discusses the cache aging process, calculation of its refresh time, and the removal of stale cached entries.

IVR Cache

Because the HTTP client cache is responsible for caching HTTP URLs, what handles URLs that resolve to TFTP or Flash? The IVR Media Player is responsible not only for playing the prompts from all of this, but also for caching the media files. As noted earlier, the audio playing process is completely separate from the file downloading process, regardless where the source file is and cached.

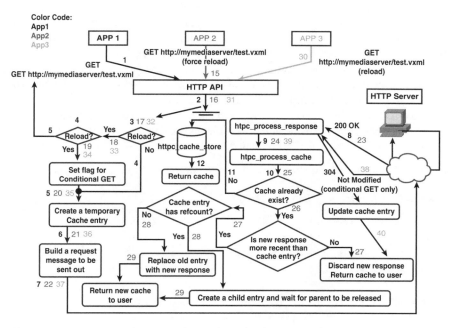

Figure 5-2   *How Caching Works with Multiple HTTP Clients*

As soon as the file is downloaded, the IVR Media Player tries to cache the file. However, before caching it, if the file is an HTTP file, the HTTP client is contacted to determine whether the IVR Media Player should cache the file. If the response from the HTTP client is positive, the file will be cached. So what happens if during the file download process the caller hangs up? The IVR Media Player notifies the HTTP client to abort the download and remove the partial data file saved in the cache. When using HTTP nonstreaming mode, the entire audio file is downloaded and stored in the HTTP client cache. Only after it has been downloaded and cached can the IVR Media Player then start to play the audio file from the VXML Gateway's memory.

In HTTP streaming mode things work a little differently. The IVR Media Player can "stream" voice from the HTTP server without the entire audio file inside the VXML Gateway's memory. This approach requires a great deal of interaction between the IVR Media Player and the HTTP client. For example, the HTTP client must notify the IVR Media Player when a "chunk" of audio is ready to be played and which party caches which part of the audio file.

IVR Cache Control

The IVR Cache is controlled by two parameters: the file count and the IVR cache memory pool size. These parameters apply to HTTP streaming mode and imply that if a file has already passed the HTTP client cache control test described earlier in this chapter, if the files cached in the IVR have not reached a preset limit, and if there is still enough memory space left in the pool, the file can be saved in the IVR cache. The term "can be saved" is used simply because if the file count limit has been reached or the IVR cache runs out of memory space, the IVR must do some shuffling to free up space for the new file. This is accomplished using a First In First Out (FIFO) algorithm, which basically removes the oldest prompt currently not used from the cache. It continues executing this algorithm until there is enough room for the newly arrived file. In the rare case that this attempt to free up space fails, the new file will not be cached.

Example 5-4 illustrates how to configure these parameters for the IVR cache.

Example 5-4   *Configuring the IVR Cache*

```
myrouter#configure terminal
Enter configuration commands, one per line. End with CNTL/Z.
myrouter(config)#ivr prompt memory ?
  <128-16384>  memory in Kbytes

myrouter(config)#ivr prompt memory 16384 ?
  files  configure number of files that can stay in memory
  <cr>

myrouter(config)#ivr prompt memory 16384 files ?
  <20-1000>  number of files
```

The default value for the IVR's prompt memory is 2 Mb, and the default for the total number of files stored by the IVR cache is 200. Following best practices for a VXML Gateway with a constant load, the maximum values should be set for these parameters. More specifically, the following command should be issued on the VXML Gateway:

```
myrouter(config)#ivr prompt memory 16384 files 1000
```

This command will set the IVR's cache pool memory to 16 Mb and the maximum number of files cached in the IVR cache to 1000.

Caching in Streaming and Nonstreaming Mode

It is worth revisiting how caching differs in streaming and nonstreaming mode. More specifically, the HTTP client does behave differently depending on what mode is used, even though caching and streaming are fundamentally two separate processes that enable them to be configured differently. Following is a recap of the characteristics of nonstreaming and streaming mode and their relationships to caching:

- **Nonstreaming mode:** In this mode the HTTP client is the owner of the cache entry, and the entire audio file is cached and stored in the HTTP client cache. The file size displayed in Figure 5-2 is the actual file size that is cached. In addition, the HTTP client is responsible for the management of this cached entry when the following events occur:

  - The cached entry has become stale.

  - The cached entry has a ref count of zero (0), which indicates that no application is currently using this entry.

  - Memory space is needed to make room for other entries.

Note   As depicted in Figure 5-2, Step 26 during application #2's fetch, if the audio file in the HTTP client cache already exists and does not require a refresh, the HTTP client transfers the audio data to the IVR Media Player from its cache. This enables the IVR Media Player to immediately start playing the prompt even in nonstreaming mode. If the file is either stale or unstable, the HTTP client would reload the audio file from the HTTP server, and the IVR Media Player must wait for the entire file loading process to complete before it can play the prompt.

- **Streaming mode:** In this mode, the HTTP client only caches the first "chunk" of the audio file. It then sends the first "chunk" of the audio file and subsequent "chunks" to the IVR Media Player for playing. The IVR Media Player becomes the owner and is responsible for caching the entire audio file. The only reason the HTTP client caches the first "chunk" of the audio file is to give it the capability to manage that entry in the cache, for example, entry age update, entry removal, and so on. By examining the HTTP headers located inside the first "chunk" of HTTP server's response data, the HTTP client can determine the "freshness" of a cached entry on behalf of the IVR Media Server Player. The HTTP client cannot clear the cache entry on its own because the IVR Media Player is still the owner of the entry and must notify the HTTP client when the entry needs to be cleared.

Note   The file size depicted in Example 5-3 is only the file size for the first "chunk" of the audio file retrieved and cached by HTTP client. In streaming mode, this value is different than that of a nonstreaming mode output; the nonstreaming mode's file size is the entire cached file size and not just the first "chunk" of the audio file.

When the VXML application script requests a prompt to be played, the IVR Media Player looks this prompt up in its own cache. If the requested audio file is already in the cache, the IVR Media Player checks with the HTTP client to see if the file is still fresh. If so, the IVR Media Player can start playing the prompt from its own cache. However, if the HTTP client reloads the audio file from the server, the IVR Media Player must wait for first "chunk" of the audio file to be retrieved before it can start playing the refreshed prompt.

Cache Aging Process

As mentioned, the HTTP client is responsible for the "freshness" of its cache. So how does the HTTP client determine whether a cached entry is "fresh" or "stale"? This is determined by two numbers as illustrated in Example 5-5: Age and FreshTime.

Example 5-5 *Age and FreshTimer Values from* **show http client cache** *CLI Command*

```
myrouter#show http client cache
HTTP Client cached information
==============================
Maximum memory pool allowed for HTTP Client caching = 20000 K-bytes
Maximum file size allowed for caching = 400 K-bytes
Total memory used up for Cache = 3558 Bytes
Message response timeout = 10 secs
Total cached entries     = 4
Total non-cached entries = 1

          Cached entries
          ==============

entry 141,  1 entries
Ref    FreshTime   Age          Size         context
--     -----.      --.          --           ---.
0      86400       126358 *     465          67518CDC
url: http://mymediaserver/script/test.vxml


entry 156,  1 entries
!"FreshTime" is the life expectancy of this URL

!"Age: is how long it has been since it was downloaded

Ref    FreshTime   Age          Size         context
--     -----.      --.          --           ---.
1      3031573     208          151          0
url: https://mymediaserver/script/firstpage.vxml

entry 158,  1 entries
Ref    FreshTime   Age          Size         context
--     -----.      --.          --           ---.
1      3334260     63           0            0
```

```
url: http://mymediaserver/audio/dir_menu.au


entry 167,  1 entries
Ref    FreshTime   Age         Size        context
—·     ————·       —·          — —         ———·
2      49982       208         455         0
url: http://mymediaserver/script/playprompt.vxml


        Non-cached entries
        ==================


Ref    Size
—·     — —
1      324
url: http://mymediaserver/audio/toolongprompt.au
```

The Age value is defined as the elapsed time because the file was last downloaded from the HTTP server. The FreshTime is the duration that the file is expected to stay fresh in the HTTP client cache. This duration is based on when the file was last downloaded from the HTTP server.

There are several variables that impact the FreshTime of a file; some include the HTTP message headers from the server and the cache refresh value configured on the VXML Gateway via the CLI. So what is the decision process for determining the FreshTimer of a file? The following steps are followed in their presented order when determining the FreshTimer value of an audio file:

Step 1. When the file is downloaded from the HTTP server and one of the HTTP message headers contains the following:

```
Cache-Control: max-age = <value in seconds>
```

then <value in seconds> will be used as the FreshTime for the file.

Step 2. If Step 1 does not hold true, but the following two headers are included in the HTTP message:

```
Expires: <expiration date time>
Date: <Current date time>
```

then the difference of <expiration date time> - <Current date time> will be used for the FreshTime for the file.

Step 3. The HTTP/1.1 spec, RFC 2616 ("HyperText Transport Protocol"), recommends that either of the HTTP message headers as described in the preceding Steps 1 and 2 be present. If the HTTP server fails to send both of these items in its

HTTP response, the VXML gateway takes 10 percent of the difference between Date and Last-Modified from the message headers:

```
Last-Modified: <last-modified date time>
Date: <Current date time>
```

So the FreshTime for this file is calculated as

```
FreshTime = 10% x ((Last-Modified) - (Date))
```

Step 4.   The last step in this process involves the CLI command for setting the HTTP client cache value. This CLI command enables the user to assign a FreshTime to the files as a provisional value in case none of the previous steps or message headers are provided:

```
myrouter(config)#http client cache refresh ?
        <1-864000> Time value in seconds
```

The default refresh value is 86400 seconds or 24 hours!

Note   The configured HTTP client refresh value has no effect on when any of the message headers interrogated in Steps 1 through 3 are present. In addition, when adding this CLI configuration, it does not become retroactive. This means that the newly configured refresh value applies only to new incoming files and has no effect on the entries already in the cache.

What happens when a file becomes stale? Does the VXML gateway automatically remove it? Quite the contrary; the VXML gateway never refreshes any stale files on its own. Stale files are refreshed only on an as-needed basis. It is not recommended to have the VXML Gateway spend its valuable CPU cycles updating files in the cache without knowing whether those files will be used. The implication of this is that a stale cached entry can stay in the cache for a long time until it is removed to make room for either a fresh copy of the same file or another file that just needs its memory space in the cache. This brings up another important point: A stale cached entry can still be usable if its age and staleness have not exceeded the maxage and maxstale value specified by the application. What if the application provides only one or none of these attributes?

In general, when the HTTP client issues a GET request to the HTTP server, it uses a "conditional" GET to minimize its impact on network traffic. What this entails is that an If-Modified-Since is included in the headers sent to the sender. With this header, the server either replies with a 304 response code (Not Modified) or returns the entire file if the file was indeed recently updated.

Note   This conditional GET applies only to nonstreaming mode. Under streaming mode, the http client always issues unconditional GET, that is, no If-Modified-Since header will be

> included in the GET request, thus resulting in an unconditional reload for each GET in streaming mode.

It was mentioned earlier that the HTTP client and IVR Media Player must manage and control their cache entries. But what if the HTTP client needs to cleanup some stale entries to regain space in the cache memory pool but it is not the owner of those files? Enter on the scene the HTTP client cache background ager.

HTTP Client Cache Background Ager

As mentioned earlier, in streaming mode, the IVR Media Player owns the cached entries. When some of those entries have "expired," the http client has no privilege to remove them because it has no ownership on those files. In normal operation, this may not be a problem because the stale entries are removed when they are refreshed with updated copies received from the server. But in certain scenarios, some new files may not get cached because of this disconnect in ownership. Consider a corner case such as the following example:

```
http client cache memory pool = 20 Mb
Memory in use for cached entries = 19 Mb
Memory taken up by stale entries = 5 Mb
Newly arrived file size = 2 Mb
```

The example details that the newly arrived file cannot be cached because the http client does not have enough memory left to accommodate the file. For a normal file request, the http client can notify only the IVR Media Player if that file is still fresh or usable. It cannot ask the Media Player to remove any other expired files. A separate communication channel is put in place for the http client to notify the Media Player that it is time to clean itself up.

The http client cache background ager wakes up every 5 minutes. If the total memory used for the cached entries exceeds 70 percent threshold of the configured cache memory pool size, the ager "walks" through every cached entry. If the entry is still fresh, it leaves it alone. If the entry is stale and has no reference to it, that is, ref count = 0, the http client deletes the entry on its own because it is the legitimate owner of that entry. If the stale entry has a reference count 1 on it and it has no parent or child linked to it, meaning the file is not in the middle of refresh download, the http client calls back to notify the Media Player to release this stale entry.

Setting the Entire HTTP Client Cache to Stale

One of the biggest issues with previous versions of Unified CVP has been the capability to refresh prompts on the VXML Gateway. In the situation in which the customer's VXML application scripts do not provide a <maxage> attribute/ property, the cached entries in the HTTP client cache are not refreshed until they expire. In the past, if a customer wanted to modify the file on the HTTP server to correct a prompt or to provide additional guidance or options for a caller, they would have only the following options for their updated prompts into the HTTP client cache on the VXML gateway:

■ Change their VXML scripts, which would never work in a large deployment.

■ Reload the VXML gateway, which could be accomplished only via a maintenance window causing a potential outage while the VXML gateway reboots.

■ Use **audio-prompt load <URL> CLI** command on the VXML gateway console for each file needed to be refreshed. This would never scale for enterprise deployments that have numerous VXML Gateways with the potential of several prompt files that need to be refreshed.

A new CLI was introduced starting in IOS version 12.4(17.5)T or later that allowed a user to manually set all the entries in the HTTP client cache as "stale":

`myrouter#`**`set http client cache stale`**

This forces the HTTP client to check with the server when any of the cached entries are requested by the VXML application. A conditional reload will be sent to the server if the router is in nonstreaming mode. Otherwise, an unconditional reload will be used for the refresh. Either way, the application will be guaranteed with a most up-to-date file after the CLI is issued.

After the CLI is issued, each of the http client cache entries will be marked as "stale" with a pound sign (#) to differentiate from the natural aging processing. Example 5-6 illustrates the effect of issuing this command:

Example 5-6 *Verifying the* http client cache stale *Entries*

```
myrouter#set http client cache stale
HTTP Client cached information
===============================
Maximum memory pool allowed for HTTP Client caching = 20000 K-bytes
Maximum file size allowed for caching = 400 K-bytes
Total memory used up for Cache = 3558 Bytes
Message response timeout = 10 secs
Total cached entries     = 4
Total non-cached entries = 0


        Cached entries
        ==============


!"#"indicates that this entry has been marked as "stale"

entry 141,  1 entries
Ref   FreshTime   Age         Size        context
```

```
—·   ———·          —·         ——       ———·
0     86400      126358     #  465      67518CDC
url: http://mymediaserver/script/test.vxml


entry 156,  1 entries
Ref   FreshTime   Age        Size       context
—·   ———·          —·         ——       ———·
1     3031573       208     #  151      0
url: https://mymediaserver/script/firstpage.vxml

entry 158,  1 entries
Ref   FreshTime   Age        Size       context
—·   ———·          —·         ——       ———·
1     3334260        63     #   0       0
url: http://mymediaserver/audio/dir_menu.au


entry 167,  1 entries
Ref   FreshTime   Age        Size       context
—·   ———·          —·         ——       ———·
2     49982         208     #  455      0
url: http://mymediaserver/script/playprompt.vxml
```

However, be aware that sometimes replacing a file on the HTTP server will not update the file modify time stamp to the current date and time. When using a UNIX-based HTTP server, use the **touch** and **cp** commands to ensure that the modified date and time stamp is updated. For IIS-based deployments, a similar command is provided named *touch* with usage help being provided with the command **touch -?**.

In some situations it may be required to simply reload a prompt, manually, to a VXML Gateway. In addition, there may be a circumstance in which a large audio file should be preloaded to a VXML Gateway to avoid a delay when the file is initially accessed by a caller. In either case the following command enables a particular audio file to be loaded into an HTTP client cache and requires the cache to be properly configured.

`myrouter#`**`audio-prompt load`** *`url`*

The <url> parameter is the full URL of the audio file located on a HTTP server. This is a great command to use to confirm that a VXML Gateway can fetch audio files from a particular HTTP server.

Streaming and Caching Call Flows

Now that a basic understanding has been established for the definition of streaming and caching and how each can be configured and controlled, it is time to take a closer look at some call flows using both of these concepts. Earlier in this chapter it was mentioned that streaming modes can be mixed and matched with different modes of caching. Each of these matches represents a slightly different interface between the IVR Media Player and the HTTP client. Following are the four calls flows that were mentioned earlier:

■ Streaming from cache

■ Streaming without cache

■ Nonstreaming from cache

■ Nonstreaming without cache

Figure 5-3 provides a ladder diagram that represents the call flow and interactions between the HTTP client and the IVR Media Player.

The key takeaway from this ladder diagram is that the HTTP client saves only the first "chunk" of the audio file but continues to deliver subsequent "chunks" of audio data to the IVR Media Player. The IVR Media Player saves the entire file at the end of the transaction if the HTTP client indicates that the file should be cached.

A similar process is followed when using streaming mode with no caching. Figure 5-4 provides a closer look at this call flow.

At the end of the call flow, the IVR Media Player is notified by the HTTP client that this particular audio file is not a cacheable. In response the IVR Media Player deletes the file.

Figure 5-5 provides details of the call flow when using a nonstreaming mode from a cache.

What is interesting about this set of transactions is that the HTTP client caches the entire file before it notifies the IVR Media Player that it is ready to be played. Furthermore, the HTTP client also determines if the file is cacheable, and if so, it saves the file after the IVR Media Player finishes playing it. If the file is not cacheable, the HTTP client deletes the file from memory.

The final call flow deals with a slight variation of the previous one in that it provides nonstreaming mode without a cache. Figure 5-6 provides a detailed ladder diagram for this call flow.

Although this call flow is similar to the one presented in Figure 5-5, the file step instruction is requesting to delete the file because an HTTP client cache has not been configured or un-usable.

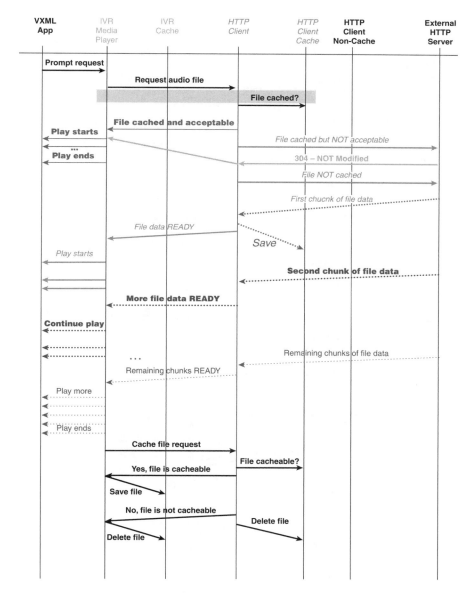

Figure 5-3 *Streaming From Cache Call Flow*

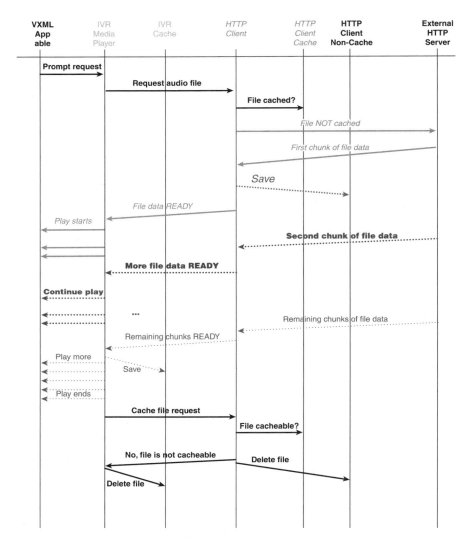

Figure 5-4   *Streaming Without Caching Call Flow*

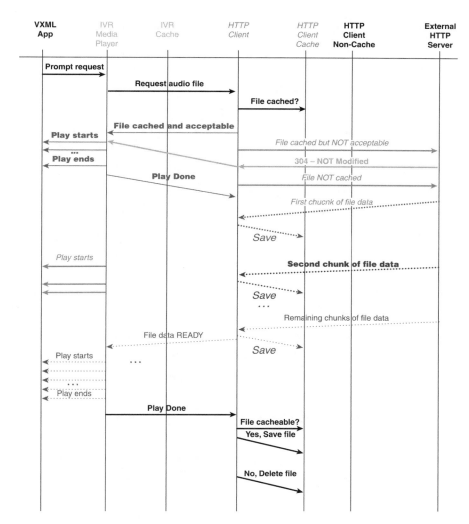

Figure 5-5 *Nonstreaming from Cache Call Flow*

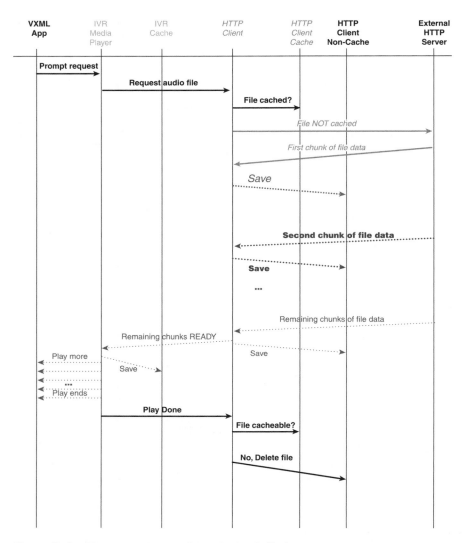

Figure 5-6   *Nonstreaming Without Cache Call Flow*

HTTP Connection

In a typical HTTP communication transaction, the HTTP client is always the party that initiates the request to communicate with an HTTP server. It accomplishes this by starting up an HTTP handshake via a TCP socket connection request to the HTTP server. After the server grants the connection request, a connection between the HTTP client and the HTTP server is established. The HTTP client sends a request, usually in the form of a VXML document, or an audio prompt file fetch, on behalf of the application to the server.

However, as soon as the client receives the response from the HTTP server, the HTTP client closes the TCP socket connection.

Sounds good, doesn't it? Not so fast. Imagine what happens to the performance of a VXML Gateway that is already under a decent amount of load while the HTTP client is simultaneously servicing multiple applications. The additional overhead for opening and closing all the TCP sock connections can take a toll on the performance of the VXML Gateway. This further complicates the issue if these HTTP client requests are small in nature and issued one after another.

Persistent Connections

To reduce the socket connection overhead, the client can keep the socket open after a previous application request is fulfilled for the next application to "reuse" the same connection. This is feasible as long as the two connections have the same host IP address and port number. This kind of connection is referred to as *persistent connection*. As the name implies, the connection can last over a long period of time without being shut down.

To establish a persistent connection, both the client and the server must agree that the connection is going to be a "persistent" one. It is initiated by the client by using the following http header:

```
Connection: Keep-Alive
```

If the server agrees to keep the connection open, it includes the same http header in the response message. The server may optionally send a timeout value and maximum of requests with the header above:

```
Connection: Keep-Alive, timeout=500, max=100
```

The server instructs the client that it agrees to keep the connection open. But if there aren't additional requests after 500 milliseconds, or the number of requests has reached 100, the connection shuts down. The default persistent connection timeout on the client is 800 milliseconds.

On the other hand, if the server responds with the following header

```
Connection: close
```

it means the server denies the client's request to keep the connection open after the application's http request is fulfilled. The server either cannot handle this kind of connection or is not configured to handle this kind of connection. The client must abide by the server's instruction to close down the connection after the server's http response data for the application request is received.

There are certain advantages to using persistent connections on the VXML Gateway. The obvious one is to reduce connection overhead and keep the router CPU usage lower. Of course, there are some situations in which the client does not allow multiple applications to share the same connection for security reason. Some "unsafe" methods such as POST as indicated in RFC 2616, do not allow persistent connection. Also in streaming mode, every

TCP socket connection is used exclusively by a single media player application. This is purely for data integrity reasons because in streaming mode audio prompt data cannot be interleaved by multiple application sessions.

The following CLI is used to enable persistent connections on the VXML gateway for the HTTP client:

```
myrouter(config)#http client connection persistent
```

The default should have persistent connections turned on; however, to disable persistent connections for the HTTP client on the VXML gateway, use the following command:

```
myrouter(config)#no http client connection persistent
```

As with any TCP handshake or transaction, there are always timeouts that play an important role about to how the transaction is completed or dropped. With HTTP connections there exists three timeouts worth mentioning.

■ **Connection timeout:** The HTTP client waits for the server to establish the TCP socket connection before it gives up. Default is 5 seconds.

■ **Connection idle timeout:** The HTTP client waits if there is no data sent before shutting down the TCP socket connection to the HTTP server. Default is 2 seconds.

■ **HTTP response timeout:** The duration that the HTTP client waits for receiving the response data from the HTTP server. The default is 10 seconds. If after waiting for this duration of time, the HTTP client fails to receive any response from the HTTP server, the HTTP client gives up and returns an "internal error" code to the application. The internal error code is usually a negative number, as opposed to the HTTP server response codes that are positive numbers.

The following CLI commands in Example 5-7 show how to configure each of the connection timeouts and the HTTP response timeout values on a VXML Gateway.

Example 5-7 *Configuring HTTP Client Timeout Values*

```
myrouter(config)#http client connection ?
  idle       Configure connection idle time allowed
  persistent Enable HTTP persistent connections
  timeout    How long HTTP Client waits for a server connection to
             establish before giving up
myrouter(config)#http client connection idle timeout ?
  <1-60>     HTTP connection idle time-out value (1-60) in seconds

myrouter(config)#http client connection timeout ?
  <1-60>     HTTP connection time-out value (1-60) in seconds

myrouter(config)#http client response timeout ?
  <1-300>    HTTP Response time-out value (1-300) in seconds
```

To display the active HTTP client connections, issue the following CLI command on the VXML Gateway, as shown in Example 5-8.

Example 5-8 *Displaying the Active HTTP Client Connections*

```
myrouter#show http client connection
     HTTP Client Connections:
     =========================
Persistent connection  = enabled
Initial socket connection timeout = 5 secs (default)
Connection idle timeout = 2 secs (default)
Connection to host mymediaserver, IP = 10.1.1.200 :
  fd = 0, state = PERSISTENT,
  Keep-Alive: timeout = 0, max = 0
  Persistent connection expired = FALSE
  Outstanding Requests = 0, Pending Requests = 0,Total Requests = 0


Total HTTP server connections = 1
```

This particular connection has a state = PERSISTENT with no timeouts or outstanding or pending requests.

Secure HTTPS Connections

Some voice applications require secure connections to the HTTP server, such as financial institutions that collect caller's personal information. This type of application can take advantage of the HTTPS support starting in the 12.4(15)T release.

To the user, there will be no distinctions between an HTTP connection and an HTTPS connection. After the VXML Gateway system administrator has configured the necessary crypto PKI trust point and certificates for the HTTPS connection, users can use an HTTPS connection just like the way they uses an HTTP connection. This similarity applies to all command-line interface (CLI) commands and all URLs used in Voice XML application documents. For more details, refer to IVR Secure HTTPS Configuration Guide located at Cisco.com or via this URL:
http://www.cisco.com/en/US/docs/ios/voice/ivr/configuration/guide/ivrapp02.html#wp1114712.

HTTP Server Response Codes

During normal operation, if for some reason, the HTTP server is unable to fulfill the HTTP client's request, the HTTP client relays the HTTP server error or status code back to the application. For example, if the application makes a request to download a file that does not exist on the HTTP server, the HTTP server responds with the error code 404 (file not found) to the HTTP client. When VXML application receives this return error code, it can throw an error event like error.badfetch.http.404. It is then up to the VXML application script to handle this event, if there is an event handler included in the application script. Otherwise, the call is disconnected in this scenario.

Example 5-9 shows the server response codes that are extracted from RFC 2616.

Example 5-9   *RFC 2616 Server Response Codes*

```
Informational 1xx:
         "100" Continue
         "101" Switching Protocols

Successful 2xx:
         "200" OK
         "201" Created
         "202" Accepted
         "203" Non-Authoritative Information
         "204" No Content
         "205" Reset Content
         "206" Partial Content

Redirection 3xx:
         "300" Multiple Choices
         "301" Moved Permanently
         "302" Found
         "303" See Other
         "304" Not Modified
         "305" Use Proxy
         "307" Temporary Redirect

Client Error 4xx:
         "400" Bad Request
         "401" Unauthorized
         "402" Payment Required
         "403" Forbidden
         "404" Not Found
         "405" Method Not Allowed
         "406" Not Acceptable
         "407" Proxy Authentication Required
         "408" Request Time-out
         "409" Conflict
         "410" Gone
         "411" Length Required
         "412" Precondition Failed
         "413" Request Entity Too Large
```

```
            "414" Request-URI Too Large
            "415" Unsupported Media Type
            "416" Requested range not satisfiable
            "417" Expectation Failed

Server Error 5xx:
            "500" Internal Server Error
            "501" Not Implemented
            "502" Bad Gateway
            "503" Service Unavailable
            "504" Gateway Time-out
            "505" Version not supported
```

HTTP Client Internal Error Codes

Sometimes, the HTTP client fails to establish a connection with the HTTP server, or it fails to receive any response data from the HTTP server. In some situations, errors can be caused by VXML Gateway system failures. In all these cases, the HTTP client uses an internal error code as the request status. The following is a list of HTTP client internal error codes:

```
#define HTTPC_CLIENT_ERROR              -1
#define HTTPC_CLIENT_TIMEOUT_ERROR      -2
#define HTTPC_CLIENT_MSG_DECODE_ERROR   -3
#define HTTPC_CLIENT_MSG_ENCODE_ERROR   -4
#define HTTPC_CLIENT_MSG_XMIT_ERROR     -5
#define HTTPC_CLIENT_WRITEQ_FULL_ERROR  -6
#define HTTPC_CLIENT_CONN_ERROR         -7      (translated to 404)
#define HTTPC_CLIENT_UNSUPPORT_ERROR    -8
#define HTTPC_CLIENT_SOCKET_RCV_ERROR   -9
#define HTTPC_CLIENT_OUT_OF_MEM         -10
```

HTTP Client Cookies

The support for HTTP client cookies stored and located on the VXML Gateways are compliant to RFC 2109 with the following exceptions:

■ Cookies are not cached. RFC 2109 section 4.5 says that cookies can be cached even though they should usually not be cached.

■ A maximum of 10 cookies are allowed to exist simultaneously per session. RFC 2109 section 6.3 says that in general, user agents' cookie support should have no fixed limits.

■ Cookies are maintained only for the duration of the VXML session. All associated cookies are destroyed when the session is terminated. A VXML session is not the same duration as the call. A VXML session may terminate after transferring the call to a different router or handing off the call to a different application such as TCL and so on. The call still exists but not the VXML session.

The following CLI is used to enable or disable HTTP client cookies on the VXML Gateway:

```
myrouter(config)#[no] http client cookie
```

The default setting is that this support is ON. Example 5-10 shows that the CLI can also be used to show a particular HTTP client cookie.

Example 5-10   *Displaying an HTTP Client Cookie*

```
myrouter#show http client cookie ?
  id Display only cookies with specified id
  ¦ Output modifiers
  <cr>

myrouter#show http client cookie id ?
  <1-2147483647>  call identifier
```

However, because cookies are maintained only for the duration of the call session, this CLI command shows only a "snapshot" of the active cookies at the moment that the command was entered.

HTTP Client Statistics

Sometimes it is necessary to determine if the communication between the HTTP server and the HTTP client is experiencing any difficulties. The HTTP client automatically collects some relevant data for this purpose in the background without any special configuration. This data may help the network administrators to find if their network topology between the HTTP server and the client is properly designed and configured.

For example, if there are any switches, proxy servers, or other network devices placed in between the HTTP server and the HTTP client, they may cause the HTTP network traffic to slow down. This could lead to HTTP badfetch error events because of network packet delay exceeding time out values. You might argue that the time out values can be increased to a point that the packets would not get dropped. The downside is that the caller can hear dead air or no prompts for an extended period of time.

Example 5-11 shows the **http client statistics** command and the meanings of the counters. This command is available in IOS 12.4T or later.

Example 5-11   *Displaying HTTP Client Statistics*

```
myrouter#show http ?
  client  Display HTTP Client info
```

```
myrouter#show http client ?
  cache       Display HTTP Client cache in details
  connection  Display HTTP Client connection info
  cookie      Display all the cookies
  history     Display the last 20 HTTP message transactions
  statistics  Display the HTTP Client statistics

myrouter#show http client statistics
    HTTP Client Statistics:
    =======================
Elapsed time: 759962960 msec   (1)


Load Count:
  total load count = 6899220        (2)
  total byte count = 26028731394    (3)
  largest file size = 624742 bytes  (4)
  smallest file size = 374 bytes    (4)


Server Response Time to Connect:
  longest response to connect = 10484 msec   (5)
  shortest response to connect = 24 msec     (5)


Server Response Time to Load:
  longest response to load = 11936 msec   (6)
  shortest response to load = 20 msec     (6)


File Load Time from Server:
  longest load time = 13124 msec   (7)
  shortest load time = 56 msec     (7)


Server Connection Count:
  max connections = 23                 (8)
  established connections = 6901185    (9)


Load Rate:
  1 hour : 123300000 bytes    (10)
  1 min  : 2055000 bytes      (10)
  1 sec  : 34250 bytes        (10)
  1 msec : 34.25 bytes        (10)
Individual Counts:
  app_requests = 8538451   (11)   app_callbacks = 8538451   (12)
  200_OK_rsp = 8512959     (13)   other_rsp = 0             (14)
  total_errors = 25492     (15)   client_timeouts = 25470        (16)
```

```
client_errs = 0              (17)   connect_errs/_timeouts =7    (18)
msg_decode_errs = 0          (19)   msg_encode_errs = 0          (20)
msg_xmit_errs = 15           (21)   write_Q_full = 0             (22)
socket_rcv_errs = 0          (23)   supported_method_errs = 0    (24)
retries = 4645               (25)   late_responses = 0           (26)
out_of_memory = 0            (27)   mem_reallocs = 1206          (28)
msg_malloced = 0             (29)   event_malloced = 45          (30)
cache_freed_by_ager = 1565   (31)
```

Decoding this output can be tricky, so following are some important observations and definitions pertaining to the values previously presented and their reference numbers in parentheses:

1. **Elapsed time:** In milliseconds since the first HTTP request

2. **Total load count:** Number of API event count

3. **Total byte count:** Downloaded from the server by API requests

4. **largest/smallest file size:** Downloaded from the server

5. **longest/shortest response to connect:** Taken by the server to establish network connection requested by the client

6. **longest/shortest response to load:** Taken by the server to fulfill a download request from the client

7. **longest/shortest load time:** Taken by the server to complete downloading the entire file

8. **max connections:** Concurrent connections

9. **established connections:** The number of currently active and previously established connections

10. **Load Rate:** Downloading rate in bytes/hour, bytes/minute, bytes/second, and bytes/msec

11. **app_requests:** Total number of GET/POST requests

12. **app_callbacks:** Total number of callbacks to application

13. **200_OK_rsp:** Total number of server messages with response code **200 OK or 304 Not Modified**

14. **other_rsp:** Total number of server messages with response code other than **200** and **304**

15. **total_errors:** Total number of errors encountered by the HTTP client

16. **client_timeouts:** Number of time outs the HTTP client has experienced, for example, response time out

17. **client_errs:** Number of HTTP client internal errors, for example, software errors, and so on

18. **connect_errs/_timeouts:** Number of failed or broken connections

19. **msg_decode_errs:** Number of server response messages that the client failed to decode the headers

20. **msg_encode_errs:** Number of send messages that the client failed to encode the head

21. **msg_xmit_errs:** Number of send messages that the client failed to transmit to the server

22. **write_Q_full:** Number of occurrences that the client failed to enter into the transmit queue a send message requested by application

23. **socket_rcv_errs:** Number of socket read error events returned by TCP

24. **supported_method_errs:** Number of unsupported methods requested by application

25. **retries:** Number of message retransmission count

26. **late_responses:** Number of messages that were decoded successfully but exceeded timeout

27. **out_of_memory:** Number of occurrences that the client failed to allocate memory from IOS

28. **mem_reallocs:** Number of occurrences that the client needed to readjust its buffer size because server response message size exceeded the allocated buffer

29. **msg_malloced:** Number of message buffers currently allocated for receiving messages from the server

30. **event_malloced:** Number of event buffers currently allocated for API requests

31. **cache_freed_by_ager:** Number of http client cache entries freed up by the background ager process

To reset all the counters listed here for the HTTP client, issue the following CLI command on the VXML Gateway, as shown in Example 5-12.

Example 5-12   *Resetting HTTP Client Statistics*

```
myrouter#clear http ?
  client  HTTP Client

myrouter#clear http client ?
  statistics  Clear the HTTP Client statistics

myrouter#clear http client statistics
```

Frequently Asked Questions

Following are the most frequently asked questions and answers about the HTTP client, the IVR Media Player, and their interaction with media files on the VXML Gateway:

What are the proper sizes for configuring the HTTP Client cache and the IVR cache memory pools?

For normal operations, the default sizes, 10 Mb for the HTTP client cache and 2 Mb for the IVR cache, should be sufficient to support a VXML Gateway playing a light load of prompts. If the VXML Gateway is constantly under a heavy load of calls with many audio prompt requests, it is recommend to use higher numbers for these two memory pools, such as 20 Mb to 30 Mb for the HTTP client cache, and a full 16 Mb for the IVR cache.

If the VXML Gateway is configured with nonstreaming mode, the HTTP client cache memory pool size should be configured with an even larger number. This is because under nonstreaming mode, the HTTP client is the owner of all audio prompt files, and it caches the entire file contents in its cache. In this case, if the VXML Gateway has ample RAM on board, it is advisable to configure the HTTP client cache memory pool to its maximum (100 Mb).

What is the proper number for configuring the HTTP client cache file size?

The default for HTTP client cache memory file size is 50 Kb. This size is approximately equal to 6 seconds of prompt playing, assuming the file is in g711uLaw CODEC format. If all the customer's files are no larger than this size, the default should work fine. But if the customer has audio files that are larger than this size, those files will not be cached by the HTTP client. Every reference to those files result in a reload.

As mentioned, the optimal audio file size is 1 minute (~500 Mb in g711uLaw) or less; it is recommended that the HTTP client cache file size should be 600 Kb. If some of the files cannot be trimmed down to 1 minute or smaller, the user can configure the number up to 10 Mb. But if the large files are seldom used, the user needs to balance between the overhead in the cache memory space and the overhead of CPU cycles for reload.

Does configuring large HTTP client cache file size waste space?

No. The size is just a limit for checking to see if a file should be cached. This configured number is used for memory allocation.

What is the proper number for configuring the IVR prompt file count?

The default for IVR memory file count is 200. This limit is the upper bound that the IVR can store up to this many audio prompt files in its own cache. When this number is reached and new files need to be cached, some swapping needs to take place before the new files can be cached. This swapping process adds overhead to the system performance.

For a lightly loaded system, 200 should be sufficient. If a customer's voice browser is constantly under load, and the total number of frequently used audio prompts is much higher than 200, a higher number should be configured. In this case, the customer should be encouraged to configure this number to the maximum of 1000 files.

How do I know if a cached file is fresh or stale?

Compare the FreshTime and the Age of the file. If the Age is smaller than the FreshTime, the file is still fresh. Otherwise, it is stale. In some cases, a stale file is still usable if the application specifies a maxstale value that is larger than the difference (Age − FreshTime).

I see an asterisk (*) next to the Age of a cached file in show http client cache. What does it mean?

It means the entry has already expired, that is, the file is stale.

I updated an audio prompt file on the HTTP server, but the http client cache does not refresh that file. Why?

Several things need to be looked at. First, the router does not automatically refresh stale files on its own. The stale files are refreshed when new incoming calls reference them.

Next, if a call were already made in an attempt to force a refresh of the audio file but the file was not refreshed, the VXML application script should be checked. How are the two attributes <maxage> and <maxstale> defined in the script? And what are the Age and FreshTime of the file in the http client cache? These numbers are all used to determine whether the http client needs to do a reload for this file from the server. See the previous section "Calculating the FreshTime" for more details.

I configured the http client cache refresh value to be 900 seconds. Why don't the cached entries expire after 15 minutes?

First, this CLI, if in effect, is not retroactive. It has no effect on the entries already in the cache. Second, the user-configured http client cache refresh value has lower priority than the FreshTime values given by the HTTP server. Server provided values are used first to calculate for the FreshTime. The user-configured refresh value is used only if the server did not specify any values for this file. Please refer to the section "Cache Aging Process" in this chapter for more details.

Which is better, streaming or nonstreaming?

For prompt playing, if the user has configured sufficient memory pool and file sizes for the http client cache so that most frequently used files can be cached, then using non-streaming mode should be more efficient. Streaming oversized audio files without enough memory space for the cache can result in multiple copies of the file in the noncached entries. Because noncached entries are temporary and nonsharable, this is a performance hit that the user needs to be aware of.

The guideline is that if the audio file can be preloaded and cached in the http client cache, the system performance would be better if nonstreaming mode is used versus streaming mode. Of course, streaming mode is the only way to go for playing huge size audio prompts.

I made a call that played a prompt, but the audio file is not being cached in the http client cache. Why?

There are several factors that can cause this effect if an audio file can be cached in the http client cache. The user can check against the following:

- Is the prompt an http prompt? The http client caches only files downloaded from HTTP servers.

- Is caching disabled by the following CLI? Check the router config for

  ```
  http client cache memory pool 0
  ```

- Has cache memory pool run out of space?

- Is the file too big to be cached in the cache? Check the following config:

  `http client cache memory file` *size*`

- If the file is okay, check for the remaining size in the cache memory pool. Is there still enough room for this file?

- Was there a fresher copy of the same file being downloaded into the cache?

- Did the audio file finish downloading?

- Has the number of IVR cached files already reached the maximum?

- The server may have instructed the client not to cache this file or cache it with a zero FreshTime. You can turn on the following **debug**:

  ```
  myrouter#debug http client socket
  ```

- Check if the server's response message contains any of the following headers:

  ```
  - Cache-Control: no-cache
  - Cache-Control: private
  - Cache-Control: no-store
  - Cache-Control: max-age = 0
  - Pragma: no-cache
  - Expires: 0
  ```

I made a call to play a fresh prompt already in the cache, but the http client cache still issued a conditional GET request to the server. Why?

In some cases, the server insists that the http client must revalidate the freshness of a file each time the file is to be used. For example, if a file contains one of the cache control headers as follows, the client checks with the server even when the cached file is still fresh:

```
- Cache-Control: must-revalidate
```

I see multiple identical audio prompts being cached in the http client cache. Why?

This can happen in streaming mode when several applications are simultaneously down-loading the same audio file. All the cached entries with the same URL are linked together in a parent-child relationship. This relationship is only brief and temporary. As soon as the child is done with its file download process, the parent is removed from the cached entry.

I see two identical query URLs being cached in the http client cache. Why?

The two query URLs may look identical but they are totally different. Query URLs are listed in the cached entries with their attribute values masked out for privacy protection. For example, consider the two query URLs with different attribute values as follows:

http://www.myserver.com/app/query.php?id=john

http://www.myserver.com/app/query.php?id=jane

These two URLs will be displayed as the following in the cached entries of **show http client cache** output:

http://www.myserver.com/app/query.php?id=******

http://www.myserver.com/app/query.php?id=******

Why is the file size listed in the http client cache smaller than its actual size?

In streaming mode, the HTTP client does not save the entire audio file in its cache; rather, the IVR Media Player does. The HTTP client caches only the first chunk of data that it receives from the HTTP server. So for a large audio file that cannot be sent to the client in one chunk, you can see this situation. In this scenario, the file size in the http client cache output reflects only the data content size of the file in the first chunk. Of course, if the file is small enough, you will not see this discrepancy.

What is the maximum URL length supported by the http client during an http get operation?

There are no standards as to what the maximum URL length should be. On the other hand, common sense should be observed that excessively long URLs are most likely constructed by mistake. VXML application scripts should yield URLs as short as possible to minimize communication overhead. In some occasions, query strings must be appended to URLs to identify certain actions for callers' transactions. As VXML applications get more sophisti-cated, URLs in the http get operation have a tendency to grow longer. As a result, the maximum URL length supported by the IVR http client has been increased from 2048 characters to 4096 characters. This upgrade applies to 12.4(15)T7.

Any attempt to send a URL longer than the maximum length can cause an error such as the following to display, if debug voip application error is enabled:

```
status=httpc error -5=internal client transmit error
```

or the following, if debug http client error is enabled:

```
iostream_write_line FAILED - URL too long or system out of memory
```

Summary

This chapter focused on a subject that is not well covered in existing Unified CVP documentation. Although some perceptions exist around streaming and nonstreaming modes and their behavior with and without caches, the reality of their behavior is quite different. The mystery of how the IVR cache works together with the HTTP client cache was solved. This chapter also provided some good insight as to how the HTTP client and IVR Media Player maintain their caches for modes where they are truly the owner.

In addition to gaining more knowledge around how VXML Gateways behave with media files in different streaming and nonstreaming modes, this chapter included some great CLI examples on how to configure, verify, and maintain each client and their respective caches.

The most important takeaways in the chapter were provided in the form of frequently asked questions. By including some detailed answers to these common questions, the key points of the chapter were summarized for future reference.

Understanding how a VXML Gateway interacts with media files and the option available for configuring its behavior is a critical skill set to comprehending the entire Unified CVP solution. At the end of the day, the delivery to and the quality of a callers experience while in the IVR is the responsibility of the VXML Gateway. It must be correctly configured to ensure the quality results that callers expect.

The next chapter addresses networking and security concerns for the Unified CVP solution. It also examines the metrics that should be implemented to conduct sizing exercises around the solution.

Recommended Reading and Resources

Cisco Documentation, *Cisco Unified Customer Voice Portal (CVP) 8.x Solution Reference Network Design (*SRND), http://www.cisco.com/en/US/docs/voice_ip_comm/cust_contact/contact_center/customer_voice_portal/srnd/8x/cvp8xsrnd.pdf.

Cisco Documentation, *Cisco Unified Customer Voice Portal Configuration Guides*, http://www.cisco.com/en/US/partner/products/sw/custcosw/ps1006/products_installation_and_configuration_guides_list.html.

Cisco Documentation, *User Guide for Cisco Unified CVP VXML Server and Cisco Unified Call Studio*, Release 8.0(1), http://www.cisco.com/en/US/docs/voice_ip_comm/cust_contact/contact_center/customer_voice_portal/cvp8_0/user/guide/cvp_801_vxml.pdf.

Cisco Documentation, *Cisco IOS TcL IVR and VoiceXML Application Guide—Release 12.3(14)T and later*, http://www.cisco.com/en/US/docs/ios/voice/ivr/configuration/guide/ ivrapp02.html.

Kristol, D. RFC 2388, "HTTP State Management Mechanism," http://tools.ietf.org/html/rfc2109, February 1997.

Fielding R., Gettys J., Mogul J., Frystyk H., Masinter L., Leach P., and Berners-Lee T., RFC 2388, "Hypertext Transfer Protocol—HTTP/1.1," http://tools.ietf.org/html/rfc2616, June 1999.

Chapter 6

Sizing, Networking, and Security Considerations

This chapter covers the following subjects:

- **Unified CVP sizing:** Sizing approaches relating to native and non-native components.

- **Quality of service:** Traffic classification, marking, and its relevance to Unified CVP.

- **Network latency:** The impact of latency with Unified CVP and mitigation techniques.

- **Security:** Ports, communication models, and server hardening available with Unified CVP.

Unified CVP Sizing

To effectively size a contact center, an engineer must first consider all calls, their types, and states they currently operate in. These considerations must also be performed with the worst case or busiest hour in mind. In other words, consider the busiest hour of operation for a contact center. What would the call volume look like, and how would it be distributed between different call states? Furthermore, how do these call states impact or use native and non-native components? Begin by examining the call states to get a feel for what the call state refers to. Following are three basic call states that are a good start that represent most calls that should be considered for sizing:

- **Self-service:** Defines calls executing applications using the Unified CVP VXML Server.

- **Queue and collect:** Defines calls in queue for an agent or executing prompt and collect type self-service applications.

- **Talking:** Defines calls connected to agents or to third-party Time-division Multiplexing (TDM) Voice Response Unit (VRU) applications.

When counting calls that fall into these different calls states, consider only calls using the Unified CVP components. Following are some additional considerations when trying to decide whether a call should be counted:

- **Calls transferred using VoIP to VRU or agent:** These calls should be counted as being in a state of "talking." These types of calls continue to use a port on the Ingress Gateway and a port on the Unified CVP Call Server because the Call Server continues to monitor the call for take back and transfer purposes.

- **Calls transferred using TDM to VRU or agent:** These calls should also be counted as being in a state of "talking." As previously stated for VoIP transfers, these types of transfers also use a TDM port on the Ingress Gateway and potentially a TDM port on the Egress Gateway with the Unified CVP Call Server still providing call control using a port on the Call Server.

- **Blind or warm transfers:** These are call legs that may have been transferred back into Unified CVP for queuing or self-service via either a blind or warm transfer mechanism. When a warm transfer is implemented, this can actually use two ports on the Unified CVP Call Server; one for the originating call leg and one for the transfer call leg because the Call Server can treat these as two distinct call control sessions. Because these calls are usually small in volume, they are overlooked during sizing exercises. These types of transfers usually account for only 5 percent to 10 percent of the total call volume. However, some customers may have transfer volumes as high as 20 percent.

- **Other transfers:** If the call is transferred using a different mechanism such as *8 Take Back and Transfer (TNT), hookflash, Two B Channel Transfers (TBCT), or an Intelligent Contact Management (ICM) Network Interface Controller (NIC), neither the gateway nor the Unified CVP can play a role in the call. Because both resources have reclaimed their means, these types of transfers should not be counted as talking calls.

> **Note**   When determining the call state, it has nothing to do with whether the agents are Unified CCE or ACD agents. It doesn't it matter whether the customer intends to use the Unified CVP's capability to retrieve and redeliver the call to another agent or back into self-service. The solution must be sized for the number of ports in use for calls in a talking-to-agents state. Even though licenses for those ports do not need to be purchased when using Unified CCE agents, TDM agents do require a Call Director license, as described at the end of Chapter 2, "Unified CVP Architecture Overview."[1]

Figure 6-1 shows how a typical inbound call occupies a VXML gateway for queuing, a Unified CVP port for call control, and eventually a Unified CCE agent during the "talking" state of a call. This same scenario applies to a transferred call.

Any ring delay must be calculated and added to the ingress port occupancy when calculating total ingress port usage. Furthermore, when the Unified CCE agent is in a state of wrap-up, the call has already been disconnected, and ports are not in use for the ingress and Unified CVP Call Server's perspective. Lastly, prior to being transferred to a live agent, a VXML gateway port is used for call treatment on the VRU leg of the call. All these segments must be taken into account when considering how to size the Unified CVP solution, in addition to devices such as load balancers, media servers, and even Session Initiation Protocol (SIP) proxy services.

After you have the contact center call state profile collected and accounted for, consider the busiest period call arrival rate in terms of calls per second (CPS). This is commonly referred to as the Busy Hour Call Attempts or BHCA.

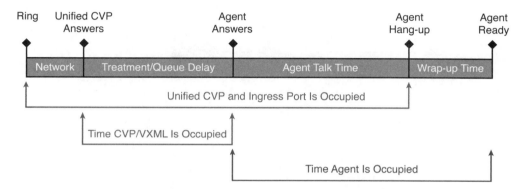

Figure 6-1   *Unified CVP Inbound Call Resource Occupancy*

Erlang Traffic Models

The Erlang traffic models were invented by a Danish mathematician named Agner Krarup Erlang (January 1, 1878–February 3, 1929). The goals of these traffic models are to determine exactly how many service-providing elements should be provided to satisfy users without wasteful over-provisioning. The Erlang Traffic Models focuses on two basic formulas: Erlang-C and Erlang-B.

Erlang-C is used when sizing call center agents where calls are queued in and no agents are available. This module does have some assumptions:

- Calls are presented randomly to the servers.

- Callers finding all agents busy will be queued, not blocked.

Erlang-B is used when sizing Interactive Voice Response (IVR) ports and Gateway ports such as Public Switched Telephone Network (PSTN) trunks. This module also makes some assumptions about the traffic:

- Calls are presented randomly.

- A percentage of calls are lost or blocked, not queued.

Figure 6-2 shows where each model is applied to calculate how many Erlang units would represent traffic at the depicted components.

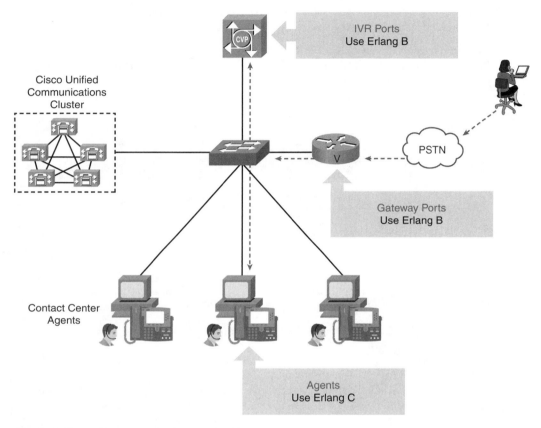

Figure 6-2   *Erlang-B and Erlang-C Traffic*

You can find several decent Erlang Calculators on the web. However, following are a few examples:

■   VOIP Calculator: http://www.voip-calculator.com/calculator/

■   Erlang-B Calculators: http://www.erlang.com/calculator/erlib/

■   Erlang-C Calculators: http://www.erlang.co.uk/ccc.htm

Use the calculators to execute a simple use case for sizing a contact center for ACME Company. For this use case, assume some basic parameters provided by the customer:

■   Service Level Goal: 90 percent of calls answered within 10 seconds

■   Maximum number of calls received during the busiest time: 10,000 calls

- Busiest time: 8 a.m. until 9 a.m. in the morning

- Call Talk Time: 3 minutes with no after-call work time

- Time to wait before abandoned: 30 seconds

Figure 6-3 shows what occurs when these values are plugged into a Erlang-C calculator providing total agents, Ingress Gateway PSTN trunks, and CVP IVR queue ports required to meet these requirements.

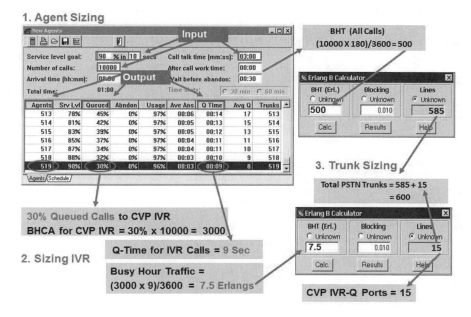

Figure 6-3 *Erlang-B and C Calculations for Agent, Queue Ports, and PSTN Trunk Sizing*

During Step 1, agent sizing, the Erlang-C calculator outputs the total number of agents required to meet the expected service level for the call volume and talk times provided by the customer. By taking the total number of expected calls and their number of seconds per call that the agent will be talking to the caller and then normalizing this back to hourly units, you can calculate the Busy-Hour Traffic (BHT) for all calls as 500 Erlang units. By plugging this back into the Erlang-B calculator (refer to Figure 6-3), you can calculate the ports required on the Ingress Gateway minus ports used by queued calls.

In addition, the output from the Erlang-C calculator provides additional information used during Step 2: sizing the Unified CVP IVR. For example, the average queue time per call and the percentage of calls expected to be queued are used to determine how many Erlang units are represented by queued calls. By taking this value and plugging it into the Erlang-B calculator, the number of lines or ports required to handle this traffic when it is queued is calculated. In Figure 6-3, 15 Unified CVP Queue ports are required to handle the calls expected to be queued. This is different than the average queue size of 9 reported by the Erlang-C calculator.

The final step is to add the values calculated in Step 1 and Step 2 to complete the Ingress Gateway port sizing. This calculation is 585 ports from Erlang-C calculation combined with 15 ports from the Erlang-B calculation for Unified CVP Queue ports, providing a total ingress port requirement of 600 (refer to Figure 6-3).

Cisco also provides an alternative tool to sizing call centers resources including Unified CVP, Unified IP Interactive Voice Response (IP-IVR), Unified CCE, and Unified CM. This tool is located on the web at http://tools.cisco.com/cucst. However, it is only accessible by registered Cisco partners and their resources. Figure 6-4 shows this tool with the customer requirements that were provided earlier plugged in.

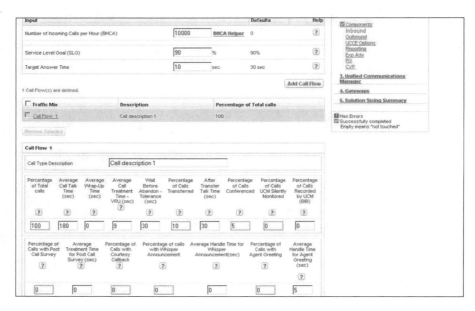

Figure 6-4   *Cisco Unified Communications Sizing Tool*

The Cisco sizing tool provides sizing pertaining to the entire solution and not just agents, Unified CVP Ports, and Ingress Gateway ports. One immediate observation is the capability to accommodate individual call treatment characteristics per call flow instead of treating all calls the same. This is something that the standard Erlang calculators don't provide. They simply leave it up to the operator to split up the call treatment characteristics and manually align them with the call volumes. (It's not to say that the same calculation could not be performed by doing the math.) However, by segmenting the call flows and applying a percentage, the usability of the tool increases. This tool has quite a few options based on individual product sizing and solution-level sizing. It requires some time to learn and understand how these options apply to different solution requirements.

It is not always possible to collect specific call volumes from all customers. Most customers won't have any of their call volumes. For those that do, just be sure to trust but verify the call volumes they report. In situations in which the customer cannot provide any call volumes, the best action is to provide a capacity model for the customers solution. A capacity model approach to sizing simply says that by implementing a bill of materials for the Unified CVP solution, the customer has "X" capacity. This approach places the customers on notice that if they exceed this capacity, they need to add more capacity to the solution.

The following are additional considerations and best practices when provisioning a call center:

■ It is always better to over-provision Unified CVP and Ingress Gateway ports. The cost of this extra capacity will be much less than the cost of lost revenue, bad service, or even potential legal risk of not meeting an SLA.

■ If applicable, always consider seasonal busy hours versus average busy hours. In addition, take into account marketing campaigns in which call volumes can dramatically increase.

■ Consider agent-related issues pertaining to staffing, availability, attendance, adherence to their schedule, occupancy, different shifts, different time zones, and even the reuse or consolidation of facilities.

■ Always make sure to provision extra Unified CVP IVR and Ingress Gateway ports for growth and unforeseen fluctuations. A good rule of thumb is to reserve approximately 20 percent extra capacity.

■ Take into account any high-availability roles that the location may be responsible for. In other words if you size a backup data center location for a contact center, be sure to provide enough capacity to meet the disaster recovery role of the location. Take heed in preventing a disaster to occur that could leave one side of the solution overwhelmed because it was not correctly sized to accommodate the additional call volume.

Sizing the Unified Call Server

Unified CVP Call Servers are sized based on two elements, the number of calls they handle and their maximum call arrival rate or calls per second (cps). Each Call ServerCall Server can handle 1200 SIP calls or 500 H.323 calls. Each Call Server is further limited to a sustained call arrival rate of 14 calls per second (cps) for SIP and 7 cps for H.323. However, these numbers apply only to deployment models where the Call Server actually performs call control duties with respect to SIP or H.323. The larger of these two calculations determines the number of Unified CVP Call Servers required for the solution:

```
((Self Service)+(Queue and Collect)+Talking)/1200[or 500 doe  H.323], rounded up
```

or

```
(Average call arrival rate)/14, rounded up [7 for H.323]
```

If a Call Server provides both H.323 and SIP call control services, prorate the performance used for each call type. For example, assume if 70 percent of the call will be H.323 and 30 percent SIP, the maximum load in terms of active calls would be

```
70%*(500 H.323 calls)+30%*(1200 SIP calls) = 780 active calls
```

Caution   Calls delivered to the Cisco Unified Communications Manager (CUCM) cluster must be load balanced among the subscribers that have been designated to handle inbound agent calls. These inbound calls must not exceed two calls per second (cps) per subscriber. It is also a good idea, if possible, to designate a pair of subscribers to handle all inbound calls that need to be delivered to Unified CCE agents. It can segment this type of call load away from subscribers responsible for the registration and control of Unified CCE agent IP Phones.

Table 6-1 summarizes the Call Server rates by server model and number.

In addition to sizing the actual Call Server, the storage allocation for log files on the Call Server must also be correctly set to accommodate the estimated calls per second. It is considered best practice to reserve enough storage space to accommodate between 5 and 7 days of logs. Following is the formula used to calculate the estimated space per day (in Gigabytes) for the Call Server Directory log file:

```
3.5 * R
 Where: R = number of calls per second (cps)
```

Tip   You can configure the log directory size via the Operations Console's Infrastructure tab for a specific Unified CVP Call Server. This size must be set individually for each Call Server and cannot be set globally for all Call Servers.

Table 6-1   *Call Server Call Rate by Server Model Number*

Server Model	MCS-7845-I3-CCE2	Supported UCS Hardware
Maximum SIP Calls	1200	900
Maximum H.323 Calls	500	—
Sustained Calls per Second (SIP)	14	10
Sustained Calls per Second (H.323)	7	—

Sizing the Unified CVP VXML Server

When sizing the Unified CVP VXML Server, first consider whether the request will use HTTP or Hypertext Transfer Protocol Secure (HTTPS). If HTTP is used, sizing the VXML Server is simple. One Unified CVP VXML Server can handle up to 1200 calls. Following is a simple formula for sizing the VXML Server:

```
Number of VXML Servers needed = Calls / 1200 (rounded up)
 Where the Calls = the number of calls that are in the VXML Server
```

Remember that the value of "Calls" should represent only the calls currently in the Unified CVP VXML Server via a self-service application at the busiest moment for the contact center. Table 6-2 summarizes this capacity when using HTTP.

Table 6-2 *Unified CVP VXML Server HTTP Rates by Server Model Number*

Server Model	MCS-7845-I3-CCE2	Supported UCS Hardware
Maximum Simultaneous Calls	1200	900

So what are the impacts of using HTTPS rather than HTTP? Because of the large processing overhead of HTTPS, the Tomcat application server can achieve a maximum of only 100 simultaneous connections, depending on its configuration. Table 6-3 provides these limits based on different Call Server Types, Applications, and Call Flow Models discussed earlier in this book.

Following are some addition considerations when using HTTPS with Unified CVP:

■ Cisco IOS Release 12.4(15)T5 or later release is required on the VXML gateway to support the HTTPS option. (Mainline Cisco Internetwork Operating System [IOS] currently is not supported.)

■ The HTTPS option has not been tested with co-resident Unified CVP Call Server and Unified CVP VXML Server and hence is not a supported configuration.

Table 6-3 *Call Server Call Rate by Server Model Number*

Unified CVP Call Server Type, Application and Call Flow Model	MCS-7845-I3-CCE2	Supported UCS Hardware
Unified CVP VXML Server Max Simultaneous HTTPS Connection with WebSphere (Standalone Call Flow Model)	250	275 @ 3 cps
Unified CVP VXML Server Max Simultaneous HTTPS Connections with Tomcat (Standalone Call Flow Model)	100	275 @ 3 cps
Unified CVP VXML Server Max Simultaneous HTTPS Connection with WebSphere (Comprehensive Call Flow Model)	100	275 @ 3 cps
Unified CVP VXML Server Max Simultaneous HTTPS Connections with Tomcat (Comprehensive Call Flow Model)	100	275 @ 3 cps

Caution   Cisco recommends the following configuration on the Cisco IOS VXML gateway when using HTTPS:

```
http client connection persistence
http client cache memory pool 15000
http client cache memory file 1000
```

Not having these configuration settings can severely impact the performance and sizing of the VXML Gateway and the over solution for HTTPS.

Sizing the Unified CVP Reporting Server

When determining how to size a Unified CVP Reporting Server, you must take several variables into account. Because a deployment can have different requirements for how the VXML application is designed, which impacts the amount of reporting data it may generate, you should consider the following factors:

- Types of elements used in the applications

- Granularity of data required

- Call flow users take through the application

- Length of calls

- Number of calls

To accurately size the reporting server, estimate the total amount of reporting data generated by the VXML applications. A Cisco MCS-7845 server can handle 420 messages per second. To determine the total messages per second for all the VXML applications, complete the following steps:

Step 1.   Estimate the number of minutes customers will spend receiving VXML call treatment by the application.

Step 2.   Estimate the calls per second (cps) the application will receive.

Step 3.   Estimate the number of reporting messages for the application. Later in this section these reporting messages are outlined and correlated with different scripting elements for reference.

After the data noted in the Steps 1 through 3 is collected, use the following formula to estimate the number of reporting messages generated per second, per call, for each VXML application:

$$A\# = (((\%CPS * CPS * MSG)/MIN)/60)$$

Where:

A# = The number of estimated reporting messages per second for an application. Complete one calculation per application (A1, A2, A3,...,An)

CPS = The number of calls per second.

%CPS = The percentage of calls that use the VXML application.

MSG = The number of reporting messages this application generates. Refer to Table 6-4 for reporting message details per VXML application element or activity.

Min = Amount of time spent in the application (in minutes).

60 = The number of seconds in one minute.[2]

Table 6-4   *Number of Reporting Messages per Element or Activity*

Element or Activity	Number of Reporting Messages (Unfiltered)
Start	2
End	2
Subdialog_start	2
Subdialog_return	2
Hotlink	2
HotEvent	2
Transfer without Audio	2
Currency without Audio	2
Flag	2
Action	2
Decision	2
Application Transfer	2
VXML Error	2
CallCMInfo (per call)	2
Session Variable (per change)	2
Custom Log (per item)	2
Play (Audio file or TTS)	2
Get Input (DTMF)	5
Get Input (ASR)	9
Form	10
Digit_with_confirm	20
Currency_with_confirm	20
ReqICMLabel	30

After collecting the reporting messages per minute for each of the applications, add them all together to provide the total reporting messages per minute for the deployment.

$$A(total) = A1 + A2 + \ldots + An^3$$

This produces the total number of reporting messages per minute for your deployment. If this value is less than the capacity of a single Unified CVP Reporting Server, 420 reporting messages per minute, you can use a single reporting server. However, if the value of A(total) exceeds 420 reporting messages per minute, you must use multiple reporting servers and partition the VXML applications to use different reporting servers. For details on how to partition the VXML applications to use multiple reporting servers, refer to the *Cisco Unified Customer Voice Portal (CVP) Solution Reference Network Design (SRND), Release 8.x*, page 14-9.

Tables 6-4 through 6-8 are also found in *Chapter 14* of the *Cisco Unified Customer Voice Portal (CVP) Solution Reference Network Design (SRND), Release 8.x.* However, they are included here for your reference pertaining to the number of reporting messages per minute certain VXML application elements generate and some simple examples of how to estimate messages per minute for applications that vary in complexity.

One of the big challenges of sizing the reporting server is that most implementations take place with the reporting server being deployed before any VXML application design or development occurs. This presents an issue because the impact of the VXML applications on the reporting server is unknown until the applications are laid out and can account for the amount of reporting messages per minute that will be generated. With that said, use the following tables to estimate this capacity by classifying the VXML applications into four categories of complexity:

- Low

- Medium (Dual-Tone Multifrequency [DTMF] Only)

- Medium (ASR)

- High (ASR)

Tables 6-5 through 6-8 provide examples and calculations for these complexity levels.

Table 6-5   *Low Complexity (16 Reporting Messages per Minute per Call)*

Element or Activity	Approximate Number of Reporting Messages
Start	2
Subdialog_start	2
Play element	2
Play element	2
Play element	2
Play element	2
Subdialog_end	2
End	2

Table 6-6   *Medium Complexity DTMF (39 Reporting Messages per Minute per Call)*

Element or Activity	Approximate Number of Reporting Messages
Start	2
Subdialog_start	2
Play element	2
Get Input	5
Play element	2
Get Input	5
Form	10
Input	5
Transfer with audio	2
Subdialog_end	2
End	2

Table 6-7   *Medium Complexity ASR (51 Reporting Messages per Minute per Call)*

Element or Activity	Approximate Number of Reporting Messages
Start	2
Subdialog_start	2
Play element	2
Get Input	9
Play element	2
Get Input	9
Form	10
Input	9
Transfer with audio	2
Subdialog_end	2
End	2

Table 6-8 *High Complexity ASR (107 Reporting Messages per Minute per Call)*

Element or Activity	Approximate Number of Reporting Messages
Start	2
Subdialog_start	2
ICMrequestlabel	30
Form	10
ASR capture	9
Digit with confirm	20
Form	10
Digit with confirm	20
Subdialog_end	2
End	2

Sizing Unified CVP Co-Residency

As discussed in previous chapters, you can install several native Unified CVP components on the same Unified CVP Call Server in a co-resident deployment model. In review, the three components found in a typical co-resident Call Server deployment are as follows:

■ Unified CVP Call Server (Call Control)

■ Unified CVP VXML Server (Self-Service VXML Applications)

■ Media Server (Web Server using IIS or Apache)

This creates some unique challenges when trying to size a co-resident Unified CVP Call Server because of all the limitations that each component may have pertaining to its own individual sizing requirements. Following are some co-resident sizing limitations to consider when attempting sizing for a co-resident server:

- A SIP-based co-resident server can handle 1200 SIP calls and 1200 VXML Server sessions while maintaining its previously mentioned call arrival rate of 14 calls per second (cps). This implies that each server would require only one 1200 port server license to license this type of deployment.

- An H.323 co-resident server can handle 500 H.323 calls and 500 VXML Server sessions while maintaining a call arrival rate of 6 calls per second (cps). This implies that each server would require only one 500 port server license to license this type of deployment.

For the co-resident media server, it can service the same number of calls as those mentioned for SIP and H.323. More specifically, when using SIP, the co-resident media server can handle up to 1200 calls. Similarly, when using H.323, the co-resident media server can simultaneously handle up to 500 calls. These limits require that prompt caching is enabled on the VXML gateways. Furthermore, the use of a load balancers should be a consideration for larger deployments to ensure that media fetch requests are load balanced across multiple co-resident media servers.

It is time to analyze a simple co-resident sizing example and put all these numbers to work. Assume that a deployment required the following sizing requirements:

- 1000 self-service ports
- 500 queue and collect ports
- 3000 simultaneous calls to agents

Note   Self-Service refers to a call that uses SIP or H.323 call control and runs an application on the VXML Server. Queue and collect refers to a call that uses SIP and H.323 call control, yet runs an application using Microapps only on the Call Server via Unified ICM.

Use the following formula to calculate the number required of Unified CVP Call Servers:

```
((Self Service)+(Queue and Collect)+Talking)/1200 [500 for H.323]
((1000)+(500)+3000)/1200 = 4 Call Servers (Rounded Up)
```

In addition, you can place the reporting server as co-resident with the Unified CVP Call Server, but only for Standalone VXML deployments. Typically, a Call Server is not needed in a standalone deployment. However, if reporting is necessary, a reporting server needs to be deployed. Furthermore, because the Call Server does not process any SIP or H.323 calls from a call control perspective, the reporting server is the only application using resources on the co-resident server because it is relaying reporting data from the VXML Server. This is the only role offered by the Call Server. It does not significantly impact the performance in this model. The sizing information for a co-resident reporting server is the same as presented later in this chapter when discussing sizing a Unified CVP Reporting Server.

Note   An additional sizing consideration for VMWare deployments using the UCS hardware platform is Input/Output Operations per Second (IOPS). This is critical when virtualizing and sizing Unified CVP components because the hardware hosting the components must meet their specific IOPS specifications. Following is the IOPS required when virtualizing these Unified CVP native components:

Call Server with VXM Server co-resident:

> Average IOPS: 380
>
> Max IOPS: 1536
>
> 95th Percentile: 797

Reporting Server:

> Average IOPS: 692
>
> Max IOPS: 3403
>
> 95th Percentile: 2024

For more details on performance numbers pertaining to the UCS platform, refer to the Cisco docwiki site for *Virtualization for Unified CVP* located on the web at http://docwiki.cisco.com/wiki/Virtualization_for_Unified_CVP.

Sizing SIP Proxy Servers (CUPS and CUSP)

The key variable to sizing any SIP Proxy server is calls per second (cps). Both Cisco Unified Presence Server (CUPS) and Cisco Unified SIP Proxy (CUSP) are sized based on the calls per second using the SIP Proxy service. However, there is one important caveat that usually is dismissed when performing this calculation. A typical ingress call can actually generate four calls into the SIP Proxy server. This is because an ingress call must use the SIP proxy to connect to Unified CVP on the switch leg, process ringback, connect to the VRU, transfer to an agent, and even handle subsequent transfers. A typical incoming call is transferred by Unified CVP four times, so the inbound PSTN call rate should be multiplied by four when calculating the calls per second using the SIP Proxy server.

Table 6-9 outlines the Cisco Unified Presence Server's (CUPS) capacities based on the server model.

Table 6-9   *Call Handling Capacities of Cisco Unified Presence Servers*

Cisco Server Model	Recording Function	UDP	TCP
MCS-7825	Record-Route On	200 cps	100 cps
	Record-Route Off	300 cps	300 cps
MCS-7835	Record-Route On	200 cps	100 cps
	Record-Route Off	300 cps	300 cps
MCS-7845	Record-Route On	600 cps	200 cps
	Record-Route Off	1100 cps	500 cps

One significant factor in sizing for a SIP Proxy server is whether Record-Route is enabled or disabled. Record-Route informs the SIP Proxy to insert the call route history into the SIP header, which obviously increases the overhead of the SIP Proxy server while reducing its overall performance and capacity. It is for this reason that Record-Route must be disabled when deploying a SIP Proxy server for Unified CVP. As previously displayed, following are similar capacity numbers for the CUSP (see Table 6-10).

Table 6-10   *Call Handling Capacities of Cisco Unified SIP Proxy*

CUSP Feature License	NME-CUSP-522	
	Standard SIP Mode (SIP Requests/Sec)	Lite Mode (SIP Requests/Sec)
FL-CUSP-10	10	10
FL-CUSP-30	30	30
FL-CUSP-100	100	450
	SM-SRE-700-K9	
Standard SIP Mode (SIP Requests/Sec)	Lite Mode (SIP Requests/Sec)	
FL-CUSP-2	2	5
FL-CUSP-10	10	25
FL-CUSP-30	30	75

Table 6-10 *Call Handling Capacities of Cisco Unified SIP Proxy*

CUSP Feature License	NME-CUSP-522	
	Standard SIP Mode (SIP Requests/Sec)	Lite Mode (SIP Requests/Sec)
FL-CUSP-100	100	450
	SM-SRE-700-K9	
	Standard SIP Mode (SIP Requests/Sec)	Lite Mode (SIP Requests/Sec)
FL-CUSP-2	2	5
FL-CUSP-10	10	25
FL-CUSP-30	30	75
FL-CUSP-100	100	450
FL-CUSP-200	200	750

The same rules apply to CUSP as CUPS for each ingress call being the equivalent of four SIP requests. Performance is limited by both the number of incoming SIP requests specified in the feature license and module processing capability. With Cisco Unified SIP Proxy version 8.5 and onward, Cisco Unified SIP Proxy can be operated in Standard and Lite modes. Standard mode provides the standard performance described by the feature license installed. Lite mode enables Cisco Unified SIP Proxy to run at a higher SIP requests/second rate when the Record-Route feature is disabled.

Sizing Ingress and VoiceXML Gateways

As discussed in previous chapters, gateways can be implemented with Unified CVP either as Ingress, Egress, dedicated VoiceXML or even a combination of and the three capabilities. Sizing these gateways is mostly dependent on their dedicated roles or their combined roles in a solution. In addition, if Automatic Speech Recognition (ASR) or Text To Speech (TTS) is introduced as a feature for the gateways to contend with, their capacities should be adjusted accordingly. For standalone Ingress or Egress Gateways, it is fair to say that they can be sized based on the number of TDM cables that can be connected to them. However, for gateways combined or VoiceXML-only, you must ensure that the overall CPU usage is less than 75 percent on average. The following factors affect CPU usage:

■ Calls per second (cps)

■ Maximum concurrent calls

■ Maximum concurrent VoiceXML sessions[4]

However, before attempting to size a gateway, make sure to apply the techniques discussed earlier in this chapter to accurately estimate the maximum number of PSTN trunks or Digit Signal 0s (DS0s) and VoiceXML IVR ports needed to support the call volume generated by the entire solution. After the call volume requirements have been nailed down, the next step is to decide what roles the gateways play in the solution. Tables 6-11 through 6-14, also found in Chapter 7 of the *Cisco Unified Customer Voice Portal (CVP) Solution Reference Network Design (SRND), Release 8.x*, provide details for different hardware and software versions for their tested capacity against different roles that could potentially run on the gateway. These tables are provided again here for reference and consumption. Table 6-11 references the newer version of the IOS software 15.1.1.T, whereas the other three tables examine older Series Integrated Services Router (ISR) platforms running IOS 12.4.15 or greater, excluding 15.1.1.T.

Table 6-11   *VoiceXML Gateway CPU Capacity for IOS 15.1.1T*

Platform	VoiceXML Only		VoiceXML+PSTN		Memory
	DTMF	ASR	DTMF	ASR	Recommended
1861	5	3	4	2	256 MB
2801	7	4	5	3	256 MB
2811	30	20	23	15	256 MB
2821	48	32	36	25	256 MB
2851	60	40	45	30	512 MB
3825	130	85	102	68	512 MB
3845	160	105	125	83	512 MB
AS5000XM	200	135	155	104	512 MB
2901	12	8	9	6	2 GB
2911	60	40	47	31	2 GB
2921	90	60	71	48	2 GB
2951	120	80	95	64	2 GB
3925	240	160	190	127	2 GB
3945	340	228	270	180	2 GB
3925E	700	470	570	375	2 GB
3945E	850	570	680	450	2 GB

The capacity illustrated in Table 6-11 is based on the use of Internetwork Operating System (IOS) 15.1.1T with basic calls utilizing G.711 codec and egressing out the Ethernet port. Obviously, if transcoding is a requirement and the expectation is that this transcoding will be accomplished using Digital signal processors (DSP) that are not dedicated via a DSP farm, the capacity of the router will be impacted. To avoid this, it is best practice to build a dedicated DSP farm that would be implemented for transcoding between different codecs. This dedicated DSP farm enables the Ingress, Egress, and VoiceXML gateways to deliver on these capacity numbers without having to provide transcoding services. The numbers illustrated in Table 6-11 also assumes that the CPU should never exceed 75 percent for ISR routers and 80 percent for 5000XM series routers.

Prior to IOS release 15.0.1M or 15.1.1T, most gateways in the Unified CVP solution were based off the 1800, 2800, 3800, and 5000XM route series and used IOS Release 12.4(15)T or greater but prior to 15.0.1M or 15.1.1T. Table 6-12 provides capacity information for these older hardware and software platforms.

Table 6-12   *VoiceXML Gateway CPU Capacity for IOS 12.4(15)T5 and Greater but Prior to IOS 15.0.1M or 15.1.1T*

Platform	VoiceXML Only		VoiceXML + PSTN		Memory
	DTMF	ASR	DTMF	ASR	Recommended
1861	5	4	4	2	256 MB
2801	7	6	6	4	256 MB
2811	30	24	25	20	256 MB
2821	45	36	36	30	256 MB
2851	60	56	56	48	512 MB
3825	180	140	210	130	512 MB
3845	200	155	230	145	512 MB
AS5000XM	240	192	240	160	512 MB (Default)

Tables 6-13 and 6-14 illustrate the impact of complex VoiceXML applications executing on the gateway. They also show the impact of HTTPS transactions on their overall capacity by role. These numbers are based on the assumption that additional activities on the gateways consist of basic routing and IP connectivity. If other integrated services are provided such as fax, security, nonagent normal business calls, and so forth, the capacity numbers provided should be adjusted accordingly to accommodate the additional overhead.

Another key observation is that the capacity numbers provided for the Cisco 3825 and 3845 ISRs are higher when the Ingress and VoiceXML roles are co-resident, both existing on the same router. When using separate routers to provide the Ingress and VoiceXML role for the solution, the routers must packetize and depacketize conversations that require valuable CPU cycles. However, when these roles exist on the same router, the packets never leave the router. They are simply handled by the router internally, saving on valuable CPU cycles, which can be used to service additional VoiceXML sessions. As before, these capacity numbers assume that the CPU of an ISR and AS5000XM router should never exceed 75 percent and 80 percent, respectively.

Table 6-13   *VoiceXML Gateway CPU Capacity for IOS 12.4(15)T5 and Greater but Prior to IOS 15.0.1M or 15.1.1T Executing Intense JavaScript Applications*

Platform	VoiceXML Only		VoiceXML + PSTN		Memory
	DTMF	ASR	DTMF	ASR	Recommended
1861	2	2	2	2	256 MB
2801	3	2	2	2	256 MB
2811	10	5	10	5	256 MB
2821	20	15	15	15	256 MB
2851	30	25	25	20	512 MB
3825	70	55	85	50	512 MB
3845	80	60	96	60	512 MB
AS5000XM	105	85	110	70	512 MB (Default)

Table 6-14   *VoiceXML Gateway CPU Capacity for IOS 12.4(15)T5 and Greater, but Prior to IOS 15.0.1M or 15.1.1T Using HTTPS*

Platform	VoiceXML Only		VoiceXML + PSTN		Memory
	DTMF	ASR	DTMF	ASR	Recommended
1861	3	2	2	2	256 MB
2801	4	4	4	2	256 MB
2811	15	10	15	10	256 MB
2821	30	20	20	15	256 MB
2851	40	35	30	25	512 MB
3825	115	90	125	75	512 MB
3845	125	100	135	85	512 MB
AS5000XM	155	120	138	95	512 MB (Default)

Because the infinite combinations of traffic mixes and subsequent tests, Cisco does not specifically test or qualify every possibility. The capacities provided should be used as guidelines and adjusted accordingly depending on additional services or traffic that gateway may be expected to process. As always, use a worst-case scenario to size gateways if you cannot predict or calculate what kinds of calls will be offered to the VoiceXML gateway. In addition, when running VoiceXML services on one of the Cisco 1800, 2800, 3800, 2900, or 3900 Series gateways, purchase an additional license such as FL-VoiceXML-1 or FL-VoiceXML-12.

The following links should also be reviewed to ensure the concurrent call load or arrival rates do not exceed the listed capacity:

■   Model Comparison:
     http://www.cisco.com/en/US/products/ps10536/prod_series_comparison.html

■   Gateway Sizing for Contact Center Traffic:
     http://cisco.biz/en/US/docs/voice_ip_comm/cucm/srnd/8x/gateways.html#wp1043594

■   One final note: Do not overlook the recommended memory values and consider how much DRAM and flash memory to order. In most situations, the memory provided with the router as a default is sufficient. However, based on what was discussed in Chapter 5, "Working with Media Files," there are a few additional considerations pertaining to media files:

    ■   Increase the DRAM if there is a large number of .wav files or unusually large .wav files. This allows the provision of more cache space for the gateway.

    ■   Increase the gateways flash memory if you plan to use the flash memory located locally on the gateway to store media files rather than a media server.

Sizing Load Balancers

In most situations, the capacity of a load balancer, such as the Content Services Switch (CSS) or Application Control Engine (ACE), far exceeds the call arrival rate of even the largest Unified CVP implementations. The use of configuration techniques such as "redirects" further reduce the amount of traffic that a load balancer actually processes because only the first fetch is handled by the load balancers. This enables subsequent fetches to be handled directly between the HTTP client and the server that offered the response to the initial fetch. However, the load balancers might not be specifically dedicated to Unified CVP traffic. If this is the case, their capacity must be prorated in such a way that all traffic is accounted for.

Table 6-15 provides some staggering application-level switching values for ACE.

The Cisco CSS product has some similar capacity numbers. However, they are based per I/O module, in which an I/O module could be Fast or Gigabit Ethernet and so on in nature. Table 6-16 provides a simplified look at the capacity of the Cisco CSS.

Table 6-15   *Cisco ACE Load Balancer Application Switching Capacity*

Application Switching Performance	Maximum Performance
Maximum Connections per Second	100,000 complete transactions sustained rate (Layer 4) 30,000 complete transactions sustained rate (Layer 7)
Concurrent Connections	1 million

Table 6-16   *Cisco CSS Load Balancer Application Switching Capacity*

Application Switching Performance	Maximum Performance
Maximum Connections per I/O Module	200,000 with 256 MB RDRAM
Maximum supported keepalives	2048

An additional observation for the CSS capacity numbers is the maximum number of keepalives. This infers that only 2048 servers can be verified from a single CSS as being alive and capable of processing a fetch. This number may seem large at first glance and most likely is for only the Unified CVP solution components. However, if the CSS is used to load balance additional server farms and the Unified CVP solution, care should be taken to understand this limitation.

Sizing Bandwidth Requirements

One area of capacity planning usually overlooked pertains to providing a bandwidth budget for the network team. This addresses the amount of bandwidth the Unified CVP solution consumes. Bandwidth sizing is a critical component when determining how much network bandwidth should be allocated in support of the Unified CVP solution. Sizing for bandwidth becomes more critical when dealing with distributed branch deployments where a WAN is provisioned to deliver a mix of traffic to and from the branch location. In a centralized deployment usually over a LAN, bandwidth sizing is less of a concern because of larger bandwidth allocations provided by a LAN versus a WAN. In the next few sections, you can find guidance for the calculation of bandwidth requirements for different Unified CVP traffic types.

Note   The following guidelines are also presented in Chapter 9 of the *Cisco Unified Customer Voice Portal (CVP) Solution Reference Network Design (SRND), Release 8.x.*

VoiceXML Documents

As discussed earlier in this book, VoiceXML documents are generated and processed by the VoiceXML gateway when executing a script developed as a Micro-Application or as a Cisco Unified Call Studio application. A VoiceXML document is generated for every prompt played to the caller. These documents vary in size, depending on the type of prompt used. For example, menu prompts with many selections are much larger than a basic prompt that simply plays an announcement. On average, these VoiceXML documents are approximately 7 kilobytes in size. By using the number of prompts used per call and also knowing the number of calls per second, you can calculate the total bandwidth budget for a branch pertaining to these VoiceXML interactions. Following is the formula to use for this calculation:

```
7000 bytes * 8 bits = 56,000 bits per prompt
(cps)*(56,000 bits/prompt) * (# of prompts / call) = kbps/branch
```

What if there is a more complex application using multiple menu prompts or a more accurate bandwidth calculation is wanted? Table 6-17 provides guidance pertaining to the exact sizes per VoiceXML document types found within Unified CVP.

Table 6-17 *Approximate Size of VoiceXML Document Types*

VoiceXML Document Type	VoiceXML Document Size (Approximate)
Root document (one required at beginning of call)	19,000 bytes
Subdialog_start (at least one per call at beginning of call)	700 bytes
Query gateway for Call-ID and GUID (one required per call)	1300 bytes
Menu (increases in size with number of menu choices)	1000 bytes + 2000 bytes per menu choice
Play announcement (simple .wav file)	1100 bytes
Cleanup (one required at end of call)	4000 bytes

Media File Retrieval

Chapter 5 revealed that Media Files (prompts) can be stored locally in flash memory on each router. This method eliminates the concern about bandwidth consumption. This is because the media file retrieval occurs locally on the router and does not generate any traffic to a HTTP server. However, this method does not scale for large implementations. It introduces significant maintenance overhead for maintaining large pools of media files scattered across numerous VoiceXML gateways. However, if the files are fetched from an HTTP server and cached locally by the VoiceXML gateway, the impact against the bandwidth budget is only the first time the media file is fetched prior to it being cached, in addition to periodic updates after the expiration of the refresh interval.

> **Caution**   Not caching prompts at the VoiceXML gateway causes significant Cisco IOS performance degradation as much as 35 percent to 40 percent, directly impacting the overall bandwidth budget for the solution.

Following is a simple formula for calculating bandwidth requirements pertaining to media file retrievals:

```
(# prompts) * (size (bytes)/prompt)*(8 bits/byte) = Total bit
(Total bits) / (cache refresh interval) = Average kbps per branch⁵
```

Assuming there is a total of 25 prompts with an average size of 50 kb each and a refresh interval of 15 minutes (900 seconds), following is how to apply the formula to calculate the bandwidth requirements for this branch for retrieving media files:

```
 (25 prompts)*(50,000 bytes/prompt)*(8 bits/byte) = 10,000,000 bits
(10,000,000 bits)/(900 secs) = 11.1 average kbps per branch
```

Call Signaling and Voice Bearer Traffic

For H.323 call signaling, every call into a branch gateway requires 6000 bytes plus 1000 bytes for each transferred call to an agent, giving a total of 56,000 bits per call (7000 bytes *bits). The following formula can calculate the bandwidth required for H.323 call signaling:

```
(7000 bytes/call) * (8 bits/byte) = 56,000 bits per call
(cps) * (56,000 bits/call) = Average kbps per branch⁶
```

Session Initiation Protocol (SIP) is a text-based protocol; therefore, the packets used are larger than with H.323. The typical SIP call flow uses approximately 17,000 bytes per call. Using the previous bandwidth formulas based on calls per second, the average bandwidth usage for SIP would be

```
(17,000 bytes/call) * (8 bits/byte) = 136,000 bits per call
(cps) * (136,000 bits/call) = Average kbps per branch⁷
```

These call control calculations are cumulative to the overall bandwidth budget for previous bandwidth requirements for VoiceXML documents and media file retrieval operations.

Unified CVP can support both G.711 and G.729 voice codecs. However, the switch and VRU leg of a call must use the same codec. As illustrated in the next section, there are some special considerations when dealing with ASR/TTS transactions. For the most current bandwidth information on voice Real-time Transport Protocol (RTP) streams always refer to the latest version of the *Cisco Unified Communications SRND* located at Cisco.com.

ASR and TTS

Because Unified CVP does not support ASR/TTS interactions over a WAN, the ASR/TTS servers must be centrally located to provide RTP and Media Resource Control Protocol (MRCP) traffic via the WAN. To support this model, quality of service (QoS) must be enabled with bandwidth specifically reserved for the ASR/TTS RTP and MRCP traffic. ASR/TTS cannot use silence suppression and must use the G.711 codec; therefore, ASR/TTS is bandwidth-intensive. Further challenges arise because ASR/TTS RTP and MRCP traffic is not tagged with QoS Differentiated Services Code Point (DSCP) markings, making it necessary to use access control lists to classify and re-mark the traffic at the remote site and central site.

Note   80 kbps is the rate for G.711 full-duplex with no Voice Activity Detection (VAD), including IP/RTP headers and no compression. 24 kbps is the rate of G.729 full-duplex with no VAD, including IP/RTP headers and no compression. Cisco provides a nice VoIP bandwidth calculator, Voice Codec Bandwidth Calculator, located at http://tools.cisco.com/Support/VBC/do/CodecCalc1.do.[8]

Although you should calculate the RTP requirements using tools such as the one provided in this chapter, classifying RTP traffic with an ASR/TTS implementation can be tricky. Different ASR/TTS server implementations may choose to deviate from the port range used by the Cisco IOS VoiceXML gateway range of 16384 to 32767 for User Datagram Protocol (UDP)-based RTP traffic. If this occurs, you can use access control lists to match the nonstandard port ranges between the ASR/TTS servers and the VoiceXML gateways. After this traffic has been classified, it should be marked with a DSCP of EF (Express Forwarding) so that it is placed in the priority queue with other voice traffic. In calculating the bandwidth to deliver regular IP phone calls mixed with ASR/TTS RTP streams, for each ASR/TTS RTP stream, you must provide 80 kbps from the centralized location to the branch location. The non-ASR/TTS RTP streams are dependent on what codec is used and the number of calls expected to transverse the WAN. Following is a simple formula to total up the RTP bandwidth requirements per branch:

```
(# of ASR/TTS Calls)*(80 kbps G.711 codec) = ASR/TTS RTP BW
(# of IP Voice Calls)*(80 kbps G.711 codec) = IP Voice RTP BW G.711
(# of IP Voice Calls)*(24 kbps G.729 codec) = IP Voice RTP BW G.729
```

Most if not all implementations can standardize on a codec for IP Voice Real-time Transport Protocol (RTP) traffic. Rarely does G.711 and G.729 RTP traffic exist for IP Voice to a branch office. By simply adding the ASR/TTS and respective IP Voice RTP bandwidth calculations, you can calculate the RTP portion of the bandwidth budget.

Because MRCP traffic is much easier to classify because ASR/TTS servers listen on TCP port 554, building an access control list to classify the traffic is trivial. The bandwidth used by MRCP can vary depending on how often the application uses ASR/TTS resources. MRCP uses approximately 2000 bytes per interaction. Following are the formulas that calculate the bandwidth budget additions for MRCP signaling:

```
(2000 bytes/interaction)*(# interactions/min)*(8 bits/byte) = # bits per minute
per call
(# bits per minute per call)/ (60 seconds/minute) = Average kbps per branch
```

This provides the average kbps per branch for a single ASR/TTS transaction. To calculate the total kbps of bandwidth consumed for all ASR/TTS transactions, use this calculation:

```
(# of ASR/TTS Transactions)*(Average kbps per branch) = Total kbps per branch
```

QoS

The communications network used to deliver the Unified CVP solution is truly the backbone of any successful implementation. These networks transport a multitude of application data, realtime voice, call signaling, and application signaling data. The backbone for this transport provides predictable, measurable, and sometimes guaranteed services by managing bandwidth, delay, jitter, and loss parameters on the network. Although a comprehensive discussion pertaining to QoS is beyond the scope for this book, mapping the Unified CVP solution into a workable QoS Class and defining how Unified CVP data should be classified is not. This section provides some best practices regarding mapping Unified CVP traffic into a standard four class-based QoS model. Table 6-18 provides detailed information about how traffic sourced from native and non-native CVP components should map to a QoS queue.

Figure 6-5 illustrates how a standard four class QoS model accommodates the queues outlined in Table 6-18. The Unified CVP Call Server marks only DSCP for SIP messages and not H.323. If QoS is needed for the Unified CVP H.323 signaling and data traffic across a WAN, configure the edge routers to correctly mark and classify that traffic using the ports previously provided and the IP addresses of the Call Servers. In addition, make sure that QoS markings are honored end to end throughout the network. The best way to verify this is to use a sniffer on each end of the conversation to capture and verify that the DSCP values set for traffic leaving the Unified CVP components in the data center retain those same values when they arrive at the edge. It is critical to trust but definitely verify that the DSCP markings are honored throughout the entire network, all segments, end to end. In the past, poorly configured QoS or high-latency networks have contributed to a significant number of outages and customer satisfaction issues pertaining to the Unified CVP solution even though the customer ensured that their network was rock solid. Trust what the customer is saying but verify that it is correct!

You need to understand that neither Call Signaling nor CVP-Data traffic is placed in a priority queue. The priority queue is used strictly for voice and other realtime traffic. It is illustrated in Figure 6-5 as Realtime. Call Signaling and CVP-Data traffic must have ample bandwidth reserved based on call volume and the calculations presented earlier in this chapter.

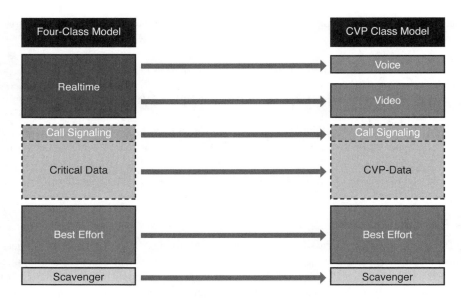

Figure 6-5 *Unified CVP Traffic Mapping into a Four-Class QoS Model*

Table 6-18 *Recommended Port Usage and QoS Settings*

Component	Port	Queue	PHB	DSCP	Maximum Latency (Round Trip)
Media Server	TCP 80	CVP-Data	AF11	10	200 ms
Unified CVP Call Server	TCP 1720 (H.323) TCP/UDP 5060 (SIP)	Call Signaling	CS3	24	200 ms
Unified CVP IVR Service	TCP 8000 (HTTP) TCP 8443 (HTTPS)	CVP-Data	AF11	10	200 ms
Unified CVP VoiceXML Server	TCP 7000 (HTTP) TCP 7443 (HTTPS)	CVP-Data	AF11	10	200 ms
Ingress Gateway	TCP 1720 (H.323) TCP/UDP 5060 (SIP)	Call Signaling	CS3	24	200 ms
VoiceXML Gateway	TCP 1720 (H.323) TCP/UDP 5060 (SIP)	Call Signaling	CS3	24	200 ms
H.323 Gatekeeper	UDP 1719	Call Signaling	CS3	24	200 ms
SIP Proxy Server	TCP/UDP 5060	Call Signaling	CS3	24	200 ms
MRCP	TCP 554	Call Signaling	CS3	24	200 ms

For more details on designing an enterprise-wide QoS strategy, refer to Cisco Enterprise QoS Solution Reference Network Design Guide located at www.cisco.com/en/US/docs/solutions/Enterprise/WAN_and_MAN/QoS_SRND/Enterprise_QoS_SRND.pdf.

Network Latency

When proper application bandwidth and QoS policies are in place, another important consideration in a distributed CVP deployment is that of network latency. With sufficient network bandwidth, the primary contributor to inactivity is distance. In distributed CVP deployments, you must minimize this latency and also understand its effect on solution performance.

The primary effect of network latency between CVP components is on the end user's calling experience. Call signaling latency, either SIP or H.323, between the CVP Call Servers and voice gateways affect the call setup time and may add a period of silence during the setup. This includes the initial call setup and subsequent transfers and conferences that are part of the final call flow. VoiceXML application document download time is also significantly affected by network latency and can have a pronounced effect on the ultimate caller experience.

For the best caller experience, network latency of less than 200 ms round trip is recommended. However, the solution can tolerate round-trip times of up to 400 ms, but with an impact on caller experience. The solution also makes heavy use of the HTTP protocol to transfer Voice XML documents and other media files that are ultimately played to the caller. For the best end user calling experience, the HTTP traffic should be treated with a priority higher than that of normal HTTP traffic in an enterprise network. It is recommended to treat this HTTP traffic the same as CVP call signaling traffic if possible.

Tolerance for call connection delays and periods of call silence are subjective and vary based on culture and/or region. The sections that follow describe a basic CVP call flow scenario and the impact of network latency on the end user experience.

Figure 6-6 outlines a basic SIP call flow with distributed voice gateways where the Ingress Gateway also hosts the VoiceXML browser capabilities.

The remote Ingress Gateway communicates with a centralized CVP environment with a 250 ms round-trip delay across the WAN. To keep the flow high-level and simple, no SIP proxy is shown, but it is part of the end solution. The purpose here is to demonstrate the effect of network latency on CVP call setup times.

After the SIP/H.323 call setup phase completes, the gateway downloads the appropriate VoiceXML application documents. The documents must be downloaded prior to the caller hearing specific prompting from the application. If possible, in high-latency situations, a ring-back or other tone should be played during this download phase.

In its comprehensive deployment model, CVP provides two distinct application types that must be examined independently when estimating call connect times in a high-latency environment. ICM-based Micro Applications provide VoiceXML documents through the

CVP IVR Service. Cisco Unified Call Studio-based applications deliver VoiceXML documents via the CVP VoiceXML Server component.

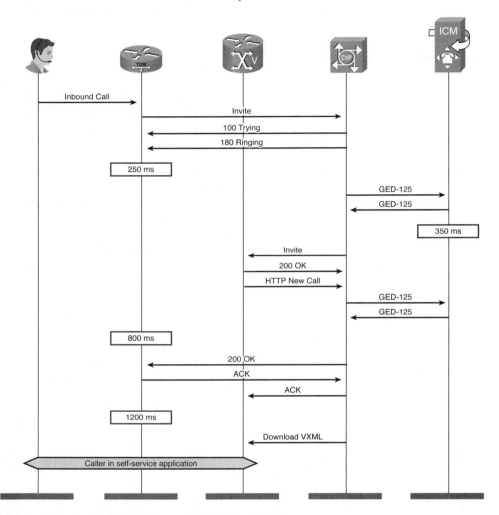

Figure 6-6 *Basic SIP Call Setup with 250ms RTT Latency*

To provide guidelines on the effects of network latency on distributed ingress CVP environments, the following sections demonstrate estimated call setup, VoiceXML download, and time-till-prompt call times. These test scenarios are simplified and provided to support customer calculations of estimated call setup times. Every network environment and solution architecture is different and impacts the final calculations. Examples include variations in QOS policies, additional solution components such as SIP Proxy servers, load balancers, and so on. Take these variations into account when applying to specific Unified CVP-based solution architectures.

Table 6-19 outlines the estimated full call setup times when deploying CVP VoiceXML applications using ICM-based micro applications. Micro applications involve fewer HTTP sessions than similar CVP studio applications. As a result it leads to faster VoiceXML transfer times and smaller first prompt delay times.

Table 6-20 outlines the estimated full call setup times when deploying CVP VoiceXML applications using Cisco Unified Call Studio. The estimated call times are longer for Cisco Unified Call Studio applications because they are typically more complex, and the solution could require interaction with both the CVP IVR service and CVP VoiceXML server when downloading VoiceXML documents.

Table 6-19   *VoiceXML Call Prompt Setup Times—ICM Micro Application*

WAN RTT Latency	SIP Call Setup	Micro App Download (initial VoiceXML)	Time Until Prompt Plays
50 ms	0.5 seconds	1.0 seconds	1.5 seconds
100 ms	0.7 seconds	1.5 seconds	2.2 seconds
150 ms	0.9 seconds	2.0 seconds	2.9 seconds
200 ms	1.1 seconds	2.6 seconds	3.7 seconds
250 ms	1.3 seconds	3.2 seconds	4.5 seconds
300 ms	1.5 seconds	3.8 seconds	5.3 seconds
350 ms	1.7 seconds	4.3 seconds	6.0 seconds
400 ms	1.9 seconds	4.8 seconds	6.7 seconds

Table 6-20   *VoiceXML Call Prompt Setup Times—Cisco Unified Call Studio*

WAN RTT Latency	SIP Call Setup	Micro App Download (initial VoiceXML)	Time Until Prompt Plays
50 ms	0.5 seconds	2.0 seconds	2.5 seconds
100 ms	0.7 seconds	3.3 seconds	4.0 seconds
150 ms	0.9 seconds	4.7 seconds	5.6 seconds
200 ms	1.1 seconds	5.9 seconds	7.0 seconds
250 ms	1.3 seconds	7.3 seconds	8.6 seconds
300 ms	1.5 seconds	8.6 seconds	10.1 seconds
350 ms	1.7 seconds	10.0 seconds	11.7 seconds
400 ms	1.9 seconds	11.2 seconds	13.1 seconds

Applications designed with Cisco Unified Call Studio inject additional delay into the solution simply because there are two additional TCP sessions as compared to ICM-based Micro Applications (refer to Table 6-20). The following sections apply to applications developed via ICM Micro Applications or Cisco Unified Call Studio. The following sections examine the causes of the delays and how they can be mitigated.

Understanding the Source of Delays

Five interactions are required before the Cisco Unified Call Studio-based VoiceXML is fully delivered to the VoiceXML gateway allowing the gateway to play prompts to the caller. Each of these contributes to the overall delay before the VoiceXML gateway plays prompts to the caller:

- SIP signaling

- Unified CVP Call Server ping

- Unified CVP Call root doc fetch

- Unified CVP VoiceXML Server root doc fetch (Cisco Unified Call Studio only)

- Cisco Unified Call Studio-based VoiceXML fetch (Cisco Unified Call Studio only)

SIP Signaling

When the call arrives at the gateway, the first thing the gateway does is send a SIP INVITE to the SIP Proxy to reach CVP. CVP, in turn, asks ICM how to handle the call, resulting in ICM returning a "temp or dummy label" that maps to the vru-leg application on the gateway. This is referred to as the SIP call setup time.

Modifications to **survivability.tcl** enable media to play during this SIP call setup time.

Unified CVP Call Server ping

Shortly after the vru-leg dial-peer is triggered, the VoiceXML gateway sends an application-level ping to verify that the Unified CVP Call Server is alive and online. The Unified CVP Call Server replies back with VoiceXML requesting the VoiceXML gateway to contact the Call Server again with the data it needs to process the call.

Modifications to **bootstrap.vxml** enable media to play during this fetch time.

Unified CVP Call Server Root Document

As part of the reply to the ping, Unified CVP Call Server sends VoiceXML a message that instructs the VoiceXML gateway to contact the Call Server again with the information required to handle the call. This is sent within the Unified CVP Call Server's root document. This is one of the larger data transfers in the call process, which means it is one of the larger sources of delay in a high-latency scenario.

Modifications to the **SubmitNext.template** enable media to play during this fetch time.

Unified CVP VoiceXML Server Root Document Fetch (Cisco Unified Call Studio Only)

If the deployment uses Cisco Unified Call Studio (instead of ICM-based Micro Applications), additional steps are required to fetch the root VoiceXML document for the Cisco Unified Call Studio application. As part of the VoiceXML sent, the Unified CVP Call Server initiates a VoiceXML subdialog to the Unified CVP VoiceXML Server. The VoiceXML Server replies with the root document for the Cisco Unified Call Studio application specified. As with the Unified CVP Call Server's root document, this is a relatively large transfer, which is composed of the largest amount of delay for the five phases.

Modifications to **GetSpeech-External.template** enable media to play during this fetch time.

Cisco Unified Call Studio-based VoiceXML Fetch (Cisco Unified Call Studio Only)

After fetching the Cisco Unified Call Studio application's root document, the final step is to retrieve the VoiceXML required for the first interaction with the caller. This enables the VoiceXML gateway to play the first prompt. This is typically a relatively small fetch, resulting in minimal delay. As such, it is unnecessary to inject audio during this phase of the call.

Mitigation by Injecting Audio

Now that the various components of delay have been covered, it is time to examine the configurable components that permit any changes from an audio standpoint. By injecting audio the perceived delay is masked, and the caller cannot notice it.

This section is intended to explain only the possibilities that exist for injecting audio into the call flow, and concepts behind why such a change to the system should occur. You can find the details of how to implement those changes in the next section. Read this section to understand how those changes can affect the overall caller experience.

There are five places in the Unified CVP Solution Set where configuration changes can be made to inject audio. They are listed in the order they are invoked during the call flow:

- Survivability.tcl

- Bootstrap.vxml

- Unified CVP Call Server VoiceXML Template: SubmitBack.template

- Other Unified CVP Call Server VoiceXML Templates (vary depending on the use of ICM-based Micro Applications or Cisco Unified Call Studio Applications)

- Within a Cisco Unified Call Studio Application

Each of these files are executed concurrent with each of the five phases in the call flow. For example, changes in survivability.tcl enable audio to play during the SIP signaling phase of the call. Changes in bootstrap.vxml enable audio to be played during the application-level ping to Unified CVP Call Server and so on.

With the exception of survivability.tcl, all the changes are to VoiceXML templates. The VoiceXML template changes enable control of not only what prompt plays during the fetch, but also how early in that phase to play the prompt and a minimum time to play the prompt—even if the fetch finishes prior to that minimum time. This is useful in scenarios in which a spoken prompt (for example, "Please hold while we connect your call") is played. By setting a minimum amount of time to play the prompt, it ensures that the prompt is not clipped off. But this is done at the cost of adding to the overall delay in getting to the first application prompt.

For survivability.tcl, there is no control over how long the prompt plays, as detailed in the next section.

Understanding Changes to Survivability.tcl

After the call gets through the PRI/CAS (Channel-Associated Signaling) setup, one of the first pieces of code to trigger on the IOS gateway is survivability.tcl. As such, survivability.tcl is the earliest stage at which you can inject audio into the call.

Changes to survivability.tcl provides the option to play a prompt from just immediately after the time the gateway receives the call from the carrier until the time that the call lands on the VRU-leg dial peer. This is referred to as SIP call setup previously defined.

There is an important caveat when modifying survivability.tcl. Unlike the VoiceXML templates, there is not a programmatic way to specify a minimum amount of time for the prompt to play.

When coupled this with the fact that SIP call setup time is under 1 second at 200 ms round-trip delay, it is suggested to either implement a short prompt or no prompt at all in this phase of the call, as a long prompt is clipped.

An example of a viable prompt for this phase of the call is a ring back tone. Ring back cadence is typically short (around 1 second for the U.S./Canada), so it makes for a good candidate change in survivability.tcl. Callers naturally expect to hear ring back at the beginning of the call, so they are typically insensitive to ring back cadence being cut short. Also each IOS gateway used in the Unified CVP solution already has a ring back prompt in flash on the gateway. This means the prompt can be fetched on the gateway itself rather than pulling it from a media server across the WAN.

Another important caveat when modifying this TCL file is that by playing audio, a call immediately connects. Normally with SIP, the call does not connect until after talking to the ICM and VoiceXML gateway. This could potentially have an implication on billing.

Understanding Changes to Bootstrap.vxml

Modifications to bootstrap.vxml, which also resides in the gateway's flash, allow media to be played during the time that the ping begins until Call Server completes its send of the first VoiceXML document. Out of all the sources of delay, this is by far the smallest.

As such, any media played would be short-lived. Because of this and because there is no capability to parameterize this change, it is recommended that modifications to boot-strap.vxml not be made.

Understanding Changes to SubmitNext.template

By modifying the SubmitNext.template, you can specify what prompt to play while the gateway fetches the Unified CVP Call Server root document. You can also specify the length of waiting time and prompt play time.

Changes to SubmitNext.template allows media to play to the caller from the time that the gateway receives a reply to the ping until the time that the gateway completes its fetch of the CVP Call Server root document.

The exact prompt to play depends on a few factors:

- Length of the delay in the environment

- Whether a spoken message is played (for example, "Please hold while we service your call.")

- Wanted sound of the overall caller experience

An example of a typical prompt used in this scenario would be fetchaudio tones, typically heard when an IVR performs a database dip or other such delay-intensive activity.

You can use music or a spoken phrase, but realize that the prompt plays only for a few seconds. Consider how the prompt will sound with other prompts in the entire call flow. Using the same music prompt for multiple phases of the call flow will likely sound dis-jointed as the prompt starts and restarts while progressing through the stages of the call flow. This is another reason why fetchaudio tones work well for this phase of the call because it is difficult to discern two instances of the prompt played back-to-back.

As with any of the prompts, it is recommended to deploy the target prompt in flash or have a media server local to the gateway to avoid any delays in downloading and caching the prompt.

Understanding Changes to Other Unified CVP VoiceXML Templates

Depending on whether an ICM-based Micro Applications, Cisco Unified Call Studio applications is running, or a mix of the two, you can modify different VoiceXML tem-plates on the Unified CVP Call Server.

If using Cisco Unified Call Studio to generate all the VoiceXML—or the Cisco Unified Call Studio-based VoiceXML is the only source of delay preferred—then only changes to **GetSpeech-External.template** are required.

If using ICM-based Micro Applications, there is a separate VoiceXML template for each of the Micro Applications. For example, PlayMedia.template can generate VoiceXML when using the PM Micro Application.

Cisco Unified Call Studio Only: Understanding Changes to GetSpeech-External.template

Modifications to GetSpeech-External.template on the Unified CVP Call Server allows media to play for the caller from the time that Unified CVP Call Server replies with the subdialog until the VoiceXML gateway completes the fetch of the Cisco Unified Call Studio application's root document. As mentioned previously, this is typically the step that experiences the longest delay.

The guidelines for what prompt to play during this phase are the same as with the Unified CVP Call Server root document fetch. Again, consider how the prompt fits in with the other prompts used and the length of delay anticipated, based on the performance of the WAN as it relates to these VoiceXML fetches. As mentioned, using a fetchaudio prompt is typically a good choice because callers are unlikely to notice that the prompt has restarted because the warbling nature of these types of prompts.

The changes made here affect any time a new Cisco Unified Call Studio application launches. For example, if the call flow is for a Cisco Unified Call Studio-based self-service application to launch at the beginning of the call, changes to GetSpeech-External.template must be used while fetching the Cisco Unified Call Studio application's root document. However, this also means that any time it is necessary to return to Unified ICM and launch another Cisco Unified Call Studio-based application, for example, a Queue Treatment application, the same fetchaudio prompt is played during that Cisco Unified Call Studio-based application's root document fetch, as well.

To avoid this, use ICM-based Micro Applications for the Queue Treatment scenarios. If the .template file corresponding to the Micro Application used (for example, PlayMedia.template) is modified, it would be similarly affected.

ICM-based Micro Applications: Understanding Changes to the Other .template Files

In the interest of brevity, this section covers only modifications to the GetSpeech-External.template. Because there is no need for a second root document because the VoiceXML Server is not involved with ICM-based Micro Applications, and there is one less set of TCP sessions required to get to the VoiceXML document, ICM-based Micro Applications do not typically require a fetchaudio prompt. The delay is similar to that of the fifth phase of a Cisco Unified Call Studio-based application. It is typically not long enough to warrant injection of audio.

However, if it is necessary to implement a fetchaudio prompt for an ICM-based Micro Application, the templates for those ICM-based Micro Applications can be modified using the exact same guidelines and procedures covered for the GetSpeech-External.template file. Be aware that implementing the change for the ICM-based Micro Application must be made *prior* to where the delay is expected. Changing the template affects all instances in which calling the ICM-based Micro Application is associated with that template.

Understanding Changes to Cisco Unified Call Studio Application Root Documents

You can insert audio globally within a particular Cisco Unified Call Studio application. You can accomplish this by setting the same properties as in the Unified CVP Call Server's VoiceXML templates. Set these within the properties of the Cisco Unified Call Studio application.

This permits the injection of audio between each VoiceXML fetch within a Cisco Unified Call Studio application. When these fetches occur depends on the application. One example of when a fetch is required is any time the Cisco Unified Call Studio application requires input from the customer (for example, Menu element, Number element, and Digits element). This is because Unified CVP VoiceXML Server does not render out a massive VoiceXML document that covers all the scripted scenarios in the Cisco Unified Call Studio application. Rather, the Unified CVP VoiceXML Server pushes just enough VoiceXML to the gateway to the next decision branch. This enables the Cisco Unified Call Studio application to change based on customer input, data dips, and other real-time information.

Be aware that if fetchaudio is implemented within the Cisco Unified Call Studio application's root document, the caller hears fetchaudio between each of these fetches, which are typically short. Consider how the selected prompt can fit within the overall application behavior because the caller will hear fetchaudio both between intra-Studio application fetches, but also as the transition from one Cisco Unified Call Studio application to another (assuming that the implement changes are made in the GetSpeech-External.template).

Implementing the Changes

The changes discussed in the previous section can be implemented for each of the five areas that were also identified earlier in this section.

Modifying survivability.tcl

The following steps detail how to modify the survivability.tcl file:

Step 1.   First, obtain a copy of the survivability.tcl script. It is typically best to pull this from one of the production gateways. Although rare, there are instances in which customers have modified survivability.tcl, so pulling a copy from the gateway ensures that existing changes are not lost when making modifications. If there is confirmation that the survivability.tcl has not been modified, pull a copy from the C:\Cisco\CVP\OPSConsoleServer\GWDownloads folder from the Unified CVP Operations Console Server.

Step 2.   After survivability.tcl is located, open the file using the text editor of your choice. Find the text *# Procedure Star*, which leads to the comments just above the Start procedure in the tcl script.

Step 3.   A few lines under this comment, the following block of code appears:

```
init_CallVars
leg proceeding leg_incoming
leg connect leg_incoming
set isIncomingLegConnected 1
```

Modify this block to look like the following (changes highlighted in bold):

```
init_CallVars
leg proceeding leg_incoming
# - - Next line added to play ringback while fetching VoiceXML
media play leg_incoming flash:ringback.wav
# - - Next line commented out to allow ringback while fetching
# - - leg connect leg_incoming
leg connect leg_incoming
set isIncomingLegConnected 1
```

Step 4.   The changes above cause survivability.tcl to play the file ringback.wav, which is stored in flash on the gateway, to play from the time that the call triggers survivability.tcl until the call lands on the vru-leg dial-peer.

Step 5.   After the modified survivability.tcl is uploaded, run *call application voice load survivability* to force the gateway to load the new changes. Alternatively, the gateway can be reloaded.

This change must happen on all affected gateways in the solution.

Understanding VoiceXML Template Modifications

You can make three specific modifications to any of the VoiceXML Templates detailed in the remainder of this section. Again, these changes do not apply to survivability.tcl.

The modifications are as follows:

- **Fetchaudio:** This is the prompt necessary for the gateway to play while it is fetching VoiceXML for a particular portion of the call flow.

- **Fetchaudiodelay:** This provides the ability to configure the length of time after this particular VoiceXML fetch starts before the prompt specified in the fetchaudio tag is played, specified in seconds. The default value in IOS is 2 seconds. This means that if a fetch takes longer than 2 seconds, the gateway starts playing the prompt when it reaches the 2 second mark. If a fetchaudio prompt is chosen, it would be advisable to set this value to 0 seconds. This means that the prompt begins playing as soon as the gateway starts the fetch. Also if implemented in both SubmitBack.template and GetSpeech-External.template, setting this value to 0 allows for a fetchaudio prompt to be played back-to-back to sound like one cohesive prompt. Again, this would not be suggested with music prompts because the restart of the prompt is noticeable. However, with typical fetchaudio tones, the restart is not perceptible.

- **Fetchaudiominimum:** This provides the ability to configure a minimum amount of time wanted for the fetchaudio prompt to play, specified in seconds. This is a minimum, which means the prompt can play for at least this number of seconds. For example, if a fetchaudiominimum of 4 seconds is specified and it takes 2.5 seconds for the fetch to complete, the prompt continues playing for a total of 4 seconds. Conversely, if a fetchaudiominimum of 4 seconds is specified and it takes 5 seconds to complete the fetch, the prompt plays for the full 5 seconds. By specifying this minimum, the gateway must wait for the prompt to complete before it can fetch the next portion of VoiceXML. Thus, if the value is set too high, it can add to the overall delay before the application's first prompt. However, in the case of a spoken prompt (for example, "Please hold while we connect your call"), this might be required to prevent clipping of the prompt. If a fetchaudiodelay value is specified, you must set fetchaudiominimum, as well. Otherwise, the default value of 5 seconds is applied, which can lead to unwanted delays. It is recommended to set this value to greater than or equal to 2 seconds because setting it to 1 second can result in no audio under certain conditions.

Modifying bootstrap.vxml

If a change to that file is wanted, you can make three changes in bootstrap.vxml, as shown in the following three steps. Again, it is advised not to modify bootstrap.vxml because the portion of the call flow bootstrap.vxml has control over is typically a low-delay portion. Also changes to bootstrap.vxml cannot be parameterized and might be overwritten in subsequent upgrades.

Step 1. Set the fetchaudiodelay and fetchaudiominimum VoiceXML properties by adding them just after the section that sets all the variables, as shown here (additions highlighted in bold):

```
<var name="PRIMARY_CVP_URL" expr="PROTOCOL + '://' +
 PORT + '/cvp/VBServlet'"/>
<var name="BACKUP_CVP_URL" expr="PROTOCOL + '://' +
 + BACKUP + ':' + PORT + '/cvp/VBServlet'"/>
<property name="fetchaudiodelay" value="0s" />
<property name="fetchaudiominimum" value="2s" />
```

These changes specify that the fetchaudio prompt must be played immediately when the fetch starts (fetchaudiodelay = 0) and that the fetchaudioprompt should play for at least 2 seconds (fetchaudiominimum = 2).

Step 2. Specify the prompt to be played. To do that, add the following code, highlighted in bold, to the <submit> tag, near the end of bootstrap.vxml:

```
<submit expr="PRIMARY_CVP_URL"
  namelist="MSG_TYPE CALL_DNIS CALL_ANI ERROR_CODE RECOVERY_VoiceXML
```

```
CLIENT_TYPE CALL_ID SIP_CALL_ID CALL_UUI VERSION"
fetchaudio="flash:ringback.wav"
fetchtimeout="7s"/>
```

To summarize the example in Step 2, the changes cause ringback.wav to play immediately when the fetch starts, and it plays for either 2 seconds or when the fetch is complete, should the fetch take longer than 2 seconds.

Step 3.   After the change is made, bootstrap.vxml must be uploaded to all gateways affected. Run **call application voice load new-call** on the gateway to load the new changes. Alternatively, you can reload the gateway. This change must occur on all affected gateways in the solution.

Modifying SubmitBack.template

The process to modify SubmitBack.template is similar to the process listed for bootstrap.vxml. There are some slight changes as to where to place the modifications. All the .template files reside on the Unified CVP Call Server in the C:\Cisco\CVP\conf\VoiceXMLTemplates folder. This modification is required on every Call Server involved with the affected call flow. The Call Server service needs to be restarted after all .template modifications have been made.

Step 1.   Open SubmitBack.template using a text editor. Just after the vars and properties are set, add the following code (highlighted in bold):

```
<var name="DEBUG" expr="%ClientDebugLevel%" />
<property name="com.cisco.media-logging-id"
  value="'%Call_Identifier%'" />
<property name="fetchaudiodelay" value="0s" />
<property name="fetchaudiominimum" value="2s" />
```

These changes specify that the fetchaudio prompt be played immediately when the fetch starts (fetchaudiodelay = 0) and that the fetchaudioprompt should play for at least 2 seconds (fetchaudiominimum = 2).

Step 2.   In the <submit next> tag near the bottom of SubmitBack.template, add the following text (highlighted in bold):

```
<block>
  <submit next="%ServletPath%" namelist="MSG_TYPE CALL_DNIS CALL_UUI
    CALL_ANI RECOVERY_VoiceXML CLIENT_TYPE CALL_ID ERROR_CODE"
    fetchaudio="flash:FetchPrompt.wav" fetchtimeout="%FetchTimeout%s"/>
</block>
```

These changes cause the gateway to play a prompt named FetchPrompt.wav, which has been uploaded to flash on all the affected gateways and played from the time that the fetch starts until the time that the Unified CVP Call Server root document has been successfully fetched.

Step 3.   The Unified CVP Call Server must be restarted for these changes to take effect. If modifying multiple .template files, wait until they have all been modified before restarting the Call Server. This change must happen on all affected Call Servers in the solution.

Modifying GetSpeech-External.template

As mentioned earlier, this section focuses only on modifications to GetSpeech-External.template. The process for modifying the ICM-based Micro Application-specific templates (for example, PlayMedia.template) is exactly the same, should modification be necessary. In most cases, there is no need to modify the ICM-based Micro Application templates. However, because the resulting VoiceXML is small, it makes fetch times short.

The process here is similar to that of modifying SubmitBack.template, except that GetSpeech-External.template launches a subdialog to the VoiceXML Server to ensure that Unified CVP (and by extension, ICM) maintains control over the call. As such make changes to the <subdialog> tag instead of the <submit> or <submit next> tags, as shown in the following steps:

Step 1.   Open GetSpeech-External.template using a text editor. Just as with SubmitBack.template, add the following code (highlighted in bold):

```
<var name="DEBUG" expr="%ClientDebugLevel%" />
<property name="com.cisco.media-logging-id"
 value="'%Call_Identifier%'" />
<property name="fetchaudiodelay" value="0s" />
<property name="fetchaudiominimum" value="2s" />
```

These changes specify that the fetchaudio prompt should be played immediately when the fetch starts (fetchaudiodelay = 0) and that the fetchaudioprompt should play for at least 2 seconds (fetchaudiominimum = 2).

Step 2.   Approximately 10 lines below the text in Step 1, notice the submit tag. Add the fetchprompt property, highlighted in bold here:

```
<subdialog name="%ExternalName%" fetchaudio="flash:FetchPrompt.wav"
src= "%ExternalPath%" %ExternalVoiceXMLNamelist%>
```

These changes cause the gateway to play a prompt named FetchPrompt.wav, which has been uploaded to flash on all of the affected VoiceXML gateways. This plays from the time the fetch starts until the time that the Unified CVP Call Server root document is successfully fetched.

Step 3.   As mentioned, the Unified CVP Call Server must be restarted for these changes to take effect. If modifying multiple .template files, you can wait until they are all modified before you restart Call Server. Again, a change to this template causes the fetchaudio prompt to be played anytime the call flow triggers a new Cisco Unified Call Studio application (for example, when exiting a Self Service app and launching a Queue Treatment app). This change must happen on all affected Call Servers in the solution.

Modifying the Cisco Unified Call Studio Application's Root Document

If adding fetchaudio between elements within a Cisco Unified Call Studio application is considered, set this within the properties of the Cisco Unified Call Studio application. Making these changes causes fetchaudio to play anytime there is a new fetch for VoiceXML, which can occur quite often in a Cisco Unified Call Studio application.

Step 1.   Open the application in CVP Studio.

Step 2.   Right-click the application and select **Properties**.

Step 3.   Navigate to **Call Studio > Root Doc Settings**.

Step 4.   In the VoiceXML Properties column, set the appropriate values for the following values found in the VoiceXML Property window:

- fetchaudiodelay = 0

- fetchaudiominimum = 2

- fetchaudio = flash:FetchPrompt.wav

Step 5.   Save the changes. Small changes may be necessary such as moving an element to save the project and redeploying the application to all Unified CVP VoiceXML Servers in the solution.

Troubleshooting and Tuning the Changes

Perform a network capture or gateway log capture prior to implementing any changes. This reveals the various conversations between the gateway and Unified CVP Call/VoiceXML Server. Armed with this information, you can determine where it makes the most sense to inject audio to improve the caller experience and, more important, where it does not.

Following is a breakdown of the conversations for one call, when looking solely at the traffic in/out of the gateway (for example, does not include CVP to ICM traffic, just to cite one example):

Step 1.   Ingress Gateway sends SIP INVITE to SIP Proxy. The call is processed through Unified CVP and ICM, returning the temp label, which lands on the gateway's new-call dial-peer.

Step 2.   The gateway makes an initial application-level ping to Call Server. Call Server replies back, based on configuration of SubmitBack.template asking the gateway to reply back to the Call Server with the information it needs to handle the call.

Step 3. The gateway submits the information requested as a NEW_CALL and gets the CVP Call Server root document back in return, which includes any changes in GetSpeech-External.template.

Step 4. The gateway next talks to Unified CVP VoiceXML Server and receives the Cisco Unified Call Studio application's root document, plus a request to submit back for the next instructions.

Step 5. Gateway submits another request to the Unified CVP VoiceXML Server, at which point the VoiceXML Server returns the VoiceXML created as a result of running the Cisco Unified Call Studio application. This includes the initial prompts that the caller hears.

Sample Network Capture

Example 6-1 is a network capture taken from Wireshark that details each of these five call flow steps along with timestamps of each of these interactions. Knowing the time spent in each phase of the flow is critical to crafting an overall design for how (or if) it is determined to inject audio during any of these phases of the call flow.

Each step is called out, along with the configurable component that enables the injection of audio during that phase of the call flow. The IP addresses of the endpoints follow:

- 10.88.194.6: Ingress/VoiceXML gateway

- 10.89.28.69: CUPS SIP Proxy

- 10.89.28.86: CVP Call Server / VoiceXML Server

Example 6-1 *Simple Network Capture with Modifications for Latency Mitigation*

```
| Time      |  10.88.194.6     | 10.89.28.69      |  10.89.28.86     |
< Step 1: Start of SIP signaling - Survivability.tcl invoked>


| 3.872    |  Request: INVITE sip   |         |SIP/SDP: Request: INVITE
sip:57013015060, with session description     (application/gtd)
| 4.075    |  Status: 100 Trying    |         |SIP: Status: 100 Trying
| 4.109    |  Request: INVITE sip   |         |SIP/SDP: Request: INVITE
sip:8777777777111625060;transport=tcp, with session description (application/gtd)
| 4.120    |  Status: 100 Trying    |         |SIP: Status: 100 Trying
| 4.124    |  Status: 200 OK, wit   |         |SIP/SDP: Status: 200 OK, with session
description
| 4.332    |  Status: 200 Ok  , w   |         |SIP/SDP: Status: 200 Ok  , with ses-
sion description
| 4.339    |  Request: ACK sip:10   |         |SIP: Request: ACK
sip:10.89.28.86:5060;transport=udp
| 4.549    |  Request: ACK sip:87   |         |SIP: Request: ACK
sip:8777777777111625060
<End of SIP signaling - 4.549s - 3.872s = 677ms>
```

```
< Step 2: Start of Call Server "ping" - Bootstrap.vxml invoked>


|5.160    |  36764 > irdmi [SYN]  |         | TCP: 36764 > irdmi [SYN] Seq=0
Win=65535 Len=0 MSS=536
<Small VoiceXML reply to "ping"; includes changes to SubmitBack.template>


|6.157    |  36764 > irdmi [FIN,  |         | TCP: 36764 > irdmi [FIN, PSH, ACK]
Seq=651 Ack=2405 Win=64204 Len=0


<End of Call Server "ping" - 6.157s - 5.160s = 997ms>
< Step 3: Start of request for Call Server Root doc - SubmitBack.template invoked>
|6.166    |  48423 > irdmi [SYN]  |         | TCP: 48423 > irdmi [SYN] Seq=0
Win=65535 Len=0 MSS=536


<...Fetch of Call Server root doc; includes changes to GetSpeech-External.tem-
plate...>
|7.787    |  48423 > irdmi [FIN,  |         | TCP: 48423 > irdmi [FIN, PSH, ACK]
Seq=569 Ack=8983 Win=64058 Len=0


<End of Call Server root doc fetch - 7.787s - 6.166s = 1621ms>
< Step 4: Start of VoiceXML Server subdialog - GetSpeech-External.template invoked>


|11.579   |  46881 > afs3-filese  |         | TCP: 46881 > afs3-fileserver [SYN]
Seq=0 Win=65535 Len=0 MSS=536


<...Fetch of Studio application's root doc; includes changes to Studio app's root
doc...>


|13.717   |  46881 > afs3-filese  |         | TCP: 46881 > afs3-fileserver [FIN,
PSH, ACK] Seq=553 Ack=19090 Win=65207 Len=0


<End of Fetch of CVP Studio application's root doc - 13.717s - 11.579s  = 2138ms>
< Step 5: Start of fetch for Studio application's VoiceXML - Studio Application's
root doc invoked>


|16.172   |  38277 > afs3-filese  |         | TCP: 38277 > afs3-fileserver [SYN]
Seq=0 Win=65535 Len=0 MSS=536


<... Fetch of CVP Studio VoiceXML...>


|16.782   |  38277 > afs3-filese  |         | TCP: 38277 > afs3-fileserver [FIN,
PSH, ACK] Seq=480 Ack=1161 Win=65448 Len=0


<End of fetch for CVP Studio application's VoiceXML to be rendered to the caller -
16.782s - 16172s = 510ms>


<Caller now hearing the first prompt from the CVP Studio application>
```

Note   The capture from Example 6-1 is a system with modifications detailed in this document in place. As such, notice some extra delay added as a result (for example, between the end of Step 3 and start of Step 4).

IOS Logging

Example 6-2 is a sample of logging from an IOS gateway showing the various stages of the call, similar to Example 6-1. In this example, the solution uses ICM-based Micro Applications, so Steps 4 and 5 are not represented. The logging is the same, except the URL points to TCP Port 7000 to talk to the Unified CVP VoiceXML Server (which may or may not be co-resident with the Unified CVP Call Server).

Example 6-2   *IOS Logging with Modifications for Latency Mitigation*

```
Step 1: +0.00 seconds - Call arrives at gateway. gateway matches dial-peers.

Oct 15 17:47:51.782: //-1/B1377E9E8036/DPM/dpMatchPeersMoreArg:
Result=SUCCESS(0)
List of Matched Outgoing Dial-peer(s):
1: Dial-peer Tag=302
2: Dial-peer Tag=303


+0.08 seconds - gateway sends SIP INVITE to CUPS proxy, which forwards it on to CVP

Oct 15 17:47:51.786: //-1/xxxxxxxxxxxx/SIP/Msg/ccsipDisplayMsg:
Sent: INVITE sip:21484525060 SIP/2.0


+0.304 seconds - gateway receives SIP TRYING from CUPS proxy

Oct 15 17:47:52.086: //-1/xxxxxxxxxxxx/SIP/Msg/ccsipDisplayMsg:
Received: SIP/2.0 100 Trying

+0.376 seconds - gateway receives SIP INVITE for Network VRU Label + correlation ID

Oct 15 17:47:52.158: //-1/xxxxxxxxxxxx/SIP/Msg/ccsipDisplayMsg:
Received: INVITE sip:9999999999118455060;transport=udp SIP/2.0


+0.384 seconds - gateway sends SIP OK message for Network VRU Label + correlation ID
```

```
Oct 15 17:47:52.166: //-1/xxxxxxxxxxxx/SIP/Msg/ccsipDisplayMsg:
Sent: SIP/2.0 200 OK
```

+0.692 seconds - gateway matches dial-peers for Network VRU Label + correlation ID

```
Oct 15 17:47:52.474: //-1/xxxxxxxxxxxx/DPM/dpMatchPeers:
Result=SUCCESS(0)
List of Matched Outgoing Dial-peer(s):
1: Dial-peer Tag=302
2: Dial-peer Tag=303
```

+0.884 seconds - gateway sends SIP OK for Network VRU Label + correlation ID

```
Oct 15 17:47:52.666: //-1/xxxxxxxxxxxx/SIP/Msg/ccsipDisplayMsg:
Sent: SIP/2.0 200 OK
```

+0.956 seconds - gateway receives SIP ACK for Network VRU Label + correlation ID

```
Oct 15 17:47:52.738: //-1/xxxxxxxxxxxx/SIP/Msg/ccsipDisplayMsg:
Received: ACK sip:9999999999118455060 SIP/2.0
```

Step 2: +1.384 seconds - gateway hands call off to bootstrap.vxml

```
Oct 15 17:47:53.166: //343//AFW_:/vapp_vxmldialog: After DNIS Map URI=flash:boot-
strap.vxml, Code = {
```

+1.404 seconds - gateway sends application-level PING to CVP

```
Oct 15 17:47:53.186: //343//AFW_:/vapp_bgload:
url=http://10.22.194.20:8000/cvp/VBServlet?MSG_TYPE=PING&CALL_DNIS=999999999911845&
CALL_ANI=sip:10.22.194.20:5060&ERROR_CODE=0&RECOVERY_VoiceXML=flash:recovery.vxml&C
LIENT_TYPE=IOS&CALL_ID=B1377E9EB8E911DE8036002545FC58C0&SIP_CALL_ID=B1377E9EB8E911D
E8036002545FC58C0-1255628871983255@10.22.194.20&CALL_UUI=&VERSION=7.0.2
```

**Step 3: +2.600 seconds - gateway sends a NEW CALL request to CVP. At this point,
the gateway will download the Call Server Root Doc.**

```
Oct 15 17:47:54.382: //343//AFW_:/vapp_bgload:
url=http://10.22.194.20:8000/cvp/VBServlet?MSG_TYPE=CALL_NEW&CALL_DNIS=999999999911
845&CALL_UUI=&CALL_ANI=sip:10.22.194.20:5060&RECOVERY_VoiceXML=flash:recovery.vxml&
CLIENT_TYPE=IOS&CALL_ID=B1377E9EB8E911DE8036002545FC58C0&ERROR_CODE=0
```

+4.473 seconds - gateway plays announcement WAV file out to caller.

```
Oct 15 17:47:56.155: //343//AFW_:/vapp_media_play: prompt=http://mediaserver/en-
us/app/e_StandardHoldMessage1.wav:
Oct 15 17:47:56.155: //71//HTTPC:/httpc_cache_isfresh: cachep(66A5163C) fresh(Yes)
lifetime(1265985) age(82663)
Oct 15 17:47:56.155: //71//HTTPC:/httpc_cache_is_acceptable: cachep(66A5163C) max-
age(-1) maxstale(-1) status(TRUE)
```

The sample logging in Example 6-2 was enabled with the following commands:

- **debug voip dial-peer**

- **debug isdn q931**

- **debug voip application vxml application**

- **debug ccsip messages**

Although injecting audio is considered a mitigation technique, it truly masks only the problem introduced with high-latency networks. The best approach where possible is to reduce the latency of the network to levels acceptable for the required customer experience. However, when latency cannot be reduced, masking is an effective way to hide the delays that become obvious when the caller hears only dead air. In addition, moving Unified CVP VoiceXML servers and media servers closer to the edge is also an effective way to bypass high latency links, especially for the conversations previously outlined that introduce the most delay. Care must be taken when considering moving key infrastructure components closer to an edge, simply because the cost of doing so can be a deal killer.

Security Considerations

Customer security teams can be a challenge when dealing with any complex voice application that uses several different TCP and User Datagram Protocol (UDP) ports to communicate and some protocols that are not deemed as secure protocols. Most of the challenges with security teams boil down to educating them on the solution for the ports and communication models used by the Unified CVP components. After this educational process is complete, most security teams are satisfied to know that there are no skeletons in the closet that they should be concerned with, or at the least they can articulate the risk and provide a mitigation plan to management. Most security teams are generalists when it comes to complex technologies, and although they understand the basic principles of security, they forget to recognize that security is an adjective applied to a noun (the solution) and should not be considered the center of the universe. It is easy to over complicate a solution in the name of security rendering it completely useless from a usability and manageability perspective. It is still necessary to acknowledge that some customers require higher levels of security. The implementations supplied in this section should provide some decent coverage about the Unified CVP solution to adequately describe it to any persistent security team that feels the need to secure it.

One of the most commonly used approaches to secure voice and data networks is the placement of firewalls to control access to and from solution components. Some implementations take this approach to an extreme putting up firewalls wherever a trust boundary is thought to exist or a different group in the same company should be "walled" off from access to the solution. Firewalls are unavoidable. However, with some careful planning and documentation, these firewalls can be correctly configured to transport voice and data for the Unified CVP solution. Table 6-21 provides the details pertaining to the components that use certain protocols to communicate on specific ports. The Reference Figure column references figures provided later in this section where these communications are visually illustrated.

Table 6-21   *TCP/UDP Ports Used by Unified CVP Native and Non-Native Components*

Server / Application	Remote Device	Server Protocol/Port	Notes	Reference Figure
VoiceXML Server: HTTP	IOS VoiceXML Gateways	TCP 7000	VoiceXML over HTTP. Calls/sessions answered on port 7000 by HTTP server, which relays request to WAS on local system port 9080.	Figure 6-7
VoiceXML Server: HTTPS	IOS VoiceXML Gateways	TCP 7443	VoiceXML over HTTPS. Calls/sessions answered on port 7443 by HTTPS server.	Figure 6-7
CVP IVR Subsystem: HTTP	Voice Browsers	TCP 8000	VoiceXML over HTTP.	Figure 6-7
CVP IVR Subsystem: HTTPS	Voice Browsers	TCP 8443	VoiceXML over HTTPS.	Figure 6-7
H323 H225 RAS	H.323 applications (like H.323 Gateway and H.323 terminals)	UDP 1719	Gatekeeper H225 RAS.	Figure 6-7
H323 H225	H.323 applications (like H.323 Gateway and H.323 terminals)	TCP 1720	H.225 signaling services.	Figure 6-7
CVP SIP Subsystem, SIP Proxy Server, Gateway, Unified CM: SIP	SIP Endpoints	TCP 5060 UDP 5060	Listen port for incoming SIP requests. Port is configurable.	Figure 6-8

Table 6-21   *TCP/UDP Ports Used by Unified CVP Native and Non-Native Components*

Server / Application	Remote Device	Server Protocol/Port	Notes	Reference Figure
CVP ICM Subsystem	IPCC Enterprise VRU CTI (ICM/IVR message interface)	TCP 5000	Between CVP ICM Subsystem (Call Server) and Unified ICM VRU PG. Port is configurable.	Figure 6-9
CVP Resource Manager	CVP OPS Console	TCP 2099	JMX communication from OPSConsole to CVP Resource Manager on remote device.	Figure 6-10
CVP OPS Console: HTTP	Web Browser	TCP 9000	Web-based interface for configuring CVP components.	Figure 6-10
CVP OPSConsole: HTTPS	Web Browser	TCP 9443	Web-based interface for configuring CVP components with SSL.	Figure 6-10
Support Tools NodeAgent	Support Tools Application Server	TCP 39100, 39101	Support Tools Node Agent service request from the Support Tools Application Server.	Figure 6-11
Support Tools Server: HTTP	Web Browser	TCP 8188	Support Tools Server services HTTP requests from web browser.	Figure 6-11
Support Tools Server: HTTPS	Web Browser	TCP 8189	Support Tools Server services HTTPS requests from web browser.	Figure 6-11
CVP Messaging Layer	CVP Subsystem	TCP 23000-28000 (First Available)	CVP Message Bus communication.	Figure 6-12
IBM Informix	CVP Reporting Subsystem	TCP 1526	Database Connection.	Figure 6-12

Caution   Because the Unified CVP Operations Console Server uses dynamic ports for communication with other components, it cannot be deployed outside a firewall while the rest the Unified CVP components reside inside the firewall.

As mentioned earlier, sometimes a table such as Table 6-21 is not enough to satisfy the security team. In addition the next few sections provide some visual representations as to how these ports communicate between the Unified CVP components. Figure 6-7 illustrates the port and communication model for the Unified CVP Call Server, VoiceXML Server, and Ingress/VoiceXML gateway using H.323.

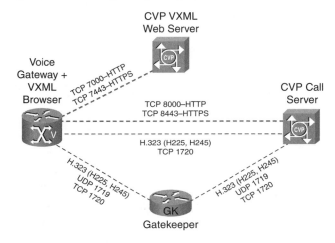

Figure 6-7   *Unified CVP H.323 Port and Communication Model*

Figure 6-7 shows the same model using SIP illustrated in Figure 6-8.

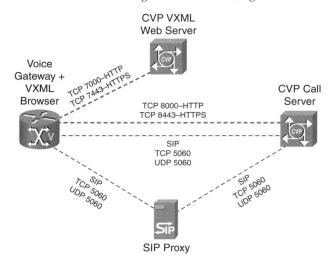

Figure 6-8   *Unified CVP SIP Port and Communication Model*

A simple but important illustration shows how the Unified CVP ICM Subsystem communicates to the Unified ICM PG that hosts the VRU PIM. Figure 6-9 provides a basic illustration of this relationship.

Figure 6-10 shows the port and communication model for the client and server interaction with the Unified CVP Operations Console.

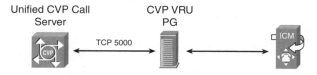

Figure 6-9   *Unified CVP ICM Subsystem Port and Communication Model*

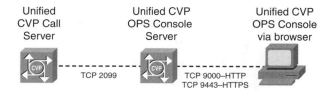

Figure 6-10   *Unified CVP Operations Console Port and Communication Model*

Although the Support Tools server is more commonly found in Unified ICM deployments, it offers some nice interfaces to the Unified CVP server for log collection and troubleshooting. Figure 6-11 illustrates the port and communication model for the Support Tools server for Unified CVP.

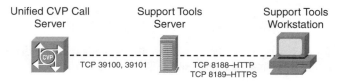

Figure 6-11   *Unified CVP and Support Tools Port and Communication Model*

Wrapping up the port and communication models, this chapter concludes with the Unified CVP Reporting Server and its relationship with the Informix Database. Figure 6-12 illustrates the port and communication model for this relationship.

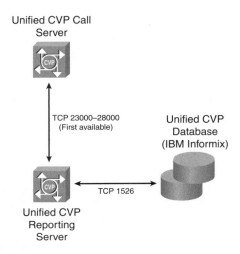

Figure 6-12   *Unified CVP Reporting Server Port and Communication Model*

Summary

In this chapter you examined three important topics:

- Sizing
- Networking
- Security

The intent for each was to boil the painful details down into content that is important to present but not overwhelming to comprehend.

Beginning with some magic regarding sizing, you examined some simple approaches to calculating the call volumes for a contact center. When armed with those call volumes, applying them to individual Unified CVP components allowed for a direct correlation between those call volumes and the sizing exercises required for native and non-native components.

This chapter also covered networking issues such as quality of service and network latency considerations. Although the best practice is to keep network latency within acceptable ranges for the solution, the impact of not doing so was presented and details around mitigating high-latency network links by injecting audio to mask the issue from the caller.

In conclusion, this chapter completed the examination of the center of the universe: security. By providing details on what ports are used by different native and non-native components, you are now armed with information that surely satisfies even the most demanding security team. However, just in case it falls short of those expectations, detailed illustrations are provided to visually depict these communication models further by clarifying how the solution communicates with key components.

The next chapter examines how to upgrade a Unified CVP solution. Important considerations about upgrading Unified CVP are discussed, along with some methodologies pertaining to upgrading native and non-native components. A protocol comparison and feature mapping are provided for H.323 and SIP and some good case studies for performing a flash or migration production cut over.

References

1. Cisco Documentation, *Cisco Unified Customer Voice Portal (CVP) 8.x Solution Reference Network Design (SRND)*, 2010: 14–2.

2. Cisco Documentation, *Cisco Unified Customer Voice Portal (CVP) 8.x Solution Reference Network Design (SRND)*, 2010: 14–8.

3. Cisco Documentation, *Cisco Unified Customer Voice Portal (CVP) 8.x Solution Reference Network Design (SRND)*, 2010: 14–9.

4. Cisco Documentation, *Cisco Unified Customer Voice Portal (CVP) 8.x Solution Reference Network Design (SRND)*, 2011: 7–6.

5. Cisco Documentation, *Cisco Unified Customer Voice Portal (CVP) 8.x Solution Reference Network Design (SRND)*, 2011: 9–6.

6. Cisco Documentation, *Cisco Unified Customer Voice Portal (CVP) 8.x Solution Reference Network Design (SRND)*, 2011: 9–7.

7. Cisco Documentation, *Cisco Unified Customer Voice Portal (CVP) 8.x Solution Reference Network Design (SRND)*, 2011: 9–7.

8. Cisco Documentation, *Cisco Unified Customer Voice Portal (CVP) 8.x Solution Reference Network Design (SRND)*, 2011: 9–7, 8.

Recommended Readings and Resources

Cisco Documentation, *Cisco Unified Customer Voice Portal (CVP) 8.x Solution Reference Network Design (SRND)*, http://www.cisco.com/en/US/docs/voice_ip_comm/cust_contact/contact_center/customer_voice_portal/srnd/8x/cvp8xsrnd.pdf.

Cisco Documentation, *Cisco Unified Contact Center Enterprise Solution Reference Network Design(SRND)*, http://www.cisco.com/en/US/products/sw/custcosw/ps1844/products_implementation_design_guides_list.html.

Cisco Documentation, *Cisco Unified Customer Voice Portal Configuration Guides*, http://www.cisco.com/en/US/partner/products/sw/custcosw/ps1006/ products_installation_and_configuration_guides_list.html.

Cisco Documentation, *Hardware and System Software Specification for Cisco Unified Customer Voice Portal (Unified CVP)*, Release 8.0(1), http://www.cisco.com/en/US/docs/voice_ip_comm/cust_contact/contact_center/ customer_voice_portal/cvp8_0/reference/guide/cvp_801_bom.pdf.

Cisco Documentation, *Cisco Unified Communications System Release 8.x SRND*, January 2011, http://www.cisco.com/en/US/partner/docs/voice_ip_comm/cucm/srnd/ 8x/uc8x.html.

Cisco Documentation, *Cisco ACE 4710 Application Control Engine Datasheet*, http://www.cisco.com/en/US/partner/prod/collateral/contnetw/ps5719/ps7027/ Data_Sheet_Cisco_ACE_4710.html.

Cisco Documentation, *Cisco CSS 11500 Series Content Services Switch Datasheet*, http://www.cisco.com/en/US/partner/prod/collateral/contnetw/ps5719/ps792/ product_data_sheet0900aecd800f851e_ps4565_Products_Data_Sheet.html.

Cisco Documentation, *User Guide for Cisco Unified CVP VoiceXML Server and Cisco Unified Call Studio, Release 8.0(1)*, http://www.cisco.com/en/US/docs/voice_ip_comm/ cust_contact/contact_center/customer_voice_portal/cvp8_0/user/guide/cvp_801_vxml.pdf.

Cisco Documentation, *Enterprise QoS Solution Reference Network Design Guide*, http://www.cisco.com/en/US/docs/solutions/Enterprise/WAN_and_MAN/QoS_SRND/ Enterprise_QoS_SRND.pdf.

Cisco Documentation, *Cisco 3900 Series Integrated Services Router Series Comparison*, http://www.cisco.com/en/US/products/ps10536/prod_series_comparison.html.

Cisco Documentation, *Cisco Unified Communications Sizing Tool*, http://tools.cisco.com/cucst

Internet Resource, Free VoIP Calculators, http://www.voip-calculator.com/calculator/.

Internet Resource, Westbay Online Traffic Calculators, http://www.erlang.com/calculator.

Internet Resource, Call Center Calculator (Windows Application), http://www.erlang.co.uk/ccc.htm.

Chapter 7

Upgrading

This chapter covers the following subjects:

- **Why upgrade?** What are the compelling reasons to consider for upgrading to Unified CVP 8.x?

- **Unified CVP upgrade strategies:** Native component upgrade methodology and supporting strategies.

- **H.323 protocol migration to SIP:** H.323 and SIP feature parity mapping with configuration considerations and protocol migration approaches such as flash cuts and phased migrations. In addition, GKTMP replacement with SIP is also discussed for implementations heavily focused on GKTMP.

Why Upgrade?

Although the old saying, "If it's not broke, why fix it?" seems to ring true in most situations, in the next few sections, you see a compelling case for why an upgrade to a newer version of Unified CVP may be justified. As with all hardware and software products, items are marked for End of Sale, End of Life and are replaced with newer products that have key feature enhancements and improved scalability. As outlined in previous chapters, Unified CVP integrates with several other non-native components including Unified ICM and Cisco Unified Call Manager. These integrations create incompatibility concerns when either of these components is upgraded or when considering upgrading Unified CVP. Just like everything in life, timing is important. If an enterprise is considering a hardware refresh or virtualizing its Unified CVP solution, upgrading to a newer version of Unified CVP could potentially make sense.

What Are End of Sale and End of Life?

Both hardware and software can fall into categories defined by Cisco as End of Sale (EoS) and End of Life (EoL). Table 7-1 outlines the definition of these categories and some equally important milestones in the life cycle of hardware and software.

Table 7-1   *End of Life Milestones and Definitions*

Platform	Total Capacity
End of Sale Date	The last date to order the product through Cisco point-of-sale mechanisms; the product is no longer for sale after this date.
End of Software Maintenance Release Date	The last date that Cisco Engineering may release any final software maintenance releases or bug fixes; after this date Cisco Engineering will no longer develop, repair, maintain, or test the product software.
End of New Service Attachment Date	For equipment and software not covered by a service-and-support contract. This is the last date to order a new service-and-support contract or add the equipment and software to an existing service-and-support contract.
Last Date of Support	The last date to receive service and support for the product; after this date all support services for the product are unavailable, and the product becomes obsolete.

Because the Unified CVP releases follow these categories, it becomes obvious as to why you need to pay attention and track these dates as earlier releases of the solution slowly approach end of life, become obsolete, and drop all supportability by Cisco. The Unified CVP solution should be upgraded in a timely fashion to avoid a mission-critical solution becoming obsolete and lacking support. Table 7-2 illustrates some important dates pertaining to older versions of Unified CVP.

Table 7-2   *End of Life Milestones for Previous Versions of Unified CVP*

End of Sale Product Part Number	End of Sale Date	End of SW Maintenance Release	End of New Service Attachment Date	End of Service Contract Renewal Date	Last Date of Support
Unified CVP 4.0	02/10/2009	11/12/2009	11/12/2009	02/08/2011	11/12/2011
Unified CVP 4.1	08/10/2010	08/10/2011	08/10/2011	11/05/2012	08/31/2013
Unified CVP 7.0	05/20/2011	05/19/2012	05/19/2012	08/15/2013	05/31/2014

It is apparent that some releases of Unified CVP will be End of Life later this year with other releases still a few years out. However, to successfully perform an upgrade, you must consider the amount of effort required to migrate a large Unified CVP deployment to a new version. This effort includes the migration of native components but can also require upgraded non-native components such as IOS gateways.

Figure 7-1 illustrates that 40 percent of an upgrade's effort is spent in planning for the upgrade. An additional 20 percent is spent preparing to perform the upgrade. Planning includes mapping out the upgrade methodology, native and non-native component migration approaches, and call control protocol conversions from H.323 to Session Initiation Protocol (SIP). Therefore, performing an upgrade requires a significant amount of planning and time, further emphasizing the importance of the awareness surrounding the critical life-cycle milestones for aging versions of Unified CVP.

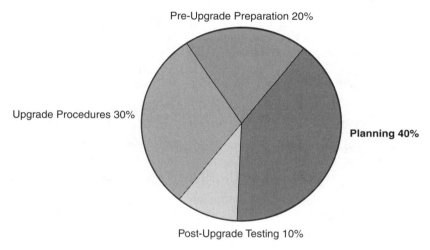

Figure 7-1   *Typical Effort Allocation for Unified CVP Upgrade*

Unified CVP 8.x Feature and Scalability Enhancements

Another compelling reason to consider upgrading Unified CVP to the latest and greatest release comes in the form of new features and increased scalability. Starting in Unified CVP 8.x, the following new components are supported:

- New G2 ISR Routers greatly increasing the capacity and performance of ingress, egress and Voice Extensible Markup Language (VoiceXML) routers

- Support for new IOS software version 15.0(1)M as part of the first generation of new IOS software release strategy from Cisco

- Support for virtualization using VMWare to virtualize the Unified CVP native components using the Cisco Unified Computing System's hardware platform

- Support for the new Cisco Unified SIP Proxy server hosted running on an IOS-based ISR router

- Support for Cisco Application Content Engine (ACE), the next generation content engine

In addition to these new components, version 8.x of Unified CVP also provided some key improvements in the area of scalability. Following are some of the more significant improvements pertaining to scalability:

- Increase in total number of SIP sessions that a single call server can terminate. At the time of this writing, 1200 sessions per server are supported with a goal to support at least 1500. These sessions can be achieved even when the call server and VoiceXML server is co-resident on the same physical server.

- The new virtualization feature also improves scalability. By providing virtualization support on the Cisco UCS hardware platform, the overall footprint of large Unified CVP deployments is greatly reduced. Cisco UCS also provides a single point for the management of all physical and virtual assets providing a compelling case for Unified CVP's usability and serviceability.

- Increase in the size of Unified CVP's reporting database also lends to creditability to increase scalability.

- As discussed in Chapter 6, "Networking, Security, and Sizing Considerations," by introducing the ISR G2 routing platform, the number of calls that a single ISR G2 can process compared to the previous ISR platform has basically doubled in capacity.

- Support for co-resident Peripheral Gateway (PG) and Unified CVP call server on the same physical server, reducing the overall hardware footprint of Unified CVP and building the case for increased scalability.

If the previous short list of components and scalability improvements are not compelling enough, take a look at the improvements added to Unified CVP version 8.x in the realm of SIP:

- Dynamic Routing Support when using SIP on a Unified CVP Call Server.

- Location Based Routing and Call Admission Control (LBCAC). As discussed in previous chapters, LBCAC is a great feature to provide Call Admission Control (CAC) and edge queuing for call origination and transfers.

- Passing and receiving SIP headers. The ability to use customized SIP headers for passing and receiving data is a significant improvement exercised by applications developed with Unified CVP.

- Supports the use of a mixture of G.711 and G.729 Coder-Decoders (CODEC) on different legs of the same call, as long as the user has allocated and configured sufficient resources in the solution for transcoding.

- Unified ICM Re-query support on SIP "Refer" transfers.

- Improved UUI processing.

- SIP support for KPML.

- Hookflash transfer support.

- SIP Sig Digits enhancements as discussed in previous chapters.

- Post Call Survey Support.

A final area that is critical to new releases of software is the increase of product usability and serviceability. The following list outlines some key areas in which version 8.x of Unified CVP has risen to this challenge:

- Improved licensing and enforcement. As discussed early, there has been a great deal of improvements around licensing including the installation and enforcement of licenses.

- Improvements around System Call Tracking, which places a conference ID and aggregation of data on the reporting server. The System Call Tracking tool uses CVP call data for creating and end-to-end call summary report.

- Improvements around the infrastructure logs. More specifically, Unified CVP 8.x now supports the Cisco Log Format and a common infrastructure code base across the majority of the CCBU products, such as Unified CVP, Expert Advisor, and CUIS. The look and feel of all logs will be similar across all CCBU products.

- Launch of the Unified CVP troubleshooting guide hosted on docwiki.cisco.com for edits by the general public. Access to this wiki is installed during all Unified CVP installations, and a pointer to this troubleshooting guide is also available at the top of each log file.

- LBCAC when calls are routed over SIP and H.323 trunks and IP Originated calls.

- Location-based routing to route the calls (including IP Originated) to the same branch VoiceXML Gateway where the switch leg or transfer originated.

- Multicast Music on Hold (mMoH).

- Distributed Music on Hold (dmMoH).

- Creation of new Web Services Manager (WSM), which enables consistent API for the development of additional tools and integrations into Unified CVP. An example tool included in Unified CVP is the new Unified System CLI tool, which provides a global command-line interface (CLI) for all Unified CVP components deployed and is configured via the Unified CVP Operations Console.

- Updated version of the Cisco Log Visualization Tool. This tool provides log files from native and non-native components generating a visual ladder diagram of the call flow found in the input files.

Challenges with Unified Contact Center Product Version Compatibility

Throughout this book, it is apparent that Unified CVP is a solution that integrates with many different products such as Cisco Unified ICM, Unified Call Manager, and CTIOS desktop clients, and so on. How can the upgrade of different components directly impact the solution? In other words, if users upgrade Unified CVP to the latest and greatest release, would they need to consider whether the current Unified ICM or Call Manager cluster will continue to work?

Version compatibility is a huge issue when performing a solution-level upgrade. The lack of accounting for these compatibility challenges when planning for an upgrade can definitely derail or delay an upgrade in it tracks. When considering whether to buy into upgrading Unified CVP, you should consider all the current integration points with the current system, which could require that other components also benefit from their own upgrade. Figure 7-2 illustrates a basic compatibility matrix for a Unified Contact Center Enterprise solution.

Although this book is focused primarily on Unified CVP, this matrix illustrates how important it is to research compatibility and dependencies when considering or planning an upgrade. For example, Unified CVP 8.x can integrate only with Cisco Unified Communications Manager 7.1 and later. Suppose a Unified CVP version 7.x integrated with a CUCM cluster running version 4.x; just to upgrade to 8.x of Unified CVP would require three major release upgrades for CUCM and one for Unified ICM. Furthermore, Unified CVP 8.5(1) can integrate only with version 7.1(5) of CUCM whereas version 8.5(1) of CUCM integrates only with Unified CVP version 8.x and Unified ICM version 8.5. CUCM and Unified ICM upgrades both take a decent amount of planning and time to complete, further complicating the need to get to Unified CVP 8.x.

Another factor comes into play when considering which previous versions of Unified CVP and Unified Call Studio can be upgraded to Unified CVP 8.x. Figure 7-3 provides the supported upgrade paths from these previous versions.

One important observation from Figure 7-3 is that version 3.x of Unified CVP and the Universal Edition of Call Studio are not supported as an upgrade to Unified CVP 8.0(1). For Unified CVP 3.x, the most likely strategy is to perform a fresh install of Unified CVP 8.x using the "technology refresh" upgrade option discussed in the next section. Universal Edition of Call Studio needs to be reinstalled with current studio applications backed up and imported into the new version of Call Studio and verified as properly working.

	Unified CM	CVP [formerly ISN])	PG/CAD/ CTI OS Server	CTI OS Desktop	IP Phones
Unified CCE 8.5(x) Product Sets	8.5(1)	8.5(1) 8.0(x)	**PG** 8.5(1) **CAD** 8.5 **CTI OS Server** 8.5(1)	8.5(1) 8.0(x) 7.5	99xx series 89xx series 69xx series 797x 796x 794x 793x 792x 791x IP Communicator
	8.0(x)	8.5(1) 8.0(x)	**PG** 8.5(1) 8.0(x) 7.5 **CAD** 8.5 **CTI OS Server** 8.5(1) 8.0(x) 7.5	8.5(1) 8.0(x) 7.5	
	7.1(5)	8.5(1) 8.0(x)	**PG** 8.5(1) 8.0(x) 7.5 **CAD** 8.5 **CTI OS Server** 8.5(1) 8.0(x) 7.5	8.5(1) 8.0(x) 7.5	

Figure 7-2   *UCCE 8.x Compatibility Matrix*

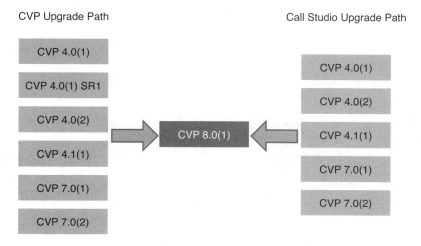

Figure 7-3   *Unified CVP and Call Studio Upgrade Paths*

Unified CVP Upgrade Strategies

You must consider factors such as dependent technologies and upgrade requirements when planning an upgrade. You also must focus on some strategies and methodologies for conducting upgrades. In most cases a significant upgrade of Unified CVP requires an equally significant upgrade for Unified ICM and potentially Unified Communications Manager. Some of the content in this section also references these additional products. However, for a more comprehensive discussion regarding upgrading Unified ICM and Call Manager, access the Cisco documentation located at Cisco.com.

To develop an upgrade strategy for Unified CVP, you need to define what key elements are parts of the strategy. Figure 7-4 provides three categories for different elements of an upgrade strategy.

Options	Base Line	Planning

• Common Ground
• Technology Refresh
	• Hardware
	  • Bill of Materials
	• Software
	  • 3rd Party
	• Compatibility
	  • ACD
	  • CUCM
	  • CTI
	  • CVP
		• Database
		  • Disk Space
		  • Cleanup
		• Backup
		• Default Routing
		• Test Plan
		  • Pre/Post
		• Schedule
		• Notification

Figure 7-4   *Unified Contact Center Upgrade Strategy Elements*

Following are the three categories:

■ **Options:** Common ground is defined as upgrading Unified CVP on the existing hardware platform that the current version of Unified CVP is hosted on. A technology refresh usually refers to new hardware staging for the hosting of the new version of Unified CVP. This new hardware can also exist in the form of a Cisco UCS cluster for the virtualization of Unified CVP.

■ **Base Line:** These elements are where all the research goes in to determine the dependencies for upgrading from an older version of Unified CVP to a current version. Elements that live in this category are items such as existing and new hardware requirements, third-party software integrations, which include the current and future host OS, and compatibility research for all solution components, even if they are not considered native to the Unified CVP solution.

- **Planning:** Although all these categories could be deemed as part of planning, this specific category hosts elements that are focused on the tactical processes of preparing for and executing the upgrade. For example, performing backups, understanding your default routing policies for calls, creating and approving your pre- and post-implementation test plans, applying and socializing the upgrade schedule all make up a major part of planning the upgrade.

Common Ground Upgrades

Looking at the major components in a Unified Contact Center Solution, as illustrated in Figure 7-5, common ground upgrades can still have some caveats you must address.

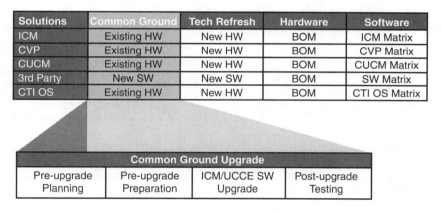

Solutions	Common Ground	Tech Refresh	Hardware	Software
ICM	Existing HW	New HW	BOM	ICM Matrix
CVP	Existing HW	New HW	BOM	CVP Matrix
CUCM	Existing HW	New HW	BOM	CUCM Matrix
3rd Party	New SW	New SW	BOM	SW Matrix
CTI OS	Existing HW	New HW	BOM	CTI OS Matrix

Common Ground Upgrade			
Pre-upgrade Planning	Pre-upgrade Preparation	ICM/UCCE SW Upgrade	Post-upgrade Testing

Figure 7-5   *Common Ground Upgrade Considerations*

For example, a common ground upgrade is performed on existing production equipment, which implies that the pre-upgrade planning and preparation must be accurate. It must also include a detailed plan for backing out the upgrade when things don't turn out the way you envision. This backup plan can be complicated because it is basically rebuilding and upgrading the application software previously hosted on the same hardware. One strategy that works well is to perform a common ground upgrade in a small lab environment before attempting it in a large production environment. This can detect any issues with the in-place upgrade with little to no risk on the production systems. Furthermore, an upgrade such as this performed in a lab can also enable testing a backout plan, ensuring its validity. Although Figure 7-5 indicates that a common ground upgrade would use the existing hardware, this observation comes with one caveat. The existing hardware must meet the Hardware and System Software Specification or what was previous coined as the "Bill of Materials" for Unified CVP. If these requirements are not met, a common ground upgrade is not a viable upgrade option.

Note Upgrades to Unified CVP 8.x usually require additional hardware, depending how old the existing hardware is. In addition, The third-party OS may also require upgrading, which should be accounted for in both the time and cost budgets. As of this writing, Unified CVP 8.x requires Microsoft Windows 2003 running Service Pack 2 or needs to be installed as version R2. Because of the likelihood that hardware must be upgraded to support an upgrade and the overall risk of an in-place upgrade failing, common ground upgrades are less common in production contact centers than technology refresh upgrades.

Technology Refresh Upgrades

A more common approach to performing upgrades falls into the technology refresh category. The reason for this is simple; it is less risky to simply build a parallel system, implement it next to the current production system, and deal with only cutting over the incoming Dialed Number Identification Service (DNIS) numbers, agents, and data. This approach enables a fairly straightforward backout plan and enables the enterprise to flash cut or migrate agents. The downside to this approach is the cost of purchasing new hardware and in some cases new software to support the technology refresh. Figure 7-6 illustrates the main areas of concentration when performing an upgrade using the technology refresh option.

Solutions	Common Ground	Tech Refresh	Hardware	Software
ICM	Existing HW	HW & SW	BOM	Matrix
CVP	Existing HW	HW & SW	BOM	Matrix
CUCM	Existing HW	HW & SW	BOM	Matrix
3rd Party	Existing HW	HW & SW	BOM	Matrix
CTI OS	Existing HW	HW & SW	BOM	Matrix

Technology/ Refresh Upgrade			
Hardware	Software	Data Transfer	BOM

Figure 7-6 *Technology Refresh Upgrade Considerations*

As in common ground upgrades, the Unified CVP Hardware and System Software Specifications document must still be consulted when purchasing the new hardware. The key to a technology refresh is to secure the new hardware and potential software, build and test the system in parallel, and then migrate the data.

Tip During the planning process of technology refresh, you should consider virtualization of Unified CVP using the Cisco Unified Computing System (UCS). UCS is discussed in Chapter 9, "Virtualization." However, if new hardware is purchased and a parallel build is used to migrate an older version of Unified CVP to a newer version, consider virtualizing the upgrade, reducing its hardware footprint while increasing its manageability.

With Unified ICM, data migration is accomplished using the Enhanced Database Migration Tool (EDMT). However, with Unified CVP each new call, VoiceXML, and reporting server should be reconfigured and added to the new Operations Console. There is no tool to export the current Unified CVP configuration and apply it to the new call server farms. In a technology refresh upgrade the new Unified CVP call servers are implemented with different IP addresses and hostnames than those that currently exist in production. Exporting data from the old Unified CVP deployment would be difficult to reuse because such a tool would not have the capability to acknowledge which call server configuration should be applied to which one of the new call servers as part of the technology refresh. Unified ICM's EDMT tool migrates the old ICM database into a format that can be placed into the new Unified ICM database, enabling call routing scripts and configuration data to be copied. Because of the simplicity of setting up the new Unified CVP Servers, it is much more common to reconfigure them and add them to the new instance of the Operations Console.

Caution   When in Doubt, Patch It Out!

Whether building a new Unified CVP deployment or upgrading an existing one, one thing is for sure: Be sure to apply all software engineering patches for the Unified CVP applications provided by Cisco. It is a common mistake to not apply these Engineering Special (ES) patches, which enable issues to creep into the deployment that have already been addressed by a Cisco ES. The old-school mentality on this topic tends to use logic that says, "Unless I have a need for an ES or a match from a behavior or bug, I don't need to load any ES patches." The problem with this approach is that a significant amount of time may be spent on bugs or issues that have already been addressed by an ES patch. By loading all the ES patches provided for the platform, time can be spent troubleshooting real issues and not ones that have already been fixed. In addition, ESs are version-specific just like service releases, and subsequent service releases usually contain the previous ESs. A majority of ESs cannot just be downloaded from Cisco.com, but rather they need to be made available to the engineer, typically on request. End customers can find out about ESs by reading through the release notes via the bug tracking tool provided by Cisco.

Hardware and Software Considerations

Whether performing a common ground or technology refresh upgrade, hardware still plays a significant role for both native and non-native Unified CVP components. Figure 7-7 continues to build on some key considerations pertaining to hardware when performing an upgrade.

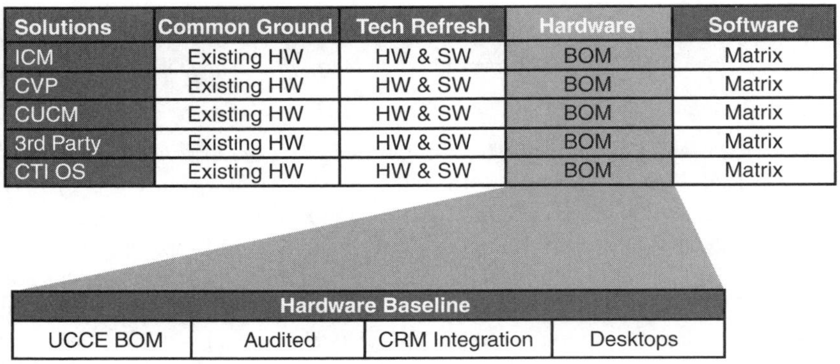

Solutions	Common Ground	Tech Refresh	Hardware	Software
ICM	Existing HW	HW & SW	BOM	Matrix
CVP	Existing HW	HW & SW	BOM	Matrix
CUCM	Existing HW	HW & SW	BOM	Matrix
3rd Party	Existing HW	HW & SW	BOM	Matrix
CTI OS	Existing HW	HW & SW	BOM	Matrix

Hardware Baseline			
UCCE BOM	Audited	CRM Integration	Desktops

Figure 7-7   *Hardware Upgrade Considerations*

If you are interested in performing a common ground upgrade, you need to audit the existing Unified ICM/CVP/CUCM platform to ensure that its current performance enables enough head room to host the newer software. Following are some simple metrics to verify:

- CPU utilization should not exceed 50 percent.

- Physical RAM utilization should not peak over 75 percent.

- Hard disk (C:) should have a minimum of 1 GB of free disk space.

- Maximum Concurrent calls on the Unified CVP Call Server. Understanding this determines the current load for the Call Server farms.

- IOS version currently installed on all Ingress, VoiceXML, and CUSP Gateways.

As mentioned earlier, checking the software compatibility matrices for each component in the overall solution is critical to determine what type of upgrade to perform but also to ensure that all dependencies are met. Figure 7-8 illustrates some of the dependencies for these matrixes.

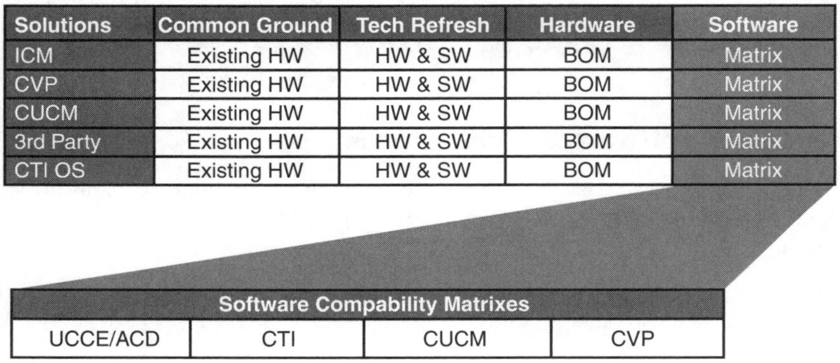

Solutions	Common Ground	Tech Refresh	Hardware	Software
ICM	Existing HW	HW & SW	BOM	Matrix
CVP	Existing HW	HW & SW	BOM	Matrix
CUCM	Existing HW	HW & SW	BOM	Matrix
3rd Party	Existing HW	HW & SW	BOM	Matrix
CTI OS	Existing HW	HW & SW	BOM	Matrix

Software Compability Matrixes			
UCCE/ACD	CTI	CUCM	CVP

Figure 7-8   *Software Compatibility Dependencies*

Unified CVP Native Component Upgrade Strategies

Now that the general strategies around performing an upgrade have been covered, it is time to focus on strategies that apply directly to upgrading the native components of a Unified CVP. As stated earlier, the native components of Unified CVP consist of the Call, VoiceXML, and Reporting Servers. The challenge when upgrading these native components is that you must perform upgrades within a limited maintenance window, usually too small to upgrade a medium to large Unified CVP deployment. Most contact centers are either 24/7 or have a subset of agents and skill groups that function in a 24/7 manner. Suggesting to the business that its critical functions will be down during an upgrade is not acceptable. Furthermore, most organizations avoid performing upgrades because they cannot determine a rational approach to upgrading mission-critical systems without having to deal with an outage. However, this section includes some great approaches to segmenting the contact center into units that can be individually upgraded during smaller maintenance windows, enabling the business to continue operating.

A CVP Unit is a logical group of VoiceXML servers, Call Servers, and Reporting Servers that can be involved when processing a call. The division of an entire Unified CVP deployment would result in multiple but logical CVP Units. By using this approach, each unit can be independently upgraded using separate maintenance windows. In other words, a maintenance window can be assigned per CVP Unit. After the CVP Units are determined, each unit can be upgraded individually, one per maintenance window, or using a multiphase upgrade approach. Certain servers grouped in multiple units could be upgraded during the same maintenance window.

A multiphase upgrade refers to the ability to upgrade a subset of Unified CVP Servers and resume call processing. The key to this approach is that all native components of a certain type (Call Server, VoiceXML Server, Reporting Server, and so on) must be upgraded at the same time. The most important caveat to this approach is the order in which native components within a CVP Unit are upgraded. Unified CVP native components must be upgraded in the following order:

1. Support Tools Server

2. Operations Console Server

3. Reporting Servers

4. Call Servers

5. VoiceXML Servers

However, not all servers of the same type need to be upgraded in a single maintenance window. As previously mentioned, there is a single Operations Console per Unified CVP deployment. Therefore logic would say that it is the first native Unified CVP component that should be upgraded. So what happens to newer fields in the Operations Console user interface for servers that have not been upgraded? In other words, if the Operations Console has UI fields that are new to the newer version of Unified CVP, how does it handle those values for servers that have not been upgraded yet? The answer is clear. The newer fields stored by the upgraded Operations Console server are simply ignored by the older servers. However, if the Operations Console is used to perform an online view for a device type of an older release version, defaults will be used for the new properties.

Use Case 1: Upgrading CVP Units Without Multiphase

Figure 7-9 provides an illustration on the segmentation process of a Unified CVP farm into two logical CVP Units.

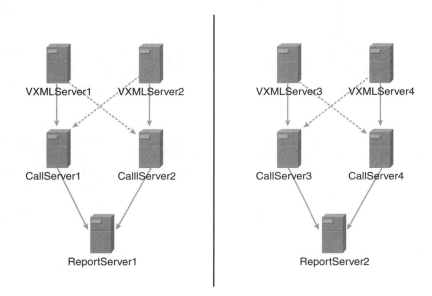

Figure 7-9 *Unified CVP Unit Partitioning Example*

In this example, two units are created (where VS = VoiceXML Server, CS = Call Server, RS = Reporting Server):

- **CVP Unit 1:** VS1, VS2, CS1, CS2, RS1

- **CVP Unit 2:** VS3, VS4, CS3, CS4, RS2

These are considered logical CVP Units because there is no path for a call to move from one unit to the other. Because the plan is composed of upgrading each unit entirely per a maintenance window, it is critical to logically partition the CVP Units in such a way that calls never cross from a native component in CVP Unit 1 to CVP Unit 2 because Unit 1 could be on a newer version of Unified CVP before Unit 2 is.

Another advantage of this approach is for the case of co-resident installations. This is the preferred and only supported use case for upgrading a CVP Unit that has native components installed co-resident with other native components. The caveat is that the co-resident native components must be part of the same CVP Unit and cannot be partitioned into different CVP Units. The upgrade process for Unified CVP upgrades *all* native components on a server when it is executed. Therefore, there is no way to upgrade only some native components on a server and leave others for a different maintenance window focused on a different CVP Unit.

Use Case 2: Upgrading CVP Units Using Multiphase Approach

What if there were much smaller maintenance windows that would not enable an upgrade for an entire CVP Unit or the approach were more focused around first upgrading certain types of native components? If these were the requirements, you need to examine the performance of a multiphase upgrade across multiple CVP Units. Using the same CVP Units partitioning illustration provided in Figure 7-9, following are a few examples of how to perform a multiphase upgrade (where VS = VoiceXML Server, CS = Call Server, RS = Reporting Server):

- **Example 1:** Upgrade a subset of server types from a CVP Unit in a maintenance window.

    - Maintenance Window 1: RS1, CS1

    - Maintenance Window 2: CS2,VS1,VS2

    - Maintenance Window 3:RS2,CS3

    - Maintenance Window 4:CS4,VS3,VS4

- **Example 2:** Upgrade all servers of a certain type in a maintenance window.

    - Maintenance Window 1: RS1, RS2

    - Maintenance Window 2: CS1,CS2,CS3,CS4

    - Maintenance Window 3:VS1,VS2,VS3,VS4

- **Example 3:** Upgrade all a subset of a server type in a maintenance window.

    - Maintenance Window 1: RS1, RS2, CS1

    - Maintenance Window 2: CS2, CS3, CS4, VS1

    - Maintenance Window 3:VS2, VS3, VS4

Example 2 is the most logical because it is required to deal with only troubleshooting a certain type of native component after the maintenance window is over. In Examples 1 and 3, some call servers have been upgraded, whereas others have not. In the rare situation that a user must troubleshoot calls when some of the call servers have been upgraded and others have not, determining which call server could be causing the issue can be difficult. Because Ingress Gateways are load balancing all calls to each of the Unified CVP Call Servers, the problem can manifest itself only when the call hits the call server in question. It is because of this uncertainty that Example 2 gives the most consistent results when troubleshoot the solution after an upgrade.

As noted in Use Case 1, be aware that co-resident native components will be upgraded when the server is upgraded. Therefore, multiphase upgrades are not recommended if dealing with a deployment with heavy reliance on co-resident native components.

Unified CVP Upgrade Methodology

It is advised that all other components in a Cisco Unified Contact Center solution be upgraded before Unified CVP. After the other components are at acceptable compatibility levels, use the high-level methodology, illustrated in Figure 7-10, with the native component partitioning strategies provided in the previous section.

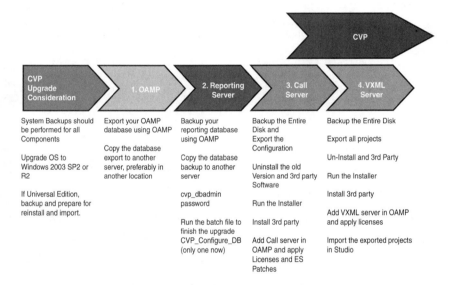

Figure 7-10   *Unified CVP Upgrade Methodology*

To re-emphasize a few observations from Figure 7-10, first, applications developed with the Universal Edition need to be exported so that they can be imported during the VoiceXML Server upgrade or phase 4. Second, depending on the type of upgrade performed, some of these steps apply, and some do not. It all depends on whether it will be a common ground or a technology refresh upgrade. Finally, be sure to pay close attention to custom Java elements and Say It Smart plug-ins because they may need to be recompiled with a newer version of a JDK. After the VoiceXML applications are imported to the upgraded servers, execute the post upgrade application tests, and verify what components still work and which may need some attention.

As this chapter concludes with upgrade strategies, one important best practice lingers. You should break down upgrades into manageable milestones, allowing for progression to occur without injecting too many changes and variables into the process overwhelming the support staff and impacting business. With that said, it is a good idea to first look at performing upgrades to native Unified CVP components before attempting to migrate non-native components, such as the call protocol from H.323 to SIP. The reason for this approach is simple: After the Unified CVP Call Servers have been upgraded and are working with existing non-native components and call control protocol, the second part of the upgrade should be to build a strategy around the migration of H.323 to SIP.

> **Caution**   After the native components of the Unified CVP solution have been upgraded, you need to upgrade the Ingress Gateway and VoiceXML Gateway support files to the new versions that are now available as part of the call server upgrades. These new files should be placed on the gateways only after the gateways' hardware and software have been upgraded to versions supported by the new version of Unified CVP. This should already be the case; otherwise, the upgrade would already be suffering from interoperability issues. It is best practice to upgrade all the TCL and support files provided by Unified CVP on the solutions' gateways to avoid any interoperability issues with the newer version of Unified CVP and new features that have dependencies on the newer versions of the gateway TCL files.

H.323 Protocol Migrations to SIP

Majorities of existing Unified CVP deployments that are candidates for upgrades were deployed using the H.323 call control protocol and not SIP. Migrating from H.323 to SIP in a Unified CVP solution can be a complex undertaking without some careful planning and feature mapping. Quite a few migrations are stalled or delayed simply because the migration engineers do not have any guidance or ideas on how to migrate H.323 deployments to SIP, or they are uncomfortable with the SIP protocol. This section tries to remove some of the spookiness around protocol migrations and provide some guidance on how to prepare and plan for a conversion. You must address some caveats when considering what approach to take when migrating your call control protocol.

An H.323 to SIP migration strategy must meet some basic requirements for it to be accepted as best practice. It must provide a quick-and-simple rollback procedure if problems arise after the migration has been completed. The strategy should also provide flash and phased migration methodologies according to the customer's preference and should limit the amount of new hardware required to perform the migration except for the introduction of Cisco Unified SIP Proxy (CUSP) chassis and blades. In addition, the strategy should maintain feature parity between H.323 and SIP with minimal changes to the solution to achieve this parity. Obviously, your strategy must focus on migrations to Unified CVP 8.x and beyond; however, as discovered earlier, customers may find it important to first migrate to Unified CVP 7.x prior to executing a protocol migration strategy. If a customer has implemented Gatekeeper Transaction Message Protocol (GKTMP), this investment should also be preserved where ever possible because it is most likely that there will be significant dependencies on GKTMP for call routing. Finally, any preparation work in advance of executing the protocol migration can be executed on production systems but cannot change or impact the behavior of the production systems.

Following is a protocol migration checklist that should exist prior to executing the migration strategy:

- Gather system configurations from all migration touch points including servers, devices, and gateways.

- Itemize a list of features that the customer uses in H.323, and map them to the SIP equivalents.

- Determine the customer's tolerance for phased versus flash cut migration methodologies. Include a general timeline for the migration plan with potential maintenance window opportunities.

- Prepare simple topology diagrams showing SIP and H.323 call paths for the first and subsequent migration nights. This information should include the following:

  - Each night of the migration

  - The part of the call path that will change

  - The components to be modified to complete the change

- Prepare a spreadsheet based on GK configuration to aid in creating the CUSP or Cisco Unified Presence Server (CUPS) dial plan, depending on which proxy server has been deployed.

- Create the production CUSP or CUPS configuration and dial plan.

- Prepare a list of every system component with detailed actions to be taken prior to the migration night and the actual night of the migration.

- Prepare a detailed rollback plan.

H.323 to SIP Feature Parity

An important area of consideration when migrating H.323 to SIP falls in the realm of feature mapping. To migrate a call protocol the features used by the protocol are mapped in to a "like" feature offered by the destination protocol. Otherwise, the solution will be operationally at risk. Table 7-3 provides an overview of feature mapping between H.323 and SIP.

These feature mappings are discussed in more detail to better understand how they are implemented in H.323 and what must be modified for SIP.

- **setTransferLabel:** Used to provide edge queuing support similar to sendToOriginator functionality found with Unified CVP and SIP. If issuing the command **showTransferLabel** via the vbadmin console on a Unified CVP Call Server displays a value that is not blank, that deployment is using **setTransferLabels** to by-pass the gatekeeper during the Voice Response Unit (VRU) leg of an H.323 call. In addition, the values used in the **setExcludeIP** do not need to be mapped into a SIP equivalent command simply because SIP uses the SIP header to determine if the device is capable of processing the VRU leg of a call. That is, is this a VoiceXML Gateway or a Call Manager subscriber?

Table 7-3 *H.323 to SIP Unified CVP Feature Parity*

H.323 Feature	SIP Feature
setTransferLabel	SendToOriginator
TBCT	N/A (set CVP dial peer session transport tcp)
Hookflash	OAMP SIP Tab; use commas to match VB ShowTakebackDelay
H.323 Refer	SIP RFXXX and SIP ECC user.sip.refertransfer
CLI Override	SIP ECC method call.user.microapp.override_cli ECC
DTMF *8	N/A (set CVP dial peer session transport tcp)
Survivability	Same for SIP; consider converting any H.323 recovery dial peer(s) to SIP
Post Call Survey	Map showSurveyDnis to OAMP SIP tab Post call survey; Set ICM script for SIP; set user.microapp.isPostCallSurvey to y
Customized RNA Timeout	Map VB showRnaTimeout equates to RNA section of OAMP SIP Tab. SIP default is 60 seconds; H.323 default is 15 seconds
UUI	Map VB showUUIParams to OAMP SIP tab GTD Parameter Forwarding
showDiscCauseCode	On SIP Gateway: set sip-status 404 pstn-cause <whatever is in vbadmin> set sip-status 503 pstn-cause <whatever is in vbadmin>
Gatekeeper Features	See detailed section next
Significant Digits	LBCAC or traditional Significant Digits supported in SIP
CAC	LBCAC

- **TBCT (TBCT):** A call-transfer standard for ISDN interfaces. This feature enables a Cisco voice gateway to request an NI-2 switch to directly connect two independent calls. The two calls can be served by the same PRI or by two different PRIs on the gateway. This feature is based on Telcordia GR-2865-CORE. TBCT makes efficient use of resources by releasing two B channels after a call transfer. Blind transfer of PSTN calls can happen outside the Cisco gateway without tying up gateway resources. Although the gateway is not involved after calls are transferred, billing continues as though the calls are still connected to the gateway. Customers using this feature need to have special agreements with their ISDN service provider for billing. Another option is that the gateway can subscribe to get notification from the switch when a transferred call clears. By examining the survivability service configured on the Ingress Gateway, it can be determined if the deployment uses TBCT. If a parameter has been configured for the survivability service in the form of **param icm-tbct 1**, be sure to add the command **session transport tcp** to the Unified CVP dial peer to avoid digits occasionally getting out of order.

- **HookFlash:** Configured via the HF configured via an ICM script. Assume the customer had an H.323 label HF1234 in its ICM application script. The H.323 default is 500 msec between sending the hookflash and sending the 1234. However, five commas should be placed between the HF and the numeric portion of the label when configuring this label for SIP, for example HF,,,,,1234. In addition, delay showed from vbadmin when executing **ShowTakebackDelay** should match the comma duration configured on the SIP tab via the Operations Console. Also remember that the command **param icm-hf** cannot be added to the survivability service assigned to the pots dial peers until the night of the cutover.

- **H.323 Refer:** If the following parameter **param icm-rf 1** is configured for the survivability service on the Ingress Gateway, the deployment uses H.323 Refer. To map this over to SIP, first configure the Expanded Call Context (ECC) variable in ICM **user.sip.refertransfer**, which replaces **user.h323.rftransfer**. In addition, when using SIP, RFXXX replaces RF88#XXX#. The dial peer for XXX on the gateway needs to be adjusted to support SIP as well. Interesting enough, the H.323 survivability service configuration **param icm-rf 1** can be left in the configuration even after migrating the gateway to SIP.

- **CLI Override:** If the deployment has either the ICM ECC variable **call.user.microapp.override_cli** set in any ICM script, or if some of the labels configured contain CLI=, this feature is used. Using the ECC variable of **call.user.microapp.override_cli** is the only method support by SIP. So if labels are discovered that contain CLI=, they need to be converted to all use the ECC method.

- **DTMF*8:** If any ICM scripts contain a DTMF*8 label, be sure to set the Ingress Gateways' CVP dial peer with the following command **session transport tcp** to avoid digits from occasionally getting out of order.

- **Survivability:** Should continue to work transparently between both H.323 and SIP. However, if your deployment uses H.323 recovery dial peers, you should consider converting them to SIP.

- **Post-call Survey:** If accessing vbadmin and executing the following command **showSurveyDNIS** provides a nonblank value, this feature is used by H.323. The value displayed by the **showSurveryDNIS** vbadmin command should be mapped to the SIP tab's Post call survey section via the Operations Console. In the ICM scripts for SIP, set **user.microapp.isPostCallSurvey** to a y because H.323 did not have a way to execute the survey on a call-by-call basis.

- **Customized RNA Timeout:** If the result of executing the command **showRnaTimeout** via the vbadmin console displays a value other than 15 seconds, the deployment uses customized RNA Timeout values. The value outputted by this command should be mapped to the SIP tab's RNA section via the Operations Console. The default for H.323 is 15 seconds and 60 seconds for SIP.

- **UUI:** If accessing vbadmin and executing the following command **showUUIParams** provides a nonblank value, this feature is used by H.323. This nonblank value should be mapped to the SIP tabs' "GTD Parameter Forwarding" section via the Operations Console. There should be no changes to any ICM scripts required to support this feature in SIP.

- **showDiscCauseCode:** If accessing vbadmin and executing the following command **showDiscCauseCode** provides a value other than 34, this feature has been customized for this deployment. By accessing the SIP gateway under the sip-ua (SIP User Agent) configure the following commands:

  - **set sip-status 404 pstn-cause** <value found in vbadmin>

  - **set sip-status 503 pstn-cause** <value found in vbadmin>

- **Gatekeeper to SIP Proxy parity:** Some features are implemented via an H.323 gatekeeper that cannot be mapped directly to a feature provided by a SIP Proxy server such as CUSP. As part of the discovery process performed during a migration, these features should be discussed to determine if any are currently configured and used:

  - **Billing to a Radius Server:** Not available in CUSP.

  - **Gatekeeper CAC:** If the CLI commands **endpoint max-calls** or **bandwidth** is present in the gatekeeper configuration, GK-based CAC is configured. There is no such feature in CUSP until release 8.6 and beyond.

  - **GKTMP:** If the CLI command **server trigger** is present in the gatekeeper configuration, GKTMP is configured with H.323. Using the Unified CVP Call Server as a redirect server for GKTMP replacement is discussed later.

  - **techPrefix:** If issuing the CLI command **show gatekeeper gw-type-prefix** on the gatekeeper results in numerous devices registered with different technology prefixes than the default technology prefix, technology prefixes are a major concern. This feature should be checked against significant digit stripping to determine if technology prefixes are being used to route calls to edge routers for treatment. If so, these technology prefixes should be replaced with a SIP site code or LBCAC configurations.

  - **Directory Gatekeeper, Alternative Gatekeeper, Gatekeeper Cluster, and HSRP:** CUSP offers only basic failover with no SIP static route replication. Although HSRP is supported with CUSP, it has not been tested with Unified CVP and is therefore not supported. As previously discussed, CUPS does provide redundant servers with static route replication.

■ **Significant Digits:** As noted in previous chapters, a similar technique can be used in SIP to support Significant Digit stripping. The major difference is that in H.323 the digits stripped and saved by Unified CVP are prepended to subsequent ICM labels as technology prefixes. In SIP they are simply prepended as site codes.

■ **CAC:** To avoid some of the more creative approaches used in older versions of Unified CVP and H.323 to implement CAC, Locations Based CAC should be used with SIP deployments to move to a more manageable implementation of CAC. As mentioned in previous chapters, LBCAC can be used to achieve CAC requirements and an edge queuing technique.

GKTMP Replacement with SIP

It's likely that some deployments must continue to use an equivalent of GKTMP scripts in the world of SIP. This is because contact center personnel who are not allowed to access data center equipment such as gatekeepers and SIP Proxy servers still need the ability to adjust routing decisions via a back-end database (time-of-day routing, holiday/weather routing, and so on). In addition, some dial plans continue to be noncontiguous and require tens of thousands of individual dialed numbers that simply cannot be entered into a SIP Proxy server in any feasible manner. Therefore, you need to engineer a plan to use a SIP Proxy server like CUSP in place of a gatekeeper but continue to use the existing GKTMP scripts for the bulk of the dial plan route resolution. The challenge is that CUSP does not provide an equivalent of a gatekeeper's **server trigger** command to hook into the GKTMP scripts.

What if a design were provided that would use Unified CVP as a SIP Redirect Server behind a SIP Proxy like CUSP but in front of the ICM GKTMP scripts? Essentially, Unified CVP would take the place of the GKTMP Network Interface Card (NIC) when using SIP. Figure 7-11 provides an illustration of this concept.

Examine the call flow for a traditional H.323 GKTMP implementation. Figure 7-12 provides an illustration of this call flow followed by the detailed steps.

The following steps detail the process of the call flow:

Step 1.   The Ingress Gateway sends a call Admission Request (ARQ) to the gatekeeper.

Step 2.   The gatekeeper sends a request to the GKTMP NIC and runs and ICM Script.

Step 3.   ICM returns a selected label (and optionally the destination endpoint IP address) in the GKTMP Response ARQ/ACF response via the GKTMP NIC. For this step assume that the Unified ICM script returns a label and the modified GKTMP Response with the IP address of the Unified CVP Call Server.

Step 4.   The gatekeeper sends a call Admission Confirm (ACF) to the Ingress Gateway with the Unified CVP Call Server IP Address.

Step 5.   The Ingress Gateway sends a setup to the Unified CVP Call Server's H.323 Service.

Step 6.   The Unified CVP queries ICM for instructions using the GED 125 protocol.

Traditional H.323 GKTMP

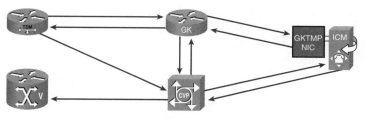

Unified CVP as SIP Redirect Server

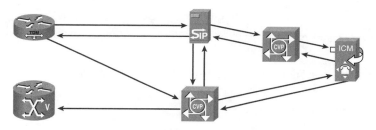

Figure 7-11   *Unified CVP as a SIP Redirect Server for GKTMP NIC Replacement*

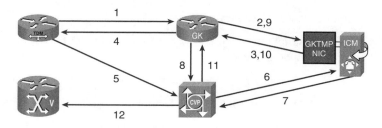

Figure 7-12   *Traditional H.323 GKTMP Call Flow*

Step 7.   ICM provides a VoiceXML gateway DN label to the Unified CVP Call Server assuming the Voice Response Unit (VRU) leg needs to be engaged.

Step 8.   The Unified CVP sends ARQ to the gatekeeper.

Step 9.   The gatekeeper sends a GKTMP request to GKTMP NIC.

Step 10.   ICM returns a selected label (and optionally the destination endpoint IP address) in the GKTMP Response ARQ/ACF response via the GKTMP NIC. Assume that the Unified ICM script returns a label and the modified GKTMP Response with the IP address of the VoiceXML Gateway.

Step 11.   The gatekeeper sends the ACF to the Unified CVP Call Server with the VoiceXML Gateway IP address.

Step 12.   The Unified CVP sends a call setup message to the VoiceXML Gateway.

How does this call flow change when the gatekeeper and GKTMP NIC are removed and a Unified CVP Call Server is put in place for the role of a SIP redirection server? Figure 7-13 provides the modified call flow when using Unified CVP with SIP as a front end to the GKTMP scripts located in Unified ICM.

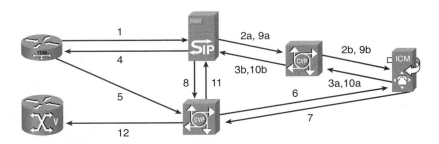

Figure 7-13   *Unified CVP as a SIP Redirect Server Call Flow*

The following steps detail this process:

Step 1.   The Ingress Gateway sends the INVITE to CUSP.

Step 2.   CUSP sends the INVITE to the CVP Redirect Server.

Step 2b.   The Unified CVP Redirect Server sends New Call dialog to Unified ICM. The modified GKTMP script runs.

Step 3a.   The ICM script returns label such as **RFsip:1234@10.1.1.10** (IP address of the Unified CVP Call Server).

Step 3b.   Unified CVP sends a 302 Moved Temporarily SIP message to the CUSP.

Step 4.   The CUSP returns the 302 Moved Temporarily message to the Ingress Gateway.

Step 5.   The Ingress Gateway processes Redirect and sends INVITE to Unified CVP Call Server.

Step 6.   The Unified CVP queries ICM for instructions using a GED 125 protocol.

Step 7.   ICM provides a VoiceXML Gateway DN label to the Unified CVP Call Server assuming the VRU leg needs to be engaged.

Step 8.   The Unified CVP sends the SIP INVITE to CUSP.

Step 9a.   The CUSP sends the SIP INVITE to the Unified CVP Redirect Server.

Step 9b.   The Unified CVP Redirect Server sends the New Call dialog to the Unified ICM. The modified GKTMP script runs.

Step 10a.   The ICM script returns label such as **RFsip:99999999999@10.10.10.1** (IP address of the VoiceXML Gateway).

Step 10b. The Unified CVP sends a 302 Moved Temporarily SIP message to the CUSP.

Step 11. The CUSP returns the 302 Moved Temporarily message to the Unified CVP Call Server.

Step 12. The Unified CVP sends the SIP INVITE to the VoiceXML Gateway.

For this to work, the GKTMP scripts must be modified to build the label referenced in Step 3a and Step 10a. For example, suppose the original Set Variable node in the script had a formula such as:

```
Call.PeripheralVariable1 = icce_site_info.host_ip_address
```

It would need to be modified as such:

```
Call.PeripheralVariable1 =
concatenate("RFsip:",Call.DialedNumberString,"@",icce_site_info.hos t_ip_address)
```

This simple modification would enable labels such as RFsip:1234@10.1.1.10 and RFsip:99999999999@10.10.10.1 to be generated and the call to be correctly routed to the endpoint similar to how it was routed with H.323 and GKTMP.

This solution comes with a substantial list of caveats and considerations.

- To use this solution for the migration GKTMP-dependent deployments to SIP, version 8.5(1) of Unified CVP must be used. There is a fix in version 8.5(1) that instructs Unified CVP to not resolve a Dialed Number passed from Unified ICM if that label already contains a URL that is fully qualified, for example, 1234@10.1.1.10.

- The Unified CVP redirect servers must be physically separate from the call processing Unified CVP servers, as shown in Figure 7-13. This is because a call with the same GUID can route through the redirect server. Unified CVP rejects a SIP call when it already has a call active with the same GUID.

- Gateways, CUCM, and even Unified CVP all honor the contact header in the redirect without additional dial peer or route table resolution. It is unclear, however, how the other SIP user agents may handle these redirects. Therefore, it there are other types of SIP user agents in the solution, they must explicitly be tested with redirect.

- The Unified CVP redirect servers should be sized by call rate and not call volume. Unified CVP 8.0 can handle 15 calls per second.

- The Unified CVP redirect server cannot replace all GKTMP functionality. The following constraints include

  - Inability to process a CLI modified by the GKTMP script. Customers that use a modified CLI for trunk group reporting would need to switch from GKTMP to the Unified CVP trunk group reporting feature.

  - Inability to process a list of IP addresses generated by the GKTMP script. It can handle only a single IP address and not multiple.

■ Because the Unified CVP redirect server can process only a single IP address, failover capabilities are limited. The GKTMP script picks the route without knowledge of the up/down state of the target server. Arguably this solution is no worse than for current H.323 GKTMP deployments.

■ Ideally, the CUSP would honor the contact header in the 302 Moved Temporarily redirect SIP message. However, CUSP attempts to re-resolve the dialed number according to its own dial plan. This defeats the purpose of having the Unified ICM scripts determine the target IP address. To get this to work with CUSP, the user must disable route recursion in CUSP so that CUSP simply passes the 302 message back to the calling user agent.

Finishing this discussion on GKTMP, following are the devices that need to be configured with some specifics:

■ Unified CVP

   ■ Configure at least two new Unified CVP SIP Call Servers sized for the customer calls per second. There is no special configuration required on these servers.

   ■ Install Unified CVP 8.5(1), which has the necessary fix for DN processing where a fully qualified URL has been provided.

■ CUSP

   ■ Configure a "no route recursion" so CUSP can pass through the redirect instead of processing it.

   ■ Create a server group for the Unified CVP redirect servers.

   ■ In the CUSP route tables, route DNs that previously went to the GKTMP NIC configured in the gatekeeper to the Unified CVP redirect server group. If there are a significant number of these DNs, it might be better to route all non-GKTMP DNs specifically and then use a wildcard "*" for the remainder.

■ Unified ICM

   ■ Make a copy of all the GKTMP scripts.

   ■ Assign to the default call type under PG Explorer->RoutingClient the Unified CVP redirect servers. This can eliminate the need to configure every GKTMP DN.

   ■ Modify the scripts as previously described.

■ Ingress Gateway: via the CLI interface on the router issue the following commands:

```
voice service voip
  no notify redirect ip2ip
  no supplementary-service sip moved-temporarily
```

Protocol Migration Approaches

The important considerations around protocol migrations have been outlined. It is time to examine some migration approaches that you can use to migrate the entire solution to SIP. Migration approaches fall into two generally accepted categories:

- **Flash cutover:** This approach requires that all configuration work be completed prior to switching the solution over to SIP. These changes to support SIP should not impact the production system and should lie dormant until the evening of the cutover.

  - **PROS:** Three simple steps need to be executed the evening of the cutover and can be easily and quickly rolled back if problems arise.

  - **CONS:** Customers typically perceive this option as too risky especially for large complex deployments. Furthermore, you cannot validate the actual dial plan with call testing before the cutover unless the customer has a lab environment that duplicates its production system.

- **Phased cutover:** This approach enables more controlled testing of an enterprise segment as it is converted. Configurations are implemented and aligned per maintenance window and cut strategy.

  - **PROS:** Limits the risk to only call flows that are being converted to SIP at the time of the maintenance window. Customers perceive this as a more acceptable approach pertaining to risk against their production system. In large complex deployments, a rollback plan can be executed against a smaller set of dialed numbers, agents, and devices because the migration is focused on smaller groups of DNs, agents, and devices.

  - **CONS:** Requires a great deal more planning and complexity around call and device partitioning. This complexity also increases the amount of device configuration because some devices will service both H.323 and SIP calls. The entire process requires more maintenance windows, time, and communication.

Flash Cutover

To perform a flash cutover, all the configurations must be completed on all native and non-native components prior to the evening of the cutover. If you choose this approach, try to use a lab to verify the configuration and dial plan modifications before the configurations are placed on to the production system. Although adding these configurations may not affect the production system, trusting but verifying the accuracy of the configurations can save a significant amount of time during the evening of the flash cut in the realm of reconfiguration and troubleshooting. Figure 7-14 provides a high-level illustration of the configuration touch points that should be considered if you choose to perform a flash cutover.

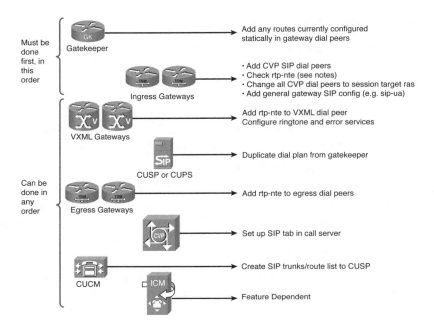

Figure 7-14 *Flash Cutover Configuration Touch Points*

The following discusses the configuration touch points in more detail:

- **Gatekeeper:** Prior to the cutover all zone prefixes sourcing from or terminating to the Ingress, Egress, or VoiceXML Gateways should be added to those respective gateways as SIP dial peers. These new dial peers should be set up with a preference allowing the existing H.323 Registration, Admission, and Status (RAS) dial peers to service production calls. The reason for these additions is that on the night of the cutover, the user must do a "shut" on the gatekeepers to flip all incoming calls on all the gateways over to SIP. This approach enables deployments with a significant number of gateways to rely on removing the gatekeepers as the tipping point to switch over to SIP without having to touch each of those gateways at the time of the flash cut. Alternatively, if there is an insignificant number of gateways, on the night of the cutover, the user could execute a **no h.323-gateway voip interface** command that would accomplish the same thing.

- **Ingress Gateways**

  - **Add Unified CVP SIP dial peers:** Add the SIP dial peers using a dial peer preference that is higher in numeric value than the existing H.323 dial peers. The higher the numeric value of the preference, the lower the actual preference is on the gateway to engage the respective dial peer. Make sure to point the dial peer to the SIP Proxy server, either CUSP or CUPS, and add support to these new dial peers for dtmf-relay using rtp-nte.

- **Check for rtp-nte:** This step could impact production if not completely understood. Next you add rtp-nte support for DTMF relay to the VoiceXML Gateways, however, it is a good idea to take a peek at those VoiceXML Gateways and verify if rtp-nte is already configured as the method for delivering DTMF relay on those gateways. If it is determined that rtp-nte has already been configured on the VoiceXML Gateways, the work is complete for the Ingress Gateway and DTMF relay configurations. Otherwise, remove rtp-nte from the H.323 Unified CVP dial peers on the Ingress Gateway. Leaving it can cause DTMF to be negotiated inband (RFC2833) after rtp-nte is added to the VoiceXML Gateways. This would then cause features such as DTMF*8 or TBCT transfers to fail.

- **Change all H.323 CVP dial peers to "session target ras":** The importance of this step is to move all H.323 static dial peers, ones that do not currently use the gatekeeper, to use RAS and the gatekeeper for routing decisions. This enables the ability to control all existing H.323 dial peers and static dial peers via the gatekeeper **shutdown** command the night of the cutover. This is another area that should be approached with caution. Be sure that the prefixes or dialed numbers that these static dial peers use have been added correctly to the gatekeeper configuration before changing these dial peers over to use the command **session target RAS**. If there are too many static H.323 dial peers or the business deems this as too risky to perform during production, opt to make the changes to these dial peers during the night of the cutover, converting them to SIP dial peers with a target pointing to the SIP Proxy servers. Make sure that their dialed numbers are part of the SIP Proxy dial plan.

- **Add general gateway SIP configurations:** Be sure to add best practice configurations to the gateways to support SIP in a Unified CVP environment. Commands that configure **sip-ua** and **voice service voip** settings should be researched and added prior to the night of the cutover. Example 7-1 shows some of these commands.

Example 7-1 *SIP User Agent and Service Configuration*

```
sip-ua
 retry invite 3
 timers expires 60000
 sip-server ipv4:<IP of SIP Proxy or Call Server>:5060
 reason-header override
!
voice service voip
 allow-connections h323 to h323
 signaling forward unconditional
 h323
 modem passthrough none codec g729r8 pre-ietf
 sip
  min-se 360
  header-passing
```

- **VoiceXML Gateways**

  - **Add "rtp-nte" for VRU leg voip dial peer DTMF relay support:** If this does not already exist, it needs to be added so that when the switch over to SIP occurs on the Ingress and VoiceXML Gateways, RFC2833 DTMF relay signaling can be negotiated.

  - **Configure ringtone and error services:** Because SIP uses the gateway to play ringtone and error messages using a combination of dial peers and application services, you must be sure to add these configurations to the VoiceXML Gateway. In addition, make sure that the gateways have the ringtone.tcl, cvperror.tcl, and critical_error.wav stored in their flash memory; if not copy these files from your Unified CVP Call Server. Example 7-2 shows how those configurations would look.

Example 7-2 *SIP Ringtone and Error Dial Peer and Service Configuration*

```
Application
 service cvperror flash:cvperror.tcl
  paramspace english index 0
  paramspace english language en
  paramspace english location flash
  paramspace english prefix en
!
service ringtone flash:ringtone.tcl
  paramspace english language en
  paramspace english index 0
  paramspace english location flash
  paramspace english prefix en

dial-peer voice 9191 voip
 description SIP ringtone dial-peer

 service ringtone
 voice-class codec 1
 voice-class sip rel1xx disable
 incoming called-number 9191T
 dtmf-relay rtp-nte no vad

!
service cvperror
 voice-class codec 1
 voice-class sip rel1xx disable
 incoming called-number 9292T
 dtmf-relay rtp-nte h245-signal h245-alphanumeric
 no vad
```

- **SIP Proxy:** Prior to cutover, define the proxy redundancy model and platform. If you use CUSP, build those configurations in the lab because they will be imported later into the production CUSP routers. Using the gatekeeper configuration and the CUCM route lists as a guide, build the CUSP triggers, server groups, and route tables. The ultimate goal is to replace any CUCM hard-coded route list targets with a SIP Proxy route. This places all SIP routing squarely on the shoulders of the SIP Proxy. If the current solution used GKTMP, implement the previously discussed solution for GKTMP replacement with SIP and create the appropriate routes in the SIP Proxy. A set of Unified CVP call servers are needed to act as SIP redirect servers. Finally, when the production sip proxy servers are in place, for CUSP, copy the configuration created in the lab into the production modules and place them in a shutdown state. This can prevent any SIP calls from accidentally being processed prior to the cutover.

- **Egress Gateways:** Prior to the cutover make sure that you have configured rtp-nte support on void dial peers to allow the negotiation of RFC2833 DTMF relay support.

- **Unified ICM:** Changes are dependent on which H.323 features the solution currently uses. By referencing the earlier discussion and Table 7-3, a list of tasks can be generated. Be careful to assess the changes required for this feature parity mapping to ensure that those changes do not impact the current production scripts or environment. If they do impact the current production system, they may need to be handled the night of the cutover.

- **Unified CVP**

  - From the Operations Console, under System->SIP Server Groups:

    - Create a proxy server group.

    - Add each SIP Proxy Server IP address and adjust their priority accordingly.

    - Enable heartbeating, which starts sending Options ping messages on the network every 5 seconds when the call server process restarts.

    - Associate to all Unified CVP call servers.

  - From the Operations Console on the SIP Tab:

    - Enable Outbound Proxy.

    - Use DNS SRV.

    - Resolve SRV locally.

    - Place the domain name used when creating the SIP Server group as the Outbound SRV domain name.

    - While this section is discussing Flash Cutover, if executing a Phased Cutover, add CSeq under the SIP header passing parameter. This can indicate a SIP call to the ICM script if there is a need in the script to determine what type of call was received by Unified CVP and ICM.

■ Depending on the customer's feature set, various portions of the Unified CVP Call SIP tab may need to be modified. By referencing the earlier discussion and Table 7-3, a list of these modifications can be generated. Following are some of the most common:

- ■ GTD for UUI parity with H.323.

- ■ Prepend digits for Significant Digit parity with H.323.

- ■ Post Call Survey DNIS mapping for Post Call survey parity with H.323.

- ■ Patterns for sending calls to the Originator for parity with SetTransferLabel in H.323.

- ■ Patterns for RNA Timeout for parity with SetRNATimeout in H.323.

■ **Cisco Unified Communications Manager:** Prior to cutover, remember to create a pair of redundant SIP trunks pointing toward the SIP Proxy and be sure to reset them. These SIP trunks should also be placed into a Route Group using the Circular type for load balancing. The Route Group should then be placed into a Route List with the Route List being assigned to any outbound CUCM Route Patterns. This includes patterns generated by Unified ICM to CUCM as the routing client for warm transfers. These route patterns should not be rerouted until the night of the flash cutover. This approach assumes that warm transfers will be load balanced between CVP call servers without regard to which CUCM subscriber sources the warm transfer. A single label is returned for the entire CUCM cluster because it is recognized as a single routing client from Unified ICM's perspective. As discussed in Chapter 4, "Designing Unified CVP for High Availability," the guidance provided around SIP high availability for the VRU leg applies here for how the CUCM cluster is configured. In other words, if you want to transfer the call into Unified CVP call servers local to the CUCM subscriber handling the warm transfer, the cutover plan should also include the respective partitioning with the effective use of Calling Search Spaces (CSS) to ensure that the warm transfer label is delivered to the local SIP proxy server with a dial plan that favors a local Unified CVP Call Server. In the end, the current warm transfer approach used by H.323 should be taken into consideration and if possible replicated with SIP and CUCM configurations.

On the night of the flash cutover, if all the previously prep work and configurations were successful, you should execute the following tasks to move calls from H.323 to SIP:

■ Point CUCM Unified CVP Route Patterns to the SIP Proxy Route List.

■ Do a service module reset if using CUSP to bring it online.

■ Do a shut on the gatekeeper, forcing H.323 calls to use the SIP dial peers.

If, however, things do not work quite as planned, and a decision is made to return to H.323 until issues are addressed, the following tasks should be sufficient to back out of the migration:

- Point the CUCM route patterns back to the original targets such as the gatekeeper trunks or route lists.

- Do a "no shut" on the gatekeeper's to bring the gatekeeper's services back online.

- Do a "shutdown graceful" on the CUSP, if you use one, to remove the SIP Proxy from processing SIP calls.

Phased Migration

The key when using a phased migration approach to upgrading the solution to SIP is call partitioning. Call partitioning is defined as partitioning the calling space into partitions such as Partition A and Partition B in such a manner that all existing calls, H.323 in nature, may use Partition B while Partition A is upgraded to SIP. After Partition A is upgraded to SIP, all incoming calls can be placed over on Partition A while Partition B is then upgraded. When both Partitions are upgraded, all the calls are allowed to use both partitions with SIP.

The general procedure for call partitioning is as follows:

Step 1. Partition the calling space into Partitions A and B. Some calls go to Partition A, and some calls go to Partition B.

Step 2. Ensure that calls are running properly in the partitioned space.

Step 3. Prevent calls from being received in Partition A.

Step 4. Upgrade or migrate Partition A's gateway configurations, Unified CVP Call, and VoiceXML servers to support SIP. All the previous steps for the flash cut approach apply here.

Step 5. Allow calls to return to Partition A.

Step 6. Ensure that calls are running properly in partition A.

Step 7. Prevent calls from being received in partition B

Step 8. Upgrade or migrate partition B's gateway configurations, Unified CVP Call, and VoiceXML servers to support SIP. All the previous steps for the flash cut approach apply here.

Step 9. Upgrade shared components: Media Resource Control Protocol (MRCP) servers, CSS, ACE, and so on. These are all typically redundant components, so it should be possible to take one side offline to upgrade while the other side continues to handle calls. Then reverse the process.

Step 10. Allow calls to return to Partition B.

Step 11. Ensure that calls are running properly in both partitions.

Step 12.   If required, remove partitioning and legacy configurations such as support for H.323 after the solution has stabilized on SIP.

Following is an example of how to partition an existing H.323 environment using technology prefixes:

Step 1.   Choose a new tech prefix that is not currently in use, such as 7.

Step 2.   Configure half the VoiceXML Gateways to register the gatekeeper with tech prefix 7#.

Step 3.   Configure half the CVP voice browsers to register to the gatekeeper with a tech prefix 7#.

Step 4.   Configure half of the Ingress Gateways to register to the gatekeeper with a tech prefix of 7#.

Here is how it works. Calls that arrive in the Ingress Gateways that are registered as 7# will be sent only to CVP voice browsers in the same partition. When those calls are transferred to VoiceXML gateways, they will also be sent to only those that are registered as 7#. This is one way to partition the call space, but it assumes that the gatekeeper is used for all H.323 transfers, and it assumes fairly simple gatekeeper usage. In more complex situations, customers may actually need to be more creative with dialed numbers and VRU transfer labels. Or they may want to make the contact center completely aphasic by simply separating the redundant gatekeepers and registering half the devices to each gatekeeper.

However, not all deployments have enough capacity to split their data centers in half to perform a Side A and Side B upgrade. In addition, the business may deem such an approach as too risky because during the upgrade Side B has no failover capacity. So to accommodate both approaches support H.323 and SIP calls simultaneously in different call partitions (Side A and Side B), there are a few caveats with this approach that need to be discussed.

For the partitioning approach to work, be sure that a particular call will never be handled by both SIP and H.323 components. Although this sounds simple, it can become a nightmare when dealing with transfers. For example, if an agent is talking to a customer via the H.323 call partition, it must also be allowed to transfer only to Unified CVP Call Servers and agents that are also routed over the H.323 partition. If this basic requirement is not met, when the warm transfer is connected between SIP and H.323 call legs, and the transferring agent steps out of the transfer, the call will disconnect because CUCM is no longer part of the conversation. This requires discovery around transfer dependency between agents and skill groups to ensure they all exist in the same call partition.

Caution   If the upgrade strategy involves using the Cisco Unified Computing System (UCS) to virtualize the Unified CVP solution, only SIP is supported on this platform. In other words, call partitioning cannot be used with UCS to run both call control protocols on the UCS platform.

To combat this issue, there are a few approaches depending on your environment. Assume there is an ability to determine dependencies between agent and skill group transfers. In other words, it can recognize which set of agents can transfer to other agents and skill groups. Because CUCM is deemed as a single Routing Client from Unified ICM's perspective, during a warm transfer, depending on the method used and configured in Unified ICM (Route Points or ICM Dialed Number Plan), usually a single routing client label will be returned for all Unified CCE agents when a transfer needs to be processed by Unified CVP.

In the case where route points are used on the CUCM cluster to get transfer instructions from Unified ICM pertaining to the transfer, the routing of this label must be unique and based on the call partition of the transferring agent. In other words, if the transferring agent is in the H.323 partition, the transfer label must use a Route List that resolves to a gatekeeper to keep the transfer in the H.323 partition. This implies that after the skill group and agent transfer dependencies are determined, additional Calling Search Spaces with identical routing client labels, for example, 8888888888<correlation ID>, must be created. Each of these duplicate Route Patterns should then use different Route Lists that resolve to either a SIP Proxy or gatekeeper trunk depending on whether they are part of the SIP or H.323 partition, respectively. The disadvantage of this approach when using route points during transfers is that duplicate dial patterns and partitions assigned to unique Calling Search Spaces must be created on CUCM, and agents must be assigned to the correct CSS to ensure that the call stays in the respective call partitions setup for SIP and H.323.

If however, the ICM Dialed Number Plan (DNP) is used to intercept the dialed number to determine which label ICM should return to CUCM, the approach is different. For example, you can define the transfer numbers within ICM DNP to return a different transfer label to CUCM based on the transfer number dialed and whether that transferred number should be treated as part of the H.323 or SIP partition. For example, if 1234 were dialed to transfer a caller to a different skill group that currently is part of the same H.323 partition as its origination, ICM DNP could match that DN 1234 and translate it to a DN of 1111, which in CUCM would resolve to a gatekeeper trunk and eventually a Unified CVP Call Server also partitioned into the H.323 partition. Similarly, assume that the transferring agent was in the SIP partitioned call space and dialed 5678 to transfer a caller that also originated from the SIP partition to a skill group for further support. ICM DNP could match that DN 5678 and translate it to a transfer label 55555, which in CUCM would resolve to a SIP trunk pointing at the SIP Proxy servers and eventually a Unified CVP Call Server also partitioned into the SIP partition. The advantage of this approach is that the dial plan segmentation would be handled in ICM DNP and not CUCM, making it easier to map the DNs to transfer labels.

Both of the previous examples for transfers using route points and ICM DNP sound achievable, but they suffer from a single point of concern. How easy is it in a large deployment to determine all the dependencies between agent to agent and skill group transfers? This is a nightmare. Even if you can create such a dependency map, validating that the dependencies on that map are the only ones that exist is equally frustrating. So what if the transfer partitioning could be handled by modifying the scripts in Unified ICM?

The concept is simple, for the originating leg of the call (that is the leg that gets to the transferring agent but has not been transferred) some call information needs to be saved that will be used during the transfer leg and script to determine whether the transferring call were H.323 or SIP. By simple adding a Set Variable node right after the Start node of the originating call script, the needed information could be stored:

```
Call.PeripheralVariable9 - Call.SIPHeader
```

If the originating call is indeed a SIP call, Call.PeripheralVariable9 will not be an empty string. However, if it is an H.323 call, this variable will indeed be an empty string. Fast forwarding to the transfer leg, when the transferring agent initiates the warm transfer, the warm transfer script is modified to insert an If node checking the same variable stored previously, Call.PeripheralVariable9. If a nonempty string is found, it is understood that the transfer leg should use SIP; otherwise, it should use H.323. In the case of SIP, a Translation Route to VRU node is used, which would return a label from a translation pool configured within Unified ICM. This translation label would then be routed by CUCM via a SIP trunk to a SIP Proxy server eventually landing on a Unified CVP Call Server via SIP. In the case that the transfer needs to use H.323, the script would use a standard Send to VRU node and return the default routing client label to CUCM, which likely is how the current transfers were configured, with CUCM matching this label and routing it via a H.323 trunk to a gatekeeper and eventually into a Unified CVP Call Server via H.323. This approach avoids dependency mappings for transfers and also is transparent to the agents allowing the originating gateway to decide which call control protocol a dialed number should use throughout the life of the call. However, the disadvantage of this approach is the requirement to configure all Unified CVP Call Servers that process SIP calls for translation routing. When the solution has been migrated to SIP, these configurations should be removed from Unified ICM, CVP, and CUCM to move the solution away from translational routing.

Whatever configuration approach is taken, be sure to allow for additional maintenance windows to clean up old configurations on the gateways and in the ICM scripts. By addressing the hygiene of the upgrade, confusion can be avoided about which configurations are needed and which are leftovers. After all, who likes eating leftovers?

Summary

In this chapter an important topic was covered: upgrading. You cannot avoid upgrades, and as mentioned, they require a great deal of focus, planning, and consideration when dealing with Unified CVP. Because of the multiple integration points and dependencies between native and non-native CVP components, upgrades can become one of the most complicated set of tasks you experience with the Unified CVP solution.

Quite often customers avoid upgrading their solutions simply because of the amount of work and risk involved. However, a strong case was crafted in this chapter as to why upgrades are an important part of a healthy Unified CVP solution. This case was solidified by examining the new features found in Unified CVP 8.x and defining what happens when older versions of the software go into an End of Sale or End of Life state. Some great methodologies were provided about applying upgrade strategies for native Unified CVP components setting the stage to deal with protocol migration approaches.

With the recent announcement of H.323 supportability for upgrades only, soon Unified CVP will no longer support any H.323. This will force enterprises to convert to SIP. This conversion can be complicated and risky depending on which approach you choose. To tackle this feat, H.323 feature parity with SIP and a detailed solution for deployments that rely heavily on GKTMP for call routing was provided. It is apparent that not all H.323 features can be mapped to an equivalent SIP feature. But over time more and more SIP features will be added to and supported by the solution, enabling additional mapping.

The next chapter examines the process to troubleshoot a Unified CVP solution. It focuses on troubleshooting techniques and tools provided for native and non-native components and provides examples of how these tools work. Troubleshooting Unified CVP can be daunting at times. However, with a good plan, a strong hypothesis, and the right tools, success if not far behind.

Recommended Reading and Resources

Cisco Documentation, *Cisco Unified Contact Center Enterprise (Unified CCE) Software Compatibility Guide*, http://www.cisco.com/en/US/docs/voice_ip_comm/cust_contact/contact_center/ipcc_ enterprise/compatibility_matrix/ipcccompat.pdf, May 10, 2011.

Cisco Documentation, *Cisco Unified Customer Voice Portal (CVP) 8.x Solution Reference Network Design (SRND)*, http://www.cisco.com/en/US/docs/voice_ip_ comm/cust_contact/contact_center/customer_voice_portal/srnd/8x/cvp8xsrnd.pdf.

Cisco Documentation, *Cisco Unified Contact Center Enterprise Solution Reference Network Design(SRND)*, http://www.cisco.com/en/US/products/sw/custcosw/ps1844/ products_implementation_design_guides_list.html.

Cisco Documentation, *Cisco Unified Customer Voice Portal Configuration Guides*, http://www.cisco.com/en/US/partner/products/sw/custcosw/ps1006/products_ installation_and_configuration_guides_list.html.

Cisco Documentation, *Hardware and System Software Specification for Cisco Unified Customer Voice Portal (Unified CVP), Release 8.0(1)*, http://www.cisco.com/en/US/ docs/voice_ip_comm/cust_contact/contact_center/customer_voice_portal/cvp8_0/ reference/guide/cvp_801_bom.pdf.

Cisco Documentation, *Cisco Unified Communications System Release 8.x SRND*, January 2011, http://www.cisco.com/en/US/partner/docs/voice_ip_comm/cucm/srnd/ 8x/uc8x.html.

Chapter 8

Troubleshooting

This chapter covers the following subjects:

- **Troubleshooting strategies and checklists:** Some good troubleshooting strategies paired with checklists to allow efficient fault isolation.

- **Device status and detailed troubleshooting:** Verifying device status to determine what is working and what is not working before executing more detailed troubleshooting exercise. In addition, details are provided for troubleshooting the native and non-native components of the Unified CVP solution. Topics included are Ingress, VXML Gateways, Unified CVP Call, VXML, Reporting server, Unified Intelligent Contact Management (ICM), and Load Balancers.

Troubleshooting Strategies

So far, this book has covered the different call flow models, native and non-native components that make up those calls flows, and strategies on how to build high availability into the Unified CVP solution. However, the more complex a solution becomes, the more challenging it surely will be to fix when it breaks. Unified CVP is no different because of its complex integrations with Unified ICM and Call Manager coupled with its use of non-native components such as Gatekeepers, Session Initiation Protocol (SIP) Proxy servers, load balancers, and even IOS ingress and VXML Gateways. No wonder an entire chapter is dedicated to troubleshooting the solution. To effectively troubleshoot Unified CVP, the user must have thorough knowledge of the solution and its current state pertaining to the following areas:

- Know the call flow in terms of how the call is expected to ingress and be treated during the troubleshooting process.

- Understand the default routing and survivability behavior when a fault occurs in the solution.

■ Be sure that all devices in the call flow are plugged in, turned on, and in an UP or operational state.

■ Start at the entry point of the call, and follow it to where the issue is, and verify components along the way. Determine if the issue can be isolated. Create a testable hypothesis on why the issue is manifesting.

■ Have an understanding of the tools needed to troubleshoot the solution. In other words, be proficient with IOS Debugs, Cisco Log Visualization Tool, Windows Event Viewer, network tools such as ping and such, Unified ICM Call Tracer, Unified ICM Process windows, Unified ICM Script Editor's Real-Time Monitor mode, Unified CVP's Operations Console, Real-Time Monitoring Tool (RTMT), and so on.

At first glance, the previous list can be quite overwhelming. However, this chapter provides ideas and tools with the attempt to increase confidence levels in each of these major areas. A few things should be considered before dismantling the solution looking for the problem. This checklist can help isolate the part of the solution that should be examined first, which is critical because of its potential size and complexity.

■ Trust but verify the exact supported software versions and compatibility matrices for solutions components such as Unified CVP, IOS, Unified ICM, Communications Manager, and so on.

■ Trust but verify the Unified CVP Deployment Model used for the deployment (Standalone, Call Director, and Comprehensive). When confirmed, refer to the call flows provided earlier in this book to understand the configuration touch points for native and non-native components in the solution. Use the respective call flow to create testable hypothesis on why the call is failing.

■ Understand the Physical Model of the solution (Centralized or Branch Office/Distributed).

■ Understand the VoIP protocol call flow also discussed earlier in this book. Is the solution doing H.323, and SIP with/without a proxy, and what edge queuing technique is used?

■ Understand the resources available for troubleshooting. This includes human resources, tools, mock labs, and maintenance windows.

■ Understand recent changes to the solution. Did the call flow in question ever work, sometimes work, or just stop working all together. If so, what changed?

Note My favorite question to ask when troubleshooting a problem is, "What Changed?" A majority of troubleshooting issues that I have seen throughout my career manifested from what I also deem as "self-inflicted wounds," whether they are in the form of adding call flows and agents that exceed a solutions capacity or changing a configuration on a gateway and introducing new versions of IOS, and so forth that were not tested or supported in the solution. If your customer or organization does not currently practice change management, they should. It can be a lifesaver when you have to ask this magical question.

So where is the problem? In other words, what component is suffering and what could be causing the agony? Start looking at the basic troubleshooting flowchart for performing fault isolation during a comprehensive Unified CVP call flow. The comprehensive Unified CVP call flow has been chosen because its name implies that it is comprehensive and is the most difficult of all call flows to troubleshoot. In addition, as seen in previous chapters, the native and non-native components engaged during a comprehensive call flow are found throughout other call flows and models, allowing the strategies provided here to be applied to any Unified CVP call flow.

This fault isolation discussion is broken into three general areas of the overall call flow: the switch leg, the Voice Response Unit (VRU) leg, and the subsequent transfer leg. Figure 8-1 provides the first of the three fault isolation flowcharts, the switch leg. It is followed by a detailed discussion.

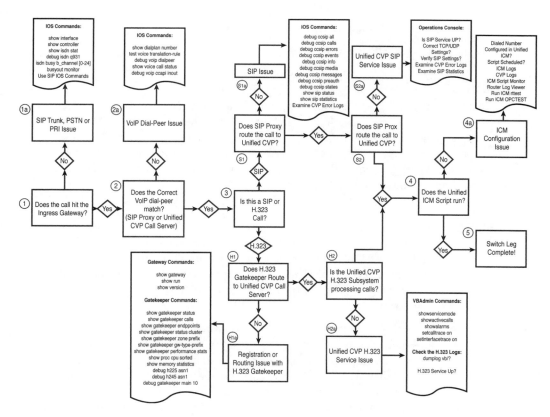

Figure 8-1 *Unified CVP Comprehensive Switch Leg Fault Isolation Flow Chart*

The following steps provide additional detail for Figure 8-1:

Step 1. Has it been confirmed that the call has arrived at the Ingress Gateway? Does the PSTN deliver the call as expected via the PRI, (SIP) Trunk, and so on to the Ingress Gateway?

Step 1a. Whether a fast busy occurs or inactivity on the Ingress Gateway, you need to verify that the PRI or SIP Trunk is correctly working. If a call cannot be seen arriving at the Ingress Gateway, the carrier must be contacted to find out if the PSTN connections are in service. Another option is to busy out certain PRIs in an attempt to further isolate the PRI that may be causing an issue. Following is a list of common commands that are useful during this step:

- show interface

- show controller

- show isdn status

- debug isdn q931

- isdn busy b_channel {0-24}

- busyout monitor

- IOS SIP commands

Note   When troubleshooting ISDN PRIs and Layer 2 does not transition to a state of MULTIPLE_FRAME_ESTABLISHED, there could be an issue between the router and the switch. However, if Layer 2 is in a state of TEI_ASSIGNED, the router and the PRI switch are not communicating at all. Furthermore, the Terminal Endpoint Identifier (TEI) value will always be 0 for ISDN PRIs. This is because there is no TEI on a PRI; therefore a value of TEI=0 displayed with the **show isdn status** IOS command doesn't indicate that there is a problem with the connectivity to the switch.

Step 2. After there is confirmation that the call is correctly delivered via the PSTN, examine where the correct voip dial-peer is matched to deliver the call to a Unified CVP Call Server. Depending on which call control protocol used, these dial-peers can be H.323 or SIP in nature, and their destination could be a Gatekeeper, SIP proxy, or the Internet Protocol (IP) address of a Unified CVP Call Server.

Step 2a. If it is suspected that the dial-peer is not matched, debug the dial-peers, and look more closely at what digits are delivered by the PSTN, and why they may not be matching a configured dial-peer. In addition, translation rules can cause issues if they are translating the dialed number breaking the routers; capability to match on an outgoing dial-peer. A great IOS command to use is **show dialplan number.** This actually shows the results of a dialed number for which translations were applied, what dial-peer was matched, and its target. Following are some additional IOS commands that are also useful during this step:

- **show dialplan number** {*Number to be dialed*}

- **test voice translation-rule** {*Rule Number*}

- **debug voip dialpeer**

- debug isdn q931

- show voip call status

- debug voip ccapi inout

Step 3. At this point a dial-peer on the Ingress Gateway is correctly matched. Define whether the call is an H.323 or SIP call. Depending on which call protocol is used, fork the fault isolation strategy to look at issues that can exist with each. Another observation: The fault isolation flow chart provided in Figure 8-1 assumes that a Gatekeeper or proxy is used. However, in the case of SIP, a proxy server is not required, and the call can be directly placed with a Call Server. Be sure to understand how the solution is routing inbound calls. Now take a look at the SIP call flow first.

Step S1. Is the call hitting the proxy server and being delivered to Unified CVP? This can be verified by using some of the commands listed in Step S1a. However, if the call seems to be routed correctly to the Call Server, proceed to Step S2.

Step S1a. By using some of the commands listed for this step, you can isolate specific SIP issues related to call setup and negotiation. Also use these commands to verify that the call is correctly set up and to the correct endpoints. Following are some additional IOS commands and guidance that are useful during this step:

- debug ccsip all

- debug ccsip calls

- debug ccsip errors

- debug ccsip events

- debug ccsip info

- debug ccsip media

- debug ccsip messages

- debug ccsip preauth

- debug ccsip states

- debug ccsip status

- show sip statistics

- Examine CVP Error Logs

Step S2. After the call is set up via the SIP proxy server but the Unified CVP SIP Service is simply not accepting the call, the issue could be local to that specific Unified CVP Call Server and its SIP configuration or lack of. Another technique is to try to move the call to a different Unified CVP Call Server to see where the issue still exists. You can do this by configuring a dial-peer on the Ingress Gateway that targets a specific Unified CVP Call Server's IP address or attempt to modify the dial plan in the SIP proxy for a specific DNIS.

Step S2a. By verifying the SIP configuration via the Operations Console and examining the CVP Error log files, an answer should be available as to whether any SIP calls are processed by the Unified CVP Call Server. Do not forget to check the Unified CVP Call Server statistics via the Operations Console to verify if the Call Server is processing any SIP calls. Following are some items to verify:

- Is the SIP Service UP?

- Are the correct TCP/UDP settings configured?

- Verify the SIP Settings.

- Examine the CVP Error Log.

- Examine the SIP statistics.

Step H1. If the call is indeed an H.323 call, you can confirm that it is processed by the H.323 Gatekeeper where the Gatekeeper provide an admission control confirmation message to the Ingress Gateway to contact the Unified CVP Call Server. Is the Gatekeeper providing the correct IP address of the Unified CVP Call Server?

Step H1a. This is where you need to verify that the Ingress Gateway and Unified CVP Call Server are registered with the Gatekeeper, have the correct technology prefix, and are correctly represented in the correct zone with the correct prefix. By running some Gatekeeper debug commands, the issue with a call can quickly be isolated and corrected. Start with the basics first and verify the registration, technology prefixes, zones, and prefixes for each device in the call leg. After you verify the basics, turn to the more advanced debug commands to sort out the real issue. Following are some additional IOS commands that are useful during this step:

- Gateway Commands

  - **show gateway**

  - **show run**

  - **show version**

- Gatekeeper Commands

  - **show gatekeeper status**

  - **show gatekeeper calls**

  - **show gatekeeper endpoints**

  - **show gatekeeper status cluster**

  - **show gatekeeper zone prefix**

  - **show gatekeeper gw-type-prefix**

  - **show gatekeeper performance stats**

- **show processes cpu sorted**
- **show memory statistics**
- **debug h225 asn1**
- **debug h245 asn1**
- **debug gatekeeper main 10**

Step H2. After you verify that the call is indeed routed correctly by the Gatekeeper, it's time to verify that the H.323 subsystem running on the Unified CVP Call Server correctly processes the call. The H.323 log files are accessed differently than other log files located on the Unified CVP server.

Step H2a. Using VBAdmin commands can verify any issues with the H.323 subsystem accepting the call. If however tracing is turned on, remember to revert them when done tracing a problem to avoid performance issues with the Unified CVP server. Following are some additional vbadmin commands and guidance for this step:

- Unified CVP vbadmin Commands
    - **showservicemode**
    - **showactivecalls**
    - **showalarms**
    - **setcalltrace on**
    - **setinterfacetrace on**
- Check Interface and H.323 Logs
    - **dump vb /?**
    - Is the H.323 service UP?

Step 4. Everything is looking good up to the point that Unified CVP must now communicate with Unified ICM via the Peripheral Gateway (PG) and the VRU Peripheral Interface Manager (PIM). If the default Unified CVP error message is played to the caller, there is definitely an issue with getting the call to Unified ICM, or the call is failing on the VRU leg of the call, which is examined in the next section. For now, assume that there is a fundamental issue with Unified ICM.

Step 4a. The first place to start is to check the Unified CVP error logs to see if Unified CVP is logging any dialog issues with Unified ICM. Next, check the PIM status on the PG. Does it look healthy? Be sure to verify that the PIM is ACTIVE in the title bar of the window, and use dumplog to export the PIM log to enable easier reading. Examine Unified ICM via the RouterLog Viewer to see if Unified ICM sees the correct incoming DNIS value. Finally, check the ICM Script Monitor to see if the incoming dialed number is actually matching the script, and if so, where is the script failing? Following is a summary of items to check:

- Is the dialed number configured in Unified ICM?

- Is the script scheduled?

- Examine the Unified ICM logs.

- Examine the Unified CVP logs.

- Use the real-time monitor mode in the Unified ICM Script Editor to trace the call.

- Examine the Router Log Viewer utility.

- Run and examine the output of RTTEST.

- Run and examine the output of OPCTEST.

Step 5.   Verification that the Unified ICM script is invoked by using the Script Monitor tool indicates that the switch leg is correctly completing for the solution. However, the call is still having issues when the VRU Leg is invoked to treat a call. Another flow chart is necessary to examine potential issues on the VRU Leg of this call. At least for now, the switch leg works.

Tip   If using a telnet session to debug devices such as the IOS Ingress Gateway, IOS VXML Gateway, IOS Gatekeepers, IOS-based CUSP, and so on, don't forget to issue the command **terminal monitor** before beginning the debug session. By default, all debugging output is sent to the IOS router's console port and not virtual terminal ports like those used by telnet. This command must be issued or debug messages will not be seen.

Assuming the call is now completing its switch leg, examine the flow chart for fault isolation during the VRU leg of the call. Figure 8-2 provides the second of the three fault isolation flowcharts, the VRU leg. This is followed by a detailed discussion.

Following are the detailed steps illustrated in Figure 8-2 with some additional guidance on their application:

Step 1.   After agent availability is determined, the call is either sent to a Unified Contact Center Enterprise (CCE) agent or out to the VRU for treatment. Assume that an agent is not available, so the script attempts to execute the Send to VRU node to kick off the VRU leg of this call. By using the real-time monitoring mode in the Unified ICM Script Editor tool, this behavior you can visually track as the call enters the VRU for treatment.

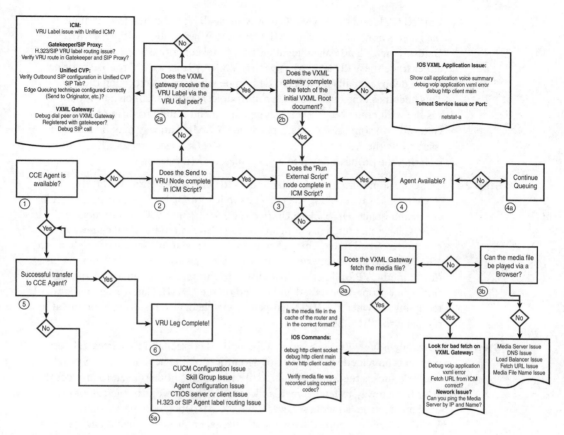

Figure 8-2 *Unified CVP Comprehensive VRU Leg Fault Isolation Flow Chart*

Step 2. By examining the Send to VRU node in the Unified ICM script, determine if a VXML Gateway was engaged by the Ingress Gateway and a VXML request for further instructions is present back to Unified ICM by Unified CVP. However, failure during the execution of a Send to VRU node within a Unified ICM script is most commonly caused by a misconfiguration of the VRU label returned by Unified ICM or ingress and VXML Gateway issues. To rule out the gateways, the VRU label presented to the VXML Gateway and its behavior is represented in the next step.

Step 2a. By examining the incoming call from the Ingress Gateway to the VXML Gateway, you can verify the VRU label that is presented and whether it is correctly configured from Unified ICM's perspective and assuring that the correct application dial-peer is matched and subsequent Tool Command Language (TCL) script invoked. If however an incoming call from the Ingress Gateway with the expected VRU label as the DNIS is not seen, Unified ICM,

Unified CVP, and the VXML Gateway must all be examined to determine why the label is not routed to a VXML Gateway. When using multiple VXML Gateways with load balancing at either a Gatekeeper or SIP Proxy, be sure to either force the VRU label to a specific VXML Gateway for troubleshooting or run debugs on all gateways to determine which one is receiving the call. This becomes quite a challenge when troubleshooting a call on a production system with numerous VRU labels generated and routed to different VXML Gateways. In some situations, a particular VXML Gateway may be having an issue while the rest of the VXML Gateways behave as expected. This requires isolating the problem down to a particular VXML Gateway.

Step 2b.   There are some situations in which the VRU label does correctly hit the VXML Gateway invoking the correct application dial-peer resulting in a fetch command being sent back to Unified CVP for further VXML instructions, only to have that fetch result in an error message on the VXML Gateway represented as a bad fetch. This behavior can also result in a failure of the Send to VRU node and is usually tied to an issue with the Tomcat service running on the Unified CVP Call Server. In addition to this rare situation, if the application is not properly installed and loaded on the VXML Gateway, it cannot correctly invoke when the VRU dial-peer is matched, also resulting in failure at the Send to VRU node.

Step 3.   After any issue with the Send to VRU node is correct and its successful completion is indicated with the Script Monitor tool, the next area that typically causes issues is the Run External Script node. This node is used to instruct the VXML Gateway to fetch a media file, that is, instructions to the call or on hold music, from a media server. Using VXML debug commands on the VXML Gateway coupled with a few other techniques, you can quickly isolate the source of the fetch issue.

Step 3a.   By examining the VXML Gateways http client cache, you can determine whether the VXML Gateway actually fetched the media file, cached it, and attempted to play it to the caller. If the media file has been cached and was successfully fetched from the media server, the possibility that any issues exist with accessing the media server or load balancers with the correct Uniform Resource Locator (URL) are nonexistent. However, this does not rule out the requirement to verify that the media file was recorded in the correct format using a supported audio codec.

Step 3b.   However, if the media file is not in the HTTP client cache on the VXML router and VXML debugs indicate a bad fetch when attempting to fetch the media file, the first thing that you must do is to examine the URL provided in the VXML instructions, which can be found by examining the VXML debugs, to determine if the format of the URL is correct. All parts must match for how the media server is configured. For example, it must have the correct hostname, file folder, and filename. To verify that the URL is correct, try placing the same URL into a web browser on a client or server machine to see if the audio file is correctly fetched. If it is not, the URL provided by the Unified ICM script is incorrectly configured, or there is an issue on the media server pertaining to the audio filename and its relative location as configured by its HTTP web services. If the file does successfully fetch from a browser with the URL that was extracted from the VXML debugs, there is a transport or reachability issue for how the VXML Gateway is resolving and requesting the same URL file from the media server. You must examine the host entries on the routers to verify that they match the hostname provided by the URL embedded within the VXML instructions. If a load balancer is used, the hostname's IP must match the one configured for the load balancers. It is common to also remove the load balancers from the equation and point the host entries for the media servers to the IP addresses of the actual media servers to rule out the possibility of a bad load balancer configuration.

Note   Never rule out using the **ping** command; by pinging the media servers' ip address and its hostname, you can ensure that the VXML Gateway can reach the media server.

Caution   If the first host entry for the media server fails, the IVR service attempts to correct this failure by sending additional VXML instructions augmenting the hostname that failed with -backup and instructing the VXML Gateway to try a second fetch operation from mediaserver-backup (assuming the original media server hostname is mediaserver and it is in comprehensive mode). This may result in the call receiving treatment with no indication that there is a failure on the first media server. Keep this behavior in mind when troubleshooting media servers and load balancers during the VRU leg of a call. In other words, just because the call receives treatment doesn't mean that the primary media servers are operational. Furthermore, the Unified ICM script must provide a URL with the same hostname configured on the VXML Gateway or there will be name resolution issues and media fetch instructions will fail. By using the command **debug voip application vxml**, both of these situations can be identified. A detailed debug illustrating these issues is provided in Example 8-30, found later in this chapter and takes a closer look at debugging the VXML Gateway.

Step 4.   After call treatment is underway, an agent could become available requiring Unified ICM to provide the agent label to the Unified CVP Call Server so that it may communicate to the Ingress Gateway to connect to the call to an agent.

Step 4a.   However, if an agent is unavailable, the Unified ICM script continues to execute and in some cases, different media files may get fetched and played. If this is the case, troubleshooting those subsequent fetches is handled by repeating Steps 3 and 3a. Potential filenames have changed. If a load balancer is used, different media servers could be engaged to handle the HTTP fetches. This should be considered if troubleshooting production systems that use load balancers and multiple media server farms.

Step 5.   If an agent becomes available, Unified ICM returns that agent label or number to Unified CVP, which then resolves this against any static routes, Gatekeeper, or a SIP proxy depending on how the solution is configured and what call control protocol it uses. Be sure to understand the outbound routing configuration used by Unified CVP. It is critical to solving VRU and agent label routing issues.

Step 5a.   If the transfer to the available agent fails, several areas need to be examined. First, verify that the outbound routing used by the Unified CVP Call Server is correctly configured to route a call to the CCE agent. If using a Gatekeeper or SIP proxy, be sure that the agent labels or numbers are statically configured either as a prefix (Gatekeeper) or as a route (SIP Proxy). In the case that a Gatekeeper is in use, verify that the CUCM subscribers' trunks are correctly registered with the Gatekeeper and that the Gatekeeper is correctly routing the call to these H.323 endpoints. If this all checks out, the agent configuration for Unified ICM and their respective agent desktop software need to be verified. Issues in these areas will usually result in agents not being reserved correctly or their inability to log into their agent desktop and change their current state. If the call is going to an agent that should not be receiving the call, check the skill group configuration within Unified ICM because it is Unified ICM that returns the agent label. Unified CVP simply resolves the agent label and instructs the Ingress Gateway to connect to the endpoint responsible for that agent label, in this case a Unified Call Manager subscriber trunk.

Step 6.   After an agent successfully answers the call, the VRU leg of a call is complete.

Assuming the call is now answered by a Unified CCE agent, examine the flowchart for fault isolation when the first Unified CCE agent initiates a subsequent transfer to a secondary skill group or agent. Figure 8-3 provides the last of the three fault isolation flowcharts and the subsequent transfer leg. This is followed by a detailed discussion.

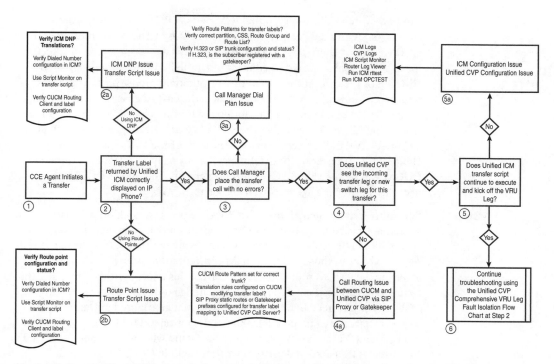

Figure 8-3 *Unified CVP Comprehensive Subsequent Transfer Fault Isolation Flowchart*

Following are the detailed steps illustrated in Example 8-3 with some additional guidance on their application:

Step 1.   Unified CCE Agent initiates a subsequent transfer by either dialing a Cisco Unified Communications Manager (CUCM) route point or a Dialed Number Identification System (DNIS) controlled by the Unified ICM Dialed Number Plan (DNP). In either case, the resulting transfer script should return a label or DNIS for processing by the CUCM cluster.

Step 2.   If the transfer script were correctly invoked and completed its "switch" leg, the IP phone of the CCE Agent usually displays this transfer label. In most cases it looks similar to a VRU label when using a correlation ID. However, depending on what label the transfer script has been instructed to return determines what label the IP phone attempts to dial. By inspecting the IP phone's display, you can determine whether the transfer label returned is correct for the transfer initiated.

Step 2a.   If a label were not returned, or if the label returned were incorrect and the transfer was initiated using ICM DNP, a closer look at the translations and Unified ICM configuration is warranted. As with previous troubleshooting flow charts, this stage of the transfer is the same as the switch leg of a new call because CUCM treats all subsequent transfers as a new call leg, which equates to a new switch call leg for Unified ICM and CVP. The only significant difference is that with a subsequent transfer initiated by CUCM, the routing client is CUCM and not Unified CVP. Therefore, the transfer script returns a label to the CUCM request it used to connect to Unified CVP for processing on the VRU leg of the call. At this point, the script monitor must verify if the label is returned via a Send to VRU node. If that is the case, the issue could be related to the CUCM configuration for routing the returned label. Remember, this label should be routed to either the SIP Proxy or Gatekeeper and eventually to a Unified CVP Call Server to process the start of the VRU leg of a call. If the Unified ICM transfer script determines that an agent is, the label returned to CUCM will be the Unified CCE agent extension. This allows CUCM to connect the transferring agent to available agent.

Step 2b.   Similar to Step 2a, Step 2b uses CUCM route points to kick off a transfer script hosted in Unified ICM. In addition to guidance provided in Step 2a, the route points should be verified within CUCM as being registered. If they are not in a registered status, there is Unified ICM configuration issue. In some cases, resetting the CUCM route point may correct this issue. In other rare cases, the route point may also need to be disassociated and then re-associated with the PGUSER or Java Telephony API (JTAPI) account configured in Unified CM. At worse, restart the Computer Telephony Integration (CTI) Manager process on the Unified CM servers. Bottom line: Understand what route points are dialed for different transfers, and verify their status within CUCM.

Step 3.   Assuming that the correct transfer label is returned to CUCM as expected, does CUCM dial the transfer label without an errors?

Step 3a.   In situations in which the dial plan is incorrectly configured in CUCM, the resulting transfer label cannot be dialed from the IP phone and results in either the dreaded "Your call cannot be completed as dialed." or a fast busy. In either case the route pattern for the transfer label, its partition, calling search space, route group, and resulting route lists must be verified to ensure it is correct and that the transferring Unified CCE agent's IP phone has access to this dial plan. For example, does the IP phone use the correct calling search space? Furthermore, check the trunk configurations for H.323 or SIP to verify that the transfer label is correctly configured in either the H.323 Gatekeeper or SIP Proxy server. Is there a prefix or static route that resolves to a Unified CVP Call Server or Egress Gateway? If using H.323, are the CUCM H.323 trunks registered with the Gatekeeper?

Step 4.   Assuming that the subsequent transfer is going to a Unified CVP Call Server, does the H.323 or SIP service accept this new transfer switch leg?

Step 4a.   In situations in which the call still does not correctly land on a Unified CVP Call Server, there still may be a routing issue between the CUCM subscriber and the Unified CVP Call Server. The CUCM dial plan must be inspected to verify that no translation rules exist that could be hijacking the outgoing transfer label and the transfer label's route pattern is pointed to the correct outgoing SIP or H.323 trunk. As in Step 3a, the dial plan configured in the SIP proxy or H.323 Gatekeeper must be verified as well. The Unified CVP Call Server logs must be inspected to see if the call is received by Unified CVP and rejected when Unified ICM is placed into the call flow.

Step 5.   Using Unified ICM's script monitor tool, does the transfer script invoked in Step 2 continue to execute kicking the VRU leg of the call off?

Note   When constructing a Unified ICM transfer script, it is best practice to use a single Send to VRU node. However, this brings up an interesting point. Won't the script need two Send to VRU script nodes because two labels are returned during a typical subsequent transfer initiated via CUCM? The first label is returned to CUCM as the routing client, which is then routed back into a Unified CVP Call Server, where the transfer script is continued within Unified ICM. Assuming an agent is still not available, a second label, the VRU label, is generated and sent back to Unified CVP to kick off the VRU leg of the transfer. The answer to this question is no. A single Send to VRU node is sufficient in a Unified ICM subsequent transfer script. The reason this works is simply because in the scenario just described, Unified ICM receives two route requests from two different routing clients. The first is CUCM and the second is Unified CVP. A single Send to VRU script node identifies the different routing clients and returns to each a unique VRU label without having to place two Send to VRU nodes in the transfer script.

Step 5a.   The first place to start is to check the Unified CVP error logs to see if Unified CVP is logging any dialog issues with Unified ICM. Next check the PIM status on the VRU PG. Does it look healthy? Further troubleshooting should include the examination of Unified ICM via the router log viewer to see if Unified ICM is seeing the correct incoming DNIS value. Finally, check the ICM Script Monitor to see if the incoming dialed number is actually matching the transfer script. If so, where is the script failing?

Step 6.   After the transfer script continues to execute, depending on whether an agent is available, the troubleshooting flow from this point is identical to the flow presented and discussed earlier in Figure 8-2, beginning with Step 2. If the transfer is failing after the transfer script is re-engaged with Unified CVP as the routing client, the issue is directly related to VRU leg of the transfer. The only difference between this VRU leg and others that are initiated by the PSTN is the source of the switch leg of the call. Remember, CUCM initiated the transfer and is the source of the switch leg of the call, which means that it must connect to any VXML or Egress Gateway that Unified CVP instructs it to connect its voice bearer channel to. Keep this in mind when troubleshooting the VRU leg of a transfer initiated via CUCM.

Although it is clear that not all deployments use the Unified CVP comprehensive model, the strategies provided can be independently used to troubleshoot other deployment models such as standalone, call, and VRU-only. The key is to understand which native and non-native components are engaged during the call flow and which troubleshooting strategies apply to those components. The next section examines techniques to verify the status of different components and details about troubleshooting. It is still recommended that the fault isolation strategies provided in this section be used first to isolate the problem to a specific component before attempting any detailed troubleshooting efforts.

Device Status and Detailed Troubleshooting

Now that guidance has been provided about isolating faults within the Unified CVP solution, it is time to provide some additional guidance on how to verify the status of different native and non-native components. During fault isolation exercises, device status must be verified first before detailed troubleshooting exercises are performed. This is to ensure that an issue actually exists. Several types of critical issues can be simply resolved by just verifying the status of the device. In cases where the device status checks out, move into more detailed troubleshooting exercises to isolate more complicated configuration issues that are not visible from surveying the status of the solution.

Ingress and VXML Gateways

In a fully functioning environment, the customer would dial a phone number, and the call would be routed through the gateway to a Gatekeeper (H.323) or SIP Proxy and onto Unified CVP/ICM, which would kick-off a script. The customer would receive some form of prompting or queue music, or the call would be routed directly to an agent. When calls fail to route properly, one of the first places to start troubleshooting is the ingress circuits to the Unified CVP Solution. The most common delivery method of customer calls in the United States is T1/PRI circuits, with E1 circuits being predominately used outside the United States. There may also be a scattered amount of T1/CAS (E&M) trunks still in use, but this section focuses on PRI/CCS.

T1 Status (Ingress Only)

Depending on the reported calling issues, checking the T1 status is recommended. Confirm that the T1 properly connects to the carrier and that the T1 is clean, no errors. Use the following IOS command to check the status of the T1. Example 8-1 provides an example of how to verify the T1T1 status on an Ingress Gateway.

> **Note**   T1 port numbers vary based upon the hardware used. This output was taken from an AS5400XM.

Example 8-1   *T1 Status Using* **show controller** *IOS Command*

```
myrouter# show controller t1 7/0
T1 7/0 is up.
```

```
    Applique type is Channelized T1
    Cablelength is long gain36 0db
    Description: MY DS3
No alarms detected.
    alarm-trigger is not set
    Soaking time: 3, Clearance time: 10
    AIS State:Clear  LOS State:Clear  LOF State:Clear
    Version info of slot 7:  HW: 1032, PLD Rev: 6
    Framer Version: 0x9
...
...
    Framing is ESF, Line Code is B8ZS, Clock Source is Line.
    Data in current interval (784 seconds elapsed):
0 Line Code Violations, 0 Path Code Violations
0 Slip Secs, 0 Fr Loss Secs, 0 Line Err Secs, 0 Degraded Mins
0 Errored Secs, 0 Bursty Err Secs, 0 Severely Err Secs, 0 Unavail Secs
    Total Data (last 24 hours)
      0 Line Code Violations, 0 Path Code Violations,
      0 Slip Secs, 0 Fr Loss Secs, 0 Line Err Secs, 0 Degraded Mins,
      0 Errored Secs, 0 Bursty Err Secs, 1 Severely Err Secs, 0 Unavail Secs
```

As illustrated in Example 8-1, the T1 is up, and there was a single-errored second in the last 24 hours. If the T1 were down, check the following:

■ Verify cabling between the gateway and the carrier demarcation device.

  ■ T1 circuits use pins 1–2 and 4–5 to communicate. Ninety-nine percent of the time, a straight-through cable will be used. A T1 x-over cable may be needed if connecting the gateway to another "user-side" T1 interface, such as a customer PBX or another gateway.

■ Use a loopback plug to test gateway T1 interface. Cut an RJ-45 patch cable, strip back the insulation, and connect Pin 1 to Pin 5 and Pin 2 to Pin 4. Use an 8-Pin female "coupler" to loopback the T1 from the demarc to the gateway.

■ Open a ticket with the carrier or Cisco TAC for further testing.

■ Check the gateway T1 interface configuration.

  ■ Ninety-nine percent of T1 circuits in the United States use Framing: ESF (Extended Super Frame) and Linecoding: B8ZS (Binary 8 Zero Suppression). If these settings do not match with the carrier, a Line code violations and errored seconds appears and the T1 does not come up.

■ Make sure that the T1 is enabled on the gateway. If the T1 status is "administratively down," use the **no shut** command under the controller configuration to enable the interface.

If the T1 is up, but is taking errors, reports of "static" on calls or intermittent dropped calls may appear. Check for the following types of errors:

- Slip Secs (Clock Slips) indicate that there is a timing issue between the gateway and the carrier. Carriers usually provide clocking to the gateway. AS5350 and AS5400 gateways do not have the capability to provide clock and can use only "line side" clocking. This means that they use the clock received from the carrier as their transmit clock. IOS 28xx, 38xx, and 39xx gateways have the capability to use internal, line, or loop clocking.

- Other errors, such as line code, path code violations, frame loss, or errored seconds can result from a T1 bouncing up and down. It is normal for a T1 to take a small amount of errors as the circuit is activated or deactivated but should not take large amounts of errors during normal operations. Use the following process to remediate errors:

  - Check cabling.

  - Open a ticket with Carrier for BERT (Bit Error Rate Testing).

  - Replace gateway hardware, more specifically only the T1 line card may need to be replaced.

  - Check the Gateway logs to see if the T1 has been "bouncing" up and down.

PRI Status (Ingress Only)

If the T1 is properly functioning, the next step is to check the status of the PRI D-Channel. The D-Channel provides the call signaling for all the B-Channels. This is referred to as Common Channel Signaling (CCS). The ISDN Switch-Type defines the D-Channel protocol for communication with the carrier's switch. Example 8-2 provides an IOS command to check the PRI status:

Example 8-2 *PRI Status Using* show isdn status *IOS Command*

```
myrouter# show isdn status
Global ISDN Switchtype = primary-ni
ISDN Serial 7/0:23 interface
     dsl 0, interface ISDN Switchtype = primary-ni
   Layer 1 Status:
     ACTIVE
   Layer 2 Status:
    TEI = 0, Ces = 1, SAPI = 0, State = MULTIPLE_FRAME_ESTABLISHED
   Layer 3 Status:
     1 Active Layer 3 Call(s)
     CCB:callid=AF3D, sapi=0, ces=0, B-chan=8, calltype=VOICE
     Active dsl 0 CCBs = 17
   The Free Channel Mask:  0x807E0000
   Number of L2 Discards = 0, L2 Session ID = 48
```

The output of the command shows that the D-Channel is up and the connection is established with the carrier's switch (Multiple_Frame_Established). There is an active call on B-Channel 8 (CCB:callid=AF3D, sapi=0, ces=0, **B-chan=8**, calltype=VOICE). The other Layer 2 states would include the following:

- **TEI_ASSIGNED:** This state indicates that the D-Channel is not active. It may be in the process of trying to connect to the carrier.

- **AWAITING_ESTABLISHMENT:** This state indicates that the D-Channel is not active. It may be in the process of trying to connect to the carrier.

If the T1 is up, but the D-Channel cannot be established, issue a **show interface** command. Verify that the interface is up and transmitting packets. Clear the counters before issuing this command. Example 8-3 provides the result of this command with some content omitted.

Example 8-3   *D-Channel Troubleshooting Using* **show interface** *IOS Command*

```
myrouter# show interface s1/0:23
Serial1/0:23 is up, line protocol is up (spoofing)
Encapsulation HDLC, loopback not set
Last clearing of "show interface" counters 00:02:00
0 packets input, 0 bytes, 0 no buffer
53 packets output, 159 bytes, 0 underruns
```

In this case the following should be verified:

- Verify with the carrier that it has the correct ISDN switch protocol. These may include the following:
  - primary-ni
  - primary-ni2
  - primary-4ess
  - primary-5ess
  - primary-dms100 among others
- Verify with the carrier that the D-Channel is active on their side. If the D-Channel on the gateway is sending packets, but not receiving any, the carrier may have their D-Channel turned down.

PRI Debugs (Ingress Only)

The **debug** command illustrated in Example 8-4 detects the incoming call and the digits sent by the carrier. Use this **debug** with the other VOIP debugs to troubleshoot the Unified CVP call flow from the gateway perspective.

Caution   Be careful when using **debug** commands because they may add CPU overhead to the gateway and under heavy loads could cause the gateway to reboot. Debug outputs are not sent to VTY (Telnet) connections. Use the **terminal monitor** command to allow console messages to be passed to a VTY session. It may be necessary to configure the console to log debug messages. Use the configuration command **logging console debug**.

Example 8-4   PRI q931 IOS *Debug Command*

```
myrouter# debug isdn q931
Mar 14 11:36:19.018: ISDN Se1/0:23 Q931: RX <- SETUP pd = 8  callref = 0x0011


          Bearer Capability i = 0x9090A2
                    Standard = CCITT
                    Transfer Capability = 3.1kHz Audio
                    Transfer Mode = Circuit
                    Transfer Rate = 64 kbit/s
          Channel ID i = 0xA98381
                    Exclusive, Channel 1              Progress Ind i = 0x8583 -
Origination address is non-ISDN
          Display i = 'Joe Customer'
          Calling Party Number i = 0x2180, '8006661212'
                    Plan:ISDN, Type:National
          Called Party Number i = 0xA1, '8005551212'
                    Plan:ISDN, Type:National
Mar 14 11:36:20.415: ISDN Se1/0:23 Q931: TX -> CALL_PROC pd = 8  callref = 0x8011


          Channel ID i = 0xA98381
                    Exclusive, Channel 1
Mar 14 11:36:20.415: ISDN Se1/0:23 Q931: TX -> CONNECT pd = 8  callref = 0x8011
Mar 14 11:36:20.431: ISDN Se1/0:23 Q931: RX <- CONNECT_ACK pd = 8  callref = 0x0011
```

The output in Example 8-4 demonstrates a call received by the Ingress Gateway. The following information can be derived from the debug:

- The PRI circuit received a setup request from the carrier (RX <- SETUP).

- The call setup message is requesting Channel 1 (Exclusive, Channel 1).

- The Calling Line ID (CLID) name is Joe Customer (Display i = 'Joe Customer').

- The Calling Party Number (Calling Party Number i = 0x2180, '5085559999').

- The Called Party Number (Called Party Number i = 0xA1, '5085550002').

- The call was accepted for further processing (TX -> CALL_PROC).

- The call connected (TX -> CONNECT).

- The carrier acknowledged the connection (RX <- CONNECT_ACK).

PRI Busyout (Ingress Only)

As part of the gateway troubleshooting process, it may become necessary to "busyout" circuits on a gateway. This would allow for calls to be processed on another circuit within the same gateway or move calls off to another gateway. There are two common methods to accomplish this task:

- **Option 1:** Use a loopback interface as a busy out trigger.

  - Create a software-based loopback interface.

  - Configure voice-port to monitor the loopback interface.

  - Configure the voice-port busy out action (graceful, alarm, or shutdown).

  - Shut down the loopback interface to trigger the busyout.

    Example 8-5 illustrates how to monitor a loopback interface for PRI Busy Out functionality. Other interfaces found and configured on the router such as the Gigabit or Fast Ethernet interfaces can also be monitored in a similar fashion in situations in which the PRI(s) need to be placed into a busyout state if the connection to the LAN or WAN is lost.

Example 8-5 *Sample Configuration for Loopback-based Busy Out*

```
interface Loopback10
 description Loopback interface for PRI 1/0
 no ip address
voice-port 1/0:23
 busyout monitor action graceful
 busyout monitor Loopback10
```

- **Option 2:** Busy out directly from the D-channel interface.

Example 8-6 shows how to busy out a PRI using the direct D-channel busyout approach.

Example 8-6 *Sample Configuration for Direct D-channel Busyout*

```
interface serial 1/0:23
 isdn busy b_channel 0
```

Note The **isdn busy b_channel** IOS command can take a specific channel for its parameter in situations in which it is believed that a certain channel on a T1 causes an issue. By providing an "0", all b-channels are placed into a busy status. In addition, it is possible to provide a range of b-channels to busyout such as "1–10."

Option 1 is the preferred method as the carrier is sent an "out-of-service" message when the loopback interface transitions from up to down. This allows the carrier to reroute calls to another available circuit in the trunk-group. The carrier is also sent a subsequent "in-service" message when the interface transitions from down to up.

Option 2 simply busies out the b-channel, and calls continue to arrive from the carrier. These calls receive a "CHAN_UNAVAILABLE" response from the gateway, and the carrier may continue trying other b-channels within the same circuit before providing the caller with a "busy" treatment.

Dial-Peers (Ingress and VXML Gateways)

POTS dial-peers provide numerous configuration parameters. But for an ingress and VXML Gateways they terminate the call from the PSTN, which enables the ability to collect DNIS and in the case of a VXML Gateway, fire off a TCL script. Although this section and some subsequent sections fall under Ingress Gateways, the commands provided also apply to VXML Gateways for troubleshooting dial-peers and call control protocols such as SIP and H.323. Example 8-7 provides an IOS command that you can use to verify that inbound calls are matching the correct dial-peer:

Example 8-7   *Dial-peer Verification via* **show voice call status** *IOS Command*

```
myrouter# show voice call status
CallID     CID  ccVdb      Port        DSP/Ch  Called #    Codec    Dial-peers
0x4B       11F6 0x84B2964C 1/0:23.1    1/5:1   8005551212  g711ulaw 1/555121
1 active call found
```

The output of the command in Example 8-7 illustrates that the call was using dial-peers 1 and 555121 and the DNIS was seen as 8005551212. The first dial-peer listed under the dial-peers column references the incoming POTS dial-peer matched for this call. In this example POTs dial-peer 1 was matched for the incoming call leg. The second dial-peer listed is the outgoing VoIP dial-peer that was matched. In this example, VoIP dial-peer 555121 was used to connect the call to Unified CVP via H.323 or SIP. This command does not show active calls that originate via a SIP trunk. Later in this section additional commands to verify if a call has been established via SIP are examined.

A common configuration issue with Ingress Gateways is reports of inbound calls receiving dial tone. Inbound calls receiving dial tone may have matched a Pots dial-peer that does not have direct-inward-dial configured, or the call matched a default system dial-peer.

Pots dial-peers also provide a good point for digit manipulation. If the DNIS delivered by the carrier needs to be modified before sending the call on to Unified CVP, use a translation rule and profile to match and change a digit pattern. Example 8-8 is a simple model of manipulation and testing the translation rules and profiles. For more detailed information on translation rules and patterns, refer to Cisco.com.

Example 8-8 *Sample Translation Profile Configuration*

```
translation-rule 1
 rule 1 /^555/ /800555/
!
voice translation-profile prepend
 translate called 1
!
dial-peer voice 1 pots
 description All Incoming PSTN Calls
 translation-profile incoming prepend
 incoming called-number .T
 direct-inward-dial
```

Assume the following:

- Carrier DNIS = 5551212

- Unified ICM Dialed Number needs to be 8005551212

Use the following test IOS command in Example 8-9 to verify that the translation profile will do exactly as expected.

Example 8-9 test voice translation rule *IOS Command*

```
myrouter# test voice translation-rule 1 5551212
Matched with rule 1
Original number: 5551212        Translated number: 8005551212
Original number type: none      Translated number type: none
Original number plan: none      Translated number plan: none
```

Note The **test voice translation rule** IOS command applies to any translation-rule whether it is applied to a POTs dial-peer or a VoIP dial-peer. In addition, this command only provides the result of a translation rule.

Dial-peer matching is another area that is critical to debugging where a call is going. For both ingress and VXML routers, POTs, VoIP and application dial-peers make up a critical part of how the solution works. So debugging their decision process is equally important. Example 8-10 provides a commonly used debug for determining which dial-peer was match for the incoming and outgoing dial-peer legs.

Example 8-10 *Dial-Peer Debugging IOS Command*

```
myrouter# debug voip dialpeer
*Jun  6 20:06:25.238: //-1/xxxxxxxxxxxx/DPM/dpMatchPeersCore:
   Calling Number=5338, Called Number=5338, Peer Info Type=DIALPEER_INFO_SPEECH
*Jun  6 20:06:25.238: //-1/xxxxxxxxxxxx/DPM/dpMatchPeersCore:
   Match Rule=DP_MATCH_DEST; Called Number=5338
*Jun  6 20:06:25.238: //-1/xxxxxxxxxxxx/DPM/dpMatchPeersCore:
   Result=Success(0) after DP_MATCH_DEST
*Jun  6 20:06:25.238: //-1/xxxxxxxxxxxx/DPM/dpMatchPeersMoreArg:
   Result=SUCCESS(0)
   List of Matched Outgoing Dial-peer(s):
     1: Dial-peer Tag=5338      }
```

Although this output has been abbreviated, it clearly shows what to look for when trying to determine if a dial-peer were matched and if so which one. As stated earlier, this command works for types of dial-peers and is used by turning it on during a debug session. However, wouldn't it be nice to have a command that would show all translations and subsequent dial-peer matching? What if such a command could also invoke any debugging that was currently turned on for the router to provide debugs for how the test command arrived at its conclusions for a provided DNIS? Indeed there is such a command; one that is commonly overlooked when testing and turning up Ingress and VXML Gateways. Example 8-11 provides a model of this gem.

Example 8-11 show dialplan *IOS Command*

```
myrouter# show dialplan number 5338
Macro Exp.: 5338


VoiceOverIpPeer5338
        peer type = voice, system default peer = FALSE, information type = voice,
        description = ` — — Comprehensive SIP calls from IP — —',
        tag = 5338, destination-pattern = `5338',
...
...
<Debug VoIP dialpeer was turned on>
*Jun  6 20:14:56.378: //-1/xxxxxxxxxxxx/DPM/dpMatchPeersCore:
   Calling Number=, Called Number=5338, Peer Info Type=DIALPEER_INFO_SPEECH
*Jun  6 20:14:56.378: //-1/xxxxxxxxxxxx/DPM/dpMatchPeersCore:
   Match Rule=DP_MATCH_DEST; Called Number=5338
*Jun  6 20:14:56.382: //-1/xxxxxxxxxxxx/DPM/dpMatchPeersCore:
   Result=Success(0) after DP_MATCH_DEST
*Jun  6 20:14:56.382: //-1/xxxxxxxxxxxx/DPM/dpMatchPeersMoreArg:
   Result=SUCCESS(0)
...
...
```

```
Translation profile (Incoming):
Translation profile (Outgoing):
incoming call blocking:

   translation-profile = `'
disconnect-cause = `no-service'
advertise 0x40 capacity_update_timer 25 addrFamily 4 oldAddrFamily 4
mailbox selection policy: none
   type = voip, session-target = `ipv4:192.168.1.218',
   technology prefix:
settle-call = disabled
   ip media DSCP = ef, ip media rsvp-pass DSCP = ef
ip media rsvp-fail DSCP = ef, ip signaling DSCP = af31,
ip video rsvp-none DSCP = af41,ip video rsvp-pass DSCP = af41
ip video rsvp-fail DSCP = af41,
   ip defending Priority = 0, ip preemption priority = 0
ip policy locator voice:
ip policy locator video:
UDP checksum = disabled,
   session-protocol = sipv2, session-transport = system,
req-qos = best-effort, acc-qos = best-effort,
req-qos video = best-effort, acc-qos video = best-effort,
req-qos audio def bandwidth = 64, req-qos audio max bandwidth =    0,
req-qos video def bandwidth = 384, req-qos video max bandwidth = 0,
   dtmf-relay = rtp-nte,

   dtmf-relay = h245-alphanumeric,
...
...
Matched: 5338   Digits: 4
Target: ipv4:192.168.1.218
```

Although Example 8-11 has been abbreviated, the shaded areas show some of the more useful outputs of the command. Any translations are illustrated at the top of the output, and the final target is noted at the bottom and the number of digits matched. As illustrated if any debugs are enabled on the router such as **debug voip dialpeer** the output is also provided as part of the command. This command verifies how a DNIS presented to the gateway via a POTs or VoIP dial-peer will be handled, all without making a real call. Another great command for generating a call on an Ingress or VXML Gateway to test dial-peer matching is illustrated in Example 8-12.

Example 8-12   csim start *IOS Command*

```
myrouter# debug ccsip error
myrouter# debug voip dialpeer
myrouter# csim start 5338
csim: called number = 5338, loop count = 1 ping count = 0

csim err csimDisconnected recvd DISC cid(102)
csim: loop = 1, failed = 1
csim: call attempted = 1, setup failed = 1, tone failed = 0

myrouter#
*Jun  6 20:36:32.390: //-1/xxxxxxxxxxxx/DPM/dpMatchPeersCore:
   Calling Number=, Called Number=5338, Peer Info Type=DIALPEER_INFO_SPEECH
*Jun  6 20:36:32.390: //-1/xxxxxxxxxxxx/DPM/dpMatchPeersCore:
   Match Rule=DP_MATCH_DEST; Called Number=5338
*Jun  6 20:36:32.390: //-1/xxxxxxxxxxxx/DPM/dpMatchPeersCore:
   Result=Success(0) after DP_MATCH_DEST
*Jun  6 20:36:32.390: //-1/xxxxxxxxxxxx/DPM/dpMatchPeers:
   Result=SUCCESS(0)
   List of Matched Outgoing Dial-peer(s):
     1: Dial-peer Tag=5338
*Jun 6 20:36:32.394: //102/7F9B24FA8112/SIP/Error/sipSPIOutgoingCallSDP: Could not
create source SDP for Outgoing Call
*Jun  6 20:36:32.394:
//102/7F9B24FA8112/SIP/Error/sipSPICreateOutboundSDP: Error in
creating an SDP for the outbound call - Check for supported codecs
*Jun  6 20:36:32.394: //102/7F9B24FA8112/SIP/Error/preprocessSetup:
Error during outbound SDP creation
*Jun  6 20:36:32.394: //-1/xxxxxxxxxxxx/SIP/Error/sipSPIGetContentQSIG: No Inbound
Container Created !!!
*Jun  6 20:36:32.394: //-1/xxxxxxxxxxxx/SIP/Error/sipSPIGetContentQ931: No Inbound
Container Created !!!
*Jun  6 20:36:32.394: //-1/xxxxxxxxxxxx/SIP/Error/ccsip_spi_process_ccapi_event:
CCAPI Event Preprocessor Failure
```

Although an actual call was attempted by the gateway, it could never be set up via SIP because of issues illustrated in the last two shaded areas of the output. However, both debugs that were enabled on the router provide their respective output just as if this were a real call.

In addition to the commands provided, there is a more specific debug used for VoIP connections. Use the command illustrated in Example 8-13 to verify that calls flow properly within the gateway. This debug can produce a high volume of debug messages, and it may be necessary to log your VTY session or make use of a syslog server to capture all the information. Example 8-13 has also been edited to show only pertinent information with real numbers masked to protect the innocent.

Example 8-13   debug voip ccapi inout *IOS Command*

```
myrouter# debug voip ccapi inout
<Note: Call Arrival from PSTN>
1/67A61A1E8115/CCAPI/cc_api_display_ie_subfields:
    cc_api_call_setup_ind_common:
    cisco-username=##########
    — —- ccCallInfo IE subfields — —-
    cisco-ani=sip:xxxxxxxxxx@xx.xx.xx.xx
    cisco-anitype=0
    cisco-aniplan=0
    cisco-anipi=0
    cisco-anisi=1
<Note:Incoming SIP Trunk provider and DNIS>
dest=sip:5338@xx.xx.xx.xx
    cisco-desttype=0
    cisco-destplan=0
    cisco-rdie=FFFFFFFF
    cisco-rdn=
    cisco-lastrdn=
    cisco-rdntype=0
    cisco-rdnplan=0
    cisco-rdnpi=-1
    cisco-rdnsi=-1
    cisco-redirectreason=-1    fwd_final_type =0
    final_redirectNumber =
    hunt_group_timeout =0
<Note:Calling and Called Number information>
*Jun  6 20:50:11.202: //-1/67A61A1E8115/CCAPI/cc_api_call_setup_ind_common:
    Interface=0x472B330C, Call Info(
Calling Number=sip:##########@##.##.##.##,(Calling Name=)(TON=Unknown, NPI=Unknown,
Screening=User, Passed, Presentation=Allowed),
Called Number=sip:5338@##.##.##.##(TON=Unknown, NPI=Unknown),
    Calling Translated=FALSE, Subscriber Type Str=Unknown,
FinalDestinationFlag=TRUE,
<Note: Call matched default dial peer>
Incoming Dial-peer=0, Progress Indication=NULL(0), Calling IE Present=TRUE,
    Source Trkgrp Route Label=, Target Trkgrp Route Label=, CLID Transparent=FALSE),
Call Id=103
<Note:Call has now matched outgoing voip dial peer 5338>
*Jun  6 20:50:11.214: //103/67A61A1E8115/CCAPI/ccCallSetupRequest:
    Destination=, Calling IE Present=TRUE, Mode=0,
Outgoing Dial-peer=5338, Params=0x48522C2C, Progress Indication=NULL(0)
*Jun  6 20:50:11.214: //103/67A61A1E8115/CCAPI/ccCheckClipClir:
In: Calling Number=sip:##########@##.##.##.##(TON=Unknown, NPI=Unknown,
 Screening=User, Passed, Presentation=Allowed)
*Jun  6 20:50:11.214: //103/67A61A1E8115/CCAPI/ccCheckClipClir:
```

```
Out: Calling Number=sip:##########@##.##.##.##(TON=Unknown, NPI=Unknown,
Screening=User, Passed, Presentation=Allowed)
*Jun  6 20:50:11.214: //103/67A61A1E8115/CCAPI/ccCallSetupRequest:
Destination Pattern=5338, Called Number=5338, Digit Strip=FALSE
*Jun  6 20:50:11.218: //103/67A61A1E8115/CCAPI/ccCallSetupRequest:
   Calling Number=sip:##########@##.##.##.##(TON=Unknown, NPI=Unknown,
Screening=User, Passed, Presentation=Allowed),
   Called Number=5338(TON=Unknown, NPI=Unknown),
   Redirect Number=, Display Info=7208751243
   Account Number=##########, Final Destination Flag=TRUE,
   Guid=67A61A1E-8FB5-11E0-8115-974FC4741272, Outgoing Dial-peer=5338
*Jun  6 20:50:11.218: //103/67A61A1E8115/CCAPI/cc_api_display_ie_subfields:
   ccCallSetupRequest:
   cisco-username=##########
   — —- ccCallInfo IE subfields — —-
   cisco-ani=sip:##########@##.##.##.##
   cisco-anitype=0
   cisco-aniplan=0
   cisco-anipi=0
   cisco-anisi=1
   dest=5338
   cisco-desttype=0
   cisco-destplan=0
   cisco-rdie=FFFFFFFF
   cisco-rdn=
   cisco-lastrdn=
   cisco-rdntype=0
   cisco-rdnplan=0
   cisco-rdnpi=-1
   cisco-rdnsi=-1
   cisco-redirectreason=-1    fwd_final_type =0
   final_redirectNumber =
   hunt_group_timeout =0


*Jun  6 20:50:11.218: //103/67A61A1E8115/CCAPI/ccIFCallSetupRequestPrivate:
   Interface=0x472B330C, Interface Type=3, Destination=, Mode=0x0,
   Call Params(Calling Number=sip:##########@##.##.##.##,(Calling
Name=##########)(TON=Unknown, NPI=Unknown, Screening=User, Passed,
Presentation=Allowed),
   Called Number=5338(TON=Unknown, NPI=Unknown), Calling Translated=FALSE,
   Subscriber Type Str=Unknown, FinalDestinationFlag=TRUE, Outgoing Dial-peer=5338,
Call Count On=FALSE,
   Source Trkgrp Route Label=, Target Trkgrp Route Label=, tg_label_flag=0,
Application Call Id=)
*Jun  6 20:50:30.906:  vsacount in free is 0
```

Example 8-13 illustrates only what happens during the processing of the switch leg of a call and the Ingress Gateway. The same debug occurs when the VRU leg of the call is presented to the VXML Gateway. The DNIS value for the called number or destination is the VRU label generated by Unified ICM. So it is fair to say that you can use this debug command to validate the delivery of the VRU leg onto a VXML Gateway from a voice bearer perspective. It should be used before using the VXML Gateway-only debugs listed later in this chapter.

SIP Related (Ingress and VXML Gateways)

Both the Ingress and VXML Gateways use SIP for terminating either the switch or VRU leg of a call. It is critical to understand how to verify the status of the gateways' SIP configuration and troubleshoot. Start by looking at some commands that focus on the status and configuration of the gateway for SIP.

Example 8-14 illustrates the **show sip status** IOS command.

Example 8-14   show sip status *IOS Command*

```
myrouter#show sip status
SIP User Agent Status
SIP User Agent for UDP : ENABLED
SIP User Agent for TCP : ENABLED
SIP User Agent for TLS over TCP : ENABLED
SIP User Agent bind status(signaling): ENABLED  192.168.1.11
SIP User Agent bind status(media): ENABLED  192.168.1.11
SIP early-media for 180 responses with SDP: ENABLED
SIP max-forwards : 70
SIP DNS SRV version: 2 (rfc 2782)
NAT Settings for the SIP-UA
Role in SDP: NONE
Check media source packets: DISABLED
Maximum duration for a telephone-event in NOTIFYs: 2000 ms
SIP support for ISDN SUSPEND/RESUME: ENABLED
Redirection (3xx) message handling: ENABLED
Reason Header will override Response/Request Codes: DISABLED
Out-of-dialog Refer: DISABLED
Presence support is DISABLED
protocol mode is ipv4

SDP application configuration:
 Version line (v=) required
 Owner line (o=) required
 Timespec line (t=) required
 Media supported: audio video image
 Network types supported: IN
```

```
Address types supported: IP4 IP6
Transport types supported: RTP/AVP udptl
```

As shown the SIP User Agent is enabled for both User Datagram Protocol (UDP) and TCP with bindings for signaling and media to the IP address of 192.168.1.11, which is assigned to a local interface on the ingress router. With an SIP call placed through the ingress router, using the **show sip connections** and assuming that UDP is used. Example 8-15 provides the detailed version of this command with some addresses masked.

Example 8-15   show sip connections *IOS Command*

```
myrouter# show sip connections udp detail
Total active connections       : 2
No. of send failures           : 0
No. of remote closures         : 0
No. of conn. failures          : 0
No. of inactive conn. ageouts  : 17


Remote-Agent:192.168.1.218, Connections-Count:1
  Remote-Port Conn-Id Conn-State  WriteQ-Size

  =========== ======= =========== ===========
        5060       2 Established            0

Remote-Agent:# #.##.##.##, Connections-Count:1
  Remote-Port Conn-Id Conn-State  WriteQ-Size

  =========== ======= =========== ===========
        5060       3 Established            0
```

Example 8-15 shows that two SIP call legs are active. The first is a connection between the Ingress Gateway and the Unified CVP Server's SIP Service located at address 192.168.1.218. The second connection, with the masked remote agent IP address, is between the Ingress Gateway and the SIP trunk provided by the PSTN carrier.

One final note is that the **show** command that is for evaluating how SIP is engaged on a router is the **show sip statistics** command. Example 8-16 provides a sample of this command's output.

Example 8-16   show SIP statistics *IOS Command*

```
myrouter# show SIP statistics
SIP Response Statistics (Inbound/Outbound)
    Informational:
        Trying 22/31, Ringing 0/1,
        Forwarded 0/0, Queued 0/0,
        SessionProgress 0/0
```

```
        Success:
OkInvite 22/166, OkBye 46/1,
        OkCancel 0/0, OkOptions 0/37,
        OkPrack 0/0, OkRegister 0/0
        OkSubscribe 0/0, OkNotify 16/0, OkPublish 0/0
        OkInfo 0/0, OkUpdate 0/0,
        202Accepted 0/8, OkOptions 0/37
      Redirection (Inbound only except for MovedTemp(Inbound/Outbound)) :

        MultipleChoice 0, MovedPermanently 0,
        MovedTemporarily 0/0, UseProxy 0,
        AlternateService 0
      Client Error:
        BadRequest 0/80, Unauthorized 0/0,
        PaymentRequired 0/0, Forbidden 0/0,
        NotFound 0/0, MethodNotAllowed 0/0,
        NotAcceptable 0/0, ProxyAuthReqd 0/0,
        ReqTimeout 0/0, Conflict 0/0, Gone 0/0,
        ConditionalRequestFailed 0/0,
        ReqEntityTooLarge 0/0, ReqURITooLarge 0/0,
        UnsupportedMediaType 0/0, UnsupportedURIScheme 0/0,
        BadExtension 0/0, IntervalTooBrief 0/0,
        TempNotAvailable 0/0, CallLegNonExistent 2/1,
        LoopDetected 0/0, TooManyHops 0/0,
        AddrIncomplete 0/0, Ambiguous 0/0,
        BusyHere 0/0, RequestCancel 0/0,
        NotAcceptableMedia 0/0, BadEvent 0/0,
        SETooSmall 0/0, , RequestPending 0/0
        UnsupportedResourcePriority 0/0
      Server Error:
InternalError 0/3, NotImplemented 0/0,
        BadGateway 0/0, ServiceUnavail 0/0,
        GatewayTimeout 0/0, BadSipVer 0/0,
        PreCondFailure 0/0
      Global Failure:
        BusyEverywhere 0/0, Decline 0/0,
        NotExistAnywhere 0/0, NotAcceptable 0/0
      Miscellaneous counters:
        RedirectRspMappedToClientErr 0

SIP Total Traffic Statistics (Inbound/Outbound)
      Invite 31/26, Ack 61/22, Bye 1/78,
      Cancel 0/0, Options 37/0,
      Prack 0/0, Update 0/0,
```

```
    Subscribe 1/0, Notify 0/16, Publish 0/0
    Refer 8/0, Info 0/0,
    Register 80/0

Retry Statistics
    Invite 1, Bye 29, Cancel 0, Response 138,
    Prack 0, Reliable1xx 0, Notify 0, Info 0
    Register 0 Subscribe 0 Update 0 Options 0
    Publish 0

SDP application statistics:
 Parses: 53,  Builds 90
 Invalid token order: 0,  Invalid param: 245
 Not SDP desc: 0,  No resource: 0

Last time SIP Statistics were cleared: <never>
```

The statistics have never been cleared for this gateway, as illustrated by the last highlighted line in the output. The SIP statistics can be cleared simply by issuing the command **clear sip statistics** on the gateway. This summary report is great for determining if any messages are responded to by the gateway and if so, which ones.

Now switching gears, take a look at some simple debugs used to troubleshoot SIP in more detail. One observation with debug commands presented on an IOS device is that the variations and output of the command can be overwhelming at times, with SIP debugging being no different. However, the next few examples focus on the more common commands used to debug SIP issues without having to turn on every SIP debug supported by the router. Remember, the more complex debug commands that are enabled on a router, the more impact it has on performance.

Example 8-17 provides some sample output from using the **show ccsip calls** IOS debug command.

Example 8-17   debug ccsip calls *IOS Command*

```
myrouter# debug ccsip calls
SIP Call statistics tracing is enabled
myrouter#
*Jun  6 22:33:10.006: //122/CA6C8F8E8154/SIP/Call/sipSPICallInfo:
<Switch Leg to Unified CVP Call Server's SIP Service>
The Call Setup Information is:
Call Control Block (CCB) : 0x47F71C20
State of The Call        : STATE_ACTIVE
TCP Sockets Used         : NO
Calling Number           : ##########
```

```
Called Number            : 5338
Source IP Address (Sig  ): 192.168.1.11
Destn SIP Req Addr:Port  : 192.168.1.218:5060
Destn SIP Resp Addr:Port : 192.168.1.218:5060
Destination Name         : 192.168.1.218


*Jun  6 22:33:10.006: //122/CA6C8F8E8154/SIP/Call/sipSPIMediaCallInfo:
<VRU Leg to Standalone VXML gateway>
Number of Media Streams: 1
Media Stream             : 1
Negotiated Codec         : g711ulaw
Negotiated Codec Bytes   : 160
Nego. Codec payload      : 0 (tx), 0 (rx)
Negotiated Dtmf-relay    : 6
Dtmf-relay Payload       : 101 (tx), 101 (rx)
Source IP Address (Media): 192.168.1.11
Source IP Port    (Media): 18408
Destn  IP Address (Media): 10.1.10.2
Destn  IP Port    (Media): 28440
Orig Destn IP Address:Port (Media): [ - ]:0


*Jun  6 22:33:29.534: //122/CA6C8F8E8154/SIP/Call/sipSPICallInfo:
<Results of call being disconnected from Unified CVP Call Server>
The Call Setup Information is:
Call Control Block (CCB) : 0x47F71C20
State of The Call        : STATE_DEAD
TCP Sockets Used         : NO
Calling Number           : ##########
Called Number            : 5338
Source IP Address (Sig  ): 192.168.1.11
Destn SIP Req Addr:Port  : 192.168.1.218:5060
Destn SIP Resp Addr:Port : 192.168.1.218:5060
Destination Name         : 192.168.1.218


...
...


*Jun  6 22:33:29.534: //122/CA6C8F8E8154/SIP/Call/sipSPICallInfo:
Disconnect Cause (CC)    : 102
Disconnect Cause (SIP)   : 200
```

The debug Switch and VRU leg of the call are clearly represented with the Unified CVP Call Server configured with IP address 192.168.1.218 and the standalone VXML gateway at 10.1.10.2. The state of the call is also represented after the call disconnects, and even the codec used between the ingress and VXML Gateway is provided in the debugs. A slight variation of this command is the **debug ccsip error** IOS command, which will display only SIP error messages. Example 8-18 provides a sample output of this command when a **csim start** command is issued on a router causing SIP to error out because of the lack of a source for SDP.

Example 8-18   debug ccsip error *IOS Command*

```
myrouter# debug ccsip error
myrouter# csim start 5338
csim: called number = 5338, loop count = 1 ping count = 0
csim err csimDisconnected recvd DISC cid(102)
csim: loop = 1, failed = 1
csim: call attempted = 1, setup failed = 1, tone failed = 0
myrouter#
*Jun  6 20:36:32.394: //102/7F9B24FA8112/SIP/Error/sipSPIOutgoingCallSDP: Could not
create source SDP for Outgoing Call
*Jun  6 20:36:32.394: //102/7F9B24FA8112/SIP/Error/sipSPICreateOutboundSDP: Error in
creating an SDP for the outbound call - Check for supported codecs
*Jun  6 20:36:32.394: //102/7F9B24FA8112/SIP/Error/preprocessSetup: Error during
outbound SDP creation
*Jun  6 20:36:32.394: //-1/xxxxxxxxxxxx/SIP/Error/sipSPIGetContentQSIG: No Inbound
Container Created !!!
*Jun  6 20:36:32.394: //-1/xxxxxxxxxxxx/SIP/Error/sipSPIGetContentQ931: No Inbound
Container Created !!!
*Jun  6 20:36:32.394: //-1/xxxxxxxxxxxx/SIP/Error/ccsip_spi_process_ccapi_event:
CCAPI Event Preprocessor Failure
```

This debug command focuses purely on SIP errors generated by the gateway, which enables filtering, showing only SIP error messages all these commands can be enabled together on a router, which mixes the output together for a more complete picture of any SIP issues. Another nice SIP debug command that filters for events specific to SPI is the **debug ccsip events** IOS command. Example 8-19 provides a sample of this debug.

Example 8-19   debug ccsip events *IOS Command*

```
myrouter# debug ccsip events
SIP Call events tracing is enabled
myrouter#
*Jun  6 22:54:34.482: //-1/xxxxxxxxxxxx/SIP/Event/sipSPIEventInfo: Queued event
from
SIP SPI : SIPSPI_EV_CC_CALL_PROCEEDING
*Jun  6 22:54:34.486: //-1/xxxxxxxxxxxx/SIP/Event/sipSPIEventInfo: Queued event
from
SIP SPI : SIPSPI_EV_CC_CALL_SETUP          *Jun  6 22:54:34.490:
//124/C81AF3ED815B/SIP/Event/sipSPICreateRpid:
```

```
Received Octet3A=0x81 -> Setting ;screen=yes ;privacy=off
*Jun  6 22:54:34.614: //-1/xxxxxxxxxxxx/SIP/Event/sipSPIEventInfo:
Queued event from SIP SPI : SIPSPI_EV_CC_NEW_MEDIA
*Jun  6 22:54:34.618: //-1/xxxxxxxxxxxx/SIP/Event/sipSPIEventInfo:
Queued event from SIP SPI : SIPSPI_EV_CC_CALL_CONNECT
*Jun  6 22:54:34.626: //123/C81AF3ED815B/SIP/Event/sipSPICreateRpid:
Received Octet3A=0x00 -> Setting ;screen=no ;privacy=off
*Jun  6 22:54:35.126: //123/C81AF3ED815B/SIP/Event/sipSPICreateRpid:
Received Octet3A=0x00 -> Setting ;screen=no ;privacy=off
*Jun  6 22:54:36.126: //123/C81AF3ED815B/SIP/Event/sipSPICreateRpid:
Received Octet3A=0x00 -> Setting ;screen=no ;privacy=off
*Jun  6 22:54:38.126: //123/C81AF3ED815B/SIP/Event/sipSPICreateRpid:
Received Octet3A=0x00 -> Setting ;screen=no ;privacy=off
*Jun  6 22:54:42.126: //123/C81AF3ED815B/SIP/Event/sipSPICreateRpid:
Received Octet3A=0x00 -> Setting ;screen=no ;privacy=off
*Jun  6 22:54:46.126: //123/C81AF3ED815B/SIP/Event/sipSPICreateRpid:
Received Octet3A=0x00 -> Setting ;screen=no ;privacy=off
*Jun  6 22:54:50.126: //123/C81AF3ED815B/SIP/Event/sipSPICreateRpid:
Received Octet3A=0x00 -> Setting ;screen=no ;privacy=off
*Jun  6 22:54:54.130: //-1/xxxxxxxxxxxx/SIP/Event/sipSPIEventInfo: Queued event
from
SIP SPI : SIPSPI_EV_CC_CALL_DISCONNECT
*Jun  6 22:54:54.130: //-1/xxxxxxxxxxxx/SIP/Event/sipSPIEventInfo: Queued event
from
SIP SPI : SIPSPI_EV_CC_CALL_DISCONNECT
```

Example 8-19 illustrates the SPI events indicating call setup, proceeding, and disconnecting. However, use caution when enabling different debugs because of their performance impacts and the readability of the debug captures.

H.323 Related (Ingress and VXML Gateways)

Some deployments still use H.323 as their call control protocol. This section examines verification and debugging H.323-related configurations and issues. Begin with some simple verification commands to verify that H.323 is correctly configured on the ingress or VXML Gateways. Example 8-20 illustrates the **show gateway** command, which provides a status of the gateway from an H.323 perspective.

Example 8-20   show gateway *IOS Command*

```
myrouter# show gateway
H.323 ITU-T Version: 4.0   H323 Stack Version: 0.1

 H.323 service is up
```

```
Gateway  INGRESS_R2800-VG  is registered to Gatekeeper INGRESS_PRI

Alias list (CLI configured)
 H323-ID INGRESS_R2800-VG
Alias list (last RCF)
 H323-ID INGRESS_R2800-VG

H323 resource thresholding is Disabled
Permanent Alternate Gatekeeper List
 priority 0 id INGRESS_SEC ipaddr 10.1.112.2 1719 register needed
 priority 120 id INGRESS_PRI ipaddr 10.1.112.1 1719 register needed
 Primary gatekeeper ID INGRESS_PRI ipaddr 10.1.112.1 1719
```

The first items that need to be verified are the gateway to ensure it is registered with a gatekeeper and using cluster of Gatekeepers and the primary Gatekeeper to ensure it is as expected, while the alternative Gatekeeper is also configured for the gateway to use if the primary goes away. If the gateway is not registering with a Gatekeeper, it cannot process the switch leg of the call (Ingress Gateway) or treat the VRU leg (VXML Gateway). Common issues with registration are incorrect Gatekeeper IP addresses or zone names also referred to as the Gatekeeper ID, as shown in Example 8-20 as INGRESS_PRI and INGRESS_SEC, respectively. Also verify that the Gatekeeper can be reached by using the **ping** command and that the H.323 ID assigned to the gateway is unique.

If you cannot resolve the issue, try debugging H.225 and H.245 messages between the gateway and the Gatekeeper. Provided in these debugs are a RasMessage::= registrationReject message block with a property named rejectReason. You can now determine why the Gatekeeper rejects the gateway's registration request by viewing this property. Following are some common registration reject reasons and possible solutions. Remember to use the command **debug h225 asn1** on the gateway or Gatekeeper to collect this information.

RRJ:rejectReason duplicateAlias

Example 8-21 shows how to identify that a duplicate H.323 ID is used to register with a Gatekeeper.

Example 8-21   Debug h225 asn1 *Duplicate Alias Reject Reason*

```
myrouter# debug h225 asn1
RAS INCOMING PDU ::=

value RasMessage ::= registrationReject :
   {
    requestSeqNum 24
    protocolIdentifier { 0 0 8 2250 0 3 }
    rejectReason duplicateAlias:
```

```
    {
    }
    gatekeeperIdentifier {"GK1"}
}
```

This issue occurs because the gateway has been assigned an H.323 ID that is already registered with the Gatekeeper by another gateway or H.323 endpoint. H.323 IDs must be unique.

RRJ:rejectReason terminalExcluded

Example 8-22 provides some output that illustrates a terminalExcluded reject reason from a Gatekeeper during registration.

Example 8-22   debug h225 asn1 *terminalExcluded Reject Reason*

```
myrouter# debug h225 asn1
RAS INCOMING PDU ::=

value RasMessage ::= gatekeeperReject :
    {
      requestSeqNum 3421
      protocolIdentifier { 0 0 8 2250 0 3 }
      rejectReason terminalExcluded : NULL
    }
```

This issue can be caused by two main configuration issues. First, make sure that the Gatekeeper zone to be referenced by the Gateway has been configured on the Gatekeeper. If the zone does not exist, configure it to match the gateway. Second, if using subnet security on the Gatekeeper to deny the access of certain subnets and devices on those subnets from registering with the Gatekeeper, this error message will be returned to those devices blocked. Check the Gatekeeper configuration and be sure not to have a **zone subnet gk** command configured that matches the subnet where the gateway is hosted. If that is the case, be sure to remove or modify this command to exclude the gateway.

RRJ:rejectReason securityDenial

Example 8-23 illustrates how to isolate a securityDenial reject reason during registration.

Example 8-23   debug h225 asn1 *securityDenial Reject Reason*

```
myrouter# debug h225 asn1
RAS INCOMING PDU ::=

value RasMessage ::= registrationReject :
    {
      requestSeqNum 3010
```

```
protocolIdentifier { 0 0 8 2250 0 3 }
rejectReason securityDenial : NULL
gatekeeperIdentifier {"GK1"}
}
```

This issue can be caused by security commands enabled in the Gatekeeper, and the Gatekeeper could not match the h323-id, E164-id, passwords, or security token required by the Gatekeeper. Verify that the security commands and information required by the Gatekeeper match the configurations setup on the gateway.

RRJ:rejectReason invalidAlias

Example 8-24 shows how to isolate an invalidAlias reject reason during registration.

Example 8-24 debug h225 asn1 *invalidAlias Reject Reason*

```
myrouter# debug h225 asn1
RAS INCOMING PDU ::=

value RasMessage ::= registrationReject :
  {
    requestSeqNum 2994
    protocolIdentifier { 0 0 8 2250 0 3 }
    rejectReason invalidAlias : NULL
    GatekeeperIdentifier {"GK1"}
  }
```

This issue can be caused by no zone prefixes being defined in the Gatekeeper. In other words, before the gateway can request routing from the Gatekeeper for a DNIS, a zone prefix that matches this DNIS must be configured in the Gatekeeper.

VXML Applications (Ingress Survivability and VXML Gateways)

Although this section focuses on the details around troubleshooting applications usually hosted on the VXML Gateway, there could be VXML applications hosted on the Ingress Gateway such as survivability, for which this section also applies. Assuming the switch leg of a call works as expected and the VRU leg is connected to a VXML Gateway for call treatment, troubleshooting issues on the VXML Gateway for the invoking of certain specific VXML applications becomes critical to troubleshooting the VRU leg of a call. This section does not provide detailed configuration steps for setting up and configuring a VXML Gateway simply because you should use the Unified CVP Configuration and Administration Guide as a reference when configuring a VXML Gateway. Before attempting to debug a VXML Gateway, it should be verified from a configuration perspective. In some cases, the VXML Gateway may have never worked correctly or processed a call. It is in these situations in which most of the problems with the VXML Gateway surface. In situations in which the VXML Gateway has worked but suddenly decides to not correctly work, isolating the issue become a bit more challenging. However, assuming that the VXML Gateway has been correctly installed and configured, look at a few commands that can help verify that the VXML Gateway is configured correctly and commands to debug issues that simply cannot be found using a **show** command.

Verifying Files in Flash

Using the **show flash** command, verify the VXML, TCL, and audio files required by a VXML router depending on the Unified CVP Deployment model. Following are the required gateway files categorized by deployment model:

- Standalone Files
  - CVPSelfService.tcl
  - CVPSelfServiceBootstrap.vxml
  - critical_error.wav
- Comprehensive Ingress Gateway Files
  - handoff.tcl
  - survivabilty.tcl
  - recovery.vxml
  - ringtone.tcl
  - cvperror.tcl
  - ringback.wav
  - critical_error.wav
- Comprehensive VXML Gateway Files
  - cvperror.tcl
  - ringback.wav
  - critical_error.wav
  - bootstrap.tcl
  - bootstrap.vxml

By issuing a **show flash** it is easy to determine if certain files are missing. In addition, using the Unified CVP Operations Console, all required files can be transferred to the flash memory of a gateway. Example 8-25 shows how the router's flash memory would be populated with a comprehensive Unified CVP VXML Gateway.

Example 8-25   show Flash *IOS Command on Comprehensive VXML Gateway*

```
R2921-VXML#show flash
-#- —length— — —-date/time— — — path
```

```
1      60620924 Nov 11 2010 22:08:14 c2900-universalk9_npe-mz.SPA.150-1.M4.bin
2          2903 Nov 11 2010 22:22:18 cpconfig-29xx.cfg
3       2941440 Nov 11 2010 22:22:34 cpexpress.tar
4          1038 Nov 11 2010 22:22:46 home.shtml
5        115712 Nov 11 2010 22:22:54 home.tar
6       1697952 Nov 11 2010 22:23:10 securedesktop-ios-3.1.1.45-k9.pkg
7        415956 Nov 11 2010 22:23:22 sslclient-win-1.1.4.176.pkg
8          4987 Nov 30 2010 17:52:12 opsConsoleServerConfig-0
9         20857 May 20 2011 19:11:22 bootstrap.tcl
10         4746 May 20 2011 19:11:26 bootstrap.vxml
11        58446 May 20 2011 19:11:28 critical_error.wav
12         5415 May 20 2011 19:11:32 cvp_ccb_dial.tcl
13         6991 May 20 2011 19:11:34 cvp_ccb_poll.tcl
14         8679 May 20 2011 19:11:36 cvp_ccb_vxml.tcl
15         1829 May 20 2011 19:11:40 cvperror.tcl
16        29548 May 20 2011 19:11:42 CVPSelfService.tcl
17        10169 May 20 2011 19:11:46 CVPSelfServiceBootstrap.vxml
18         2446 May 20 2011 19:11:48 en_0.wav
19         2446 May 20 2011 19:11:50 en_1.wav
20         2446 May 20 2011 19:11:52 en_2.wav
21         2446 May 20 2011 19:11:54 en_3.wav
22         2446 May 20 2011 19:11:58 en_4.wav
23         2446 May 20 2011 19:12:00 en_5.wav
24         2446 May 20 2011 19:12:02 en_6.wav
25         2446 May 20 2011 19:12:04 en_7.wav
26         2446 May 20 2011 19:12:08 en_8.wav
27         2446 May 20 2011 19:12:10 en_9.wav
28         2406 May 20 2011 19:12:12 en_pound.wav
29         2446 May 20 2011 19:12:14 en_star.wav
30         1432 May 20 2011 19:12:16 handoff.tcl
31       126454 May 20 2011 19:12:20 holdmusic.wav
32        26582 May 20 2011 19:12:22 pleasewait.wav
33          596 May 20 2011 19:12:24 recovery.vxml
34        32110 May 20 2011 19:12:28 ringback.wav
35         4312 May 20 2011 19:12:30 ringtone.tcl
36       132467 May 20 2011 19:12:34 survivability.tcl
```

In addition to these files, other files may be required depending on what additional roles and features are expected from the VXML Gateway. In Example 8-25 the additional .wav files are for DTMF collection and the cvp_ccb_* files are used for a Unified CVP feature branded Courtesy Call Back or CCB. Be sure to understand any special roles or files required by the VXML Gateway, which makes it easier to connect the dots to a possible culprit when that feature is not working.

Stare and Compare

Another effective tool for verifying a VXML Gateways configuration can be termed "Stare and Compare." If lucky enough to have a working VXML Gateway, try to compare its configuration to the VXML Gateway that is not working. This can quickly isolate missing configurations or parameters that could be causing an issue. The Unified CVP Operations Console has canned configurations for different gateway deployment models, which can be accessed via the System > IOS Configuration > IOS Template Management menu. Templates can also be saved and managed. This enables templates to be saved for a gateway and reused for additional ingress or VXML Gateway deployments. If you use a combination ingress and VXML Gateway for the deployment, the configurations located in the Operations Console for each gateway type must be combined with the files listed earlier in this chapter when deploying a combo gateway.

Verifying VXML Applications

After the VXML application files have been verified to be in flash and the correct application dial-peer, http, and Interactive Voice Response (IVR) configurations exist on the gateway, the next step is to verify that the applications loaded correctly into the gateways memory. Using the **show call application voice summary** can immediately isolate issues with the application not loading correctly.

Example 8-26 show call application voice *IOS Command with Error*

```
R2921-VXML#show call application voice summary
 SERVICES (standalone applications):
 name                   type            description
 ipsla-responder    Tcl Script    builtin:app_test_rcvr_script.tcl
 new-call                          IncorrectFileOrMissingFile.vxml
 Loading...
 CALLIndSs_SErviCe  C Script      builtin:CallIndSs_Service.C
 RetrProxy          C Script      builtin:RetrievalProxy_Service.C
 session            Tcl Script    builtin:app_session_script.tcl
 ...
 ...
```

In the output from Example 8-26, the file name IncorrectFileorMissingFile.vxml does not exist in the flash of the router or it is incorrectly spelled. Example 8-27 shows how the new-call should look when correctly configured:

Example 8-27 show call application voice summary *IOS Command Without Error*

```
R2921-VXML#show call application voice summary
 SERVICES (standalone applications):
 name                    type             description

 ipsla-responder    Tcl Script      builtin:app_test_rcvr_script.tcl
```

```
new-call            Vxml Script      flash:bootstrap.vxml
CALLIndSs_SErviCe   C Script         builtin:CallIndSs_Service.C
RetrProxy           C Script         builtin:RetrievalProxy_Service.C
session             Tcl Script       builtin:app_session_script.tcl
...
...
```

In addition, it is a good idea to have the gateway application files copied to the router's flash memory before configuring any application services. When configuring an application service and referencing a file in flash, the IOS provides an error if the file referenced in the application service configuration cannot be found. Likewise, it can also provide a successful message if the file can be found and loaded into the gateway's memory. Example 8-28 provides the output for both of these situations, respectively:

Example 8-28 *IOS Error When Trying to Load Nonexistent Application File*

```
<Incorrect file name configured causing the gateway fail upon loading>
 *Jun  8 20:56:27.594: //-1//HIFS:/hifs_ifs_cb: hifs ifs could not open file
IncorrectFileOrMissingFile.vxml
*Jun  8 20:56:27.594: //-1//HIFS:/hifs_free_idata: hifs_free_idata: 0x29AB1A24
*Jun  8 20:56:27.594: //-1//HIFS:/hifs_hold_idata: hifs_hold_idata: 0x29AB1A24
*Jun  8 20:56:27.594: Could not load IVR script
  IncorrectFileOrMissingFile.vxml
  errno=-1=hifs Failure

<Correct File name configured and loaded into Router Memory>
 *Jun  8 21:05:39.962: //-1//HIFS:/hifs_ifs_cb: hifs ifs file read succeeded.
size=4746, url=flash:bootstrap.vxml
*Jun  8 21:05:39.962: //-1//HIFS:/hifs_free_idata: hifs_free_idata: 0x29AB6DF8
*Jun  8 21:05:39.962: //-1//HIFS:/hifs_hold_idata: hifs_hold_idata: 0x29AB6DF8exit
```

In addition to looking at all the application services configured on the router with a single command, also look at an application service to see if it is registered. Verify the loaded version of the script. Example 8-29 provides a variation of the previous command by referencing the new-call application service.

Example 8-29 show call application voice new-call *IOS Command*

```
R2921-VXML#show call application voice new-call
Script Name : new-call
       URL  : flash:bootstrap.vxml
       Type : Service
       State: Registered
       Life : Configured
```

```
        Exec Instances: 1

Script Code Begin:
— — — — — — — — — — — — — — — — —
VXML Application new-call
    URL=flash:bootstrap.vxml
    Security Level: not trusted
            0 incoming calls
            1 calls handed off to it
            0 call transfers initiated
            0 pages loaded,  0 successful
            1 prompt play attempts, 1 successful
            0 recorded messages


The VXML Script is:
— — — — — — — — —
<?xml version="1.0" encoding="iso-8859-1"?>


<vxml version="2.0">


<!— Script last modified by: pantinor —>
<!— Script Version: CVP_8_0_1_0_0_4_22 —>
<!— Script Name: bootstrap.vxml —>
<!— Script Lock Date:1/11/2007
...
...
```

Although the output of this command was abbreviated, the shaded areas outline some items of interest. First, the state of the new-call service is "Registered" indicating that it correctly loaded into the gateway's memory. Equally important are the counters that are highlighted indicating that one call has used this script with a single prompt play attempt, which was successful. These counters are a great way to determine if the application service is invoked or if the service were configured incorrectly. The final area of interest is the script version. Always verify that this version matches the version of Unified CVP running on the Call Servers. Believe it or not, people copy files from older VXML Gateways and expect them to magically work with newer versions of Unified CVP. This is a big mistake. Always copy application files from Unified CVP Call Servers either manually using TFTP or via the Operations Console regardless of whether it is an upgrade or green field deployment. If there is any inclination an older version of a script is used, immediately update it.

VXML Debugging

If there are issues with prompts or queue music being played to callers, debug what VXML instructions are sent to the gateway from CVP. Verify the source of the requested wav files and the names of the files. For example, the ICM script defines the

Call.user.microapp.media_server = "http://mediaserver:8080". This means that the gateway will be presented with a request to "fetch" files from this repository. Before turning up the VXML debugs, run through some basic checks:

Note The hostname mediaserver and mediaserver-backup are some defaults used in common Unified CVP deployments. However, it is correct to use a different hostname defined in the ICM variable previously listed, as long as the VXML Gateway also defines and uses the same hostname.

- Ping the hostname mediaserver from the gateway. Gateways can be configured with static host entries such as mediaserver and mediaserver-backup as part of the gateway configuration. Validate that the hostname of the media server defined in ICM or VXML Studio App resolves to the correct IP address.

- Use a web browser to validate that the wav files are in the correct URL path that will be sent to the gateway. (http://mediaserver:8080/en-us/sys/holdmusic.wav).

If the matter persists, use the following debug provided in Example 8-30 to diagnose the issue. Again, this debug produces a large output of data and can impact the CPU load. Try to use this during off-peak calling hours and use IOS filtering commands to search the output.

Note The output of the debug has been edited. The actually output is too large to be included. The ICM test script was intentionally configured with an incorrect wav filename Test_Missing_File to allow the debugs to illustrate a bad fetch scenario.

Example 8-30 debug voip application VXML *IOS Command*

```
R2921-VXML#debug voip application VXML
<Call is placed into Unified CVP invoking Unified ICM Script>
R2921-VXML#show log | include mediaserver
<Note: Used <pipe |> and inc (include) just to look for log entries containing the
word "mediaserver">
URI(abs):http://mediaserver:8080/en-us/app/Test_Missing_File.wav
<The gateway was instructed to "fetch" the wav file from CVP>
  host=mediaserver
  str=http://mediaserver:8080/en-us/app/Test_Missing_File.wav cachable=1 timeout4
maxage=-1 maxstale=-1

Mar 15 10:01:22.050: //23//AFW_:/vapp_media_play:
prompt=http://mediaserver:8080/en-us/app/Test_Missing_File.wav:
  URI(abs):http://mediaserver-backup:8080/en-us/app/Test_Missing_File.wav

<The initial "fetch" failed and would produce an error response from the gateway to
```

CVP (vxml_error_badfetch_event). CVP would then request another fetch to the backup media server (mediaserver-backup). Please see the note at the end of this section about the changes required for vxml version 2.0 and the fetch errors.>

   host=mediaserver-backup

   str=http://mediaserver-backup:8080/en-us/app/Test_Missing_File.wav cachable=1 timeout4 maxage=-1 maxstale=-1

Mar 15 10:01:22.278: //23//AFW_:/vapp_media_play: prompt=http://mediaserver-back-up:8080/en-us/app/Test_Missing_File.wav:

<The fetch to the backup media server would also fail if the file could not be found on that server. This would result in the call being routed out of the "failed leg" of the PlayMedia node in the ICM script.>

 URI(abs):http://mediaserver-backup:8080/en-us/app/Hold_Music_Loop.wav

<The ICM script reset the Call.PeipheralVariable and hit another PlayMedia node. Notice that the URL is still pointing to the mediaserver-backup media server. The backup media server will be used for the duration of the call unless the script hits a node that resets the media_server back to mediaserver.>

   host=mediaserver-backup

   str=http://mediaserver-backup:8080/en-us/app/Hold_Music_Loop.wav cachable=1 timeout4 maxage=-1 maxstale=-1

Mar 15 10:01:23.222: //23//AFW_:/vapp_media_play: prompt=http://mediaserver-back-up:8080/en-us/app/Hold_Music_Loop.wav:

?Show Log output to look for "fetch" errors
R2921-VXML>#show log | include fetch
        <submit>: caching=fast fetchhint=invalid fetchtimeout=7 maxage=-1 maxstale=-1
Mar 15 10:01:21.858: //23//AFW_:/vapp_stop_fetchaudio_timer:
        <submit>: caching=fast fetchhint=invalid fetchtimeout=7 maxage=-1 maxstale=-1
Mar 15 10:01:22.010: //23//AFW_:/vapp_stop_fetchaudio_timer:
   path=/en-us/app/Test_Missing_File.wav caching=fast fetchhint=invalid fetchtime-out=4 maxage=-1 maxstale=-1
Mar 15 10:01:22.110: //23/883D976B8006/VXML:/vxml_error_badfetch_event:
  CALL_ERROR; *** error.badfetch.http.404 event is thrown
        <event>: event=error.badfetch.http.404 status=0
  expr=(var _event='error.badfetch.http.404')
  name=error.badfetch count=1
        <goto>: caching=fast fetchhint=invalid fetchtimeout=0 maxage=-1 maxstale=-1
        <submit>: caching=fast fetchhint=invalid fetchtimeout=7 maxage=-1 maxstale=-1
Mar 15 10:01:22.238: //23//AFW_:/vapp_stop_fetchaudio_timer:
  path=/en-us/app/Test_Missing_File.wav caching=fast

```
fetchhint=invalid fetchtimeout=4 maxage=-1 maxstale=-1
Mar 15 10:01:22.338: //23/883D976B8006/VXML:/vxml_error_badfetch_event:
   CALL_ERROR; *** error.badfetch.http.404 event is thrown
         <event>: event=error.badfetch.http.404 status=0
   expr=(var _event='error.badfetch.http.404')
   name=error.badfetch count=1
            <goto>: caching=fast fetchhint=invalid fetchtimeout=0 maxage=-1
maxstale=-1
            <submit>: caching=fast fetchhint=invalid fetchtimeout=7 maxage=-1
maxstale=-1
Mar 15 10:01:23.182: //23//AFW_:/vapp_stop_fetchaudio_timer:
   path=/en-us/app/Hold_Music_Loop.wav caching=fast fetchhint=invalid fetchtimeout=4
maxage=-1 maxstale=-1
...
...
```

Caution By default, when a gateway is configured for VXML version 2.0, the gateway will not send bad fetch errors to Unified CVP. This will not allow Unified CVP to send subsequent fetch requests to the backup media server. Include the additional configuration command of **vxml audioerrors** when configuring the gateway. Following is a configuration snippet on how to accomplish this:

```
vxml tree memory 1000
vxml audioerror
vxml version 2.0
```

Media Files (VXML Gateways Only)

Chapter 5, "Working with Media Files," covers the basics of media files and even provides some detailed troubleshooting techniques and answers to some of the more frequently asked questions pertaining to media files and the IVR cache. However, this section summarizes the general flow of media files for interactions between a VXML Gateway, Unified CVP, and ICM. Begin by reviewing how media is fetched from the VXML Gateway. Figure 8-4 illustrates a media fetch operation at a high level followed by a detailed discussion.

Step 1. Unified ICM sends instructions back to Unified CVP to play the WAV filename specified in the Network VRU script, also referred to as the Run External Script node. This occurs as part of the VRU leg of the call.

Step 2. Unified CVP converts these instructions into VXML instructions and sends them to the VXML Gateway.

Step 3. The VXML Gateway processes the instructions, which includes the HTTP URL for fetching the media file from the media servers. Although this URL could reference a load balancer such as Application Control Engine (ACE) or Content

Services Switch (CSS), that interaction is transparent to the VXML Gateway, and steps to troubleshoot ACE and CSS are provided later in this chapter.

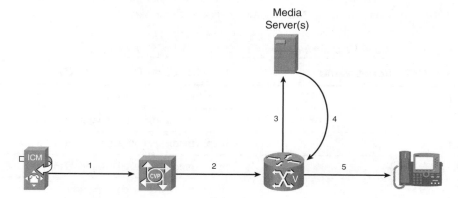

Figure 8-4 *Unified CVP Media Fetch Operation*

Step 4. The VXML Gateway receives the fetched media file from the media servers.

Step 5. The WAV file is played out to the caller. When the VXML instructions provided in Step 2 have been completed by the VXML Gateway, the process starts over with the VXML Gateway asking Unified CVP for further instructions, which indicates to Unified ICM to execute the next step in the call script.

The high-level steps involved in successfully fetching and playing a media file on the VXML Gateway have been reviewed. It's time to walk through a set of troubleshooting steps to isolate and correct any media file issues.

Step 1. Check the Unified ICM routing script and make sure the Call.user.microapp.media_server variable is set to **mediaserver**. This allows the gateway to resolve the hostname to an IP address via its local host table (see Step 5). As noted earlier, the use of a hostname **mediaserver** is not required. The only requirement is that whatever hostname is decided upon, it is necessary that the gateway and Unified ICM configurations match.

Step 2. Check the Unified ICM routing script and make sure the Call.user.microapp.locale variable is set to **en-us.** This assumes English WAV files are used.

Step 3. Check the Unified ICM routing script and make sure the Call.user.microapp.input_type variable is set to **D** for Dual-Tone Multi-Frequency (DTMF) or **B** for both DTMF and Automatic Speech Recognition/Text To Speech (ASR/TTS). Unified CVP requires this to be set, even if you are not executing DTMF or ASR/TTS.

Step 4. Check the Unified ICM routing script to ensure the Run External Script node is correctly configured. This node should "point" to the Network VRU Script name, which specifies the WAV filename. (You can find details starting on page 150 of the *Configuration and Administration Guide for Cisco Unified Customer Voice Portal*). Table 8-1 provides a few examples of Play Media Network VRU Script Names and the URLs that the CVP can generate and from which the VXML Gateway can fetch the WAV file.

Table 8-1   *Network VRU Script Names to Unified CVP URL Examples*

Network VRU Script Name	URL Generated by Unified CVP
PM,Friday	http://mediaserver/en-us/app/Friday.wav
PM,Friday.wav	http://mediaserver/en-us/app/Friday.wav
PM,Friday,A	http://mediaserver/en-us/app/Friday.wav
PM,Friday.wav,A	http://mediaserver/en-us/app/Friday.wav
PM,Friday,S	http://mediaserver/en-us/sys/Friday.wav
PM,Friday.wav,S	http://mediaserver/en-us/sys/Friday.wav

Note   WAV filenames are case-sensitive.

At this point assume the script is correctly configured and move down the line to the VXML Gateway. Although the CVP Call Server provides the interaction between Unified ICM and the VXML Gateway, there isn't a whole lot of troubleshooting that can be accomplished on that box for WAV files.

Step 5.   Verify that the VXML Gateway is configured to talk to the correct media servers by logging to the VXML Gateway and typing **show run**. Two IP host statements are located near the beginning of the output. When the VXML Gateway receives a URL to a WAV file embedded into the Unified CVP VXML instruction set, it uses its local host table (which is defined using these IP host statements) to resolve the media server's hostname to an IP address. Following is an example of two IP host statements. The IP address of the primary mediaserver is 1.1.1.1 and the secondary mediaserver is 2.2.2.2.

```
myrouter(config)ip host mediaserver 1.1.1.1
myrouter(config)ip host mediaserver-backup 2.2.2.2
```

As discussed earlier, the VXML Gateway always uses the primary media server unless it is down. Also discussed several times, if the solution uses a load balancer such as ACE or CSS, these IP addresses point to the virtual IP addresses (VIP) configured for the load balancer. This enables the load balancer to load balance HTTP requests between multiple media servers.

Step 6.   While logged into the VXML Gateway, enable monitoring from the terminal session by executing the **terminal monitor** command. Next, turn on HTTP client error debugging with **debug http client error**. Place a test call and look for errors from the http client. Example 8-31 provides output from this debug that occurs when neither the primary or backup media server can be reached by the VXML Gateway.

Example 8-31   debug http client error *IOS Command*

```
R2921-VXML#debug http client error

 *Jun  9 16:06:18.757: //58//HTTPC:/httpc_process_rsp_timeout: msg

timeout before being sent

*Jun  9 16:06:18.757: //58//HTTPC:/httpc_callback: URL:http://mediaserver/en

-us/app/CCMusic.wav, TIMEOUT(4000 msec), fd(0)

*Jun  9 16:06:22.777: //58//HTTPC:/httpc_process_rsp_timeout: msg

timeout before being sent

*Jun  9 16:06:22.777: //58//HTTPC:/httpc_callback: URL:http://mediaserver-backup/en-

us/app/CCMusic.wav, TIMEOUT(4000 msec), fd(1)

*Jun  9 16:06:44.761: //58//HTTPC:/httpc_process_read_ev: socket error, conn failed -

fd(0), errno=(257)

*Jun  9 16:06:48.781: //58//HTTPC:/httpc_process_read_ev: socket error, conn failed -

fd(1), errno=(257)
```

Step 7.   If an output from the command listed in Step 6 cannot be located but the following error message is received, verification is required to confirm that the WAV file was recorded in the correct and supportable format for Unified CVP.

```
%IVR_MSD-3-NOPROMPT: Could not create IVR prompt
http://mediaserver/path/to/WAV/file
errono=0=Can not recognize the file format
```

Log into the media server and check the audio format of the WAV file by right-clicking it, selecting **properties**, and going into the Summary tab. The format should match Figure 8-5.

Step 8.   If using a load balancer such as ACE or CSS, this would be a good time to verify server groups and the configuration of those load balancers. Refer to the troubleshooting section for load balancers presented later in this chapter for details on how to verify and troubleshoot ACE or CSS. Another option is to remove the load balancers from the fetch operation by pointing the media server host IP addresses directly at a functioning media server. If the fetch works, either it is a bad configuration in the load balancer or a particular media server is incorrectly configured from a HTTP server perspective.

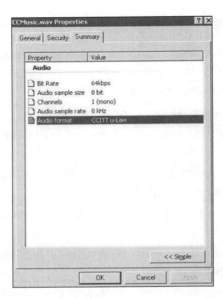

Figure 8-5   *Verifying Audio Format of WAV File*

Step 9.   Log into the media server and verify that the World Wide Web Publishing Service is running. (This assumes that IIS is used as a media server.)

Step 10.   Examine the IIS logs located in the C:\WINDOWS\system32\LogFiles\W3SVC1 directory. Navigate to and open the newest file and look for lines with the WAV file name accompanied by 404 errors. Following is an example of a log entry for a client with the IP address 192.168.1.10 attempting to get a file with the name Friday.wav, but the file did not exist in the /en-us/ directory; therefore, IIS sent a 404 File Not Found HTTP response back to the HTTP client.

```
2009-12-21 19:53:59 W3SVC1 192.168.1.200 GET /en- us/Friday.wav - 404
 -     192.168.1.10 cisco-IOS 200 0 0
```

Note   Although the media server can be colocated on a Unified CVP Call Server, it does not mean that when that same Unified CVP Call Server sends VXML fetch instructions to a VXML Gateway that the gateway will use the media server colocated on that Unified CVP Call Server. The media server used by the VXML Gateway depends on the IP host entries configured for that VXML Gateway and whether a load balancer is used to load balance to multiple media servers.

Step 11.   Verify that the IIS wwwroot directory is set to the expected location. This is the location that IIS uses as your root path to your WAV files. By default this is set to c:\inetput\wwwroot. To verify this, click **start > Programs >**

Administrative Tools > Internet Information Services (IIS) Manager. Expand the Local Computer icon, and then expand the Web Sites folder. Finally, right-click **Default Web Site** and go to Properties. Under the Home Directory tab you see the setting for your Local Path, as shown in Figure 8-6.

Figure 8-6 *IIS Default Web Site Root Directory Verification*

Following are some final tips for troubleshooting media files:

- If the WAV file is invoked from a Unified CVP Studio application, check the Audio Settings under the project properties. The Default Audio Path Uniform Resource Identifier (URI) contains a partial URI to a path containing the audio content for this voice application. If set, the designer needs to provide only the audio filename while building the application, knowing that this path will be prepended. If the audio for this application is stored in multiple areas, this field can be left blank. In that case, the developer must provide the full URI for each audio file used by the application.

- To quickly determine if the media server is up and functioning and the WAV file is in the correct location, enter the URL of the WAV file into the browser (be sure to be on the same network as the media server) to see if it downloads it and plays it. If a 404 File Not Found Error displays, the file is in a different location than what was expected. Remember to not use the hostname mediaserver in the browser's URL simply because the client machine most likely cannot resolve the hostname mediaserver as the VXML Gateway does. Replace this hostname with the IP address configured on the VXML Gateway.

- Enter the **show http client cache** command on the VXML Gateway. Is the WAV file listed?

■ Use the **audio prompt load http://mediaserver/path/to/your/wav/file** command
covered in Chapter 5 to manually download the WAV file from the media server to
the VXML Gateway. If this works, the problem is most likely in the ICM script.

Gatekeepers

This book introduces some IOS commands that are useful from the gateways perspective
when troubleshooting H.323 and Gatekeeper registrations. However, what about verifying
H.323 endpoints, prefixes, and clustering from a Gatekeeper's perspective? Although the
support for H.323 within Unified CVP will diminish going forward, having some basic
knowledge pertaining to troubleshooting Gatekeepers is important when supporting legacy H.323 deployments and equally important when building a plan to migrate H.323
deployments to SIP. This knowledge is critical when surveying the solution to understand
the endpoints and how routing is achieved by the gatekeepers.

Status

First examine the status of a Gatekeeper. Example 8-32 provides the output for the **show
Gatekeeper status** IOS Command.

Example 8-32   show Gatekeeper status *IOS Command*

```
R2800-GK1#show gatekeeper status
  Gatekeeper State: UP
  Load Balancing:    ENABLED
  Flow Control:      DISABLED
  Zone Name:         GK1
  Zone Name:         CCM_PRI
  Zone Name:         VB_PRI
  Zone Name:         VXML_PRI
  Zone Name:         INGRESS_PRI
  Accounting:        DISABLED
  Endpoint Throttling:        DISABLED
  Security:          DISABLED
  Maximum Remote Bandwidth:            unlimited
  Current Remote Bandwidth:         0 kbps
  Current Remote Bandwidth (w/ Alt GKs): 0 kbps
  Call Capacity:        0 / unlimited
  Endpoint Capacity:    4 / unlimited
  Memory Utilization:   15% / 70%
  CPU Utilization:      0% / 80%
  Hunt Scheme: Random
```

Following are some observations from the output in Example 8-32:

- The Gatekeeper is currently UP.

- Five zones are configured, one for each type of component in the solution.

- Gatekeeper-based Call Admission Control (CAC) is not configured because the Maximum Remote Bandwidth is unlimited.

- Four endpoints have registered with the Gatekeeper, and there is an unlimited number of endpoints that can register.

- Memory and CPU thresholds have been set to 70 percent and 80 percent, respectively, with load balancing configured to enable the clustered Gatekeeper GK2 to handle requests via Gatekeeper Update Protocol (GUP).

- CPU and Memory utilization are both low illustrating that this device is not overwhelmed.

Another nice show command on the Gatekeeper is the **show gatekeeper calls** IOS Command. As the output in Example 8-33 illustrates, all call legs that transverse through the Gatekeeper are represented with their respective DNIS numbers; even the VRU Label is represented.

Example 8-33 show gatekeeper calls *IOS Command*

```
R2800-GK1#show gatekeeper calls
Total number of active calls = 2.

largest hash bucket = 2
                        GATEKEEPER CALL INFO
                        ====================
LocalCallID                       Age(secs)   BW
22-5499            623            415         0(Kbps)
ConferenceID                          CallID                          SrcCRV
15E9D67B 920A11E0 81CF974F C4741272  15EB0F64 920A11E0 81D1974F C4741272  12
 Endpt(s): Alias                  E.164Addr
   src EP: INGRESS_R2800-VG        8005551313
           CallSignalAddr  Port  RASSignalAddr   Port
           10.1.11.1       1720  10.1.11.1       53924
 Endpt(s): Alias                  E.164Addr
   dst EP: VB-CVP8                 2#1212
           CallSignalAddr  Port  RASSignalAddr   Port
           192.168.1.218   1720  192.168.1.218   1719
       callstate: SEP, DEP,
LocalCallID                       Age(secs)   BW
23-5499            623            416         128(Kbps)
ConferenceID                          CallID                          SrcCRV
15E9D67B 920A11E0 81CF974F C4741272  FD6C1B3E C000001F 312CF58A FB187157  9607
 Endpt(s): Alias                  E.164Addr
   src EP: VB-CVP8                 1212
           CallSignalAddr  Port  RASSignalAddr   Port
```

```
         192.168.1.218    1720   192.168.1.218   1719
Endpt(s): Alias                   E.164Addr
  dst EP: VXML_R2921              88888888887
         CallSignalAddr   Port   RASSignalAddr   Port
         10.1.10.2        1720   10.1.10.2       50865
      callstate: SEP, DEP,
```

The output in Example 8-33 identifies two call legs, the switch leg between the Ingress Gateway and the Unified CVP Call Server and the VRU leg, between the Unified CVP Call Server and the VXML Gateway. This command is great for verifying the source and destination endpoints and the DNIS or VRU Label used to place the call.

If interested in looking at the performance of the Gatekeeper, Example 8-34 provides a sample output from the command **show gatekeeper performance stats.**

Example 8-34   show gatekeeper performance stats *IOS Command*

```
R2800-GK1#show gatekeeper performance stats

— —-Gatekeeper Performance Statistics— —-

Performance statistics captured since: 15:45:05 UTC Wed Jun 8 2011

Gatekeeper level Admission Statistics:
     ARQs received: 46
     ARQs received from originating endpoints: 23
     ACFs sent: 46
     ACFs sent to the originating endpoint: 23
    ARJs sent: 0
    ARJs sent to the originating endpoint: 0
    ARJs sent due to overload: 0
    ARJs sent due to ARQ access-list denial: 0
    Number of concurrent calls: 1
    Number of concurrent originating calls: 1

Gatekeeper level Location Statistics:
    LRQs received: 0
    LRQs sent: 0
    LCFs received: 0
    LCFs sent: 0
      LRJs received: 0
    LRJs sent: 0
    LRJs sent due to overload: 0
    LRJs sent due to LRQ access-list denial: 0
```

```
Gatekeeper level Registration Statistics:
      RRJ due to overload: 0
       Total Registered  Endpoints: 4

Gatekeeper level Disengage Statistics:
      DRQs received: 38
      DRQs sent: 0
      DCFs received: 0
      DCFs sent: 38
      DRJs received: 0
      DRJs sent: 0

Gatekeeper viazone message counters:
        inARQ: 0
        infwdARQ: 0
        inerrARQ: 0
        inLRQ: 0
        infwdLRQ: 0
          inerrLRQ: 0
        outLRQ: 0
        outfwdLRQ: 0
        outerrLRQ: 0
        outARQ: 0
        outfwdARQ: 0
        outerrARQ: 0

Load balancing events: 0        callstate: SEP, DEP,
```

You can examine the messages returned by the Gatekeeper in Example 8-35. Make note of any unusual behavior to the number of rejected messages and denials.

Endpoints and Prefixes

In most cases the gatekeeper needs to be examined to ensure that devices have registered or prefixes are correctly configured for routing calls to H.323 endpoints. There are a few simple commands to perform these validations beginning with endpoint registrations.

Example 8-35 provides some sample output for the IOS command **how gatekeeper endpoints** that returns all the H.323 endpoints registered with the gatekeeper and their flagged status. Notice the entry flagged as alternative or A. This is examined in the clustering discussion found later in this section.

Example 8-35 show gatekeeper endpoints *IOS Command*

```
R2800-GK1#show gatekeeper endpoints
```

```
                    GATEKEEPER ENDPOINT REGISTRATION
                    ================================

CallSignalAddr  Port  RASSignalAddr   Port  Zone Name        Type     Flags
--------------- ---   --------------- ---   ---------        --       ---
10.1.10.2        1720 10.1.10.2       50865 VXML_PRI         VOIP-GW
    ENDPOINT-ID: 47CC185000000004  VERSION: 4  AGE: 11 secs  SupportsAnnexE: FALSE
    g_supp_prots: 0x00000050
    H323-ID: VXML_R2921
    Voice Capacity Max.=  Avail.=  Current.= 0
10.1.11.1        1720 10.1.11.1       53924 INGRESS_PRI      H323-GW
    ENDPOINT-ID: 47C3DD1400000004  VERSION: 4  AGE: 21 secs  SupportsAnnexE: FALSE
    g_supp_prots: 0x00000050
    H323-ID: INGRESS_R2800-VG
    Voice Capacity Max.=  Avail.=  Current.= 1
192.168.1.213   44604 192.168.1.213  32799 CCM_PRI          VOIP-GW
    ENDPOINT-ID: 47CE0F6000000004  VERSION: 5  AGE: 33 secs  SupportsAnnexE: FALSE
    g_supp_prots: 0x00000050
    H323-ID: GK_TRUNK_PRI_1
    Voice Capacity Max.=  Avail.=  Current.= 0
192.168.1.213   44659 192.168.1.213  32798 CCM_PRI          VOIP-GW A
ENDPOINT-ID: 484B536C00000000  VERSION: 5  AGE: 17 secs  SupportsAnnexE: FALSE
g_supp_prots: 0x00000050
H323-ID: GK_TRUNK_SEC_1
192.168.1.218    1720 192.168.1.218   1719 VB_PRI           VOIP-GW
    ENDPOINT-ID: 4777116C00000004  VERSION: 5  AGE: 23 secs  SupportsAnnexE: FALSE
    g_supp_prots: 0x00000040
    H323-ID: VB-CVP8
    Voice Capacity Max.=  Avail.=  Current.= 1
Total number of active registrations = 5Total number of active registrations = 4
```

As shown in the output in Example 8-35, the H.323 IDs for these registered endpoints have been architected with a prefix that defines their function. This was not by accident but simply by design. By building some intelligence into the way that devices are named, searching for and finding information about them from show commands or debugs becomes much easier. For example, to learn which VXML Gateways were registered with this Gatekeeper, simply revise the show command to be **show gatekeeper endpoints | include VXML** and only the devices where their H.323 IDs contain VXML would appear. This is a nice feature when dealing with potentially hundreds of H.323 endpoints with all unique names.

Another equally interesting observation from Example 8-35 is the H.323-ID highlighted as GK_TRUNK_PRI_1. This happens to be an H.323 Trunk name hosted by a Cisco Unified Call Manager Publisher and not a Subscriber. How was that recognized by just looking at the H.323 ID? When Call Manager servers are deployed into a Call Manager cluster, they are each given a server number based on the order in which they were deployed. The publisher is always given the first number in the cluster because a cluster cannot exist without building the first server, a publisher, which happens to be 1. The first subscriber or second server to be installed is given the number 2 and so on. When H.323 trunks hosted by a CUCM cluster register with a Gatekeeper, they append their server number onto the end of the trunk name configured in the Call Manager. In the output for Example 8-35, the trunk is defined in the Cisco Call Manager as GK_TRUNK_PRI (Gatekeeper Trunk Primary). When it registers the H.323 ID becomes GK_TRUNK_PRI_1 allowing a unique name to exist per server assigned to handle a trunk. So why is this important? It is important simply because when prefixes are configured on a Gatekeeper to use the H.323 ID that is responsible for handling that prefix, it is assumed that zone routing is not used. If the H.323 ID of the H.323 Call Manager trunks were the same name as the trunk name in Call Manager, a call should never be routed to the Call Manager cluster. The server number as part of the H.323 ID must be supplied. Using the **show gatekeeper endpoints** command shows what H.323 IDs are registered and their true spelling.

H.323 edge queuing techniques such as technology prefix stripping and the call flows with their complexity for assigning technology prefixes were discussed in previous chapters. However, in large deployments that use this model, accessing each endpoint to verify technology prefixes can become a time sink. Luckily, the gatekeeper has a nice IOS command that can sort all the registered H.323 endpoints by technology prefix. Example 8-36 provides a sample output of this command.

Example 8-36   show gatekeeper gw-type-prefix *IOS Command*

```
R2800-GK1#show gatekeeper gw-type-prefix
buffer used: 386, size: 20480
GATEWAY TYPE PREFIX TABLE
==========================
Prefix: 2#*    (Default gateway-technology)
  Zone VB_PRI master gateway list:
    192.168.1.218:1720 VB-CVP8
  Zone INGRESS_PRI master gateway list:
    10.1.11.1:1720 INGRESS_R2800-VG
  Zone VXML_PRI master gateway list:
    10.1.10.2:1720 VXML_R2921
Prefix: 1#*
  Zone CCM_PRI master gateway list:
    192.168.1.213:33143 GK_TRUNK_PRI_1
```

Example 8-36 illustrates that three of the four devices registered use a technology prefix of 2#, whereas the Call Manager publisher uses a technology prefix of 1#. In larger deployments using technology prefix routing, this command can save a significant amount of time when trying to verify if an endpoint S registers with the correct technology prefix.

Finally, verifying the Gatekeeper's routing table for its zones and prefixes is one of the most common and significant exercises when troubleshooting H.323 call flows. Example 8-37 provides output for the command **show gatekeeper zone prefix** IOS command.

Example 8-37   show gatekeeper zone prefix *IOS Command*

```
R2800-GK1#show gatekeeper zone prefix
      ZONE PREFIX TABLE
      ==================

GK-NAME                   E164-PREFIX
- - - ·                   - - - - - ·

CCM_PRI                   1*
INGRESS_PRI               2070*
INGRESS_PRI               21*
VB_PRI                    3*
VB_PRI                    5*
INGRESS_PRI               81*
VXML_PRI                  88*
```

In addition to building intelligence into H.323 IDs, it is also best practice to do the same for H.323 zones. As illustrated in the output in Example 8-38, its easy to figure out what zone is used for what traffic. For example, CCM is used for the Unified CCE agents with agent extensions starting with 1. Unified CVP Voice Browser (aka H.323 Service) registers in the zone named VB_PRI, which stands for Voice Browsers on Primary Gatekeeper. And the VXML Gateways all register with a H.323 zone ID of VXML_PRI, which obviously stands for VXML Gateways registered to the Primary Gatekeeper. This naming convention enables the focus to be set to figure out what DNIS or label is routed where versus decoding what is registered in which zone and what the actual zone name means. As shown in the next few examples, these zone names are replicated to gatekeeper two in the cluster with a slight change in the zone name to append a _SEC for the Secondary Gatekeeper.

Clustering

The detailed configurations for setting up a Gatekeeper cluster is beyond the scope of this book. It is not because it's a difficult task, but simply because it is well documented throughout several overlapping resources. A good resource for voice gateways and Gatekeepers is the Cisco Press book *Cisco Voice Gateways and Gatekeepers* written by Denis Donohue, David Mallory, and Ken Salhoff. This book covers all the previously presented IOS commands pertaining to voice gateways and Gatekeepers and great insight about their design. However, in this section examples are provided to assist in identifying any potential clustering issues between Gatekeepers, which may warrant deeper research on their configuration.

First, the status of a Gatekeeper cluster should be verified, as illustrated in Example 8-38. Two Gatekeepers are participating in a cluster with each named GK1 and GK2, respectively.

Example 8-38   show gatekeeper status cluster *IOS Command*

```
R2800-GK1#sh gatekeeper status cluster


              CLUSTER INFORMATION
              ====================

                        Active   Endpoint   Last
Hostname      %Mem  %CPU  Calls    Count    Announce
- - - -        - -   - -   - - -    - - - -   - - - -

R2800-GK1      15    0     1        4         Local Host
R2921-GK2       7    0     0        0                    26s
```

The second Gatekeeper R2921-GK2 checked in with first Gatekeeper R2921-GK1 26 seconds ago indicating that the cluster is up and healthy. If there were a configuration issue, the remote Gatekeeper in the cluster would not have checked in leaving the field for Last Announce empty or unknown.

As shown in the next section, each zone configured on the Primary Gatekeeper is placed into a cluster with a partner element configured on the Secondary Gatekeeper in the cluster. By issuing the command **show gatekeeper cluster** it becomes apparent how these clusters are configured virtually across the two Gatekeepers, as illustrated in Example 8-39.

Example 8-39   show gatekeeper cluster *IOS Command*

```
R2800-GK1#show gatekeeper cluster


            CONFIGURED CLUSTERS
            ====================

Cluster Name    Type    Local Zone    Elements        IP
- - - - - -      - -     - - - - -     - - - -

GK_Cluster      Local                 GK1GK2          10.1.112.2 1719
CCM_Cluster     Local                 CCM_PRICCM_SEC    10.1.112.2 1719
VB_Cluster      Local                 VB_PRIVB_SEC      10.1.112.2 1719
VXML_Cluster    Local                 VXML_PRIVXML_SEC  10.1.112.2 1719
INGRESS_Cluster Local                 INGRESS_PRIINGRESS_SEC  10.1.112.2 1719
```

The idea is that when an endpoint registers with the primary zone name on the Primary Gatekeeper ending with _PRI, GUP also places an alternative registration on the Secondary Gatekeeper into the partner element or zone located on the Secondary Gatekeeper with an IP address of 10.1.112.2. The zone prefixes should be configured identically because they are on the Primary Gatekeeper in the Secondary Gatekeeper using similar zone names but ending with _SEC. This allows for routing to continue working when the Primary Gatekeeper fails. Example 8-40 shows the output of the endpoints registered with the Secondary Gatekeeper. Some are flagged as alternative, and some are primary, meaning they registered with the Secondary Gatekeeper as their Primary. An example of this is the CCM Trunk. There is now one trunk for each Gatekeeper as primary with the other trunk listed as an alternative on each Gatekeeper, respectively. Refer to Example 8-36 for registrations on the Primary Gatekeeper.

Example 8-40   *Secondary Gatekeeper Endpoints and Cluster Status*

```
R2921-GK2#show gatekeeper endpoints
                    GATEKEEPER ENDPOINT REGISTRATION
                    ==================================

CallSignalAddr  Port  RASSignalAddr   Port  Zone Name        Type     Flags
--------------- ----- --------------- ----- ---------------  --------  -----
10.1.10.2       1720  10.1.10.2       50865 VXML_SEC         VOIP-GW A
    H323-ID: VXML_R2921
10.1.11.1       1720  10.1.11.1       53924 INGRESS_SEC      H323-GW A
    H323-ID: INGRESS_R2800-VG
192.168.1.213   33143 192.168.1.213   32799 CCM_SEC          VOIP-GW A
H323-ID: GK_TRUNK_PRI_1
192.168.1.213   33144 192.168.1.213   32798 CCM_SEC          VOIP-GW
H323-ID: GK_TRUNK_SEC_1
    Voice Capacity Max.= Avail.= Current.= 0
192.168.1.218   1720  192.168.1.218   1719  VB_SEC           VOIP-GW A
    H323-ID: VB-CVP8
Total number of active registrations = 5
R2921-GK2#show gatekeeper status cluster
                    CLUSTER INFORMATION
                    ===================

                        Active  Endpoint  Last
Hostname      %Mem  %CPU  Calls   Count   Announce
--------      ----  ----  -----   -----   --------
R2921-GK2     7     0     0       1       Local Host
R2800-GK1     15    0     1       4       2s
R2921-GK2#show gatekeeper cluster
                    CONFIGURED CLUSTERS
                    ===================

Cluster Name      Type    Local Zone    Elements        IP
------------      ----    ----------    --------        --
GK_Cluster        Local   GK2GK1                10.1.112.1 1719
CCM_Cluster       Local   CCM_SECCCM_PRI        10.1.112.1 1719
VB_Cluster        Local   VB_SECVB_PRI          10.1.112.1 1719
VXML_Cluster      Local   VXML_SECVXML_PRI      10.1.112.1 1719
INGRESS_Cluster   Local   INGRESS_SECINGRESS_PRI  10.1.112.1 1719
```

The endpoints that registered with the Primary Gatekeeper show as registered endpoints on the Secondary Gatekeeper with a flag of "A," meaning it's an alternative registration. In some situations, especially in which Resource Availability Indication (RAI) is used on the gateways to signal the Gatekeeper when they are out of resource, an "O" flag may show up or in addition to the "A" flag. An "O" flag basically means that resource has been flagged by the Gatekeeper as being out of resources and calls will not be sent to it unless all endpoints of that type are also flagged as "O" or the endpoints recover below their configured high resource water mark.

Before moving on to SIP proxy troubleshooting, Tables 8-2 through 8-7 summarize the commands referenced in this section and some extras for quick reference, organized by their relevance and utility.

Table 8-2   *PSTN Related IOS Commands*

Command	Description
show controller t1 x/y/z	View the status of the T1 circuits. AS5XXX (x/y :slot/port) 28/38/39xx (x/y/z : slot/module/port) may vary depending on network module.
show isdn status	View the status of the PRI.
show isdn service	View the status of the PRI B-Channel.
show isdn serial x/y/x:23	Check the status of the PRI D-Channel. AS5XXX (x/y:23) 28/38/39xx (x/y/z:23)
show busyout	Show channel busy out status.
busyout monitor isdn busy b_channel 0	Used to configure busyout for PRI.
debug isdn q931	Provide layer 3 debugging for PRI.

Table 8-3   *Dial-peer-Related IOS Commands*

Command	Description
show voice call status	View status of voice call.
show dial-peer voice summary	Shows a list of configured dial-peers and their status.
show dial-peer voice #	Shows information for a specific dial-peer.
test voice translation-rule	Verify outcome of voice translation rule.
debug voip dialpeer	Turn on dial-peer debugging.
show dialplan number	Test the gateways dial plan against a dialed number.
csim start	Simulate a call on the gateway.
Debug voip ccapi inout	Debug voip calls that are flowing through the gateway.

Table 8-4 *SIP-Related IOS Commands*

Command	Description
show sip status	Display the status of SIP UA on gateway.
show sip connections (udp/tcp) detail	Show existing SIP connections on gateway.
show sip statistics	Show SIP statistics for SIP calls on gateway.
debug ccsip calls	SIP Call statistic debugging.
debug ccsip errors	SIP Call Error debugging.
debug ccsip events	SIP SPI Event debugging.

Table 8-5 *H.323-Related IOS Commands*

Command	Description
show gateway	Display status of gateway and H.323 registration.
show gatekeeper status	Show status of Gatekeeper.
show gatekeeper calls	Display active call legs managed by Gatekeeper.
show gatekeeper performance stats	Display the Gatekeeper messaging statistics.
show gatekeeper endpoints	Display registered H.323 endpoints.
show gatekeeper gw-type-prefix	Display the registered H.323 endpoints sorted by technology prefix.
show gatekeeper zone prefix	Display the configured zones and their associated prefixes.
show gatekeeper status cluster	Display the current status of the Gatekeeper cluster.
show gatekeeper cluster	Show the configured clusters for a Gatekeeper.
debug h225 asn1	H225 message debugging.
debug h245 asn1	H245 message debugging.
debug gatekeeper main 10	Gatekeeper debugging.

Table 8-6 *VXML Gateway-Related IOS Commands*

Command	Description
show flash	Display the contents of the gateways flash memory.
show call application voice summary	Display the status of configured voice applications.
show call application voice <app name>	Display voice application details for a specific configured voice application.
debug voip application vxml	Debug VXML interactions on the gateway.
vxml audioerror	Enables gateways using VXML version 2.0 to send fetch errors to the Unified CVP Call Server.
debug http client error	Debug HTTP client issues when fetching media files.

Table 8-7 *General IOS Commands*

Command	Description
clear counters	Clears the interface counters.
clear log	Clears the log.
show log | inc mediaserver	Shows the log entries that include the word mediaserver.
show log | inc fetch	Shows the log entries that include the word fetch.
show log | inc error.badfetch	Shows the log entries that include the word error.badfetch.
show log | inc <your ANI or DNIS)	Shows the log entries that match your digit string.

SIP Proxy Servers

As discovered earlier in this chapter, there is a significant amount of support built into the IOS software running on the gateway to allow for effective debugging for SIP. As mentioned in later sections, Unified CVP also provides some nice debugging tools to troubleshoot calls that may or may not use a SIP Proxy. However, just like the H.323 Gatekeeper, the SIP proxy is still responsible for routing calls whether it for the switch or VRU leg of the call. This section focuses mostly on the verification of best practice configurations for Cisco Unified Presence Server (CUPS) and Cisco Unified SIP Proxy (CUSP). Where possible it provides sample debugs for more detailed troubleshooting.

Note If at any time during the troubleshooting process it is suspected that the SIP proxy server (CUPS or CUSP) causes an issue, first try removing it from the call leg to validate the suspicion. For the switch leg, you can configure an SIP dial-peer for a specific test DNIS that routes directly to the Unified CVP Call Server. For the returning VRU leg, disable the outbound SIP option in the Unified CVP Call Server via the SIP tab and configure a static route for the VRU label pointing to an available VXML Gateway. If the call proceeds as expected, the issue to your SIP proxy server is isolated.

Cisco Unified Presence Server (CUPS)

The major challenge for CUPS is that it runs as an appliance and not as an IOS device. Furthermore a Unified CVP solution uses only CUPS as a SIP Proxy server via static routes configured in CUPS. The additional Presence features supported by CUPS is not used by a Unified CVP solution at this time. Most of this section focuses on the verification of key configuration elements of CUPS and its role with Unified CVP. Before any troubleshooting is attempted, it is a good idea to trust but definitely verify that CUPS has been configured to work properly with Unified CVP.

Verification of Best Practice Parameters

Below is a list of service parameters that should be configured for the Cisco UP SIP Proxy service. You can access these parameters via the System > Service Parameters; then select your CUPS server name followed by the Cisco UP SIP Proxy service.

- **Server name (supplemental):** If there are issues with the Unified CVP Call Server using CUPS for outbound SIP calls including the routing of the VRU leg of a call, the field should be inspected. It should contain the host portion of the FQDN used when configuring local SRV records either locally on the router or via SIP Server Groups in Unified CVP. For example, if the SRV record or SIP server group has been configured with the name myproxy.mydomain.com, make sure the value of this field is myproxy, especially if the real hostname of the CUPS server is different than myproxy. This allows CUPS to recognize its supplemental name in the Request URI and avoid dropping the request.

- **Maximum INVITE retransmissions:** This parameter specifies the maximum number of INVITE message retransmissions. When this limit has been reached, the next "route to" attempt will be chosen by evaluating highest priority routes first and then the highest weight within that priority.

  Default: 3

  Recommended: 2

- **Maximum non-INVITE retransmissions:** This parameter specifies the maximum number of non-INVITE message retransmissions.

  Default: 6

  Recommended: 2

- **Maximum TCP connection timeout(ms)**

  Default: 10000

  Recommended: 1500

- **Add Record-Route header:** This parameter specifies whether to have the Proxy add the Record-Route header

  Default: On

  Recommended: Off

- **Transport preferred order:** This parameter specifies the preferred transport type order whenever NAPTR cannot be used or is unsuccessful.

  Default: TLS-TCP-UDP

  Recommended: UDP

- **Maximum MTU size upconvert (bytes):** If the SIP service receives a UDP SIP message exceeding this value, it converts the packet to TCP before forwarding it on to the next hop. Per the CVP 7.0(2) release notes, this generally happens when "signaling forward unconditional" is used on the Ingress Gateway. To preserve UDP transport usage, you may change the CUP service parameter setting up conversion for Maximum Transmission Unit (MTU) to 1800 instead of 1300.

  Default: 1300

  Recommended: 1800

- **Privacy module status:** Controls whether the SIP Proxy Privacy module is enabled (or disabled).

  Default: On

  Recommended: Off

- **Privacy with PAI:** When On, the Proxy accepts the P-Asserted-Identity (PAI) header in the INVITE request received from a trusted address and removes the PAI header from the INVITE received from an untrusted address. When authentication is on, the Proxy adds its own PAI header to an authenticated INVITE. When Off, the Proxy passes along any PAI header in the INVITE request as-is without any processing.

  Default: On

  Recommended: Off

  Privacy use PAI domain: When On, the Proxy always uses Proxy Domain when building the PAI header. When Off, the Proxy uses the value specified by the Proxy Address Resolution Type parameter.

  Default: On

  Recommended: Off

Incoming and Outgoing ACLs

CUPS requires that incoming and outgoing Access Control Lists (ACL) be configured for all devices that either communicate with CUPS as an incoming connection or receive an invite as an outgoing connection from CUPS' perspective. This is an area commonly missed during configuration and essentially blocks route requests from occurring. If experiencing issues with some devices and not others, be sure to check the ACLs in the CUPS server to ensure that the subnets or IP addresses for those devices are included and allowed to communicate with the CUPS server.

Access the incoming and outgoing ACL menus from within CUPS by accessing the System Menu and then choosing either the incoming or outgoing ACL menu accordingly. The default behavior of CUPS is to drop any traffic not specifically defined as allowed.

System Troubleshooter

Another nice tool built into the CUPS product is the System Troubleshooter. You can access this tool from the Diagnostics menu and provides a significant amount of information above what is needed to troubleshoot CUPS for Unified CVP. Figure 8-7 highlights the area that is important to the SIP Proxy functionality of CUPS.

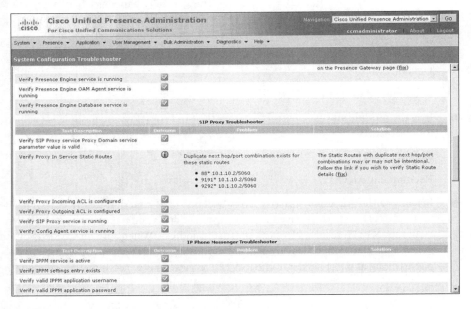

Figure 8-7   *CUPS SIP Proxy Troubleshooter*

Although the SIP Proxy Troubleshooter section of the Figure 8-7 complains about duplicate static routes, it also acknowledges that this may not be an error but completely intentional. In this case, its intentional because 10.1.10.2 is a standalone SIP-based VXML Gateway. Furthermore, the SIP Proxy Troubleshooter verifies that incoming and outgoing

ACLs have been configured, but it does not correlate this verification with data configured in the static routes. The assumption is to add a static route to a host that is not allowed via the incoming or outgoing ACLs. Then run the SIP Proxy Troubleshooter tool only to find out that the ACLs have passed the test and are "configured." Responses to and from that host would still drop.

Console Tools

So far all the troubleshooting tools provided for CUPS have been based off access to a web browser. However, CUPS is unique in that it also has a console interface that can be accessed via secure shell (SSH). When at the interface, the amount of options and commands is vast and far too great to cover in this book. However, this section examines a few of the more interesting ones.

Chapter 4, "Designing Unified CVP for High Availability," discusses static route replication for CUPS and outlines different architectures that support such a replication within a CUPS subcluster. The console interface has a decent list of commands to check the status of a CUPS server and verify any replication events. Example 8-41 provides a list of the commands that are used to verify server replication.

Example 8-41 *CUPS Database Replication Commands*

```
admin:utils dbreplication
     utils dbreplication clusterreset
     utils dbreplication dropadmindb
     utils dbreplication forcedatasyncsub
     utils dbreplication quickaudit
     utils dbreplication repair
     utils dbreplication repairreplicate
     utils dbreplication repairtable
     utils dbreplication reset
     utils dbreplication runtimestate
     utils dbreplication setrepltimeout
     utils dbreplication status
     utils dbreplication stop
```

The console interface also has a diagnose command run some simple tests for the platform and provides a report similar to the one in Example 8-42.

Example 8-42 *CUPS Console Diagnostics Test Ouput*

```
admin:utils diagnose test

Log file: platform/log/diag4.log
```

```
Starting diagnostic test(s)
============================
test - disk_space          : Passed
skip - disk_files          : This module must be run directly and off hours
test - service_manager     : Passed
test - tomcat              : Passed
test - tomcat_deadlocks    : Passed
test - tomcat_keystore     : Passed
test - tomcat_connectors   : Passed
test - tomcat_threads      : Passed
test - tomcat_memory       : Passed
test - tomcat_sessions     : Passed
test - validate_network    : Passed
test - raid                : Passed
test - system_info         : Passed (Collected system information in diagnostic log)
test - ntp_reachability    : Failed
The NTP process is stopped. Please contact Cisco Support.
test - ntp_clock_drift     : Warning
The NTP process is stopped. Please contact Cisco Support.
test - ntp_stratum         : Warning
The NTP process is stopped. Please contact Cisco Support.
skip - sdl_fragmentation   : This module must be run directly and off hours
skip - sdi_fragmentation   : This module must be run directly and off hours
test - ipv6_networking     : Passed

Diagnostics Completed
```

As with Cisco IOS routers, CUPS also supports a **show tech all** ACLs command. Be warned: The output of this command is massive and should be used sparingly. There are targeted **show tech** commands more suitable for gathering data.

Debugging CUPS

Debugging calls on CUPS requires two main steps. The first is to turn on the appropriate level of tracing using the Trace menu from the Cisco Unified Serviceability web interface. This trace menu provides options for turning on tracing for the CUPS Proxy server. The second step requires downloading and installing the Cisco Unified Presence Real Time Monitoring Tool (RTMT) from the Applications > Plugins submenu located from the main CUPS web interface. RTMT monitors the CUPS cluster and accesses the log files where the output of the trace settings will be stored. After the wanted trace levels are set for the proxy service and are installed RTMT, you can run a few test calls through CUPS and capture the results in the log files viewable by RTMT.

Cisco Unified SIP Proxy (CUSP)

The web interface introduced in version 8.5 of CUSP has greatly improved the serviceability of the module both from a configuration management and troubleshooting perspective. More specifically, version 8.5.2 of the CUSP software included enhancements specifically targeted at troubleshooting SIP calls. Immediately upon logging into the web interface, a screen similar to Figure 8-8 appears.

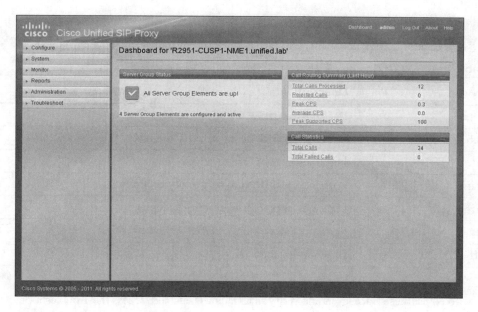

Figure 8-8   *CUSP Dashboard View*

Figure 8-8 illustrates the current status of the CUSP module with respect to its peak, average, CPS, and the number of calls processed and the number of those calls dropped. The Server Group status is also shown making it possible to determine if there are any issues with the servers that have been configured for routing calls to and from.

The next section illustrates the interface used to debug requests that pass through the CUSP module. The CUSP module supports tracing for the following areas:

- Base Tracing
- Routing
- Proxy-Core
- SIP-Wire-Log
- Normalization
- Proxy-Transactions

- SIP-Ping
- License-Mgmt
- Trigger-Conditions
- Accounting
- SIP-Search
- Config-Mgmt

For each of these components you can set the levels of tracing, as shown in Table 8-8:

Table 8-8   *CUSP Tracing Levels*

Level	Description
default	Uses the trace level of the parent
debug	Logs messages of debug severity or higher
info	Logs messages of info severity or higher
warn	Logs messages of warning severity or higher
error	Logs messages of error severity or higher
fatal	Logs messages of fatal severity or higher
off	Does not log messages

To adjust these trace levels and verify that tracing is enabled, access the Troubleshoot > Cisco Unified SIP Proxy > Traces menu, as shown in Figure 8-9.

In addition the log file can be viewed and downloaded as well by using the Troubleshoot > Cisco Unified SIP Proxy > Log File Menu. Figure 8-10 illustrates the output of turning on the SIP-wire-log trace via the Log File. Make sure when viewing the Log File to navigate to the last page of the log file for the most recent trace information.

The Troubleshoot > View submenu provides additional options for troubleshooting CUSP. The first is the ability to generate a Tech Support report similar to the IOS command **show tech** available on other IOS routers.

As noted earlier, version 8.5.2 of the CUSP software provides enhancements to debugging SIP messages and failed calls. To enable SIP Message logging, first enable the logging via the SIP Message Log > Controls submenu. When enabled, search all calls placed through the CUSP module, as shown in Figure 8-11. This example filters the Request-URI for the incoming DNIS of 5338, essentially filtering out all switch call legs. This field can also be changed to reference a VRU label, such as 8888, filtering to display only VRU call legs.

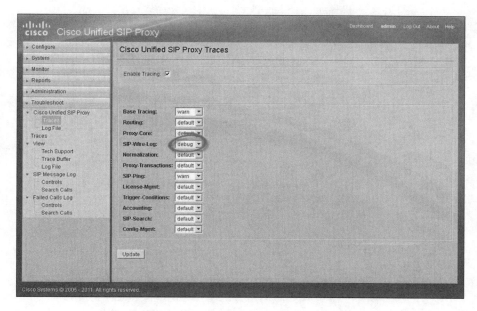

Figure 8-9   *Enabling Tracing and Setting Component Levels on CUSPModule*

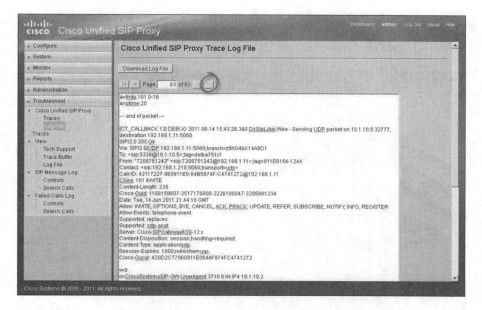

Figure 8-10   *Viewing the Log File for SIP-Wire-Log Captured Traces*

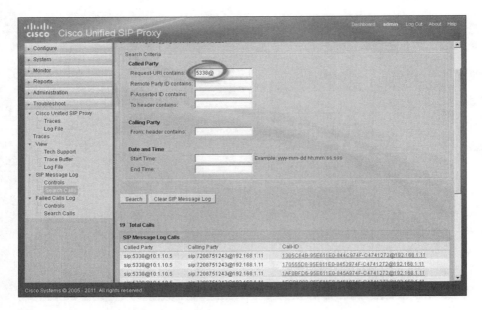

Figure 8-11   *Searching SIP Message Log for Switch Call Leg*

By clicking the Call-ID, any SIP Messages that relate to this call leg appear. It is an effective way to determine what may not correctly work from the switch or VRU leg of a call. Figure 8-12 provides a sample of the SIP detailed messaging for a call.

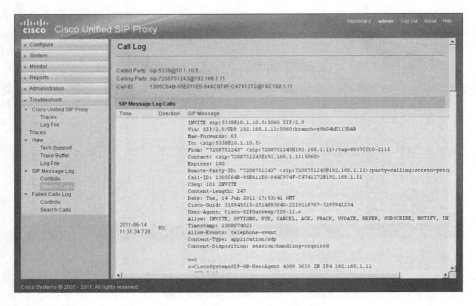

Figure 8-12   *Detailed SIP Messaging for a Specific Call-ID*

If the target of the investigation is to look at failed calls, version 8.5.2 of the CUSP software provides specific logging for just failed calls. First, access and enable logging for failed calls by accessing the Troubleshoot > Failed Calls Log > Controls, and enable logging. When logging is turned on, reproduce the failed call leg, and then access the Troubleshoot > Failed Calls Log > Search Calls submenu where an interface similar to the one shown in Figure 8-13 appears.

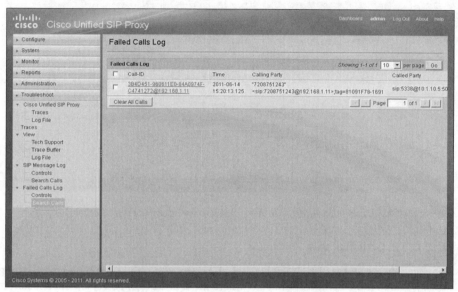

Figure 8-13 *Viewing the Failed Calls Log*

Clicking the failed call's Call-ID link shows the detailed messages for that specific failed call leg, as shown in Figure 8-14.

In general, setting the correct trace level or using the SIP Messaging and Failed Call logging options allows for capturing and tracing issues important to the call flow. As noted several times throughout this book, if the problem is because of incorrect configuration of a CUSP module, it is recommended to reference the Documentation Roadmap for Cisco Unified SIP Proxy Release 8.5 located at http://www.cisco.com/en/US/docs/voice_ip_comm/cusp/rel8_5/roadmap/cuspdocguide.html#wp1063495.

The Configuration and Administration Guide for Cisco Unified Customer Voice Portal, April 2010 document provides a sample CUSP configuration beginning on page 348. In addition, the Cisco DocWiki also provides some light coverage on the subject of CUSP, which you can access via http://docwiki.cisco.com/wiki/Cisco_Unified_SIP_Proxy.

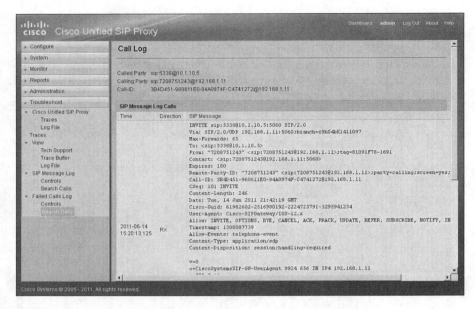

Figure 8-14 *Detailed Failed Call Messages for a Specific Call-ID*

Unified CVP Call Server

For checking the status of a Unified CVP Call Server, you should examine several different areas. Begin in the Operations Console, where the status of the server should be analyzed. Figure 8-15 provides the Operations Console's view via the Control Center menu option.

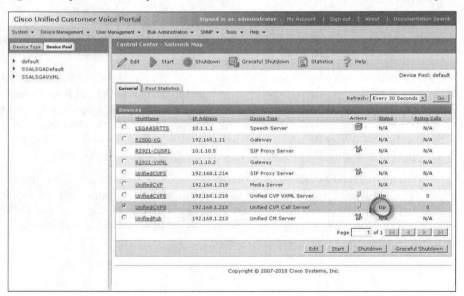

Figure 8-15 *Verifying Unified CVP Call Server Status via the Operations Console*

If any of the following threads miss a heartbeat, the subsystem transitions to a PARTIAL_SERVICE status.

- Heartbeat Monitor
- Message Bus Listener
- Message Bus Publisher
- PIM Listener
- PIM Publisher
- Admin Monitor
- Garbage Collector

To verify that the Unified CVP Call Server receives calls, access the Call Server statistics page by first selecting the Call Server from the Control Center menu and then selecting the statistics link at the top of the page. Figure 8-16 shows this interface, which provides some values that should be verified.

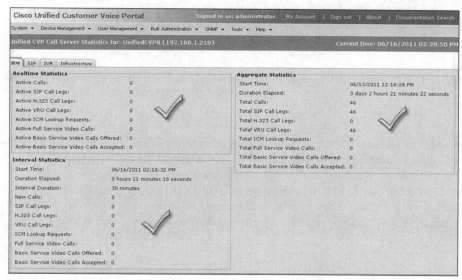

Figure 8-16 *Unified CVP Call Server Statistics*

In addition, statistics specific to SIP calls, IVR messages, and Infrastructure statistics can also be examined. The term Infrastructure is used in various document sets provided by Cisco for Unified CVP and references the Unified CVP Call Server and its operational state from a port, memory, threads, and Java Virtual Machine (JVM) perspective. Before attempting to perform any detailed troubleshooting always verify the devices status to determine where a fault may occur and what the next steps should be. When the status of the Unified CVP Call Server is surveyed, look closely at the log files. Table 8-9 provides details pertaining to where the log files for Unified CVP are stored on each Call Server and a description for what each log file contains.

Table 8-9   *Unified CVP Log Files*

Log File Name	Location	Description
CVP.YYYY-MM-DD.###.log Error.YYYY-MM-DD.###.log	%CVP_HOME%\logs	CVP and error log files for ICM, SIP, IVR, and Infrastructure events/traces
Multiple formats	%CVP_HOME\logs\SNMP	SNMP-related log files
CVP.YYYY-MM-DD.###.log Error.YYYY-MM-DD.###.log	%CVP_HOME\logs\ORM	CVP and Error logs for the Operations Resource Manager
CVP.YYYY-MM-DD.###.log Error.YYYY-MM-DD.###.log	%CVP_HOME\logs\VXML	CVP and Error logs for the VXML-related events
CVP.YYYY-MM-DD.###.log Error.YYYY-MM-DD.###.log	%CVP_HOME\logs\OAMP	CVP and Error logs for the Operations Console
CVP.YYYY-MM-DD.###.log Error.YYYY-MM-DD.###.log	%CVP_HOME\logs\WSM	CVP and Error logs for the Web Services Manager
Perflog_	%CVP_HOME\logs\PERF	Performance logs in CSV format
VB_YYMMDD_HHMMSS.ems	%CVP_HOME\VoiceBrowser\logfiles	CVP H.323 Service log files

> **Tip**   The reference to %CVP_HOME% is an environment variable set when Unified CVP is installed on a server. Typically, the value of this variable is C:\Cisco\CVP, assuming the default installation directory was chosen during installation, which completes the root directory for log files to C:\Cisco\CVP\logs (refer to Table 8-9). To verify the value of this variable on the Call Server, start a command prompt and entire the command **set**. The output lists all the environment variables stored on your server.

One important observation from Table 8-9 is that the H.323 log files are located in completely different location than the other log files. In addition, to view the H.323 log files, use a tool named dumplog with a syntax of dumplog Process Name /of <output_filename>. Example 8-43 provides the syntax for this command. Keep in mind that this command is also used to examine and dump Unified ICM logs.

Example 8-43   *Dumplog Command-Line Options*

```
C:\Cisco\CVP\VoiceBrowser\logfiles>dumplog /?
Version: Release 4.6 CISCO service pack 0+, Build 08419
Usage: dumplog [ProcessName(s)] [/dir Dirs] [/if InputFile] [/o]
[/of OutputFile] [/c] [/bd BeginDate(mm/dd/yyyy)]
          [/bt BeginTime(hh:mm:ss)] [/ed EndDate(mm/dd/yyyy)]
```

```
[/et EndTime(hh:mm:ss)] [/hr HoursBack] [/all] [/last] [/prev]
[/bin] [/m MatchString] [/x ExcludeString] [/ms] [/mc]  [/debug]
[/help] [/?]
```

The Process Name for the Unified CVP H.323 Services is VB, which stands for VoiceBrowser. Example 8-44 provides an output for executing the dumplog utility against the H.323 log files used by Unified CVP. Notice the directory from which the command is executed and the command line options used. By using a begin time of 15:50:00, log information found in the log files starting at this time for the current date can be extracted.

Example 8-44   *H.323 Log Extraction Example Using Dumplog*

```
C:\Cisco\CVP\VoiceBrowser\logfiles>dumplog VB /bt 15:50:00 /of UnifiedCVP.txt
Events from June 16, 2011:

15:50:04 VoiceBrowser-VB Trace: ERROR INTERNAL: QueryPerformance: Failed
Performance Query

15:50:09 VoiceBrowser-VB Trace: ERROR INTERNAL: QueryPerformance: Failed
Performance Query


— — —-Voice Browser Interval Statistics— — —-
15:52:47 VoiceBrowser-VB Trace: Calls:
15:52:47 VoiceBrowser-VB Trace:    Interval Statistics:
15:52:47 VoiceBrowser-VB Trace:       Interval size:                       1800

15:52:47 VoiceBrowser-VB Trace:       New calls this interval:            0
15:52:47 VoiceBrowser-VB Trace:       Max call arrival per second:        0
15:52:47 VoiceBrowser-VB Trace:       Calls transferred this interval:    0
15:52:47 VoiceBrowser-VB Trace:       Max IP Transfer per second:         0.
15:52:47 VoiceBrowser-VB Trace:       Calls redirected this interval:     0
15:52:47 VoiceBrowser-VB Trace:       Transfers not completed this interval: 0
15:52:47 VoiceBrowser-VB Trace:       Prompts not found this interval:    0
15:52:47 VoiceBrowser-VB Trace:       Calls using critical media:         0
15:52:47 VoiceBrowser-VB Trace:       Calls finished this interval:       0
15:52:47 VoiceBrowser-VB Trace:
— — —-Voice Browser Snapshot Statistics— — —-
15:52:47 VoiceBrowser-VB Trace:    Snapshot Statistics:
15:52:47 VoiceBrowser-VB Trace:       Calls In Progress:                  0
15:52:47 VoiceBrowser-VB Trace:       Calls Waiting for VXML:             0
15:52:47 VoiceBrowser-VB Trace:       Calls Playing Prompts:              0
15:52:47 VoiceBrowser-VB Trace:       IVR Ports in use:                   0
15:52:47 VoiceBrowser-VB Trace:       Calls Waiting for DTMF:             0
15:52:47 VoiceBrowser-VB Trace:       Calls Transferring:                 0
15:52:47 VoiceBrowser-VB Trace:       Calls Transferred:                  0
15:52:47 VoiceBrowser-VB Trace:       Calls Disconnecting:                0
15:52:47 VoiceBrowser-VB Trace:       Calls Disconnected:                 0
```

```
15:52:47 VoiceBrowser-VB Trace:        New calls:                        0
15:52:47 VoiceBrowser-VB Trace:        Other:                            0
15:52:47 VoiceBrowser-VB Trace:        Internal Call count:              0
15:52:47 VoiceBrowser-VB Trace:        System memory in use (percent):
543519598
15:52:47 VoiceBrowser-VB Trace:
— — —-Voice Browser Total Statistics— — — —-
15:52:47 VoiceBrowser-VB Trace:   Since Startup:
15:52:47 VoiceBrowser-VB Trace:        Total Calls:                      7
15:52:47 VoiceBrowser-VB Trace:         Disconnect Disposition:
15:52:47 VoiceBrowser-VB Trace:          Redirected:                     2
15:52:47 VoiceBrowser-VB Trace:          Caller Hangup:                  2
15:52:47 VoiceBrowser-VB Trace:          Called Party Hangup:            3
15:52:47 VoiceBrowser-VB Trace:          ICM Release:                    3
15:52:47 VoiceBrowser-VB Trace:          Critical Media:                 3
15:52:47 VoiceBrowser-VB Trace:        Max Simultaneous Calls:           6
15:52:47 VoiceBrowser-VB Trace:        Max IVR Ports:                    5
15:52:47 VoiceBrowser-VB Trace:        Total prompts not found:          0
15:52:47 VoiceBrowser-VB Trace:        Total transfers not completed:    1
15:52:47 VoiceBrowser-VB Trace:          Busy:                           0
15:52:47 VoiceBrowser-VB Trace:          Ring-no-answer:                 0
15:52:47 VoiceBrowser-VB Trace:          Gatekeeper problem:             0
15:52:47 VoiceBrowser-VB Trace:          Destination problem:            1
15:52:47 VoiceBrowser-VB Trace:          Other:                          0
15:52:47 VoiceBrowser-VB Trace:        System Startup Time:          Jun 09

2011, 13:26:59
15:52:47 VoiceBrowser-VB Trace:        System UpTime:                    7
Days,
02 Hours, 25 Minutes, 48 Seconds
15:52:47 VoiceBrowser-VB Trace:        Current State:                   In
Service
15:52:47 VoiceBrowser-VB Trace:        Packets Transmitted(approx):     0.
15:52:47 VoiceBrowser-VB Trace:


— — — —- Current Alarms — — — —-
15:52:47 VoiceBrowser-VB Trace:   None
```

Basically, four sections are listed in the Unified CVP Voice Browser (H.323) log files:

- Interval Status

- Snapshot Statistics

- Total Statistics

- Current Alarms

What about accessing the other Unified CVP log files? One option is to open the log files in notepad and read them. However, that method can be cumbersome and problematic when dealing with a large amount of entries. Fortunately, Unified CVP provides a diagnostic URL, which you can use to troubleshoot several areas of the solution, one being the review of CVP log files.

Diagnostic Servlet

In the early days of Unified CVP, the infamous Diagnostic Servlet URL (accessible on each CVP server via the URL http://<CVP-IP-Address>:8000/cvp/diag) was in the same category as Area 51. It just didn't exist; even though engineers and customers all knew that Cisco Technical Assistance Center (TAC) (as well as other resources that were in the know) used some tool to quickly set tracing levels, gather solution status, and directly view log files. The reality is that the Diagnostic Servlet did indeed exist, and with the recent releases of Unified CVP, it has been officially exposed with the expectation that the end user should use it as a viable tool when troubleshooting Unified CVP. However, before this secret weapon is examined, take a bit of time to understand how the Servlet is structured for its user interface. This is critical because depending on what accomplishments are attempted, different view panes are used for both initiating the request and displaying the results. Unfortunately, the panes used for output are not intuitive. It is the responsibility of the user to realize that an action has be completed and the data is now in one of the panes displayed in the browser. Figure 8-17 provides a basic illustration defining the areas that can be expected to see input or output from the Servlet.

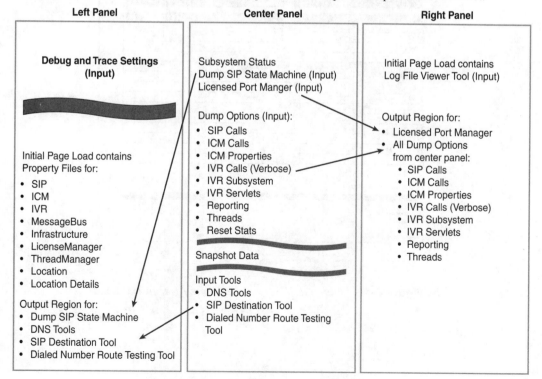

Figure 8-17 *Diagnostic Servlet Input and Output Regions*

Now that there is a good understanding of where data can be placed into the tool and the pane that displays the results, this section disassembles the Diagnostic Servlet and provides some examples on how its content can be used to troubleshoot Unified CVP.

Left Panel Breakdown

As Figure 8-17 illustrates, the left panel of the Servlet is where the Debug and Trace levels are set for the Unified CVP Server. It should be noted that these settings are only for the server that provide the URL and Servlet. If it is wanted to set debug or trace levels for all servers, it is necessary to access their Diagnostic Servlet individually. In addition, when initially loading the Servlet page, this panel also displays the values of important Unified CVP property files. These files map directly to fields that are configurable via the Operations Console's UI but are only representative of the server hosting the Servlet displayed.

If any of the tools available in the center pane are invoked, such as dumping the SIP state machine, invoking a DNS tool, registering a SIP Destination, or testing a route for a dialed number, the lower part of the left panel will be updated to represent the respective output. The arrows displayed in Figure 8-17 represent which tools from the center pane place their output into the left pane. Figure 8-18 shows the left pane after the initial load of the Servlet.

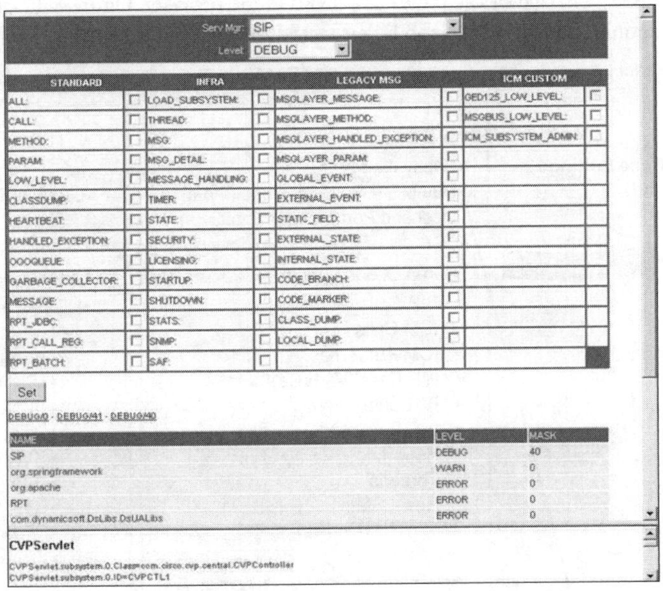

Figure 8-18 *Diagnostic Servlet Left Pane After Initial Load*

Center Panel Breakdown

The center panel provides some nice tools and snapshot statistics on how this particular Unified CVP Call Server performs. The center panel also uses both the left and right panels for output depending on which tool are invoked (refer to Figure 8-17). Figure 8-19 provides the initial state of the center panel immediately after the Servlet has been loaded.

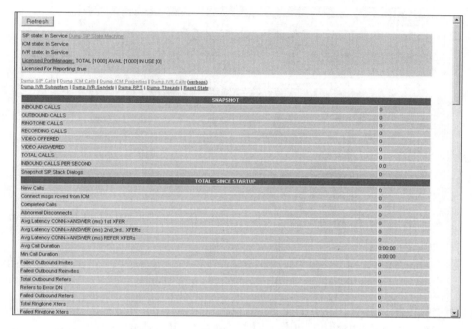

Figure 8-19   *Diagnostic Servlet Center Pane After Initial Load*

Although Figure 8-19 displays the top part of the center panel, don't forget to scroll down to the bottom of the center panel for additional tools. Later in this section the output of the DNS and SIP tools located at the bottom of the center panel are examined. Now the emphasis is on the important tools located at the top of the center pane. These tools include the following:

- **Dump SIP State Machine:** This tool dumps the current state of the SIP state machine. The output is placed in the lower portion of the Servlet's left pane. Figure 8-20 offers some sample output when the link is clicked in the center pane.

  This output is useful when verifying the reachability of SIP endpoints configured via the Operation Console with in a Server Group. In this example, two server groups are defined for this Unified CVP Call Server: one for CUPS and one for CUSP, both showing a green status with the endpoints in both groups reachable by TCP and UDP. Although not shown in Example 8-20, at the bottom of this output is the SIP state machine history providing valuable information when troubleshooting the state of the SIP service.

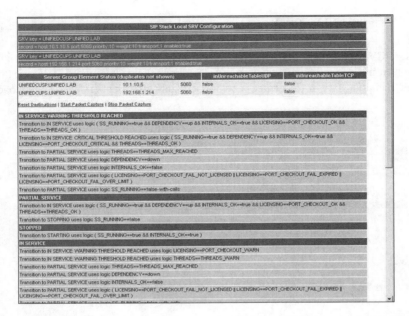

Figure 8-20   *Diagnostic Servlet Dump SIP State Machine Left Panel Output*

- **Dump SIP Calls:** This tool dumps information about active SIP calls and endpoints that have been seen in previously connected and disconnected calls. Figure 8-21 provides shows the output of both the switch and VRU leg of a call and which SIP invites the Unified CVP track. Toward the bottom of the output are the connection keys or endpoints that Unified CVP is aware of and tracking as well.

- **Dump ICM Calls:** This tool dumps the current active ICM dialogs including deleted dialogs. Figure 8-22 shows this output, which provides the current ICM dialogs for both the switch and VRU leg of an active call.

- **Dump IVR Calls (verbose):** This link enables the active calls processed by the IVR subsystem to display in the right panel. Figure 8-23 shows this output. The current IVR Calls display at the lower portion of this output with details pertaining to the VXML Gateway treating the call and the VRU label (DNIS) used to route the call.

Further down the center panel are a set of tools that are not clearly visible when initially loading the Servlet but worth taking a few moments to discuss. Figure 8-24 shows these three tools followed by a short discussion how they are used.

The first tool is a DNS lookup tool that enables the lookup of a hostname against a DNS server. This tool also checks to see if a SIP SRV entry exists for the hostname in question. This is a useful tool when troubleshooting DNS and SIP and enables verification that the host is resolvable and that the correct SRV records have been configured on the DNS server for the host in question. The second tool, Register Destinations, gathers SIP statistics for endpoints provided and separated by a comma. The last tool, Test DN, tests how this

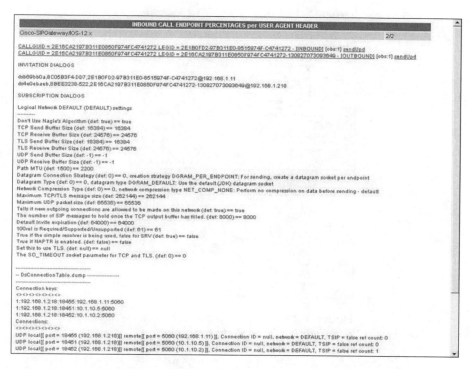

Figure 8-21   *Diagnostic Servlet Dump SIP Calls Right Panel Output*

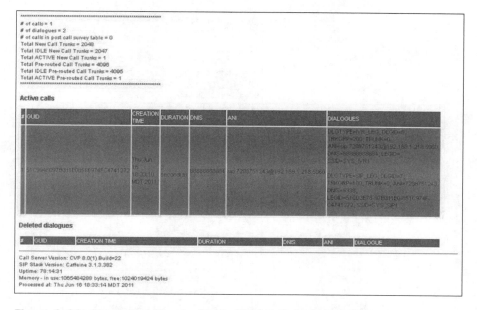

Figure 8-22   *Diagnostic Servlet Dump ICM Calls Right Panel Output*

```
Call Controller (Calls enumerated):
    ICM SS timeout secs: 5
    Client Map: numClients=2
        CVPVBClient - Name: 192.168.1.218 Type: ISN
            LongPollVBClient - Name: 192.168.1.218 Type: ISN
                timeLastAccessed: Thu Jun 16 18:45:51 MDT 2011
                timeFirstAccessed: Mon Jun 13 12:18:46 MDT 2011
                Active: true
                Timeout(ms): 120000
                LongPoll size: 0 Max size: 0
                LongPoll total added: 0
        IOSVBClient - Name: 10.1.10.2 Type: IOS
            timeLastAccessed: Thu Jun 16 18:45:52 MDT 2011
            timeFirstAccessed: Thu Jun 16 18:15:19 MDT 2011
            Active: true
            Timeout(ms): 7320000
    Max call sessions=4
    Call sessions completed=51
    Last garbage collection done at=Thu Jun 16 18:45:53 MDT 2011
    Call Sessions=1 (IVRCalls in Call Sessions: 1)
        CallSession - CALLGUID=170FC99097B511E08524974FC4741272
            callStartTime: Thu Jun 16 18:45:52 MDT 2011
            duration: 3 secs
            bMultipleLegsBySameVBClient: false
            IVRCalls: 1
                IVRCall - CALLGUID: 170FC99097B511E08524974FC4741272
                    DNIS: 88888888886
                    ANI: sip:72087512438192.168.1.218:5060
                    UUI:
                    LOCATION:
                    CALL LEG ID:
                    CALLER TYPE: UNKNOWN
                    seqNum: 1
                    callStartTime: Thu Jun 16 18:45:52 MDT 2011
                    timeLastAccessed: Thu Jun 16 18:45:52 MDT 2011
                    duration: 3 secs
                    client: 10.1.10.2 clientType: IOS
                    slot: 0
                    isVideoCall:false
                    routerCallKey:null
```

Figure 8-23   *Diagnostic Servlet Dump IVR Calls (verbose) Right Panel Output*

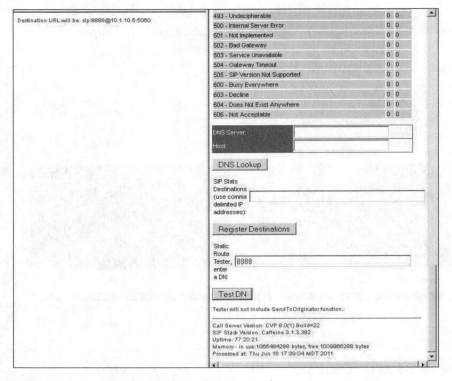

Figure 8-24   *DNS and Dialed Number Test Tools*

individual Unified CVP Call Server routes a dial number or label outbound. Whether static routes, a SIP Proxy, or Server Groups are configured, the tool works with all three. As shown in the left pane of Figure 8-24, if this particular Call Server were to receive a label or DNIS targeted for outbound routing (most likely a VRU label), the CUSP SIP Proxy server at IP address 10.1.10.5 would be asked to route the call as indicated by the output in the top of the left pane:

You can find the destination URL at SIP:88885060.

Right Panel Breakdown

The last panel in this discussion of the Diagnostic Servlet is the right panel. This portion of the Servlet is dedicated to searching and viewing CVP log files. Not all CVP log files can be viewed from this tool. Only the primary log files for the Unified CVP Calls Server located in the directory %CVP_HOME%\logs are directly accessible. The additional subdirectories that contain other log files such as Operation Console (OAMP), Resource Manager (ORM), Web Services Manager (WSM), and so on appear in the tools dropdown menu. But the tool is not designed to navigate to this subdirectory for further log file processing; at least not at this time or for version 8.0.1 of Unified CVP. This feature could be fixed in future releases of Unified CVP. But for now those other log files still need to be viewed the old fashion way—manually using an application such as notepad. Figure 8-25 shows a Unified CVP Error log file directly viewed using the tool.

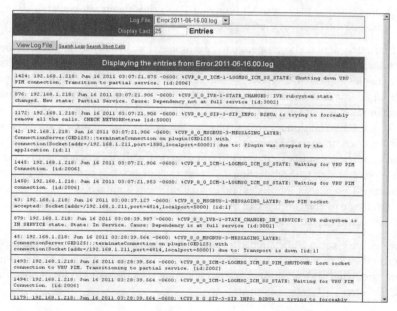

Figure 8-25 *View Unified CVP Log Files Using the Diagnostic Servlet*

Note Another option for collecting log files with Unified CVP is to use a product that was originally targeted to support Unified ICM: Support Tools. Although Support Tools does support Unified CVP, its future is unknown and most likely will not support versions of Unified CVP 8.5 and beyond. Because of this, most deployments do not depend on or use Support Tools as a legitimate troubleshooting tool for Unified CVP. Outlined at the end of this chapter are additional tools that have some promise for their capability to troubleshoot Unified CVP. Although the discussion is brief, the key takeaway is that tools will continue to evolve; some will survive whereas others will disappear. Keep a pulse on which tools are invested in and which ones are not to avoid committing to tools in a troubleshooting tool kit that won't exist in the near future.

Unified System Command Line Interface (CLI)

Unified CVP version 8.x introduced a new and unique tool for accessing information managed by ORM and the Operations Console. This new interface is the Unified System CLI and is accessible via the Cisco Unified Customer Voice Portal windows menu. After the Unified System CLI tool launches, you must enter a set of credentials. The default username is wsmadmin, which stands for Web Service Manager Administrator. The password for this account was set up during the installation of Unified CVP matching the Operations Console password and can be managed via the Operations Console via the User Management > Users web UI submenu. After this, the initial login places the user at a command-line interface focused on local collection.

The Unified System CLI can operate in two modes: local and system. Local mode returns only information that is local to the machine that the CLI runs on. However, the system mode enables a query to all devices configured as part of the Operations Console with a single CLI command. In other words, the job of the Unified System CLI when running in system mode is to normalize a CLI command such as **show version** for all devices part of the Unified CVP solution regardless of what the syntax maybe for a **show version** output on different components. This powerful CLI enables an engineer to quickly pull version, licensing, technical support information, and so on for all devices configured via the Operations Console without having to access each device and compile the information by accessing different user interfaces and issuing different commands. You can access the "system" mode of the Unified CLI by typing the word **system** followed by pressing the Enter or Return key at the admin: prompt.

Before viewing some CLI examples running in system mode, this section focuses on a granulated structure for CLI for the local or system mode. Example 8-45 shows a **show config** command with additional options allowing the command to focus specifically on the Call Server's SIP subcomponent.

Example 8-45 *Unified System CLI* show conf *Example*

```
admin:show config component CallServer subcomponent SIP
Downloading Configuration file: [SIP: srv.xml] ...
— — — — — — — — — — — — — — — — — — — — — — — — —
NAME: UNIFIEDCUPS.UNIFIED.LAB
WEIGHT   PRIORITY        DESTINATION     PORT
— — — — — — — — — — — — — — — — — — — — — — — — —
10       10              192.168.1.214   5060
— — — — — — — — — — — — — — — — — — — — — — — — —
NAME: UNIFIEDCUSP.UNIFIED.LAB
WEIGHT   PRIORITY        DESTINATION     PORT
— — — — — — — — — — — — — — — — — — — — — — — — —
10       10              10.1.10.5       5060

Downloading Configuration file: [SIP: location.properties] ...

#Properties for locations
#Examples:
#Location.1.name=loc-1
#Location.1.pkid=12345
#Location.1.siteid=444
#Location.1.ip=2.2.2.2,3.3.3.3
Downloading Configuration file: [SIP: sip.properties] ...

SIP.Ringtone.DN : 91919191
SIP.handleGWOptionsRouting : true
SIP.HeaderValue :
SIP.QOSLevel : cs3
SIP.ServerGroupHeartbeats : true
SIP.ServerGroupHBTransportType : UDP
SIP.GTDParamForwarding : UUS
SIP.UUSHexToAscii : true
SIP.ServerGroupHBLocalListenPort : 5067
SIP.ServerGroupHBNumTries : 1
SIP.SigDigits : default
SIP.UseOutboundProxy : true
SIP.RingtonePatterns :
SIP.RejectOnTclVersionMismatch : false
SIP.UseSRV : true
SIP.SessionExpires : 1800
SIP.ServerGroupHBTimeout : 500
SIP.Tone.Duration : 100
SIP.RetryCount : 2
SIP.ServerGroupOverloadedResponseCodes : 503,480,600
```

```
SIP.Error.DN : 92929292
SIP.SendToOrigin :
SIPStack.logLevel : ERROR
SIP.UseSimpleRecording : true
SIP.ServerGroupHBMethod : OPTIONS
SIP.Proxy.Port : 5060
SIP.UseSessionExpires : true
SIP.logLevel : DEBUG
SIP.Comma.Duration : 100
SIP.UseCCMCAC : true
SIP.MTU : 2200
SIP.UseErrorRefer : true
SIP.PostCallSurveyWait : 2000
SIP.UseLocalSRV : true
SIP.OptionsOverrideHost : cvp.cisco.com
SIP.Incoming.Transport : TCP+UDP
SIP.traceMask : 0x00000041
SIP.ServerGroupDownInterval : 5000
SIP.PostCallSurvey.DN :
SIP.Terminating.Pause : 2000
SIP.Outgoing.Transport : UDP
SIP.Incoming.Port : 5060
SIP.Proxy.Route :
SIP.Proxy.Host : UNIFIEDCUSP.UNIFIED.LAB
SIP.handleGWOptionsReporting : true
SIP.skip18XWithSDP : true
SIP.RejectCallOnRecordingFailure : false
SIP.UseSymmetricPorts : false
SIP.ServerGroupUpInterval : 5000
SIP.UseRingtone : true
SIP.ZombieCheckCallLength : 120
SIP.OutboundInviteTimeout :
SIP.RecordingServerDN : 93939393
```

By using the ? after each level of commands provided by the Unified CLI, it becomes obvious as to how powerful this new CLI is. The number of options and granularity that can be built into local and systemwide searches is too extensive to completely cover in this chapter. But the Unified System CLI interface is an extremely effective tool for quickly collecting information required during troubleshooting the entire Unified CVP solution. Example 8-46 shows the output of a **show version** command issued from the System CLI while in system mode.

Example 8-46 *Unified System CLI* show version *Command in System Mode*

```
admin(system):show version

Retrieving [version] data from device [192.168.1.218] ProductType [cvp] ...

CVP CVP 8.0(1)  SR=0 ES=0 Drop Number=4 Build Number=22 Build Date=Wed Jan 13 21:
44:22 MST 2010
CallServer CVP 8.0(1)  SR=0 ES=0 Drop Number=4 Build Number=22 Build Date=Wed Jan
 13 21:44:22 MST 2010
OAMP CVP 8.0(1)  SR=0 ES=0 Drop Number=4 Build Number=22 Build Date=Wed Jan 13 21
:44:22 MST 2010   .
VXMLServer v8.0(1)
Reporting CVP 8.0(1)  SR=0 ES=0 Drop Number=4 Build Number=22 Build Date=Wed Jan
13 21:44:22 MST 2010
VMS CVP 8.0(1)  SR=0 ES=0 Drop Number=4 Build Number=22 Build Date=Wed Jan 13 21:
44:22 MST 2010
ORM CVP 8.0(1)  SR=0 ES=0 Drop Number=4 Build Number=22 Build Date=Wed Jan 13 21:
44:22 MST 2010


Retrieving [version] data from device [192.168.1.214] ProductType [cup] ...

Product Version List:
Active Server Version: 7.0.5.10000-26
Cisco Unified Presence
7.0.5.10000-26
Common Services
7.0.5.10000-26


Retrieving [version] data from device [192.168.1.213] ProductType [ucm] ...

Product Version List:
Active Server Version: 7.1.3.10000-11
Cisco Unified Communications Manager
7.1.3.10000-11
Common Services
7.1.3.10000-11


Retrieving [version] data from device [192.168.1.11] ProductType [ios] ...

Cisco IOS Software, 2800 Software (C2800NM-IPVOICEK9-M), Version 12.4(24)T2, REL

EASE SOFTWARE (fc2)
Technical Support: http://www.cisco.com/techsupport
Copyright (c) 1986-2009 by Cisco Systems, Inc.
Compiled Mon 19-Oct-09 17:38 by prod_rel_team
```

```
ROM: System Bootstrap, Version 12.4(13r)T, RELEASE SOFTWARE (fc1)


R2800-VG uptime is 4 weeks, 2 days, 20 hours, 50 minutes
System returned to ROM by reload at 20:18:39 UTC Fri May 20 2011
System image file is "flash:c2800nm-ipvoicek9-mz.124-24.T2.bin"
Cisco 2811 (revision 53.51) with 249856K/12288K bytes of memory.
Processor board ID FTX1208A2EN
2 FastEthernet interfaces
2 Voice FXO interfaces
2 Voice FXS interfaces
DRAM configuration is 64 bits wide with parity enabled.
239K bytes of non-volatile configuration memory.
62720K bytes of ATA CompactFlash (Read/Write)
Configuration register is 0x2102


Retrieving [version] data from device [10.1.10.2] ProductType [ios] ...


Cisco IOS Software, C2900 Software (C2900-UNIVERSALK9_NPE-M), Version 15.0(1)M4,

 RELEASE SOFTWARE (fc1)
Technical Support: http://www.cisco.com/techsupport
Copyright (c) 1986-2010 by Cisco Systems, Inc.
Compiled Thu 28-OcT10 18:32 by prod_rel_team


ROM: System Bootstrap, Version 15.0(1r)M9, RELEASE SOFTWARE (fc1)

R2921-VXML uptime is 4 weeks, 2 days, 20 hours, 24 minutes
System returned to ROM by reload at 20:24:50 UTC Fri May 20 2011
System image file is "flash0:c2900-universalk9_npe-mz.SPA.150-1.M4.bin"
Last reload type: Normal Reload
Last reload reason: Reload Command
Cisco CISCO2921/K9 (revision 1.0) with 483328K/40960K bytes of memory.
Processor board ID FTX1446AJKL
3 Gigabit Ethernet interfaces
DRAM configuration is 64 bits wide with parity enabled.
255K bytes of non-volatile configuration memory.
250880K bytes of ATA System CompactFlash 0 (Read/Write)
License Info:
License UDI:
- - - - - - - - - - - - - - - - - - - - - - - - - -:
Device#
```

```
                PID                 SN
       ------------------------------.
*0         CISCO2921/K9         FTX1446AJKL


Technology Package License Information for Module:'c2900'
-------------------------------------------
Technology    Technology-package        Technology-package
              Current     Type          Next reboot
-------------------------------------------
ipbase        ipbasek9     Permanent    ipbasek9
security      None         None         None
uc            uck9         Permanent    uck9
data          None         None         None
Configuration register is 0x2102
```

The Unified CLI queried all devices that were configured via the Operations Console and correctly returned each device's output from its version of **show version**. For this to work, make sure that the serviceability for the device is enabled and supply correct user credentials via the Operations Console. The **show version** command can be further refined to show only device types that are IOS in nature using the command **show version devicetype ios**. Other commands are equally interesting such as **show debug devicetype ios**, which outputs the active debug commands for all IOS devices configured in the Operations Console. Some commands output a significant amount of data such as the **show tech-support** command, especially if it is issued in system mode against numerous devices. In this case, the Unified CLI saves all the output from such a command and places the output into a compressed zip file, as shown from the output in Example 8-47.

Example 8-47   *Unified System CLI* show tech-support *Command Output*

```
admin(system):show tech-support devicetype ios
Warning: Because running this command can affect system performance,
Cisco recommends that you run the command during off-peak hours.
Do you want to continue? [y/n]: y
Retrieving [version] data from device [192.168.1.11] ProductType [ios]
Retrieving [version] data from device [10.1.10.2] ProductType [ios] .
Retrieving [component] data from device [192.168.1.11] ProductType [ios]
Retrieving [component] data from device [10.1.10.2] ProductType [ios] .
Retrieving [log] data from device [192.168.1.11] ProductType [ios] ..
Retrieving [log] data from device [10.1.10.2] ProductType [ios] ..
Retrieving [trace] data from device [192.168.1.11] ProductType [ios]
Retrieving [trace] data from device [10.1.10.2] ProductType [ios] ...
Retrieving [configuration] data from device [192.168.1.11] ProductType [ios]
Retrieving [configuration] data from device [10.1.10.2] ProductType [ios]
Retrieving [debug] data from device [192.168.1.11] ProductType [ios]
```

```
Retrieving [debug] data from device [10.1.10.2] ProductType [ios] .
Retrieving [license] data from device [192.168.1.11] ProductType [ios]
Retrieving [license] data from device [10.1.10.2] ProductType [ios]
Retrieving [perf] data from device [192.168.1.11] ProductType [ios]
Retrieving [perf] data from device [10.1.10.2] ProductType [ios] ..
Retrieving [platform] data from device [192.168.1.11] ProductType [ios]
Retrieving [platform] data from device [10.1.10.2] ProductType [ios]
Retrieving [sessions] data from device [192.168.1.11] ProductType [ios]
Retrieving [sessions] data from device [10.1.10.2] ProductType [ios] .
Output is saved to "C:\Cisco\CVP\wsm\CLI\.\download\clioutput3.zip"
```

As the example output highlights, be careful when and against which devices are executed as a **show tech-support** command, especially when running in system mode. As with debug commands, issuing this command during periods of high call volumes can be a disaster for any production Unified CVP deployment. Example 8-47 also shows additional granularity with any of the CLI commands because the output was filtered down to just IOS devices. As a final caveat, as of this writing, the Unified System CLI does not natively support accessing it via telnet or SSH. The implication is that it is required to access the console of a server that has the tool directly installed to run the CLI. This limits how, where, and from what client the CLI can be accessed.

Unified CVP VXML Server

Most of the processes and tools illustrated for showing device status and troubleshooting the Unified CVP Call Server also apply to the VXML server. However, some differences exist that should be pointed out for the VXML server. First, to verify that the basic functionality of the VXML is up and working, point a client browser at the following URL http://<IP Address of VXML Server>:7000/CVP/Server?application=HelloWorld. If the browser retrieves a VXML document, odds are that the VXML server is correctly set up. You can configure a VXML Gateway to place a call into the HelloWorld application via self-service to provide additional confirmation that VXML instructions are retrieved and correctly interpreted by the VXML Gateway. As with Unified CVP, always verify the status of the VXML server via the Operations Console in a similar fashion, as illustrated earlier in this chapter for the Call Server.

Table 8-10 provides the filenaming convention, location, and description for the VXML server log files.

Table 8-11 provides some of the common error codes that may occur with a VXML application hosted on the VXML server:

Table 8-10 *Unified CVP VXML Server Log Files*

Log File Name	Location	Description
activity_logYYYY-MM-DD-HH-MM-SS.log	%CVP_HOME%\VXML Server\applications\<App Name>\logs\ActivityLog	Activity Log for VXML application
admin_historyYYYY-MM-DD.txt	%CVP_HOME%\VXML Server\applications\<App Name>\logs\AdminLog	Administrative log for VXML application
error_logYYYY-MM-DD.txt	%CVP_HOME%\VXML Server\applications\<App Name>\logs\ErrorLog	Error log for VXML application

Table 8-11 *Common VXML Application Error Codes*

Error Code	Name	Description
40	System Unavailable	Returned if the application server is unavailable (shutdown, network connection disabled, and so on).
41	App Error	Returned if some Cisco Unified CVP VXML Server-specific error (for example, java exception) occurs.
42	App Hangup	Returned to Cisco Unified CVP if the Hang Up element is used without being preceded by a Subdialog_Return element.
43	Suspended	Returned if the Cisco Unified CVP VXML Server application is suspended.
44	No Session Error	Returned when an emergency error occurs. (For example, an application is called but has not been loaded in the Cisco Unified CVP VXML Server application.)
45	Bad Fetch	Returned when the Cisco Unified VXML Server encounters a bad fetch situation. This code is returned when either a .wav file or and external grammar file is not found.

In addition to checking the status of the server and visiting the application log files, there are also some batch files specifically written for the administration of applications. By accessing the following directory via a command prompt, you can run the status.bat file to get a status on a specific application:

`%CVP_HOME%\VXMLServer\applications\<App Name>\admin`

Example 8-48 provides the output of this command when executed against the HelloWorld VXML application:

Example 8-48 *Status.bat output for Sample HelloWorld VXML Application*

```
C:\Cisco\CVP\VXMLServer\applications\HelloWorld\admin>status
- Application 'HelloWorld' is running.
- There are no active callers and no sessions waiting to end for the application
Press any key to continue . . .
```

Unified CVP Reporting Server

Most of the issues found for the Unified CVP Reporting Server are associated with authentication. However, the log files for the Reporting Server is located at the following directory:

`%INFORMIXDIR%` which is defaulted to `"c:\db\informix"` with the log file format being: `%INFORMIXSERVER%.log`

By examining these files, authentication errors can be seen with -951 errors, the cvp_dbuser cannot login. Most of the time this issue is associated with either a bad or expired password that can quickly be corrected by using the User Management interface on the server to set the cvp_dbuser account to never expire and that the user does not need to reset their password the next time they log in.

Unified ICM

This section focuses on some key tools and concepts regarding troubleshooting Unified ICM and its relationship with Unified CVP. To understand how to troubleshoot Unified ICM in its entirety is well beyond the scope of this book. However, you can use some simple tools to isolate any faults that occur with elements such as the Unified ICM script, PG, and VRU PIM status.

As noted earlier in this chapter, the Operations Console should always be used to check the status of the ICM subsystem and statistics pertaining to its operations. The statistics for the ICM subsystem can be accessed via the Statistics options when configuring a Call

Server (refer to Figure 8-16). This provides a great snapshot for starting the process of troubleshooting Unified ICM's interaction with Unified CVP. However, if it is determined that there is potentially a PG or VRU PIM issue with Unified ICM, you can use additional tools to verify and isolate such an issue. This section examines the tools that verify the status of the PG and the VRU PIM.

Peripheral Gateway (PG) and Peripheral Interface Manager (PIM) Status

Unified ICM provides some nice tools for checking the status of a PG, its processes, and the status of a particular PIM hosted by the PG. This section examines the output of two tools specifically designed for this purpose: RTTest and OPCTest.

ICM Call Router Test Utility (RTTest:status)

The RTTest utility provides status and debugging information for the overall system status including PGs and Peripheral status. Example 8-49 provides a sample output of the command.

Example 8-49 RTTest:status *Command Output*

```
C:\WINDOWS>rttest /system UNIFIED-ICMSPRW /cust cisco
RTTEST Release 7.5.1.0 , Build 23684
rttest: status
Router Version: Release 7.5.6.0 , Build 25951
Release Date:   08/13/2009 16:41:44

Current Time:   06/20 19:18:17
Local Time:     06/20 13:18:17 (-6.0 hr)
Router Up:      06/16 09:31:05 (4.4 day)
Router Sync:    —
State size now: 752,768 bytes
State size max: 757,296 bytes

Process            LastStateChange              LastHeartBeat
A agi              - —                           —
A basv             - —                           —
A cic              - —                           —
A clgr             OK MH 06/16 09:31:44 (4.4 day) 06/20 19:18:04 (13 sec)
A crpl             - —                           —
A csfs             OK M- 06/16 09:31:26 (4.4 day) —
A dba              OK MH 06/16 09:31:05 (4.4 day) 06/20 19:18:05 (12 sec)
A dbw              - —                           —
A hlgr             OK MH 06/16 09:31:44 (4.4 day) 06/20 19:18:04 (13 sec)
A nrpl             - —                           —
A rcv              OK M- 06/16 09:31:38 (4.4 day) —
A rtr              OK MH 06/16 09:31:06 (4.4 day) 06/20 19:18:05 (12 sec)
```

```
A rts          OK MH 06/16 09:31:05 (4.4 day)    06/20 19:17:58 (19 sec)
A ssim         -  —                               —
A tsyr         OK M- 06/16 09:31:06 (4.4 day)    —
```

Controller	LastStateChange	LastHeartBeat
PG1A,1	CFO 06/16 09:32:06 (4.4 day)	06/20 19:18:08 (9 sec)

Peripheral	LastStateChange	LastHeardFrom
PG1A_CCM	COS 06/16 09:32:23 (4.4 day)	06/20 19:17:56 (21 sec)
PG1A_CVP7	CO —	06/16 09:32:08 (4.4 day)
PG1A_CVP8	COS 06/16 09:32:21 (4.4 day)	06/20 19:18:08 (9 sec)

From this example, it is clearly noted that the PG is healthy and was heard from 9 seconds ago. In addition, both the CUCM and Unified CVP VRU PIMs are active and healthy reporting in 21 and 9 seconds ago, respectively. In the Controller section of Example 8-49, a status code of CFO is listed just to the left of the LastStateChange column. The following list defines possible values for the LastStateChange status code:

- C: Signifies that the Unified ICM PG server has successfully downloaded a configuration from the ICM Controller

- F: Signifies that the Unified ICM PG is fully configured and that the configuration is valid

- O: Signifies that the Unified ICM PG is online and communicating with the Unified ICM Router

For the section labeled Peripheral in Example 8-49, the status code COS found just left of the LastStateChange column has the following meaning:

- C: Signifies that the peripheral is correctly configured to communicate with the ICM PG.

- O: Signifies that the peripheral is online, for example communications have been established with the Unified ICM PG.

- S: Signifies that the peripheral is in service, for example agent and call data are sent to the Unified ICM PG.

The system's name and the Unified ICM customer instance name must be known to correctly launch the tool. In addition it must be launched on the Unified ICM router because the tool is not installed on other ICM nodes. For more specifics on how to interrupt the output of the tool or initiate debugging via the tool, access the Cisco Document, *The Cisco ICM* rttest Utility located at http://www.cisco.com/en/US/products/sw/custcosw/ps1001/products_tech_note09186a00800ac69b.shtml.

Open Peripheral Controller Test Utility (OPCTest)

To gather more detailed information about the PIM and Peripheral status, OPCTest is invoked. As with rttest, the customer instance and the PG node name is required, which can be gathered when using the **rttest:status** command. Figure 8-26 provides a sample output from the execution of the OPCTest command highlighting key areas of the output.

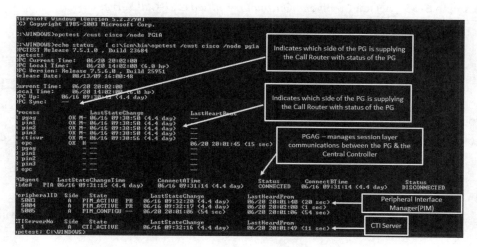

Figure 8-26   *Output of OPCTest Command Line Tool*

Figure 8-26 clearly illustrates the status of each PIM running on this PG and the state of the PIM sorted by its PeripheralID shared with Unified ICM's configuration. Because this particular deployment of Unified ICM is simplex and not duplex, the OPC Sync value is empty because syncing is not occurring because of the lack of a Side B PG.

For more specifics on how to interrupt the output of the OPCtest tool, access the Cisco Document, *Using the OPCTest Command-Line Utility*, located at http://www.cisco.com/en/US/products/sw/custcosw/ps1001/products_tech_note09186a0 0800acafa.shtml.

In some situations calls reach the Call Server but do not reach the intended VRU PIM. This can either be caused by the PIM not being in the correct state to pass traffic or the ICM service on the Unified CVP Call Server being connected to another VRU PIM on another PG. Example 8-50 and 8-51 show a sample output illustrating how to use the **netstat** command to isolate this issue:

Example 8-50   netstat *Command Output for Unified ICM PG*

```
C:\WINDOWS>netstat -a | find "5000"
    TCP    UNIFIED-ICMSPRW:1233    UNIFIEDCVP8:5000    ESTABLISHED
    TCP    UNIFIED-ICMSPRW:4398    UNIFIEDCVP7:5000    ESTABLISHED
```

By accessing the Unified CVP Call Server and issuing a similar command, it can be confirmed which machine has port 1233 open with the Unified ICM PG. Although the naming convention here makes it obvious which machine is communicating to PG on port 1233, sometimes machine naming issues require the port to be verified using the **netstat** command.

Example 8-51 netstat *Command Output for Unified CVP Call Server*

```
C:\WINDOWS>netstat -a | find "5000"
  C:\Cisco\CVP\VXMLServer\applications\HelloWorld\admin>netstat -a | find "5000"
  TCP    UNIFIEDCVP8:5000         UNIFIEDCVP8.unified.lab:0    LISTENING
  TCP    UNIFIEDCVP8:5000         UNIFIED-ICMSPRW:1233         ESTABLISHED
```

Router Log Viewer

To validate that calls are received by Unified ICM, the Router Log Viewer should be used from an Admin Workstation (AW). The Router Log Viewer displays any dialed numbers received by Unified ICM, their corresponding Automatic Number Identification (ANI), Caller Entered Digits (CED), and even a label that was returned to the routing client. In addition, error messages display for the Unified ICM Script. Figure 8-27 provides a sample the Router Log Viewer tool, which can be found via the ICM Admin Workstation windows menu.

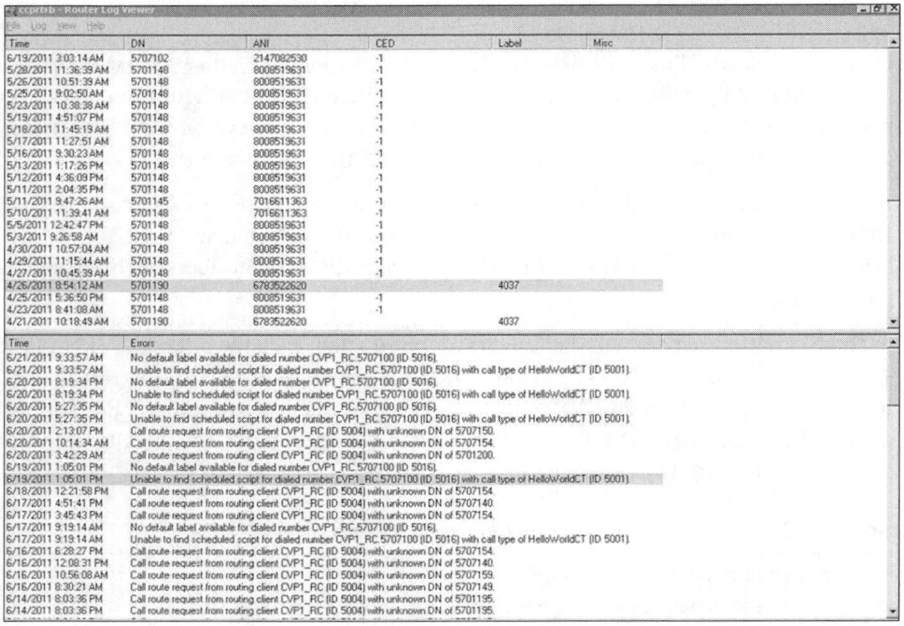

Figure 8-27 *Unified ICM Router Log Viewer*

Script Editor (Real-time Monitor Mode)

A common area of misconfiguration lies in the Unified ICM Script. After the Router Log Viewer has confirmed that the dialed number is seen, depending on how far the call is getting between the switch and VRU legs, the Scrip Editor can be invaluable in debugging the Unified ICM Script. Figure 8-28 shows a script that has been placed in Monitor mode.

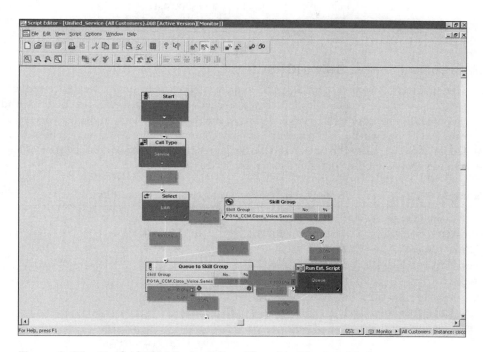

Figure 8-28 *Unified ICM Script Editor Placed in Monitor Mode*

By placing the script into Monitor mode, all incoming calls that have been mapped to this script by their dialed numbers will be tracked by Unified ICM incrementing counters for each step (highlighted in the green boxes), which allows troubleshooting how far the script is or is not executing. If the counters are incremented up to but not including the Send to VRU node, there is either a label issue in Unified ICM, routing issue for Unified CVP, or potentially a VXML gateway configuration issue. You need to complete all the success and failed exit legs of the scripts to determine which leg the node is exiting during different conditions. Counters appear each time a call uses a leg allowing errors to be tracked each time they occur in the script. Do not forget to clear the counters by resetting the script via the Script > Monitor Options > Reset Current Script menu option.

Additional Unified ICM troubleshooting content can be accessed via the Cisco DocWiki at http://docwiki.cisco.com/wiki/Troubleshooting_Unified_CCE.

Load Balancers

Although the use of load balancers such as the CSS or ACE is optional with the Unified CVP solution, as noted early on, they are invaluable for larger deployments when large media server or VXML Gateway farms exist. Therefore, the basics for troubleshooting load balancers is a topic worth covering in this chapter. This section examines the commands employed to troubleshoot a CSS switch, which are fairly basic and simple. However, Cisco has published a more comprehensive guide for troubleshooting the ACE, which is also covered.

Cisco Content Service Switch (CSS)

The first steps to troubleshooting a CSS implementation are to survey the device status, its version, interfaces, and circuits. It is critical to check all IP connectivity first before spending time troubleshooting services and groups, simply because without the network, services and groups will not be up and operational. Example 8-52 provides an output of three commands that verify the version of CSS, its current interface status, and the state of any circuits that have been configured using interfaces.

Example 8-52 *Cisco CSS* show run, interface, *and* circuits *Commands*

```
CSS11501# show version
Version:              sg0810106 (08.10.1.06)
Flash (Locked):       08.10.1.06
Flash (Operational):  08.10.1.06
Type:                 PRIMARY
Licensed Cmd Set(s):  Standard Feature Set
CSS11501# show interface
  Name            ifIndex    Type    Oper   Admin    Last Change
  --              ----.      --      --     --.      -----.
  Serial-Mgmt     1          console Up     Enable   06/10/2011 06:23:34
  Ethernet-Mgmt   2          fe      Down   Enable   06/10/2011 06:23:34
  e1              3          fe      Up     Enable   06/10/2011 10:03:25
  e2              4          fe      Down   Enable   06/10/2011 06:23:35
  e3              5          fe      Down   Enable   06/10/2011 06:23:35
  e4              6          fe      Down   Enable   06/10/2011 06:23:35
  e5              7          fe      Down   Enable   06/10/2011 06:23:35
  e6              8          fe      Down   Enable   06/10/2011 06:23:35
  e7              9          fe      Down   Enable   06/10/2011 06:23:35
  e8              10         fe      Down   Enable   06/10/2011 06:23:35
  e9              11         ge      Down   Enable   06/10/2011 06:23:35
CSS11501# show circuits
                                                              Operational
  Circuit name  Circuit State    IP Address     Interface(s)  Status
  ------        ------.          -------.       ------        ------
  VLAN1         active-ipEnabled 10.89.28.199   e1            Up
```

As shown in Example 8-52, the interface e1 used for the circuit named VLAN1 is up and enabled, allowing for traffic to be handled by the services and groups configured on this particular CSS. Next, verify the status of the CSS services handling two media servers. Example 8-52 provides a summary of the services followed by their configuration details.

Example 8-53 *Cisco CSS* **show service summary** *and* **show service** *Commands*

```
CSS11501# show version
CSS11501# show service summary
Service Name                   State     Conn  Weight  Avg   State
                                                       Load  Transitions
mediaserver1                   Down       0     1      255      1
mediaserver2                   Alive      0     1      2        2
CSS11501#  show service
Services (2 entries):
 Name: mediaserver1      Index: 1
  Type: Redirect          State: Down
  Rule ( 10.89.28.84   ANY   80 )
  Session Redundancy: Disabled
  Redirect Domain: 10.89.28.84
  Redirect String:
  Prepend Redirect with "http://": Enabled
  Keepalive: (HTTP-80:HEAD:/index.html   5   1   2 )
  Keepalive Error: General failure
  Keepalive Encryption:       Disabled
  Last Clearing of Stats Counters: 06/10/2011 10:12:12
  Mtu:                    1500     State Transitions:          1
  Total Local Connections:    0    Total Backup Connections:   0
  Current Local Connections: 0     Current Backup Connections:  0
  Total Connections:          0    Max Connections:        65534
  Total Reused Conns:         0
  Weight:                     1    Load:                     255
  Weight Reporting:        None


 Name: mediaserver2      Index: 2
  Type: Redirect          State: Alive
  Rule ( 10.89.28.123   ANY   80 )
  Session Redundancy: Disabled
  Redirect Domain: 10.89.28.123
  Redirect String:
  Prepend Redirect with "http://": Enabled
  Keepalive: (HTTP-80:HEAD:/index.html   5   1   2 )
```

```
Keepalive Encryption:       Disabled
Last Clearing of Stats Counters: 06/10/2011 10:19:14
Mtu:                   1500    State Transitions:          2
Total Local Connections:   0    Total Backup Connections:   0
Current Local Connections: 0    Current Backup Connections: 0
Total Connections:         0    Max Connections:        65534
Total Reused Conns:        0
Weight:                    1    Load:                       2
Weight Reporting:        None
```

The output in Example 8-53 shows that the media server located at IP address 10.89.28.94 is down. This could be because of a few reasons, such as an incorrect IP address or the web server such as IIS is not running or responding to the CSS keepalive: HTTP-80:HEAD:/index.html also noted by the output. When the services have been confirmed, the next step is to verify the group for which those services are configured. The group basically maps the services or real servers into a group that employs the VIP for the group. This enables all the services (real servers) to be accessible from a VXML Gateway via the CSS VIP. Example 8-54 provides the output for verifying the status of a group called mediaservers.

Example 8-54   *Cisco CSS* show group *Command*

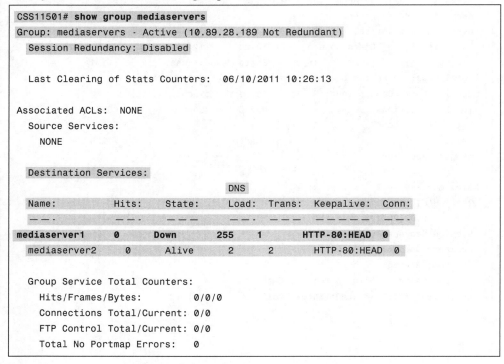

```
CSS11501# show group mediaservers
Group: mediaservers - Active (10.89.28.189 Not Redundant)
  Session Redundancy: Disabled


  Last Clearing of Stats Counters:  06/10/2011 10:26:13

Associated ACLs:  NONE
  Source Services:
    NONE


  Destination Services:
                                    DNS
    Name:       Hits:     State:    Load:  Trans:  Keepalive:   Conn:
    — —.        — —.      — — —     — —.   — — —   — — — — —   — —.
mediaserver1     0        Down       255     1       HTTP-80:HEAD   0
    mediaserver2     0        Alive        2      2       HTTP-80:HEAD   0


  Group Service Total Counters:
    Hits/Frames/Bytes:         0/0/0
    Connections Total/Current: 0/0
    FTP Control Total/Current: 0/0
    Total No Portmap Errors:   0
```

In addition, Cisco has compiled a list of Troubleshooting TechNotes specifically for the Cisco CSS 11500 Series Content Services Switches at cisco.com via the following URL: http://www.cisco.com/en/US/products/hw/contnetw/ps792/prod_tech_notes_list.html.

Cisco Application Content Engine (ACE)

Cisco has produced an excellent guide to troubleshooting the Cisco Application Control Engine (ACE) covering all topics ranging from basic to more advanced troubleshooting topics relating to Redundancy and Compression. This guide is located on the Cisco DocWiki at http://docwiki.cisco.com/wiki/Cisco_Application_Control_Engine_%28ACE%29_Troubleshooting_Guide.

This same link also provides some additional links at the bottom of the page for ACE configuration, command references, and even a CSS to ACE Conversion Tool User Guide.

Matching a Symptom with a Resolution: A Final Thought

Another approach to troubleshooting a Unified CVP solution is to work on matching a certain symptom to a known and documented resolution. Cisco provides an excellent set of troubleshooting documents structured around matching a symptom with a resolution. You can access these documents via the Cisco DocWiki URL: http://docwiki.cisco.com/wiki/Troubleshooting_Unified_Customer_Voice_Portal as well as the general Cisco documentation URL for troubleshooting Unified CVP at: http://www.cisco.com/en/US/partner/products/sw/custcosw/ps1006/prod_troubleshooting_guides_list.html.

The number of symptoms provided by this wiki is too massive to cover in this chapter. However, it is a good idea to become familiar with the common symptoms found on this wiki just in case there is a situation where any one of these problems can be matched, allowing for a quick resolution. In addition, this wiki is periodically updated, providing an up-to-date source on symptoms and their common resolution.

Furthermore, the Cisco Document published for troubleshooting version 7.0, *Troubleshooting Unified Customer Voice Portal, 7.0(2), January 2011,* provides some excellent appendixes that outline common error messages found throughout the log files discussed in this section. Although the targeted version of this document is Unified CVP 7.0(2), the error codes presented are still accurate for newer versions of Unified CVP.

Summary

Previous chapters examined the complexities of Unified CVP for its design and implementation models. This complexity becomes even more apparent when attempting to troubleshoot the solution because of the number of integrations and platforms involved in making the solution work.

To be successful during detailed troubleshooting exercises, it is critical to have a solid plan for isolating faults. This chapter began by providing some fault isolation flow charts to aid in isolating faults with the solution. After you isolate the fault to a more specific area of focus, you should invoke detailed troubleshooting exercises to find the root cause of the fault.

Device status and detailed troubleshooting techniques were presented and organized for non-native and native devices following a similar flow as the fault isolation flow charts providing a logical flow between isolating the fault and resolution. Although the commands, tools, and techniques to troubleshoot different components are immense, this chapter provided some of the more commonly used ones and provided links to others for reference.

Troubleshooting a Unified CVP deployment is one of the most difficult skill sets to acquire, and it should also be no surprise that it is also the most important. With a massive number of integrations supported by Unified CVP driving a significant number of configuration sets, isolating issues can be daunting and time-consuming, which is why having a solid troubleshooting methodology becomes key to successfully navigating Unified CVP call flows and their respective dependencies.

The next chapter examines the virtualization of the Unified CVP solution using the Cisco Unified Computing System platform (UCS). An overview of UCS and a discussion pertaining to blade cohabitation and sizing is provided. The future of Unified ICM and CVP deployments is no doubt hinged around virtualization; making it necessary to establish some ground rules on how to provide a virtualized Unified CVP solution without sacrificing performance.

Recommended Reading and Resources

Cisco Documentation, *Cisco Unified Customer Voice Portal (CVP) 8.x Solution Reference Network Design (SRND)*, http://www.cisco.com/en/US/docs/voice_ip_comm/cust_contact/contact_center/customer_voice_portal/srnd/8x/cvp8xsrnd.pdf.

Cisco Documentation, *Cisco Unified Contact Center Enterprise Solution Reference Network Design (SRND)*, http://www.cisco.com/en/US/products/sw/custcosw/ps1844/products_implementation_design_guides_list.html.

Cisco Documentation, *Cisco Unified Customer Voice Portal Configuration Guides*, http://www.cisco.com/en/US/partner/products/sw/custcosw/ps1006/products_installation_and_configuration_guides_list.html.

Cisco Documentation, *Hardware and System Software Specification for Cisco Unified Customer Voice Portal (Unified CVP), Release 8.0(1)*, http://www.cisco.com/en/US/docs/voice_ip_comm/cust_contact/contact_center/customer_voice_portal/cvp8_0/reference/guide/cvp_801_bom.pdf.

Cisco Documentation, *Cisco Unified Communications System Release 8.x SRND*, January 2011, http://www.cisco.com/en/US/partner/docs/voice_ip_comm/cucm/srnd/8x/uc8x.html.

Cisco Documentation, *Cisco Customer Voice Portal Troubleshooting Guide*, http://www.cisco.com/en/US/products/sw/custcosw/ps1006/prod_troubleshooting_guides_list.html.

Cisco Documentation, *Cisco Unified Presence Troubleshoot and Alerts*, http://www.cisco.com/en/US/products/ps6837/tsd_products_support_troubleshoot_and_alerts.html.

Cisco Documentation, *Documentation Roadmap for Cisco Unified SIP Proxy Release 8.5*, http://www.cisco.com/en/US/docs/voice_ip_comm/cusp/rel8_5/roadmap/cuspdocguide.html#wp1063495.

Cisco Documentation, *Cisco Unified SIP Proxy via Cisco DocWiki*, http://docwiki.cisco.com/wiki/Cisco_Unified_SIP_Proxy.

Cisco Documentation, *Troubleshooting Cisco Unified Voice Portal via Cisco DocWiki*, http://docwiki.cisco.com/wiki/Troubleshooting_Unified_Customer_Voice_Portal.

Cisco Documentation, *The Cisco ICM rttest Utility*, http://www.cisco.com/en/US/products/sw/custcosw/ps1001/products_tech_note09186a00800ac69b.shtml.

Cisco Documentation, *Using the OPCTest Command-Line Utility*, http://www.cisco.com/en/US/products/sw/custcosw/ps1001/products_tech_note09186a00800acafa.shtml.

Cisco Documentation, *Troubleshooting Unified CCE via Cisco DocWiki*, http://docwiki.cisco.com/wiki/Troubleshooting_Unified_CCE.

Cisco Documentation, *Cisco Application Control Engine (ACE) Troubleshooting Guide via Cisco DocWiki*, http://docwiki.cisco.com/wiki/Troubleshooting_Unified_CCE.

Cisco Documentation, *Cisco CSS 11500 Series Content Services Switches Troubleshooting TechNotes*, http://www.cisco.com/en/US/products/hw/contnetw/ps792/prod_tech_notes_list.html.

Chapter 9

Virtualization

This chapter covers the following subjects:

- **The new data center challenges:** New challenges present in today's data centers for server management and how virtualization solves these challenges.

- **Overview of the Cisco Unified Computing System (UCS):** UCS and the deployment models used by Unified CVP.

- **Unified CVP components supported for virtualization:** Components supported when virtualized, capacity guidance, and caveats.

- **Performance requirements:** Key performance requirements when virtualizing Unified CVP.

- **Use cases:** Several Unified CCE use cases are provided and discussed. Each case provides key virtual machine cohabitation on physical UCS hardware for an entire Unified CCE solution including Unified ICM, Unified Call Manager, and CVP.

New Data Center Challenges

In the early 1990s, the focus was on building monolithic servers that provided the capability to scale up data centers. These servers usually had a large number of CPUs running on proprietary platforms and operating systems. Typically, a large number of applications were hosted per server. This approach created an expensive environment with a large failure domain. Later in the early 2000s, the focus switched to scaling out servers because the hardware had evolved to a commodity model with fewer CPUs. It focused mostly on the x86 platform using commoditized operating systems hosting a single application per server. This approach caused an increase in power and cooling requirements and produced underused servers. In today's environment the focus is on scaling in by deploying blade servers with multicore CPUs running on an x86 platform. At present, the operating system has been commoditized and supports virtualization. However, this current approach creates a great deal of complexity around all aspects of management including deployment, configuration, and troubleshooting with limits on how much it can scale.

By focusing the computing resources of a server in a blade form factor within an enclosure, administrators gain additional advantages:

- Maximum use of physical space

- Shared power distribution

- Shared networking and storage access

- More efficient power and cooling

Today, server processors are multicore, offering multiple processing cores in the same space previously used for single-core processors. In addition, many vendors have created memory controllers that can address large amounts of RAM well into the tens of gigabytes. Although blade server sizes have remained the same, the processing and memory has increased significantly, enabling blade servers to run processing and memory-intensive applications.

Virtualization has enabled companies to more easily consolidate servers in the data center. Instead of the standard one-to-one server model, many servers, each running in independent virtual machines (VM), can run on a single physical server.

Virtualization is achieved by creating virtual representation of physical hardware components. A number of advantages exist for using virtualization, including better use of computing resources, greater server densities, and seamless server migrations:

- **Virtual machine:** A virtualized set of hardware that can operate in a similar fashion to a physical server.

- **Virtual server:** A virtual set of hardware along with the operating system, applications, and files that can operate comparable to a physical server.

- **Hypervisor layer:** A software layer that abstracts the physical hardware and creates individual virtual hardware for each VM; for example, VMWare ESX, Microsoft Hyper-V, Xen, and so on.[1]

The data center of today is the product of multiple evolutions in thinking and architecture. The scale-out x86 architecture is currently undergoing another evolution through the use of blades, virtualization, and Input Output (I/O) consolidation. New technologies and architectures such as Unified Computing System (UCS) can add infrastructure and management complexities in the name of virtualization.[2]

Overview of the Cisco Unified Computing System

This section examines the UCS deployment models supported by Unified CVP. However, a detailed discussion on what and how UCS works is not provided because there is an underlying expectation that the reader should have some basic knowledge about the UCS architecture and virtualization. As discussed at the end of this chapter, a great book for introducing UCS is the *Cisco Unified Computing System (UCS)* published by Cisco Press (ISBN 1-58714-193-0) with authors Silvano Gai, Tommi Salli, and Roger Andersson. This book provides a complete reference guide to the Cisco Data Center Virtualization Server Architecture. The UCS architecture coupled with VMWare ESXi is the only virtualization architecture supported by Unified CVP.

Starting with Unified CVP Release 8.0(1), virtualization of the following deployments and Unified CVP components on Cisco UCS hardware is supported:

- Unified CVP Call Server

- Unified CVP VoiceXML Server

- Unified CVP Reporting Server

- Unified CVP Operations Console

However, the following deployments and Unified CVP components have not been qualified and are not supported in virtualization:

- H.323 Call Flow Deployment

- Distributed VoiceXML Server and Call Server deployment (where each server runs in a separate virtual machine).

- All-in-one lab deployment with a small reporting server

The first two bullets are worth noting. For upgrades from a nonvirtualized deployment of Unified CVP in which you want to consolidate hardware and virtualize onto a new version of Unified CVP, H.323 deployments must be migrated to SIP and all distributed Voice Extensible Markup Language (VoiceXML), and Call Server deployments must consolidate and size to run on a single virtual machine. These two caveats alone can make migrating and virtualizing Unified CVP problematic.

In addition the following VMWare features are also not supported with Unified CVP:

- VMware Physical to Virtual migration

- VMware Snapshots

- VMware Consolidated Backup

- VMware High Availability (HA)

- VMware Site Recovery Manager

- VMware vCenter Update Manager

- VMware vCenter Converter

> **Note**   Unified CVP components are supported on the UCS platform only in a virtualized environment with VMWare ESXi.

UCS Hardware Requirements

Following are two supported hardware deployment models for which Unified CVP components can be virtualized onto:

- UCS B200 M1 hardware using a UCS chassis, controller, and SAN

- Standalone UCS C210 hardware not using any UCS controllers or SAN

UCS B200 M1

This deployment model is the classic model that uses the following components to deliver the hardware platform onto which Unified CVP can be virtualized:

- Cisco UCS Management and Switching
  - Cisco UCS 6100 Series Fabric Interconnects
- Cisco UCS Blade chassis
  - Cisco UCS 5100 Series Blade chassis
- Compute Nodes
  - Cisco UCS B Series Blade Servers (UCS B200 M1)
- Chassis Network Distribution
  - Cisco UCS 2100 Series I/O Modules
- Server Network Distribution
  - Cisco UCS VIC M81KR Virtual Interface Card
  - Cisco UCS VIC M71KR Converged Network Adapter
  - Cisco UCS VIC 82598KR 10-Gigabit Ethernet Adapter

Table 9-1 provides additional specifications for the UCS B200 M1 server blade.

This hardware deployment model uses the UCS 5100 chassis populated with the UCS B200 M1 blades, which are actually half-length blades. At the time of this writing, the full UCS B250 full-length blades are not supported by Unified CVP. The advantage of this model is that the chassis can be centrally controlled and managed via the UCS 6100 controllers, enabling a significant efficiency gain pertaining to the management and configuration of all blade servers. Providing a single touch point for management is an important advantage when using the B-series to host virtualized Unified CVP servers.

Table 9-1 *UCS B200 M1 Server Blade Specifications*

Base Server Model and Generation	Total Capacity	RAM	Storage	Adapters
UCS B200 M1 Blade	Dual E5540 (eight physical cores total)	36 GB (6x2GB + 6x4 GB)	DAS (RAID1) for VMware, FC SAN for UC apps	Third-party CNA
	Dual E5540 (eight physical cores total)	36 GB (6x2 GB + 6x4 GB)	Diskless—FC SAN for VMware and UC apps	Third-party CNA

UCS C210 Standalone

This hardware deployment model uses the new UCS C210 servers to provide a standalone rack mountable server that has been optimized to support both bare metal server Software-only or a virtualized server. Mixing virtualized servers hosted on a UCS C210 server with nonvirtualized UCS C210 servers is also supported.

The key takeaway with this deployment model is that as of this writing the UCS C-series is actually a replacement server for the older MCS models. This means that although they are truly UCS servers, there is currently no support for centrally managing a UCS C210M2 via a UCS 6100 controller as done with the B-Series. Some sources indicate that there should be no issue enabling the UCS 6100 controller the capability to control the UCS C210M2 server using direct network connections by passing the non-existent UCS 2100s. However, it has not currently been tested or announced as a supported hardware deployment model.

Table 9-2 provides the tested and supported server specifications for the UCS C210 M2 server:

UCS Hardware Caveats

As illustrated with both the B- and C-Series, only certain hardware sets have been tested and announced as supported. In addition to those considerations, when virtualizing Unified CVP keep the following caveats in mind:

- Unified CVP can be virtualized only using VMWare ESXi 4.0.

- Unified CVP can be virtualized only using SIP and not H.323.

- UCS Hardware must be used.

- Always use specific VM configurations and templates outlined on the docwiki.

- Quite a few key VMWare features are not supported.

- Off-box storage is support only with the UCS B-Series and not the C-Series.

- Currently on the UCS B-Series, half-width blades are supported (B200M1).

- SAN storage is accomplished via Fiber Channel only; no support for NAS or iSCSI.

Table 9-2　*UCS C210 M2 Rack Mount Server Specifications*

Base Server Model and Generation	CPU	RAM	Storage	Adapters
UCS C210 M2 General-Purpose Rack-Mount Server	Dual E5640 (eight physical cores total)	48 GB (12x4 GB)	DAS (two disks RAID1) for VMware + DAS (eight disks RAID5) for UC apps	1 GbE NIC

Unified CVP Component Capacities and VM Configuration Requirements

The VMWare requirements for Unified CVP are fairly straightforward. Version 8.0(1) and later or 8.5(1) and later are supported on VMWare vSphere ESXi 4.0 or 4.0 with Update 1 applied. However, as of this writing VMWare vSphere ESXi 4.1 is not supported. Table 9.3 shows the supported Unified CVP components, their capacities, and the VM computing resource requirements. You must use the OVA virtual machine templates to create the Unified CVP component virtual machines.

Note　A virtual machine template defines the configuration of the virtual machine's virtual hardware. Open Virtualization Format (OVF) is an open standard for describing a virtual machine template, and Open Virtualization Archive (OVA) is an open standard to package and distribute these templates. Files in OVA format have an extension of .ova. By using an OVA template, the setup and configuration of a virtual machine is not only easier but also consistent for critical hardware settings required to support the virtualization of Unified CVP and ICM applications.

The OVA templates can be accessed via the Cisco Unified Customer Voice Portal Download Software URL at http://www.cisco.com/cisco/software/release.html?mdfid=270563413&catid=278875240&softwareid=280840592&release=8.0(1)&relind=null&rellifecycle=&reltype=null&i=rp.

You can have one or more Unified CVP Virtual Machines co-resident on the same ESXi server. However, you must adhere to the following rules:

- Any number of Unified CVP virtual machines and combination of co-residency of Unified CVP virtual machines with other UC applications are possible on an ESXi server as long as the sum of all the virtual machine CPU and memory resource allocation is not overcommitted on the available ESXi server computing resources.

- The CPU must not be overcommitted on the ESXi server running Unified CVP application components. The total number of vCPUs among all the virtual machines on an ESXi host must not be greater than the total number of CPUs available on the ESXi server. In the case of the Cisco UCS B-200 M1, the total number of CPUs available is 8.

- Memory cannot be overcommitted on the ESXi host running UC real-time applications. Allocate a minimum 2 GB of memory for the ESXi kernel. For example, if an ESXi server on B-200 M1 hardware has 36 GB of memory, after allocating 2 GB for the ESXi kernel, 34 GB are available for the virtual machines. The total memory allocated for all the virtual machines on an ESXi server must not be greater than 34 GB in this case.

- VM co-residency with third-party applications is not supported. Currently, the Media Server for Unified CVP is not recommended to be coloaded on the Unified CVP call server/VoiceXML server VM.

Furthermore, the Media Server virtual machine can use a 2-vCPU virtual machine profile. Refer to the Unified CVP Operations Console profile in Table 9-3. However, this is a third-party virtual machine and can be tailored to have a different virtual machine profile to satisfy a particular Unified CVP deployment requirement.

Table 9-3 *Supported OVA Templates: Unified Customer Voice Portal*

Component	vCPU Cores	vRAM/ Memory	vDisk	vNIC	OVA Name
Unified CVP Call Server + VoiceXML Server (colocated Call Server and VoiceXML Server). Media Server is optionally included depending on the conditions.	4	4 GB	1x146 GB	1	Template Name: Cisco Unified CVP Call Server-VoiceXML Server.ova
Unified CVP Reporting Server (Large).	4	4 GB	Disk 1 – 72 GB, Disk 2 – 438 GB	1	Template Name: Cisco Unified CVP Reporting Server.ova
Unified CVP Operations Console.	2	2 GB	1x20 GB	1	Template Name: Cisco Unified CVP Operations Console.ova

On the other hand, the Unified CVP Media Server can be on the Unified CVP call server/VoiceXML server virtual machine, providing that the following conditions are met:

- Internet Information Server (IIS) is used and not Tomcat.

- Audio prompts are cached on the voice gateway.

- Logging is turned off on the IIS media server.

Tables 9-4 and 9-5 summarize the capacity with the virtual machine requirements to support such holding capabilities for both Unified CVP and Unified ICM. Although this information is different than what is provided by the OVA templates, it illustrates what is required for the specific component, whereas the content provided in Table 9-3 outlines what each OVA template can build when used to set up the virtual machine.

The CPU referenced in Tables 9-3 through 9-5 are based on a 2.53GHz Xeon, E5540 using RAM with a speed of 1066 MHz. All UCCE components listed in Table 9-5 require two vNICs, whereas all other components in Tables 9-3 and 9-4 require only a single vNIC.

Table 9-4 *Unified CVP Supported Capacity and VM Requirements*

Component and Scale	vCPU	vRAM (GB)	vDisk (GB)
Call+VoiceXML+Media (1200 Calls)	4	4	1 x 80
Reporting(Medium) (840 Msg/Sec)	4	4	1 x 364
Reporting(Large) (840 Msg/Sec)	4	4	1 x 510
Operations Console	2	2	1 x 18

Table 9-5 *UCCE Supported Capacity and VM Requirements*

Component and Scale	vCPU	vRAM (GB)	vDisk (GB)
Router 8000 Users	2	4	1 x 80
Logger 8000 Users	4	4	1 x 150
Agent PG 2000 Users	2	4	1 x 80
VRU PG 9600 ports	2	2	1 x 80

Performance Requirements

Some of the data discussed in this section was provided earlier in Chapter 6, "Sizing, Networking, and Security Considerations." However, it is worth reviewing because of its relevance when virtualizing Unified CVP. The following performance considerations should be addressed:

- CPU usage (average) should not exceed 60 percent for the ESXi Server and for each of the individual processors and for each virtual machine.

- Memory usage (average) should not exceed 80 percent for the ESXi Server and for each of the virtual machines.

- Virtual machine snapshots are not supported in production because they have significant impact on system performance.

- The SAN must handle the Unified CVP application disk I/O characteristics as shown in Table 9-8.

- Be sure to enable hyperthreading on all ESXi servers.

Now look at the HTTP, HTTPS, and virtual machine I/O per second (IOPS) requirements when virtualizing Unified CVP components.

The metrics outline in Tables 9-6 and 9-7 are measured with full reporting. HTTPS degrades the solutions performance. It is a critical component to virtualization, especially when a SAN used to host the virtual machine image is I/O per second or IOPS. If a SAN is used, it must meet the IOPS specifications of all virtual machines for which it is hosting the images for. Table 9-8 provides the specific virtual machine IOPS for Unified CVP components.

Table 9-6 *HTTP Performance Metrics*

Call Flow	Simultaneous Calls Supported	Calls Per Second
SIP Comprehensive	900	10
VoiceXML Standalone	900	10
VoiceXML Standalone with Req ICM Label (VoiceXML Server on Tomcat)	900	10
VoiceXML Standalone on WAS	900	10
VoiceXML Standalone with Req ICM Label on WAS	900	10

Table 9-7   *HTTPS Performance Metrics*

Call Flow	Simultaneous Calls Supported	Calls Per Second
SIP Comprehensive	275	3
VoiceXML Standalone	275	3
VoiceXML Standalone on WAS	275	3

Table 9-8   *Unified CVP Component IOPS Summary*

Unified CVP Server	Average	MAX	95th Percentile
Call / VoiceXML Servers	380	1536	797
Reporting Server	692	3403	2023

Use Cases

It is now time to look at some sample use cases on how to build a virtualized CCE deployment using either the B- or C-series servers. Although this chapter focuses on Unified CVP virtualization, most deployments are Unified CCE in nature; therefore, you need to provide complete samples for how each of the components in a Unified Contact Center Enterprise (CCE) solution would co-habitate and share ESXi Servers. Furthermore, the following considerations apply to all the use cases presented here:

- You can deploy the ESXi Servers listed in these use cases on either a B-Series or C-Series hardware platform.

- Although the sample deployments in these use cases reflect the C-Series restriction that the HDS cannot co-reside with a Router, Logger, or a PG, this restriction is not present on a B-Series hardware platform.

- For deployments in which Historical Data Servers (HDS) are co-resident; two Redundant Array of Independent/Inexpensive Disks (RAID) 5 groups (one for each HDS) are recommended.

- Any deployment > 2 k agents requires at least 2 chassis when using B-Series hardware.

- It may be preferable to place the domain controller on bare metal rather than in the UCS B-series chassis. When a power failure occurs, the vCenter login credentials are dependent on Active Directory, leading to a potential chicken-and-egg problem if the domain controller is down as well.

- ACE and CUSP (for CVP) components are not supported virtualized on UCS. These components are deployed on separate hardware. Please review the product SRND for more details.

Use Case: Rogger Example 1

This use case provides the following:

- Up to 450 CTIOS Agents or 297 CAD Agents

- 150 IPIVR or 150 CVP ports (N + N)

- Optional 50 CUIC reporting users

Tables 9-9 and 9-10 provide the specifics for each virtual machine where shaded cells are optional components.

Table 9-9 *Chassis A (B Series)/Rack of C Series Rack Mount Servers*

ESXi Server	Component	# vCPU	RAM (GB)
ESXi Server A-1	Rogger A	4	4
	Agent PG A (Generic PG with optional VRU, CTIOS/CAD, optional MR PG)	1	2
	Domain Controller A	1	2
	Support Tools	1	2
ESXi Server A-2	AW-HDS-DDS 1	4	4
	CUIC 1	4	6
ESXi Server A-3	UCM Subscriber 1	2	6
	UCM Publisher	2	6
	IPIVR 1 or CUP Server 1	2	4
ESXi Server A-4	CVP Call Server + VoiceXML Server 1	4	4
	CVP Reporting Server 1	4	4

Table 9-10 *Chassis B (B Series)/Rack of C Series Rack Mount Servers*

ESXi Server	Component	# vCPU	RAM (GB)
ESXi Server B-1	Rogger B	4	4
	Agent PG B (Generic PG with optional VRU, CTIOS/CAD, optional MR PG)	1	2
	Domain Controller B	1	2
	CVP Operations Console Server	2	2
ESXi Server B-2	AW-HDS-DDS 2	4	4
	CUIC 2	4	6
ESXi Server B-3	UCM Subscriber 2	2	6
	IPIVR 2 or CUP Server 2	2	4
ESXi Server B-4	CVP Call Server + VoiceXML Server 2	4	4
	CVP Media Server	2	2

Use Case: Rogger Example 2

This use case provides the following:

- Up to 2000 CTIOS Agents or 1000 CAD Agents
- 600 IPIVR or 900 CVP ports (N + N)
- Optional 200 CUIC reporting users
- 1500 CCMP users

Tables 9-11 and 9-12 provide the specifics for each virtual machine where shaded cells are optional components.

Use Case: Rogger Example 3

This use case provides the following:

- Up to 4000 CTIOS Agents or 2000 CAD Agents
- 1200 IPIVR or 1800 CVP ports (N + N)
- Optional 200 CUIC reporting users
- 1500 CCMP users

Table 9-11 *Chassis A (B Series)/Rack of C Series Rack Mount Servers*

ESXi Server	Component	# vCPU	RAM(GB)
ESXi Server A-1	Rogger A	4	4
	Agent PG A (Generic PG with optional VRU, CTIOS/CAD, optional MR PG, SIP Dialer)	2	4
	Domain Controller A	1	2
	Support Tools	1	2
ESXi Server A-2	AW-HDS-DDS 1	4	4
	AW-HDS-DDS 3	4	4
ESXi Server A-3	UCM Subscriber 1	2	6
	UCM Subscriber 2	2	6
	UCM Publisher	2	6
	IPIVR 1 or CUP Server 1	2	4
ESXi Server A-4	CVP Call Server + VoiceXML Server 1	4	4
	CVP Reporting Server 1	4	4
ESXi Server A-5	CUIC 1	4	6
	CVP Media Server	2	2

Table 9-12 *Chassis B (B Series)/Rack of C Series Rack Mount Servers*

ESXi Server	Component	# vCPU	RAM(GB)
ESXi Server B-1	Rogger B	4	4
	Agent PG B (Generic PG with optional VRU, CTIOS/CAD, optional MR PG, SIP Dialer)	2	4
	Domain Controller B	1	2
ESXi Server B-2	AW-HDS-DDS 2	4	4
	AW-HDS-DDS 4	4	4
ESXi Server B-3	UCM Subscriber 2	2	6
	UCM Subscriber 4	2	6
	CVP Operations Console Server	2	2
	IPIVR 2 or CUP Server 2	2	4

Table 9-12 *Chassis B (B Series)/Rack of C Series Rack Mount Servers*

ESXi Server	Component	# vCPU	RAM(GB)
ESXi Server B-4	CVP Call Server + VoiceXML Server 2	4	4
	CVP Reporting Server 2	4	4
ESXi Server B-5	CCMP (All in one)	4	4
	CUIC 2	4	6

Tables 9-13 and 9-14 provide the specifics for each virtual machine where shaded cells are optional components.

Table 9-13 *Chassis A (B Series)/Rack of C Series Rack Mount Servers*

ESXi Server	Component	# vCPU	RAM (GB)
ESXi Server A-1	Rogger A	4	4
	Agent PG 1A (CTIOS/CAD, optional MR PG, SIP Dialer)	2	4
ESXi Server A-2	VRU PG A	2	2
	Support Tools	1	2
	Domain Controller A	1	2
ESXi Server A-3	Agent PG 2A (CTIOS/CAD, optional MR PG, SIP Dialer)	2	4
	CVP Reporting Server 1	4	4
ESXi Server A-4	AW-HDS-DDS 1	4	4
	AW-HDS-DDS 3	4	4
ESXi Server A-5	UCM Subscriber 1	2	6
	UCM Subscriber 3	2	6
	UCM Publisher	2	6
	IPIVR 1	2	4
ESXi Server A-6	UCM Subscriber 5	2	6
	UCM Subscriber 7	2	6
	IPIVR 2	2	4
	CUP Server 1	2	4

Table 9-13 *Chassis A (B Series)/Rack of C Series Rack Mount Servers*

ESXi Server	Component	# vCPU	RAM (GB)
ESXi Server A-7	CVP Call + VoiceXML Server 1	4	4
	CVP Call + VoiceXML Server 3	4	4
ESXi Server A-8	CVP Media Server	2	2
	CUIC 1	4	6

Table 9-14 *Chassis B (B Series)/Rack of C Series Rack Mount Servers*

ESXi Server	Component	# vCPU	RAM(GB)
ESXi Server B-1	Rogger B	4	4
	Agent PG 1B (CTIOS/CAD, optional MR PG, SIP Dialer)	2	4
ESXi Server B-2	VRU PG B	2	2
	CVP Operations Console Server	2	2
	Domain Controller B	1	2
ESXi Server B-3	Agent PG 2B (CTIOS/CAD, optional MR PG, SIP Dialer)	2	4
	CVP Reporting Server 2	4	4
ESXi Server B-4	AW-HDS-DDS 2	4	4
	AW-HDS-DDS 4	4	4
ESXi Server B-5	UCM Subscriber 2	2	6
	UCM Subscriber 4	2	6
	IPIVR 3	2	4
ESXi Server B-6	UCM Subscriber 6	2	6
	UCM Subscriber 8	2	6
	IPIVR 4	2	4
	CUP Server 2	2	4
ESXi Server B-7	CVP Call + VoiceXML Server 2	4	4
	CVP Call + VoiceXML Server 4	4	4
ESXi Server B-8	CUIC 2	2	6
	CCMP (All in one)	4	4

Use Case: Router/Logger

This use case provides the following:

- Up to 8000 CTIOS Agents or 4000 CAD Agents

- 3600 CVP ports (N + N)

- Optional 400 CUIC reporting users

- 8000 CCMP users

Tables 9-14 and 9-15 provide the specifics for each virtual machine where shaded cells are optional components.

Table 9-15 *Chassis A (B Series)/Rack of C Series Rack Mount Servers*

ESXi Server	Component	# vCPU	RAM (GB)
ESXi Server A-1	Router A	2	4
	Agent PG 1A (CTIOS/CAD, optional MR PG, SIP Dialer)	2	4
	Agent PG 3A (CTIOS/CAD, optional MR PG, SIP Dialer)	2	4
	Domain Controller A	1	2
	Support Tools	1	2
ESXi Server A-2	Logger A	4	4
	Agent PG 2A (CTIOS/CAD, optional MR PG, SIP Dialer)	2	4
	Agent PG 4A (CTIOS/CAD, optional MR PG, SIP Dialer)	2	4
ESXi Server A-3	HDS-DDS 1	4	4
	AW-HDS 1	4	4
ESXi Server A-4	AW-HDS 3	4	4
	AW-HDS 5	4	4
ESXi Server A-5	UCM 1 Subscriber 1	2	6
	UCM 2 Subscriber 1	2	6
	UCM 1 Subscriber 3	2	6
	UCM 2 Subscriber 3	2	6
ESXi Server A-6	UCM 1 Subscriber 5	2	6
	UCM 2 Subscriber 5	2	6
	UCM 1 Subscriber 7	2	6
	UCM 2 Subscriber 7	2	6

Table 9-15 *Chassis A (B Series)/Rack of C Series Rack Mount Servers*

ESXi Server	Component	# vCPU	RAM (GB)
ESXi Server A-7	UCM 1 Publisher	2	6
	CUP Server 1	2	4
ESXi Server A-8	UCM 2 Publisher	2	6
	CVP Report Server 1	4	4
ESXi Server A-9	CVP Call + VoiceXML Server 1	4	4
	CVP Call + VoiceXML Server 3	4	4
ESXi Server A-10	CVP Call + VoiceXML Server 5	4	4
	CVP Call + VoiceXML Server 7	4	4
ESXi Server A-11	CVP Media Server A	2	2
	VRU PG A	2	2
ESXi Server A-12	CUIC 1	4	6
	CUIC 3	4	6
ESXi Server A-13	CCMP Database	8	4

Table 9-16 *Chassis B (B Series)/Rack of C Series Rack Mount Servers*

ESXi Server	Component	# vCPU	RAM (GB)
ESXi Server B-1	Router B	2	4
	Agent PG 1B (CTIOS/CAD, optional MR PG, SIP Dialer)	2	4
	Agent PG 3B (CTIOS/CAD, optional MR PG, SIP Dialer)	2	4
	Domain Controller B	1	2
ESXi Server B-2	Logger B	4	4
	Agent PG 2B (CTIOS/CAD, optional MR PG, SIP Dialer)	2	4
	Agent PG 4B (CTIOS/CAD, optional MR PG, SIP Dialer)	2	4

Table 9-16   *Chassis B (B Series)/Rack of C Series Rack Mount Servers*

ESXi Server	Component	# vCPU	RAM (GB)
ESXi Server B-3	HDS-DDS 2	4	4
	AW-HDS 2	4	4
ESXi Server B-4	AW-HDS 4	4	4
	AW-HDS 6	4	4
ESXi Server B-5	UCM 1 Subscriber 2	2	6
	UCM 2 Subscriber 2	2	6
	UCM 1 Subscriber 4	2	6
	UCM 2 Subscriber 4	2	6
ESXi Server B-6	UCM 1 Subscriber 6	2	6
	UCM 2 Subscriber 6	2	6
	UCM 1 Subscriber 8	2	6
	UCM 2 Subscriber 8	2	6
ESXi Server B-7	CVP Operations Console Server	2	2
	CUP Server 2	2	4
ESXi Server B-8	CVP Report Server 2	4	4
ESXi Server B-9	CVP Call + VoiceXML Server 2	4	4
	CVP Call + VoiceXML Server 4	4	4
ESXi Server B-10	CVP Call + VoiceXML Server 6	4	4
	CVP Call + VoiceXML Server 8	4	4
ESXi Server B-11	CVP Media Server B	2	2
	VRU PG B	2	2
ESXi Server B-12	CUIC 2	4	6
	CUIC 4	4	6
ESXi Server B-13	CCMP Web/Applications Server	4	4

Summary

Virtualization is unavoidable and continues to be the standard used by companies to consolidate their assets and reduce their total cost of ownership. Unified CVP does support virtualization. However as discussed in this chapter, it comes with some serious caveats and considerations.

Unified CVP can be virtualized only on Cisco Unified Computing System (UCS) hardware with specific hardware specifications. In other words, not all configurations available with UCS are supported or tested with Unified CVP. The specifications were pointed out earlier in this chapter. Furthermore, not all the cool features provided by VMW are supported or tested with Unified CVP components

On a positive note, OVA templates have been built and provided by Cisco to help provide a simple process for setting up a virtual machine that can host a Unified CVP component. By using these templates, the correct virtual machine settings can be realized, enabling a smooth installation of the host OS and application software into the virtual machine.

Valuable use cases were also included in the chapter. Upon examining the cases provided, it became apparent as to how well virtualization can scale to meet larger solution requirements. This is accomplished without having to significantly increase the footprint of the physical solution. After all, this is one of the most important strengths of virtualization.

The physical hardware and virtualization software limitations were illustrated for the Unified CVP solution throughout this chapter. Yet, the advantages of virtualizing during an upgrade or a green field deployment remain attractive and should be given serious consideration. With careful planning pertaining to solution sizing and a strong cohabitation plan running Unified CVP in a virtualized environment is more than just a possibility.

References

1. Cisco DCUCI Training, "Cisco Data Center Unified Computing Support Specialist," Volume 1, Version 3.0, 1–9.

2. Cisco DCUCI Training, "Cisco Data Center Unified Computing Support Specialist", Volume 1, Version 3.0, 1–15.

Recommended Reading and Resources

Cisco Documentation, *Cisco UCS B-Series Servers Documentation Roadmap*, http://www.cisco.com/en/US/docs/unified_computing/ucs/overview/guide/UCS_roadmap.html.

Cisco Documentation, *Cisco UCS C-Series Servers Documentation Roadmap*, http://www.cisco.com/en/US/docs/unified_computing/ucs/overview/guide/UCS_rack_roadmap.html.

Cisco Documentation, *Cisco UCS C-Series Integrated Management Controller*, http://www.cisco.com/en/US/products/ps10739/tsd_products_support_series_home.html.

Cisco Documentation, *Cisco UCS Manager*, http://www.cisco.com/en/US/products/ps10281/tsd_products_support_series_home.html.

Cisco Documentation, *Unified Communications VMWare Requirements*, http://docwiki.cisco.com/wiki/Unified_Communications_VMWare_Requirements.

Cisco Documentation, *Cisco Unified Customer Voice Portal (CVP) 8.x Solution Reference Network Design (SRND)*, http://www.cisco.com/en/US/docs/voice_ip_comm/cust_contact/contact_center/customer_voice_portal/srnd/8x/cvp8xsrnd.pdf.

Cisco Documentation, *Cisco Unified Contact Center Enterprise Solution Reference Network Design(SRND)*, http://www.cisco.com/en/US/products/sw/custcosw/ps1844/products_implementation_design_guides_list.html.

Cisco Documentation, *Cisco Unified Customer Voice Portal Configuration Guides*, http://www.cisco.com/en/US/partner/products/sw/custcosw/ps1006/products_installation_and_configuration_guides_list.html.

Cisco Documentation, *Hardware and System Software Specification for Cisco Unified Customer Voice Portal (Unified CVP), Release 8.0(1)*, http://www.cisco.com/en/US/docs/voice_ip_comm/cust_contact/contact_center/customer_voice_portal/cvp8_0/reference/guide/cvp_801_bom.pdf.

Cisco Documentation, *Cisco Unified Communications System Release 8.x SRND, January 2011*, http://www.cisco.com/en/US/partner/docs/voice_ip_comm/cucm/srnd/8x/uc8x.html.

Index

PEARSON IT Certification

Browse by Exams ▼   Browse by Technology ▼   Browse by Format   Explore ▼   I'm New Here – Help!

Store   Forums   Safari Books Online

Your Publisher for IT Certification

Pearson IT Certification is the leader in technology certification learning and preparation tools.

Visit **pearsonITcertification.com** today to find

- **CERTIFICATION EXAM** information and guidance for IT certifications, including

  CISCO.   CompTIA.   Microsoft·

- **EXAM TIPS AND TRICKS** by reading the latest articles and sample chapters by Pearson IT Certification's expert authors and industry experts, such as

  - Mark Edward Soper and David Prowse – CompTIA
  - Wendell Odom – Cisco
  - Shon Harris – Security
  - Thomas Erl – SOACP

- **SPECIAL OFFERS (pearsonITcertification.com/promotions)**

- **REGISTRATION** for your Pearson IT Certification products to access additional online material and receive a coupon to be used on your next purchase

Be sure to create an account on **pearsonITcertification.com** and receive member's-only offers and benefits.

Pearson IT Certification is a publishing imprint of Pearson

Apps

Articles & Chapters

Blogs

Books

eBooks

eBooks (Watermarked)

Cert Flash Cards Online

Newsletters

Podcasts

Question of the Day

Rough Cuts

Short Cuts

Videos

Connect with Pearson IT Certification

pearsonITcertification.com/ newsletters

 twitter.com/ pearsonITCert

 facebook.com/ pearsonitcertification

 youtube.com/ pearsonITCert

 pearsonitcertification. com/rss/